# Folktales and Society

## STORY-TELLING IN A HUNGARIAN

## PEASANT COMMUNITY

# Folktales and Society

## STORY-TELLING IN A HUNGARIAN PEASANT COMMUNITY

## Linda Dégh

Translated by Emily M. Schossberger

INDIANA UNIVERSITY PRESS

Bloomington / London

Based on the original German edition, *Märchen, Erzahler und Erzählgemeinschaft dargestellt an der ungarischen Volksüberlieferung,* copyright 1962 by Akademie-Verlag GmbH, Berlin

Published in Canada by Fitzhenry & Whiteside Limited,
Scarborough, Ontario

Library of Congress catalog card number: 69-15994
Manufactured in the United States of America

# CONTENTS

# ILLUSTRATIONS

*(following page XIV)*

Mrs. Zsuzsánna Palkó
György Andrásfalvi
Mrs. Anna Sebestyén and Mrs. Bode
Mrs. Erzsi Mátyás
Mrs. Zsók and daughter-in-law
Map of the Szekler Settlements

# PREFACE

THIS BOOK PRESENTS AN INVESTIGATION OF STORYTELLING BY THE correlation of oral folk narratives, their creators and performers, and the participant audience as a complex whole in the expression of culture. Choosing a transplanted Bucovina Szekler community now residing in the village of Kakasd (County Tolna, Hungary) as a point of departure, I have aimed at reaching general conclusions about the social role and cultural values of narration. This study of the Kakasd people emphasizes the interaction of personality and community in oral creation. It is based primarily on field research materials, recorded oral narratives, oral statements from the villagers, and minute observation of their actions and functions. To achieve a thorough comprehension of the ideology of the Kakasd folk as expressed in oral narration I relied heavily on the original statements of the informants. In the elaboration of a research method I was stimulated by studies in personality and culture written by American anthropologists. However, I did not find much to rely on in the utilization of their experiences concerning folklore materials. Acknowledging earlier accomplishments of disciples of Franz Boas, E. Wolf rightly pointed out that "American anthropologists have tended to neglect the individual artist and his relation to his audience, in favor of the study of technique and art object. . . . Americans deserted the problem of creativity for the more mechanical study of the products of creativity."[1] I am dealing with creative individuals and their repertoires, that is, the formation of the narrative stock socially acknowledged, during the period of investigation.

The peculiar culture of the Bucovina Szeklers has for a long time attracted the attention of folklorists and ethnologists, representing as it does not only the influence of two definite historical phases but the impact of a new environment, to which these people are still adapting. A cultural situation in which interethnic traits enter into archaic and modern stages of the same culture offers the researcher a unique opportunity to observe a process of rapid cultural adjustment. This acculturative process, if not stimulated by outside forces, would normally be extremely slow and extended over many generations.

A plan to undertake ethnographical research among the resettled Bucovina Szeklers was first outlined in 1941, immediately after the Szeklers had left the Bucovina. According to the project, a team of collectors was to follow, step by step, the gradual transformation of the ethnic group over a period of six to eight years.[2] During the war, however, the Bácska settlement was destroyed, and the project was abandoned. In 1947 staff members of the Folk-Life Research Institute at Budapest (closed in 1949) explored the brand-new Szekler settlements in the Transdanubian area. A considerable amount of folklore materials were amassed at that time. Dances and ritual performances were filmed, while songs, ballads, instrumental music, and dialectological items were recorded. Little of this exploratory fieldwork was ever published.[3] I visited the Szeklers for the first time in 1948 with a group of students enrolled in my fieldwork seminar at the Eötvös University, Budapest. The students, some of my colleagues, and I cooperated in investigating various aspects of folk culture in six different villages in which the population of the five original Bucovina Szekler communities had made their new home. As a community study of the whole ethnic culture, the fieldwork was carried out very methodically. It is regrettable that most of the collected raw materials remain unpublished; they are now preserved in the Archives of the Ethnographical Museum, Budapest, and the Folklore Department of the Eötvös University.[4]

My Kakasd field collection deals in the main with storytelling of the former residents of Andrásfalva, one of the five Bucovina villages. It does not offer a complete picture of the Bucovina Szekler storytelling, nor does it reflect the narration of all the former Andrásfalva inhabitants. Storytelling situations found in Kakasd during the period of research,

however, produced generalizations that also applied to the old Andrásfalva, as a result of several favorable conditions:

1. the majority of the population, including the most prominent families
   and leading personalities, had moved to Kakasd;
2. the most representative storytellers and their supporting audience had
   likewise moved to Kakasd;
3. the occasions and customs of storytelling were uniform among all
   Andrásfalvers during the period of observation;
4. the Kakasd settlers retained the Andrásfalva pattern of strong clan,
   family, and neighborhood ties, a solid basis for the maintenance of
   storytelling customs.

Materials for this study were gathered in the course of twelve field
trips between December 1948 and November 1960. Besides tales collected
from the most distinguished narrators[5] and analyzed in this work, I have
recorded a large amount of miscellaneous folk narrative materials from
different informants. At the time of the fieldwork, storytelling in Kakasd
was still a significant and characteristic social institution. Almost all in-
telligent adults were able to tell a good many tales from the community
repertoire and they also knew the favorite pieces of the recognized
raconteurs. However, the stories treated here came exclusively from outstanding personalities and acknowledged entertainers whose performance
attracted a larger public. In other words, their functional role was linked
with socially important communal activities. I also collected many other
ethnographical items pertaining to storytelling. The study of culture
change within the course of the last eighty years was based on the information of representatives of three subsequent generations. The key
areas of our interest were basic economy, social cooperation, division of
labor, social stratification, kinship, family life, education, folk history,
moral code, folk religion, and world view as expressed in belief, custom,
ritual, and dramatic performance. The Szeklers characteristically emphasize their own past, and the unconscious systems of meaning that characterize them aided our understanding of Szekler narration, narratives,
and narrators.

The first edition of this book was issued by the Publishing House of
the German Academy of Sciences, Berlin, in 1962, under the title *Märchen, Erzähler und Erzählgemeinschaft*. It grew out of folktale collections recognizing the importance of creative storytellers and their social
function, a point of view initiated by Gy. Ortutay and elaborated by his
students and disciples. The method of monographic collection and analy-

sis worked out for the Kakasd study utilized the experiences accumulated by this group of folktale scholars. In a critical evaluation of the series *New Collection of Hungarian Folklore* (*Uj Magyar Népköltési Gyüjtemény*) representative of this trend,[6] I pointed to certain dangers in the method of approach, which had become repetitious and sterile. Useless details were presented without proper synthesis and analysis. Having completed the Kakasd monograph, I fully recognize the necessity of further improvement in research techniques. More exact means of exploring ideas, symbols, and images in the folktales and simultaneously in the conscious and unconscious layers of the mind of the narrators and their listeners would grant us better insight into the secrets of the cultural performance of taletelling. Methodical questioning of informants about the meaning of their tales immediately after storytelling sessions, with the participation of their audience, seems to open a wider perspective into the matter, especially if combined with psychological inquiries. I have been experimenting with this idea for some time. However, I was unable to carry out the major changes necessary to introduce the results of this experimentation in revising this edition of the original Kakasd manuscript. Additional fieldwork would be needed, although, even if I could visit Kakasd now, the situation would be quite different from what I formerly knew, and there would be no way to recapture what had vanished. Nevertheless, there are considerable alterations in the text, reflecting changes in my own conviction on these matters. I also took advantage of recent research results in international folktale scholarship. The bibliography has been brought up to date.

Finally, I wish to express my deep gratitude to all the friends and colleagues who gave me help at different stages of the preparation of this work. My warmest thanks go first of all to the people of Kakasd, my hosts and hostesses, who invited me into their homes and were generous enough to acquaint me with their way of life, who taught me the wisdom of the simple folk, and who helped me in every possible way. I will always remember and cherish their loyalty and the warm friendships that developed between me and my informants and involved me even more closely in their lives. All of them are referred to between these pages. The memory of Mrs. Susan Palkó, the great storyteller and magnificent personality who is no longer among us, is and always will be a source of inspiration.

Furthermore, I am grateful to those dear colleagues who joined me in field research and shared their ideas with me in heated discussions: Ferenc Bakó, Márta Belényesy, Tekla Dömötör, and László K. Kovács. I am particularly thankful to my teacher, Gyula Ortutay, who was a patient adviser throughout the preparation of the manuscript; and to Károly Marót (d. 1963), the great classics scholar, whose theory of oral literature inspired Hungarian folklorists and whose kindly criticism helped me. The tragic news of Wolfgang Steinitz's untimely death reached me as I wrote these words of thanks. He accompanied me on one of my field trips to Kakasd. It was due to his keen interest and enthusiasm that I submitted the book for publication to the Institute of German Folklore (Institut für deutsche Volkskunde) he headed. My best thanks are due to scholars who have aided me with valuable advice, sending articles and books that were hopelessly out of my reach during the time of writing: William R. Bascom, Paul G. Brewster, Séamus O'Duilearga, Sabin V. Drăgoi, József Faragó, Irving A. Hallowell, Martti Haavio, Gottfried Henssen, Pjotr V. Lintur, Erna G. Pomerantseva.

I was greatly honored by the Pitré award jury that granted me a prize for the book in 1963, as well as by the appreciation of reviewers in the professional journals. I am especially grateful to Francis Lee Utley[7], whose evaluation was instrumental in securing the American publication and to Richard M. Dorson, who generously went through the translated manuscript. I wish to thank the Indiana University Foundation for a grant to cover the expenses of translation, and Emily M. Schossberger for her expert translation and her indulgence.

**L.D.**

*Bloomington*
*1968*

*Folktales and Society*

STORY-TELLING IN A HUNGARIAN

PEASANT COMMUNITY

Mrs. Zsuzsánna Palkó

György Andrásfalvi *(left)*

Mrs. Anna Sebestyén and Mrs. Bode

Mrs. Erzsi Mátyás

Mrs. Zsók and daughter-in-law

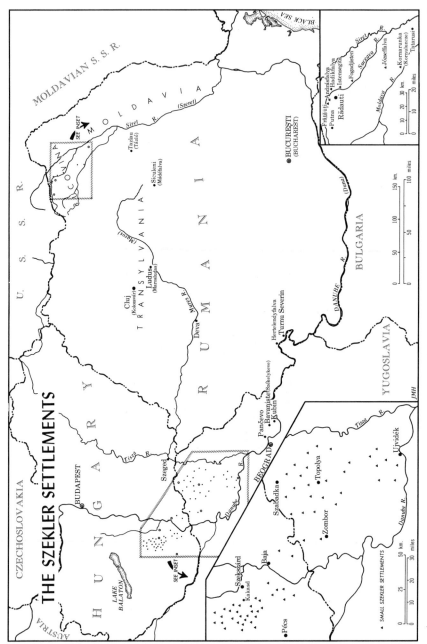

Map of the Szekler Settlements

# PART ONE

---

# *The Szeklers in Kakasd*

# 1

# History of the Szeklers

THE MAJORITY OF THE SZEKLERS (HUNGARIAN, *Székely*) INHABIT THE southern part of Transylvania, an area that was once a borderland but today is an autonomous Hungarian territory in Rumania. This particular ethnic group is distinguished from other Hungarian ethnic groups by its racial origin, history, and legal codes and by the geographical position of its settlement.

The question of the origin of the Szeklers has never been completely clarified. Some historians are of the opinion that they are the descendants of a Bulgarian-Turkish tribe, and that their culture corresponded, at the time of the original settlement of the Magyars (960 A.D.), to that of the Hungarians. Others hold that their descent cannot be traced to a single source, but that their historic task of guarding the frontier formed them into a unit. The Szeklers themselves have preserved many legends regarding their origins, legends which, however, lack any historic foundation. Our informants from Andrásfalva are in complete accord, telling us that their ancestors were the Huns, that the Szeklers are "Attila's descendants" and had settled the Danube basin before the Hungarians. The narrator György Andrásfalvi, for instance, reported:

> We are descendants of the Huns. Hunor[1] said to Magyar: "Here is the land of the Szeklers." Magyar moved on, because there was not room enough for both. We are the older settlers.

The Szeklers first appear in history as a nomadic tribe of cattlebreeders. Their society was based on a clan organization, and land was communally owned. During the Middle Ages, however, this warlike people formed an important military contingent for the Hungarian kings, a fact which explains the privileges granted them. The Szeklers, in contrast to the Hungarian serfs, paid no tribute but absolved their obligations to the crown through military service. The Szekler soldiers were awarded military rank according to their property holdings, which later formed the basis for their permanent social structure. The leading group were the Primores, who provided the chief officers. Second in importance were the Primipili (in Hungarian "horses' heads"), each of whom owned a horse as part of his military equipment; and third were the Pixidarii, the common or foot soldiers. During their wars the Szeklers took prisoners and looted conquered territories, and as reward for their deeds, were given land by the kings.[2] Even though individual land ownership came about in later times, the former system, based on sib organization and common ownership of land, persisted well into the fifteenth century, and the broad social stratum of soldiers continued to exercise their privileges.[3] The sibs formed the foundation of the later social order based on units called *széks* (literally "chairs"), units of public administration, which in turn were abolished during the nineteenth century. A so-called Szekler *szék* combined six extended families, and was divided into two branches. This peculiar social structure, and the fact that the development of feudalism among the Szeklers lagged centuries behind that among Hungarians generally, was decisive for the culture of this ethnic group.

Feudalism brought about a stronger societal grouping among the Szeklers. The members of the upper classes who had acquired property moved up into the ranks of the landed aristocracy, while those who had not became poorer. Among the lower classes ("foot-Szekler," or common freedman) poverty was especially great, since in addition to military service, this class, during the second half of the sixteenth century, was also burdened with taxation. Many of the Szekler freedmen retrogressed to serfdom, though not to the same degree as occurred elsewhere. Only 38 per cent of the Szekler population became serfs, whereas in Hungary and the rest of Transylvania the percentage was 81.[4] At the beginning of the eighteenth century, a number of Szeklers took part in the Rákóczi revolt against the Hapsburgs. After the defeat of the revolt the government of Vienna dissolved the military order of the Szeklers and ordered universal taxation.[5]

Though the particular social order, and the privileges, of the Szeklers had practically ceased to exist by that time, the memory of it and the proud knowledge of their former freedom and privileges continued to remain alive among the inhabitants of the Szeklerland. These memories are particularly vivid in the tradition of the Szeklers who left their homeland during the second half of the eighteenth century and moved into the Moldavia region or Bucovina, and from there during 1946-47 to Hungary, to the counties of Tolna and Baranya.

Since this work is concerned with a part of this ethnic group, in what follows we have consulted not only historical data but the present-day Szeklers of Kakasd.

The history proper of the Bucovina Szeklers begins during the time of the Empress Maria Theresa (1740-80), when they emigrated from the Szekler lands. The immediate reason for emigration can be found in the organization of the Szekler border guards. The Empress of Austria and Queen of Hungary placed particular importance on strong military forces to safeguard her empire and her throne and as a result decreed the organization of a border guard along the southern border of her empire. As there had been no organized border guard in Transylvania since the Szeklers were demilitarized, the Empress in 1761 dispatched the Austrian Quartermaster General, Buccow, to carry out the task there.[6] The Szekler border guard was to consist of 15,000 men.[7] But the recruiters everywhere encountered heavy resistance. As one man the Szeklers refused military service, invoking their old privileges and pointing out that they would not tolerate the violation of their rights. They would be ready to take up arms, but only according to their own customs, under their own officers, in their own uniforms, and only in defense of their own soil. For years promises and threats were in vain; very few of the Szeklers took the oath to serve under the Empress. But peace in the Szekler lands was disturbed by these events, social contrasts were sharpened, and violence occurred daily in the villages. This anarchical state of affairs was worsened by the conflict between the partisans of the Austrians, who had entered military service, and the population who resisted in order to safeguard their rights. All this finally erupted in open conflict. On the morning of January 6, 1764, the soldiers stationed in Mádéfalva surrounded a throng of 2,500 assembled there and opened fire. This tragic moment in Hungarian history, which took the lives of 200 people,[8] is still considered, in the consciousness of the people, the event which triggered the mass emigration of the Szeklers:

They had to leave Mádéfalva because the Austrians had opened fire upon the community. It was because the Austrian Emperor Joseph[9] wanted to force them that Hungarian rose against Hungarian. Three times they [the regular troops] were asked to rise and cut down the Hungarians. But they preferred to leave the land. The Austrian army dispersed them; they hurried into woods and the mountains and those who returned were felled by ax and mowed down by scythe.

In fact, it was the sum of all this—the consequences of establishing a border guard, the fear of serfdom and of being taken prisoner—which forced the Szeklers to take to wandering about the country. Wherever they went, they proclaimed: rather death or emigration than forced military service. Misery, great poverty, and hopelessness added to their burden. Taxation enslaved the lesser nobility as well as the serfs, and the obligation to provide room and board for the military and to render special services added to their worries. The unsettled state of affairs kept them from tilling their fields, and there was no security anywhere. Serfs and freemen alike decided upon escape.[10] Sántha writes: "At the time of Mádéfalva's peril, the struggle for border protection was shot through with the dissatisfaction of the poor and with revolutionary atmosphere."[11] Most of the inhabitants of the Csík emigrated because of poverty; they could scarcely feed their families from the yield of the barren land, to say nothing of paying taxes and doing military service.[12] Under these circumstances it was impossible to prevent their flight; in vain were village guards installed and heavy penalties threatened. Not even the promise of going scot free on their return could stem the swelling tide of refugees. In the spring of 1763, 278 families left the Csík, and more followed later.[13] Even though a group here and there was enticed to return, the Szeklers continued to flee in a constant stream toward the Moldavia region.

The refugees were welcomed by the governor of the fertile Moldavia lands, which were under Turkish sovereignty, and received land and taxation privileges. Some of the Szeklers settled in Hungarian villages along the river Szeret (Siret), villages founded by Hungarians who, for one reason or another, had fled the arbitrary reign of the Hapsburgs. Another group founded new villages along the rivers Tatros (Trotus), Tázló (Tazlau), and Beszterce (Bistriza).[14] Some of these families were able to amass in this new environment the material goods that were a prerequisite for social advancement, and that enabled them to return to the land of the Szeklers. But the inhabitants of Kakasd today have bitter memories of those days, as if their ancestors had been wandering the empty tundras.

"They crossed the frontier towards Rumania," an informant related.[15] "They were not received in Transylvania anymore, because this province was a part of the Austrian state; they had become homeless, and for a long time, maybe fifteen or twenty years, they wandered around in the Moldavia regions. But they did not like the conditions there." In general, the people of Kakasd felt that the big landowners (Boyars) of Moldavia made them work for a pittance.

Finally, in 1774, the Austrian government promised the ethnic groups of the monarchy all kinds of privileges—among them freedom from serfdom—in exchange for settling the uninhabited regions of North Moldavia (Bucovina). It was here that the Ruthenian, Polish, Slovak, Czech, and other settlers converged. The Szekler deserters were promised amnesty. In those days the Bucovina was "an uninhabited place, a wooded region; nobody lived there and then the Austrians occupied it," an informant accurately related.[16]

According to Kis-Várday, General Splényi, the conqueror of the Bucovina, himself originally from Transylvania, brought the first Szekler settlers into the country. After the founding of Fogadjisten[17] and Istensegits[18] in 1776-78, András Hadik, Governor of Transylvania and Commander-in-Chief of Galicia and the Bucovina, suggested a mass settling of the deserters.[19]

Seven years later Józseffalva was founded, taking its name from the Emperor; then followed the two villages named after András Hadik, Hadikfalva and Andrásfalva. This sequence determined the ranking positions of the five Szekler villages, awareness of which is alive today in the consciousness of their former inhabitants.[20]

In the year 1786, there were 800 Szekler families—a total of 2,500 persons—living in the Bucovina. The largest village was Istensegits, with 275 families, while the smallest was Andrásfalva, the last to be founded, with only 75 families.[21] Many of the Szekler refugees remained in their Moldavia settlements, but some of them joined the Bucovina settlers. Here a different cultural development took place, and as a consequence the present day Szeklers deny any relationship with the Hungarians of the Moldavia region, where the increasing Rumanian influence and the precarious economic conditions caused a decline in the ethnic unity of the Szekler settlers. The Bucovina-Hungarians, on the other hand, remained in a closed social complex and grew into a strong ethnic group.[22]

For purposes of comparison with the historical facts, we shall recount here the legend of the flight into the Moldavia region and the settling of the Bucovina as János Mátyás, the "judge" (burgomaster) of Kakasd, has related it. In this legend is anchored the concept of Szekler unity and the explanation of the origin of the five Bucovina villages.

They ran until they were driven into the region of Moldavia, to the domain of a baron, or that of a duke. They passed the Rumanian border,[23] and the duke saw them, some with a wagon, the others with a pair of oxen. He asked them, "How long? Where to?" "Well, we don't know. They have driven us from our homeland." "Do you understand something of agriculture?" "Yes!" "Do you like to work?" "Yes." "Well, don't go just any place. I have all this land, I shall settle you here. I have a brother and we can settle the others there." Thus it came about that the Andrásfalvers who came from Csík settled with the first count, those of Hadikfalva with his brother, those of Istensegíts with a third, those from Józseffalva with the fourth, and those of the Fogadjisten with the fifth.

During five years they built their nests.[24] After that they had enough. "Let us abandon everything, leave the Rumanian landlord." They held their council and went away along another river. This was the river Siret. They wandered with poor oxen and bad wagons. In Karnarunka there was the passage to the Austrian border. They asked the customs officers to allow them to go to the other part of the country, but there were the Austrians. They were there in such masses—the devil with them!—and who among them really wanted to work? At the Austrian border a general stopped them: "Where are you going? Austria is not a state in which so many people could just wander around!" So András Hadik told them where they came from. They looked at each other. There were plenty of places. They should go to the river Szucsáva (Suceava), to the lands that lay fallow there, and should search for a place where they could live. When they arrived there they saw that it was good fertile land and the best of it along the river. They reported this to András Hadik and he begged the general: "I am their leader, permit me to divide the people. One part comes from Mádéfalva, a part from the Csík, and each should be settled in its own village." The general permitted this. Hadik first selected those from Fogadjisten and there he began: "Fogadj Isten—God take us all." "Well," he said, "let us proceed." "Well," he said, "this name should be vowed to God. Let us settle the Istensegítser." Those were from Csíkszentmárton. "Now, friends, to my own name." They went on some ten kilometers and he said: "We shall perpetuate its memory—Hadikfalva [Hadik village] it should be named." They gave it the name of Hadikfalva. Then they went on for eight more kilometers and there were still eighty-one families left. "Now, my given name—Andrásfalva [András village] it should be called."[25] And thus he divided his people into five communities. And when they were settled, what then? Do you know anything about agriculture? Can you plow? Can you clean the seed? "Well," they answered, "well," and when they were put to the test they passed it well. Well, how they received the land, built homes—but not they themselves but the emperor, the Austrian emperor. He appointed the houses, told them where to put in street crossings, chose the eighty-one numbers. They started to build. When they had erected the buildings and whitewashed them and set the ovens, they received furniture. Also cattle. They received everything.

Kis-Várday considers the settlement of the Szeklers very advantageous. Not only did they receive the promised amnesty, but they were given everything necessary for a new settlement. They were given fields and lots. To help them over the difficulties of starting anew, every peasant received from government revenues, and with no obligation to repay, six crowns, every farmer's wife received three crowns, and two crowns were allotted per day for each child. Each family received a tax-free stipend of fifty forints—a sum which could be repaid according to each family's financial circumstances—toward the cost of building a house. Each family was entitled to twenty forints toward the acquisition of farm equipment, if they needed it, and this loan was to be repaid, without interest, within four years. The settlers were exempted from taxes for five years, and every community of more than fifty families was provided, at government expense, with a church and its own priest.[26]

In spite of these favorable conditions, it was only a few years before the Bucovina settlers were once again heavily burdened. The Szeklers who had looked for a new home in order to safeguard their independence found themselves reduced in many ways to the status of serfs. The informants of Kakasd were unanimous in describing the enforced labor and tithing imposed on their ancestors.

János Mátyás related:

Here they received land, the state contributed the material for each building, and by and by every family received twelve acres of land. They were glad to receive so much land . . . but for this they had to do forced labor. How many eggs they had to contribute for each hen, how much milk for each cow, had been calculated. For five days they were working for themselves; the sixth day's work was for the landlord. The women were organized and it was decided how many measures, equivalent to spans of fingers, they had to spin each week during the winter. Whoever did not comply was taken away and received twenty-five whippings. . . .

Antal Molnár related, "I have heard that there was much forced labor because the land belonged to the master; about four days they had to work for him and two days for themselves."

Gergely Fábián said, "When they were settled, our ancestors were given land, but they had to work for it. They were divided into three classes: according to the strength each had, he received land and had to work for it—first farmer, second farmer, third farmer."

Antal Zsók related, "For twelve acres they had to work twelve days."

The many complaints that arose in spite of the favorable settling conditions can easily be understood if we add that at the very time when the Szeklers were being settled, landed estate proprietors began to buy extensive holdings in the Bucovina. It quite often happened that one of the newly erected villages was discovered to be on the land of some property owner's family, who would attempt to force the new settlers into serfdom. Even though the Emperor Joseph II had abolished serfdom by decree in the crownlands, in fact the economic status of the former serfs had changed very little. Thus the situation of the Szeklers in the Bucovina before 1848, the date of the abolition of serfdom in Hungary, was neither worse nor better than that of other serfs in the Austrian monarchy. Those who lived near the landowners fared much worse than those who were able to work independently. The rapaciousness of the lords of the manor is remembered even today by the people.[27] The situation of the inhabitants of the five villages varied according to the attitude of the lords of the manor. Life was more difficult in Istensegits and Fogadjisten than in Andrásfalva, Hadikfalva, and Józseffalva. "Three years after settling they were obliged to do forced labor and tithing on the property of the Greek-Orthodox Church."[28] Forced labor had to be done one day, using the oxen if necessary. Tithing meant giving over one tenth of the field harvest and the livestock.[29]

Having briefly surveyed the history of the Szeklers and the settlement of the emigrants, we shall concentrate our study on the Szeklers of Andrásfalva who live today in Kakasd. Their information and narrations give us a reasonably truthful picture of the old Andrásfalva, which had been their home for 160 years.

# 2

# Social and Economic Life
# in Old Andrásfalva

NDRÁSFALVA WAS FOUNDED ON THE BANKS OF THE RIVER SUCEAVA.
When Szeklers today recalled the old Andrásfalva it seemed to
them a veritable fairyland. The little river became a mighty
stream, the small spot of land a land of abundance, the log houses spacious
palaces; even the air and the water seemed better there, in retrospect,
than anywhere else in the world. Andrásfalva today appeared to them in
this light because the times preceding World War II were comparatively
peaceful, even though life in the village had always been hard. The other
villages in the Bucovina had always regarded Andrásfalva, the most isolated of the four villages, as the most backward, especially in regard to
education. Undoubtedly the culture of the people living at Andrásfalva
even today shows the least evidence of outside influence. The soil was of
poor quality and the inhabitants in general were poor; their lives were
filled with the struggle for a bare living, even in comparatively peaceful times.[1]

In the following pages we shall see what the former Andrásfalva inhabitants said today about the economic life and the social structure of
their Bucovina community.

Although the Szeklers took possession of the Bucovina as free men,
they were soon burdened with the obligations of serfdom that prevailed
throughout the Austrian monarchy. Only after 1848 were these obliga-

tions lifted. Agrarian capitalism developed here exactly as it did in the other eastern European states. Banking capital made common cause with agrarian industries and the landed proprietors, farmers constantly slid back into debt, and the small plots of land under their feet dwindled to nothing. The great population increase resulted in partitioning of the plots, which began very early. Oberding writes that at the end of the last century nearly every family in the Bucovina possessed twenty to thirty acres of land, but before World War II only a few families possessed that much. The average at Hadikfalva was two to four acres. No new land could be acquired; the borders of the villages were narrow, and more and more Szeklers became landless agricultural laborers.[2] When the Bucovina was settled there were scarcely seven inhabitants per square kilometer; by 1890 the number had risen to sixty-two.[3] The population of Andrásfalva grew proportionately. The village originally consisted of seventy-three families, but when it was evacuated in 1941, there were 700 houses. From a letter written by a Presbyterian minister of Andrásfalva we know that the number of inhabitants in 1842 was 1,879.[4] Kis-Várday gives the following figures for the year 1930: 3,680 Szeklers, about 200 Germans, 80 Rumanians, 180 Poles, and 16 Ruthenians.[5] The agrarian proletariat was quickly swelled by the great population increase. Generally, industrial development lags in underdeveloped countries and is so slow that an important body of industrial workers cannot be formed; the majority of the rural population remain agricultural workers. This was true of the Bucovina. Since rail services in that part of the country were very poor, the populace had some opportunity to haul for profit, though this varied greatly. Thus, for example, Szekler haulers were used to transport victuals during the Rumanian-Turkish-Russian war in 1877. They received in advance money to buy wagons and horses, but were not paid for the hauling. Many of them fled the scene of the battle, leaving their wagons behind. When three decades later the state recovered the advances, the interest had accumulated to the point that the descendants of the carters had to repay forty to fifty times the original amount. They were able to do so only by asking for new loans.[6]

In view of these economic conditions, the distribution of property had settled by the 'twenties and 'thirties into a pattern which was to remain stable throughout this period, according to our informants in the fifty-to-seventy age group. During this time there were very few big landholdings. Our informants indicated that Sándor Ömböli, with sixty acres, and Antal Kerekes, with fifty-seven acres, were the biggest farmers. Kerekes was an innkeeper as well as a landowner. At the time when their forefathers had acquired the land, they would have been "judges" (i.e. prominent community leaders). Collecting the facts cited by all informants, there were, aside from three or four larger farms, only twelve farmers with twenty to twenty-five acres and thirty families with eight acres. These were the only well-to-do farmers.

How could a peasant increase his holdings in the face of the partitioning of his land that resulted from the increase of his family? Our informants, in general, were of the opinion that impoverishment was avoidable only if the farmer was extremely lucky. Mostly, they reported, "If the family was big he had to partition." Young people often married without a penny and waited for their inheritance. Ambrus Sebestyén had to wait twenty-nine years for it. Many informants talked of the considerable holdings of some relative who in the end, through partitioning, was left with nothing. "The Szeklers were very fertile, like rabbits. The father distributed the land which he had inherited among sons and daughters; he had to give so much away that he lost twenty to thirty acres." "The same thing happened to us," Mrs. Juhász related. "The father of my husband was well-to-do, but he had six sons and daughters, and we remained poor."

Only one who was very lucky could become a "happy man," that is a rich man, our informant Mrs. Palkó related. For example, a farmer "was well-to-do because his wife had been a widow; the plot of her husband was in one piece and he had a bigger parcel of land . . . he brought up his sister's orphan, which brought him her land, and so they became rich." Another had worked in a factory in America for eight years and had made considerable money. He had returned before World War I and had bought land and a threshing machine. Other Szeklers, of course, had made money through selling or hauling produce. They in turn bought land cheaply from those who were in distress or who wanted to emigrate to America. But a merely diligent man could never acquire land. "He who had many children and worked like my father, never could get rich," said János Mátyás. "For he who has a lot of yeast his dough will rise; he who has no yeast cannot bake bread." When the conversation got around to how to become rich, one often heard picturesque examples: "The poor man had nothing he could hold on to; he liked to work but he could not. Where there is no root, no second crop of hay will sprout. How often did I go to hack wood at my rich brother-in-law's, Anti Zsók, but nothing came of it because poverty devoured what I earned," related György Andrásfalvi.

A man who had little land was forced to take up additional work, or else he could not make a living. The informants were unanimous in their statements. "I had four acres of land, but my wife worked the land, not I. I had a contract for hauling and that is what kept us alive." "The farmer with six or seven acres went to the one with twenty-five. How I started? My wife received an acre and I got one, and so my life started. I could not wait to go to work for Anti Zsók, for the farmer who had six to seven also went there for hire. We preferred to go into the Moldavia region to earn our living," related János Mátyás.

The smaller farmers tried to look for work with the bigger ones in the village; but anyone who had less than five acres was forced to distribute the work among the members of his family. One tended the fields, another took work outside the village—the whole family had to work for a living.

Most of the inhabitants of the village, however, had only dwarf farms and possessed no land of their own. "The Magyars were not farmers, because agriculture sustained only a fourth of them; so everybody went where there was work to be found," we were told. "Three quarters of the village depended upon the city; only a small part could be called farmers."

Seasonal labor for four to seven months became the basis of the Szekler's livelihood. A man who possessed land left its cultivation to his wife or neighbor, to other relatives, or to the children, and went to work in the Moldavia region. During spring the poor part of the village was nearly deserted. Oberding describes in the following passage the fate of the seasonal laborer, which had become general since the eighties.

> . . . more and more people become dependent on going to the Moldavia region for work. But even the seasonal work in Moldavia would not assure a living wage if the head of the family could not send into service his wife and the children who are able to work. Work contracts are signed during the winter under the worst conditions. Employers tie down people during the hard winter months by giving advances which force them to sign even the most pitiful contract in order to free themselves from misery. The average pay of the seasonal worker contracted for four months usually does not surpass 1800 to 2000 leu advance and seven hundred weights of corn.[7]
>
> The poor families from the Bucovina often hire out their ten-year-olds for seasonal labor in the Moldavia, where the inhuman treatment, the mass quarters, and the bad food hardens not only the children's souls but also those of the grownups. Unfortunately,

more and more people were forced to seek work in the Moldavia region.[8]

The Moldavia landowners, with the permission of the Austrian au-. thorities, imported cheap labor from the Bucovina. As the landed proprietors developed more economic management of their big properties according to capitalistic principles, the numbers of workers increased proportionately. The more openings for work there were, the better use the landowner could make of the labor potential of one family: from the feeble child to the feeble grandparent, everyone was given some task. One member of the family took care of the labor in the fields; another worked as a farmhand on the farm itself; another was cook, night watchman, or factory worker; and some carted with their own wagons.

The grief and sorrow which the laborers experienced as a result of the months away from home left a deep impression, especially on those over forty years of age. Remembering the strange surroundings and the treatment they received, the Szeklers recalled the sad songs of the time of exile:

> Andrásfalva, what have I done
> That I cannot live in you.
> Others live well
> Only I weep bitter tears.
> The Moldavia region is vast—
> Dear Lord, take me away from here.
> If you don't take me away
> I am doomed to die from grief.[9]

The Andrásfalva people never ran out of breath when they talked about the times they spent in the Moldavia region:

When the Bucovina did not yet belong to Rumania,[10] they got themselves a passport and the landlords hired from three to four hundred people. They came at Christmas and the drums rolled: who wants to work may come. They took the advances, then spring came, they went to the lords, boyars. Cart after cart, thus they started out. In the fall they returned full of lice. All through winter they starved; thus lived these many poor people.

Before Christmas the drums were rolling—the agreement between the Austrian and the Rumanian consuls was made regarding border passage—for farmhands, seasonal laborers, and labor for the turnip harvest and maize harvest. I too made the bargain. I too went because our livelihood was so uncertain. I had four holds of land. I had to go.

It happened that three hundred or four hundred people went at the same time. They worked on the count's property. If anyone worked in the factory, he received 2,000 to 3,000 kilograms of wheat and corn, he received money, he bought clothes for the whole family. They took the children with them—the count came and got them and brought them back at his own expense. They were used for hacking vines, maize, for harvesting, on the threshing machines, for any kind of field labor. Another went to work in the factory, one served as a night watchman . . . whoever had a few horses brought them along and hauled lumber, turnips, and corn for the count.

One informant, reminiscing about his youth, related:

"I could hack two rows of sugar beets when I was fourteen. For this I received 800 leu, 1,200 leu, whatever the money was worth then. In addition money for tobacco and 20 leu a week for expenses. This is as much as 20 forints [about eighty cents] now. The girls bought soap with it, bought thread. I also helped my brother-in-law, so I got a few hundred more. My brother-in-law assigned the rows. There were girls of fourteen, of ten, even of nine years. There were also children who had two rows, or one row, according to how old they were. We ranged in one line and the girls had to sing, the boys also. The children had to hack sugar beets, harvest rape, and set up the sheafs behind the threshing machine."

Not only the poor went into the Moldavia region, but the children of the rich as well. Mrs. Palkó recalled that "even the daughters of the large-scale farmers went, and thus the poor hardly found places; they were envious."

Agriculture offered a sure income only to a few in Andrásfalva, and consequently many tried vegetable gardening, the most reasonable kind of farming for the fertile strips along the bank of the river Suceava. The harvest was copious, and since vegetables were in great demand, the Szeklers reverted to vegetable gardening.

Cucumbers, onions, and cabbage grew best. The people of Andrásfalva preferred to grow cucumbers and onions; those of Hadikfalva, cabbage. The Rumanians, who celebrated many feasts and frequently fasted, liked onions very much and bought them to store. When Rumania signed a trade agreement with Finland, more onions were needed for preserving sardines.

The Szeklers were well known in the Moldavia region for growing onions, cabbage, and potatoes. When they left the Bucovina, the Rumanians said, "There will be nobody left from whom to buy cabbage and potatoes."

The Szeklers not only sold their produce for money but bartered it for other produce which they could not grow economically. In particular, they took onions and cabbage to Old Rumania and brought back corn and wheat in exchange.

One of the most important products of Andrásfalva was the colored runner. From the wool of the long-haired Racka sheep the villagers not only provided for their own clothing needs but made products for the Rumanian villages surrounding them. The women manufactured bedspreads, cloth for men's clothing, fur coats and vests, and the attractive embroidered parts of the colorful Szekler national costume. In winter, when there was no other work to do, the men helped with the weaving. The poor who had no sheep "bought the wool at the market of Rădăuti, combed it out, bought dyes, and worked up hemp vests. They also wove runners and earned a pretty penny with them. Then the rich got envious, and quickly took over, had the poor work for them, so they could bring merchandise to the market twice and three times, while the poor could not produce them so fast," said Mrs. Palkó. "Even the rich were weaving. They were envious of the poor."

"These women brought hundredweights of carpets for sale. They all came from Andrásfalva. Everywhere the Rumanians bought these carpet runners. There was no need to take them far. In the neighboring villages lived many rich Rumanians, and with them it was fashionable. When one of their daughters got married, she needed two or three such runners because she used them to protect the walls instead of paper, and they were hung on rods all around the walls. Even the beams were covered and the Andrásfalva people produced them because the Rumanians bought so many of them."

The poor of Andrásfalva tried all sorts of work to carry them through the wintertime and until the next harvest. They were never idle; they were always working at something. "When there was nothing else to do," Andrásfalvi said, "I took my knife, went to the Suceava, and fetched a bundle of rushes. Twelve baskets resulted from it; even when they were only six, it was nice money. Or I took my ax, the fork, cut holes into the ice, and looked out where the fish were sitting. I threw the fork after the fish, for the fish comes close to the hole, and speared it to see which was the best. . . . When the ice melted, the river was closed off; a barrier was laid and the booty brought to the elegant section of Rădăuti where the gentlefolk bought fish. There were also the big woods where one could look for mushrooms."[11]

Carting counted among the most preferred sources of income during the winter. We have noted elsewhere that since the times of serfdom, freighting had played an important role in this area because of the sparsity of the railway network. Most of the carters of the five Bucovina villages came from Andrásfalva. Anyone who had no land but who could get some money together bought a horse and wagon; he never thought of buying farmland.

"We people here would like to buy a small horse, because we are carters," said Andrásfalvi. In Kakasd such work was rare, although it was available at the neighboring state farm. Freighting had indeed become part of the villagers' way of life in old Andrásfalva. Mrs. Palkó's excellent gift for storytelling was especially brilliant when she related details from her own experience. She and her son had done hauling into the Carpathian mountains. The snowstorms and their encounter with wolves she describes so vividly that the listeners share the experience with her. The experiences and sufferings of the Szekler haulers have found an echo in the folktales as well.[12] That they met other ethnic groups and became acquainted with the customs of people who lived far away from them is due, above all, to the hauling trade.

We have already mentioned that many Szeklers took their horses and wagons with them for summer labor; after the beet harvest they hauled the sugar beets back to the factory or performed similar tasks. Most of the Szekler haulers had contracts for hauling with the factories.

They worked with the Ruthenian woodsmen and haulers and transported timber to the timberyards:

> With us the freight was this way: it was not economic for me to stay at home to mow or hack, for by hauling we made so much money; after three days I got more money than I would have made if I had worked on daily labor all summer long. Later we made hauls of over one hundred kilometers [sixty miles]. We transported timber into the interior of the country. There was also a spirit factory; we took the spirit from the refinery and brought it to the refinery in Rădăuti. In one day we made 500 to 600 leu, if we stepped on it. The haulers felled the trees in the forests and cut them up. When they had 3,000 or 4,000 cubic meters, the haulers came and loaded the timber on our wagon, and we secured it. We went

down and unloaded and went back again. We made daily round trips five or six times.

Freighting became such good business that the carters in time became independent businessmen and hauled their own merchandise to market. When our storyteller, Mrs. Palkó, was widowed, she made regular freight runs. As long as the children were small she went by herself. Later she took the two oldest sons with her:

> I, too, made hauls. I collected towels, bedspreads, and bed linens and went to sell them. At home I bought them cheap, then I sold them in the Carpathian mountains. I also took onions, cabbages, cucumbers, and fruit with me. I went to Putna. There were big factories. There we sold our merchandise and bought wood. Then I bartered onions for wood. We got an amazing amount of wood. When I had loaded, I started back home. Another time we fetched boards; in one autumn I fetched fourteen loads of boards. Once I took six onions for wood. We also brought dried fruit.

Because of their work the Szeklers visited distant regions—Transylvania, Rumania, Galicia, even Russia. Necessity sharpened their skills; there was no work which they would not accept, and everyone tried, according to his own skill, to become "lucky."

The varied activities of the Szeklers also showed how the different ethnic groups worked together. The Rumanians bartered their surplus corn and wheat for the Szeklers' vegetables and woven goods; the Szeklers, in exchange for freighting for Ruthenians, were able to secure dairy products and fruit from the Lipovanis.[13]

The relationships of the Szeklers with people of other nationalities were of two types: one was that with Andrásfalva inhabitants of different nationalities; the other was that which came about through work outside the village. Relationships within the village were for the most part good, for the other small ethnic groups were, like the Szeklers, foreigners who had come to the Bucovina and had no special privileges. Mutual understanding was the first condition for peaceful coexistence. Although the joining of the Bucovina to Rumania after the dissolution of the Austro-Hungarian monarchy did not remain without consequences for these relationships, in general friendship among the Bucovina inhabitants was not influenced one way or the other.

Living in Andrásfalva with the Szeklers were not only Rumanians but Poles and Germans. That the Szeklers were numerically the strongest is best shown by the frequent marriages among themselves. As can be seen in names, many people from other ethnic groups were absorbed by the Szeklers.

It was easiest for the Szeklers to form family links with Germans, who were closest to them culturally. In Kakasd today we find Szekler families whose names reveal German antecedants (Rózsa-Rancz, Gábori-Gruber). But the Szeklers also accepted the native Rumanians into their families. The following song clearly shows that they felt deeply the difference between the Szeklers of the Moldavia region and those from the Bucovina:

> Hey, Moldavia is a land
> That makes a Walach of the Hungarian.
> Bucovina is a land
> That makes a Hungarian even of a Walach.[14]

We hear of marriages with Poles,[15] and in these mixed families, too, there is complete harmony. As for the Rumanians, the Szeklers lived peacefully with those both within and around Andrásfalva. Unanimously they related that they never had any difficulties with the Rumanians of the Bucovina, only with those of the old Kingdom of Rumania.

"We were sisters and brothers," said Mrs. Szakács. "They were not the same kind of people like those from the Kingdom of Rumania. They had round, rosy faces, the Bucovinians. They liked the Hungarians, wept when we had to leave. Those from the kingdom are dark-skinned like Italians, and they talk different, too." Mrs. Palkó often relates how hospitable and friendly the Rumanians were when a snowstorm forced her to seek shelter with horse and wagon with a Bucovina–Rumanian family. She also told of other nationalities with which she came into contact through her work or through barter. Each nationality respected the customs of the other. The Szeklers came to know the Lipovanis, for example, as itinerant vegetable and fruit vendors.

"Vegetables came in; they [the Lipovanis] went with apples, cherries, and plums. At every street corner they cried out, '*Hai la mere.*' [Buy apples!]. They also took up farm labor."[16] The Ruthenians "lived in the mountains; they were sheep and goat farmers; they made cheese; they bartered milk, brought cream, milk, and cheese—that's what they lived off. They burnt peat for coal; many worked in the sawmills and in the timberyards."[17]

The different folk costumes were also described. Dénes Sebestyén related that on Fridays, at the market in Rădăuti, they met all sorts of ethnic groups from the neighboring villages; they could distinguish the groups by their national costumes:

> The Hungarian: white stockings with black or red tassels, low cut boots, smooth furs or, in summer, cloth coats, wide linen trousers. The Walach: shirts so long that they came down over their knees; their stockings were just white, but they had so many folds that they could not wear boots over them. Their sandals were made of leather strips. They wore their hair long. The Ukranians had long kilts, like the Rumanians, but their foot coverings were red and their fur coats were embroidered with other flowers. The Germans: long trousers and fine shoes. Then we knew immediately with whom we were talking. . . .
>
> The Lipovanis wore beards which came down to their breasts and a flannel shirt; the shirt was of a different color red and reached down to their shoes, hung over them; they wore half-high boots; the pants were of black velvet, of cloth, and the coat was quilted. . . .[18]

This accurate observation of national costumes proves the Szeklers' keen interest in other people's customs. In describing these costumes the Szeklers stressed, above all, how they differed from their own. The reason for this can be found in the Szeklers' constant preoccupation with their own tradition. Their aim in comparing their own and other peoples' customs and usages is to stress their own characteristics.

Economic relations and collaboration among the many ethnic groups in the Bucovina contributed not only to mutual understanding and recognition, but to intercultural relationships. Belényesy points out quite graphically how one could gauge the shift of political power in those regions where state power had changed in the course of time by the changed relationships within the power structure during the different stages of cultural development. Thus two important influences stand out within the culture of the Szeklers. During the time of the Austro-Hungarian monarchy, the neighboring Germans who were in contact with the Szeklers imparted to them the provincial bourgeois culture of the civil service class. After World War I, however, beginning with the 'twenties, the Szeklers were increasingly influenced by the Rumanians. But the Szeklers made a distinction between the Rumanian civil servants and the inhabitants of the friendly neighboring Rumanian villages; the Rumanian civil servants, as far as the Szeklers were concerned, were a different people.[19]

Having discussed the economic conditions of the people of András-falva, we will now examine their social development.

After the freeing of the serfs, the disintegration of society in András-falva went through the same stages as it did in the villages of Central Hungary: the difference in material possessions resulted in class distinctions among the peasantry. But in Andrásfalva, this disintegration was tempered by special circumstances. The reason is to be found in the Szeklers' conscious upholding of their tradition of freedom and in the fact that in a multi-ethnic country they formed a strong ethnic island. On the other hand, the rapid social division according to property was retarded by the fact that the greater farm properties were often split up in consequence of the population increase, whereas the owners of smaller farms could sometimes recover by turning to different sources of income (hauling, vegetable gardening). The owners of medium-sized farms and the families of the big farmers went out for seasonal labor, did freighting, and sold colored carpets just as the poor. In order to increase their fortunes, the well-to-do farmers took the path that the poorest had to take in order to keep their self-respect. We may well say that there was no really visible difference between the well-to-do farmers, the farmers with eight acres, the haulers and traders, and the day laborers. This too had its roots in the fact that, historically, the Szeklers were a closely-knit group, on both the clan level and the kinship level.

This unity, or clannishness, in the Bucovina turned its face outward. In both words and deeds were stressed the firm, unmovable brotherhood of the Szeklers and the conservation of all ethnic distinctions. The Szeklers' behavior is characterized by the continuation of their old national traditions and the preservation of knowledge about their privileges. Both these traits are evidence of a certain nationalism. From the words of our informant we can see that this unity was consciously stressed:

> The Szeklers clung together. Even if they quarreled among themselves one always stood up for the other. Our tribe is united. . . . Our people are so closely knit together that no one would abandon another. When he sees a man from the Bucovina quarreling with a Szekler, he will kill the stranger.
>
> The Szeklers clung together; even if one of them would have killed my father, we still would be united. At the time of the Austrian monarchy they told us: "You are so clannish, you don't want to know any other people but Szeklers."

A separate study of the Szekler kinships would be well justified. The emigrant Szeklers in Bucovina reactivated, in their isolation, their institution of the sibs. The strong ties of kinship preserved the sib system intact, as the words of our informants prove. Mátyás Mátyás, for example, said, "The Szekler people observed their kinship, not only with the first grandchild, the second, but also the one of the seventh generation. When one would fall sick, a relative went to him to help; whether he would be repaid did not matter. We helped each other through common work; we hauled fertilizer, worked the fields, so strong was our unity."

Family relationships were always strong. Helping out on the farms was the custom among neighbors as well as relatives. They were rewarded with dinner or a drink after work, and there was dancing for the girls. There were seldom differences in this regard between poor and rich relatives; both could be invited for the slaughtering of the pigs or for a wedding feast. "The relative was invited for the wedding no matter how poor he was; or the godfather, if he was a good worker, was respected and never looked down upon."

In Kakasd today kinship is still highly cultivated, even when a part of the family group has settled elsewhere. As long as it was possible, the Szeklers went as far as Rumania and Yugoslavia to see their relatives. Even today a family is able to maintain relations with 180 to 200 members of the sib.[20] János Mátyás related that his father and his three brothers had quarreled bitterly over a broken-down, ramshackle house, and as a result did not speak to each other for seven years:

> They fetched their water from the same well, but they did not speak to each other. Once my father heard that there was a brawl in the tavern. He heard the voice of his brother. My father was a carpenter and was just covering a roof with shingles. He covered the uppermost row. He thought that they might club his brother, so he threw away his ax and jumped down. He landed on his feet and ran as fast as he could. "Who is harming my brother? I shall beat him to a pulp!" "Well, dear brother, you did this for my sake?" They shook hands, asked forgiveness, drank three times twenty-four hours long and ate together; since then there was no quarrel between them.

Thus relatives helped each other out, mostly when one or the other was badly off, when he had not inherited anything or had mismanaged his property. On the other hand, conflicting material interests also separated relatives; kinship did not mean material security in every case.

The Szeklers' unity splits over the most delicate topic, marriage between rich and poor. The example of András Jordáki is typical. His case shows that although a poor boy may occasionally marry a rich girl, it seldom turns out well:

> When someone had fallen in love with a farmer's daughter, they gave her to him. But he did not want such a one, because, if he had been embarrassed in the house, they always said: "You nothing, you beggar!" For seven years I had served a farmer. He had four daughters. For nothing all those riches; I did not like them, none of them was good-looking. They wanted to unload one on me. I didn't want to say anything against her, I was only eighteen years old. On some occasion the mother of the girl was asked: "Well, are they already betrothed?" "The pearl is not for the pig." She was not even at home yet when I knew about it. I married a poor girl.

Even when they did not let the hired man feel his low position, as soon as the subject of marriage was broached, the situation changed.

"If he did not belong to a sib that was as respected as theirs, they did not give the girl to him, under no circumstances; they would rather have seen her dead," said Mrs. Juhász. "They were all cutthroats, but by belonging to powerful families they were all elevated."

This is where the traditional Szekler "bride rape" had its origin. Because of the great economic differences, the parents' permission could only be obtained by force, so the boy, with the girl's consent, kidnapped her. After a week the young people returned, and the family had no choice but to prepare the wedding. Elopement also occurred in poor families, usually with the knowledge and consent of the parents. There was a different reason for elopement in this situation: a girl who had covered herself with shame was only entitled to a small dinner party within the family circle and thus the bride's parents were saved the cost of the otherwise obligatory wedding feast.[21]

In the long run, material interests weighed more heavily than kinship considerations: this was stressed above all by the poor Szeklers.

"Well, the poor man hung back, he did not have such distinguished clothing, and in many cases he was rebuked when he tried to get a word in edgewise: 'You beggar!' That was the worst expression. Maybe he had more brains, but the rich man had more rank. Just as with the landlords who had rank, there were people who said what others wanted to hear." It is true "that they were together at the dances, but the poor went with the poor, and the rich went with the rich. Whoever is well to do thinks himself to be something special and the poor man humbles himself knowing that he is poor. It is the same the world over."

In Andrásfalva the poor population inhabited a separate quarter of the village, living on homesteads which had been divided from the land of the judge for that purpose. Here the day laborers lived, in huts which they had erected on parcels of land two hundred to six hundred square meters in area. This part of the village emptied every spring. Since this neighborhood was on the edge of the village nearest the Rumanian village of Frătăuti, it was at one time named Border Street, and later Rose Street, but everyone called it by the nicknames of Hucsény and Lükütyest. Here, near one another, lived three of our narrators—Mrs. Palkó, György Andrásfalvi, and Márton László. The best storytellers lived in this quarter. The role that the rich had destined for the poor is revealed in a satirical remark in Márton László's ritual *Book of the Dead*, which we shall discuss later: "When are the poor from Rose Street respected most? When hacking diligently, when collecting potatoes, when electing a judge; and when this is over they say, 'Go jump in the lake! Kiss my —!'"

This street of the poor, which connected Andrásfalva and Frătăuti, had seven crossroads. "The big farmers and the medium-sized farmers never took this street." Those who lived there rarely advanced to the level of the well-to-do farmers: "Here live only poor people." In general one spoke of this part of the village only in terms of "poor quarters," and those who lived there were "those from the poor quarters." The poor were badly educated; many were illiterate, and conditions made school attendance difficult.

In the eyes of our Kakasd informants, social conditions of Andrásfalva were shot through with contradictions which increased as capitalism developed. The increase in farm laborers and seasonal and migrant workers was accompanied by an increase in social ills; families were looking for a more secure life.

# 3

# Resettlement Procedures
# (1883-1941)

THE TREMENDOUS INCREASE IN THE BUCOVINA SZEKLER POPULATION led to a gradual carving up of the land; and the number of those whom the land could no longer maintain kept growing. Seasonal and day laborers possessed no more than the houses they lived in and perhaps a few square meters of land. Because of the constant fluctuations of landed property, not even this situation was permanent. The land changed hands from time to time, as a result of the success or failure of various agricultural enterprises.[1] As we have seen, the Szeklers' livelihood was not based on the soil alone. They had adapted to the cultivation of root and other vegetables for marketing, which meant that they concentrated not only on growing but on transporting these products. Since many of the well-to-do people gained material advantages by skillful investments and became rich through good crops, thus advancing socially, the landless Szeklers had no means of bettering themselves. They worked all summer with their families in the Moldavia region, and in winter, to make a living, they worked at lumbering. The need for land was constantly increasing, and within the narrow confines of Andrásfalva not even those who were able to pay a high price could buy arable land. The only way out was resettlement.

A succession of drought years beginning in 1864 and the resulting famine and cholera epidemics contributed to the success of the Hungarian government's resettlement action in 1883. The regions which became arable after the lower part of the Danube had been regulated became government property, and a movement began for the resettlement of the Bucovina Szeklers. A commission was set up to win one thousand one Szekler villagers for resettlement, but more than two thousand volunteered immediately. During the period from 1883 to 1888 they were settled near Pancsova in Hertelendyfalva and Sándoregyháza, and later in the region of Balvanistie on the lower Danube (the place was called Székelykeve after the castle Keve). Altogether four thousand Szeklers settled within three communities.[2]

But there were hardships ahead of the new settlers. Although they transformed into arable land a wilderness of marshland overgrown with bullrushes and eventually succeeded in erecting villages on the bare ground, this work, which had taken many years, was destroyed by the innundations of the Danube floods.[3]

For many this meant bitter disillusionment; in the face of overwhelming difficulties, their only recourse was to return to Andrásfalva. Many families had lost everything in the flood; they returned without a penny and had to live on what neighbors and relatives gave them. The case of the Zaicz family, who tried to tempt fortune, was typical. It not only reveals the character of the proceedings, but it shows the way of life of the Andrásfalva poor in a new light. György Andrásfalvi narrated the moving of his grandfather, the famous storyteller József Zaicz, who was the father of our narrator Mrs. Palkó:

> The father of my father worked a half acre of land, and he had three children. In winter he did not have work; he went over the Rumanian border. During the night he smuggled tobacco and sold it in the well-to-do Rumanian villages for victuals. He said, "Woman, I can't make out any more. I shall volunteer for labor on the Russian railroads." That was under the Czar before 1914. My grandfather had just recently got married. Then he went to Russia, to the railroad. He made good money, bought two horses, and did hauling; with this he made his living. When he thought he had made enough for a living, land was parceled out in the neighborhood of Kubin. He brought news of this. He and many of his comrades listed their names in order to go home [i.e., resettle in Hungary]. They went by train or with their wagons. Since he had sold his horse, he took the train. He had sold his land and his house to a German. About spring the surveyors came and each head of family was supposed to see where he was getting land. He received eight acres of land, eight covers woven of rushes, and sixteen stakes; from

this he was to build a house and cover it with the rush covers. Then they marked: here is the community, here is the road. He put the sixteen stakes together and covered them, but so that they dug deep into the ground; then they took turf and covered them, so it was warm inside. For a tripod they took a three-branched stick, wound wire all around, then hung the kettle upon it to cook. The families of Györfi, Rancz, and Zaicz went together. They were relatives, godfathers. They asked for it so the kinship could be maintained, a neighborhood could be maintained, and so they were given parcels of land.

When they were settled, a landlord appeared at the hut: "If you like we shall provide a master, or will you build it yourself?" My grandfather took over the ground, but not the framework. Everything was built from earth and clay. After two years everybody was in his house. When they received the parcels of land, everybody worked together; all put their backs to the work. The state contributed wheelbarrows, spades, axes, and saws. They built the houses; then the state gave them wood, so they got the beams up; then the state gave them bricks and they got houses covered with bricks. One got eight acres, the other nine—land was parceled out according to the family. He who had come with his own wagon did not get any, but he who had not brought one was given a wagon, horse, and whip by the state. It also gave them seeds for wheat and other things. "Why did you go back to a garden of 600 square meters?" I asked my grandfather. He said, "See, my boy, we got all sorts of things there, and I also took up a scythe. Seven hats I bought for my seven sons, just for a keepsake, for everything grew well, so high that you could have hidden in it. The wheat was so high it would have reached the sky. We needed only a sack and could have reached God's hand. Well, the state did not wait for the two, three years until we had found a firm foothold. I went bankrupt and Grandmother had to go and beg with little János. Everything they took away to pay our debts. I still would have tried again," he said, "in spite of the high taxes and the repayment burdens, but two years later the Danube flooded. The Serbs had dynamited the dam below Kubin, and we nearly drowned. We burnt torches to beat back the waters of the Danube. We did drive back the waters of the Danube, but it was years before everything dried. Giant weeds grew there so we could not build a house. I was so bitter, I thought to myself: I toiled and suffered enough in the Bucovina; I go, I pull myself together, on the Suceava I live better." There he became a fisherman; then he worked as a cook, went to work for the Count.

In spite of this, resettlement progressed. From 1888 until the outbreak of World War I in 1914 various groups tried their luck.[4] They moved for the most part to Transylvania, settling at Déva, Marosludas, Csernakeresztúr, and elsewhere. Many returned—there was constant coming and going. The biggest and most viable settlement was on a strip of land belonging to the city of Déva. Here 248 people settled in 1888[5] and many smaller groups between 1892 and 1910. The favorable conditions, the nearness of the city, the labor possibilities in the salt mines and in the industrial plants increased the education of the Andrásfalvers who settled there; very soon began the process of transformation into a middle class. According to statistics of the year 1939, 278 families in Déva were farmers while 132 worked in industry.[6] Beginning in 1906, many left to seek their fortunes in Canada. Although some returned, many Andrásfalva families still have relatives in America. In Canada the Bucovina Szeklers joined three older Hungarian settlements.[7]

The unity so characteristic of the Szeklers was not impaired by emigration. Those who remained in the Bucovina maintained their connections with their relatives. The new settlers continued their old way of life in the new environment, just as they had done before in the Bucovina. One proof of this is that Márton László copied for those who emigrated his *Book of the Dead*, which was indispensable for the traditional wake, the characteristic ritual of the Szeklers. We know from his son that he made ten copies for the inhabitants of Déva, two for those of Marosludas, and one each for the inhabitants of Csernakeresztúr and Székelykeve.

In the meantime the situation of the Szeklers who had remained behind in the Bucovina went from bad to worse. The factories which slowly developed could not provide enough work for those without land, and while the farmers' wealth continued to increase, the situation of the poor became more and more hopeless. To the social crisis was added political tension: the nationalities which had lived together peacefully were now roused against one another.[8] It is not surprising that the Bucovina Szeklers' resettlement in Hungary in 1941 met little resistance. Nevertheless, it was not easy for the Szeklers to leave the soil where father and grandfather had been born. Although the procedure instituted by the Hungarian government was less pleasant for those who were better off,[9] the poor were glad to move; they hoped that they would at last get land. The resettlement action could therefore be carried out quickly. The inhabitants of the five Hungarian villages in the Bucovina were settled in the Bácska, in the midst of peoples of many nationalities. This unusually fertile territory, allotted to Yugoslavia after World War I, had been partitioned to Hungary by Nazi Germany on the eve of World War II. In twenty-eight villages, altogether 2,828 families, consisting of 13,198 persons, were settled. The Andrásfalvers founded seven townships around Topolya.[10] Since every settler received, over and above his holdings in the Bucovina, five acres of land and an additional acre for every member of his family, the process of equalization of the social differences so acute in the Bucovina had a headstart. The former large landholder with a small family received less land than the small farmer with many children. Even though the social distinctions were blurred with respect to material things, however, the attitudes of the well-to-do and the poor toward one another were sharpened—a fact which M. Belényesy notes. The word of those who had been well off in the Bucovina carried more weight than that of those who had just received land; the formerly well-to-do Szeklers chose the best houses and distributed them among themselves, pushing the poorer family members into the background.[11] The unity of the sib, which had been strengthened in the Bucovina by the multi-ethnic environment, started to dissolve. The newly formed social conditions were not strong enough, however, to form the basis for a new societal hierarchy. When the war in 1944 forced the evacuation of the Bácska, the differences among the refugees disappeared; they formed new groups along kinship lines and wished to settle according to these new groupings.

The four years of settlement in the Bácska were too brief to permit the Szeklers to adapt to new living conditions, and when they looked back to it, this time meant little to them. But even today they stressed that they were not happy to be settled in a region inhabited by another nationality, and for the return of which the Serbians clamored. They would have preferred to be settled—as was the Hungarian government's original plan—somewhere deep in the center of Hungary.[12] György Andrásfalvi remarks on this point:

> The big lords did not want us to have a good place. The Szeklers increased like rabbits. Thirteen and fourteen persons there were in a family. Give them room in the Fejér county;[13] they need room to grow in. The lords looked at each other and said, "That is not possible." To the priest they said, "Well, holy father, well, our governor[14] cannot get along with his ministers, the sainted father should pity the country people and give them land from the property of the parish." But he did not have any pity on us either. The ministry should have been ashamed, they said, and the Church should set a good example. Every Szekler has money. They make

shingles, they make bricks from clay, they can work wood, are masons; they should be given room and materials. Not eight to ten years pass and they have a village. One does not need to send them among minorities, on the bear's back. The Bácska was a beautiful place, but full of hostilities. Well, then, it happened: the bear shook himself and shook us all loose.

On October 8, 1944, the Bácska became a battle field, and the Szeklers on two hours notice fled their villages, taking only what they could hastily pack. The Hungarian villagers were full of sympathy toward the homeless villagers, who took refuge for a while in their stables or barns, and here and there were given a plate of hot soup or a few potatoes. Mrs. Sebestyén told how the refugees were addressed on the highway:

> "Where do you go, brother?"
> "Towards ruin!"
> "Where is this?"
> "Where we are going."

Like their ancestors 160 years ago before in the Moldavia region, the Szeklers wandered aimlessly along the river Tisza as far as Szeged, traveled from there to the Duna, crossed the Duna, and wandered through the county of Zala until finally, in 1946-47, they settled in what is now their home.

# 4

# The Settlers of Kakasd

THE INTERNATIONAL AGREEMENTS AFTER THE WORLD WAR II CON-cerning the exchange of populations and the soil reform laws had far-reaching consequences in Hungary. The apportioning of the great landholdings among Hungarian peasants who previously had possessed either no land or very little, together with the population exchange, led to ethnic changes of major dimensions. In the course of these events, the Szeklers were definitely settled during 1946-47 in thirty-eight villages in the counties of Tolna and Baranya, an area formerly known as *die Schwäbische Türkei* (Swabian Turkey).[1] The great majority of the German (Swabian) colonists, who had been there since the early eighteenth century, had been moved to Germany because of their collaboration with the Nazis. The Szekler's traditional, legendary sense of unity and the strength of kinship once again came to the fore. Although it meant swapping their settlement plots, the clans succeeded in staying together, and the settlers from the Bucovina tried to reunite with groups of Szeklers that had split off from them in the past. When news of the settlement in Transdanubian lands leaked out, even the Szeklers from Transylvania and the lower Danube tried to take part in it. One group which settled in the new territory was the kin of the Andrásfalvers who had settled in Déva. Despite the renewed contact between these relatives, it was unavoidable that the forty to fifty years' separation cause a certain estrangement. The Andrásfalvers did not take part in the community projects of the settlers from Déva. The groups kept apart, and there was little contact even among siblings. Those from Déva, who well remembered the seasonal labor in the Moldavia region which caused them to leave Andrásfalva, contended that the "big clans" even today form a common front against them, the "poor folks" of the past. The Andrásfalvers, on the other hand, prentended that the Déva group looked down their noses at them and thought themselves better educated.

After settlement in Transdanubian lands the old social and economic differences once again became acute. The Kakasd people said (around 1955): "The richest families were settled in Lengyel, in Kakasd there are the most respected Catholics, in Hidas the reformed (Calvinist) families, whereas the smaller families have found homes in Tabód, Mucsfa, and Závod."[2] But even the differences within the separate clans were very clear. The reputation of those who were the big farmers in the Bucovina prevailed to this day to a certain extent, even though the foundation for their standing no longer existed. Those who had been able to take along to the Bácska their threshing machines and corn mills had had to leave them behind in 1941, and now had to be content with the same as everyone else: two acres of land plus an additional acre for every member of the family. Thus it came about that the married children of formerly wealthy farmers had become small farmers, while others who formerly possessed no land now owned 15 to 20 acres because of their large families.

The social change is characterized by a song sung, according to Mrs. Erzsébet Molnár, by the poor people during the settlement of Kakasd:

> Thanks to God, the world has turned;
> From poor people, big farmers have grown.[3]

But the esteem founded on the old economic system had been kept alive until the present. This was the bitterest complaint of the young, energetic, and ambitious former farm hands. The narrator György Andrásfalvi said, "Even today there are people who think they are big because they were big in the Bucovina."

Mrs. Juhász said, "Even today they look down their noses; there are a few who are wealthy here, who have received land. But it does not help them to be wealthy—the former rich ones still look down upon those who at home were the last. In the neighborhood, there is a man who has a beautiful horse, because he was very diligent, and at home he did not inherit anything, he did not have anything, but today they look down upon him." András Jordáki, from Déva, whose son was the founder of the Cooperative for Agricultural Production, complained, "What kind of people are these? My son is not good enough to become a judge, for they say: 'Who was your father, you vagabond?' "

Even though the distribution of land in Kakasd was intended to create equal opportunities for the farmers, some of the formerly well-to-do farmers succeeded in gaining for themselves special advantages—better fields, better housing. Deep rifts were visible in the relationship between the rich and the poor members of the respected families during the settlement process, even though on the whole the spiritual links remained. Some sisters and brothers had still not overcome the anger caused by inequities and injustices during the settlement. The respected farmers who had a voice in the resettlement favored each other rather than their poor relations. György Andrásfalvi lamented this in his own family. His wife Erzsi came from the Mátyás family, who were very wealthy and greatly respected in the Bucovina. Erzsi, the youngest daughter, who married late because of an eye ailment, became the wife of the poor Andrásfalvi, who also had a deformity. During the settlement process the Mátyás family, because of their former economic power, were allotted some of the better fields and houses. Erzsi Mátyás, however, had lost standing when she married and moved to the poor part of Andrásfalva, and for this reason, she and her husband did not get one of the better places in Kakasd. "A man who had a big farm at home, plays a big part here, too. The families of Fábián, Csakír, and Sebestyén closed ranks, and the poor, the little ones, were shouldered out. . . . I was here at the same time with them, but I was less than they. When we arrived only the relatives, the in-laws, and the godfathers were on the list. . . . I am related to half of Andrásfalva, but I am living like a swineherder. . . ."

Yet with all this, the influence based on old reputations was on the wane. The difference between those who formerly were wealthy and those who were no longer poor was diminishing, and for several reasons. The most important may be the confrontation with strange, new surroundings, which forced the settlers to assume, for the sake of appearances, an attitude of unity. In the settlements of the Transdanubian area the researcher was immediately struck by the specific features of the Szeklers culture, by the adherence to tradition and the backwardness compared to the Hungarian ethnic groups surrounding them. This striking backwardness was especially strong in the older generation who had lived in Andrásfalva; even in the Bucovina they were among the most backward of the five villages, and of all those who were resettled, the

Andrásfalvers had most faithfully retained the old culture characteristics.

The culture of the former Bucovina Szekler settlers represents the interplay of various elements: the historic development of this ethnic group and the influences upon it of the sojourns in the Moldavia region, in the Bucovina, and in the Bácska.

> With them we still find a stage of community life based on blood relationship which is deeply rooted in feudalism. It is a lingering residue of feudalism which can be found not only with our peasantry, but especially with the Szeklers and the small group from the Bucovina. . . . Their cultural profile retains many of the old characteristics which show a strong similarity to the culture of Transylvanian Szeklers. This may be a consequence of the fact that feudalism was to die much later in Transylvania and the lands east of it, than in the countries which made the classical ascent to a capitalistic society.[4]

The characteristic features of Szekler solidarity were particularly evident in the ethnic groups resettled in Transdanubia because, though their language is the same, these groups differed greatly from those of the new environment. The original and the resettled populations in Kakasd belong to different ethnic groups; the Szeklers were aware of the fact that they were considered backward, and for this reason they placed great stress on community spirit—the unity of the Szeklers and the unity of kinship.

Elements of the "Szekler freedom" still lived in the consciousness of the people. The people of Kakasd considered themselves the descendants of the privileged soldier class and were correspondingly haughty. As a result of their contacts with other ethnic groups, their powers of observation were extremely sharp in this regard; as in old Andrásfalva, they compared their own qualities with those of other peoples and took advantage of the comparison to stress their own unique traits. All informants said such things as "Our people don't do things like that." The individual was a spokesman for the entire group. This outspoken spirit of unity led, even in Kakasd to a reserved attitude toward the other inhabitants, and contributed to the conscious preservation of folk traditions and historic memories, as well as to conscious care of the Szekler language. This extremely colorful dialect—which is also spoken today by the people in the Csík—may be considered the most archaic Hungarian dialect. In the view of our informants, the Szekler language is an expression of the Szekler freedom. They related how strangely they were impressed by the language of the Hungarian lords in the Bácska, and how much they felt the servility in the language of Hungarian politeness: "The Szeklers do not beg; when they have a right to it they say, 'Give it to us.'" "This is how we are," the eighty-year-old Ferenc Farkas said. "Our people do not like the command. We do not say, 'Please.' That's how the Szeklers are. Democracy is innate with them; they dislike courtesy before a lord." Another informant, Mátyás Mátyás, said, "We have retained the simple speech. We cannot talk fancy as the Hungarians. We speak a little like the old writings, as it is in the books."

The feeling for unity in the Szekler ethnic group is revealed in another context as well. Even the young people who worked in industrial centers outside the village came home to get married; they married only one of their own people.

Knowledge of their common origins plays a great part with the Szeklers. According to tradition, in the "original home" they lived in independent units, and this old Szekler sib had survived in the form of kinship ties. According to Szekler tradition, each family clan once founded a village; they congregated in several groups when they fled Transylvania, and the individual clans were settled in the Bucovina and the Moldavia region. The clans hung together even when they came to Hungary, and even though economic differences led to contrasts within the same families, the feeling of family solidarity was stronger than the temporary economic differences. When the people of Kakasd talked about themselves, they always said, "We belong to this family, they belong to that family. . . ." In Andrásfalva, relatives often were also neighbors; they lived close to one another. In Kakasd, where these neighborly family ties no longer exist, new ties had taken the place of the old ones. Being a neighbor in the Bucovina meant almost as much as being a relative, and through marriage and by becoming god-parents, neighbors actually become relatives. It was the neighbors who were called in first to give aid, to help in the work, or to celebrate family feasts. A dead man was laid to rest not only by the immediate family but by the godfathers and by the neighbors "above" and "below." Neighbors were often in the same economic circumstances, which provided another basis for this close relationship. That the old neighborly connections were still valid is borne out by the fact that the narrator Mrs. Palkó attended the funeral of a woman who had been her neighbor, but did not attend the wake of an old man. Her reason was that "We were not neighbors in Bucovina, and I am ashamed to go."

The source of the Szeklers' awareness of old ties lay in their active preservation of historical traditions. No other Hungarian ethnic group has such a well-established historic consciousness.

This historic sense is derived from three sources: from the old Csík-Szekler tradition; from the conscious and cherished Bucovina tradition springing from this; and from a newer, literary interpretation of history.

The first may be traced to the privileged position held by the Szeklers when they were border guards during the Middle Ages. The educated and the uneducated, the "lord" and the "peasant," for centuries were not distant from each other socially. The rift between them was not as great and irreconcilable as that between the serfs and the nobility of Hungary proper. The Szeklers derived their tradition from the privileged standing of the heroic defenders, the border guards, of the fatherland. The past of independent Transylvania showed up in the pride and the consciousness of these late descendants.

Because of their origins in the Csík, the Szeklers feel a close association with Transylvania. Again and again they pointed to the fact that not Hungary but Transylvania was their land of origin, mistakenly believing that Transylvania was an independent country and did not belong to Hungary. In truth Transylvania was an independent duchy only for 150 years, from 1526 on, during the time that Hungary was occupied by the Turks.

The old tradition was not interrupted by emigration but continued to develop along new paths. This is the second source of the Szeklers' historic consciousness—the feeling of being torn away from their moorings, the isolation which strengthened the ethnic consciousness. It was also significant that the relationship of the emigrants with the Szeklers of Transylvania was not interrupted. The people from the Bucovina were constantly on the move and visited many, many times the villages of the Szeklers in Transylvania. During these visits they exhibited their vivid interest in historical matters, always asking who their forebears were, and from whom they were descended. And when they succeeded in discovering a "relationship"—which generally consisted only in a similarity of names or a common memory of the peril of Mádéfalva—they reported to their children at home, "We have our origins in such and such a village." Everyone who lived in the Szekler villages was considered a relative. There was scarcely a family in Andrásfalva which could not trace their descent "with certainty." Whenever they carted the Andrásfalvers tried to establish connections in the land of the Szeklers and to discover their origins. Said Mátyás Mátyás,

It was from my uncle that I heard what kind of Mátyás we are.
I did freighting in Madaras, Karcfalva, and Rákos. There they
showed me a house, where my great-grandfather had lived. They
were highborn Szeklers . . . as far as I know we came from
Karcfalva. In 1936 I carried freight there. There I sold my horses.
At that time the house of my great-grandfather was an official
residence. It was covered with woven thatch and about eight
centimeters of moss was growing on it. The neighbors still knew
it this way, that István Mátyás had lived there.

The third source, the literary interpretation of history, has now become
folk tradition. There was an independent Hungarian church in every
village in the Bucovina, even though Rumanian had been the language
of instruction in the schools there since 1920. On the Hungarian grade-
school level, the priests, teachers, and church singers played the greatest
role. The Presbyterian and Catholic authorities, through the parochial
schools, tried to make the connection with the Hungarians of Transylvania ever closer.[5] Within and outside school, particularly before World
War I, the teachers would relate stories about Hungarian and Transylvanian history:

Teacher János Molnár read to us at least twice a week from
Hungarian history: where we come from, who we were. He alone
taught four classes. Thus I know how Kossuth started. This children do not know any longer, for the Rumanians wanted for them
not to learn this. This János Molnár was the son of my great-grandfather; he went to school in Pest.[6]

The teachers, priests, and lay church singers who came from the ranks
of the settlers not only taught Hungarian history in school but ministered
to the villagers' inexhaustible thirst for learning. They lent to the villagers historical novels, short stories, and textbooks, especially after 1920
when Hungarian history was dropped in the schools. The men, in particular, were interested in history, and many sent to Hungary and Transylvania for books whose titles they had copied from the jackets of cheap
series. As a result, Hungarian or Transylvanian nationalistic traditions
penetrated the Szekler consciousness, for the literary output had purposely fostered their pride.

By means of tradition and of historical reading matter, a knowledge
of history was transmitted to those in the Bucovina. Information from
both these sources had now passed into popular tradition, slowly taking
on the characteristics of the epic style of folk prose and becoming legends.
It was no longer passive knowledge but a narrative fabric that played a

role in the community and had a function. But this role was different from the roles of other narrative genres. Discussion of history, of the deeds of one's forefathers, was not entertainment but a recollection of credible events. Older and reputable men discussed history when they got together in winter for a drink and talk—quite often for the education of the younger men and their own enjoyment. Such conversations often turned to current political topics and their relationship to historical events. Thus the men of Kakasd who were generally respected—not necessarily the storytellers—would talk, one after another, about Hungarian history. Each of them related the details in the light of his own opinion. These narratives did not have a specific form, nor was the delivery standardized— they were considered as adult male entertainment. Everyone could take part, making additions or corrections to the part of the history he himself knew. In this respect, such narration is similar to that of the belief legends, though it differs somewhat in its makeup (see Chapter 7).

All the peculiarities that characterized the ethnic group settled in Transdanubia contributed to the conservation of oral folklore. Even though the old folk costume, for example, had lost much of its glamor owing to a shortage of materials, the Kakasd Szeklers even today attracted attention because of their colorful dress when they met at the markets of the nearby cities of Bátaszék or Szekszárd. One of the traditional festivities was the Nativity Play, which was performed every two or three years. In it several of the actors wore animal masks. Other great rituals were the wake, the New Year's Greeting, and the Feast of Epiphany. The Kakasd settlers' stock of folksongs is exceptionally rich and, in all of Hungary, has preserved the most songs in the old pentameter. The degree to which folk belief, folk religion, and the magic-ritual customs influenced the imagination of the people of Kakasd will be examined more closely later on, since these are intimately connected with the body of the folktales. In the following, however, we shall examine the settling of the Szeklers in Kakasd and their relations with the groups already living there.

About two thirds of the former inhabitants of Andrásfalva—Catholics— were now living in Kakasd. They represented the overwhelming majority—about 80 per cent—of the Kakasd population. The other groups were small by comparison, and it was only natural that the Szeklers should set the tone and play the leading part in the community.

There are three ethnic groups besides the Szeklers in Kakasd: (1) the so-called Swabians who had remained when the majority were moved to Germany; (2) Hungarians from West Slovakia (from the ethnic group of Csallóköz who were settled here); and (3) poor peasants from county Tolna who were given land in the village.

Because of their size, these three groups could not be considered ethnic unities. They were also more civilized, even urbanized, and much better schooled than the Szeklers. The Szeklers' ethnic peculiarities— the clothing, the language, the customs, the feasts, the faith and behavior —were more obvious as a result. This was felt not only by the ethnic groups living around the Szeklers, but by the Szeklers themselves, and they, in fact, deliberately clung to these peculiarities. Adaptation to the new surroundings was just beginning. Their acculturation progressed slowly, and they had difficulty accepting some of the prevailing customs; they consciously hung on to the old. They retained the old type of dress, even though they had to use new materials: they lacked the long-haired Racka sheep; looms were difficult to construct; and the old furriers were dead and gone. They adhered to their old culture self-consciously and viewed the customs of others critically. Since they were in the majority, they did not mind if others viewed them critically, particularly with respect to the Szekler dialect, a dialect so strange to the other groups that they considered it primitive.

That does not mean, however, that the Szeklers did not maintain good relations with the other groups in the village. They had come to know many different neighbors in the Bucovina, and were gradually beginning to strike up friendships in Kakasd. They took part in their mutual customs and exhibited interest in the agriculture, crafts, cooking, and national costumes of the other groups. There was much they found strange, but also much that they adopted.

The Szeklers had become particularly good friends with the Swabians. The memory of their German neighbors in the Bucovina predisposed them to sympathy for this ethnic group. They regarded with compassion the *Volksbund* Germans who were moved to Germany, and felt guilty about occupying their former property. They paralleled their own fate to that of the Germans. This connection was especially strong among the young people: the Swabian girls were invited to dances by Szekler boys, and Szekler boys visited the spinning bees of the Swabian girls. They began to become familiar with the way of life, getting accustomed to tilling the hill country. They borrowed from the Swabians the knitted stocking with the inlaid sole, and learned from them vine culture, which they did not know before.

Making friends with the Hungarians from Slovakia was more difficult, for the Hungarians, largely from the lower middle class, imagined themselves much better educated and did not encourage contact with the "peasants."

We should add, regarding the situation of the Kakasd people today, that while the settlers of Déva founded an agricultural cooperative in 1950, individual farming in Kakasd was maintained until the government forced the inhabitants in 1962 to convert individual farms into cooperative farms. Many people in Kakasd have taken up vegetable gardening, and many hire out as seasonal labor on the state-owned farms in the neighborhood; others for a while tried freighting and hauling lumber and coal. Since the establishment of farm cooperatives, many try to leave the land and seek labor in industrial plants outside the village. Many of the young people of Kakasd are employed in the nearby coal mines of Hidas and Pécs; but many work farther away and come home only once a week. More and more young people now continue their education and acquire special work skills. Those who attend the Szekler boarding school go on to the Szekszárd high school, and generally turn to an intellectual profession.

# PART TWO

# The Tale, the Community, and the Narrators

# 5

# *Survey of the Results in Folktale Research to the Present*

ROM ITS INCEPTION, FOLKTALE RESEARCH HAS HAD A TWO-PRONGED aim: it has been interested, on the one hand, in the nature and origins of oral narration not fixed in writing; and it has been interested in folk culture as expressed in the content and form of the folktale. These two points of view have resulted in two different kinds of research methods. One has sprung essentially from comparative literature and has been established as a new branch of that discipline; the other has developed from the French sociological and the British anthropological schools, which consider folk tradition—to which the folktale belongs—merely as a means, a point of departure, for researching the folk community.

These differing methods and points of view have split the community of scholars into two camps. The Folklore Fellows Association, active since the beginning of this century, investigates international folk narratives through comparative analyses of texts and has achieved indispensable results. Among groups of a different nature are the Russian scholars, whose interests lay for a time in the sociological-historical analysis of folklore. Though individual methods of research are not fully developed, and though these groups start from different points of view, it cannot be denied that both are constantly coming up with new results.[1]

In our opinion these two methods and aims—philological analysis of texts and sociological text interpretation—are not incompatible. Isolating them from one another in fact results in one-sidedness which is an obstacle to the true understanding of the folktale and its place in culture and hinders the continuing healthy development of folktale research, the most highly developed field of folklore. We can hope to advance only if we succeed in uniting the two directions, in putting the textual analyses on the right socio-cultural basis. To realize this goal is no mean task. The foundations of a more perfect method will be recognizable only after many detailed studies, careful observations, and experiments. Today the available material appropriate for scientific research is very limited, and the material collected at Kakasd by no means fulfills this need. However, we kept this aim in mind while working on this study, and should we succeed even in pointing out the necessity for uniting the two methods, our work has not been in vain.

The key questions in folktale study are these: How was the tale shaped, and how does its form originate? The search for answers focuses on the creative person, or, in a given case, the person at hand who passes on the tradition.

Even before folktales were systematically collected, the talents of extraordinary storytellers—servants, nurses, soldiers, etc., who told stories as part of their professional pursuits—were known.[2] Authors of storybooks and editors of literary folktale collections, however, preferred to credit some imaginary storyteller with telling the tales.[3] Although even the first collectors, such as the brothers Grimm, who deemed it necessary to rework the material stylistically, expressed their admiration for the storytellers, it is not rare to find in later folktale collections that the storyteller is mentioned.[4] It should be noted here that Săineănu, one of the pioneers in classifying folktales according to their types, makes a strong plea for the collectors of folktales to gather the material of good storytellers and to describe the qualities of the narrators. His admonition was heeded.[5]

In Hungary, too, the narrator is mentioned early. Kriza, for example, mentions the names of several narrating peasants and artisans.[6] The pioneers of the systematic collection of folk narrative and poetry drew attention to the person of the narrator: "Much depends on whether we have heard a folktale from the lips of an excellent storyteller or an unskilled one. Therefore collectors should try to find outstanding narrators," Greguss wrote.[7] Sándor Pintér characterizes the village storytellers in detail, and lists the names of two whom he met during a feather-stripping bee.[8] These examples, which could be duplicated at will, show that the discovery of the storyteller's role in folk narrative is nothing new.

The representatives of the Finnish school have likewise cited their informants as sources,[9] and, in addition to the German folklorists who concerned themselves with the form and structure of the folktale, other scholars have also noted the individual character that makes itself felt in the form and structure of the folktale.[10] Even Albert Wesselski, who stated that folklore is the corrupted recreation of literature, recognized that it is the individual alone and not the masses who can be creative in transforming literature into folklore.[11]

The Hungarian scholars, who in part are following the positivist German method of comparative philology and in part the Finnish school, recognize the role of the narrator. Béla Vikár states that his folktales are of greater value because he had taken them down from outstanding narrators;[12] Gyula Sebestyén[13] discovered "numerous individual nuances" in the renditions of his storytellers; János Berze Nagy draws evidence from the way in which the storyteller enraptures his audience. In his collection, however, Berze Nagy notes only briefly the individual personalities of his narrators. In several studies he speaks of the qualities of storytellers and accepts the principle of categorization according to the personality of the narrator when outstanding talents are involved.[14] But even in this he goes no farther than other representatives of the Finnish school; he maintains that it is neither worthwhile nor possible to penetrate more deeply the problem of the narrator's personality.

The folklorists mentioned there, therefore, are cognizant of the narrators and of the circumstances in which a story is told, but they do not attribute great importance to them nor consider them factors which touch the essence of the folktale.[15]

Why is it that the majority of folklorists concerned with the folktale have neglected the question of narration, of the creative process of storytelling? The reason must be sought in the development of the discipline itself. The scholars of the philological school were for the most part concerned with finding a system for the classification of the mass of materials accumulated up to the beginning of the twentieth century—a system somewhat similar to that used by botanists in classifying plants[16] —in order to gain access to the bewildering mass of types and motifs and make scientific evaluation possible. The scientific work thus was begun with the establishment of types and motifs. Through this work, new fields were being opened to research and at the same time the old material was constantly being replenished.[17] Necessary as this classification is, it caused research to become more or less formalized and onesided. By the ordering of narrative materials, by the establishment of the different genres, types, and incidents, the researchers abstracted the tales from their natural environment and tried on the basis of dead material, to get to the bottom of the origin of archetypes. As a way out of this formalized research, many folklorists began to search for new ways and methods. In particular Carl Wilhelm von Sydow,[18] one of the founders of the Finnish school, at the beginning of the 'thirties scored the weak points of the Finnish methods. His investigation led him to a vivid, sociological consideration of the folktale. Thus he pointed out, in connection with a critique of Aarne's tale types, that folktales should be investigated only within the framework of their living surroundings. He did not believe in the possibility of reconstructing the "archetype."[19] He thought it necessary, however, to identify the local redaction within a language or ethnic area and to discover the regular rhythm between traditional sequence and variation.[20] From our point of view it is important that he insisted on observation of the folktale-bearing individual as essential for solving the problem of folktale transmission, which was considered by the Finnish school to be a mechanical act. He says, "It is not enough to study folktales only, it is also necessary to make oneself familiar with the use of folktales, their life in tradition, their transmission and spread."[21] He explains in detail that it is necessary to have listened to many narrators of diverse talents in order to determine origin, development, retention, and spread of the folktale, and he insists that the circumstances of the tale transmission must be noted.[22] He stresses the decisive roles of the active and passive bearers of tradition and the importance of outstanding narrators in the preservation of the folktale stock.[23] Taking a stand against the methods of the Folklore Fellows, von Sydow realizes the importance of the sociological approach.[24]

The direction taken first by von Sydow and later by many other researchers brought new life to folktale research. The von Sydow research principles were realized in the start of the collections by the Irish Folklore Commission,[25] in the work of his disciples,[26] and in the short but compact study by Christiansen.[27] Quite independent of this, we find similar conclusions in the various essays by Károly Marót and other Hungarian scholars.[28] Eberhard and Boratav[29] were critical of the Aarne-Thompson system, into which they could not fit Turkish tales. They used their own system and expressed the view that even those who approach the folktale from the philological viewpoint recognize that the folktale has to be understood in its own environment, and that any kind of research has to start with the present.

Three principal factors are equally essential to the existence of the folktale, and their interrelationship forms the core of our own research: (1) tradition, or the communal contribution of past bearers of tradition; (2) the present storytelling community; and (3) the narrator.

Simultaneous interaction of these basic factors is essential for the creation of the folktale.

Research, to a great extent, stresses the communal character of folklore. This concept is valid for both traditional collaboration or past bearers of tradition and the collaboration of the present folk community. Let us first consider the meaning of tradition.

Though the myths of communal creativity or collective authorship of works were quickly exploded, and though it has been proven beyond any doubt that there is no one work which cannot be traced back to a single individual, even though during the course of time many others have added to and continued the work, many researchers still believe that emphasizing individual contributions to folklore would be opposed to the real aim of the discipline—that is, the understanding of the traditional substance of culture.[30]

Every invention in art is individual; the only question to be raised is whether it is possible to localize the first author as an individual in folklore. Can he be called "popular," since the forms of folklore are not individual but form a link in the chain of tradition?[31]

Neither in literature nor in folklore does it make sense to overestimate the "original concept," though we have to take its existence into account.[32] By paying attention to the limited possibilities of folklore, by considering its forms of existence and the variations of a certain theme, we must state carefully the relationship of the individual to the community, and determine what is contributed by tradition and what by the individual. This is the problem which confronts the researcher.

Doubtless the individual is the point of departure, be he a creator of folklore or of literature, or simply the individual who first gave words to a certain story at a certain moment.[33] It is certain that, without his contribution, the text would have been formed differently or would not have been created at all. But it is equally certain that his work was not created in isolation and independent of the community.

A new form does not emerge through the sudden rearrangement of motifs on the basis of a new and original idea, but rather by the gradual addition of scarcely conceivable components by various unknown individuals. In contrast to all those who say that the first individual alone, the one who conceived the material, should be designated as the author, and that all others should be designated only as passive bearers and preservers of tradition (Wesselski), we must state that there is no essential difference.

When we contemplate the series of traditions which pass on the theme from mouth to mouth, we have to agree with the argument of Sharp, who sketches the passage of transmission of a work by a chain of individuals as follows: "The authorship belongs equally to all those who have taken part in the transmission. Thus the authorship, originally individual, has become communal. The individual has vanished, and the community has slipped into his shoes. . . ."[34]

The traditional folktale, which enters the life of a community at a given moment, thus acts as a model. It does not have an author; the folk community—or, as Anikin calls it, the chain of "collective authorship"—has produced it.[35] Many texts have been lost in the course of transmission, but what has survived has become increasingly richer and more beautiful.[36]

Thus, tradition originated through the chain of individual contributions which, at the very moment when the folktale is being narrated, comprise the substance as well as the immediate situation of a given community. Tradition which has become latent continues to live and work as the property of a community and determines the creator and the audience in the present moment.[37] Gorki speaks several times of this collective substance when he mentions that every creation of a great artist is at the same time the creation of the people, for in it the entire culture of a people has resonance. Some Russian authors stressed the significance of tradition with the outstanding storytellers.[38]

The traditional material fetters the creative individual.[39] A group's common traditional stock of oral literature—which distinguishes it from other groups—usually manifests itself not in the creations but in communal knowledge.[40] The average person knows the communal stock of folktales, the tale body; he may be able to narrate but he is not accustomed to doing so, and he is not able to perform fluently in public. The narrators choose from this communal and well-known material the parts they want to narrate and which the audience likes to hear over and over again, and which as a result become more and more polished. These narrators, always unusually gifted,[41] stand at the center of our study, and with them rests the actual fate of the folktale. It is upon their shoulders that the narration in the community devolves.

Wisser[42] and other researchers distinguish between regions which are "rich in folktales" and those which are "poor in folktales." Experience has shown that folktales flower where there have been, until recently, good storytellers, or where good ones are still about.[43] Clearly, social circumstances exert an influence on the folktale, but this in itself is not decisive. Where there is no true storyteller, the function of the folktale may be fulfilled by legends or stories—any kind of oral narrative—or even by reading aloud from a book at communal work. A change in social circumstances may cancel out an occasion for storytelling; it can abolish the old working communities, and storytelling may thus lose its natural prerequisite. Such cases are well known to contemporary folktale collectors.

I myself was able to observe this phenomenon in Sára (Zemplén county) between 1943 and 1954. During this time, as a consequence of the parceling out of land from the manorial estates among the population, the principal occupation changed from fishing to farming. Since storytelling was a pastime at communal get-togethers of the fishermen, it was discontinued after fishing itself was given up. Some of the old storytellers still preserve their tales, but without an audience, they no longer function.

It is hard to find a narrator who keeps the folktale alive, embroiders it, and popularizes it in the community. What is required is not only a good memory—so that no details are omitted from the long narration—but the ability to compose, a rich vocabulary, dramatic power, etc. Many researchers,[44] Tillhagen[45] in particular, have stressed this. The position of the narrator within the village community in general differs very little from that of the creative artist: he either enjoys great respect or is shunned as an outsider. We shall return to the social position of the narrators and to the different types of narrators later. Here we shall state only that for the most part, the narrators are poor people who have been around, who have learned their folktales in various working communities and have narrated them there, and who, in their declining years, have settled in a village—if they were lucky, in the village of their origin—and have become a member of the village community. The individual situation, then, accounts for the narrator's remaining active or becoming passive.

Even though there seem to be some points of resemblance between village narrators and the vagrant students of the middle ages,[46] even though stylistic features of medieval entertainers can be traced in the performance of village narrators, it is scarcely possible that anything like a "narrative order" of professional storytellers could have existed in Europe.[47] With the people, storytelling was associated with certain occupations; we find it among wandering apprentices, craftsmen, soldiers, and landless peasants. We do not think that the assumption that storytelling has been a continuing institution in the villages has ever had any foundation. Even though we know of villages where storytelling is alive, we must still consider the existence of many good storytellers and the handing down of narrative talent as a sudden flowering, a lucky accident, rather than as the continuation of a past natural state.

From the above, it is clear why we are centering our attention upon the storyteller. We are convinced that social recognition of a folktale depends above all on the storyteller's ability to formulate it.[48] In view of the fact that the individual can develop only with the cooperation of the community, researchers have been correct in observing the limits of individual capabilities and in constantly stressing the importance of the community where the tales are told.[49] Every narrator is the vessel for the tradition of the community which he represents.

Since the new creation which develops during storytelling and the telling performance itself (since folklore is not written down, both of them develop at the same time—re-creation and performance are simultaneous) can happen only publicly, the importance of the audience must not be overlooked. Functionally, both the individual telling the story and the listeners take part in the new creation. The structure of the community, its attitudes and moods, the nature and the time as well as the place of the gathering can influence the narrator fashioning his text in such a way that one and the same folktale, recorded under different conditions, often shows decisive modifications.[50] This relationship between narrator and audience has also been recognized by Ortutay, who cites the observations by Sharp.[51]

Even the folklorists who focus their attention on the storyteller do not consider the individual alone to be responsible for the creation of the folktale. And it is precisely the casting of light upon this ambiguity which they consider to be the aim of folklore research. Such research can be practically carried through only by actual observation of outstanding storytellers in the midst of their audiences. We are thus equally interested in tradition, narrator, and the community attending storytelling sessions: all three combined should yield the key to the origin of the folktale, to the ethnic and individual changes in it, and to the role and the essence of the community. The concurrent relationship between individual and community is a much better guide to the variations and the formation of ethnic subtypes of orally transmitted folklore than the whole of the international narrative material evaluation by formal, statistical comparison.

The new trend in folktale research, as outlined above, is working with fundamentally new methods: it wants to capture the nearly palpable social function of storytelling on the basis of intensive collecting in the field. Such collecting should not stop at the literal transcript of the text, but should consider the close relationship between the text and the individuals and should record the general atmosphere in which the text is transmitted. Such collecting must be carried out with highly authentic scientific thoroughness in order to serve as a basis for scholarly analysis of the material. The folklorist must be an experienced fieldworker, whose starting point in building up a study would be his own collection.

The classic folktale collectors in Hungary and elsewhere, following the principles of the Grimm brothers, had esthetic viewpoints in mind and stylized the texts.[52] Later, the researchers of a preponderantly philological orientation did not care for and even objected to recording the embroidering of the individual storytellers, because the individual characteristics of style would have "watered down" the "pure" type sketches.[53] As long as attention was not focused on the person of the narrator, it was less the individual variant developing at the moment (with a few early exceptions)[54] than the subject itself on which all interest was centered. Only when the social role of storytelling replaced the dead text of the folktale as the object of research did it appear necessary to scrutinize the occasions for storytelling. In the face of the new requirements, most of the older collections are unauthentic.

Thus the researchers were confronted with the problem of finding a way to observe folktale creation as undisturbed as possible. This had to be done without impairing the natural development of the narrator's performance or the enjoyment of the audience, and leaving undisturbed the collaboration of narrator and audience.[55] Many have pointed out that the text is nothing more than the skeleton of the performed folktale, and that it is necessary to fill out this skeleton by recording the inflection, cadence, and tempo—the rhythm—of the narrator. Gestures, facial expressions, and dramatic interplay must be retained.[56] By means of the technical props which are at our disposal today, we have been able to come much closer to knowledge of folktale creation; the individual and communal stylistic forms are recognizable, and the recorded tale texts are much more complete than they were before.[57] A comparison of old and new collections from regions where the storytellers are still at work is most illuminating. During the last twenty-five years, folktales have been collected in Hungary which are much more beautiful and varied than the old, monotonous, routine abstracts of their contents. The reason for this is probably not to be found in a new flowering of the art of story-telling, but in the literal and exact tape recording of folktales of the best Hungarian storytellers.

Completeness, always relative, is also a facet of the reliability of re-cording texts. It is essential that the complete tale stock of the commu-nity examined be recorded without regard to the categories or qualities of the texts, and without conscious choice. The complete material of the narrators permits conclusions as to their personalities, and the material of the community in which they live leads us to recognize the local and ethnic character of the tale tradition.

If we succeed in reaching this degree of reliability by collecting mate-rial and by observing the folktale in its function as communal folklore, we shall also succeed in uncovering the inner cohesion of folk culture.

The functional approach to folkloristic phenomena follows the prin-ciples of the French sociological and the British anthropological schools. Of the greatest importance for folktale research were the theoretical spec-ulations of Emile Durkheim and Lucien Lévy-Bruhl and the methodo-logical references of Bronislaw Malinowski. The latter, who collected the narrative material of the Melanesian aborigines, makes statements which are of great consequence for the nature of the collective phe-nomenon. The mere text of a folktale, he says, is lifeless and can be truly observed only during the telling and in the presence and with the co-operation of the audience.[58] As a conclusion to his considerations, Malin-owski recommends "a new method of treating the science of folklore, for we have shown that it cannot be independent of ritual, or sociology, or even of material culture. Folktales, legends, and myths must be lifted from their flat existence on paper and placed in the three-dimensional reality of full life."[59]

The functional research of folklore continues to develop along the lines of Malinowski's postulates. English and American anthropologists[60] and above all the German folklorists[61] have repeatedly stressed the impor-tance of this question. Friedrich Ranke,[62] Mackensen, Peuckert, and the Swiss Richard Weiss,[63] in addition to the Schwietering school and to Henssen and his disciples, have frequently reiterated that it is important to research the social conditions of folklore. Thompson and the conserva-tive folktale scholar von der Leyen also stress the importance of such examinations.[64] Sokolov, in turn, confirms the social character of the folktale.[65] Though there is a definite tendency toward functional, planned investigation, the sparsity of knowledge as to the results of such investigation is pointed up in a remark of W. Eberhard: "The whole problem of the function of the tale is not explored enough in spite of Azadovsky's and Sydow's studies."[66]

More and more groups of folktale scholars are today applying the new methods in folktale research. The collection and ordering of folklore material according to informants was introduced by the nineteenth century Russian collectors. Dobroliubov's criticism of Afanasjev's *märchen* collection was a milestone: "Anyone who is busy recording and collecting the creations of folklore would indeed do something very useful if he would also record the inner as well as the outward circumstances in which he heard the story or the song, instead of confining himself to recording only the text of the tale or the song itself."[67] Later collectors, particularly Russian scholars who collected the Russian heroic epics (*bylini*), have essentially built on these foundations.[68] Following Onchukov (1908), the first collector of tales of identified narrators, extensive collecting activity was initiated in 1914 in the northern part of Russia. Miller at Moscow and the disciples of Oldenburg at Petersburg began to elevate this research method into a school,[69] which since the Revolution has been improved in various ways.

The Russian scholars have at their disposal various folktale collections with reliable texts arranged according to narrators and containing biographies of the narrators and notations about the type of storytellers, their repertoire, their environment, and their social standing.[70] As time passed, the horizon of the researchers widened and folklorists became interested in the whole tale body of a larger community, of a village, of a region.[71]

Among other theoretical works, Azadovski's monograph *Eine sibirische Märchenerzählerin* deserves special mention. Through this study the Russian method exercised a tremendous impact on international folklore research.[72] Important studies were also published in the Soviet folklore journal *Russkij Folklor*. Studies concerned with the new development of the folktale in the Soviet era and with the role of the narrator's personality or the relationship of tradition and authorship in folklore were especially impressive.[73] Lintur devoted ten years to studying this problem among the narrators of Gorinchevo in the sub-Carpathian Ukraine. He not only recorded the tales of a great narrator but analyzed the way in which the folktales of the village, the village environment, and the environment of the whole region were mirrored in the tale body of a given narrator.[74]

The greatest achievement of the Russian school is the introduction of personality research and the establishment of a model method for analyzing the tales of individual narrators, a method based on sociological, stylistic-critical, and esthetic principles.

In the early 'fifties, however, exaggerations of a twofold nature were noticeable in the personality research. One is a consequence of the fact that storytelling itself, as well as the status of the storyteller, has undergone a great change under the new social order of the Soviet Union. Narrators have become known all over the country, enjoying respect and popularity. Through the general upgrading of education, the art of the storyteller has undergone a slow transformation from folklore to literature. This is revealed in the very lively critical discussions aroused by the voluminous work of Astakhova-Dmitrakov and Lozanova.[75] Several researchers, in particular Nechaev and Rybakova, are unanimous in stressing the collective aspect of folklore. They exclude from folklore the individualistic creations of today's storytellers and pseudo-folklore creations encouraged by political impulses, since these lack the characteristics of folklore.[76] The same opinion has crystallized in the discussions of the Soviet Academy Institute of Literature. The essence of folklore in the Soviet epoch has still to be clarified.[77]

Criticism has even been leveled at folklorists who, like Sokolov, have gone so far in stressing the importance of personality that they evaluate each weak variant as an artistic fact of independent importance.[78] However, contemporary Russian folklorists have discontinued development of the method their classic forerunners initiated. Their interest has turned toward the comparative-historical analysis of narrative texts, which was initiated by the great nineteenth century scholar, Wesselovski. Azadovski and his disciples have even been criticized for their concern with master storytellers.[79] The most recent word in the matter of oral creation has tried to discredit the narrator's individual contribution, emphasizing "collective" creation.[80] Russians have at the same time returned to analysis of impersonal tale texts for esthetic values.

In addition to the Russian approach, the activity of the German sociological school and its precursors needs attention.

As stated above, the German folklorists early had their attention drawn to the tale-creating role of the individual storyteller. The first collector who mentioned the circumstances of the narration and the depth of the repertoire is Ulrich Jahn.[81] Bünker's collection, the first to publish the material of one single storyteller, made a tremendous impression.[82] Wisser,[83] G. F. Meyer,[84] and Hertha Grudde[85] offered interesting observations when they gave an account of their folklore collections. During the 'thirties, the collecting activity increased,[86] and the storytellers received more attention. But in spite of this we find a methodological evaluation only with Julius Schwietering and his disciples, who analyzed the creations of folklore not from the viewpoint of the individual but from that of the community.

Rejecting the outmoded romantic idea of the *Volksgeist* and continuing on the sociological premises of Durkheim and Lévy-Bruhl, the Schwietering school regards the collective essence of folk culture as the decisive factor.[87] Their circumspect manner of collecting is exemplary; even though the role of the individual is minimized, their monographs contain important methodological results.[88] Sister Mechtilda Brachetti exhaustively treats the question of whether the folktale is a communal creation. Even though originally created by an individual, "the folktale is collective lore not according to its origin but according to its fate . . . because it mirrors the collective psyche of a community."[89] She considers all collections which had so far appeared unreliable and therefore unusable for her purposes. Of extreme importance are her views on the methodology of collecting:

> Whoever wants to capture the folktale as communal lore would have to consult the storytelling folk . . . would have to gain knowledge of the inner and outer structure of the community from which the tale arises. For a complete understanding of the folktale it would be necessary to compare the repertory of similar as well as of different communities.[90]

Henssen[91] harshly criticizes an overappreciation of the community to the detriment of the individual.[92] He himself had found a different path: in one of his earlier works he publicized the material of narrators living in a village where storytelling is popular, whereas in a later publication he treats the relationship of a very gifted narrator to tradition.[93]

A similar direction is taken by Leza Uffer[94] and Karl Haiding.[95] The circle around Henssen and the German Folktale Archives which he established in Marburg is responsible for several excellent works. Langstroff and Sareyko,[96] to name only two, have made exemplary use of their material concerning the relationship between the individual and tradition.

The new method eased somewhat the work of the German researchers, although the old, living narration of folktales has more or less passed away in highly urbanized Germany. Some fine individual storytellers and even storytelling villages still crop up.[97] However, in most cases folklorists find themselves compelled to evaluate, from different viewpoints, the existing reliable collections: Merkelbach-Pinck, Grudde, or even classics like that of the Grimm brothers. This was done by Langstroff, Sareyko, and others[98] who examined and investigated the folkloristic and philological reliability of the collections and re-recorded the materials after many years, in order to conduct the investigation on a live and varied body of narratives. This entailed the uncovering of ethnic characteristics of the areas in question, of the environment, often by means of comparison with neighboring areas. The result of the German research indicates that folktale monograph studies must be more daring in the quest for local characteristics. The study of the tale body of a local group as compared to these of neighboring groups and the larger national unit of a people may possibly lead us to the solution of the question of the transmigration of the folktale. Research in interethnic relationships of the folk narrative has only recently been opened up as a field of general interest. The study of ethnic characteristics and national features as the cause of specific variations in the spreading international tale seems to be a successful innovation in the historical-geographical approach. However, although the importance of such study has been emphasized, not much has been accomplished as yet.[99]

In addition to attempts to observe changes in the tales of bilingual or multilingual narrators in mixed ethnic regions and attempts to establish the ethnic subtype of a tale by comparison with tales of neighboring peoples,[100] Kurt Ranke's edition of the Schleswig-Holstein *Märchen* merits attention. He endeavors to determine the specific folktale dialect of an ethnic region and brings together philological and biological viewpoints.[101] This provides a basis of comparison for a definitive regional type formation.

Special attention must be paid to the Irish Folklore Commission, which was established in the 'thirties.[102]

The I.F.C. was founded in 1935 with the help of government funds. Delargy's paper at the International Folklore Conference at Tours was very effective since he reported about a folk tradition of a richness until then unheard of.[103] The survival of the mythical Celtic tradition and the literary tradition of the Middle Ages was helped by the geographic isolation and the economic backwardness of the Gaelic-speaking southwest region of Ireland. But there are other considerations, too, which make it urgent to collect and evaluate the Irish material. This relict region, preserved in its peculiarities, is one of the key points of the European tale treasure.[104]

The collecting technique of the Irish Folklore Commission is highly developed.[105] The very carefully determined principles for collection and subsequent use of the material are founded in the main on von Sydow's theories[106] and were transformed into practice in the rich Irish folktale region.[107]

Many scholars[108] and research groups in various countries have in recent years come closer to this direction of folktale research.[109] It is especially heartening to know that the long stagnant Rumanian sociological school, which once was so active within the Rumanian Folklore Institute, is once more growing.[110] American folklorists, who in the past had paid little attention to studying in depth their own regional and ethnic body of narratives, have in the past decade made increasing efforts to collect and analyze folktales, and have exhibited interest in the personality of the narrators.[111]

In Hungary a volume by Lajos Kálmány containing the complete tale body of the hired man Mihály Borbély of Temesköz was published rather early, in 1914-15.[112] Kálmány probably followed the example of Radloff and Bünker. In some instances, of course, researchers have referred to individuals and their qualities without making the person of the narrator the focal point of the investigation.

The Hungarian representatives of the new trend have been directly influenced by the Russian research methods. Azadovski's monograph about the Siberian storytelling woman, Vinokurova, led Ortutay to collect the complete material of his narrator Mihály Fedics and to record his life story. Nor should we underestimate the influence of Malinowski's functional research method and the theoretical considerations of Károly Marót and his interpretation of the ambivalence of "survival" and "revival" in oral tradition.[113] These influences prevented Hungarian folklorists from overemphasizing the importance of the individual in folklore. Even inactive narrators were observed not in isolation but in relation to their communities.

In the introduction to his work, Ortutay sums up the aim of his research as follows:

> I made it my task to observe the fate of the creative individual which was formed in the old, strict communal order of the Hungarian peasantry and culture. How far can the individual develop his creative powers within a tradition circumscribed and approved by the community? How far can the individual influence the formation of the epic tale transmitted from generation to generation? This is a talent whose creative role we must not neglect

within a culture which is growing and changing in an environment where the strict order of the community is hostile to the individual. It is precisely this strange tension between tradition preserved by the individual and the one preserved by the community which is a key to the understanding of the nature of folklore, and any kind of one-sidedness can lead to gross errors.[114]

This aim has been upheld as a principle in the works that followed and has been realized with more or less success. The single volumes have appeared in the *Uj Magyar Népköltési Gyüjtemény* (*New Collection of Hungarian Folk Literature*). The first volume of the collection is the tales of M. Fedics, the Ortutay work already mentioned; the second volume contains the materials, put together by István Banó, of the narrators of an ethnic group.[115] The third and fourth volumes contain the tales of Péter Pandur.[116] The fifth and sixth volumes are those in which Ágnes Kovács[117] published material of the narrators in the village of Ketesd. In most of the volumes are given characteristic traits of the narrators and biographical and sociological data. Ortutay has summarized the methodological considerations and the principles and results of these volumes, and the discussions which were triggered by them.[118]

In keeping with the nature of the given material, in these volumes every researcher explored the relationship between the storyteller and the community. He proceeded, for example, from the ethnic and general anthropological point of view to the art and style of the individual, his tale structure, and tradition; and he investigated how the community received the narrative and which part the community itself had in its formation.

After the appearance of the first six volumes of this series, the researchers tried to refine their method. They set out, in their monographs, to examine and evaluate the various types of narrators and of storytelling within certain periods of different length, as well as to evaluate outstanding narrators. The present aim of research is to get to the bottom of the continuing process of preservation, transmission, variation, innovation, and decay, as well as the ethnic cohesion of the tale body, by examining narrating families in the villages where storytelling is still in existence.[119] This leads to the basic question of the science of the folktale. Most important in this connection are the investigations concerned with the folktale body of recently resettled ethnic groups and with the change of the folktale through the influence of a new environment.

Hungarian folklorists succeeded in the elaboration of an anthropological–sociological basis for the study of the folktale. However, they were less successful in working out a consistent method for content and style analysis. There are very few examples available that permit examination of narrative style or techniques of composition. If the researcher is to profit by the results of the Hungarian research method, he must pursue intensive collecting of material and then evaluation of it.

Intensive collecting involves (1) reliable recording of the material—taping and recording of the entire material of the individual narrators; (2) gaining a conception of the life and the type of the creative narrator based on sociological and on exact psychological observations; (3) examination of the storytelling community from the viewpoint of the local narrative tradition, with attention to its structure and composition; (4) observation of the narrative process—the simultaneous cooperation of the narrator and his community; (5) repeated recording of this procedure over a span of several years. Each creative individual is a good object, whether he lives in a storytelling community or has dropped out of it.

Raw material collected according to these principles is apt to throw light on different types of creative tale-tellers as well as on the ethnic features of the tale variations. It is not of decisive importance whether the tale stock is elicited from a displaced narrator who had lost his audience or from one of a smaller or larger, still viable, taletelling community. Evaluation centers on the question of the traditional and individual contributions in the tale formulations of individual narrators. Investigations will thus stem primarily from analysis of style; this means that, among other things, the composition technique of the narrator will have to be closely examined.

The investigation will uncover first of all the local status of the tale body; it is quite certain that only material evaluated in such a minute manner can provide the foundation for the solution of further questions, for example, international comparison along synchronic and diachronic bases.

As far as local circumstances permitted, we have ordered and evaluated the material for Kakasd according to these principles. This brings us back to our point of departure, the demand for a new basis for the comparative analysis of folktale texts. Within the framework of the present study, we have followed the system of the international classifications of folk narratives. Concise references are made to Hungarian and international parallels, while the national, local, and individual modifications are emphasized and detailed. This, however, is only one step in the direction we hope international folklore research will take in the future.

# 6

# The Tale Occasions

THE FOLKTALE ARISES FROM A NEED EXPERIENCED AT A CERTAIN STAGE of development in human society. It is the circumstances which generate a folktale, which form its conception, its shape, and its narrative style; as long as these circumstances prevail, the folktale will endure.

Evidences of the folktale can be found all over the world; they are quite ancient, and even if these narratives arise from different conditions, depending on place and time, they all have something in common: they have their origin in a social need.[1]

The oldest written records contain indications of the function of folktale narration. People everywhere have listened to storytellers with the greatest of interest. They brought news of exciting events, praised heroic deeds, and thus aroused interest in history; they provided models of religious and ethical perfection for the people to emulate. The narrators banished the drab monotony of everyday life by entertaining their hearers with exciting, adventuresome, and highly imaginative stories. It was from these premises, before the invention of written literature, that oral narrative forms originated.

The same stock of motifs from the narrative elements formed the heroic legend, the myth, and the folktale.[2] It has not yet been clarified when the completed form of the tale, which served mainly for entertainment, actually originated. Nor can it be determined whether this form antedates the other narrative genres which were a living part of the primitive rites of society before class distinctions developed, though narratives of these genres often correspond to folktale episodes in content.[3]

It will be difficult to shed any light on this question, as written records from the past are scarce, and have not only proceeded from different points of view in determining the different narrative genres, but have used different terminology.[4]

It may well be impossible to clarify the origins of the folktale or of a related genre. Certainly we will encounter cases where the transition from one type to another can be traced as a series of moments in which the legend or myth turns into a folktale, but we cannot and must not generalize. In full agreement with Thompson, we would not dare trace the origin of the folktale to times so far removed that we would not have sufficient documentation.[5] That kind of investigation has not furthered folktale research in the least.

The age of the folktale can be fixed, or rather, can be traced, only insofar as it is first discernible in the form, aim, and function of folktales known today. When we make this statement for the European folktale—and we shall restrict ourselves to this in the following work—we refer to the development of the folktale which is similar from Ireland to India,[6] and of which our knowledge dates, at best, from the nineteenth century.

Very often the question is posed whether the prose narratives of the early Egyptian, Greek, or Roman sources, which contain folktale motifs or even the more complex folktale incidents, were really *märchen* in the modern sense. It is not difficult to find parallels in classical literature,[7] but this does not mean that we are dealing with true folktales or that they are the prototypes of the present European folktale. Marót, too, disagrees with the view that traces of the folktale as a separate, complete art form can be found in the Odyssey.[8] This does not exclude the possibility that some European folktale type actually is the end product of a two-thousand-year process of development. But the question would remain whether this really is a folktale, or a myth, or an antique novella which at some later date was transformed into a folktale. It has been assumed that one means of folktale formation consists in transforming a different kind of narrative into a folktale.[9] This does not mean that myth and legend are lost as soon as the folktale emerges from them. They could easily have existed side by side in classical antiquity, as they do in today's primitive societies.[10] Contemporary development of oral narratives[11] in Western

Europe and America indicates that where folktales became extinct, diverse forms of legends can still flourish.

Our knowledge of European folktale material stems from two sources: literary works and oral tradition. The most striking characteristic of the traditional tale lies in the fact that the social institutions and concepts which we discover in it reflect the age of feudalism. Thus the question of the origin of the folktale coincides with that of the origin of literature in general.

When the European tale body was formed, a close connection still existed between the epic material fixed in writing and the oral tradition.[12] It is significant for the incipient literary life that the poetic works reached the public not in written form but by word of mouth, not only because interpretation was part of the author's task, but because so much of society was unable to read.[13]

The literature of the Middle Ages was in the main ecclesiastic.[14] This, however, was interspersed in many countries with orally transmitted poetry which "still was common property even in the different strata of society, so that the traditional popular elements and forces in the individual creations of the singers played a major part."[15]

Even though we do not possess much documentation of the early existence of the folktale in Hungary, we may be permitted to assume that for a long time it took the place of secular prose lore for all classes of society. Of its existence we know little more than what the clerical chroniclers remarked about the folktale: that it was a lie, empty talk, garrulity.[16] Storytelling was general until the scope of the written word forced it into a more restricted circle, until the upper classes gave preference to written literature.

We have ample evidence for the fact that storytelling in the Middle Ages existed at the courts of the dukes as well as in the highway inns, the manor houses, and the village taverns. But storytelling as an activity was not highly regarded and increasingly became the occupation of hired hands, servants, and wet nurses.[17]

The function of the folktale in the houses of the monarchs, the nobility, and the well-to-do burghers is documented not only in the Oriental world but, starting with the twelfth century, in Europe as well. All through the Middle Ages we hear about storytelling "buffoons" in Russia, who were itinerant folk entertainers[18] and whose style was maintained even by some of the nineteenth century storytellers.[19] Equally popular were the storytellers of the French, Polish, and Irish courts.[20] The reigning classes accepted storytelling to distract them, entertain them, and lull them to sleep.[21] Storytelling in these circles was considered not an art but a service to be expected from the serf and from the entertainer, and it was valued as such.

The double standard of feudalism with regard to storytelling is quite characteristic, as Pomerantseva so aptly points out. While the folktale was the best-loved entertainment at ducal banquets and in the bedrooms of the big landowners, the tales circulating among the people were branded by both the clerical and the secular powers as damnable and inspired by the devil.[22] We may assume that the courts of dukes and noblemen became veritable transshipping points for the international tale body. Folktales which were brought into a country by the servants, entertainers, and nurses who formed part of the retinue of a sovereign or a queen were assimilated by the local populations, and population migration caused by warfare likewise provided, very early, an important means of folktale exchange.[23]

The Hungarian folktale body stands between the East European and the West European;[24] the West European folktale has come mainly through Germany, the East European through Slavic transmission.

With the spread of literacy, the growth of urban life, and the development of cultural and educational class distinctions, the European folktale became one of the most important means of artistic expression for the lowest strata of society, since education of the people progressed only very slowly as a result of increasingly stronger distinctions among the educational elite. The fundamental feudal aspect of the folktale did not change, or changed only slightly. Though elements of modern technology penetrated the folktale, they did not essentially transform it. The uneven industrial and urban development in Europe had its effect upon the existence of the folktale: the mighty industrial evolution in Western Europe made peasants into a middle class. The folktale remained within the lower middle class and retired to the nursery.[25]

In Eastern Europe the day laborers on the estates of the rich landowners were the carriers of the folktale; their living conditions differed qualitatively very little from those they had experienced under the patriarchal conditions of feudalism. Thus the folktale, which had provided entertainment for all classes of society, became, in its entirety, the property of the lowest classes. With this its functional content changed. It lost its purely entertaining character and became a reflection of the hopes and desires of its bearers.[26]

The material which we shall examine in the following pages originates in accurate and reliable folklore collections and was recorded in the second half of the nineteenth century and the first half of the twentieth. This period coincides, all over Europe, with the era of developing capitalism. Every statement, every generalization, will relate only to the material available for the period. We have disregarded the evaluation of earlier, unreliable sources because this would lead us too far astray.

In view of the many remarks and documents regarding the form of European popular narration, and of field experiences in Hungary, we can say that, generally, the folktale lives in the poorest strata of the people, though there are of course exceptions. Storytelling, according to its essence—and we do not want to deal in detail with the essence of the folktale—may have different tasks and may carry different messages. It can ease work, it can serve as recreation after work, or it may simply be an entertaining pastime. It occurs generally on occasions which make possible or necessary the narration of a lengthy oral prose.[27] Let us examine the professions which offer possibilities for storytelling.

We can classify the following types of storytelling communities according to occupation:

1. Migrant working communities outside the village.
   a. Nonpeasant groups:
   craftsmen
   soldiers
   sailors
   fishermen; other professions depending on mobility
   b. Landless peasants:
   construction laborers
   seasonal laborers in agriculture
   day laborers, hired hands
   lumbermen
   herdsmen
2. The village. Opportunities occur for storytelling in the village during
   a. communal work, and
   b. winter entertainment.
3. Involuntary work communities of short duration.
   a. hospital
   b. jail
   c. military service, including those
      (1) drafted in war, and
      (2) prisoners of war.

In examining these groups we are struck first of all by the fact that the great majority of storytellers come from the poor segment of the people, and that their professions and places of work provide the opportunity to exercise their faculties. Students of folklore are unanimous on this point. According to F. Ranke, the narrators everywhere are poor people: day laborers, hired hands, sailors, itinerant journeymen, shoemakers, tailors, etc.[28] Mackensen, in his list of narrator types, stresses the small village craftsmen.[29] Langstroff sums up the results of the German researchers by saying, "There is a preponderance of the small peasants and peasant-craftsmen of lesser means."[30] Zender is the only researcher whose statistics show 34 per cent of peasantry, 20.5 per cent of workers, and 17.5 per cent of craftsmen to be narrators,[31] but he also points out that his experience is different from the usual one.[32] A similar picture is presented in other regions. The teachers of the gifted Estonian storyteller Jürgensen are shepherds, day laborers, cotters, discharged soldiers, village smiths, village tailors, night watchmen, millers, bricklayers, and hired hands.[33] The Czech narrators, too, were mostly craftsmen and small merchants[34]; in Western Prussia, cobblers, night watchmen, migrant workers, and poor people who were "experienced."[35] Bîrlea, in evaluating Rumanian material, says in conclusion that the narrators are to be found among the poor: village craftsmen, bricklayers, shoemakers, furriers, etc.[36] The part which well-to-do peasants have played in forming the folktale body is negligible.[37]

Storytelling is a very old tradition with craftsmen. When the different crafts began to organize their guilds, each apprentice was obliged to go out wandering. The village craftsman went out not only to learn his craft, but he went from village to village and accepted work to make a living. All wandering apprentices were obliged to entertain their landlord; thus some folklorists believed that storytelling was decidedly a nonpeasant occupation. Uffer builds upon the examples quoted above as well as on his own experiences collecting with Rätoromans to arrive at the following conclusion:

> Is it a coincidence that the conscious raconteur always is a craftsman? My best narrators are craftsmen—shoemakers, tailors, cabinet makers, bricklayers. It is certain that the professional activity influences the talent for narration. The peasant, as I see it, is too earthbound . . . the craftsman sits at his workbench, stands at the file stock, often for days on end at the same spot. There is always somebody around who observes his work and who talks. He always knows all the news because relatively more people come and go in

his shop. Or then he went—or goes—on his rounds which gives him an occasion to enter all the houses, getting to know all the households better than a peasant. . . . The craftsman—and I am especially thinking of the cobbler, the tailor, or the house painter—is surrounded by children in whom he finds a grateful public. The fact, too . . . that the craftsman goes through a period of apprenticeship which takes him, for a few years, to another village or another region, may be of importance. In former times the craftsmen took off for their wandering years, met here and there with colleagues, and everywhere heard the telling of stories, folktales, and folk legends.[38]

Henssen cites proof for Uffer's opinion from the pertinent literature and his own experience: "I found these excellent narrators so far only among the craftsmen; on account of their mobility this type seems to develop best among them. The talented narrators of other collectors confirm my experience."[39] The observations of Henssen from Westphalia coincide with those of Kurt Ranke from Schleswig-Holstein[40] and with those of Haiding from Austria.[41]

Elsewhere, too, we hear of storytelling tailors,[42] icon painters,[43] boatwrights,[44] itinerant tinkers,[45] shoemakers,[46] and construction workers.[47] Although researchers have not yet seriously examined this question, one thing can be stated: Hungarian informants are most explicit about the narrating of the shoemakers, both at their workshops and in the village.[48] Of special interest is the role of the Hungarian bricklayers as bearers of folktales—the little we know so far indicates that we can expect much new evidence in this regard.[49] When factory- and city-building activity increased in Hungary in the 'eighties, many peasants, and in some cases whole villages, went into the construction trade. The men worked as bricklayers, joiners, and construction workers and took their wives and daughters along as helpers.[50] New narrative communities developed, and the folktale tradition of the craftsmen and peasant traditions became intertwined.

Many researchers have noted that the heroes of European folktales often are craftsmen by profession.[51] Most frequently they are tailors, joiners, basket weavers, potters, painters, and broom makers. Since the Hungarian tales are usually told in a rural milieu, it is not the craft itself which is in the foreground but the circumstances connected with the craft, as for instance a period of wandering, which often forms the basis for the magic tale. The prince must "try his luck," he must wander along the highways, must "take up his staff and wander, must ask asylum in strange houses and can become king only after completing a heroic deed just as the apprentice can be released only after his wandering years."[52] It does not seem improbable that the peculiar incident of choice of profession of the three brothers and the tests in the Hungarian variant of the *Master Thief* tale (AT 1525) originated among the guild craftsmen. We could cite numerous other examples, and it would be a worthy task to disentangle from the content of the folktales the close connection of the folktale public with the activities and the way of life of the craftsmen. Let us first investigate the wandering apprentice.

The craftsmen, regardless of the group to which they belonged, finished their schooling with a year of wandering. They traversed far-away regions and traveled to foreign countries, stopping here and there with a master and then continuing on their way. In the workmen's hostels they rested from the rigors of their wanderings. These hostels, too have played an important role in the interchange of the European folktale treasure. Apprentices from the Austro-Hungarian monarchy learned and told their folktales in the hostels.[53] On their way home to their native villages they gathered great repute in workshops and hostels by relating folktales.[54] The narration of the wandering apprentices is repeatedly mentioned. Of special interest are Haiding's records from neighboring Austria.[55] He speaks of several village storytellers who had learned their tales in their youth or at work from itinerant apprentices: ". . . the itinerant apprentices . . . related countless tales with many variants. They were honest people—it is true that the masters kept the best of them over winter. When they told stories they got liquor."[56] Haiding also says that through the influence of the wandering apprentices different variants of one and the same folktale would be spread through the villages.[57]

Like the apprentice, the soldier, too, left his native village. The serf's son who became a soldier was sent to distant regions either to fight or to man a garrison city. Many who had been called into the service as young men did not return until they were discharged twenty years later. Several folklorists point out that the soldier played an important part in the transmission and spread of the folktale.[58] His adventures and his boasting are known all over Europe. He himself has even assumed the proportions of a folktale hero. Many folktales and anecdotes begin with the statement that a soldier, discharged from service after many years, starts on his way home—and here the plot begins. In Hungary the pioneer tale collectors, among others János Mailáth and György Gaál,[59] recorded the texts of soldiers. Kálmány's narrator Mihály Borbély was a popular storyteller during his military service in Vienna.[60] In his introduction to the

tale collection edited by Kropf-Jones, Lajos Katona points out the soldiers among the narrators: "He mentions the greatest raconteur and tale
transmitter, one of the most active wizards of the tale migration and tale
exchange, the discharged soldier, just as if the playful goblin of folklore
would have chosen him on purpose to nullify any one-sided tale analysis
by his baggage collected here and there and everywhere."[61]

Though we have categorized under the heading "involuntary communities" the tale occasions of the man called to military service, we
want to treat these here. All narrators who were soldiers are unanimous in
stating that they heard a considerable number of their folktales in the
barracks. It seems to have actually been a requirement to know tales.
Some remembered having received an order of the day that after "lights
out" at night, each one, following the sequence of their beds, had to tell
a tale; anyone who was not able to do so was the butt of scorn.[62] The
father of a narrator from the Burgenland boasted that whenever it was
his turn to tell a story when he was a soldier, the room filled and even
officers came in and gave him money and tobacco.[63] Thus the elements
of the tale body which originated in different regions were exchanged
and spread.

Although war prisoners' tales have not been recorded as yet, I feel
certain that this involuntary extension of service also provides storytelling opportunities for soldiers.[64]

Among the itinerant storytellers we must also count sailors, boatmen,
and fishermen, especially where people lived along the coasts, since they
often spent weeks on the water. Jahn has observed that fishermen and
sailors are good narrators.[65] Lajos Katona cites Lönrot's entries from
1855, according to which a Finnish fisherman had learned his tales ship-
ping on Norwegian and Russian fishing boats. "Sometimes a storm kept
us from fishing," he says, "and then we passed the time telling tales."[66]

"Fishermen engaged in salmon fishing off the rocky coast of Sliabh
Liag, Southwest Donegal, used to say their night prayers while waiting
for the haul, and these were followed usually by storytelling. It is on
record that so attentive were the fishermen on one occasion to the folktale being told that the look-out abandoned his post to listen, and the
boat had a narrow escape from being rammed by a steamer," Delargy
writes and also notes: "Fishermen mending their nets have been known
to send for a storyteller to help while away the time."[67] Sokolov reports
that fishermen told stories while waiting for the wind to blow from the
right direction, and "he who told the most beautiful tale received half of
the catch."[68] We also heard of storytelling among the river fishermen in

Hungary. Storytelling in the village of Sára in Zemplén County is influenced to a great extent by the living conditions of the fishermen. Tales are told not only during summer, around the campfires along the riverbanks, but also in winter, when the nets are weighted down with irons, the baskets woven, and the tools mended.[69] The same happens with the fishermen of Kopács.[70]

To this group belong the narrators for whom the art of storytelling has become a valuable trade. The itinerant apprentice, the discharged soldier, and the peddler are typical folktale tellers.[71] The storytelling of water-power station workers is worth mentioning here: often more than thirty people lived together on the floating barges.[72] When they arrived in a village, they sought shelter for the night, and in exchange for this, told their tales. Sokolov and Azadovski have thoroughly investigated the so-called *Brodjaga* (vagrant) narrators, who have formed an individual storytelling style. In the second half of the past century there were several thousand vagrants loose in Siberia; many endeared themselves to the inhabitants through their tales; in return for narrating on successive evenings, a vagrant would enjoy the hospitality of a family.[73] The Irish counterpart of the *Brodjaga*, the *Bacaigh* (itinerant people) can look back upon a tradition possibly even older. They found open doors wherever they went, received shelter and food, and in exchange brought news and information and told their stories. Many of them were widely known and people from near and far converged upon the house where they usually stayed. These itinerant beggars were for centuries the most respected narrators.[74] But storytelling was also of great importance in countries, unlike Russia and Ireland, where no traditional practice was emerging. In Austria the telling of folktales was considered an occupation for beggars. Gypsy women on their begging tours entertained their hosts all over Eastern Europe.[75] In Lorraine, the itinerant peddlers who stayed with the well-to-do peasants during the winters were the center of winter entertainment, as Meckelbach-Pinck notes. In Transylvanian villages, Slovak pottery vendors and itinerant tinkers were known as popular narrators.[76]

In a wider sense, the tale-telling opportunities which result when people travel in a group, as in Chaucer's *Canterbury Tales*, also belong in this category. Since the times when transportation and communications were unreliable, we have heard of storytelling by Hungarian miners. The miners from Kishartyán in Nógrád county had to walk twelve miles to work. In 1953, a miner told me that they started out in the middle of the night, their hurricane lamps in hand, so as to begin work at six o'clock in the morning. They tried to shorten the walk by telling stories. On the way to market or to the mill, or on the return from working in the fields, storytelling went on.[77] As B. Gunda states, storytelling while traveling is general with Gypsies, tinkers, horse dealers, and the like in Hungary, Bucovina, and Rumania. Groups of eight to ten Gypsies, riding wagons, would also tell stories.[78] So far we have only a few indications of the manner of storytelling among earth movers. Bereczki notes that earth movers from Dévaványa told tales for his colleagues after dinner in 1948. Another informant reports that after work in Rézbánya people had to listen to storytelling.[79] The next day the young workers were asked whether they had stayed awake, and were quizzed about the fate of the tale hero. If one of them did not know the exact answer, the money for the storyteller's liquor was deducted from his pay on Saturday.

Narration among the agrarian proletariat, which plays a decisive part in Hungary as well as in agricultural countries, is as important as that of the groups mentioned so far. Here, too, the learning of the folktale and its narration occurred at the place of work outside the village, a fact which determined the nature of narration. Since the majority of Hungarian narrators come from this group, they usually learned their folktales in work communities on the estates of the landowners, where agricultural workers who had no land were able to perform all kinds of occasional work.

Nearly every kind of work in the fields which is not excessively strenuous can be an occasion for storytelling—hacking, weeding, cutting roots, gathering potatoes, planting, sheafing.[80] Storytelling is done during work like this by one of the workers, who sits down near a ditch and entertains the others. The inhabitants of Sára had their most important storytelling occasions while they worked in the vineyards. From spring until vintage time, every phase of work was accompanied by storytelling. "This is possible with quiet work, such as planting," storyteller András Kormány says. "When we grafted the vine, that is the best occasion: fourteen to fifteen men are grouped together and they always tell stories. This is the easiest work, a kind of quiet work, only you have to pay attention." "Ax and hatchet are noisy, but it is quiet here. And they call: 'Czapár come here, Czapár come there!' " the forty-three-year-old Ferenc Czapár relates. It is not unusual in the vineyards for a narrator to spin out a tale over two days.[81]

Another occasion for storytelling in the village is the stringing, smoothing, and sorting of the tobacco leaves. On the estate farmsteads, the families of the hired tobacco growers did this work, and anyone who could tell stories did so to keep the others from falling asleep in the big, dark barns. Mihály Borbély has also told stories for tobacco workers: "The narrator was in great demand, greatly sought after, because he entertained those who worked as well as those who just listened; wherever such a narrator was available, everybody liked to go and work," he said.[82] Good raconteurs are famous in the regions where tobacco is grown, particularly Szabolcs county.[83] Publishing the tales of the flax manufacturers of Trégor in Lower Brittany, G. Massignon describes how tales are told by men while the work is divided among the men, women, and children.[84]

Seasonal labor provides other occasions for storytelling. Although storytelling is not of minor importance for seasonal workers, tales cannot be told during work—only after dinner at night in the communal barracks or hostels. The good storyteller will keep on telling his story, regardless of how tired he himself may be, until all his listeners have fallen asleep.[85]

In wooded areas, the most important storytelling occasion is woodcutting and sawing. This is reported by Azadovski from Vercholensk in Siberia.[86] The Sokolov brothers, in the introduction to their collections of the year 1915, report that in the huts of the timber workers, men, women, and children listened to the storyteller together.[87] The Mari (Cheremis) narrator, Bogdanov, states that after 1920, as a worker in the woods, he told tales to the other workers for weeks on end, and that other people from the village and workers from other areas of the woods came to listen to him. He was so highly respected for his knowledge that he did not have to worry about food or tobacco, and he was even given lighter work. Once an overenthusiastic listener offered him his horse in exchange for the tale of *Prince Bova*.[88] Haiding mentions similar storytellers from the Böhmerwald, from Styria and Upper Austria,[89] and we know that they are also common among the Rumanian timbermen.[90] Mihály Fedics learned his tales while clearing woods: "There is a big hut—it contains seventy men, this hut. We told stories all night long."[91]

Storytelling was a favorite pastime with the Szekler woodsmen. The daily laborers for the timberyards, since the end of the last century, had worked all winter long in the woods. During the evenings, after dinner, narration went on in the huts for fifty to sixty people until bedtime. In this connection a tale told by the woodcutters from Hétfalu (Transylvania) is worth mentioning. The diction and rhythm of the tale recital correspond perfectly to the rhythm of their work. Zsigmond Szendrey was attracted by the tale of *The Little Serpent, the Cat, and the Worm* (AT 560), which follows the rhythm of woodcutting and sawing. Gyurka Móki and István Szakáll told their tales alternately to the rhythm of the ax and the saw.[92] That storytelling is vital for the woods people is shown in József Faragó's description of the typical circumstances of work outside the village.

Faragó, who examined the storytelling of the woodcutters of Marosmagyaró in the neighborhood of Szászrégen, states:

> The majority of the male inhabitants in a vast region have spent all their lives, from childhood until old age, as daily laborers in these factories in the woods. They returned home only for high holidays or for a few days of agricultural work. In the mountains they lived under inhuman conditions in patched-up huts, without a place to sleep; around the open fire they vegetated, dirty and full of lice. . . . Since the nationalization of the timber industry their lives have changed radically: they are living in stone houses, have beds with sheets and covers, have stoves and oil lamps for illumination; sanitary facilities are to be found all over without exception. One thing, however, has not changed: the folktale. We can hardly find a form of life where the tale has become such an indispensable spiritual nourishment. From fall through winter they have nothing to do from five in the afternoon until morning. They could not live without the folktale. The narrator is greatly honored. They encourage him with cigarets and other small favors, so that he will talk; however, if he teases them, they seize him and throw him into the snow, locking him out until he promises to tell a story. When he is ready, the listeners take it easy; they sprawl around, sitting, lying, supported on their elbows, smoking and listening to him. The narrator, too, takes his ease and calls, "Bones, people," and the chorus answers, "Soup," which means that the audience is ready to listen to a tale.[93] From then on nobody can make the slightest noise, and if anyone wants to say something the others wave him aside. If anyone starts snoring he is silenced. They all hang on the lips of the narrator, more than on the word of the priest in church. . . .

This is from a study by J. Faragó[94] of the lumbermen-storytellers in Transylvania, in which he gives an account of the narration of Minya Kurcsi, who worked at different places during the past thirty years.

Here we must also refer to the storytelling of the mountain shepherds in the pastures which János Mailáth (1786–1855) mentioned.[95] Gyula Ference, a shepherd from Csikmenaság (Transylvania), told me in 1943 about the storytelling of the shepherds, which seems to be identical in form with the storytelling custom of the Hungarian lumbermen and of the Rumanians.[96] Throughout the Hungarian language territory, on the dairy farms, in the stables, and outside in the meadows herding cattle, people pass the nights in storytelling. Young people, too, tell stories while thus occupied.[97]

As we turn to the examination of the village storytelling communities, we must state right from the start that fall and winter are the main seasons for storytelling, when the strenuous work in the fields is interrupted. There are two occasions for storytelling: (1) communal work connected with entertainment and (2) festive or regular get-togethers during the evening.

On both occasions storytelling is enjoyed as an agreeable pastime, an entertainment. However these occasions do not necessarily demand a folktale or a long prose narration; the folktale is one among many kinds of entertainment on such occasions—party games, dancing and singing, riddle telling, question and answer games, and the telling of anecdotes or scary stories. The folktale, of course, is not prevalent when there is no specially gifted raconteur. But even when a good narrator is available, such communities cannot tolerate an overlong folktale, as Ágnes Kovács has observed.[98] The good narrator tries to adapt himself to these circumstances. He narrates shortened fairy tales, entertaining fables, or short horror or prank stories, but not the voluminous magic tales. In general, however, the great and talented narrators are not as popular during the winter tale occasions as the articulate funny men, who not only tell stories but sing and crack jokes. These men always have a stock of jokes or stories about magic experiences, and although they also know the folktale body and can narrate a tale on request, they tell only short excerpts. The average village narrators belong in this category. A typical example of such a narrator was Henssen's singing and narrating Egbert Gerrits, at least at the time when Henssen collected his stories. It is this kind of man a collector usually meets. He likes to narrate because he loves to play a role, but it soon becomes apparent that he merely reproduces what he knows and that his knowledge is quickly exhausted. There are many such men in the village, and they hold the threads of the entertainment in their hands. The situation is quite different when a definite narrator is invited to be present during communal work, as was the custom when spinning and quilting were occupations for women as well as for the young.[99] Yet these narrators belong for the most part among the entertainers at communal agricultural work outside the village (in Hungary they are of the agrarian proletariat), and they take over the role of narrator during the winter when there is nothing to do. "The narrator is always the center of the community and enjoys the rights of a sib elder. The place of narration is the house or the stable around the fire. He is the first to drink from the bottle and he is offered the best tobacco. When an old woman tells stories, the whole household is at her command, even when she is not in her own house. This is her right."[100]

Storytelling in winter is customary all over Europe, and likewise in Hungary, when everyone returns to the village; it lasts all during the winter, when the outdoor work is finished and a quiet existence is possible.[101] During the day stories are told while the villagers are shucking corn, quilling feathers, and spinning; during the evening the family and their guests sit on the benches around the stove and listen in the dark. In former times stories were told in the heated stables and in the spinning rooms as well as in the family circle.[102] Á. Kovács sums up the different kinds of communal labors and the tale occasions in a village,[103] describing the communal work of the men and women which furnishes occasions for storytelling from November until February. She details festive occasions and occasions for spur-of-the-moment gatherings and the gatherings of families. Worth mentioning is the narrating of men such as the storytelling tavern host, of which there are many examples, especially in Western Europe.[104]

Since traditional communal work has faded into the background, the folktale has been restricted to the family circle and is told only when company comes. Uffer writes that while storytelling formerly went on while corn was shucked and hemp skeined, today it occurs only on holidays and, even more rarely, on Sundays.[105] Brinkmann relates that since the disappearance of the spinning rooms stories are told at the family table and on summer evenings when the old people take their coffee in the open air.[106] Zenker-Starzacher,[107] Cammann,[108] and von Sydow[109] also mention storytelling within the family circle, and we hear that on the high feast days, stories were told for entertainment.[110] Since in Hungary, too, the spinning rooms have lost their former importance for the creation of tales, the folktale assumes an important role only when the families and neighbors gather from the village for a so-called "evening-making."

On some isolated farmsteads today, storytelling is still carried on as Tömörkeny described it forty-five years ago: "Darkness is necessary which gives wide scope to phantasy and everybody can see in it the magic figures the way he images them. Thus it is being done on winter afternoons when dusk comes fast, in the heated farm rooms where—one day here, one day there—the neighbors get together. There is no light and we do not even smoke a pipe, [because] its smoke cannot even be seen."[111] The folktale requires a certain receptiveness such as is found in the atmosphere of the old spinning rooms and stables, mentioned by Fedics:

> Formerly there were no lamps in the spinning rooms and stables, the fire was blazing and around it sat women . . . and the men too gathered there. Everyone had a felt coat which was folded and put on the floor, and they sat down upon it. Whoever liked it better, spread it out and laid upon it. There, on the floor, the men sang and told stories. It was quiet. The most of it I heard sitting quietly on the floor; then I collected everything into my head. The men were talking; one of them just said, "Well, now it's my turn." When he had done with his story, another started, or if he did not start, they admonished him, "Now, it's your turn."[112]

This is a classic description of a storytelling occasion in a village where storytelling is practiced.

Similar in form are the "involuntary" storytelling groups, in hospitals, jails, and military barracks. With the sole exception of Dragois' notes from Rumania, we have only Hungarian examples at our disposal for storytelling in hospitals and jails. But it can be assumed with certainty that a true storyteller, if he finds himself in such a place, will entertain those around him with his tales. Storytelling in the hospital is widespread. The sick have time on their hands, and when their illness is of a lighter nature they like to be entertained by folktales in the big wards. Péter Pandur, who had often been in the hospital because of his eye ailment, related how delighted people were with his tales. He himself asked other patients about folktales and learned a great deal. Here we wish to mention Mrs. Tóth, the excellent storyteller from Dunaujváros, a newly built industrial city, who told stories while peeling potatoes and washing dishes in a plant community kitchen. When she had to go to the hospital she continued her storytelling there: "They cried when I had to leave, they liked my tales so much."[113] In the county jails, too, tales are swapped during work in the work halls. Péter Pandur also related that when he was in the county jail of Gödöllö, even the daughter of the jailer listened to him. She put a ladder outside the jail and stepped up to the window.[114] Péter Pandur even remembered which tales he was narrating in 1919 when he spent eight months in the jail of Vác for participating in the first Communist revolution. The three distinguished storytellers from Sára, János Nagy, József Fejes, and Ferenc Czapár, heard their most beautiful tales in the jails of Salgótarján and Sátoraljaujhely: "In the work room, weaving baskets, there were seventy to eighty of us. We were not allowed to speak. We were ten to twenty men at long tables, and then I started storytelling in a soft voice," says Czapár.[115] We might include here the storytelling that goes on in old folks homes, where retired people kill the time with, among other pastimes, narration, and where folklorists like myself have been successful in collecting.

These examples permit the conclusion that the conditions which foster narration are not necessarily connected with village or farm. Good narrators bring the folktale from outside work communities into the village. The narrators who retain the folktale tradition which survives in the consciousness of the peasants, and bring it to new flowering, usually learn their tales outside the village, and the storytelling opportunities in the village are of only secondary importance for them. We are therefore faced with the same question which János Honti asked himself when he examined the life conditions of the narrators Péter Pandur and Mihály Fedics.

> Both Péter Pandur and Mihály Fedics are rootless wanderers, half-peasants, agriculturists; they told their tales to the researchers when the tales already had lost their original function. . . . It may well be that the narrators who really command a rich treasure of folktales do not belong to a locally rooted rural community. Is it not possible then that the narrator, like every true entertainer, is necessarily a wanderer—a vagabond who does not belong anywhere?"[116]

International evidence indicates that Honti's assumption is right. Storytellers usually are the "experienced" people, who have traveled through "ninety-nine villages" and settled only when old in the village community.[117] As the work opportunities for the wandering apprentices and the migrant agricultural workers change, communities are formed within which the folktale comes into existence and is needed. As a consequence of the close connection of these professions with village life, the folktale attains a place within the village entertainment. But the folktale has remained only one among many entertainments. Most of the communal work of the autumn and winter season involves the social life of the village young people, whose attention is distracted by many trifles, and who do not feel the isolation of the men who work in groups outside the village. This does not mean, of course, that it is impossible for an excellent storyteller to develop his talents to a maximum through the storytelling opportunities presented by the village. It is possible that he succeeds, in the village, in tying down attention, and in the past there were special occasions for this, particularly at times when the villages were very much isolated. We shall find this to be true with the tale community of Kakasd. It is probably the case, however, that the villages are not the true sources of narration; the narrators do not receive their inspiration here, for they themselves bring to the villages mainly what they learned elsewhere. The storytelling occasions in the village serve, above all, as a last opportunity for the aging storytellers. They no longer work; they have lost contact with the old community, but they enjoy a good reputation as storytellers and are invited to social gatherings. They themselves seek the community. Pandur once said that the true storyteller *must* tell stories, and when he does not have listeners, he goes and looks for an audience. The storytellers' adaptability permits them to adjust to the new circumstances, and in order to please their listeners, they shorten their tales and vary their way of telling a story.

We therefore do not believe that the village type of narrator is the "original," as described by Á. Kovács at Ketesd, and that his entertaining function is the real one, whereas the other types are created by devolutionary processes. According to Banó, storytelling was the natural content of the original village get-togethers and anyone could participate in it. Distinguished storytellers emerged only later on, he explains, when the division of labor due to the bourgeois development of peasant society resulted in the destruction of old communal life.[118] Accordingly, the last stage before the complete extinction of the folktale is reached when "the tale discontinues being told in a community while the narrators still know their tales."[119]

In contrast, the examples cited seem to show that the "narrating village" is not the rule; we therefore suggest that at an earlier stage it could not have been general either. We think, rather, that the storytelling villages known to folklorists were the result of coincidence involving good narrators, and that a special situation was created by the passing on of the tale treasure through several generations, causing the folktale to become very highly regarded.

We know a few places, like Ketesd, where storytelling is still alive and where there are several good and mediocre narrators; but each example is the result of some specific development which should be investigated individually. In most of the cases, considering the economic and social conditions of the village, we arrived at the conclusion that the popularity of the custom of storytelling is due to the fact that the narrators worked with the villagers in extra-village work communities. This was the situation in the regions of the former big estates of the clergy and high nobility, where a great part of the villagers worked as day laborers on the farms or spent a part of the year as seasonal laborers in a different region, and where the winters in the village were passed in storytelling. Thus it was in Sára, a fishing village on the river Bodrog. Here a rich folktale tradition is to be found—fishing, work in the vineyards, and seasonal harvest labor were the fertile grounds for storytelling. Since the large estates were parceled out among the poor families of Sára in 1946, there have been few occasions for storytelling, and narrating itself has ceased.

## NARRATIONAL OCCASIONS

AS WE HAVE SEEN, storytelling, in the course of the nineteenth and twentieth centuries, became mainly an entertainment of the poor, of the socially underprivileged classes. This is to be seen in the content of the tales—in their social tendencies, in the message they express,[120] and in the fact that the work occasions of the poor generally furnished the storyteller with the framework of his tales which appeals to the imagination of the storytelling community. The well-to-do peasants in the village have little respect for the folktale. They will tell anecdotes during their get-togethers but only laugh at the long magic tale. The respectable peasant wants to hear something "true," a historical event; he reads newspapers and no longer listens to "lies." His way of thinking is rational. He has access to modern mass media, education, and a comfortable standard of living, and as a result he is able to seek more than oral entertainment. The women, on the other hand, tell stories to the children, as they do in the cities, and here we return to the findings of Uffer and other researchers which show that the narrators are mostly the "little people." Indeed, the working conditions of the peasants who possessed land never provided the same conditions for storytelling as occurred with the agricultural workers and other day laborers. Under these circumstances, we should not say that the folktale is alive mainly among European peasants, but rather that it lives among the lowest social ranks of the people.

## THE FUNCTIONS OF STORYTELLING

BEFORE WE CAN EXAMINE the storytelling at Kakasd, we must concern ourselves with some questions of storytelling about which folklorists have reached different conclusions, and which touch upon the basic question of the life of the tale. Clarification of these questions will aid in the evaluation of our concrete material.

The examples cited so far show that we have many proofs of the existence of the functioning tale, but because of their brevity and the haphazard manner in which the observations pertaining to storytelling were recorded, they are not sufficient to show clearly the diverse types of the communities where folktales are being told. In Eastern Europe, of which the Hungarian folktale region must be considered to be a part, tale tradition is an organic part of folk culture. Even though the tale plays an important part within the village, it is really at home in the extra-village work communities of the poor peasants. In these communities is developed the narrative talent which keeps tradition alive and infuses it with fresh blood.

Within these communities two systems of storytelling have developed: several persons may narrate one after the other, or one single individual may narrate for the whole evening. Since we have touched several times upon these two systems and have cited concrete proof for them,[121] it is sufficient to mention here only their essential elements.

Storytelling by several persons, one after the other, is the more frequent system. As if following the rules of a game, each member of the community is obliged to tell a tale, or the most skillful storytellers take turns. The former practice can be found where there are no specially good storytellers, as for example in the barracks room, where anecdotes and jokes take the place of the folktale. Usually several good or mediocre narrators can be found who alternate with each other—two or three tell tales during one evening. It may happen that there is an extremely gifted storyteller present who listens for a while and takes the stage only later, when his superiority can shine by contrast. In general, however, the outstanding storyteller does not let others take the limelight; he demands the undivided attention of his listeners.[122]

The second system of narration presupposes the presence of an outstanding narrator personality. The raconteur must have the ability to prolong his tales; he must be able to fill an entire evening and, if necessary, to continue his tales on several evenings in succession.

Both narrative methods have a strong impact on the formation of the folktale. If the narrators follow each other or if several individual storytellers take turns, the individual tale naturally is shorter, for each narrator wants to be heard. This also causes a certain kind of competition: one will try to outdo the other in telling something better, funnier, and more exciting. What is decisive is not the length of the recital but the variety, for the listeners and all those who are waiting their turn to narrate can hardly wait for each one to finish his tale. We have known many examples of this competition, whose the final phrase with its "challenge for competition"[123] has been in use in various forms in Hungary. Often a storyteller challenges another storyteller who is present to compete against him by jokingly including him in the terminal phrase of his tale, and if the other storyteller cannot rise to the challenge, he "remains in the tale," which is a great shame.

If there is an outstanding storyteller present, the long folktale will be told. It is the usual magic tale but will be lengthened or shortened according to necessity or the wishes of the audience. If the storyteller in the spinning rooms becomes aware that his listeners are not especially attentive, he can terminate his tale within half an hour, but by the same token he can add new adventures and fill a whole evening with the same tale or even continue it over several successive evenings. The conscious act of composition included in arbitrary lengthening is possible because the folktale is composed of independent, well-rounded episodes. Nearly all of the outstanding storytellers have confirmed this. To speak only of the Hungarian storytellers, Fedics, Pandur and János Nagy stated on several occasions—as we shall see later on—that they were able to make a long tale out of very little material. The virtuosity of Mrs. Palkó's storytelling in Kakasd is an example. We must, however, stress that such free handling of the folktale tradition is possible only for the consciously creative storytellers, and this only in storytelling communities where the traditional tale is not treated as holy writ.[124] Tradition must not be frozen but must still be living.

The noticeably long folktales of the Hungarian storytellers were mentioned in 1877 by László Arany: ". . . the reason for this . . . I see in the manner of life of our people, which brings with it many lazy evenings on the farms and with the shepherds, and also in the silent character of the Hungarian which gives him the patience to hear out the long tales."[125] An example of narration in installments is quoted by István Lázár: "By paying attention one could follow how a saga gleaned here and there from the tale body was forming on the lips of the skillful storytellers; the recital of it would take several evenings. This also used to be labeled a 'patience tale.' "[126]

Today we know more about the reason for this kind of Hungarian storytelling. The statement of a single storyteller proves that the creative narrator considers the tale as his spiritual property; he forms the episodes of the tale according to his own judgment, finishes it where he likes, and lengthens it as the spirit moves him:

A week passed before I had told [i.e. finished telling] a tale. One can begin with anything. With a table, a plate, whatever comes handy. The tale is just like this little sapling. It develops, you prune it, graft it, clean it, and it sprouts branches, leaves, and fruit. A life develops, just as with man. Who knows what will become of it? Thus it is with the folktale. Once I started a tale with a young girl finding a small casket. She took it up and opened it to see what was in there—and it was a dragon. He seized her and carried her away. What became of her I related for a whole week. The tale goes on as we want it to go; it only needs soil and foundation, then one can put anything into it.[127]

Since Ferenc Czapár's words might be considered exaggerated, let us also consider the opinion of József Faragó. It shows how in Marosmagyaró, among the timbermen, a tale has to develop by installments as a matter of course:

The tale runs on, time passes. Some become tired and fall asleep. The storyteller at some moment says "bones," to which the answer has to be "soup," as a sign that one is not falling asleep but is listening. Some who have already fallen asleep instinctively answer drowsily, but belatedly and very slowly. This causes loud laughter.[128] Gradually, everybody gets tired and finally falls asleep. The question "bones" is answered by "soup" by fewer and fewer people, sounds lower and lower, and finally the storyteller lets be. The next evening he seeks out the place in the narration which everybody still had heard and continues his tale from there on. . . .

Faragó's storyteller, the 56-year-old Minya Kurcsi, told stories which extended over two and three evenings.

The international examples as well as those originating in Hungary require that the question of storytelling in installments be examined seriously. It is plausible that storytelling in installments should have developed in the tale-rich regions of Europe, as results from Russian,[129] Irish,[130] Turkish, and other research show.[131] There are many indications that storytelling in installments was not quite as fantastic as it seemed from the publication of the Sára examples, the first analysis of this phenomenon in Hungary.[132] In the examples mentioned the necessity of lengthening the magic tale was quite obvious.

Each of these narrative systems modifies not only the length but the content of the tale. Of importance to us are the loose parts of the folktale, which, even though they have in part been formalized, still give more scope to the narrative inventiveness of the storyteller than the ready-made episodes. The ad hoc improvisations of the storyteller are most discernible in the introductory and the closing parts of the tale. They conform to the occasion and the audience. A few improvised remarks lead from reality to the realm of the tale or from the tale back to reality. They can make the other parts of the tale "credible" or enhance the standing of the narrator, because the listeners are guided by him through the world of the folktale. We named this the "framework" of the folktale.[133] It is immediately dependent upon the function of the folktale and surrounds the tale with reality; the nature and extent of this framework is determined by the tale community. When one story is told after another, a whole frame story might develop; however, since we can provide proof for this only by quoting the European folktale, we cannot draw any conclusions on this point.[134]

The long tale, however, is a daring flight of imagination and variety. We know the introductory and concluding formulae which, in general, answer questions about the magic tale to be told or are meant to dissolve the listeners' doubt. The narrator refers to something, confirms it, testifies for it, and wishes his listeners good luck and himself ample rewards.[135] To fashion these formulae ingeniously and to alternate them is an indispensable part of composition for narrators in work communities outside the village. The scant material garnered so far permits us to conclude that the collector will find a treasure of possibilities not yet exhausted. That we know so little about this process is the consequence of an, as yet, undeveloped methodology of collecting.[136]

Having investigated the modes of narrations, we must not neglect the atmosphere of taletelling, from which springs the need for the folktale.[137] As we have seen, there were and still are situations in which people live in small groups or closed communities, cut off from the outside world. One day passes as uneventful as the next. The folktale is the only spiritual nourishment for this kind of community, forged together by work, and is its only form of recreation and entertainment; it eases work, releases tension, and helps induce a refreshing sleep.[138] Relaxation after work, the overheated air in the hostels, the tobacco smoke, and the flickering lamp create an atmosphere conducive to the acceptance of the folktale. It forms a bridge from reality to illusion, from the state of wakefulness to that of the dream, as many folklorists have pointed out. S. Dömötör[139] refers to the festive expectation, on the part of narrator and listeners alike, which precedes the telling of a tale, but the spiritual predisposition for it is important above all. It brings the tale to mind, lends wings to the tale itself, and captivates the listener. We need not necessarily trace this behavior back to the primitive male communities only because the tale performance is dramatic or even ritualistic, or because the members of the storytelling group are all men. The peculiar physical situation of such groups, however, evokes a similar atmosphere which is an important factor in storytelling.

Here another question must be raised, that of credibility—the belief in the truth of the tale—which is closely connected with the question of atmosphere. For the folktale to be effective, the audience must be in the proper spiritual state, a state which is receptive to the message of the tale. We know very well that the folktale differs considerably from the other narrative genres in that it is a consciously entertaining art form and does not lay claim to credibility. As long as folktales have been known, they have borne the stamp of the "not true." Much folklore data show[140] that it is indeed decisive for the acceptance of a tale whether the folk consider a narrative as truth or as a *märchen*.[141] "I lied for they listened to me," ends one of the concluding formulae. "Let us lie a little bit, Gyuri," says Ágnes Kovács' narrator. "Okay, let us lie a little," his comrade assents and starts to tell a story.[142] János Nagy, a storyteller from Sára, thinks that "Every man has to have a hundred lies in his pocket, but of the very best, so that everybody will believe them." This is the key to the problem. The fundamental law of the folktale is this: Lie, narrator, but do not be found out; swear that you have dished up the truth. Berze Nagy is right when he says, "The folktale is only considered a beautiful lie by our people."[143] But as soon as the narrator enters into its spirit, his creative consciousness forgets that the tale is not the truth, and he himself shares the adventures of his imaginary heroes.[144] There is a strange ambiguity in folktale narration: the storyteller has recourse to all the tricks of the trade to make his listeners believe what both he himself and his listeners know are lies; but at the same time they are trapped by the effect of the tale and will live through it, reacting with tears and laughter to the individual situations. When they get hold of themselves, the folktale is once again just a story. But this is not only the aim of the storyteller; it also is the artistic law of the tale, which is served by the introductory and the concluding formulae. To make everything credible, the folktale has to be placed in a far, distant time,[145] and this is the reason that the storyteller uses the first person in the introductory and concluding statements.[146] To bear out the credibility of his words, he conjures witnesses, cites those from whom he has heard the tale, those who were there, and even refers to imaginary books from which he got the story. Sometimes he represents as having come from where all the action has taken place,[147] and to make this credible, he gives an exact description of the place and quotes certain statements.[148]

This ambivalence of "true" and "untrue" is shown in some of the playful introductions: "Damned be he who will not believe my stories, but he who will believe them will not be blessed;" "Who does not believe me, search for himself;" "Who does not believe my story should stay in it." Or joking statements like this: "I see it before me, as if it were happening now;" or "I myself was there when this was told."

The truly creative narrator considers the folktale as his spiritual property. The lesser talents see it as the property of the person from whom they have learned it and thus endeavor to render it without change to honor the other's creation. In sober conversation people usually talk about the folktale as Péter Pandur did: there is some truth in it, but the storyteller can shape this at will.[149] Or, they say, like Fedics: "Today the folktale is no longer true, but once it was.[150] The different evaluations of the folktale—the conscious "I don't believe it" and the unconscious "I believe it"—stem from one natural fact: the story is not just entertainment or recreation for the folk community, but more than that—contentment, an outlet for protesting social injustice and fulfillment of the hopes and wishes of man generally, especially of the poor man in backward, rural communities.[151]

Ortutay investigates the question of credibility from another point of view and poses this question for Fedics: Is the story true or not? For this creative narrator the folktale has only "mental reality," and he is trying not to involve it in contradictions, after having, in advance, taken the researcher, with the pride of an author, behind the scenes of his working methods. The "reality" of the tale is relegated by him to a far-off past, and as proof for this naive and superstitious concept Fedics cites examples in which he himself believes blindly. Fedics' explanation leads Ortutay to conclude that "the credibility of the folktale results mainly from the connection with the folk belief concepts."[152] We, however, believe that the connection between folktale and belief concepts is only one of the roots for the belief in the folktale. We shall come back to this later. Ortutay himself states convincingly that what we find in a tale has nothing to do with the conscious, rational believing of a truth, but is concerned, rather, with the unconscious participation which is a natural consequence of listening to a tale, just as it is of watching a play or a motion picture.[153]

In community storytelling we note that the narrator often has his own repertoire, which is respected by other narrators. This applies even more to the gifted raconteurs, though they, too, tell stories they originally learned from others.[154]

The narrators from Sára, János Nagy and József Fejes, who were recognized as the most outstanding there, had several tales in their repertoires which belong to the same type family but whose construction differs fundamentally, so that there is not the slightest suspicion that they used the same sources. We shall see in examining Mrs. Palkó and her nephew that their tale body originates from the tradition of their mutual ancestors, and yet their repertoires are different. What the narrator has learned during his life, what he has picked up here and there, is stored away for a long time and eventually recited in a completely new form. It is not necessary for the narrator to have had a master: often he has gleaned the foundations and the subject of his tales from the taciturn delivery of a simple, knowledgeable man within the family circle. It is unlikely that a new storyteller will have learned his tales from an older, respected narrator and then attained equal popularity within the same tale community. Within the circle of listeners there is no occasion for trying out, only for listening and learning. The gifted narrator, therefore, is both model and teacher. The new narrator can recite what he has heard only where he is the center of attention and can play a leading role. He has to seek out a new community where his master is not known, or at least is not present. Usually a gifted new storyteller learns from various masters, and in different places. For a long time he works up his material, making it his own, and only when he has reached the age of maturity necessary for the reputation of a storyteller does he come forward. We can see, therefore, that learning a story does not involve the usual learning patterns but preparation by attentive observation. New narrative talent can develop only under favorable circumstances.[155]

Like the literary work of art, the folktale, too, can be the property of an established storyteller. This occurs in primitive societies[156] and among European peoples.[157] Lajos Kálmány was the first to recognize this in Europe.[158] Berze Nagy also points out this phenomenon and says:

> Storytelling is done one after the other; everybody narrates a story which he has learned to perfection on precisely such occasions, and which he has recounted several times. Thus the narrator or the "folktale tree" who increases his skill by having been forced to be the sole storyteller during winter evenings reaches such artistic narrative perfection that people say, "That is his story." And if the person in question did not know the tale he would say, "So-and-so told this; he knows it." I had to wait a whole evening for a

man who, according to the narrators and the listeners, was the only one who could tell the story and knew the way it had to be told. The mere appearance of the man was greeted by "Ohs" and "Ahs," to say nothing of the effect the telling of the tale had on everybody."[159]

This is an excellent observation of the community in which stories are told one after the other, though it is not clear how the type of narrator who can fill a whole evening by himself fits in here. Uffer mentions that the father of one of his storytellers narrated with a friend, alternating with him on winter evenings, each one telling in turn his own stories.[160] Similar cases are cited by other researchers.[161] This shows that there is a certain right of authorship of a folktale, not only for the gifted raconteurs but for others in the community who tell stories. (We do not count among these the passive connoisseurs of stories who, if necessity demands, can repeat what they have heard; the unwritten rules do not apply to them.) In narrators who tell only a single story, as Berze Nagy mentioned, we simply have the fact of an often-told tale which is fused with the person of the narrator by constant repetition and thus is most successful when he tells it. Therefore no other person wants to spoil it, nor would the community stand for it. It is a different case, however, when a narrator infringes upon another narrator's property. In Sára it happened that János Nagy caught another fisherman, a younger, less experienced narrator, Ferenc Czapár, dictating to me one of his own tales. János Nagy sat down and listened sullenly, from time to time making condescending marginal remarks. When Czapár had finished, Nagy called, "Now I am going to tell you how it *really* goes." He had forgotten that his own version had already been recorded in writing. This time his narration produced six additional typewritten pages and was much more colorful. This new formation resulted from his being upset about the appearance of a rival. Thompson states that the Irish *shannechas* consider it one of the best tricks of the profession for the narrator to mention that a tale has already been told by another good storyteller.[162] We also have proof for the fact that a well-loved folktale is a precious treasure which is anxiously guarded. When Bladé's storyteller was dictating his story to the collector, he looked around furtively to see that nobody was listening. From this Röhrich deduced that the folktale is not always a "communal property."[163] We would rather deduce that the narrator was afraid of competition, because the tale cannot live simply in the consciousness of a person; it has to be told. Two Irish incidents bear out this conclusion. One concerns an old storyteller, who, on his deathbed, bequeathed to his friend his most beautiful tale, a tale the other had never heard before.[164] The other cites the theft of a closely guarded tale. An itinerant beggar was especially proud of one of his tales, and when he stopped at certain houses, he always told it; but he was afraid of a famous storyteller because he feared that the man might learn the tale and would become his rival. Once the other hid himself so that he could hear the tale:

> On the fall night when the storytelling was about to begin, the beggarman looked carefully at the assembled company, eager to hear him tell his jealously guarded tale. "Is Lynch here?" he asked his host. "Oh, sure, he is in Valentia and probably asleep by this time!" said the farmer. On this assurance, the tramp began his tale. When at length he came to the end, there was a triumphant shout from the storyteller who had hidden in the loft. He jumped down, in the midst of the startled audience. "I have the tale now in spite of you!" Lynch called to the poor beggarman. Lynch began to tell the tale then to prove his words, and the dawn was breaking before he finished.[165]

We must examine a final problem raised by the situation at Kakasd. Here we meet for the first time extraordinarily gifted Hungarian female storytellers. Let us see how far storytelling in Europe is limited according to sex.

There is no doubt that the earliest notes in folktale literature mention wet nurses and old women. They are the old narrators, the fictitious and the real ones, of world literature, of whom poets revive their childhood memories in the magic tales.[166] These are also the narrators whom we can find in the Grimms[167] and in Hahn,[168] Gonzenbach, and Bladé. The German women living on Hungarian soil are the family-circle storytellers mentioned by Zenker-Starzacher.[169]

The main burden of proof, however, convinces us that storytelling is not a specific occupation for women. There are stories destined mainly for children which, of course, are told by women. It is the task of women to tell stories for children, but this does not mean that women are true storytellers, recognized by the community. It is quite possible that there were among these women some extremely gifted storytellers, but this cannot be stated with certainty today due to the scarcity and stylization of the available documentary evidence. Surely we are not dealing here with the true storyteller. The Hungarian documents show clearly that the household tales for children told by women were never taken seriously by adults.[170] True storytelling is adult entertainment having an important social role. Sándor Pintér writes, "It would be a serious mistake to think that only children listened to tales; on the contrary, the tales were mostly told for the entertainment of adults."[171] In Sára the children who sneaked in and hid in corners were driven out of the room; nor did Pandur suffer any children among his listeners, except when he told stories for children only, as Novopolzev also did.[172]

Researchers are split in their opinions about which sex is prevalent among storytellers. Without critical examination of the material and solely for statistical purposes, Bolte and Poliivka register as many male as female narrators.[173] Mackensen, too, states that storytelling is neither a decidedly male nor female art.[174] Wisser, however, says something different. It is well worth quoting him:

> As to the sex of the persons who . . . contributed to my collection, the number of male narrators (190) exceeds that of the female narrators (50) to a striking extent. Therefore we have simply thrown out the dogma, prevalent until now, that female storytellers are superior to male storytellers and will assume the contrary. This assumption is borne out by the fact that the male narrators usually knew much more than the female ones. Among those only one woman knew more than 40 stories; among the rest only one more than twenty. Among the male narrators two knew more than 60 tales, one more than 50, one more than 40, five more than 30 and six more than twenty.[175]

Wisser not only bases his observation on statistics but points out that the "female" theme in the stories do not indicate female storytellers:

> It was variously stated that the true magic tale was told by women, the anecdotes by men. This statement, which is probably based only on an assumption, does not apply with regard to my own collections. In these there are only the tales about the bad stepmother, five stories in different forms . . . which were told me by women only, and only four . . . where the number of female narrators is greater than that of the male. With all other types that of the male narrators exceeds—to a great extent. . . . That women, therefore, are the guardians of the tale treasure is only a nice thought. About anecdotes we cannot say more than state the fact that they were mostly told by men.[176]

Older and newer collections show that the role of women in storytelling is less significant than that of men. Numerically, too, the male storytellers are preponderant[177] and the repertoire of the good female storytellers is much smaller than that of their male counterparts.[178]

Contrary to Boratav's statement that folktales in Turkey are developed and maintained by village women, Walker and Uysal point to the male coffee house meetings as the center of storytelling.[179]

The folklorists are unanimous in demonstrating that the tales of the women are much shorter and less colorful, that women limit themselves to the mere recital of the necessary details, that they stick to what they have learned, whereas the narration of the men is colorful and moves along well, and men recite details, describe with epic depth, and often dramatize, striving to attract the biggest possible audience through exceptionally good storytelling.[180] The women are also in the background because they are much more homebound and have very few occasions to leave the village in order to collect adventures and to learn.

The proofs are, in the main, favorable for the men, and yet we should examine the individual cases carefully: How far is it a question of gifted storytellers? What kind of narration is being investigated? Thompson says that men and women alike can be narrators, that this is determined by the prevailing customs. Yet in Ireland, for instance, storytelling is the privilege of the men.[181]

According to Cammann, storytelling in West Prussia was "Männersache" and an exception with women.[182] In principle, there can be narrative gifts in men and women alike, for true talent will always come to the fore, even under the most adverse circumstances. We have come to know excellent female storytellers among the Russians, in particular—Anna Barishnikova, Marimjana Medvedjeva, Natalia Ossipovna Vinokurova.[183] For the sake of completeness we must add here that the women excelled especially in the genre of the dirge. Until 1925 the Russian researchers had found only thirty-five females among close to one hundred storytellers.[184]

In Hungary, it is mostly the men who tell stories in public before a big audience, whereas the tales recorded by women show only that they know the stories and preserve them. By reason of their position in society and their work, women rarely become storytellers; Mrs. Palkó of Kakasd, who could vie with any man, is an exception to the rule. In general, the women remain within the family circle; they tell their stories to children or grandchildren or other adults in the family; the men, on the other hand, seek the big audiences, the publicity.[185] From what we have said about the place of the narration, it is obvious that storytelling is mostly connected with male occupations and the places of work for men. Doubtless it is the men who are the storytellers among European peoples. There have been cases where men, when telling stories, excluded not only

the children but the women.[186] The storytelling of women is only a
secondary matter in the estimation of folk society; it is limited to the
family, to the entertainment of children, and to the communal work of
the women.[187] Swahn's presentation shows that these questions are important not only from the viewpoint of the community but also with
respect to the variants of the folktale. In connection with the story of
Amor and Psyche he states:

> . . . Aa 303, in the first place, had male audiences and male tradition-
> bearers as opposed to Aa 425; which apparently developed almost
> exclusively in a female milieu. . . . It is striking, however, to see to
> what great extent this tale has been cherished by female story-
> tellers . . . it is only in the case of subtype O, the "male" form of
> the tale, that male storytellers regularly appear. This is an impor-
> tant aspect of the conditions in which the tale tradition is handed
> down and one which cannot be dismissed in a few words. Inci-
> dentally, however, I should like to point out that the male form
> of the tale is one that has made the longest "independent" wander-
> ings. This may have some connection with the fact that those
> professions which in older times forced people to travel, were
> primarily recruited among men—soldiers, apprentices, sailors,
> fishermen, etc.[188]

Although we have not been able to deal with some major and minor
problems connected with the storytelling process, we have stated our
opinion in regard to the main questions, so that we may now proceed to
the storytelling in Kakasd.

## STORYTELLING IN KAKASD

IF WE COMPARE the taletelling occasions and the narrative customs of the
Andrásfalva Szeklers with those of Kakasd, we notice changes which
were wrought within the space of time under investigation.

In both villages, the old Andrásfalva and the contemporary Kakasd,
storytelling was cultivated—that is, a tale tradition was generally known.
If necessity called for it, many villagers could tell stories; some of them
might even be creative and able to keep up the tradition of storytelling
and maintain the respected place in the tale in the social life of the community. This applies to every village which is rich in tales. Social necessity led, originally, to the cultivation of traditional material, and through
the participation of some of the villagers, this became a work of art.
The passive tradition-bearers played the decisive part—but without the

lively interest of creative storytellers within the broader community and in smaller circles the tale would not exist. The community graded its storytellers, and often the estimation of the storyteller invited would also indicate the importance of an occasion.

As for Andrásfalva, we noted, when analyzing one of its tales, that "the origin of storytelling in Andrásfalva doubtless should be sought among the poor people in the poor part of the village."[189] How the popularity of a folktale outgrows its old framework, how it achieved its present standing in the community of Kakasd, is shown in the scrutinization of the available information on narration.

Mrs. Palkó related:

> As far as I can remember, the best tales could be heard in the Moldavia region. I was still a little girl, about nine or so, when I was there for the first time, and there the people listened every evening to these tales, on the way to and also during their work, and only there. My father, too, had heard most of his stories there.

Our informants, especially the older ones, stressed this point. They unanimously declared that the most beautiful folktales were heard during seasonal labor.

"There, the men did not go out, they did not frequent the taverns, did not read; and everybody was glad when someone started to tell a story. Not an evening passed without a tale, and we all fell asleep over them," said Benedek Sebestyén. "There were still good storytellers abroad at that time and Uncle Marci was one of them."[190]

Thus it was with the Szeklers who had lived in the poor part of the village. The once well-to-do peasants, however, asserted that formerly they hardly paid any attention to folktales. "It was not the fashion then," said Ádám Sebestyén. "We did not have time for this, only those who had no work." "This is why they never amounted to anything, they only had these things on their minds," was Antal Zsók's opinion. He considered the folktale a useless waste of time and waved it off when the conversation got around to it. Lajos Farkas, Lajos Ömböli, and Mátyás Mátyás recognized those who could tell a good tale, but as far as they themselves were concerned, they took exception to the assumption that they could have taken part in such lowly entertainment. "Among the poor there were some who told so many stories that the others never could get their fill of listening. They gave the storytellers so much liquor, bacon, just so he would go on telling stories," reported Cirill Sebestyén. When questioned about how they could have learned so many tales, he answered, "Where

—well, where then? In the Moldavia region, for there the folktale grows like a weed."

We have already mentioned that each spring from three to four hundred seasonal laborers left for seven months, together with their families, to work for the big landowners in the Moldavia region. Year after year, they were accommodated in the barracks, which became their second home. Of importance for storytelling was not only the fact that these closely-knit work communities lasted for a definite time, but the fact that a part of the village, relatives and neighbors, remained together in their place of work as a storytelling community, far removed from their homes. Here originated the occasions through which storytelling became a custom, and through which the traditional tale body was elevated to a higher artistic level by the appearance of gifted storytellers. Here lies the origin of the storytelling among the Andrásfalva people; here is the place which played a major part in the development of their folktale tradition over the last eighty years. Here storytelling went on during work, and since outstanding talents appeared in this circle, the custom survived.

There were two tale occasions for the seasonal laborers who migrated to the Moldavia region. One we have mentioned in connection with field labor: in general the working groups were spurred on by the narrators. It was on such occasions that József Zaicz, Mrs. Palkó's father, who in the opinion of the people of Andrásfalva was the oldest and most famous storyteller of them all, told his stories. He died in 1938 at the age of ninety-seven. Mrs. Palkó's brother, János Zaicz, who was as famous a storyteller as his father, also told stories on such occasions, as did Marcika Pintyer (or Márton László), who also lived in the poor quarters of Andrásfalva, close by the Zaicz family. All three of them most frequently told their stories during the hacking of sugar beets; as foremen of the single groups they entertained the others during work, but they also told stories to the young people doing other kinds of work.

"My father went to Rumania," said Mrs. Palkó. "He told stories to the workmen so that time passed more quickly and work went on faster. Others can confirm this. When a month had passed they thought it had only been a week since they had arrived in the Moldavia region." László and Ambrus Sebestyén remembered that nobody wanted to remain behind with his hoe, for he would not hear the story, so they all hurried to stay behind the storyteller. Asked if they remembered what kind of folktales were being told, only two informants could answer. Mrs. Szakács said, "First of all witty ones, those that caused laughter," or "Just as they came about." Lajos Palkó said, "They asked that the tale of the *Red Cow* be told"—they ordered the tale which they wanted to hear. Erzsi Mátyás added, "Everybody was glad to work under a foreman who could tell good stories."

The other occasion for storytelling, and probably the more important one, resulted from sitting together during leisure time, after dinner. Mrs. Palkó related that her father was a good cook, so later he "was employed as a cook and cooked for the others." After dinner they all congregated around him, sitting in the yard and he started to tell stories. János Mátyás noted, "He always used to say, 'As many days as has the year, I have stories. If you like, we can divide them into months, in this month I shall tell so many stories, but you mark them, so that I would not tell it twice.' But he had so many stories that we wondered and worried where it would lead." But others, too, told stories. "Before we had regained consciousness of the outside world, the cock was crowing." Another informant remembered Marcika Pintyer's tales. People gathered in small groups, had fun, and offered the storyteller their brandy. When work during the day had been strenuous, they did not tell stories, but everybody went to bed right after dinner. When they were not too tired, they gathered around the storyteller, and the young ones especially were enthusiastic listeners. Many storytellers tried to vie with each other, to relate what they had once heard and to gather a following, for not all of the people could gather around one single storyteller. It happened that one tried to "tell a nice story, but he did not narrate, just stuttered: not everybody succeeded. Then they left him alone and went where they could hear something," Mrs. Palkó told us. But Albert Szakács also said, "When they heard laughter in some place, when the story was started, they rather went there; they wanted to hear the brother of Zsuzsi [Mrs. Palkó]." Every group thus gathered around a certain good storyteller and listened to him. Our informants confirmed that, in every case, when they came together in order to hear one specific storyteller, another never had a chance, and telling stories in turn simply did not get started. Generally long tales which filled a whole evening were told, and sometimes two short tales, but never more than two. Mrs. Palkó remembered having heard there several times the stories of *The Fawn*, or of *The Turk* or *Prince Sándor*. Very seldom were anecdotes narrated on such occasions, but it did happen that tales of a religious nature which somebody had read were narrated. Marcika Pintyer could read; he knew such stories, and he liked to tell them. Installment storytelling was seldom practiced, although Andrásfalvi said about his own storytelling, "If I could not bring it to an end one day, I finished it the next."

At the taletelling occasions in the Moldavia region, it was the men who excelled, not the women.

Judging from the childhood memories of those who today are seventy and eighty years old, a certain ranking developed during the seasonal labor in the Moldavia region. This was the stimulus for the folktale life in Andrásfalva. The audience of the individual storytellers was composed, as we have said, of the work communities and of those gathered around a storyteller after dinner, of men and women, old and young, even of ten- and twelve-year-olds, as far as they participated in the work. Here, too, as with the itinerant workers, it was mainly men who excelled. But the audience consisted partly of women, which laid the groundwork for the storytelling by women in Andrásfalva.

After seven months of working with daily storytelling, the families returned home from the Moldavia region, and in their native village they congregated on every possible occasion. The relatives and neighbors met at communal work occasions and on feast days. The entertainment of the Moldavia region was continued here and widened to include a greater part of the villagers. With this the strict rules about who told stories were not followed, for here the tale was the center of attention, and anyone who had been a listener in the Moldavia region could try his hand and see how far he got. Here appeared also the female storytellers; when none of the excellent storytellers were present, others started to narrate whatever came into their minds or what they had heard or learned during the summer.

If we consider the tale communities of Andrásfalva, we see that the folktale was most relished in the spinning rooms, especially in the spinning rooms of the married women. The young people preferred games and songs. "From Monday to Thursday there was spinning every day; on Fridays we did not go to the spinning room," said Erzsi Mátyás. "Saturday is the day of the Virgin Mary; we wash our clothes and must put the house in order. We have a lot of work which does not permit time for spinning," explained Mrs. Sebestyén-Boda. György Andrásfalvi remembered: "How we laughed! Aunt Zsuzsi [Mrs. Palkó] told tales and I told funny stories. On winter evenings when it snowed, the women congregated and sat down to spin, and the men joined them. Then they took their turns, amused themselves and laughed. Thus it was in the Bucovina. They never left me behind." Rudolf Varga related:

Then my wife said to me, "Well, let's go to the spinning room, and you come along too, my good man. The neighbor is also coming." Thus the groups got together, seven, eight, nine would go. They cooked wine with sugar; one would knit, the other sew or spin. The men told stories, and so we were entertained every evening. János Zaicz, too, told many stories in the spinning rooms, but when it was his turn nobody else told any stories.

János Mátyás gave a good picture of the atmosphere in a spinning room: "The women who were spinning started a song, the men jumped up and started to dance. Wherever they got together, stories were told. In one evening here, on another they said, 'Please be good enough and come tonight to our place.' Thus the spinning groups took turns and came to each of the houses."[191] "Most of the stories were told in the spinning rooms. Wheat was cooked; it was sweetened, and corn and wooden spoons were laid out. Everybody told what he knew. But well into one and two hours after midnight the fun went on." And as Mrs. Sebestyén-Boda added, "So that we did not fall asleep, one person told this story, another that one."

The storytelling occasions of other communal work, such as stripping feathers or shucking corn, were similarly connected with entertainment. Mrs. Rózsa related, "It often happened that we went with the neighbors to take the kernels off the cobs. There were women—young married women and older ones. Then Andrásfalvi was asked: 'Well, Gyurka, will you tell us a story?' 'All right, I shall do so.' "

Another tale occasion in the village was the gathering together on feast days. Our informants told us that the relatives and the neighbors got together on Saturday and Sunday evenings for a taste of *pálinka* (brandy), and some cake and fruit. On winter evenings the neighbors went visiting each other. Though the spinning bees had lost their importance—there were now no spinning bees among the married women and only a few girls spun together—storytelling was still alive during spinning in Kakasd. In the streets they hailed each other with "Come to our house tonight!" They sent their children or came even without being asked. When the young matron was alone at home she would pick up her distaff or her knitting and visit relatives or neighbors, taking the youngest child along. On such occasions, it depended on those present whether stories were told one after another by anyone who had a mind to do so, or whether everyone would listen to one good storyteller. This was the most frequent occasion for storytelling, but it was of no special importance for the community, even though it was informal. The house was full, the children were present; it was no offense not to listen attentively to the storyteller, and he could be left unattended. Everybody could have a try at storytelling, "and if it does not turn out well, he will be laughed at," Erzsi Mátyás said. Thus the story resulted spontaneously, without having been announced beforehand. Gergely János said: "In the evening, the whole neighborhood congregated. When they are sitting around without anything to do, one starts on one story, the other on the next." On such occasions men who could tell jokes and women who could entertain were very welcome; these are familiar types also known in the villages where no folktales are told.[192] They not only told a variety of stories, (mythical stories, true stories, erotic anecdotes, pious exampla, *märchen*), but they could sing and dance, imitate the drunks in the taverns, and describe generally known funny incidents at which everybody would laugh. Among these types were Illés Mátyás, Erzsi Mátyás, and Gertrud Szakács. The latter two deserve special attention, as they were the most popular tellers of true stories. These stories had been enriched by the countless experiences of recent years. The stories about the Bucovina had been joined by stories about the settlement and resettlement, coming to Kakasd, establishment of farm cooperatives, incidents and collisions with the Communist rule, and newly formed friendships. The satirical stories concerning personal adventures with the Communist authorities are countless. Though the stories at first were attached to the person who formulated them, the whole village community knew them by heart and requested them again and again. Thus by repeated recital the style of the stories became polished. The stories of Erzsi Mátyás and her sister Gertrud Szakács attracted special attention by the fact that they were told in alternate parts and adorned with song inserts. It was possible to record this new type of narrative genre in its improvised, natural informality only by hiding the tape recorder and films and by recording the whole performance without anybody noticing.[193]

In these social gatherings, Mrs. Sebestyén, Mrs. Kerekes, and the late Mrs. Dávid and other women whose narrative talents were a bit above what is required for the nursery were the narrators. In a word, the social gatherings were completely informal; and if folktales were not told exclusively, the tale took a subordinate position beside the other kinds of entertainment.

It was different when a true narrator could be present at the gathering, which was usually no coincidence. Someone who lived nearby would seek him out to hear his stories, or the storyteller would be invited to come to this or that house in the evening to tell his stories.[194] The storytellers were accustomed to having the same community around them every evening: the women from the neighborhood, work in hand; and later on the men and as many children as the house would hold. Some examples will show how highly respected were these old storytellers who told their tales in the evenings. Many a social gathering came about only through the desire to hear the most popular storyteller.

Mrs. Palkó said, "This is the way my father told stories; every evening the house was full. They came from all over the village, but he himself never went any place." György Andrásfalvi and Linusz Palkó still remembered the storytelling of the old Zaicz:

> On winter evenings when the wind was howling outside and it snowed, we all sat down together, children and grown-ups, and then Grandfather started a story. Even the children were silent, not a sigh could be heard. For the men, he told what suited them, not what he told others. On Sunday they went to see him to be entertained; they went to him as they would go to Church.

Mrs. Palkó's brother János, in contrast, went everywhere that people called him. "They invited him for the evening: 'Come and tell us stories.' The whole village gathered there and he told his stories," Mrs. Juhász told us. Mrs. Sebestyén also remembered János Zaicz: "My mother often gave him flour or a good hunk of bacon for his tales, so he would tell them, would come to our house. He was a good man but he cursed. Saturday and Sunday evenings, but also during the week, godfather [Zaicz] came into the spinning room and started telling stories." János Mátyás remembered that even the well-to-do had János Zaicz tell them stories, so great was his fame. "On holidays, the rich people summoned János Zaicz to come and tell stories. From ten, twenty households they came together; he sat down at the table and told stories. He never told the same story twice."

Mrs. Palkó's popularity until her death in 1965 equaled that of her father and her brother. Since both passed away she had been famous as a storyteller. She had told stories before, but then not so many people came to hear her; it is a long time before a woman can vie with the men, until the occasional storyteller in the family circle becomes a professional personality. As Mrs. Palkó herself told it, she became an acknowledged storyteller only after the death of her brother, when she lived in the Bucovina. There was hardly a winter evening that she was not asked to tell stories. When she became old, she preferred to tell them at home, surrounded by her grandchildren who "ordered" what she was to tell. In the evening the whole street would assemble at her home to be entertained; everyone would come to the small house in which she lived with her family. Rapt as children, they listened to her stories. The small room would be full to bursting; besides the immediate family there were usually ten to twenty guests. Mrs. Palkó related:

> So many people were here every evening that the house was full. Not everybody could tell a story, but even if he wanted to, they did not like to listen to just anyone. I said they should not always call on me, others too should tell stories. They did start, but soon asked: "How was it now?" Well, that was enough for me. They should not stop and ponder—once a story is started it should be told to the end. So it was in the Bácska. I then started to tell stories to the women, I was to tell them a story. Then the men fetched their chairs and came, then everybody came, even those who were playing cards, with their hands they played cards but with their ears they listened! They liked to hear what I told: "Oh, that was nice!" During the night I told the stories of *Józsi the Fisherman*, *The Psalmsinging Bird*, and *Katyika and Matyika*. I don't know any more how many I told. There are many people who tell stories, but the others do not always like to listen to them. One is slow, the other mumbles, but what I say they can understand, even those who are hard of hearing."

In 1950 Mrs. Palkó had broken her hand. Since she could not work, she had told even more stories. "Now that I cannot spin I am better at storytelling. In the evening they all come here knitting and spinning. They insist on coming here: 'Is there a story being told?'" Mrs. Palkó belonged to a rosary circle which gathered each week in a different member's house. When the service took place at her house, a tale was told after the prayer: "It was a prayer service and everybody who belongs had come, all twenty-nine of them were at my place. The house was full and I then told them a story which they liked. I told them the story of *Józsi the Fisherman* and *Prince Sándor*. We sat there until midnight."

But Mrs. Palkó narrated not only in her home. Well into her seventies, she still went out when she was invited, though not as much as before, to see relatives nearby or neighbors, or to make a sick visit. Often she would be invited to tell stories, and then she would say: "You know, on Saturdays I always go to house No. 42 to tell stories. Please come there." This was the home of Titus Sebestyén, who is married to Mrs.

Palkó's niece, who told what she learned from her father and from Mrs. Palkó. Otherwise Mrs. Palkó went only to wakes to tell stories.

We still must mention the tale occasions which are intimately connected with male occupations. In Kakasd today they are of little importance, but in Andrásfalva, where the men were a closely-knit group, they played an important part. One tale occasion arose in the forests, when the carters came for wood. Before loading, the carters gave the horses a rest and went into the timbermen's huts "for a folktale." Many in Andrásfalva still remembered that. The nightly fishing expeditions on the Suceava river presented a good occasion for tales. Old man Zaicz took his grandchild György Andrásfalvi with him to fish, and Andrásfalvi relates: "This particular tale we always told while fishing in winter—when we caught fish, around the camp fire, nights, everybody who could tell a story did so. I did not need to collect the fish from the snow when I was the narrator."

Here again we have the storyteller who makes the work of others easier and thus has an advantage. János Mátyás told the following story about János Zaicz: "Once we let the horses graze along the banks of the river and asked the old man to tell us stories. He told us such a long tale that I said it would never end!"

In former times only men would congregate in winter, younger men as well as older ones. They liked to gather at the workshop of a craftsman whose work prevented his leaving the shop. They brought with them work, news, and stories. The favorite meeting places in Andrásfalva were the shops of the shoemakers. Cirill Sebestyén said, "I lived close to the cobblestone street of the village and I worked in peace. They often brought me something to drink and talked, told stories, while I repaired their shoes." Gergely János still could remember that, in the Bucovina, Andrásfalvi used to tell stories evenings in the shoe-repair shop. Ten to fifteen men gathered while the master did his work. He said,

> I was a bachelor; there were just two of us, my mother and I. My sister had married, my brother was as good as married, and I alone had stayed at home. I was occupied raising pigs, but in the evenings I went to the shoemaker's house. That one was my friend, János Daradics. There were fifteen of us men who went to the shoemaker's. First, János said to me, "Well, Gyuri, do you entertain the people here?" "Oh, well, what do you want?" "Come," he said, "tell us something nice."
>
> So I started. When we finally came down to earth again, he had

finished a pair of shoes. When I returned home my mother was asleep. . . . I entered carefully, made a wood fire, put the rest of the bacon in the pot, and ate my supper. I blew out the lamp. Then she cried out, "Now you come! The devil get you! Was it better to look for fun, gossip from one window to the other?" . . . Thus the men got together.

All these examples show that every get-together was an occasion for the telling of folktales. For György Andrásfalvi even the twenty-four days he spent in jail in Szekszárd were an occasion for storytelling.

Twenty-four days I was a prisoner in Szekszárd. But it was my buddy's fault. We gathered kindling and the constable caught us. In jail we were sixteen to a room, and I had to tell a story every evening. When I was set free they said to the jailer, "Mister Warden, that Gyuri Andrásfalvi, the pride of our room, don't let him go," for my buddy had let it slip that I could tell stories.

The good narrators also roused the well-to-do peasants' interest in the folktale. We have already mentioned that János Zaicz had been called to the big farms to tell stories. Even among the day laborers who worked on the big farms, stories were told. Mrs. Palkó, for instance, often went to the peasants while hacking was done and entertained them with her narration. Cirill Sebestyén remembered: "She started in the morning and continued telling stories until late at night. There were twenty people; they all took it easy, and she told them stories, and all stayed into the morning." Mrs. Palkó mentioned in connection with her best story, *I Don't Know*, that she had learned it on such an occasion from Mátyás Mátyás: "I had gone to their house for the hacking. 'Wait, sister-in-law, I am going to tell a story.' 'All right, I have told enough.' And then he started. I did hacking and he told the story."

When there were many people around Mrs. Palkó it was not difficult to make her tell stories. József Sebestyén could still remember that, whenever Mrs. Palkó assisted the priests' cook in her kitchen, she told stories to all present there. He himself was then about twelve years old and tended to the ringing of the bells. Whenever he brought the key back to the pastor, he sat down with the others in the kitchen and listened to the story. Many children also came there, and some of them learned the tales from Mrs. Palkó. One such child was the fifteen-year-old Ambrus Sebestyén, who in turn told the tales to the other children. "We boys and girls then went outside and sat down at the gate, and she [Mrs. Palkó] told stories."

Here we wish to add something about storytelling for children. With the Kakasd Szeklers, this is not considered collective entertainment but one of the duties of women. Yet it is of extreme importance for the transmission of the tale tradition. Nearly every mother tells her children stories, well or badly according to her ability and as she remembers them from her own childhood. As the children ask for stories, she usually refreshes her memory with a book of magic tales. What Mrs. Sebestyén-Boda had to say about the magic tale applies to the average family:

> I was told many stories and I also had a storybook. To tell a story one has to have time. The child knows many stories and it asks over and over again: "Mommy, tell me a story!" Then I start. I was able to tell stories, but I would forget because of my many worries. When others tell stories they come back to me, but by myself I would not remember. One, maybe, I could tell. Who likes to read also knows the stories. Formerly I was able to tell stories until midnight. But you must be in the right mood for this.

It does not matter whether the children's stories are told well or badly or whether they are read. They constitute for the children the first real encounter with the folktale, and it quite often happens that it is decided then and there who will become, sometimes after many decades, a good storyteller. Excellent storytellers such as Péter Pandur[195] come from a long line of storytellers, a veritable dynasty.[196] Mrs. Palkó and Andrásfalvi learned their stories from their fathers, who were famous storytellers. In Kakasd there is a sharp differentiation of the childrens' story from the other tales, and only the smallest child at home is told children's stories. But as a matter of course the children learn not only those stories that are intended for them, but those that are not meant for their ears. Thus originates a new generation of bearers of tradition and storytellers. Most of the children never hear as beautiful stories as the children and grandchildren of narrators hear, but even a weakly told tale can rouse interest in a child.

Children, too, try to tell each other stories. We have found examples of this in Kakasd. The twelve-year-old Zsuzsi Sebestyén and eight-year-old Lajos Palkó were very skillful storytellers. It would be interesting to examine more closely how the children learn stories and how they tell them. This, too, is a key question in folktale research.[197]

From what we have shown so far, we can deduce that storytelling was, first and foremost, a pastime of the poor people of old Andrásfalva, even though the well-to-do peasants of the village invited noted narrators every now and then to their houses.

There was one occasion in old Andrásfalva on which the art of story-telling had a tremendous social importance for all levels of Andrásfalva society: the custom of the wake. It is significant for the conscious upholding of this custom that it is considered by the Szeklers to have ethnic value. No matter whom we questioned about the characteristics of the Szeklers, he sooner or later would mention that nowhere among the Hungarians could be found such a beautiful custom as the Szekler wake.

"They [the Hungarians] put the dead person into the room, close the doors, and leave him alone. But this is a great sin," said Cirill Se-bestyén. "My God, how nice it is when people assemble for the soul of the deceased. There is no counterpart for it, and they do not know this here. The Hungarians do not treat their deceased brethren as Christians. When he is dead, he is dead and that's it. He does not interest them anymore. They bury him in a hole, they don't hold a wake," said Mrs. Szakács.[198]

The custom of the wake, observed by everyone, has created an order for the narration of folktales which is an indispensable part of the ritual.[199] Here the tale has an important and recognized function. Here we have the "true" storytelling. Two things are required: first, the presence of really good and gifted storytellers; and second, the forty-eight-hour duration of the wake. The house of the deceased will be full of people, and they all have to stay awake during the night. This can be managed only when a truly outstanding storyteller is avialable, a storyteller who entertains those present and at the same time makes storytelling a constant part of the wake itself. This very custom, which was preserved after the set-tling in Kakasd, shows clearly that the tale has lost its function of being exclusively the entertainment of the poor and has assumed importance for the whole community. In old Andrásfalva games were played rather during the wakes,[200] but these have disappeared completely from wakes today. It is important for the process of narration that it is not done by just anyone but exclusively by the most gifted storyteller. The more distinguished the deceased had been, the more importance is placed by the family on the fact that the best storyteller entertains the guests. The wake is not only a special occasion which involves many people, but for the elderly and for married people it is the most important occasion for entertainment. Here existing relationships are cultivated and kinship becomes more closely knit. A well-carried out wake is discussed for years to come, and one remembers who told what stories. Such a well-managed wake was the one for Mrs. Jordáki, in 1948; six years later, it was still being mentioned by eight people. Mrs. Palkó, on that occasion, had told her story of *I Don't Know* from six o'clock in the evening until the bell-ringing early the next morning.

But in examining the wake in Kakasd, we can recognize how much the older social order has changed, and how a new situation has resulted from newly formed neighborhoods and relationships. When one considers the old role played by the folktale in the community, this development also shows clearly that the folktale has driven out the old party games during the wake and has become its unique pastime. Considering the general social and economic changes after the settlement in Kakasd, this development seems logical and a matter of course. This is the reason why we shall examine the wake more closely in what is to follow.

Mrs. Palkó related:

> When the sick person dies, he is shaved, his hair is cut; he is washed, and a white shirt is put on him, and trousers, as is the custom with an old man; and a woman also is dressed in a white shirt and a skirt which she left behind. A young woman, however, is dressed in a colored skirt, pink or blue. The dead person is lifted high upon a pedestal and is laid out there. The coffin is covered with a white embroidered sheet; for a young man a colored one; three pillows [are placed] below the head, colorful, plump cushions. Two candles are placed beside the head.

The tolling of the bells announces to the village that someone has died and that a wake will be held. It is not customary to invite people to a wake, but it is expected that the relatives, the godparents, good friends, and neighbors—those from the Bucovina and the nearby ones—will appear. "Nobody is asked to come and see the dead. When somebody has died, a relative goes to see the neighbors. Everybody comes, even strangers," said Mrs. Szakács. "Nobody is asked to the wake," Mrs. Zsók confirmed, "but it is customary for everybody to go who wants to; this is our custom, we go to each other's wakes." When the house is ready to receive the mourners, everyone comes when he has time. When a new mourner arrives, he genuflects with his face turned toward the dead and then takes a seat. During the day only the close relatives are usually present, but from afternoon to midnight the house is full. Usually couples go to the wakes and older people, regardless of whether the deceased belonged to the younger generation. The young people come because it is the thing to do, but stay only a short while. In the Bucovina the mourners were treated to *pálinka* (brandy) and cake; today wine is offered. The bottle goes from hand to hand and everyone drinks for the repose of the soul of the deceased. "May the Lord give him peace and have mercy on his soul," said Mrs. Zsók, but Dénes Sebestyén put it: "May God rest the dead! Let them rest in peace. Amen!"[201] The specially invited mourners attend the banquet after the interment. When the deceased had been young, there is music during the banquet.

In Andrásfalva the deceased used to be laid out in a room emptied for the occasion, and all the guests congregated around him. In Kakasd, in the larger houses with three to five rooms, there is much more space, and the mourners occupy three rooms. In the first room, giving on the street, the deceased is laid out between the two windows, with his face toward the door. There is also a long table in the room and chairs. Here sit the singers, the men who say the prayers, and the nearest relatives. In the second room the men play cards,[202] also at a long table, or they simply sit around, having fun and drinking. When they enter the house of the deceased, the men take off their hats but keep a fur cap on. In the third room there are only women. If the house has only two rooms, men and women sit together.

Two people, much like masters of ceremony, are a part of every wake: the singer and the narrator. Some person who specializes in the dirges of the church is invited so that he can lead the singing.[203] "Such men like to do such things. They can tell about saints and stories from Holy Writ." Every hour or every half hour the entertainment is interrupted. The singer, who is sitting at the feet of the deceased, starts the singing of the dirges, and the men who are sitting at the long tables join in. When all the verses of the song have been chanted, they say a prayer. "One of the men prays, and they stop the tale. One recites the Creed, another the Our Father, another an Ave; they recite it for the deceased and for others who have preceded him." After that they continue to drink and to be entertained, picking up where they had left off.

The song leader at a wake is always one of the most gifted men in the village. When I was in Kakasd they were Mihály Kerekes, Mrs. Palkó's son, József Palkó, and Mátyás Mátyás. Formerly they were the older József Palkó, Vince Sebestyén, and Márton László. Márton László (Marcika Pintyer) was the author of a guide for the ritual of the wake, a book which contains dirges and which also provides entertainment for the mourners during a wake. We shall examine this book more closely in connection with the tales of Marcika Pintyer, but we wish to mention here that he was the only song leader who was also a storyteller. It is rare to meet a song leader who is also a narrator, for storytelling makes different demands on a person than singing, as a singer must be a deeply religious person. Of the sons of the old Zaicz, for instance, János was a storyteller and József a song leader. Márton László's *Book of the Dead* has become the recognized ritual to follow during wakes. At the beginning of the 'twenties László began to write copies on commission. Song leaders or older men who liked to go to wakes also began to copy parts of it, such as saints' legends, songs, and prayers. During my stay, there was only one complete copy in existence in Kakasd; it was written in 1934 and belonged to Ferenc Boda. Only when a particularly respected villager died was it loaned out; otherwise it was carefully shut away. There are also a few fragments in existence from which József Palkó in turn copied his songs. The death of Marcika Pintyer has not put an end to this custom. No one knows whether anyone had written a book of the dead before. It can hardly be assumed that there had never been a model. "He has done it all by himself;" said Mrs. Palkó, "from it they used to read. Those who used to go to wakes quite frequently bought many from him. I have never heard that anybody had written anything like it."

After the singing, the praying, and the toasts, entertainment is resumed:

All through the night they take turns drinking. The men drink and eat by themselves, then they play cards, in between they joke. It is said that there is no wedding without tears, and there is no house of mourning without laughter. Nobody, though, uses foul talk. Sometimes somebody tells about his own fate; we have this now that we were refugees, and everybody knows how to tell a story, but best of all Mrs. Palkó.

Thus we see that men and women are separated during the wakes. The men play cards and in between tell jokes and anecdotes. The invited storyteller, however, sits down with the women and tells them his stories. After some time, "even the men leave their cards and take themselves over to join them."

Storytelling has an important function during wakes. If one asks about a folktale in Kakasd, nearly everybody will refer to the wakes or to an outstanding storyteller of former or present days who played the chief part during a wake, and he will mention the families of Zaicz, Mrs. Palkó, or Andrásfalvi. People even vaguely remember the titles of the stories or when and at which wake a particular story was told. A storyteller will characterize a tale as follows: "This is very long; this is fit for a house of mourning." The storytellers know very well what kind of stories are expected from them on various occasions.

Dénes Sebestyén said, "They always told stories in the house of a

dead man." Mrs. Palkó related, "With the rich peasants, stories were listened to only when one of them had died, when there was a wake. So that
nobody got too tired, stories were told by whoever could and the others
listened. I went too. I liked to go to a wake. I think that the second day
with the Jordáki family I told them the story of *The Psalmsinging Bird*."
On one occasion when she had finished a story, she told me, "I know
even longer tales, but these belong with the wakes. Two tales last from
evening to morning—*The Twelve Robbers* and *I Don't Know*—and then
I still know *The Sky-High Tree* and *The Psalmsinging Bird*."

The name of János Zaicz was mentioned most often in this connection. He never played cards, Mrs. Matyi said, and Mrs. Juhász stated:
"When somebody had died, he could tell such tales that everybody was
anxiously waiting for him to start." Antal Molnár said:

> When János Zaicz started a story during a wake, it lasted until
> morning. The father of Zsuzsi, too—[Mr. Palkó] was such a story-
> teller. When my uncle died, I went to him, he was a poor man,
> and I said, "Józsi, you will come to our house and tell the women
> stories, won't you? We'll have a glass of *pálinka* for you; there
> will be plenty of food and drinks." Thus the old man told stories
> from evening to morning.

In Kakasd, Mrs. Palkó and Andrásfalvi were best liked for wakes.
But they were never invited together, for this would be an offense, as
they could not both hold the spotlight. During a wake it is not necessary to speed up storytelling; everybody has time to listen all night long.

The kind of stories that were told during wakes—long magic tales
or coarse anecdotes—were revealed by some of the informants' statements. Among the long tales, the most adventurous and vicissitudinous
were the best liked. The wake lasts for forty-eight hours and this demands the most long-winded tales, even when only two nights are involved, from six o'clock in the evening until dawn. During the day the
young people come, and the most distant relatives, because this is the
thing to do; in the evening there is less coming and going, and the group
which gathers then will stay together until the end.

Once the mourners remained without a story during the first day of
the wake. Andrásfalvi, who had been invited as the storyteller, was
drunk. When we asked him why he had not come, he said:

> You asked my wife: "Why did your husband not come to the
> wake, Erzsi?" The people waited for me to tell stories the second
> evening, for on the first I was drunk. I had been with my brother-

in-law. We drank wine, then it was so warm during the wake, the wine got warm, I could not stay there. The other day when I went there I told the tale of *The Discharged Soldier*. Outside in the woods one tells it differently; it is different for a wake.

The folktale does not have the same importance at every kind of wake.

When old people die, the wake is not so sad, for a person who was already old is not mourned so much. This is a natural thing, this is not so sad. When a young person dies, he is greatly mourned; people weep; then it is more difficult. With an old person we sing eleven to twelve hours, they don't weep as much as with a young person. There more tales are told. Where mourning is not so bad, stories are being told more, prayers are sung, but within bounds,

Mrs. Sebestyén told us. When a child dies it is not the best narrators who are asked to come. The mourners are for the most part women, and among them can be found storytellers. They are usually women who have been telling stories to the children or within a small circle, as for example Mrs. Matyi and Mrs. Geczi. They are not invited especially to tell stories, but in between singing and praying they are asked: "Well godmother, tell us a story—we know you can do it." "Tell us a story so that the little one may hear it also."

In considering the occasion and the place of storytelling among the Szeklers at Kakasd, we may state that the importance of the folktale for the whole community has increased, while it has been transformed in its specific nature. During the last eighty years, certain changes have taken place. The stay in Moldavia, before repatriation, was the source and seed bed of the *märchen*, which provided a necessary accompaniment during itinerant work. After the return to the village, the folktale, because of the exceptional storytellers who narrated on winter evenings, gained more importance with the rest of the villagers than was usual. In addition to its function at the social gatherings in the village, the *märchen* acquired another importance: it became the exclusive entertainment during wakes. Thus through the influence of several outstanding narrators, the folktale has once again become serious entertainment, this time for the whole society.

While these changes were in process, the change in the function of the *märchen* was being shaped by another set of circumstances as well. As a consequence of the resettlement procedures, social differences were leveled, a fact which contributed to an increase in the popularity of the folktale. The two subsequent changes in the peasant economy resulted in a temporary setback in their cultural development, and continued to level the already fluid social distinctions. By this process the *märchen* was elevated from the circle of the poor people and became a natural component of the wake.[204]

Through repatriation the original source of the *märchen*—itinerant work—dried up. At the same time the communal tasks within the villages also diminished, but in their place appeared the group entertainments during the long winter evenings, which also provided an occasion for storytelling. At the time of my fieldwork, two occasions seem to prevail: wakes, and social gatherings in winter. The importance of the *märchen* for wakes is very great, for here it fulfills its function according to its essence and form, as it did in the Moldavia region. Wakes, like seasonal labor, unite people for some length of time, and therefore a similar atmosphere is created. During wakes, when tales are told, small groups participate: neighbors, relatives, the inhabitants of certain sections of the village. The respect due the deceased, and which the community harbors for him, makes it necessary that the mourners be kept together at least until the end of the wake, and therefore provisions are made for thrilling entertainment. This is why the best narrators are invited, those who can tell the most varied stories, and the longer the stories the better. There are special *märchen* for the wakes, and it is these tales which determine the status of the individual wake. Storytelling in the house of mourning has thus originated from the "true" storytelling occasions. It represents a development peculiar to the Szeklers of Kakasd, continuing as it does an old tradition while at the same time creating a new one.

Storytelling for entertainment during winter evenings is informal and loose in Kakasd just as in other villages. The *märchen* appears, if it shows up at all, among all the other narrative genres of folklore. Neither the audience nor the narrator himself pays special attention to the value of an especially intricate tale. The main purpose is to while away the time pleasantly. Only when people gather to listen to an especially gifted raconteur does the situation change.

From all this it is clear that research must differentiate between the different quality of storytelling situations, since European folklorists' data until now never permitted us to distinguish between true storytelling, and mere passive reproduction of a tale. It is important to know whether the *märchen* is accepted as a serious component of communal entertainment—if it is an important phenomenon—or whether it merely represents a pastime.[205] This distinction is made by the listeners themselves when they ask for a true raconteur, but will content themselves with the occasional storyteller when the aim is just to pass the time. But the important storytellers themselves judge the tale occasion by consciously selecting their material. The tale collecting done in Kakasd shows clearly that in the villages where folktale tradition is still alive, the existence not only of creative narrators is essential but of the tale connoisseurs labeled by von Sydow and Wesselski as passive bearers of tradition. There are many narrators like Mrs. Geczi. Her tale treasure consisted of twenty-two stories, but she told only what she has heard from the great storytellers, giving short abstracts of plots when no other narrator was present. Narrators like this tell stories at home to their children or during wakes for a child. They pass on the raw material of the tale, and their importance lies in the fact that they can inspire gifted narrators to complete their scant sketches and create something new from them.

In this connection we must mention a phenomenon specifically indigenous for the Kakasd people. We have seen that on the true tale occasions it is for the most part the men who take part, in the old days as well as today. They are the recognized raconteurs, who appear in public. In Kakasd we find an exception: the gifted female narrator, Mrs. Palkó. Her audience was hardly ever composed solely of men; women were also present, and during wakes, where, contrary to the rule, the men set the tone for singing and praying, the folktale was told for the women. So women, too, have an occasion to accumulate a certain tale body. They do not appear in public, but tell their stories within the family circle or to smaller groups during communal tasks. Mrs. Palkó herself said that she was seldom invited to tell stories during wakes while her brother was still alive, though it was generally known that she could tell stories well. She too had told her stories mainly within the family, and when she had to appear for the first time in public in 1943, she was very shy. Through the coincidence of several simultaneous events, Mrs. Palkó became a generally recognized storyteller: the old narrators had died, while she herself had the skills necessary to develop into a good storyteller, and the old social order had been dissolved through repatriation.

## THE INTERACTION OF NARRATOR AND COMMUNITY

IN CONSIDERING the tale occasions of the resettled Szeklers, we must examine another question which has frequently arisen but which has never been closely investigated: How did the community present during the telling of a tale cooperate with the narrator? Theoretical considerations concerning the roles of personality and community in folktale creation were dealt with in Chapter 5. Therefore we need not repeat the generally known fundamental criteria of folklore resulting from the oral nature of delivery, from the simultaneity of performance and creation, and from the presence of the audience. In addition to the fact that the composition of the audience, their attitude, and their attention is mirrored in the formulation of the tale, the narrator is influenced by the atmosphere of the community, in both the choice of his material and the manner of presentation. Often the smallest motion among his listeners influences the narrator and influences the shape of his narration. It may help him, but it may also destroy a variant in the making. The tale becomes more beautiful and colorful when the narrator feels that his listeners are with him, living each moment along with him; the more complete the audience cooperation, the more perfect becomes the tale. Conversely, the narrator influences his listeners. It depends on him whether they consider the *märchen* essential to their social gathering, whether they pay only cursory attention or give him their undivided attention, whether everything fades into the background except the *märchen*, and whether the narrator can attract new admirers or even disciples.[206]

To gain complete knowledge of the process of narration before the natural audience, it would be necessary to make close observations on the spot. With every single tale, the interpolated audience calls should be attentively followed, as well as the behavior of each listener, and all the reactions which change from one telling to another. Systematic observation for several years would be necessary to get to know the individual listener types and their actual attitudes. The greatest drawback of folktale collection is that the tales have seldom been recorded in the natural habitat of the community. Generally the audience gathered— and this was the case also during tape recording—because the collector was present, which created a sensation.[207] Or, as usually was the case, the folklorist recorded the tales of good informants when no one was around and they would not be disturbed by interruptions. Or the collector found it safe even to invite his informant to his office in a scientific institution, thus creating a laboratory situation which shut out the natural atmosphere of tale telling. Ideally, the collector should observe the natural setting and attend storytelling sessions unobserved, but it is no easy task. To record the tale as a complex of recital, text, accompanying body movements, gestures, mimicry, voice modulation, and audience participation is almost impossible. There are rare occasions when natural spontaneous storytelling develops because of the presence of enthusiastic individuals who urge the storyteller to narrate in the presence of the folklorist.[208]

On winter evenings the two families in Kakasd which could offer hospitality to the collector—the Zsók and Sebestyén families—vied with each other over whose house the storytelling should take place in. Each invited his own relatives and his neighbors and acquaintances as well. This all was done not so much for the sake of storytelling but to draw admiration and increased prestige. I recorded the tales of Mrs. Palkó evening after evening, by the light of the oil lamp, in the home of the Fábián family. The neighbors who had come to be entertained seldom tired of the lengthy dictating—and yet the atmosphere was not right.

Several times, however, the occasion presented itself for hearing again, in its natural context, a tale which we had already recorded. Then changes—variations in the text and the interruptions of the listeners—could be noted, and the behavior of the audience observed. Some conclusions could be drawn from these observations, it was not possible to actually record the tale but since a second time, our method did not prove sufficient. We have only one single tale text in which the cooperation of narrator and listeners—at least that apparent from the interruptions—could be fully recorded. Although not even this tale occasion was a spontaneous one, it might be well worth our effort to talk about it, since the attitude of the audience could easily be observed.

On a Sunday afternoon stories were told in the house of the Antal Zsók family. I was in Kakasd for the first time, staying with the Zsók family. György Andrásfalvi, whose living circumstances were substandard, wanted to come there to narrate so he would not have to be ashamed in front of strangers. The Zsók family, for whom the visitor from the capital city was something new, heated the big front room and invited their friends who were in the habit of dropping in on Sundays anyway. Those present were Mrs. Dobondi (sister of Mrs. Zsók); János Mátyás (brother of Mrs. Zsók); Mrs. Fábián (oldest daughter of Mrs. Zsók) and her little son; József Sebestyén with his wife (second daughter of Mrs. Zsók) and two children; György Sebestyén (a godfather) and his wife; Gergely Fábián (a godfather from Lengyel who was visiting); Albert Szakács and his wife; Illés Mátyás; György Andrásfalvi and his wife (all cousins of Mrs. Zsók who see each other only rarely); Titus Sebestyén (a neighbor); Antal Kerekes with his wife (neighbors); and Antal and Ferenc Zsók (adult son and head of the family).

Only a few of the invited had come because they had heard that Andrásfalvi would be the narrator. Titus Sebestyén, Illés Mátyás, and the Szakács family had never visited with the well-to-do Zsók family in the Bucovina, where they lived in the poor quarters, though they were related through Mrs. Zsók. With the exception of the young Zsók, all those present belonged to the older generation (over forty years of age).

The *märchen* which Andrásfalvi narrated to this elect audience was one of his most famous, *The Twin Rod*. Many people knew this tale, which he usually tells at wakes but is often asked to narrate. It is usually referred to as "his" tale. Nobody else would tell the tale, and Mrs. Palkó explained, "I know it; I have heard it from him. It is his tale."

That this unaccustomed company became a narrational community in spite of itself is apparent in the fact that during the narration there were many interruptions—fifty-nine, in fact. This is significant, for the heightened attention of the listeners, despite the many interruptions, did not enhance the *märchen*. The tale as transcribed runs to twenty-one single-spaced typewritten pages, as the narrator told his tale slowly for dictation and did not accompany it with the usual vivid pantomime. It would not have been unusual for a company thus composed to begin to become bored.

The active members of the audience, Mrs. Dobondi, Erzsi Mátyás, and Gertrud Matyi were quick witted, fun loving, and generally well liked. Dénes Sebestyén was impertinent; Illés Mátyás and Albert Szakács liked to make robust jokes. János Mátyás, a former judge, was a quiet man full of good humor, as was Gergely Fábián. The others were rather passive and rarely said a word. The commentary on the folktale told exhibited these same characteristics.

The first part of the tale was listened to in silence. The reason for this may be found in the fact that it was not a natural tale telling occasion and that those present, still shy in the beginning, did not quite know how to act. At the place where the hero meets the witch, enters her service, and receives nine eggs for diner, Mrs. Dobondi could not hold back any longer: "Was this sufficient?" To this Gertrud Matyi, who knew the rules of the game and knew that whatever good befalls the hero must also be wished for the gathering, remarked, "We would also eat the eggs now!" Here the first laughter was heard, although the company had not yet arrived at the proper mood. For a long time there were only acquiescing remarks (the narrator was not sure what name he had given the second son; he asked his listeners, and they confirmed that he called him Miska). This, of course, might also mean an attempt to get the audience to talk, to force them to participate. Sometimes they also called the narrator to order when he used drastic expressions, but this was in deference to the visitor from Budapest.

Only about the middle of the tale was the right atmosphere created, which then lasted until the end. Dénes Sebestyén could not stop marveling when he heard the beautiful descriptions of the story: "How can you keep all this in your head?" "This is prescribed for him, he takes it all from his store," Illés Mátyás answered. "This will last very long," said Erzsi Mátyás, affirming her superior knowledge. When Andrásfalvi reached the point where the three maidens are liberated, the listeners followed him enraptured. They still said "Ah!" or "What the devil?" and admired the capabilities of the folktale hero: "How he could lie!"

Then they began to comment vividly on the details; they asked questions and quarreled among themselves. In the story, the young man lives with an old woman. There he puts on his armor and goes out to fight the dragon, or he goes to the King's court, disguised as a baker's apprentice, to saw wood there. "With the old women he was in good hands," Dénes Sebestyén remarked. "A pity that the girl was not there," said Mrs. Dobondi; and Illés Mátyás added, "For sure, the arsonist will also retire there."[209]

The sawing of wood of the disguised hero remains a joke to the end. When the sawing of wood was described, Albert Szakács said, according to the rules of the game, "We could well use a cord of it ourselves," and alternating with Dénes Sebestyén he came back to it three more times, until they pointed out clearly that sawing wood is the favorite occupation of the hero in disguise.

There are occasions for funny remarks at other points in the tale, for instance when the hero strokes the princess' forehead: "Would you stroke a fifteen-year-old's forehead?" Or when the hero said to the princess, "Woman, leave me in peace tomorrow night," Mrs. Dobondi said, "I said you were going to say this to me." Striking things were explained: "In those days they still wore skirts," or "The engagement ring was immediately there." "Did they not get a drop of milk so they had to drink their coffee black?" János Mátyás asked. "They did not own a cow," Mrs. Dobondi answered. In the kitchen of the folktale orders were given by pulling a wire, so Dénes Sebestyén stated, "In those days they still were pulling wires; they did not press doorbells." She explained the expression *tent* as "a tarpaulin with which one covers the threshing machines." "He then had to do with witches?" "They destroyed it completely, then." "He had already been caught," and so forth. Such statements were made until the tale came to an end.

General interest was aroused by exclamations like "Now, something will really happen!" or "*Jujujuj!*" "Now they will start quarrelling, if not more!" When the narrator mentioned that the purse is of pure gold,

Dénes Sebestyén sighed, "Gee, that would do us good now, too." "What does he do with it?" asked Gertrud Matyi. "I would bury it so that nobody sees it!" At suggestive places the audience did not remain silent. When they heard that a sword is laid between the sleepers, János Mátyás said, "The sword was between them, so love was really great." The narrator described how the young woman turned her back, offended, and upon this Erzsi Mátyás stated, "The lean, sorry backside of the woman sighs," and thus comment followed upon comment.

The general suspense was relieved when Illés Mátyás finally remarked, "Well, that sure was a long tale! What the devil—it lasted two hours!"

Among those present only the József Sebestyén family had moved. They were bored by the tale, had constantly whispered among themselves, and had left the room and come back in again. Several times they asked if it would last long, and how long it was going to last: "We are leaving," and the narrator calmed them down: "It won't take long." "He said that before, too!" "If he wants, he still won't be finished by tomorrow morning; that was in an old story book, was it not?" Yet then they all decided to stay to the end of the tale; it was about eleven at night when the company broke up. The narrator had succeeded, in spite of the slow tempo of the second half of the narration, to rouse a true magic tale atmosphere among his listeners. Satisfied with himself, red in the face because of the effort and in the secure knowledge of his wisdom, the narrator finished his glass of wine with a gesture which was supposed to pass for modest.

During Mrs. Palkó's tales we had very few interruptions to record, but even these are worth mentioning. The most typical were the following:

1. Expressions of respect and recognition for the narrator. "Well, I could never tell such a tale!" (*The Three Princes and The Man with the Iron Hat*)

2. Unconscious exclamations, agreements which showed how the listeners were identifying with the tale. "Well done . . . how soulless he was!" "My, was he stubborn!" "What the devil!" "Oh, boy." "My, my. . . ."

3. Formalized hints at the connection between tale and reality. "Once he met up with me." Interpolation: "Like today!" (*The Three Princes*) Mrs. Palkó: "I cooked for the King, and they carried the dishes inside." Exclamation: "You saw it just like now, didn't you?" (*Prince Sándor*) The closet of the folk hero was full of clothes, and somebody exclaimed: "I could have used some of these." (*Peasant Gagyi*)

4. Questions which were answered by the narrator. "Why did she not say that she was a princess?" "She did not say who she was." "Did he know now that he was the King?" "He did not know it. The girl knew him but he did not know the girl." (*The Princess*) "Was the maiden beautiful?" "Of course she was beautiful." "She could do this so quick?" "In one night." "He did not believe it?" "No." "Did he know?" "He knew." "Did he not know that his wife drank coffee?" "No, he did not know it." "Where were all the people?" "Out, on daily labor." "Did he sleep so quick?" "They too were there." (*Peasant Gagyi*)

Often interesting details were commented upon. In the magic tale about the fairy princess, the deed of the ugly gypsy caused general outrage. Mrs. Palkó: "Had I known beforehand that I was so beautiful I would never have put down the mirror." A listener: "Then she would have become a mirror-Kate." Another listener explained the gypsy's unrest when the tale is told at the King's court: "She had noticed that they were talking about her." They pitied the King because he had such an ugly wife: "Maybe he looked at her only once a week?" They were astonished that they could not detect more sympathy at the King's court, when the heroine related her own fate: "The others were silent; did their hearts not hurt?"

Mrs. Palkó could be upset even when Lajos Ömböli, who was listening to the tale, entered and destroyed the tale of *Prince Sándor:* "I can tell a big lie; I know only one tale, *The Hair.*" He said it with an uproarious laugh like someone who wanted to attract attention, if only for a moment. The others looked at him angrily; they knew what kind of tale that was. Mrs. Palkó quickly silenced the boaster—"you be quiet now, you have already told it once, I got quite giddy listening. I don't know where you heard it; that must have been some lightweight who told you this story"— and calmly continued her tale.

When Mrs. Palkó was often interrupted in her storytelling, for instance when she narrated on Saturday nights at home while preparing dinner and at the same time looking after the children ("Now, where did I stop?"), she sometimes made a mistake or left something out, but was corrected by her daughter or the grandchildren. With the tale of the *Redbellied Snake*, for example: "You left something out, Mother! The snake taught it to her," her daughter Erzsi would remind her. But mostly she herself would discover it when she made a mistake, and with a skillful maneuver she would return to the skipped episode.

In general, the listeners are interested in the tale, and that is why they sit down together around the narrator. Those among the listeners who like to make fun and attract attention can hardly resist the temptation to interrupt. They are known for this and influence mainly the narrator, who voluntarily answers all their questions and who sees encouragement in every commentary, even if it is derisive or expresses doubt. But the listeners who follow the recital in silence also influence the narrator, by their strict attention and by the interest which is mirrored in their faces. Often it is with them that most tales are deposited, and one fine day a new storyteller from among their ranks appears in public.[210]

Of course there are things which disturb both narrator and listeners: crying children; impatient people who suddenly start laughing or whispering and thus detract the attention of others from the narrator.[211] This can be observed in the tale and in the interruptions as well. It sometimes also happens that an interruption is answered not by the storyteller but by another listener. Even a third listener may assert himself, and while the tale is being developed, a small dispute originates.

The interruptions during Mrs. Palkó's and Andrásfalvi's narrations, though few in number, may be classified as follows:

1. Spontaneous exclamations, triggered by wonder about some part of the tale.
2. Playful or serious commentary on a single episode of the tale.
3. Questions about details which were not understood, and responses to them.
4. Connecting of individual experiences with the tale elements.
5. Praise and encouragement for the narrator.
6. Playful remarks directed to the narrator or other listeners.
7. Impatience: When will the tale be finished?

In arranging this grouping, we do not aim at general conclusions but wish merely to indicate what results may come from our collection. Painstakingly accurate recording should put the researcher in a position to judge how far the individual listeners have been captured by the story atmosphere and how much they have identified with the tale. The influence of the tale on the listeners and their reactions to it are an important problem for folktale research.

# 7

# The Tale Material:

# The Narrative Body of Kakasd

## Folk Belief, *Weltanschauung*, and Practice

THE FOLK NARRATIVE GENRES COLLECTED IN KAKASD GIVE US A GOOD idea of the stock of folk literature in the possession of the community. The tales we recorded came from several outstanding narrators and are known to most of the villagers. The listeners usually indicate to the narrator what they want to hear, what they find entertaining, what interests them, and what they like and don't like. When questioned, they told us their opinions of the tales and quoted details to prove how interesting one or another was. Stories which are not folktales in the narrower sense are the most prevalent, for no special talent is needed to recite them—everyone who knows them is ready to tell them.[1]

As in every other community where tales are told, the tale body in Kakasd is not homogeneous but variable as to form, origin, and function. But, as they are an inherent part of the taletelling atmosphere, we must also have a general knowledge of other narrative genres. Only the complete, interconnected material of folk narratives can give us a true picture of the traditional wisdom and the world view (*Weltanschauung*).[2]

As to legends, folktales, and belief stories, the forms found in Kakasd do not, in the main, differ appreciably from those found in other villages. Closer investigation, however, poses the following question: What is the relationship of the *märchen*, which does not claim credibility, to the legend, which is assumed to be true? This question, which touches the essence of the *märchen*, was first raised in Hungary by Ortutay in connection with the folktale's basis in reality.[3]

Related opinions can be found in Vajkais' study about the narrative based on living folk belief.[4] In his posthumously published study, János Honti explored the question from another viewpoint: How can mythical-belief motifs be transformed into folktale motifs?[5] This is one of the key problems in the study of the relationship between the narrative genres. The dependence of the folktale on living folk belief is essential for our study, as it throws light on the background of the Kakasd tale body. However, we cannot deal here with the topic in general.[6]

The archaic belief still existing in the village is clearly mirrored in the world concept of our narrators, strong in some, weaker in others.[7] The magic belief of the people of Kakasd is a typical survival of the backward world view of the former settlers of the Bucovina, preserved by the Church. Traditional belief is continually given new meaning in the framework of the Christian religion. Catholicism helped to retain the naive folk religion of the Kakasd Szeklers and with it the whole belief system, which is shot through with the belief concepts of the Rumanians and diverges greatly from that of the Hungarian peasantry within the borders of Hungary.[8]

It is only natural that the people of Kakasd should be devout followers of their Church, and that the events prior to their settlement in new environs only strengthened them in this attitude. Religious faith offered the only refuge for the poor peasants from the misery and vicissitudes of their lives. That this feeling has not led to the other extreme, anticlericalism and the formation of sects, as happened with the Protestant landless peasantry beyond the river Tisza, or to the attitude of the "revolutionary serf," as manifested in the personalities of the outstanding storytellers Fedics[9] and Pandur,[10] can be explained solely by the influence the Church wielded in the Bucovina. The Szeklers could not turn their backs on the Church which represented the spirit of Hungary (Magyardom), of the far-off fatherland. But the impact of the Church paralyzed the activity of the people and led to a turning away from secular things, to fatalism in the face of fate—no matter what happened, it was God's will. With this fatalism grew a belief in the beauty of the Beyond. In religious services merit plays a great part; through merit one is considered worthy of beatitude after death. The obligations of the Church, attendance at services, offerings, mass, and prayer hours, are faithfully kept by young and old. The belief concepts relating to the dead and the explanations concerning life after death are abundant. Every new death affects the people —as we indicated when dealing with the customs of wakes—from the moment of death to the tending of the grave. The people knew many cases where the smallest neglect caused the wrath of God. Most of the narratives hinge on the return of the dead: the survivors must act in their behalf, the living must order their own life and be prepared, for death may come at any time. This is the reason for the calm acceptance of the death of their children. Fertility is great, and nine or ten children are no rarity; though as a consequence of ignorance or quack practices, hardly half of them stay alive. They considered this a matter of course; they could not bring up so many, in any event. It was God's blessing that He took them away. The little innocents would be much happier in the Beyond. When the people talked about adversities and vicissitudes, we often heard that "God's Will" had been worked in them, and this gave the suffering ones a certain feeling of resignation and calm. In stories of all kinds, including *märchen*, we often find the statement "God made it happen," "God paid him back," "God permitted it to happen," and when he succeeds in something the hero says: "Thanks be to God." The Kakasd people pondered deeply God's actions, His intentions, and the attitude of the souls in the Beyond. It was one of the common themes of conversation that was strengthened by sermons and religious writings; everybody liked to expatiate on it; not only the elders, but also the women, old and young. We noted down many of these argumentations when we were searching for a storyteller.

The combination of blindly zealous piety and the superstition hiding behind it is quite obvious. The women who healed with magic practices or spoke charms over the sick proudly proclaimed that they were doing God's work, not superstition, and that they invoked God's and not the devil's help. Mrs. Palkó said about the magic rites connected with water: "I do not think it is sin, for it has to be done not with soothsaying but with praying." She told how she once was called to a family to cast water over their sick daughter. The priest, too, arrived and declared that this was only superstition. "So I interrupt him: 'Reverend Father, how can this be bad if it is done while praying? I am not a fortuneteller.'" Mrs. Palkó was of the opinion that self-imposed fasting was also a pious action, as was the Mass which the people of Kakasd ask to have celebrated so that evil people will be punished by death (Appendix, No. 13).

Folk belief is a belief in life after death, a belief in compensatory justice in the Beyond. Even the poorest never missed having a Mass celebrated even for the most distant relative, godparent, or friend, and not only on the anniversary of his death, on his birthday or nameday, but also on feast days, when he dreamed of him, or when he believed that there is some reason for it. Considerable sums were spent for these purposes.[11] Thus the people of Kakasd patiently endured the tests of their earthly existence to insure for themselves the happiness of the beyond, a characteristic feature of their belief concept which has its parallels in the religious concepts of the Hungarian peasantry as a whole. The cult of the dead played a dominant role.

During his life on earth the individual—and that means a family as an economic unit with its property—according to the concept of the Kakasd Szeklers is exposed to a fourfold danger from supernatural forces:

1. God's punishment (abortions, return of the dead, sickness caused by a curse);
2. Malice, vengeance (damage caused by malicious magic powers in man and beast);
3. Involuntary, unintentional bad deed (evil eye, overpraise);
4. Sicknesses (fright, wasting away).

Protection against these damages is in part preventive: God's laws have to be kept faithfully; everything must be done for the peace of the dead. One has to know how to keep the evil away from oneself. Once the mishap has occurred, one must know the art of healing. Prevention of danger, protection of the newborn or the precious cattle, the healing of ordinary sicknesses, and the casting of magic spells can be done at home. One of the simplest methods of healing for the newborn is changing his name: the name entered in the birth register is "removed," and the child in the future will be called by another name. At home people protect themselves against the damage wrought by witches or sorcerers in the stables:

> Blessed garlic rings are hung up in the stable and a small garlic section is entwined in the mane of a living horse or into the dried mane of a deceased horse or stuck into a sick horse's shoe, because of the witches, for they saddle the horse and braid their manes. But then they do not saddle our horses but the dead horse head and our horse is protected from them,

said Mrs. Sebestyén. It is mostly the older women who attend to these things, but some of them know more than others, and their knowledge is widely known. There are specialists for melting tin, soaking, "boiling of the consumptive child," and similar methods of healing. These are pious, elderly women who have learned their art from others even older, and because they have "a good hand, God gave them the gift to make good out of evil." The Kakasd people could name many such women, and even at the time of our research these women were called to attend to sick children or precious cattle.

Our narrators Mrs. Geczi, Mrs. Szakács, and Mrs. Sebestyén also belonged to this group. The most respected and revered, however, was Mrs. Palkó. Her long and eventful life, the recovery of her own children from sicknesses, had resulted in her acquiring, over the years, a kind of folk-medicine practice. She gladly shared her knowledge with everyone, and thus acquired a reputation for sympathy. Mrs. Palkó's methods of healing corresponded to those in force in the Hungarian villages of the Bucovina. Since her magic, the casting of spells and healing incantations, formed a considerable aspect of her personality, we shall examine it more closely.

According to Mrs. Palkó's experience, it is mostly small children and young animals that are "overpraised." This is generally done not from malice but because someone liked them very much; someone looked at them "with a pure heart." There are people who have "knotted eyebrows," "some have such blood, they don't know it themselves, and they are prone to overpraise." "It is said that a child taken twice from the breast that feeds him will become a good spell-caster." "Somebody looks at it [the child], he has the evil eye that harms the heart; his nature is so bad that even an animal must die—a pig or a cow—and even a man, when he forgets to cast water afterwards." Mrs. Palkó knew many such cases. "Once they gave me a young foal. The children were happy with the foal; they fed it hay and I gave it sugar. Well, you know, some neighbors' children came and they scared it so much that the foal laid down and hung its head. I sprinkled it with water; the foal became healthy again; I washed it with the water." But one can avoid the spell. The one who admires a small child must say, "My, you ugly one!" "One who can cast a spell must put his fingers into his belt and then it won't harm the child." "When a girl marries, or when she is a young bride, she makes he sign of the cross on her forehead so that she may not catch the evil eye." The forehead of the suckling infant is smeared with soot so that "the evil eye falls on the soot, not on the child."

How did Mrs. Palkó cast her healing spell?

I learned this from older women; they spelled the water for me when I was a little girl, and it helped me. When I cast a water spell,

I first fetch the water in silence. I make the sign of the cross over the bowl, throw in three glowing pieces of coal, and say a prayer, when I give Rózsi, or whatever her name is, of the water, to the young one or the child: to the Father, the Son and the Holy Spirit. Then I say an Our Father, an Ave, and the Creed. Then I say: "I cast it for the little boy, blue eye, black eye, glazed eye, serpent's eye, cat's eye has bewitched him. Tut, tut, tut—the eye has seen it. I let it shrivel up so the spell has no power; the heart loves it so that the spell is not effective, Jesus, Mary, and Joseph please come and help the little one and comfort him." You must throw in three burning pieces of kindling. Then one must remove the coal and put it into the mouth of the little one with the ring finger. If he is bigger, he drinks it. One must rub his heart, the little eyes, the palms of his hands, then he will recover.[12]

The most popular healing method against overpraise and spell-casting is the melting of tin,[13] which Mrs. Palkó also knew how to do well. She related:

I pour tin three times. No matter what has scared the child, when I melt my tin he recovers and is not so sick any more. One has to go out to the well, fetch water without a word, and draw it in the name of the Father, the Son, and the Holy Spirit, for the child Jóska. One must pour it into the basin and say a prayer over it— the Our Father, the Ave, the Creed. I say the prayer in the Holy Name of Jesus, that he may restore health to the child, and so on. I melt the tin three times in the spoon. The plate is put over the head, and the tin is poured into it; the second time on the breast, the third time on the legs. The hands and the feet are crossed and such. Then the form which originally scared the child is moulded from the tin.

The most complicated procedure of the healing woman, however, is the "boiling of the shriveled child." In this Mrs. Palkó was an expert. The magic healing of the sickness and the symbolic boiling are known all over Hungary. The method known in the Bucovina corresponds in every detail to the procedure of the Transylvania Szeklers.[14] This sickness, as Mrs. Palkó described it, attacks only infants, or they contract it even before birth because their mother "kicked a dog";[15] or it becomes "bewitched without the mother noticing anything, and the spell goes into the bones, into the stomach, and that causes her to have a shriveled child." This opinion was also gleaned from other villagers. Many had participated in a "boiling," or they assured us that they knew from their own experience that "boiling" had helped. Let us then quote Mrs. Palkó's own words about the procedure. It is strange to note that this outstanding storyteller, when she reported her own healing methods, paid no attention to presentation; on the contrary, she talked in choppy sentences, jumped from one point to the other, and said what was passing through her head—whatever she thought it was necessary to tell the uninitiated stranger. First, she told the "why" of the boiling; then she related a concrete case:

From three springs or wells one must steal water, and three splinters from three different wooden blocks. "I draw this water for Antal in the name of the Father, the Son, and the Holy Spirit, so it will become medicine. I drew this water." One must go for it without saying a word. One must not say a word, and go fetch it only with prayers and good intentions. At dawn, before the sun has risen, before anyone is about, because he would wish you a "Good morning" and if he does his greetings receive no answer and he will think that one is mad. I pray while I walk but no one must say a word. One then fills a vessel; I fetch it from the second and the third well, with a small pot. Then I bring the water. From three woodblocks I collect splinters, and even then nobody must talk. Then I take it home and then one can boil the little one. When I do my boiling there, I put the kindling on the fire and put the kettle on the stove. First we must heat the water, for it would not be warm from the kindling. Then I hold the naked child over it. Two more Zsuzsis are necessary, or Mari, Anna, or Rózsi, all with the same name. Two walk around the house and one sprinkles water on the little one. When she comes to the door she asks: "What are you boiling, Godmother?" "Old man and old flesh!" "Boil it, boil it, until it gets thick like fat." This you do three times, but in between you must sprinkle and burn the new kindling. This must be done on Mondays, Thursdays, and Saturdays. Others can come but they all must have the same name. In the Bucovina, with the Rumanians and the Germans, I have boiled so often, they even came from our village when they had a shriveled child. Then it passed. There was an old woman. Mrs. Klári Tamás was her name. She called me for the boiling and then told me how to do it, then I could boil myself.

The little one loses weight though he eats and drinks; his mouth never stands still; he is hungry like a wolf but nothing remains with him. It becomes worse; he gets wrinkled like an ape. They brought me children that I was worried might die under my hands. There was a little girl. My God was she sick, the little one of Mari. Two weeks they talked about it and I always heard them talking. I did not want to go there. She was young and I was old, but I was on quite good terms with her mother. Well, once there was dancing in the neighborhood. My daughter went, and I also went there. It was in the evening. I looked and there was Mari with the sick little one. I asked her; "My God, I heard the little one was sick, and you are here with her?" "Oh, Godmother, I am sick and tired of all that work." "You, Mari, pick her up and take her home so it cannot be said she is dying on the dance floor. Go home with her. Shame on you!" She was really mad at me. The next day she came to me: "Godmother, do you know why I have come? Boil the little one; maybe she had a scare." Her weeping was like that of a soulful little animal. I took her out of her winding sheet; she was like a monkey child, all skin. She would not die so fast; she will first become like a stick of kindling. "Why did you not bring her yesterday, now you have to wait a whole week, if she does not die in the meantime." She did survive to the next week. "She sucked so hard she nearly broke my nipple, and yet the girl is still hungry," Mari sighed. Then she returned on Monday. I unwrapped the little one and went to fetch water, fetch the kindling. "I shall pay you for it, God-mother!" I looked for two more women with the name of Zsuzsi. In this very night she did not need to be breastfed any more, she did not cry any more but was quiet and slept the whole night through. "Well, on Thursday, I shall boil her once more—it takes time until she is all right again." I boiled her three times. You should see what a nice girl she has become! As if one had packed the meat onto her bones. She will be forever grateful to me.

As we can see, the whole disaster-preventing procedure, magic and healing, which is an integral part of daily life, is still strongly intermixed with religion: prayers, pious customs, and magic rites are interconnected.

At the other pole in Hungary there is the "wise woman"—the witch type. Here we are confronted by the evil powers within the pious world view; here help and assistance from hell is prevalent. The people of Andrásfalva said that there were "wise women" who healed not for the little gifts they received but as a vocation. These women were called in when neither homely wisdom nor the pious woman could help any longer. These wise women usually were Rumanians or had attained their wisdom from the women of that nationality. Two such women lived in An-drásfalva: Mrs. Priszekár and Mrs. Berétyi (see Appendix, No. 14). But there were also women whose reputations reached into all the five Bucovina villages, and who were called in from great distances when severe damage was caused or when there was danger to life, when a cow dried up or when an adult became seriously ill through witchcraft. But these wise women did not unveil their art, and their methods remained a secret: the villagers could only talk about their effectiveness. Mrs. Palkó said:

It occurred to the neighbor woman that the Swabians [a reference to the Kakasd German settlers in Hungary by that name], took the milk away from her cow; so she had her treated by another woman. But this is done in secret. I heard that the milk was taken from the cow, but how it was done, God forbid, I did not know. They say that when she comes home with the herd she stops at the gate and moos where her milk was taken. The grandmother of my husband told us, she had cut and torn and stamped her hoofs, but the milk was all cheesy. There lived a Mrs. Priszekár; she was a mighty wise woman, she could heal. I don't know how, but the milk reappeared. They also cast water spells; when she was bewitched it helped, but if it was something else, it didn't. My grandmother tells how Mrs. Priszekár taught her to make a big piece of iron glowing, to put it on the threshold of the stable and then pound on it. The stronger the iron is pounded, the sooner the one who caused the damage will go back there.

The witches consciously do evil, and often are identical with the wise women who understand healing. "He who has spoiled it, can also make up for it," said Mrs. Palkó, and we could witness her protest that she, too, might be suspected of understanding how to do it. While she and her like knew something about healing by the grace of God, the others have learned their practices from the devil. They do damage in order to profit from it, out of vengeance, or because others goad them into it. They heal only for profit and do both only through the help of supernatural evil art. The witches were real figures for the whole village,[16] and inserted themselves quite naturally into its life. Their suspicious, strange behavior attracted the immediate attention of the villagers. Most of the witches had an animal. Mrs. Palkó related that through a friend of hers she heard of a woman who owned a frog; the frog whispered every secret into her ear. Mrs. Palkó did not seem to believe this, because, while she was telling this story, her daughter Erzsi said, in order to bear her out:

What do you know, I have seen such a one in the Bácska. One had to pay a woman a forint and then she gave you a slip of paper. "Step down into the depth, look the women in the eye," she said, and in a glass I saw such a little devil; he danced up and down in the glass. He rose by himself and came down again. I got such a scare that I said to Anti, "Quick, let's get out of here."

Andrásfalvi, too, could tell about the devils of the witch, his mother, once while she was combing flax in the evening, was told of the following incident:

> Then Annacska Györfi began to speak, and she said, "Listen to me, Mrs. Bori. I was fifteen years old and Kati Pál called me for weaving. She went to town and I stayed at home, and I really needed flax. And flax was in the chest and I took it out, as much as I needed. And Kati Pál came home in the afternoon from town and as she entered the door she asked: "Isn't it true, Annacska, that you got into the chest?" "Kati—oh, no!" "Don't lie to me, girl!" I was astonished a thousandfold, how come she knew about it, and then I knew, she said the woman has a spell in her chest, who is a devil, she always puts two rolls into the chest. She was called witch-Kati. She was the mother of Orbán Kozma.[17]

The witch powers originating with the devil are the elements in which the helplessness of backward, agricultural man in the face of the forces of nature is best expressed. "Here in Tabód there is an old woman," said Erzsi Matyi, "who sat down on the flax stool and rode with it nights along the streets, and I have seen her hair flying. Thus she went ahead on the flax stool; she has promised her soul to the devil."

Erzsi Matyi also told an extremely interesting story, which, as far as we know, has been recorded only once in the Hungarian (by Kálmány in 1893). In it, the devil concludes a pact with a witch in order to separate a happy young couple. In vain does the devil try his luck, without success, but the witch succeeds in destroying the young couple's happiness in a few minutes.[18] The practices of witches were usually called "devilries" by the people of Kakasd.

## BELIEF LEGENDS

THESE PRACTICES were generally known, and there was hardly a family that could not tell some story about an experience that one of them had with witches. Since these experiences were most interesting, they were very popular. But the description of such experiences, by immediate or remote witnesses, never lead to a predetermined gathering. These experiences might be mentioned any time that several people gathered and alternately told stories. Conditioned by the similar evolution of the peasant's belief concepts, these "cases" develop according to the theme in a rather narrow framework following narrative patterns. But, even though stereotypes came about through constant retelling, the content, not the form is handed on, in other words, the very typical content lends them their form.[19] These narratives, usually included in the Hungarian collections under the heading "legends" or "Märchen," or sometimes listed in the form of abstracts in chapters dealing with popular belief, belong to a specific group of folk narratives which is worth special attention. Vajkai, in his study mentioned above, tried to isolate these stories as belonging to a distinct group. He called them "stories of superstition," following earlier classifications. Folklorists who stressed their fantastic character called them "miraculous stories,"[20] and those who adopted the term used by the bearers themselves called them "true stories."[21] Likewise, in the European folk narrative collections they can be found alternately under the entries "legend," "mythical legend," "Märchen," or "true story."[22] Indexes available generally do not distinguish between types and motifs of this genre. In recent years, though legend classification is under way, there still has been considerable disagreement concerning the form and content and extent of the folk legend, largely due to its great flexibility and variability and to the fact that it still functions in contemporary society. Besides Sydow's basic distinction between "Memorat" and "Fabulat" (similar to "local legend" and "migratory legend"), there is a distinction between the personal "experience story" in the first person, and the one told as though experienced by others. Even in the case of the "belief story" and the "belief legend," the distinctions are made, obviously, on the degree of the stability of the form, although the attitude toward reality and relationships with actual folk belief are also decisive factors.[23]

When considering the narrative stock of Kakasd and dealing with the narratives reflecting the living folk belief and the attitude toward the supernatural, that plays such an important role in the maintenance of the folktale, we do not propose to make suggestions about legend terminology. "Belief story," in this case is only a tentative term to encompass the oscillating Kakasd stories which carry messages about folk belief.

The greatest merit of Vajkai is that he distinguishes the "stories of superstition" (or belief legends) as a genre from other narrative genres on the basis of their function. Before he tried this himself, he evaluated the published Hungarian material, which he had to gather from different sources. For the most part he found them in studies on folk religion, since the interest of the researchers was directed to the types of belief concepts rather than to the prose narratives which contained them. This is the reason why the stories featuring belief or superstition remained unrecorded, and only their essence, the belief itself, was elicited. Though some folklorists published belief stories, these were not considered as pieces belonging to a folk narrative genre, and their relationship to *märchen* and legends was not clarified. Vajkai considered them as "real" factors of folk belief, resting on everyday experiences and living in the people "not like simple, short rules but as historic facts, with acting personages, actions and words."[24] Epic forms grow from the rules, phenomena, practices, and events of the realm of folk religion, because a people "molds each experience, each observation as much as possible into a narration which is rich in vivid and colorful pictures. . . . The narrative form, the personal experience is much closer to folk concept than the lifeless summation of the contents in a few words."[25]

Just as folk belief concepts are common among the people, the narratives informing about them are well known. What Vajkai observed in Cserszegtomaj can be summarized as follows: in peripheral, isolated, and backward areas—as is the case with the Kakasd Szeklers—stories of superstition have communal interest. This genre, too, has its proper specialists—those who like to tell about horrible events, who react more sensitively to the supernatural, who are attracted by the mythical world, whose imagination is slanted by a pseudological bent, or who are by nature neurotic, given to hallucination, and eager to attract attention. Vajkai lists the occasions which serve for the spread of such stories;[26] he underlines the fact that it is precisely the informal entertainment setting and the vivid comments which make one story generate another. This merits particular attention, since it bears out what we have said in connection with the storytelling occasions as distinguishing criteria: the opportunity for telling the belief story, as Brinkman stated, is provided by the active cooperation of the community—nearly everybody is a narrator and listener at the same time.[27]

From all this Vajkai concludes that the belief story is logically structured. Attempting an assessment of the material he knew, Vajkai established fourteen thematic cycles. The stories, known all over Hungary, which relate personal experiences or reproduce those of others are astonishingly similar:

> Belief is fused into a definite narrative form which they know intimately as a whole and in detail and faithfully repeat like a song or a *märchen*. It is only right that we treat these extensive stories, traditionally handed down by the people, in their entirety, like we

would treat the magic tale. But we must not see anything accidental in the personal experience but a firm framework which forms a strong core of unity together with the belief. Therefore we can treat the belief stories, just like the *märchen* or the song, as a separate group because they have a clearly outlined shape.[28]

When Vajkai rightly refers to the formal independence of the belief story and to the necessity for a clear-cut distinction between this and other narrative genres, he still is careful not to exaggerate. He shows—and this can be termed the starting point for further differentiation—that the essence of the belief story lies in its foundation in everyday life, and that its figures live in the village: they are essentially true, they have no beginning and no end, and their elements continue to reverberate in daily life after the end of the tale. In contrast, the *märchen* is a closed form whose world moves on another plane; even those elements which correspond to the belief stories appear here in a different light.[29]

We need not repeat here that the line of demarcation lies in the different functions of the two genres; but what they have in common is the result of a parallel historical development. The belief story, no matter in which typical form it appears before us, can never be elevated to such formal clarity as is shown in the *märchen*. It remains "a case," which presupposes unconditioned belief[30] and thus can never attain the artistic logic of the *märchen*, even when rounded out with colorful narrative additions and dialogues which follow the rules of oral narration.[31] The contents, the rules, the actions connected with magic events are typical and logical—and this is the reason that the structure of the belief story is also logical. This constitutes the decisive difference in form between *märchen* and belief story: the logic in the belief story is not anchored in the composition but springs from the similarity of cases. Obviously, then, the belief story is far from artistic in style: the texts continue to remain far behind the rhythmically pulsating prose of the *märchen*. This great difference is also evident in the fact that not every narrator can tell a belief story. Mrs. Palkó, for instance, whom we came to know as a pious, healing woman, does not belong to the category of good narrators of belief stories. She lived with these belief concepts, but she was not inclined to relate her own experiences or to tell about things she had heard of. When she did, however, she did not elaborate on her words but was intent on relating a single case with the utmost fidelity; this indicates that she did not consider this narration as belonging among the tales, but among the occurrences of everyday life.[32] Such a story would begin "My father relates . . ."; "Well now, two girls were talking . . ."; "My oldest son had died. . . ." Or, before she came to a concrete case, she would first state the principle which would be clarified in what followed: "The dead person who has hidden something in life has no rest. Here is a woman whose mother had died. . . ."

The tradition in Kakasd shows that most of the belief stories are cases or events which concern the revenant. We have included thirteen cases in our material, of which six come from Mrs. Palkó, one from Andrásfalvi, and six from Mrs. Geczi; but we might have made a whole volume of Kakasd belief stories the foundation of our research. Since they are quite similar and follow a pattern, we shall content ourselves with listing only the most characteristic plots. We could distinguish only two distinct types: the appearance of hideous apparitions; and the stories of the return of beloved deceased family members. The latter were told with special insistence by the older women of Kakasd. Thus Erzsi Mátyás described with true histrionic talent how her dead mother asked her to take care of her sister:

> At midnight I saw my mother, heard her voice and her laments. God permitted her to visit me. I look out the window. She said: "Yes, my child, my dear child, come out here!" I did not think of my mother, that she would appear; I thought of a strange woman. It was the time of the election of judge, and Sándor Geczi was made judge, my father had drunk wine and gone to sleep. Well, now they have clobbered somebody for sure, and the woman is looking for help. And again, yes, yes, I was running outside to see who it was. It was a beautiful moon and first I did not see anybody. I went to the back, nobody there; I went to the front, nobody there. Well, am I awake? Nobody here. I go near to the fence and here she stands! My mother it was, she showed her face and I saw it. She was dressed in white, just as they had buried her, in white linen. She left me her speech: "I tell you, Erzsi, you are the oldest, you are still with Marika; the others have married. Don't be bad. Young and weak is the reasoning of the young. I don't have to mention this." When I went back, my older sisters had lifted their heads: "Erzsi, tell us, why did you go out?" "It was Mother." "Oh, oh, if we had only seen her!" they said to me. Mother, my God, Mother! I did not know if I should weep, oh Mother! She was gone and I did not see her again. Oh, I started to weep that she was not there any more. Her soul had shown in the shape of her body.

Erzsi Mátyás relived it all once more. She tore her black headscarf from her head while she told her story, her hair fell into her face, her eyes filled with tears, and with loud wails she lamented the death of her mother, twenty-five years before.

Mrs. Palkó told with similar strength of dramatic expression of the apparition which her mother had after the death of one of her children. She also convincingly described apparitions which are connected with a dead person whose punishment consists of having to come back (see Appendix, Nos. 10 and 11). One must not weep over the dead, otherwise they never find rest, the rules say, and when the dead one has to come back because of the sins he himself committed while on earth, then one has to force him to confess how he could be helped. This is everybody's duty concerning the dead. Only the spectres of witches must be shunned, for they bring misfortune to men.

The stories of Kakasd which are founded on witch belief can be categorized in three types: (1) destruction of love (Appendix, No. 74, Andrásfalvi); (2) torment by a witch (Appendix, No. 14, Mrs. Palkó; No. 75, Andrásfalvi); and (3) the shoed witch (Appendix, No. 76, Mrs. Geczi). In order to illustrate clearly the formal structure based upon the sequence of the content, we quote two variants of the same story. Mrs. Palkó several times related this adventure, which had occurred while her father was fishing, and even though both variants given here contain the whole set of motifs and there are obvious similarities in sentence structure, they still differ fundamentally from the structure of frequently told folktale text.

The two texts whose introductory part we are quoting here were recorded in 1949 and 1954.

| 1949 | 1954 |
|---|---|
| My father relates, he was a fishermaster, a fisher, he liked to go catch fish in the Suceava when he still was a young man. He was not afraid no matter if it rained buckets or was dark; he came and went to the water. During the day he made a big dam and then the fish hurried to reach deep waters; he laid out a basket and then collected the fish from it. I often said, "Aren't you afraid in the dark, Father?" He often told what he had seen, | My father was a fishermaster, he always went to catch fish. Well, one day he went with his brother-in-law to dam the water. It was such a clear, clean water, like crystal was the Suceava. It was so deep it could have swallowed a horse; the ground was quite stony. In one place it divided into two forks, so they shut off one fork and there they caught the fish. They put out a basket and the fish jumped into it. He went with |

and he was not a liar. He knew so many tales, my God, how many he knew! There was an old lady who lived close to the river on the bank, she had a small house. She had neither husband nor children. Mrs. Berétyi was alone. That was her name. She went neither into the village nor to church. She had a cat, and with it she carried on conversations as if it were a child. The old woman became weaker and weaker, she became ill. There was a Rumanian; he, too, lived thereabouts near the water; Demjan Cigánás was his name. It was he who often went to Mrs. Berétyi and brought her milk, wood, and buttermilk. So this woman lamented he should bury her when she died, this Rumanian, for she had nobody and could not leave her house to anybody. So Demjan Cigánás said not to be afraid that he would bury her, not on account of the house, for he was a rich man, a carter. Well, the old woman died and the cat sat upon her breast. The man buried her and then he demolished the house. It was covered with straw and whatever fell down stayed there in a heap, and he carried the wood away. Well, so my father went to catch fish. Jóska Kozma, that was his name, he was the same kind of fisherman as my father. They both went to dam the water. This was much work, they dammed it with rushes. As soon as the

his brother-in-law; they went in the evening to watch the basket, or else the stork would have taken the fish from the basket. In the evening they went to the banks and made a fire so that the wind could not reach them, and every quarter hour they collected the fish from the basket and put them out on the covers. There, on the banks, there lived an old woman, Mrs. Berétyi. She was a witch. She had a cat, and slept with it, and ate out of the same plate with it. During the day the door was always closed. There lived a Rumanian not far away. He often fetched her flour, milk—well, he had pity on her. "Look here, auntie," he said to her one day, "you are getting weaker every day. Who will bury you when you die? What will become of you?" "I don't know, my son, as long as somebody cares for me while I am alive." "I do for you; I saw wood, I take care of you—when you die you give me the little house." He thought it would be quite good as a stable or the like. "My son, once I shall die, I won't take the house with me to my grave. I shall give it to you." Well, and so they agreed. Not much later she died. György Cigánás—that was the name of the Rumanian—he demolished the house, he took the wood, carried away the bricks—the straw he left. My father was near the house; they fetched the straw to make a fire. . . .

water was low, they laid out
their basket. These were beautiful fish, good fish, not those
with bones. They were comrades! "Come, comrade, there
the water is dammed up, there
will be many fish!" They
dammed the water and in the
evening they went out to put
out the baskets. On the bank
they made a fire to watch the
baskets so that the stork should
not eat the fish. There they
went to sleep. They made a
good fire, fetched the straw
from Mrs. Berétyi's lot, and
burnt it. . . .

It can be seen here that Mrs. Palkó did not keep in her memory firm,
formally structured motifs as she did with the folktales; she only had the
single facts of the story in mind. The form is quite informal, and Mrs.
Palkó concentrated upon the faithful rendition of the events. She introduced the story with the same words; she explained in both cases exactly
why the basket had to be watched: otherwise the stork would get the
spoils. In the first form she talked more about the damming procedures,
but it is not done cohesively; she inserted the fate of the old woman, who
asks the peasant to aid her in her helplessness. She also let the two friends
have their say. In the first variant we only hear how helpless the woman
was because she had no children, and that because of this she was spoil-
ing a cat; it results from the second variant that she was a witch. In the
second part she stressed how the old woman and the Rumanian come to
terms about the bequest of the house. Here it is not the woman who
asks for help, but the Rumanian peasant who offers it. The failing power
of recollection is especially apparent in the change of the names. Both
variants make it clear that Mrs. Palkó wanted to retain faithfully the
events often mentioned by her father. The beginning is grouped around
the most essential happenings, as they occur; the further motifs of the
narration, however—the nightmare, the frog witch, the black monster,
the woman, the gigantic spectre—dovetail with each other and do not
follow the logical structure of the *märchen*. We can find the same structure with other belief stories in Kakasd, proving again that the form
of this genre is not fixed but is dependent on content.

The first episode of this story of belief (a frog spectre jumps out of the straw of the witch) also occurs in the story of Andrásfalvi (Appendix, No. 71). We know that he had fished in the Suceava, and he may well have encountered similar "cases." Since Andrásfalvi, however, was the grandson of the old Zaicz, whom he often accompanied on fishing expeditions, we cannot help but suppose that he heard the story from him and then put his own person in the center and recited it as his own—and this in such a way that he combined the two episodes of the frog and of the spectre. From Andrásfalvi also originated stories which skirt the stories of superstition, stories which tell about somebody having a scare and then thinking it was a ghost or a witch, and in the end loud laughter would result. The story cited above also ends with the incident of the dog hiding in the sleeve of his coat and scaring him.

But this does not mean a disintegration of the old magic world view of Kakasd. The rationally thinking men waver between the "I believe" and the "I don't believe," especially when they hear the stories of somebody else. Also, when there were strangers present they hid their readiness to believe. But what is better proof for the existence of folk belief than the ghost and witch stories of Andrásfalvi (Appendix, Nos. 69 and 70a). Likewise, the explanations which Mrs. Palkó attributed to her father (at the end of Appendix, No. 14)—"Don't be scared, my girl. Time has run out and there are no ghosts any more"—do not express a conviction but would, rather, dispel worry, because the great number of belief stories and their popularity prove that archaic folk belief still lives.

The several types of Kakasd belief stories are not particularly variegated. Research has discovered few, if any, villages in which all fourteen types listed by Vajkai are known. The stories he cites are of greatly divergent origins—cycles which hinge upon local events or noted personalities, stories which go back to some literary model or generally known narrative form which is based on living folk belief. They only occur sporadically, as explanatory or historical legends, throughout the scant number of collections. Depending on local requirements, different types or cycles of belief stories become popular in different communities. The belief stories in Kakasd fall mainly into two groups: (1) the recitals of extraordinary experiences and (2) the relation of unlucky happenings. The purpose of the first group is to entertain, of the second to advise and warn the audience against supernatural danger. These are the simplest and also the most widespread forms of belief stories. Their individual components are (1) the event, (2) the healing process, and

(3) the atonement of the culprit. Instruction which can be applied to similar cases is never omitted. This shows that the belief story originates in the magical-religious belief concept without developing into an art genre.[33]

## Folk Belief and the *Märchen*

HAVING DISCUSSED the formation of the living folk belief in Kakasd and the persistence of narratives based on it, we shall now investigate its relationships to the *märchen:* To what extent do actual folk belief systems and actual stocks of *märchen* depend on each other?

We shall begin at the point where we abandoned the question in the preceding chapter: the belief story is "true," the *märchen* is "not true." Since the tale attains effectiveness through artistic means, it succeeds in making narrator and audience believe in the world of the tale as reality— at least when, during the recital, a gifted storyteller carries the audience with him. A world is created which, as Jolles says, is not identical with the world of reality but with its desired-for, better image, a world in which the elements of wonder are transformed into facts.[34] The people distinguish clearly between the belief story and the *märchen*, according to their different purposes. "We cannot stress enough the differences," Honti writes, "which exist between the transmission of the folktale and the legend which is nourished by folk belief. . . . The world of tradition is different from that of logic."[35]

Then is there no connection between these two genres other than the fact that they are both nourished by the same sources? Is the formation of the tale body not influenced to any degree by the living folk belief? On the contrary! The connection is very close; it is constantly present and clearly discernible. This results from what we have said about the epic narrative forms, about the mythical motifs and their correspondences with the tale incidents; the common motifs of the different folklore genres have developed in different directions according to their function. The elements which penetrated the *märchen* have lost their actuality and with it their credibility outside the *märchen*. Their credibility within the *märchen*, however, has widened; transformed into elements of the folktale, the elements of the different belief systems can well co-exist, and they never become anachronistic in their new forms.[36]

Ever since the *märchen* has developed into an independent genre, it has been continuously nourished by the living network of folk belief. In some of the tales, belief motifs characteristic of different ages are maintained in a loose form. They lost their original meaning due to the requirements of the *märchen* and developed into genuine tale motifs. The supernatural beings of the *märchen*—the witches, monsters, magicians, and fairies—have nothing in common with the realistic, flesh-and-blood characters of local folk belief.[37] They have early broken away from the functioning belief system to which they belonged. While the belief system continued to develop and to actualize until this day, the detached motifs remained on the level at which they once penetrated the *märchen*. Enchantment, magic, and transformation became elements of the folktale, yet are easily distinguished from the parallel phenomenon of the living belief world. It is, however, decisive that these elements of the folktale proper are present in the folktale as well as in folk belief, and that each has developed in a different direction, though they spring from the same source.[38]

Considering the contemporary stock of tales—and that is our task—we have to admit that in the folktale we are confronted not only with fossilized belief concepts but with elements which have an immediate connection with the living folk belief. We meet them in three forms: (1) as tale types, based upon belief concepts; (2) as tales, in which tale and belief motifs are on the same level (a *Märchen*-legend—a mixture of the two genres); and (3) as surface belief motifs which may occur in any folktale.

We can find examples for all three cases in Kakasd. In examining them more closely we may see what lessons can be learned from them.

## Tale Types

AMONG THE TALE THEMES we find a group which is based upon religious belief. Although we cannot deal here with the whole group, it should suffice to discuss two tales which were very popular in Kakasd and which are of different origins. One is the tale of the *Dead Bridegroom*, AT 365, closely related to AT 407. (The origin and nature of the fear of the revenant is discussed in the Appendix Nos. 8 and 9.) Both the foundation and the formation of the tale show that the *märchen* was maintained in tradition through its dependence on the living folk belief. Mrs. Palkó and Mrs. Geczi both used to tell this *märchen* in Kakasd. We know that the belief concepts and the customs which have grown up around the return of the dead are of a greatly varying nature. We also know that the forms of these concepts were influenced to a considerable extent by the Rumanian environment. Nothing is more natural, then, than that with the Kakasd variants of this type of *märchen* all the parts which coincide with the living belief concept should be so formed as to be taken as credible, corresponding to the living belief. In both variants the devil-bridegroom becomes a vampire,[39] and thus the fate of the folktale heroes develops according to corresponding "experiences" of the villagers. The two stories of Mrs. Geczi (Appendix, Nos. 73 and 74) originate from different sources; in her versions it is a ghost that visits the girl, just as in the Moldavia-Csángó version cited in the notes to tale No. 8 in the Appendix. But the words of the neighbor woman in the tale sound as if they were spoken by Mrs. Palkó. Instead of the narrator, a pious woman steps in to help the girl haunted by misfortune:

> In the neighborhood there lived an old woman. She called the girl that she should come and see her. She said, "What do you want, old mother?" She said, "I have come." "Well, now look," she said, "I have called you because I want to ask you something. I have heard that a boy comes visiting you. Whose son is he?" she said. "I asked him but he did not tell me." "And he does not tell you where he comes from?" She said, "No, but you know, he is a beautiful boy." She said, "That he might be a prince. He is so well dressed that even a prince does not have better clothes." "Well, why are you so thin then?" "My, I don't know. All I feel is that I am getting weaker and smaller every day!"

This tale is known not only in Kakasd; it is one of the most common tales in the Hungarian language territory, having been formed in the villages according to actual belief concepts. This can be proved by the other Hungarian variations of the type, especially the two which were formed according to their own belief concepts, by the reputable storytellers Péter Pandur and Mihály Fedics.[40]

Our second example shows that a *märchen* which is founded upon a belief concept may lose its tale character through the influence of the living folk belief, whereas the characteristic features of the belief story are strengthened. Mrs. Palkó's story of *The Blackfrock* (Appendix, No. 23, AT 507), as Liljeblad has noted, belongs to the tale complex originating in the concept of the returning dead.[41] The structure and tendency of Mrs. Palkó's version deviate completely from other Hungarian and even international variants. Its course is as follows:

(a) A prince is looking for a wife who is at least as beautiful as his mother. (b) On his way he pays the debts of a dead man who is being beaten up by his creditors at the burial site. (c) With the help of the dead man he gains the hand of a princess, after having fulfilled three wishes of the King. The solution of his task is essential in the tale type; however, the text of this part falls far below the other parts of the tale, for it is not the prince who carried out the tasks but the dead man. (d) The dead man does not leave him. The hero tries in vain to shake him. He travels with him; he delivers the pledge at the altar with him. The prince takes him back in vain to the cemetery, has him beaten by his soldiers. The dead man keeps returning and in the end is finally destroyed by the priest. The lesson of the tale is that it was not necessary to help the dead man because his soul was damned.

This tale considers the returning dead man as a malevolent spirit from beginning to end. Main topics are the scare and the hope for deliverance; the essential parts of the folktale type take a back seat. This is apparently a case of a story which follows the Kakasd belief of the returning dead, and took this form with Mrs. Palkó because she either could not recall the original correctly any longer, or because the story had already been transmitted to her in this form. In any case, this version is much closer to the stories of the returning dead at home in the Bucovina than to the main variants of this tale type.

## Märchen-*legends*

WE DO NOT KNOW of many stories of superstition molded into the form of the folktale, but there are many instances of *märchen* and belief story motifs occurring side by side.[42] Where a belief story narrative has slowly changed into a folktale,[43] we find it mostly to be a process of disintegration of the tale text, an unsuccessful contamination by a narrator, or simply the result of the fact that in folk life the single genres are so closely connected in function that they flow together. But there are also stories, like that of the *Dead Bridegroom*, which show an earlier phase of transition from one genre to the other. With these belong Mrs. Palkó's tale, *The Count and Coachman János* (Appendix, No. 12). The text itself, which was recorded in ten variants in Hungarian, is close to the types of *The Youth Who Wanted to Learn What Fear Is* (AT 326) and *The Servant János* (AT 1000). The story centers on a poor servant who is lured into a spooky adventure; he eavesdrops on the returning dead count in order to go with him masquerading as the dead man himself. He is successful in finding out where the dead count buried his money, and earns his reward. The folktale framework is very slight and is filled in with belief story motifs and incidents derived from living folk belief. The basis of the story is the belief in the return of the unquiet dead and in the action destined to render the dead man peace; but the form is completely fused and the story of the treasure hidden by the dead is added at random. Here again we can convince ourselves that a "true—not true" narrative, so familiar to the people of Kakasd, was confirmed through the belief in the return of the dead.

Mrs. Geczi's tale, *The Devil's Midwife* (Appendix, No. 84), is the result of the fusion of various elements taken over early from the folk belief concept into the *märchen* (the devil who is invoked by a thoughtless word, the magic power of a word and its consequences, a worthless object that turns into gold), and from narrative elements of the living belief (the changeling) into a folktale. We have learned from other variants of this tale that it is connected with *märchen* AT 765B and the other legend-like types; but even if we did not know this, we would recognize the whole structure and phraseology as folktale-like.[44]

> The devil seized knife and spoon and began to drum upon the bowl: "Nothing, nothing, nothing, nothing"; and the bowl was filled with eggs. Then he seized the pot and drummed upon it with his knife: "Nothing, nothing, nothing, nothing." Then the pot was filled with bacon. Said the poor woman, "What are you up to, my Host? Always it is "nothing, nothing, nothing,' and the pot is filled with bacon, the bowl with eggs. You should give some of it to the poor." But the devil said, "This is all for us; when the poor complain, we have nothing."

### Surface Belief Motifs

Examples from this group are the most frequent. It is characteristic that they do not touch the essence of the *märchen* but are only added on to the surface as a sign of the prevailing world view. They generally appear in religious trappings. Among them we must count Mrs. Palkó's *The Smoking Kalfaktor, Józsi the Fisherman, Killer Istéfán,* and *András Kerekes.* They may appear disguised in magic practices—*Ej Haj, Rupcsen-Hencsen*—or in the practices of old women. The role played by these motifs in the folktale is shown by the representation in the tale body of the "real" witches of Kakasd folk belief.

The description of the witches in the folktales of Kakasd is paralleled by the attitude and the activities of the "wise women" of the village. Parallel incidents taken from two different tales will show the role of village witches in tale composition. The two situations show great differences: in one tale the prince asks for advice, in the other, a woman villager. The latter asks a wise woman to help her decide which of two children is her own. Only when she has found out does the adventure of the tale start. In both cases the witch is visited in complete secrecy, and—

which proves the importance of this episode—in either tale it is the advice of the witch which introduces the action proper; her consultation is the threshhold leading from the world of reality into the world of the *märchen.*

*From* "The Snake Prince"

There was once an old woman in that neighborhood, an old witch, and the princess had heard that there lived a witch who could cast a spell on anything. Once, when the King and Queen were not at home, she went to the witch in the neighborhood. And the witch said to her: "What is the matter with you that you are so thin? You are just skin and bones, nothing but a skeleton! How come? Don't you have anything to eat, or are you sick, or worried, or what is it with you?"[45]

*From* "The Twin Rod"

In the neighborhood, there lived an old woman who knew how to tell fortunes from cards, soothsaying from beans or the palms of your hand. Pista and his wife, however, were God-fearing people and did not believe in such things, especially the man. Now he was in Church and the old neighbor woman was still at home, and the woman thought, "I'd like to try it; the old woman should read the tea leaves and maybe I can find out which of the two children is really mine." So it happened. She went there, entered, and said, "God may grant you a good day, Aunt Terka!"

"God welcome you, Mariska. Well, dogs and cats will lie down together. What shall I make of it that you come to see me? For two months you never came and we are neighbors yet!"

"Listen to me. Since this child has come to our house, I not only have more work, I am so worried that I don't care about having a good time."

"Why, my child? Aren't you glad? You have two little heroes coming up there, who will be the envy of everyone."

"All right, all right, Auntie. But I would like to know to which of them I have given birth?"

"Ah, my dear child, this can soon be remedied."

"Will you read my fortune from the leaves?"

"Leaves are not necessary. This can be done much simpler. I shall give you advice and you will see that the truth comes to light. You shall know which one is your child."

"Well, look here, my good neighbor, I would willingly give you a ham together with the pot and a good basketfull of beans if I knew which child I have put into he world, and you will also have a loaf of bread when I do my baking this week."

"You are promising me a whole carload, my child!"

"And I shall keep my promise, if I only know which of them is my own child. . . ."[46]

As we can see, the tale characters, be they princesses or peasant women of Kakasd, turn to the wise woman in difficult cases.

Our examples from Kakasd show three phases of development; they show how the elements of actual folk belief penetrate into the tale almost unnoticed. These three phases mirror the changing relationship with the living belief as it has developed in the last two hundred years; each example represents a different stage of the formation of the tale.

To start with the lowest rung, our third example shows the first stage: the incident taken from the realm of the belief world has not yet lost its original character. It is believed; it is actual and of common interest and therefore finds entrance into the folktale. This type of incident belongs among the tale motifs which make the world of the *märchen* palpable for the villagers. They serve as confirmation of the whole of the *märchen*. Therefore, although they are seemingly random motifs, their significance in the maintenance of tales is tremendous. They remain on the surface of the tale and do not effect the essentials of the action. However, they make it acceptable, credible, and actual by connecting real life with imagination. The second stage shows that the outward motifs of folk belief reality, serving the purpose of creating atmosphere for the tale, are in time transformed and absorbed by the folktale. The third phase shows that complex *märchen* type families can develop from one belief concept and that these can constantly be nourished by actual belief concepts. We are here confronted with a process which leads to the whole of history of the tale and shows the importance of exploring the juxtaposition of *märchen* and folk belief. Honti, who was deeply interested in the relationships of folk narrative, has also dealt with this theme:

> The tale tradition can constantly be increased by foreign but as-similated elements; but at the same time traditional material of a different world view can assume the outward form of the *märchen* and take over not only its motifs but the specific world view of the folktale and is also able to impose its outlooks, its form and structure, upon traditions of other origins.[47]

Honti describes in detail how the epic narratives originating in living folk belief are formed into *märchen*. The narrator tries to embroider them and introduces tale episodes; with these the *märchen*-like *Weltanschauung* affirms itself, and the tale is born. Our present knowledge of the material is insufficient to enable us to draw far-reaching conclusions: we must content ourselves with the statement that folk narratives based on living folk belief might develop into *märchen*.[48]

We cannot agree with Vajkai, who considers this question solely from the point of view of function but does not consider it historically. He denies that the belief story may present a transition to the folktale: "From the superstitious tale there never comes a *märchen:* persevering collectors may at best find more complete forms and richer variants."[49]

This is indeed the picture which confronts the researcher who today wants to record the body of folk tradition of a village. The connection between these two genres is obscured because it is the functional differences which catch the eye; the process of fusion occurs so slowly that it can be shown only on the basis of a laborius and extensive historical investigation over a considerable span of time.

We have seen that the living belief concepts have reached the tale as evidence for, and acceptance of, the message of the tales. In this respect we agree with Ortutay: he has investigated this question from Mihály Fedics' point of view and has arrived at the conclusion that the belief elements occuring in the folktale wind up by lending even the *märchen* its "credibility."[50]

We do not, of course, conclude from this that the *märchen* have originated from the belief stories. We know that there are some tales which have. Von Sydow, Liljeblad, and Lüthi[51] have quoted convincing examples. But we are likewise sure that the *märchen* did not necessarily develop along these lines.

## THE IMPACT OF LITERATURE

WHEN CONSIDERING the folk narrative body, we must not neglect the literary education of the folk. We must make careful observations to discover how far reading material has influenced the tale treasure— whether a folk prose has developed from it, and whether the style or the structure of the literary reading material has influenced folklore.

It is generally known that oral and literary traditions have, directly or indirectly, always affected each other, and that this cross-fertilization was furthered by the growth of the reading public and the appearance of chapbooks and other cheap editions. Research for a long time neglected this relationship. Folklorists excluded from consideration texts that were not completely untouched by literary influences; therefore, either the literary influences were overlooked, or everything that could be traced back to written sources was labeled as "deterioration."[52] When the informant of a folklorist referred to a book as his source, he was not listened to; and when it appeared afterward that the original of his text could be found in a calendar, it was removed from the collection.[53] The fact that we can still find much material of literary origin in folklore collections is due solely to the ignorance of the researchers concerning the field of cheap literature.

Right at the beginning of folklore collection, the influence of popular reading matter was already a factor to be taken into account. It is above all the folktale material which appeared in cheap books and popular pamphlets which had a great influence on the international folktale. In more than one case the regional redactions of certain tale types coincide with those printed in the popular publications. We certainly do not go too far in asserting that the constantly revised editions of storybooks revived the stagnant or decaying tradition, and that such collections may have inspired excellent storytellers to create new versions.[54] How important the knowledge of the various popular writings is considered to be for the tracing of folklore sources is pointed up by the Irish researchers who directed their collectors specifically toward exploring local newspapers, handbills, and pamphlets. Therefore we agree completely with Christiansen's statements:

> . . . a wider knowledge [is necessary] of the influence which printed matter—books, newspapers, and magazines—has had in the dissemination of tales, at least within the last hundred years. . . . Such information is extremely difficult to procure as it presupposes an intimate acquaintance with the bibliography, not only of books, but of such fugitive matter as newspapers and magazines—as a rule next to impossible to come by. It is well known how a printed text easily acquires a greater authority than those taken from oral tradition and all students will agree that such influence has, particularly in the last century, been ever on the increase. . . .[55]

Attention to the reading matter of narrators, even the recording of the retelling of this reading matter, became one of the most important points of departure for the examination of the narrator's personality and his narrative style. In Hungary it was Gyula Ortutay who first pointed to the reading matter of the peasant.[56] From the mouth of an illiterate woman, he recorded the tale variant of a novel by Jókai; this tale, *Turkish Rule in Hungary*, had been heard by the woman and retold.[57]

Every volume of the *New Hungarian Folklore Collection* also includes texts which can be traced to printed material, mostly for the reason that the correlation with the available original text gives a graphic picture of a narrator's creative vein.[58] Since Péter Pandur is most affected by the influence of literary style, we have also studied the different aspects of literary influences on his tales.[59]

In Europe, and especially in Germany, where literacy had an early and more direct influence on the development of the tale body, attention was soon drawn to the effect of the *Buchmärchen* on the *Volksmärchen*. It is well known that some pieces in the collection of the brothers Grimm come from older literary sources (Perrault, Musäus, etc.).[60] The influence of the oriental tales translated into European languages, above all the *Arabian Nights* collection, is very old.[61] Ulrich Jahn shows how one folktale was disseminated through a book: A servant girl came across a copy of *One Thousand and One Nights* and thus learned the tale of *Aladdin*. When she returned to her village, she related the story to a gifted storyteller. Through him it became so popular that during one generation—and in spite of the fact that the printed text was repeated faithfully—the story had changed so much that Aladdin had become an illiterate, stupid Hans.[62] Azadovski mentions a similar case. Vinokurova, during service in the city, had come across several stories from the *Arabian Nights*. Though her version comes very close to the original, she has considerably re-created and re-shaped it.[63] We may say that the influence of the tales of the brothers Grimm has continuing impact on the tale body in all of the Western World, especially in the German language, because of the innumerable editions that have appeared. Henssen compared four texts of his narrator with the original texts of the Grimm tales,[64] and K. Ranke wrote about the impact of the Grimm tales on the body of German folktales.[65] Research has also turned toward the Perrault texts.[66] Haiding stresses that those pieces for which there are literary models lend themselves well to the study of folk creation: "It is necessary to observe how printed tales are received—and transformed—through the new, oral transmission."[67] In this review of Elli Zenker's tale collection, Peuckert states that "there are hardly any tales any more which exist independently from literary sources."[68] In his review of the tale collection from Lorraine by Merkelbach-Pinck, Langstroff treats separately those tales that come from literary sources.[69] The analyses made by Friedrich Ranke, and lately also by E. Rath, of the influence of the book tale on folk tradition merit special attention.[70] When recording the complete repertoire of storytellers, Rumanian folktale experts do not distinguish between traditional texts and those of literary origin.[71]

In turning to the tale body of Kakasd Szeklers, we must refer again to the historic development of the Bucovina Szeklers in the last two hundred years. The Bucovina people, on the whole, are less literate than the peasants of central Hungary, and yet their literary tradition is older and deeper. The Szeklers, because of their privileged positions, had a rather highly developed literary knowledge which slowly penetrated their tradition. We have already dwelt on the fact that the Szeklers traveled around, that they were eager for knowledge, that they were interested in their own history as well as in the lives of other peoples, and that they assuaged their hunger for knowledge with the available reading matter. According to profession, a circle of readers—however small—developed, and would bring the knowledge attained by reading to the attention of the whole village. This was not only the foundation of the literary education of the village but the beginning of the process by which literary material penetrated traditional oral literature. We intend to demonstrate in what follows how this process developed.

What kind of literary material could be disseminated in Andrásfalva will have to be deduced only in retrospect. Nearly everything has been lost during the adventurous wanderings, and we are dependent upon unreliable information and traces found in the folklore texts themselves.

What kind of books did the people of Andrásfalva take up and how did they get them?

Traces of the old popular literature and the fact that strikingly similar tales can be found among the tales of the old Szeklers permit the assumption that this literature was well known. We assume that the tales of *The Beautiful János* (Appendix, No. 70) and *Prince Sándor* (Appendix, No. 27) originated from it, as well as a number of religious legends and exempla. Also the interest in history and search for historical documents, as well as the religious education bearing plainly the imprint of the Franciscans in the Csík, have their origin in popular literature that infiltrated the Szekler culture. It is quite possible that the form and composition of Marcika Pintyer's *Book of the Dead* may be traced to the Franciscans, since it is a guide to the customs of the wake. Unfortunately, we have until now found no proof for this assumption, and we do not know of a single written folklore creation which corresponds to the *Book of the Dead*. What is certain, however, is the fact that—to judge from old Hungarian literary parallels—we have here a late variant of the church codex containing miscellaneous literary genres. It may be that an old custom, whose developments we cannot reconstruct, is preserved here. It may well be that Márton László composed his work for the wakes all by himself and put it together according to his own concepts, using both reading matter and oral tradition. To be able to see clearly in this, we would have to know if there were, or are, similar cases to be found with the Szeklers in the Csík.

Style examinations show us that the oldest literary influence came from religious and historical material, both disseminated through the medium of the church school. This twofold influence continued in the Bucovina. Under the Austrian regime, homesickness for the fatherland grew at the same time, as we have noted, as the reputation and power of the Hungarian church in the Bucovina. The church not only administered to religious needs; it also symbolized *Magyardom*, the nation. Thus those who were interested were led by the Church to the historical and generally informative reading material and to spiritual reading. In order to satisfy the nascent interest, several "popular libraries" series appeared, as well as juvenile and popular literature, and above all writings of a religious character. All the publications of the Budapest religious publishing houses, as well as those of the dioceses of Vác and Eger, were readily available. Many Szeklers, Márton László among them, looked over the catalog and ordered the books whose titles they liked. Later, after the First World War, there appeared the chapbooks of the religious publishers of Kolozsvár, Marosvásárhely, and Brassó, three great cities in Transylvania. A considerable part of the reading matter came from the series of books which were published in Rumania for the Hungarian minority groups.

The Szeklers had access, of course, in addition to the church-oriented literature, to the secular literature in the form of chapbooks, storybooks, and juveniles. The interest in books was characteristic of the people in Andrásfalva. János Mátyás relates that everybody who crossed the Carpathian Mountains bought books, not only for himself but for others who were interested, and whose orders he was carrying out. When someone returned from his travels a veritable pilgrimage started to his house. Everyone saw the kind of book he could acquire for himself. Their first interest was in "historical novels and books about which one could weep, and those which talked about the *betyárs* [outlaws]."

The character of the books which were most in demand is a good indication of the way reading material was disseminated in the village. The Hungarian church schools taught reading and writing, and yet not all the Szeklers in Andrásfalva or in the other villages of the Bucovina could read. Actually, only the men learned to read and write. The girls, and especially the poorer ones, were soon taken from school, if their parents sent them there at all. This explains why the older women such as Mrs. Palkó, Mrs. Geczi, and Mrs. Szakács never learned to read and write. The men, who liked to think themselves superior, enjoyed reading. "When there are no such books, what is a man supposed to learn from?" asked Andrásfalvi. "He does not mind the few forints; he buys the book." These books satisfied the historical as well as the religious interests and developed two types of readers in a village who, when the occasion called for it, took a prominent role.

The "well-read man" was respected in every regard; he knew more than the others. In Kakasd all those who read constantly and who "know writing" were respected and admired. "He was always bent over books," they said with great respect about Marcika Pintyer. "I love to read," said Andrásfalvi. "I climb up the printed letters like a squirrel on a tree. We went to visit relatives in Hadikfalva; will you believe it, I stayed there for two nights so I could read all the books?" Of old József Sebestyén they said, "He did not even need to eat when he was reading." But the well-read man was not only an object of admiration; he performed a useful service in passing on the knowledge gleaned from books. In the case of Andrásfalvi this could be done only by reading aloud in public or by free interpretation.[72] The usefulness of a book was not considered to lie in its being read by one reader, but in its being read in public and in the use of what is learned from it.

Among the "well-read-men" there were some who distinguished themselves clearly from the storytellers. They did not think much of the tale; they wanted truth from a book and wanted to spread its edification. In this group belonged the younger József Zaicz. Of him Antal Molnár said, "He doesn't bother with *märchen;* he prefers to proclaim Holy Scripture. He knew it by heart and told it like a priest." To this type of personality also belonged the chanters at the wakes. They knew many edifying stories, legends, and church hymns, and the church rites, and could explain the Bible. Among them were also the respected "credible men" who liked to read historical material and to talk about historical events. János Mátyás, András Jordáki, and Rudolf Györfi-Varga did not, without exception, tell *märchen,* in spite of their excellent narrative talent, their feeling for form and style. When they were in company they told best anecdotes or stories which had "simple people" for their subjects and did not appear unreal, for they kept strictly to true happenings.

But there were also storytellers who read and then told stories: they knew the art of reading and thus acquired fame in a twofold capacity. Among them we may count the old Zaicz and his son János, as well as Marcika Pintyer, who, however, was a narrator only secondarily; and in Kakasd we may also count Andrásfalvi among them.[73] They acquired their reputation for storytelling mostly through their reading. Of János Zaicz someone once said, "He knew the Scriptures; he had a quick intelligence and a good memory for the stories," for otherwise it is inconveivable that János Zaicz could retain so many stories in his head. Some narrators enlarged their knowledge from storybooks and chapbooks.[74]

On the opposite end is the narrator, the man who narrates only *märchen* and not other stories. The book-tale influences him only indirectly; he refuses to tell anything but a genuine tale. Mrs. Palkó says, "I don't tell true stories; I know only real folktales—I have not been there; I have not seen; I only heard it from Kossuth.* Why should I tell it if it was not true? But I can tell magic tales."[75]

Different reading material was read aloud for the entertainment of the listeners or was freely interpreted. Whenever the occasion arose, older men mentioned what they had read and discussed historical and religious topics. During communal work or at social gatherings the recital of what was read alternated with storytelling. Sometimes a good narrator was asked to read aloud from a storybook or a school book, when nobody could tell a tale.[76] This was the way Mrs. Palkó learned some of her tales, for she was always eager to hear new ones. She not only had tales told to her but read to her from storybooks; her children, for example, read many tales to her. Lajos Palkó said of her, "She had such a quick perception; whatever was read to her, my mother immediately knew." And her daughter Erzsi added, "She has learned much from me as well as from storybooks." Thus literature slowly, consciously or unconsciously, erodes the folktale body through the mediation of both the narrators who can read and those who cannot. When Mrs. Palkó received her official distinction and when her volume of *märchen* had appeared, she began to learn new *märchen* purposely, for she recognized that her knowledge was appreciated outside her village as well. She was interested in new tales not only in Kakasd but when she went visiting elsewhere. She told what she had learned recently, though it would be hard to say how long the new tales stayed in her repertoire. We have

* National hero of the Hungarian War of Independence, 1848-49.

recorded seven of these tales. They are especially interesting because we can compare them with the originals and thus recognize what Mrs. Palkó added.[77]

In the Kakasd tale body can be noted the influence of storybooks, secular narratives from chapbooks, and church literature and exampla.

## Storybooks

THE NEWER EDITIONS of storybooks are those that are found for the most part today in Kakasd. A visitor who came to see Mrs. Palkó, for example, brought with him a storybook—Sándor Dömötör's *Hetedhét országon túl (Over Seven Times Seven Countries)*.[78] It was to be read from in the evening. In conversations we were able to learn that the grade school teachers had once lent many storybooks to the villagers, and that such storybooks were also bought; but no one could give any further information about these books or quote title or author. Our tale collection shows that the most important source, in addition to a few other folktale editions, was Elek Benedek's *Hungarian World of Tale and Legend*, in five volumes, published in 1894. Besides this, the influence of László Arany's folktale collection is striking—though the tales are secondhand—as is the influence of the juvenile editions of the Grimm tales.[79] Ortutay also points out their popularity.[80] Ágnes Kovács analyzes the great impact of the Benedek collection on the folktales.[81] This generally well-liked collection influenced the tale treasure of the Szeklers not only in the village of Ketesd in Kalotaszeg (a region of Transylvania) but all through Transylvania and the Bucovina. In the Appendix, which gives accounts of the variants of the tales, we have also listed the literary sources when we were able to pin-point them, as well as the subsequent changes in the text. Here is the list of the tales which can be positively traced to Benedek:

*The Iron Laci (Vas Laci)*, No. 1
*I Don't Know (Nemtudomka)*, No. 3
*Pihári*, No. 5
*The Count and the Coachman (A gróf és János kocsis)*, No. 12
*The Princess (Hercegkirály kisasszony)*, No. 16
*Józsi, The Fisherman (Halász Józsi)*, No. 22
*András Kerekes (Kerekes András)*, No. 26
*The Psalmsinging Bird (Zsoltáréneklö madár)*, No. 29
*Nine (Kilenc)*, No. 32
*Ilona the Beautiful (Tündérszép Ilona)*, No. 36

*Istéfán, the Murderer (Megölö Istéfán),* No. 37
*The Two Hermits (A két remete),* No. 38
*Anna Miller (Mónár Anna),* No. 46
*The Three Archangels (A Három Arkangyal),* No. 39
*The Shrewd Servant (A furfangos szolga),* No. 47
*Nine Wheat Kernels (Kilenc búzaszem),* No. 39
*The Beautiful János (Világszép Jánossa),* No. 70
*Jutka in Ashes (Hammas Jutka),* No. 83

These are, altogether, eighteen in number, a relatively high count. Some of them are still very close to the original—the course of action is unchanged, and only a few stylistic phrases appear. Most of them, however, were changed so drastically that we can be certain that their adaptation was not an act of conscious re-creation. The raw material stays alive for some time in the consciousness of the people; it receives its form from the storyteller and the folk tradition. The kind of opportunity the gifted narrator has is best demonstrated in the tale of *I Don't Know.* The point of departure is the tale listed by Benedek under the title *King of the Castle of Planks,* also known and popular under this title in Kakasd. When we read Mrs. Palkó's tale, which is artistically shaped and embroidered, we notice immediately that not one single line of the tale is exactly like the Benedek version. Since it is probable that Mátyás Mátyás, who was no storyteller, rendered this tale in a much more succinct form than it is found in Benedek, it is clear that Mrs. Palkó shaped her tale from a narrative which cannot have been much more than a sketch.

The tale of *András Kerekes* also shows the characteristic manifestations of literary influence. Marcika Pintyer read it and since he liked the tale, incorporated it into his *Book of the Dead,* transforming it suitably. Through this *Book of the Dead* the tale became known all over the village. Mrs. Palkó learned it and put it into her repertoire. Other tales, too, were disseminated through the storybooks. Here the obstacle of strange or involuted language, which rendered so many popular books incomprehensible for the simple man, was more or less removed. If they still reached the Szeklers in this form, these tales either were not assimilated or were completely reshaped.

## Secular Narratives from Chapbooks

Historical stories from chapbooks were very popular but were not drawn into the folktale treasure. Old Zaicz often told stories about Miklós Toldi, Pál Kinizsi, and Péter Szápári[82] and about the War of

Independence (1848–49). "This was in the reader for the fifth and the sixth grade," said Andrásfalvi. Much was read about the history of Transylvania. Andrásfalvi liked to tell about the exciting adventures of the *betyárs:*

> What is the name of the robber who sprang from a snowflake? Rinaldo! Well, that is a very thick book; I know a few verses from it. Is it available? I would like to get it. I know how he was born, how he became a *betyár;* he has wrought much justice. Sándor Rózsa and Bandi Patkó—I have read in those little pamphlets. They came from Budapest. We had a teacher and he brought them with him. He organized a library. They were also sold on the market. There was a novel, *Sarolta Tecsö* was the name, three leu apiece: it had eight pages.

Marcika Pintyer even put things worth knowing about the *betyárs* into his *Book of the Dead:*

> Rinaldo was the chief of the robbers but he did not live with them in Hungary; he lived and died on Italian soil. There he had started his life, and there he ended it. He was a famous robber; but he was not a Hungarian, he was an Italian. That is something different. The chiefs of the famous bands of robbers in the Bakony forest were first, Sándor Rózsa; second, Imre Bogár; third, Bandi Angyal; fourth, Bandi Patkó; fifth, Jóska Sobri; sixth, Józsi Savanyó; seventh, Marci Zöld—born 1780, died 1840. With the death of those seven robber chiefs the robbing in the Bakony Forest came to an end, since then there were no more good birds in the forest. The robbing came to an end but they, too, were finished; I don't know the birthdays of the others, but I was present at the wake of Marci Zöld and Sándor Rózsa with István; together we dug the ditch and we buried them.[83]

Mrs. Palkó's daughter also read such books: "Once there were stories in a book, and also Sándor Rózsa and a novel, *Brave Sons.* It was about 1848."

But we cannot find any trace of these historical reading materials in the Kakasd tale body. It was rather the tale-like chapbooks which exercised some influence. Here we must first mention the popularity of the story of *The Seven Sages of Rome.* This classic collection of novella was disseminated all over the land by the chapbooks and around the middle of the nineteenth century landed in the folklore tradition of the peasants.[84] While their influence vanished in recent years with the peasants of most of Hungary, it still lived in Kakasd, and had all its original impact. For this reason we have included four novellas in our collection.

*The Seven Sages of Rome*, or rather the *Story of Poncianus*, had once been in circulation in Andrásfalva and was among the reading material most in demand. The people of Kakasd said that both József Zaicz and Marcika Pintyer told many stories from it; that everybody in Kakasd knew a part of it—an obvious proof of its general popularity. Marcika Pintyer used two novellas in his *Book of the Dead: King Sándor and King Lajos* (Appendix, No. 97) and *The Woman Who Could Sing Well* (Appendix, No. 101). Although in former times Andrásfalvi was able to tell all fifteen novellas, when we knew him he remembered only parts of some. Those he liked best he transformed and inserted in his repertoire of tales: *The Faithful Widow* (Appendix, No. 72) and *The Young Shrew* (Appendix, No. 69). He was able to reconstruct only a short list of the contents of the others after a long search of his memory. Mrs. Palkó, too, knew these novellas, but as she did not consider them real tales she did not narrate a single one of them. When we asked about it, she said, "Mrs. Ömböli knows much about *The Seven Sages of Rome*, but she reads it from a book. She reads a story, and then she tells a tale," which means that the tale takes the place of the story. Mrs. Palkó no longer knew that *King Sándor and King Lajos* also came from this collection—she experienced this narrative completely as a folktale. With absolute certainty she said that she had learned this "folktale" from her daughter-in-law, who had read it to her ten years ago out of a storybook. It is incomprehensible that she should not have known Marcika Pintyer's variant before. It may be that Mrs. Palkó had heard it without paying much attention to it. What is certain is the fact that this tale comes from a common source and was formed by Mrs. Palkó independently of the text in the *Book of the Dead* and included in her repertoire. It is not impossible that this tale had been separated long before the Poncianus novellas and entered the folk tradition of the Szeklers in the Bucovina.

Which popular edition is at the base of the Poncianus novellas that play such a part in our collection is something that can no longer be determined, because there were numerous editions published from the second half of the last century until the beginning of World War I. It is probable that the source is an edition, edited by an unknown hand, of the publications of Bucsánszky and Rózsa, which came out in a new edition nearly every year between 1864 and 1911.[85] These voluminous and richly illustrated editions show a beautiful archaic language which is not obsolete even now. It is largely distinguished from the involuted and heavy-handed language of the chapbooks, which were translated from other languages, mainly from the German. These books found ready acceptance in Andrásfalva but had no influence on the language; the texts were adapted into the local dialect. Another fact points to these popular editions: the texts which were incorporated into the folk tradition still retain the foreign names—Guido, Florentina, Tiberis—no matter how vastly they differ from the originals. Concepts which are foreign to the people of Kakasd—knight, cup-bearer—and the sequence of the content were unaltered. The free variation of Mrs. Palkó, the conscious, artistic re-creation of Marcika Pintyer, and the weak reconstruction of the content by Andrásfalvi all agree, in that the individual incidents of the story were preserved and only the style changed into the traditional folk style. The texts which do not have folktale forms which have nothing in them which might tend toward folklore tradition and thus could be molded, absorbed, and blended with tradition, slowly disintegrate as soon as they become detached from the book original. The two handwritten variants of Marcika Pintyer represent a type of folk tradition for which there is as yet no example in the Hungarian. With *King Sándor* only the dialect is transformed, but even so it represents a most significant variation. *The Singing Woman,* however, shows another type not known before, the form of rhymed prose. Apart from the rich folk speech there are no important textual changes to be found. Each further formulation in oral tradition almost always represents an abbreviation. The knowledge and the presence of an original written text do not permit of free modification, as we can see, for example, with Andrásfalvi. His tale style, in general, shows a definite personality: he enlarges upon a tale rather than shortens it. When he recited a story which he read he became very concise. Separation from the text does not generate a free variant but rather results in destruction, as is borne out in Andrásfalvi's text after the seventh novella of Poncianus, *The Husband Who Was Shut Out.* The text limits itself to the bare facts; the best episode in the original story—the ruse of the stone thrown into the well—is even omitted. This example, on the other hand, demonstrates how massive speech and style traditions loom with the Szeklers. The strange, nontraditional text is taken over only as far as content is concerned and is restyled right from the start. Andrásfalvi translates it into his own language, and the original literary style disappears completely:

A knight married for the second time. He asked for the hand of the daughter of a burgher—today we would say of a Kulak.[86] He was a noble knight, sixty years old. She had a lover; she went out to meet him in the garden and they had a good time. The knight

did not find her during the night. "Woman, where have you been?"
She always lied to him where she had been. Evenings she put a
sleeping draught into the drink of her husband, but then the knight
found out and did not drink his tea but pretended to be asleep.
Then he went after his wife. He saw that they hugged and kissed
at the well in the street, across from the castle, and he heard: "That
the devil may get the old one so that we could stay together!" The
young woman noticed that her husband was after her, and she
hurried back quicker than he, back to the castle. The small door
that led to the street, she locked it so that her husband could not
come through it. The man was in his nightshirt only, and it was
night, about eleven o'clock. The young woman hurried to the second floor, opened a window, and cried out to her husband, "You
faithless husband who only waits until his wife is asleep, then he
goes to the well to meet his love." Then she made so much noise that
all the neighboring castles woke up and people came to the
windows. But nobody went into the street for there was an ordi-
nance that anybody who was found on the street by the watchmen between eight o'clock in the evening and six o'clock in the
morning would be pilloried. The knight knew very well that
the bailiffs would take an innocent whippingpost if he stayed outside, but he complained in vain. He desperately implored his wife
to let him in. But the young wife cried out loud, "You are the
faithless one, and want to pass it to me! You have been cheating on
me for weeks, for months!" So the old one had to stay outside, and
in the morning he was pilloried, and it was the custom that every
passer-by had to spit in his face. But as the mayor of the town was
himself acquainted with the knight, he could not believe that he
should have betrayed his wife during the night even though he was
found there. So the wife was hauled before him and the law punished her severely, first because she had tried to sully the honor
of the knight, and second for having married him. And if they have
not died, they are still living today.

In addition to other material which has penetrated the tale body from
the popular story books—similar examples are texts No. 71 and No. 100
in the Appendix—it is worth mentioning *Gábor Német* and *Bálint
Galambos*, two variations of the same tale. In No. 62 and No. 96 we
have recorded two variants known to everyone in the village. The narrative, whose origin cannot be ascertained, undoubtedly comes from the
nineteenth century. As our analyses in the Appendix for both variants
show, the specific social development of Andrásfalva made it possible
for this story to develop into a full-fledged and true new *märchen*,
in all its parts.

## Church Literature and Exempla

RELIGIOUS WRITINGS for edification circulated widely among the villagers. We could, however, find only two of them at hand: *The Life of St. George*[87] and the story of *Genoveva*,[88] the most popular and the best liked everywhere. But there are traces of many more writings in oral narratives in the *märchen*, and in the *Book of the Dead*. We shall return to the content of the latter when we examine the personality of Márton László. Here we wish only to mention that the *Book of the Dead* was a focal point which attracted all the true and apocryphal legends and miracle stories. The pious women of the village were well acquainted with the stories about the lives of the saints and their martyrdom. Some of them, such as Mrs. Szakács, often told them and said they had heard them from their fathers; for many old men, too, had an inexhaustible stock of such stories. And yet these stories had not become *märchen* and had not entered into the folk narrative body any more than had the narratives which lack tale-like characteristics. It cannot be assumed that the pious stories were spread exclusively through the *Book of the Dead*, because many people in Kakasd said that they had heard them from their parents, from János Zaicz, or from others. It is more probable that the religious writings and Marcika Pintyer's anthology were read at the same time.

The religious legends with a moral deserve special attention. In contrast to the folk legends they fulfill to a certain degree the function of the *märchen*, even though they themselves were not included in the folktale treasure. These edifying, moralizing stories, which tell about punishment for circumventing church laws and teachings, or show how a godless person is brought back to the straight and narrow path, or how he reaps well-deserved punishment, stories that talk of overcoming evil, are equally as important as the *märchen*. Their tone is didactic and they were especially favored by zealous, deeply religious women. Mrs. Palkó knew a countless number of them. We shall quote here only three: *János the Blacksmith* (No. 41), *A Mother's Atonement* (No. 42), and *Margít* (No. 63). All three are characteristic, though from a different point of view. The first story was very popular and apparently does not come directly from a literary source. The second may have its origin in an unknown pamphlet containing pious, virtuous teachings. The third, relatively the newest, may have come from one of the numerous pamphlets distributed by church publishers. Worth mentioning here also is another text of Mrs. Palkó's, *Fendrik*, a story in which a priest does not prevent the cruel annihilation of a whole family because he cannot violate the seal of confession. In another story a Protestant man is damned because he had made fun of confession; in a third a guilty soul does not find peace in the grave. Though their recital is pleasing because of the seductively beautiful language of the Szeklers, these texts are actually of little value and cannot become folktales.

When we examine the influence of this reading material upon the style of the folktale, we can truthfully say that it was not important. This is especially striking when we compare our material with narratives recorded from other Hungarian peasant communities. On the other hand, newer collections demonstrate that the literary style influenced the structure and often even the choice of words of the tale texts.[89] Modern folktale experts have called attention to the influence of new concepts which enter into the *märchen*.[90] However, this influence usually does not affect the essentials of the tales. The tale body of the narrators from Kakasd is even less affected and retains its archaic and clean style. Neither the convoluted style of the chapbooks about the turn of the century nor the language of the city environs as found in the dime novels spoiled these narrators' feeling for form nor their methods of composition. Of course, there are words to be found in the Kakasd tales which were borrowed, foreign concepts which penetrated from the outside. With Mrs. Palkó the king went to work in the "parliament"; people "telephoned" to the castle when something was out of order; the heroine had "her picture taken"; in the coach, by magic, there are "beautiful seats"; the presents which the grateful hero received from the animals are put into his "notebook." All this can be traced less to books than to the spread of technology, the proximity of other peoples, the spread of the language soldiers picked up in service, and the experiences of many trips. These foreign expressions, though rare, are not dissonant but insert themselves into the language of the Szeklers just as do the words coming from the Rumanian language. The folktale heroes, even the mightiest kings and dukes, all speak exactly like the Szeklers; the artifice, the embroidery, and the citified traits which have an adverse affect upon the most beautiful tales of Péter Pandur[91] are not to be found here. It occasionally happened that a recently heard word caught on and was used temporarily; on the whole, however, the people of Kakasd watched carefully the purity of their language—another manifestation of the self-consciousness and the pride of the Szeklers. The insidious influence of the reading material, of which Mackensen speaks,[92] had not been felt, and thus the capacity of the dialect folk style for assimilation had more rein. How linear this style is can best be seen in the *Book of the Dead* by Márton László. His texts originate in the reading materials; he wrote them down, but in such a way that the style of the Szekler language penetrated them completely and the Szekler dialect appears even in the spelling. The book stories, if they are diffused by the people, are thus significantly transformed, whether or not they enter the traditional folktale body. Ranke ably describes how the book story is shortened by transformation on the lips of the people: long-winded and cumbersome descriptions of landscapes and characterizations are dropped; not situations but only events are related, and even those are compressed to the essentials.[93] Only the names and the rhymed parts remain unchanged.[94] Through their transformation, the texts become more logical: the unessential and confusing parts of the story are omitted and are replaced by incidents which are closer to the life of the people in the village. These changes can be noted in all the texts which originate in the literary sources.

The overpowering strength of the folk style is best seen in the formation of two newer themes. The one is the story, already mentioned, of Gábor Német (Appendix, No. 62). Here the events take place in an environment which was strange for Mrs. Palkó: in the city, in the factory, and among factory workers. This atmosphere is completely transformed by Mrs. Palkó's interpretation. Before our eyes appear the world of the people in Kakasd and the magic world of the *märchen*, the pomp, the royal splendor, the folklore atmosphere which transforms the story, despite the dissonant elements, into the true folktale. A similar masterful formation can be felt in the other story, *Margit* (Appendix No. 63). This story does not become a *märchen*, but its moralizing, succinct presentation assumes weight as a result of the popular interpretation.

In addition to the 30 recorded belief stories and the 21 texts traceable to literary sources, our collection of narratives in Kakasd contains 161 *märchen* and *märchen*-incidents, falling into the following categories:

| | | |
|---|---|---|
| 1. Magic tales | 76 | |
| 2. Legends | 9 | |
| 3. Novellas | 26 | |
| 4. Jokes and Anecdotes | 30 | |
| | 161 | |

This list shows that the Kakasd tale material consists mainly of ordinary tales, among which are to be counted the legends and the novella, while the realistic peasant tales—jokes and anecdotes—are in the minority. This is further borne out by the fact that neither the fragments which are incompetently told nor the jokes narrated by weak narrators have increased this number. The world of the magic tale enjoyed undivided popularity in Kakasd, so much so that from the many joke types known in the general Szekler stock, only the most characteristic were chosen by the Kakasd narrators. These chosen types are, above all, those which are the closest to the conditions and problems of the Andrásfalva people: the vivacious, caricaturing satires; the pillorying of a bad habit, especially for the instruction of youth. The anticlerical jokes, so popular elsewhere, play only an inferior role.

The two extremes of the poetic, fantastic, adventuresome world of the magic tale and the down-to-earth, cheerful expression of the joke live side by side and complement each other; while the *märchen* is taken seriously and narrator as well as audience prepare themselves for it, the joke serves to dissolve the *märchen* atmosphere, "so that we can have a belly laugh." It is a kind of interlude, like that provided on the stage by jokes which balance the impact of the serious drama.[95]

Whenever she told a long tale, Mrs. Palkó would say, "So, now I am going to tell something short, something funny." With the words "It will only be a little nothing," she always tried to prevent me from writing it down. "That is only a joke, that is not a tale!"

These two narrative genres also existed side by side in the old Hungarian peasant community. That the balance has changed in favor of the joke in the course of the past fifty years is the result of the dissolution of the atmosphere favorable for the magic tale. The occasions for storytelling have diminished and the joke, for which much less time is required, has taken the upper hand.[96] It is more easily told; it does not require special narrative talents; it generally consists of one episode with a punchline. The gifted narrator can, of course, at will link together independent episodes, precisely because of the structural peculiarity of the genre.

A thorough analysis of the *märchen* will follow: in Chapter 8, we will consider the aspect of the personality of the individual narrators; in the Appendix we will treat the structure, style, and peculiarities of the single tales. The Kakasd tale body is archaic not only in language and style but in content and composition. The Szeklers from the Bucovina went through stages of development different from those experienced by the peasants of Hungary. Their isolated geographical situation brought to light an ancient layer of the Hungarian folk collection. Some of the *märchen* were previously known in only one or two variations or in scanty fragments. The Kakasd versions, however, indicate that these tales have not completely disappeared from the Hungarian ethnic territory. After a lapse of sixty to eighty years we encounter them again here. It must certainly be stated that many classical tales of early Szekler tradition have come back to the Szeklers through Elek Benedek's collection, although in a stylized form. But tales like *The Three Princes and the Man with the Iron Hat* (Appendix, No. 2), *The Smoking Kalfaktor* (No. 40), *The Turk* (No. 45), *The Twin Rod* (No. 64), and *The Nine Kernels of Wheat* (No. 65) prove that through the analysis of the Kakasd tale treasure we have come to know material of archaic vintage.

# 8

# *The Storytellers*

OUR STUDY SO FAR HAS SHOWN THAT PROBLEMS OF FOLKTALE SCHOL-
arship, whether structure, text, or social function is treated, can
best be approached when the role of the narrator and of the
community in which storytelling is practiced is taken into consideration.
In agreement with Lintur we abhor the neglect of the conservative
folklorists who recorded their texts from "story manufacturers" who
merely repeated tradition without any ambition to achieve an artistic
creation. "We must never forget," he writes, "that the *märchen* is above
all an artist product."[1] Therefore, research has to focus on the outstanding storytelling personalities of a given community in order to gain,
through them, an insight into the community's tale tradition. In order to
fulfill both tasks—that is, to come to know the outstanding narrators
as well as the *märchen* tradition of the group—we must also consider the
lesser talents. Ágnes Kovács follows this principle, even if she is not
always consistent.[2] Lintur's collection is outstanding in this connection,
with regard to both his methods of collecting and his evaluations.[3] Insofar as we agreed with them, we tried to apply his methods to our own
research in Kakasd.

Before we discuss our narrators, we must mention the opinions which
have prevailed so far with regard to storytellers.

Ever since research recognized that abilities are required for the recital of folktales which are not always found among those who know the *märchen*, its attention has been drawn to different problems. First of all, the person who had grown up in a book culture was struck by the vivid and excellent memory of the storytellers. Memory[4] is an essential factor of folk culture based mainly on oral education and on the transmission of oral tradition. Memory is significant for storytelling in that (1) the narrator can retain many *märchen* in his memory, and (2) he is able to preserve the individual pieces of his repertoire over a long period of time. In view of this fact, it was believed that the narrator's greatest virtue lay in his faithful adherence to the text, in keeping the *märchen* unchanged in his memory. This opinion was strengthened by the fact that the majority of the narrators themselves affirmed that nothing must be changed in a tale. They referred to respected storytellers and people who were deceased—parents or grandparents—(sometimes even to books) from whom they had taken over the tales verbatim, like sacred relics. Every tale collector encounters during fieldwork people who refer to "best storyteller," the master, who has just died. And those who see in the teller of tales the bearer of tradition and not the artist consider faithfulness to the traditional inherited text as the greatest virtue.[5]

In the meantime, research has come to the conclusion that a good memory is only one of the important virtues of a narrator, and that close adherence to the text is not in itself a guarantee of quality. We often find that those who anxiously cleave to the tradition of the past generation are weak storytellers—among them are those whom Wesselski and von Sydow labeled bearers of tradition—and are not really creative. Today, it would be difficult to discover whether the old narrators who were famous for the faithfulness of their renditions, such as Frau Viehmann of the brothers Grimm, really were outstanding storytellers. One thing is sure: Elli Zenker's Mrs. Pallanik felt herself responsible for the text which she had inherited from her parents; she did not consciously change one single word, because she would have considered any variation a falsification. Therefore she simply omitted everything she could not remember.[6] S. Erdész's outstanding storyteller, the night watchman Lajos Ámi, claimed he heard his entire repertoire of 236 tales from an Italian sergeant under whom he served during the First World War and that—some 40 years later—he had never changed a word. It may well be that the collectors accepted uncritically the declaration of the narrators that nothing must be changed in the texts and never closely controlled the possible variations. Thus we cannot know if they were concerned with simple bearers of tradition or with truly creative narrators. We cannot check the information about György Bözödi's outstanding narrator, János Bágyi,[7] because it is impossible to find out about all the variants of his one hundred recorded *märchen* and anecdotes known only in written form. Our experiences and the proof recorded further on show, however, that faithfulness to the text here means a retaining of the *märchen* theme rather than a verbatim repetition of what was heard and what was thought to be an original version. This is the case with the illiterate narrator, Tobias Kern.[8] Bünker recorded his tale of *The Rich Miller's Daughter* (AT 955) twice within ten years and stated that Kern was incredibly faithful to his text. However, the second version showed considerable variation. The distinguished master storyteller, Mihály Lacza, told Ortutay at their first meeting, in the late 'thirties: "You cannot change anying in a *märchen;* we have to tell it exactly the way we have learned it. How could you change it?" he asked. "It would no longer have its proper meaning." According to his statement, "he related the *märchen* just as, according to his best knowledge and memory, he once had heard them."[9] This example shows the growth potential of an excellent storyteller. His ninety tales retold twenty years later do not correspond in the slightest to the forms recited before. Elli Zenker, too, notes that her narrators, in striving for faithful rendering, embroider certain parts very carefully when they become aware that their listeners are paying them rapt attention.[10] What Henssen writes about Gerrits, the narrator who consciously sticks to tradition, is certainly applicable to most narrators who perform in public:

> The . . . manner of narrating permits us to recognize if the informant has grasped tradition in all its detail and is treating the material handed down to him with reverence. He does not change anything essential. . . . Wherever he did undertake changes they were, judging from the viewpoint of tradition, genuine improvements. . . . He knew that he had to guard a precious inheritance and showed a kind of artistic conscience by answering to himself for the changes.[11]

The observations which stress the inviolability of the *märchen* tradition in individual communities also recognize the individual modifications.[12]

From this it is clear that what is important is not the question of faithfulness, but the attitude of the narrator—whether he views the tale as a sacred tradition or as material he can embroider. The claim to faithfulness can be truthful as far as the content of the tale is concerned, but its formation is always variable. From the narrator's viewpoint, authority and credibility play an important part, as well as faithfulness and respect for tradition. Just as we recognized that the narrator had not learned everything he was telling from the book to which he referred,[13] so, too, we could see that the inviolability of the tales learned from the older generation is pure fiction. It is inconceivable that a narrator should repeatedly tell a long tale, letter-perfect, according to what he had heard in his childhood. The constant transformation of a tale preserved in the communal tradition is logical and follows its own law. There is no "tale of the old ones," for those from whom the old ones received the tale retained nothing but the outline of the tale. The longer the text itself and the more ambiguous the theme, the more complicated the combination of the tale theme, the stronger is the transformation. Even narrators such as Hertha Grudde's women informants who wanted to preserve their fathers' *märchen* can never adhere completely to what they have heard, even when they write down the texts so as not to spoil the *märchen*.[14] The narrator uses the traditional material consciously or unconsciously (in the former he retains tradition, in the latter he feels free to vary), and if he is gifted, his work will be excellent in either case. "Each adoption is done both on the historical plane and from the inside, according to the requirements of the psyche which meet with tradition."[15]

The repertoire of an excellent storyteller as a rule is quite voluminous. According to the general observations in the scholarly literature, there are occasional storytellers who know no more than 4 to 6 tales, though some of these, if necessary, can summarize the content of as many as 20 tales. The true storytellers generally know at least 40, and most of them know many more. The Samarian Novopolzev knew 72 tales; David Lebediev, the Cheremis storyteller whose tales were recorded by Beke, knew 78; Barishnikova from Voroniezh knew 120; and Lintur's Kalin knew 80. Henssen's and Jahn's narrators knew 50 to 60 tales. Satke's Smolka related 54; Bîrlea mentions an average of 20 to 80 among Rumanians; and the Jemenite Jewish narrator, Jefet Schwili, could tell 200, as could the Michigan Negro Suggs.[16] The Hungarian narrators are led by Lajos Ámi with 236 tales, followed by Péter Pandur with 107, and Mihály Lacza and Mrs. Julie Tóth, who come very close to this number.[17] Some Irish narrators know an astonishing number of tales—200 to 300[18]—as do the Swedish gypsy Taikon with 250 tales and the Estonian Jürgensen with 265.[19] As more recent finds suggest, anecdote tellers or those who specialize in genres other than the magic tale might know even more: O. Nagy's Mrs. Györi in Transylvania knew 400 stories and Jech's Filoména Hornychová in the Czech ethnic island of Glatz, 500.[20] These narrators did not learn all these tales at one time, but during the course of a lifetime they have absorbed the various tale elements and have become a sort of reservoir of the national tale body. Generally they heard the *märchen* during their youth, and only much later attained the rank of storyteller.[21] With few exceptions, such as Mihály Borbély, who was 32 years old when Kálmány recorded his tales,[22] only older men and women tell tales. These storytellers are usually between 60 and 80 years old, and rarely under 40.[23] But taking into consideration that, as a rule, storytellers are poor people who have become village storytellers only in their old age, and that the folklorist can encounter them only in the village, it may well be possible that our assumption that a certain age is a prerequisite for storytelling is erroneous. It is impossible that there would have been old storytellers in the barracks and youth hostels, and storytelling is best learned in youth. In spite of this, however, we think that certain qualities are necessary for becoming an authoritative storyteller. The kind of audience such a storyteller attracts indicates that he is advanced in years; for age, to this audience, indicates superior knowledge and experience and this engenders, on the part of the narrator, an attitude which demands respect.

To keep such an immense amount of material constantly in the forefront of the mind requires not only the power of recollection but the corresponding ability to narrate. And this, in turn, presupposes a thorough knowledge of the existing tale treasure. The raw material, growing wild like seeds, arbitrarily passing from mouth to mouth, needs a great storytelling personality to give it its true form. Storytellers pass on material that would be destined to oblivion without them. The storyteller attracts narrative material like a magnet. Wherever he is, he is learning, and he generally retains what he has learned to the end of his life. Many people refer to the fact that they learned this or that tale in their childhood, and they still recall on what occasion and from whom they heard it. This was the case, for example, with the Dutchman Gerrits, who came to Germany at the age of eleven. Gerrits knew many tales of his homeland, and even remembered which tale he had learned from a peasant woman when he was fourteen or fifteen.[24] A woodsman by the name of Forster, when he was seventy, told stories he had learned in his home village, which he had left at the age of eleven. The 75-year old nightwatchman Schlepp was eight years old when he learned his tales from a neighbor.[25]

The first setting for learning the tale is, of course, the home; after that, a person who has aptitude for it can learn everywhere. He stores up material gathered here and there, and if conditions are propitious, he appears much later as a creative narrator.[26] It makes no difference whether his teachers have told him corrupted tale skeletons, whether they had read the tales in books, or whether, on the other hand, they themselves were outstanding storytellers. As narrators such as Fedics, Pandur, and János Nagy have said, the gifted narrator needs nothing more than the raw material, the sketch from which he can form his tale himself.[27] Other folklorists, too, have found much evidence to support this opinion.[28] Thus the new tale naturally differs from the one the narrator had heard originally.

But the creative individual learns more than the sketch. The technique of construction, the traditional customs of storytelling, the proper presentation—all these become the narrator's own. When the storyteller has found his own public, his reputation grows with his activities. His techniques become more refined and his ambition increases. Folklorists at one time would point out that there is no aspiration to recognition of authorship in folklore creation, that the folktale narrator did not aspire to a recognition of his knowledge and would disappear, nameless, and modest, behind his work.[29] This opinion has changed since the attention of folklore scholars has been drawn to the personality of the storyteller, and it has been drawn to the personality of the storyteller, and it has been shown to be an erroneous assumption on the part of collectors who fell prey to an optical illusion. In oral tradition, in traditional folk culture, there is none of the professionalism among creative individuals that exists in highly civilized areas. But each good storyteller or folk artist seeks special recognition of his talents,[30] and the public readily complies. Károly Marót is to the point: "Just as with other artists of the mind, the folk artists are constantly driven by the ambition to outdo competitors at their own occupation. This means a striving for something 'new' just as in any other creative activity."[31]

In talking about the tales, the storytellers let it be known that they are well aware of their own capabilities. Exaggerations like the following occur: "There is not paper enough in the world that I could not fill with my stories."[32] "I know a million of them";[33] "thousands."[34] Boastful statements like that of János Zaicz that he knew a different tale for every day of the year are a good indication of this tendency.[35] A skillful narrator does not need to be urged: he likes to have his knowledge tested, even in the presence of the collector,[36] and some narrators let their "discovery" go to their heads. The exaggerated and boundless self-confidence of Fedics[37] has also appeared in other narrators. Prime examples are János Nagy, from Sára, who far overestimated his knowledge and his capabilities, and Péter Pandur, who fancied himself a writer of novels[38] and was waiting to dictate to somebody what he had imagined during sleepless nights.

From the perspective of the village, the storyteller, generally an experienced and widely traveled man, is a knowledgeable man well versed in the ways of the world. This, along with the fundamental conformity of the international tale body, is the main reason why the peculiarities of the tale body of an individual ethnic group within a country are so hard to distinguish. As many recorded life histories indicate, the life of the storyteller is colorful and varied, and he has many opportunities for transmitting tradition.[39] First, the home tradition influences the narrator; then, during his years of military service, he comes in contact with a wider national tradition. During the course of the work occasions treated earlier the variants which the narrator has accumulated are shaped by him into his own versions, and once these are congealed, he varies his own creations. If we chose at random some of the excellent storytellers of Hungary and sketched their lives in a few words, we would see how much the colorful and variable life contributes to the development of the narrator. Tobias Kern, the street cleaner from the North Hungarian city Sopron, came through Nether Austria in search of work.[40] Mihály Borbély from Temesköz (in the south of Hungary, now in Yugoslavia), despite his youth, had already tried various occupations when Kálmány met him; he was a swine herder and lamb herder, and as a hired hand he had gone from farm to farm, and then had done military service abroad.[41] Pandur, too, had covered a long stretch from the county of Arad (in Transylvania) to the village of Bag in Pest county: he had been a valet in a manor house, and during the First World War had traveled as far as the swamps of Rokitno and then fought on the northern front as a soldier in the Hungarian Red Army. He worked in Fiume, then in Styria, and later in the most widespread areas of the country as a ditchdigger, day laborer, seasonal laborer, and miner, until he finally settled on a place he selected as home.[42]

The special gift of any storyteller consists in his being able to shape a tale. He is able not only to narrate well, however, but to keep in his memory a great number of tales from the traditional supply—more than the average person could retain, and he constantly reworks them in accordance with his own artistic talents. In this he differs from—and stands head and shoulders above—the simple carriers, the passive preservers of tradition, and the type of storyteller who serves merely as a mediator of tales. The narrators can therefore be distinguished by type according to the way they proceed in shaping a *märchen*.

Since the narrator has at his disposal the ready-made traditional raw material, he does not have much choice concerning the plot—the inventory of motifs, incidents, stylistic formulae—and what he himself can add.[43] He can move only in a very restricted space; his innovations are controlled by tradition and audience and can be seemingly very slight, and yet manifold types of narrators have sprung up under such conditions. As to *märchen* themes, there is hardly anything new for the researcher to discover, even though the possibilities for the reshaping of the well-known forms are legion. They can occur in the tale structure (the possibilities for combination of motifs are infinite) or in the individual shaping, in the way the narrator actualizes the tale (whether he makes the recital epic, dramatic, or lyrical, satirical, fantastic, sentimental, or rational), and they depend on whether his manner of narrating aims at breadth, length, detail, precision, or density of content. Some narrators concentrate their attention on the embroidering of details; others follow the thread of the main action and neglect the secondary episodes or connect the magic tale with everyday life, while still others remove the action into mystical distances.

Since the attention of research has been drawn to the creative personality of the storyteller, many researchers have tried to describe the qualities of the narrators and to classify the different narrator types. Azadovski, for example, is of the opinion that the individual narrators, even beyond the necessary "acclimatization" of the tale plot to the ethnic culture, which Aarne described, have put the imprint of their own personality on each folktale.[44]

In general, the Russian folklorists who first worked out the method of personality research have not distinguished between types of storytellers; they have merely indicated the qualities of the narrative personalities. In 1903 Zelenin mentioned Lomtjev, the master of composite, colorful tales. He prefers magic tales and "watches over tradition as if it were sacred; he varies and complements only the small parts describing everyday life." Bogdanov, the narrator of the brothers Sokolov, has been most successful in combining the traditional tale forms with brilliant, individual artistry.[45]

Azadovski highlights the *brodjaga* (itinerant beggar) type of narrator, who is long-winded and devoted to detail, among the narrators of the Vercholensk region: Medvedev is of the type who are extremely accurate and strictly observe traditional forms; Vinokurova, a Siberian narrator, is the realist who tries for density and has an uncanny feeling for psychology.[46] Sokolov, in his frequently mentioned work, gives a summary treatment of the Russian narrators. Among them there are those who adapted the heroic style of the Russian *bylina*, there are fantastic dreamers, moralists who strive for edification in their stories, specialists for magic tales, and those who see the *märchen* from the point of view of everyday reality. These realists prefer the adventuresome, anecdotal, novella-like tales. They are funny storytellers, humorists who laugh loudly at their own jokes; but Sokolov also knows narrators who are bitingly satirical, who pillory the abuses of society.[47] He also lists the type of the "over-clever" and "dramatic" narrator, and gives several examples of each.[48] Similar examples are also listed by Pomerantseva, who includes the classes of nursery narrators,[49] those who continue the style of medieval buffoons, and the educated, book-reading storytellers.[50]

Chicherov lists four different types of Russian storytellers:

1. the bearer of tradition who retains the tale and passes it on;
2. the performing artist who embroiders the tales with his dramatic gift, for whom not the text but the recital (intonation, facial expressions) is important;
3. the poet, who even when he uses traditional material, changes the tale in such a way that he is essentially transforming the plot; and
4. the improviser, who breaks the plot into its constitutent motifs; that is, he destroys its sequence and freely constructs his tale according to his own ideas.[51]

Ortutay considers the attitude toward traditional material and divides the narrators, on this basis, into two groups: those who cleave as closely as possible to tradition, and those free and unhampered, who vary their manner of narration, exchange motifs, and introduce new elements. He also notes that there may be stronger or weaker narrators in either group.[52] In another connection he mentions the narrators who have specialized in one single species of *märchen*.[53] Similarly, Henssen distinguishes between those who subjectively enlarge, consciously exaggerate, are objectively faithful to what was heard, and are dramatically gifted.[54]

István Banó divides his narrators into two categories, the rich and the poor—the narrators of "anecdotes, represented by landed peasants," and the "minstrels." He speaks of the "Bohemian" carefree-storyteller type and the Münchhausen type (the lying soldier), and of the type of the literate peasant, which he bases on the type of storytelling in vogue in Baranya county.[55] Later on he mentions the realist as a new type.[56]

Leza Uffer, who classifies his Rätoroman narrators within a closed society, also deserves mention. During his activity as a collector he has noted down the material of the conscious storytellers as well as that of the people who knew tales. On the basis of his experience, he describes the bearers of communal tale tradition as follows:

1. The passive narrator, who knows the *märchen* but does not tell them. Though he remembers what he has heard from early childhood, he is not particularly interested in the *märchen* and is willing to tell a tale only when he is urged to do so.
2. The occasional storyteller. He knows tales and will tell them when the occasion arises and he is urged to do so. He notes what he once heard, but he does not create anything new; he only repeats tales he heard in his youth. He knows jokes and anecdotes as well as legends and magic tales.
3. The conscious storyteller, whose outstanding quality is his originality. He is a conscious creator and is recognized by the public. He considers it quite natural that people seek him out because of his tales; he likes to tell tales; he prides himself on his memory, and if he forgets something he improvises. In general, he tells only a certain kind of tales.

In addition to this grouping, which sheds light on the local manner of narrating tales, Uffer presents a consideration of the narrators according to type. He emphasizes the teller of anecdotes, who appears most frequently in the villages. Whereas the anecdotes of the true narrator are composed of many incidents which form links in his chain of narration, the occasional teller of anecdotes knows only short pieces lacking in motif.

Uffer also characterizes the narrator of legends, whose task is less to entertain than to teach: "He is the historian of the people, whereas the teller of folktales is an artist." While the former faithfully adheres to the text, the latter creates freely.[57] Haiding, too, touches on this when he says that the teller of legends has a special inclination for his material and that his attitude is fundamentally different from that of the teller of tales, because he does not ask his listeners to believe.[58] This is also pointed out by Henssen, Langstroff, Röhrich, and others.[59]

We have seen that there are different approaches to the classification of narrators: we have also noted that the capabilities of the narrators vary; and it is merely a matter of consideration which viewpoint is chosen for the determination of narrator types: the preference of tale genres, the manner of performance, or the psychological character of the raconteurs.[60] Hence it is unnecessary to list further attempts to classify types; every attempt is well motivated and encompasses all the most important qualities characteristic of the narrators.

This leads us to the following question: How does the narrator swing into action in front of the community, that is, how does he use his tale material, how does he form the tale, what means does he utilize in shaping the tale?

First of all, he is selective. Having heard tales since childhood, he selects from the community tradition consciously or unconsciously according to his own taste, his preference corresponding to his psychical needs. He adds certain tales to his repertoire, while he leaves out others without even considering them.[61] Then, at storytelling occasions, he selects from his repertoire only the kind of tale which fits the occasion in question. This procedure has been mentioned at various times[62] and results to a great extent from dependence on society. We have seen how the people of Kakasd "order" their tales and indicate which tale the audience wants to hear (the repertoire of the narrators is generally known); but, in addition, the narrator himself knows very well which audience will want to hear which tale. Just as Novopolzev narrates differently in the nursery and before work communities of men, Péter Pandur does not relate the same thing to women who are shucking corn and to an audience containing young men. The narrator knows what is expected from him each time. What is suitable in the barracks is not suitable in a public place of work, and what is appropriate in either of these settings does not suit in a dairy farm or in the spinning rooms. In order to gain a knowledge of the narrator's taste, it is important to note the sequence in which he presents his tales to the collector—which tale he considers the most beautiful, which he values less, or which he assumes will best please the collector.

The voluminous tale material which lives in the consciousness of the storyteller, and which he preserves in his excellent memory, is formed anew by him every time he recites it. Research has always been attracted by the constant changes of the tale texts and has been at pains to discover the essence of these changes and the laws which they follow. Nevertheless there is no penetrating research in this field. István Lázár, who earlier studied this constant changing of the tale texts, says:

> One can observe how the tale material, small at the beginning, is extended as its recital is refined. It never happens that two people tell all the parts exactly the same way: not even one person tells

the same tale the same way a second time, with the same words and the same details. Feeling and fancy render him a poet during his recital, and he embroiders the individual details according to real life. . . .[63]

That this is not a sign of a failing memory, but conscious art, has been noted by János Arany:[64] "Whatever the peasant storyteller adds to the tale through his poetic soul and creative instinct, he immediately passes on to the people. . . ."[65]

Many researchers have touched upon this point and have stated that this is not only an unconscious, unintentional change (a consequence of oral transmission) but a conscious one; the two have different results,[66] yet it is impossible to separate them, for they both appear with every storyteller. In addition, the change with which we are faced may be unessential, or it may be of great importance. This depends not only on the type of storyteller but on the nature of the tale and on the psychical circumstances, which have a hand in the adaptation or the recital of the folktale.[67]

When F. Ranke examined the changes which occurred during repeated recitals of one and the same tale, he concluded that it was for the most part the eventful part of the *märchen*, the action, which was preserved, whereas "the individual expression and the whole manner of presentation changed according to the attitude of the listeners and the mood of the narrator."[68]

Ágnes Kovács was concerned with the changes in the Ketesd tales and also observed the local book tales, which leads her to assert that the main factors of modification are to be found in the realistic view of life, in the shifting of the place of the *märchen*, in individual additions, and in the psychological capabilities and inclinations of the narrators.[69] To prove this, various experiments were carried out by different folklorists: a *märchen*, one which he had never heard before, was told or read to the narrator, and from time to time he was asked to relate it again. This made it possible to note the incidence of change. Since, as a result of oral transmission of folk narratives, the variation is hard to follow up, the laboratory experiments of Bartlett and other psychologists became attractive to folklore scholars. W. Anderson's famous experiment first described in his 1923 study of the tale *Kaiser und Abt*, which he emphasized and defended for more than thirty years against those who disagreed or reworked it, was meant to support his thesis of the "law of self correction." However, the reason he gives for the basic stability of the folktale is not convincing. Theoretical considerations and the results of my own experiments still in progress made me realize that none of these experiments were elaborate enough. The personalities of the storytellers and their cultural background, among other things, were left unconsidered. No attention was paid to whether or not they belonged to "storyteller types." No consideration was given to the tale content and its relationship to the personality of the narrators. Our investigations, which involved repeated recordings of tales by the same narrators in different situations and the recording of variants passed on to others, permit us to assume that the storytellers in question would have reproduced other texts in a different way. This means that their "memory" would have acted differently, especially if they had been given free selection, as real storytellers have in a nonlaboratory situation.[70]

It should be noted here that the alternately creative, preserving, and destructive processes of oral transmission were recently emphasized by Ortutay as of major importance in folk literature. Speaking about the laws of this procedure that can be observed in *statu nascendi* as a result of the perfect collaboration of individual and community, he points out some phenomena of special importance to folktale research. Among these is "affinity," an attractive force between certain narrative motifs which results in typical clusters, and another called the "invariant," which is significant in the process of rejection or innovation in folklore.[71] It would be gratifying to see the suggested analyses worked out by Ortutay.

Folktale variations can be observed most minutely in two ways: (1) by comparing the text of the transmitter with that of the receiver; or (2) by comparing the variants, recorded at different times, of one narrator's stories. In connection with both methods the attempt of Jech and Rychnová should be mentioned. These followed the transmittal of a tale by one narrator and the acceptance of the same tale by another narrator, as well as the recital of the same tale by the same person at different times.[72] It is very rewarding to trace variations of a stock of tales within a family, following up narrators handing over the same tales to each other.[73] Researchers have also tried to collect from the descendants of raconteurs of long ago. The variants of the same tale told by different narrators of the same community at the same time led me to some conclusions, too.[74] We have even more means at hand for the comparison of identical tales repeated several times by the same narrator. Here we are faced, as Halpert wrote, not only with the problem of individual creation but with that of the stability of the tale and, beyond this, the stability of the individual tale genres.[75] As a matter of fact, Halpert's storyteller was revisited by I. H. Brunvand, who recorded his tales seventeen years later.[76]

It is well worth citing Zs. Szendrey's opinion in regard to János Honti's comments, assuming that the great difference in the earlier of two variants of the twice-recorded tale of a Nógrádszakáll narrator is due to the falsification of the second version recorded. "Even the willing narrator is not always in the same mood. Why? There may be different reasons. This is why Lajos Katona states that the recital depends on the mood of the narrator, something that changes not only from person to person but from occasion to occasion."[77] An evidence for this is the collecting work of the Folklore Fellows. Szendrey states:

> Shorter and longer *märchen* come from same narrator. The experienced collector immediately senses that his man is not in form, and thus desists from pressing him for a tale, for he would meet with only a poor extract by which the narrator is trying to get rid of him. Therefore we never can be content with the one-time rendering of a tale, because the inexperienced "gentleman collector" only gets an "occasional tale."[78]

Ortutay makes similar statements, based on his experiences with Fedics, whose variation in the length of his stories is so blatant that the same tale once was recorded on 11 record sides (78 rpm) and later on twenty-five.[79] Ortutay notes regarding the three variants of a tale by Fedics, "He has changed their composition; in some phases (though he also changed the structural elements) stylistic elements were transformed, he hit upon new formulae; in parts he enlarged, in parts he condensed. All variants are siblings, but there are no three alike."[80] Tillhagen, too, chooses the method of manifold recording and arrives at similar results.[81]

The extent of the changes also depends on the time elapsed between the two recordings. "Each new variant of a folktale represents . . . a new redaction. One can without scruples speak of two redactions when the same narrator tells the same story again after much time has elapsed."[82] Several instances of a new recording having been made after a long time require attention. Ranke, in his complete edition of Schleswig-Holstein tales, cites examples which accorded him, as he says himself, insight into the biology and the foundation of the existence of the *märchen.*

> Thus we can follow the stability, or variability, of the personal narrative stock by checking the many variants which the same informants told over the course of many years . . . for instance,

the variation of *The Dragon-Slayer*, which was told three times within a span of twenty years by a Swedish woman domiciled in Germany, to Wisser, Meyer, and Miss Bünz. In these various forms we can very well recognize a fundamental change of the style of narration, from a loose style in youth to a dense one in advanced age, which represents a curious inversion of the principle that narrating becomes quieter and fuller in the later years than in the earlier and more active ones. We can find rigid tale forms in the variants 5 and 6 of the *Magic Flight*, which both were told by the same narrators, the first time to Wisser, the second—twenty years later—to Meyer and Miss Bünz.[83]

The observation of the creative ability of the narrator and the development stages of the *märchen* is much more fruitful for folktale research than the comparative analysis of the standard motif inventory of the tale. Even the smallest items of modification are essential signs of life; without them the whole tale treasure would long since have become extinct. Each modification in the international tale, each ethnic variation of the common European plot, infuses contemporary life into the empty form, or, when told before a certain community on a certain occasion, actualizes the performance.

Let us now investigate individual creative shaping as it occurs within the narrow framework of possibilities: (1) in the composition, in the structure of the tale, and in the technique of motif combinations; (2) through combining tale and reality; and (3) in the style and recital of the storyteller.

## Composition

As we cited examples of the technique of tale composition and motif combination in an earlier article, we will not treat it here in any depth.[84] We are well aware of the fact that the narrator who has a profound knowledge of motifs also has the themes and outline for tale structures at his disposal.

In making use of the stock of motifs when filling in countless themes living in the awareness of the narrator, there are a great many ways of formulating a tale. The tale is altered mostly by the change in motifs. The question of how the narrator uses his motif stock has been convincingly treated by Karl Spiess, who is regarded by many as more or less an amateur.[85] For Spiess it is not only a question of the narrator's combining motifs according to his memory, his actual mood, and his audience.[86] He also shows how the changes resulting from the combination of motifs can lead to an association of motifs. Using motifs that belong to the same trend of thought but to different tale sketches actually sends the tale in a completely different direction, and a consequence can be the formation of a new type.[87] The extension of the motif stock, which is a recent development observed with some outstanding Hungarian storytellers, not only causes an episodic anecdote to grow into an ambiguous chain of incidents but the magic tales to surpass their established limits and combine several types into one whole.[88] This tendency appears mainly with narrators who tell their stories continually, evening after evening, and consciously stretch and vary them.[89] We must note here, however, that the length of the *märchen* very often is caused by an *ad hoc* addition, that the storyteller often combines several tales to reward the attention of his audience, as happened with the Gaelic Irish and the Scots.[90] In the same way the narrator can shorten his tale at will by leaving out one or another event. The combining of motifs shows that the accumulated tale inventory does not live unchanged in the consciousness of the narrator. Let us give one example for this. Péter Pandur's tales were recorded between 1940 and 1942. In the intervening years we often asked him to repeat to us one tale or another. A lecture which I gave before several hundred people was illustrated by Pandur's tales. As he faced the audience and performed, inspired, we realized that a completely different *märchen* was hidden behind the title on which we had agreed upon. It came to light quite often that he did not remember the tales he had told before. Sometimes only the title remained intact—the story was so transformed in the course of the years that it was hard to recognize it. However, the variation was entirely unconscious on his part, for when he was asked from whom he had learned the *märchen*, he referred to the same person he had mentioned to me at the time of the first recording. When we told him that the tale sounded different and that it was not to be found in his tale collection in this form, he said that our memory was faulty and that he had told it the same, then and now, word for word. Other tales he had retained faithfully according to topic, as we heard them the first time—making allowances, of course, for the outward changes resulting from the changed situation.[91] This incident also shows that the narrators dispose of a stock of stable and more variable *märchen* themes. In order to be able to come to such conclusions, one has to observe a storyteller systematically over a span of many years. Such variations do not belong among conscious formation, for conscious transformation is induced by the immediate outward circumstances.[92]

Being aware of the countless possibilities for the broadening of a tale, we must give credence to the sovereign assertions of a proud narrator: "Anyone who knows just a handful of tales—maybe even ten—can make hundreds from them if he has a little sense as to how to do it."[93] Though not quite so striking, the words of Nober, the bricklayer, convey a similar meaning: "When I heard a story I could make one double in length. Gotta give them stories a good heave-up so they sound good."[94] Solymossy, whose concern is the philological examination of the tale texts, mentions the liberty of creation of the storyteller, in connection with a tale of *Cupid and Psyche* whose editing deviates considerably from the established form:

> The telling in our tales is not exactly exemplary, but it is most characteristic for the style of narration. . . . The narrators combine well-known motifs not originally belonging in the context with the well-composed magic tale at the moment of delivery; they are constructing their newly composed tale in front of the audience, so to say. . . . This kind of storytelling is quite prominent with us.[95]

The *ad hoc* tale and the structural alterations caused by frequent telling led us to the complicated question of the origin of tale oicotypes, to the question of the tale origin. Solymossy has given a thorough and plausible explanation of this problem in his well constructed monograph about the tale, *The Maple Tree*. The initial episodes of tales of different content are the same, he states; the new version originated when some old motif still present developed in a different direction.[96] He explains the formation of a new tale type by the fact that completely independent motifs, related only distantly in their general features, have formed a new tale through special combination.[97]

## Combining Tale and Reality

A NARRATIVE, no matter what the genre, which does not keep in touch with the daily life of the people, and has no connection with reality, is doomed at the outset. The main characteristic of the *märchen* is the fact that each individual variant springs from the soil on which its creator lives.[98] The narrator always has his roots in the circle of experience of his social stratum: his figures behave as he assumes the people of his village would behave under the same circumstances; their problems coincide with those of the community; and even the landscape and the surroundings conform to the milieu of the community in which the *märchen* is created.[99] Even when the talk is of great rulers or supernatural monsters, they behave like the gentlemen or the well-to-do peasants in the village[100]—in their actions and in their way of speaking. The two hostile camps, the two antagonistic worlds of the tale, express in their milieu the contrast between rich and poor between the mortal and the superhuman, the powerful and the weak. (For the narrator this is "my world," and "their world.") Correspondingly, the narrator thus identifies with the tale hero and his surroundings, and adds personal experiences and elements to the tale. The narrator is never impersonal, nonpartisan, or uninterested; he is the passionate representative of a subjective truth, and he depicts the better reality which is expected.[101] The peasant narrator takes sides when he solves the conflict between the poor hero and the might figure, who is at the center of the tale, in favor of the poor one. We do not agree with the researchers who considered the *märchen* the "wish poetry" of the poor.[102] Yet, even if the narrator embeds his wishes in his tales, it is, in reality, more than pure longing. The narrator weaves his own person into the tale, he imparts his own point of view when he tells the tale. His own fate is involved in all the situations of the tale; he identifies himself with the tale action; and he interprets all the life expressions of his people. Every narrator does this, but the means depend on his personality. This is essential, because it shows the reason why the methods of comparative tale research have produced no adequate results. The painstaking labor involved, mainly occupied with the scheme of the tales, omits all the background which leads to variations.

In the following we shall point out incidents which have attracted the attention of the researchers. We shall observe first of all the place of the tale, its geographic and sociological environment,[103] the integration of personal experiences and observations into the tale, the occupation of the tale heroes,[104] the way of life of the poor peasants,[105] and the inclusion in the tale of the narrator's experiences, opinions, and world view.[106]

These incidents are important largely because they illuminate the world view of the people. "In every folktale," Ortutay writes, "the good reader can recognize innumerable traits of peasant life, its single moments, the foundations of the peasant way of observation, and his concept of society. With the adventures of the hero, the peasant himself goes on an adventure in his peasant world, where the whole view of life, society, and customs conforms to the peasant order."[107] This is also borne out in Röhrich's book on folktale and reality, in which he outlines the reality image of the magic tale according to the best known German tale collections.

## STYLE AND RECITAL

FINALLY, the role of the individual in formation and performance, in manner of expression and delivery, deserves attention. Depending on the capabilities of the storyteller, language, style, and the dramatic recital shape the tale variants to a great extent. Given this, the manner of delivery alone can characterize the narrator's role. It is true that the *märchen* is a genre with a traditional and strictly determined style;[108] but it nevertheless depends considerably on the stylistic subtleties added by the narrator. J. Ball has stressed the necessity of distinguishing the traditional style of the folktales from the individual style of the storyteller.[109]

Interest in the tale type and the individual style of the narrator led to a lively discussion in Bloomington in 1950.[110] Here the opinion was expressed, among others, that the variations of a tale are consistent if there is a very gifted, creative storyteller in the background. Behind a certain kind of narrative style characteristic of a small circle, a community, a village, or some other unit, there always lurks a strong individuality.[111] In recent years research into the biology of storytelling has begun to shape a method for studying the narrator's style and performance. Although a well-defined approach and detailed study has not yet been worked out, the importance of such a method is clear.[112]

It is first of all the performer's language which attracts the audience and holds their attention. Narrators from different regions—though sometimes even from the same village—are distinguished by the differences in their vocabulary.[113] The vocabulary of Mrs. Palkó, for example, is much richer and more varied than that of György Andrásfalvi. Mrs. Palkó's language oftentimes is rhythmical, full of compact, expressive turns and idioms, of beautiful poetic images and alliterations. There are narrators who cling strictly to the traditional *märchen* formula,[114] and there are others who adhere only to their own formulae, as we shall see with Mrs. Palkó. There can also be many variations in the structure of the tale, depending on which incidents in the structure draw the narrator's greatest attention and which he thinks he can neglect. According to general observation, it is always the action which is the main issue, not the pauses in the action—the description of situations, moods, character, or conditions of mind. Azadovski contradicts this in talking about the artistic capabilities of Vinokurova, who describes the landscape and the different moods of her characters.[115] Similarly, with Fedics, the peculiar "inner monolugues" of his actors before they do battle have drawn attention.[116] The same is true of a number of Hungarian narrators who prefer epic width to dramatic conciseness: the Transylvania lumberman A. Albert; the sharecropper F. Kiss of County Szabolcs; L. Ámi of County Szatmár. This, too, as we shall see later, is one of the characteristics of Mrs. Palkó.

The manner of narration can be epic or dramatic. Some narrators prefer to relate the tale action in the third person; others have their dramatis personae act, and they reduce their comments to the minimum as they lead up to the climax of the plot. Here we come to the manner of narration which involves not only the words of the story but dramatic performance. In fact, there is no narration without dramatic gestures by the narrator.

It is only natural that the narrator experience the tale action as he tells it, and that he express himself with gestures as well as words. The unconscious identification and the conscious striving for credibility lead directly to this kind of experience for the narrator. Nearly every researcher has encountered the mimic-dramatic manner of narration.[117] These tricks of the trade are not always employed consistently, and in this regard, too, there are more expressive and less imaginative storytellers. Many researchers have come to the conclusion that it is no longer sufficient to retain the text alone. Henssen and others, at the same time that they recorded on tape the recital of a *märchen*, anecdote, or belief legend, also filmed with a 16 mm. camera those narrators whose dramatic talents were particularly obvious.[118]

The narrator, besides taking part in the events and imitating the gestures of the actors, dramatically shapes the appearance of the hero. "A carpenter from Upper Styria, who had started his tale sitting down, suddenly got up when the hero of the tale approached the devil, stepped over to me and demonstrated the dialogue between the misunderstood hero and the tavernkeeper who wagered with him on the occasion of the wedding feast. . . ."[119] Many similar examples could be mentioned.[120] A kind of acting is shown by Tillhagen in the tales of his Gypsy, Taikon. The individual members of the work group divide the roles of the tale among themselves and actually perform it in the true sense of the word, like a play on the stage.[121] Similar occurrences are described by Cammann in the West Prussian dramatization of tales and anecdotes.[122]

## THE STORYTELLERS OF KAKASD

OUR FOUR STORYTELLERS did not first come forward in Kakasd. They had played an important role in the life of old Andrásfalva as personalities who possessed a considerable tale stock. Every one of them told only his own tales, and each of them had his own repertoire. Only Mrs. Geczi, less gifted than the others, had a few texts which indirectly show Mrs. Palkó's influence. Each one narrated for a different audience and on different occasions, and even though the tale material comes from a common source, the tales of each individual have a different form. Every storyteller was eager to learn new tales and asked his acquaintances to tell him new ones or to read to him. Since every storyteller learned his tales long ago and had told them often, he had marked them with his own formative stamp before an audience, and everyone in the village knew which tale was whose. The individual storytellers also liked to listen to each other.

We asked Andrásfalvi if he knew Mrs. Palkó's *märchen*. Without stopping to think he rattled off the titles of the most important ones. When asked if he could tell one of them he said, "She will tell them when she wants to. I cannot tell them. I only know them—these are *her* tales."

"But she learned them from your father, from whom you heard them, too," we countered. He only shook his head.

"Those were different tales. Only the titles are similar." And, in fact, Andrásfalvi was no longer aware of the common origin but only of the new variant formed by the narrator over the years.[123]

Thus the same property rules which we mentioned in Chapter 6 apply to the outstanding narrators of Kakasd. One of the most intricate questions in the matter of the biology of the folktale is that of the transmission of the tale stock from generation to generation and its transformation through the processes of submersion, latency, revival, and addition of new materials. It is not easy to follow this up, but the resurrection of some of the old inherited pieces might permit some conclusions.[124]

The tale treasure still alive in Kakasd came from the poor people of old Andrásfalva and, more immediately, from the Zaicz family, whose knowledge of tales was a matter of legendary conjecture among the villagers. The Zaiczs were poor, but generally highly respected, and the village tried to explain their narrative gifts through their origins.

Some thought they were Slovaks; János Mátyás thought they were of "Polish nationality"; and others pretended to know that Mrs. Palkó's mother (Maria Rudik who came from Galicia) was a Jewess, and that the gift of storytelling came from her. This gift had also been transmitted to her nephews: "There are Gyurka, and Mátyás, and Zsuzsi. How they can tell a story! Well, they are clever like all Jews."

We can no longer investigate the old narrators József Zaicz and his son János. Mrs. Palkó's father and her brother (the grandfather and uncle of Andrásfalvi), and Márton László who died in 1949, for a long time narrated simultaneously. The repertoire left behind by them has become the heritage of many different narrators, who received it in many different ways. And during the time of transmittal the traditional material had undergone changes and developed in different directions.

We described in an earlier chapter the life of old Zaicz—his fate, his desperate attempts to keep himself alive and to support his family. His life is the typical life of the itinerant storyteller. A poor man, full of the will to work, he tried over and over again, and old and feeble, with a renewed spurt of energy, he returned to the gates of poor Andrásfalva to die. Wherever he was he told tales—in Russia, in Moldavia, in Rumania, in Hungary, and in Galicia. He worked as an agricultural laborer and in industry; he did some freighting. "He vegetated as a poor man and told the workmen tales during work. He did military service for twelve years and six months," Mrs. Palkó related. As a man who had experienced much and was friendly and always inclined to joke, he was welcome everywhere and was respected, though he never mastered reading or writing.

His son János surpassed him as a storyteller. He was better "educated," more agile, and could read. He loved company and told his tales not only during work but at home and in company, and when he was called he also went out to other houses. He was not as quiet, good tempered, or modest as his father. On the contrary, he was short tempered and easily aroused, and people often criticized him for his "foul mouth and sacrilegious talk." The pieces which narrators of the younger generation learned from him permit the conclusion that he was very inventive and extremely talented.

The present material surveys the narration of three generations of the Zaicz family. It is, of course, incomplete, but this in itself is an indication of the importance of research covering several generations in storytelling families.

# 9

# *Mrs. Zsuzsánna Palkó*

MRS. PALKÓ DIED IN 1964 AT THE AGE OF EIGHTY-FOUR. TEN YEARS earlier, on August 24, 1954, she received the distinguished title of Master of Folklore from the Hungarian government. When the Deputy Minister of Culture handed her the 3,000 forints (about $120), the document, and the medal bearing an inscription which she could not read, she said, completely confused: "Thank you very much, but I do not deserve this." Her soft, clear blue eyes were directed in astonishment toward the "golden pillars" of the House of Parliament, which she had described so often in her magic tales. ("There the walls are made of silk and velvet; my God, how beautiful it is there.") To the newspapermen who surrounded her she said over and over again, "My father also told tales, much nicer ones, but he never got anything for it." This modesty was characteristic of Mrs. Palkó.

On this occasion she saw Budapest for the first time, and her imagination—filled with rich magic pictures of fairy gardens and visions of lavish pomp filling the royal palaces—collided for the first time with reality. For the first time she saw a big city. Her fantasy, which knew so well how to infuse life into a world never seen, was revived by reality. She arrived at night, by car, seeing the lights of the city ("It was as if the stars had come down from heaven to light my way; there must have been hundreds of thousands") and the wonders which seemed to have been wishes fulfilled made her become silent. She proceeded without a word, letting anyone take her anywhere; she goggled at the Church of St. Matthew (Mátyás) and admired the streetcars, the underground, and the bus. The outsized statue of the rider on the monument of Duke Rákóczi and the millennium monument astonished her considerably. As if in a dream world, she observed everything from afar, was stunned into silence by the bigness of the apartment houses, of "the palaces." She asked how "anyone could get up there" and was astonished at the many people in the streets. "Where do they all come from?" Mrs. Palkó knew only small peasant mirrors, and in her hotel room she stared without comprehension into a full-length mirror. First she thought that her neighbor was coming to meet her, and then slowly she recognized herself. She showed great interest in all things technical, and asked people to explain the mechanics of the elevator and of the bridges crossing the Danube. It was as if the magic of her tales furnished her with the key for understanding reality. She saw the bridges, the prototypes of which a fairy had built in one night; she saw the "miracle garden" of St. Margaret's Island which is so similar to the magic garden in *Józsi the Fisherman*. Here we realized how right Maxim Gorki was when he saw the reason for the development of magic things in folktales in the technological thinking of man.[1]

But for the rest, too, she tried to square the "wonders" of reality with the magic of her tales. Her attention was especially captivated by the historical past. She saw the statues of the great kings with sword and helmet, astride the horses, just the way they always took shape in her tales. She saw for the first time the Parliament mentioned often in her tales, whose king puts into order the affairs of the kingdom.[2] She wandered through Pest as in the realm of the folktale. Whenever a new view opened before her, she identified it with the concept she had of it in her mind: "This is the palace of the king; in just such a one *King Lajos* lived." "Just such a flower garden was the one owned by the King who cast out *I Don't Know*." "What a beautiful equestrian statue! Such a beautiful horse! Maybe the little prince owned such a one." "You have a telephone like in the King's Palace?" and so on.

All this is characteristic of Mrs. Palkó's fantasy and her views of the world, as well as those of her contemporaries in the village. She mirrors the concept of the world and the education which developed under the old economic conditions in the Bucovina. Misery had enclosed her like plated armor, keeping her education at a very low level. Her living conditions, her illiteracy, and, during the last fifteen years of her life, her advanced age, prevented her old view of the world from being transformed, through new experiences, into a new one. Her ideas lived in the magic, religious world in which she had sought refuge from the hardships of life. Childlike, archaic ideas come to light when she looked at the wonders of the city. Ortutay reported the Budapest stay of the illiterate Fedics.[3] We ourselves still remember the attitude of the narrators from Szabolcs and Zemplén, who had never been to a city. They all showed excitement and astonishment, but none of it had a trace of the magic world of Mrs. Palkó, who in her youth had lived for years in the Bucovina cities Ćernovic and Rădăuti. The imaginary world and the events of real life give a two-fold character to the world view, both in life and in the folktale; progressive social ideas mingle with the old belief world and with superstition, surviving along with elements of the patriarchal conditions within a peasant family.[4] These are the natural consequences of conditions in the Bucovina.

Zsuzsánna Zaicz was about one year old when the Zaicz family moved to Székelykeve.[5] It was a very big family: "Józsi, Mari, I, János, my brother Marci, and two newly born ones. For six years we were in Székelykeve. There my 19-year-old brother died. My mother had ten children, but most of them died young."

After six years of back-breaking labor, the Zaicz family saw their hopes by the Danube, and the family was again uprooted.

> When one's very existence is in danger, who can think of schooling for the children? So I remained a donkey who did not learn how to write. I was six years old when we returned to the Bucovina. I was not sent to school. I went out in service as a nursemaid. There was no serious law that I had to go [to school], so I didn't go. But whatever they said by word of mouth I learned.

After his return to the Bucovina, József Zaicz continued to work in the Moldavia region. "He did not have land; he worked the land of other people." Zsuzsánna Zaicz worked in the sugar beet fields when she was eight or nine years old. When she was thirteen or fourteen she took a position as a nursemaid, in summer at home, in winter in the city with the masters:

> Thus I had my dresses provided for. I could not expect anything from my father; only when I married he helped me with my dresses. . . . I made runners, wove linen, I worked the threshing

machine in Rumania, harvested and went out to hack beets in summer. I was also in service with the merchant of the village; then I went to Rădăuti."

At eighteen Zsuzsánna married István Dobondi. After three years of marriage, she lost her husband (who died of tuberculosis) and two children within one year. Five years later she was married a second time, to the foreman of sharecroppers, József Palkó, whom she had met during seasonal work in the Bucovina.

> "My husband received two acres of land; that was enough for us, and then he got 10 kilo wool and 3000 leu. In the fall we went, cut down [the crops], cleaned up, brought it home. He got so much cheese that it was enough for the winter. He was the foremost sharecropper in the Bucovina. When the big landowners came they always looked for József Palkó; we always had it good as long as my husband was alive."[6]

When József Palkó died in 1927, life became a struggle for his widow. She went freighting like a man and transported not only wood but all sorts of goods which she sold or traded; she bought her goods cheap and sold them, at very little profit, at distant places. As long as the children were small—of the eleven children she had with József Palkó, four are still alive today—Mrs. Palkó went alone on her errands. Later she took the two grown sons, Mátyás and Linusz, along with her. In addition she went out to do daily labor, went hacking, wove runners, and hired out for spinning; she had to accept any kind of work in order to have bread for her family. When they were settled in the Bácska in 1941, the Palkó family took with them everything they had. Mrs. Palkó herself remained behind until she was able to sell her house at a good price. Then she joined her recently married daughter, Jusztina, and when her daughter died a year later, she moved in with her oldest son, Mátyás. He had received about three acres of land, and for the two children who were born later, he received two more acres. Mátyás did not return from the war, and his wife, who was a skilled seamstress, worked for the girls of the village making the traditional Szekler waistcoats and thus was able to provide for her two sons. Mrs. Palkó thought, when they were settled in Kakasd, "Here they don't need me so urgently any more as the sick Erzsi [her youngest daughter] does, where one child follows another; besides, it is the way of the world that the young woman should marry another time . . . ," and she went to live with the Fábián family. The Fábiáns, who worked nine acres, had five children, the oldest of whom was twelve when I first met the family.

From that time on the entire burden of the housework lay upon the old woman; she also did part of the outside work, since Erzsi could not perform any strenuous physical task. Mrs. Palkó did most of the cooking, and that left only sewing and mending for Erzsi. With calm serenity and an alacrity which belied her age, the old woman mastered her hard tasks. She never complained and was always friendly and polite to everyone, and when her three daughters-in-law had extra work—for example on laundry days or when the pigs were slaughtered—Mrs. Palkó arrived to help them. During the fourteen years we knew her, we did not once see her idle, and even so she was always willing and ready to tell tales. At most, when she was busy with cooking, she would ask us to wait.

Her way with children was impressive. In the tiny household of the Fábiáns, where three grown-ups and five children were squeezed together in one room during the winter, badly behaved and quarrelsome children would have been unbearable. The education of the Fábián children, however, was exemplary, and this education was directed by Grandmother, with calm words and the telling of many tales. Summer and winter these children looked clean and neat—which meant quite a bit in the village. They were quiet and modest and always polite. We still see them in our mind's eye as they listened to the words of their grandmother. They knew all her *märchen* by heart, and they could easily tell which tale should follow which; they called Grandmother's attention to the magic tale she had not told us yet. Mrs. Palkó sat on the low stool in front of the iron stove, with one of the smallest children on her lap. The infant's cradle was rocked by her foot. On one bed sat her daughter Erzsi doing some handiwork; on the other bed sat her son-in-law Antal, and the male visitors. The women sat on low stools, spinning or knitting. Thus tales were told in the evening, sometimes until midnight.

Under such circumstances Mrs. Palkó hardly ever left the house. She went out only to church or to funerals and wakes, or when she was called upon to help out in the neighborhood or among her relatives, for to deny such help would be "a great sin." This woman had gone through many tests, and was still being tried by the necessity, at her age, of doing all the housework, and yet her burden was lightened by her infinite goodness. She had learned to face her fate and created around her a serene atmosphere in which she met her family in patience and love.

Let us now consider Mrs. Palkó's tales. Her repertoire consisted of seventy-four themes (forty-five *märchen*, nineteen anecdotes, and ten stories of different genres). Today it is realized that the distinction of the state award she had received spurred her on to learn many new tales. She did so at every opportunity—when visiting relatives, in the village or the hospital, or when marketing. Of these new *märchen* we shall consider seven here. These seven, together with the fifty-two standard tales, also appear in the two-volume published text of her tales. Mrs. Palkó related these tales very often during her last years, and the texts show different stages of adaptation as well as the mark of the narrator's style. Despite these facts, however, we cannot count these *märchen* among Mrs. Palkó's regular repertoire because they were not told for a long enough time.[7]

Like other narrators,[8] Mrs. Palkó could in many cases indicate almost exactly where she had learned the individual tales. Her modesty would not permit her to claim the authorship of the *märchen*, as some of the proud and boastful narrators are wont to do, and knowing her as we did, we believe her. Having twice tested the information—in 1949 and again in 1954—and having asked the origin of all her titles, we found that she was only rarely unsure of the source. If she could no longer recall it she said so. In this connection we wish to quote her literally.

1. *The Iron Laci:* "From my sister in Mucsfa, in the fall of 1955."
2. *The Three Princes:* "I heard it from my father when I was a little girl."
3. *I Don't Know:* "From Matyicska. We went into the fields to hack beets and he told me the tale. He is my godfather. I have done much hacking for him. 'We don't want to be bored. I shall tell a story if you listen' [he said], so he told it."[9]
4. *Ej Haj!:* "From my father."
5. *Pihári:* "1955, from the lay singer. He read it from an old book."
6. *Zsuzska:* "It was read from a book and then I learned it so."
7. *The Dead Lover:* "There was a person who was not married but she was no girl, either. She came to us in the spinning rooms, then she spun and told the tale. That was when I was a girl."
8. *Death with the Yellow Legs:* "That I learned from my brother, from János."
9. *The Glass Casket:* "I heard this from a Rumanian girl in the Bucovina. We were in service together."

15. *The Beautiful Erzsébet:* "It was read to us in Mucsfa in the fall of 1955."

16. *The Princess:* "From my brother, from János."

18. *The Fairy Princess:* "From my brother, from János."

20. *The Snake Prince:* "I was a girl when I heard it from Anna Petres, maybe fourteen years. She has died already."

21. *The Fawn:* "From my father, I learned it from my father."

22. *Józsi the Fisherman:* "From Marcika Pintyer [Márton László]."

23. *The Sky-High Tree:* "From my father."

24. *Rupcsen-Hencsen:* "I don't know from whom I learned it. Maybe from my father."

26. *The Flea-Girl:* "From my sister Mári. She read it. She married into a different community; I went to visit her, then she told it."

27. *Prince Sándor:* "From my daughter-in-law, Mrs. Regina Palkó, you know, the one who sews the fur waistcoats. When we were resettled, I heard it and learned it from her."

28. *András Kerekes:* "From my brother, from János. From Marcika Pintyer."

29. *The Psalmsinging Bird:* "From my brother."

30. *Peasant Gagyi:* "From János; from my son Mátyás."

31. *The Golden Egg:* "In Mucsfa, the young people told it a year ago."

32. *Nine:* "Erzsi [Mrs. Fábián] read it from a book."

33. *The Strong János:* "From my father."

34. *The Red-bellied Serpent:* "From János."

35. *The Twelve Robbers:* "From a Rumanian girl. I also was a girl; she told it in Rumanian."

37. *The Murdering Istéfán:* "From my brother."

38. *The Two Hermits:* "From Marcika Pintyer."

40. *The Smoking Kalfaktor:* "I heard it from my father."

41. *János the Smith:* "From Marcika Pintyer."

42. *The Mother's Atonement:* "It was read to us, so I learned it."

43. *The Proud Princess:* "From my brother János."

45. *The Turk:* "From János."

46. *Anna Mónár:* "From János."

47. *The Shrewd Servant:* "At the fair in Mucsfa in October, 1955; I heard it there from my niece. She read it from a book."

48. *The Wager of the Two Chums:* "From János."

49. *The Szekler Bride:* "I heard it from the daughter of my sister in Mucsfa."

52. *Peti and Boris:* "From Erzsi Matyi."

53. *Könyvenke:* "From my mother, when I was a little girl, like this one" (she pointed to her grandchild).
54. *The Uncouth Girl:* "From a woman in Andrásfalva, I heard it; but I couldn't tell who it was."
56. *The Five Brothers:* "From János, from my brother."
57. *The Two Brothers:* "I heard it from János."
59. *The Gypsy as King:* "From my son, Jóska."
62. *Gábor Német:* "From Marcika Pintyer."
63. *Margit:* "From Marcika Pintyer."

Many conclusions can be drawn from this list. One is that the narrator can remember the origin of forty-four tales—not including the belief stories, which can be counted as true experiences. Another is that she knew from whom she had learned the individual tales, in spite of the fact that the village attributed to her a certain right of authorship. Mrs. Palkó was not aware of her right to authorship of the tales she narrated, or of her narrative talent. The self-confidence which is so often prominent with other narrators was completely unknown to her.

The list also shows that six pieces were learned from old József Zaicz. We cannot determine, of course, what the tale treasure of her father was like, nor what his capabilities were. The only thing we can conclude is that the sketches for his *märchen* form the bottom layer of Mrs. Palkó's stock of tales. Of all the tales she heard in her childhood from her father, these six stayed most clearly in her memory; these were the themes which attracted her most. It does not mean anything that among them there are both colorful tales and dull ones, and even one which can be considered weak (*The Strong János*). Over a long span of time the *märchen* could well have changed in Mrs. Palkó's memory. It may also well be that the form in which we received the weak tale for recording was strongly influenced by the mood of the narrator. In any case, we can believe the modest storyteller who had an excellent memory: these six tales came from her childhood, and they can be traced to her father. Tale No. 53 belongs to the oldest layer of her tale material. She had heard it, while still at home, from her mother, who told tales in the family circle. In her youth Mrs. Palkó heard tales No. 7 and No. 20 in the spinning rooms and the village community; when in service as a maid in the city, tales No. 9 and No. 35; when she was a grown woman, her sister told her No. 26. In the Bácska during resettlement and in Kakasd she learned tales from children, relatives, and friends, and she still remembers which were told and which were read. From Erzsi Matyi she heard the funny tale of *Peti and Boris* (No. 52), which has been especially popular since it was related by Mrs. Palkó.

Though Mrs. Palkó liked to listen to *märchen*, her repertoire, apart from the new tales already mentioned, and whose further fate we do not yet know, was slow to enlarge. She must have heard hundreds of tales during her long life; still, she adapted only a handful of them. The first encounter with these was so memorable, however, that she recalled it all her life. She made very discerning choices. Although she listened to many tales, she was inspired to adopt only a few as her own[10] Whatever she did adopt she transformed, and after a short time it became a masterpiece. A good example of this is *Prince Sándor*, which she had learned during the resettlement. Another interesting example of a quite different nature is the tale of the *Gypsy That Became a King*, which she told in 1959. She had heard it from her son József the previous winter. J. Palkó, fifty-one at that time, claimed he had heard the tale from his grandfather at twelve or thirteen, when they worked together in the fields. This piece, which belongs to the tale stock of Andrásfalva, was latent for a long time in the memory of this passive bearer of tradition, until the dedicated narrator revived it. The comparison of the variants of mother and son is a good proof of Mrs. Palkó's creative talent.[11]

We must treat separately the material which she learned from her "master," her brother János. We know that Mrs. Palkó never appeared in public as a storyteller while he was alive, and that she was a passive bearer of what she had unconsciously learned from him. She says of thirteen tales that they came from her brother. Here it is no longer a question of topics which she appropriated while still a child, but of material which accompanied her during her entire life. János Zaicz was the greatest narrator of the recent past and his tales were well known to Andrásfalva. Even today are remembered individual pieces such as *Peasant Gagyi* (Mátyás Palkó also heard it from him in the family circle), *The Murdering Istéfán, Anna Mónár* (these are tales Mrs. Palkó also tells), *The Well of Youth, The Black City, The Wedding of My Father* (these three tales do not belong in Mrs. Palkó's repertoire).

It is striking, however, that the style of the six tales which she learned from the excellent narrator Márton László, to whom she was closely related, differs from that of the others. The reason for this might be that the moralizing character of these tales and their religious coloration prevented her from transforming them freely.

The main sources for the tale body of Mrs. Palkó, therefore, are the three excellent storytellers József Zaicz, János Zaicz, and Márton

László. They were doubtless masters of their craft and had influenced the storyteller continuously since her childhood—in the family, in the life of the community, and in the work community in the Moldavia region. Since these tales were narrated before a large public, and thus also impressed other listeners and narrators, it may well be that pieces for which Mrs. Palkó quotes other sources may actually be traced back to these three narrators. In the *Book of the Dead*, for instance, we find both *Prince Sándor* and *András Kerekes*. The tale of *Prince Sándor* was read to her in 1944 by her daughter-in-law; the tale of *András Kerekes* was at times told by her brother. Since we do not possess one single tale by Márton László except the texts in the *Book of the Dead*, and since Mrs. Palkó denies direct transmission from him, we have no possibility of testing the extent of her individual transformation of his tales. All we can do is draw conclusions from the repeatedly heard variants of her own versions or from the individual method of adaptation in her different tales. But we have a good reason to point to the stylistic connection between her tales. The fact that the same phraseology and even the same idioms are used in related tales or tales that are similar in type, which she had learned from the different narrators, indicates that she has completely transformed these tales. Thus, for instance, tales No. 16, 17, 18, 21, 35, and 36, which show some relationship in spite of the fact that they came from different sources, and which show the same type of delivery over several sentences, prove that Mrs. Palkó formed them individually.

The world view of Mrs. Palkó, as it appears in her tales as well as in her daily life, correspond to the typical peasant world concept, the enduring conservative feeling for tradition which was a natural outcome of the conditions in Andrásfalva. Since we have already treated this, as well as her piety and her magic practices in connection with Szekler folk belief in Kakasd quite thoroughly, we shall note it here only in passing.[12]

Her piety is seen not only in the fact that the *märchen* texts refer to God and often ask God's justice, but in the fact that punishment of evil is seen as God's justice. In many places God aids the good and helps the poor. He is always on the side of justice, and therefore the evil and the powerful ones must perish, for they have opposed God's laws. The heavenly powers and helpers are part of Mrs. Palkó's world of naive folk belief—miraculous guardian angels like the old man in the tale of *The Twelve Robbers*, or like the Child (Christ's messenger) in the tale of the *Smoking Kalfaktor*. But when the supernatural powers turn against the people, the poor man also turns against them, as in the tale of *Death with*

*Yellow Legs* or *Two Brothers*. In this is expressed nothing other than the helplessness of the peasantry living under primitive conditions. On the same plane as the miracles are the benevolent helpers in the tales—good fairies, gray-haired old men, wise advisers—who are also beings from the heavenly sphere: God, Jesus Christ, the angels and the saints. The devil, on the other hand, takes his place in the world of the evil powers, with the witches, monsters, and dragons (*Zsuzska, The Glass Casket, The Murdering Istéfán*). This becomes quite clear in the tales with outspoken religious tendencies.

When we examine these phenomena even more closely, we see that Mrs. Palkó's piety, just as folk piety in general, was nothing but a glaze, an outward shell, under which concepts of social justice as they appear in the tales and wish for compensatory justice are still smoldering.

Church-going in the life of the tale figures takes on exactly the same importance as it does in the life of the village. It is not astonishing that the royal family in *I Don't Know* goes to church every Sunday, and that the cook wants to go there so badly that she finally leaves the preparation of the royal dinner to the boy who plays dumb. For the villager church not only represents the stage for the usual religious ceremonies, it can become one of the most important places for social contact.[13] Thus it is only natural that the tale heroes meet their loves there; that conflicts happen there, as in the tale of *The Glass Casket* and *The Murdering Istéfán*. And even in connection with difficult tasks the church plays a role: the king built a church and his sons must solve the difficult task; they must bring the bird that can sing psalms, that sings better than the chief singer and preaches better than the priest (*The Psalmsinging Bird*). This, too, is an aspect of the combination of *märchen* world and reality.

We find two tales in which the career of the hero consists in becoming a priest or ascending the ranks of the priestly hierarchy to bishop and even to pope (*András Kerekes, The Murdering Istéfán*). The denouement of another story lies in the hero's return, after a twenty-year absence, just at the moment when his twin sons are ordained priests (*The Turk*). When one knows the role of the Hungarian church in the Bucovina, no explanation is necessary. The most likely means of becoming a master for a peasant was to be found in the priesthood. This was a career open even to the poorest peasant's son—no noble descent or wealth was necessary. The priestly careers in Mrs. Palkó's tales correspond to the capturing of secular power.

In the tale of *Prince Sándor,* the way in which the King brings about the "miracle," by fasting and praying according to the rules of the church, deserves attention because it is an obvious example of the spiritual fusion of active religious belief and magic action. One of the truly religious titles in Mrs. Palkó's tale body is based upon a medieval saint's legend, *The Two Hermits.* It has its root in the search for supernatural bliss, just as does *A Mother's Atonement,* as well as the belief legends. The most interesting, however, is *Margit,* for Mrs. Palkó's piety appears clearly in the way this *märchen* has been shaped. This tale, the content of which we shall examine later, is transformed by her into a bitter accusation against the unjust social order which forces the poor peasant either to die of hunger or to steal. Which one the peasant ought to choose is prescribed to him by the other power, the church.

It is worthwhile to compare Mrs. Palkó's piety with that of other narrators. One cannot call her a moralist, as Petruschichev, who is mentioned by Sokolov. This narrator was a daily laborer, timberman, railroad worker, and for twenty-one years sacristan in his village.[14] Intentional moralizing is far removed from Mrs. Palkó. Nor does she belong to the type of narrators exemplified by Fedics, who combines in his person the devoted serf-peasant and the revolutionary. We must not forget that Fedics' background was quite different: he came from a typical region of big landowners; he spent his life as a hired hand in a region where religious fundamentalist sects flourished and where emigration was the only way out, a region where the growing discontent erupted in the rebellious agrarian movement. Even though Fedics was of the Eastern Catholic rite, the Protestant rationalism of the region from which he came is mirrored in his tales. His pious acceptance and his prayerful poetry seem to have been fruits of his old age, and they developed when he had finally had to relinquish his belief in earthly happiness.[15] But—and this he has in common with Mrs. Palkó—in his religious tales we can see, when God, Jesus, or the saints appear, the same fusion of elements from religion and the peasant world of belief. His tale heroes, too, take a stand for the protection of the people's interests, and they even go much further, as tale types from this kind would permit.[16] With Mrs. Palkó, something else is dominant. With her, piety is not an end-product which appears with age, but the natural companion of her life. Fusion with naive folk belief is actually a natural event, just as the miracles and the concepts of justice in the tales follow the Christian moral concept. By combining all these elements, the tale justice as social justice imperceptibly attains a rational plane and serves to mirror social conditions.

In this way the apparent contradiction founded in the religious-magic world view of the narrator and the actual realism of the tales is smoothed out. In the preceding chapter we have shown how belief elements penetrate into the tale from the real world of the village. It is indeed the most credible village milieu which Mrs. Palkó created for her magic tales. The Bucovina peasantry, living under the most primitive economic conditions and in search of an outlet, arrived at a quasi-mystical explanation and, through recognition of the social reality, gave expression to discontent.

We have still to examine social criticism in the tales of Mrs. Palkó. Modest and kind-hearted as she may have been, she was still the representative and the advocate of the poor of the village community. All violence, all feelings of revenge, were alien to her. She never revolted against her own condition and that of her fellow sufferers, for "God is right, he metes out justice," and the place of punishment is Hell. Her tale heroes, however, defend the right. When she was narrating, her accusing voice was like a whip, her judgment hard and implacable, her justice often without pity, even brutal at times. Mrs. Palkó is unlike the female narrators, known to Azadovski, who do not believe in punishment:[17] she even goes so far (as in the tale of the *Two Brothers*) to contradict the teachings of Christian morality in the interest of social justice in an effort to correct "God's order."

There is hardly a *märchen* in which she does not plead for the "poor people." Memories of her own girlhood arise when Zsuzska, in tale No. 4, goes into service with her sister, for "she wanted to get married but she did not have even a dress," just as was once the case with Mrs. Palkó,[18] for they were the "children of poor people." The same thing happens with the initial situation in *Rupcsen-Hencsen*. The self-confidence of the poor man reaches such dimensions with Mrs. Palkó that she opposed her own religious conviction and her fatalism. The poor man, in despair about not being able to find a godfather, stops in the middle of the highway to accost the first person he meets. And when he finds out that the two he has stopped are St. Peter and Christ, he says,

> "If this is who you are, I don't need you as godfathers. And if you want to make promises, I don't want them."
> "But why not, you poor man?"
> "Because," he said, "you have given me so many children that I don't know any more which answers to what name. There are people, Lord, who take baths in milk and butter, they do not have children. . . . I have so many that five, six are weeping in every

corner because they are hungry and I cannot maintain them with the labor of my hands. Go along. I do not need you any more."[19]

Both Mrs. Palkó and Vinokurova constantly show concern with poverty and the fate of the poor,[20] and with both the personal elements are dominant. This makes the parts in their tales which describe poverty even more stirring. Such descriptions of misery are found in *Death with Yellow Legs*, *Peasant Gagyi*, and *The Fawn*, and in the tale of the *Smoking Kalfaktor*, which is laid in peasant surroundings. Here is described the marriage between poor young people (between an orphan boy and an orphan girl, for with the Szeklers the absence of relatives was synonymous with poverty):

> "I would like to marry if I found a girl which would fit me."
> "What kind of girl do you want? There are, there truly are, rich and good girls."
> "No—just let her have a pair of hands and be good. I myself am an orphan."
> "Well, until now I have maintained myself through my own handiwork. I never had a father. I had to earn money and buy my own dresses, firewood, everything."
> "That is just why I came. If you want to come with me, I would like to marry you and have you as my wife."

The fate of the poor is still in Mrs. Palkó's mind even when her heroes are princes. On his deathbed the King admonishes his son to govern justly and in the best interests of the people: "Take care of the kingdom; be as I was so that the people love you. The people should not be angry with you, but should love you." *(The Princess)*

The people's cause is also of great concern to the factory owner in *Gábor Német*. He instructs his adopted son as follows: "Be good, my son. Don't be bad with the workers. Don't withhold their wages from them. Give to everybody what is his due so that everybody may love and won't curse you!" In another tale the hero's success also benefits the poor man: "They became rich and then they became Counts. And there was so much that it could be divided among the poor." *(The Turk)*

The justice of the poor man is essentially expressed in the character of the "obstinate lady" in the tale of the *Proud Princess*. Mrs. Palkó describes the fight for survival of the poor man and enhances the tale toward the end with her own opinions. The princess, who has to live among scullery maids and cooks, has no longer any contact with the lords who amuse themselves in the gorgeous castle; she turns down the prince who asks for her hand; she loves a poor boy.

The contrast between rich and poor[21] appears in various guises throughout Mrs. Palkó's tales. Sometimes it is a simple enumeration without a commentary and the listener can judge for himself who is the victor *(Peasant Gagyi)*; sometimes it is a battle of life and death (as in the tales of *Nine, The Strong János,* and *Józsi the Fisherman*). In *Józsi the Fisherman* the battle is especially dramatic: the lord of the manor knows very well that the rise of the serf's son will mean his own downfall, and therefore he does everything to ruin him—and precisely for this he will be ruined himself.

The antagonism between rich and poor in Mrs. Palkó's tales appears also within the framework of the village. In addition to the tales already mentioned, it appears in *Two Brothers* and in *The Red-Bellied Serpent,* where the head shepherd refuses to give the hand of his daughter to the young shepherd in the same form in which the big landowner in Andrásfalva had done it: "My daughter does not belong on the same nail with you!" *Gábor Német,* the hero of tale No. 62, also complains to the girl after the judge has refused him: "You father has jammed it down my throat that you do not fit the same nail as I do. . . ."

These few examples should be sufficient, though we could cite many similarly shaped social situations which are organic parts of the international tale variants. How unconscious this partisanship is in the tales of Mrs. Palkó may be judged from that fact that we find this point of view expressed particularly in the magic tales, and much less in the realistic tales. In the magic tales she stresses her compassion for the poor hero (or for an equivalent third, disinherited, repudiated son of a king).

Mrs. Palkó's anecdotes are for the most part social satire condemning bad qualities. We find the lords of the village pilloried for their bad conduct in *Nine, The Strong János,* and *The Two Brothers.* Her partisanship appears clearest and without contradiction in the tales adapted from literary sources, such as *Gábor Német* and *Margit. Gábor Német* is the first folktale which has fully absorbed the industrial environment of the city. The topic of this tale is the fate of a worker, and its aim is to acquire power for the child of the worker. This is a real *märchen* transposed into the industrial environment.

Ideally, a social justice is expressed here that originated in the old patriarchal system of the peasant family. We experience the career and success of an industrial worker (not the traditional tale hero) while the tale retains completely the peasant outlook on life. It is very unlikely that such a form could have developed under the circumstances inside Hungary. Our experiences so far show that the peasant, as soon as he becomes industrialized and a city-dweller, breaks completely with the peasant tradition and does not continue to live with his tales in the new environment. If he nevertheless retains them, they are meaningful as an exciting and stimulating but unbelievable entertainment. In working-men's circles the tale has actually lost the value of social justice which, in peasant circles, kept it alive for centuries. Fundamentally, *Gábor Német* has its origins in the first encounter of the agrarian proletariat with factory work, admittedly under backward economic conditions. This folktale is characteristic of the poor, seasonal-labor society of the Bucovina folk group.[22] From data I have collected we can see that it originated with the Andrásfalva seasonal laborers, who also came in contact with factory work in the Moldavia region. But this experience was not strong enough to shake the basically peasant outlook of the tales. On the contrary, the tales absorbed it. In the poor quarters of Andrásfalva, this tale was especially popular and was told by Mrs. Palkó to small circles of listeners. (See page 261 for Mrs. Se-bestyén's treatment of this tale.) The general popularity which it gained after the settlement in Kakasd is due to the fact that the social differences among the settlers were extinguished by the new distribu-tion of property, and also to the fact that the possibility of making one's fortune as a factory worker appeared very enticing. The industrialist or factory owner acts as the *märchen* king, and his fortune is also fabulous, but the atmosphere is that of an industrial city perceived through the *märchen* fantasy.

When we pass to the tale of *Margit* (a "true story," not a traditional tale), we became acquainted with Mrs. Palkó's plastic description of society. According to the concept of Andrásfalva, it is the good families that are struck by misfortune. We have already mentioned that the people of the Bucovina were rich in children. Poor as the family may have been and as many children as they may have had, they did not regret it, but on the contrary were happy about it. Such is the case with this family: the woman loves her children. She is even a tiny bit "proud" as she vaunts in front of an old woman. And the man loves his family and works for them with all his strength. But everything is in vain, their "God-pleasing" life means nothing, and there is no escaping the harsh fate. The rich man has reserves; the poor man does not even have subsistence. Nowhere can he find work. Embittered, he goes to beg for groceries to be able to feed his hungry family some bread. Mrs. Palkó's narrative makes it clear what it means for the diligent, hard-working man to beg from the rich peasants, for whom he has worked all year long, a piece of bread. But his humiliation is for nought: they turn him down. Why does he have so many children if he cannot support them? They laugh in his face. Mrs. Palkó narrates it realistically: the *via crucis* of the unemployed, the repeated attempts, the shameful rejections, the heart-rending position of the family. Who has not known similar cases? This was an everyday occurrence between the two World Wars. With skillful psychological identification Mrs. Palkó conjured before our eyes the struggles of the poor man. She showed us what happens inside the diligent man until he finally makes up his mind to steal. There is no other way out for him. Society is indifferent, even hostile, in the face of his fate, and he must go steal to assuage the hunger of his children, crying at night.

The next day the poor man becomes conscious of the enormity of his desperate action. All night long he has not closed an eye, and the next morning he wants to sell his only treasure, his winter coat, to redeem himself. The peasant in the Bucovina did not clench his fist in the face of society's injustice; he has not brought it crashing down. It was not the terror of the police that made him shrink from it; it was solely the fear of God's punishment. He took the destruction of his whole family upon himself rather than "carry the sin on his soul." The power of the church over the poor people was such that it held them fast and forced them to submit to "the inevitable social order" which meant their destruction. The poor man did not revolt against it because it was "the will of God." Purity of soul is important—but what will become of us when there is no more bread? The narrator does not have an answer for this.

Very moving in this tale is the episode concerning the watchmaker's apprentice who is suspected of the theft. The constables beat him until blood spurts from his mouth and nose, and even his mother, who tries in vain to shield her child, is hurt, since "it is only the question of poor people whose child must be rotten."

If we categorize Mrs. Palkó's tales, we see that she prefers magic tales almost exclusively. And among these, she prefers those in which the subject is the sufferings of a female hero. These heroines who "have to suffer most" are the ones with whom she identifies most readily and which she can enter into most easily. In this she resembles the Russian female narrators. And yet Mrs. Palkó cannot be identified with any other narrator type. The lyric and tender poetic feeling to be found in her tales of unhappy maidens (she told about fourteen such tales) is matched by fire, fighting spirit, and audacity in her heroic tales (sixteen in number). Of the latter she preferred *I Don't Know, Prince Sándor*, and *The Psalmsinging Bird*. And her tone changed again in adventure stories like *The Turk*, where she masterfully built up extremely complicated structures and developed her motifs very logically. Her narrative art changed once more when she related anecdotes. As we have mentioned, her anecdotes are actually, with a few exceptions, character comedies which personify qualities under criticism by the village community or public opinion. Mrs. Palkó narrated anecdotes in the intervals between magic tales or at the end of a long tale in order to dissolve the tension created by the tale and rouse healthy laughter.

The content of funny incidents—of stupid men and women, of female vanity, laziness, stupidity, slovenliness, and quarrelsomeness, of girls who cannot find a husband because of their poor qualities—which is often moralizing, is greatly disguised and makes these anecdotes doubly charming. These tales are, for the most part, laid in old Andrásfalva, where the guileless suitor comes from another village, usually Hadik-falva. Mrs. Palkó related them with magnificent humor and dramatic personification. Here she did not lose herself in descriptive particulars. She created the people of her dialogues—as we shall see later—right before our eyes. The absence of all anecdotes of an anticlerical nature is striking, since this is a type very popular in that region. The money-hungry priests, who are pilloried in so many variants even by mediocre narrators, can never be found as the dupe in the anecdotes of Kakasd. The reason for this can again be found in the respect in which the church was held in the Bucovina. Yet the piety of the narrators alone would not be sufficient explanation, because it could not prevent the development of this type in other regions nor rid other regions of it. There is another reason in the case of Mrs. Palkó: the priest anecdotes usually have erotic coloring. Coarse expressions were alien to her, and even more alien was the slimy adulterer's story.[23] When she was exposed to these tales in company she blushed and was ill at ease, and would rather not continue listening.

Mrs. Palkó was a realistic storyteller. This is shown in the way she constructed the stage for the tales from parts of her own world, form-ing the figures of the tales from her own experience.[24] She lived with the tale, she did not view its action from the outside; she suffered and fought with her heroes and was happy with them. With her there are no muddled, unclear figures: even the most fantastic mythological mon-ster behaved as people do. The ideal human qualities such as goodness, faithfulness, courage, charity, and beauty are represented in her tales, just as are nastiness, vanity, envy, and greed, the qualities she herself most condemned. With sparse means, she described people and situations so well that they materialize before us; we could almost draw them. In this connection we can note the careful treatment of certain spots—parts which seem secondary from the point of view of the action, but primary for the reality content of the tale. These passages serve to point up a situation, to describe a human character, or to create an atmosphere. Very often she went to great lengths in the treatment of these passages which are unimportant relative to the complete action, but which are related in much more detail than the tale actually seemed to require.

Some of these passages, are often to be found at the beginning of the tale, as an exposition of the initial situation. For the storyteller, the basic situation is of such importance that she wants to throw special light on it.[25] This is the case, above all, when she starts with the misery of the poor families and the village situation, as in the tale of *The Fawn*, or *Józsi the Fisherman*, *The Smoking Kalfaktor*, and *The Turk*.

Her dramatic art—for example the way in which she introduced the actors and happenings into the tale of *The Fawn*—would be worthy of a special study. The rational elements fuse so well with the magic ones that the listeners heardly notices that he is no longer in the rational world. Mrs. Palkó worked up every detail with painstaking care. There was no break, no tension, no passage which needed explanation, for all the strange and curious happenings were related in this absolutely credible manner.

The starting point of this tale is especially characteristic. Before our eyes the misery of the family, the constant hunger of the children, the desperate attempts of the woman to find something for them to eat. The situation contains much which then follows logically from it. These elements are the bricks that build the house of the tale. The hunger of the children, the desperate deed of the woman in cooking her own flesh, then the terrible thought of slaughtering their own childern and eating them. This is no dry, dreary description of "a fact," but we feel the anguish of the woman, and her plan to murder is of equal power. Mrs. Palkó developed the plan in a masterful way, and in order to increase the impact on the listeners she repeats it three times, each time from a different viewpoint: the first time when the couple discusses it after dinner; the second when the boy tells his sister about it; and the third at the end of the episode of the lucky escape. These are simple means, but over all they are exceptionally powerful artistic tools, with the help of which she succeeds in making the listener believe that he is hearing not a tale but a real event which she happened to witness. Until the point where the children flee, the realistic point of view is striking. Then follows the world of wonder—the magic forest leading to the sphere of the tale world, the transformation into an animal, the kings palace, and the realm of tale justice. Mrs. Palkó's art is also apparent in the renewal of traditional tale elements for which she created a psychological background. Not even the smallest detail remains without explanation. (When the woman cut a piece of flesh from her leg to feed her husband, she staunched the flow of blood with vinegar.)

The narrator directs attention to a seemingly unimportant point which differs from the habitual but which becomes an important link in the chain of events: the little boy is afraid to go out alone into the courtyard at night, though he was never afraid before. Ceaselessly she exploits every possibility of the tale. The single elements of the tale are generally known, and she does not even modify them but builds them into her story as they are, and she even inserts them into the structure of other tales. The sister's being called to go out into the courtyard also occurs in the tale of *Zsuzska and the Devil;* the declaration of war is also seen in *I Don't Know;* and the simulated sickness of the evil woman appears in *The Fairy Princess* and in *Rosemary*.

The village of the Szeklers in the Bucovina, with its customs and rituals, can be found in numerous tales. Let us quote as an example the following passage from the tale *Anna Mónár*, when the vengeful chief of robbers approaches the girl cunningly:

> Once he wrote a letter to the girl . . .
> "My dear Annus, I saw you at the mill. Since then I cannot eat or sleep, I am always thinking of you. I am now writing you a letter and sending a photograph and if you like me answer me quickly, whatever you want. But do not distress my heart for I am dying for you."
> Well, the girl gets the letter and reads it. She has herself a good laugh, then she runs in to the old ones to show them what kind of letter she got. The old father takes it and likes it, for it was well written.
> "Do you know him, my girl?"
> "No, but he says he saw me here at the mill."
> The old man looks at the picture, he likes it.
> "A nice, good fellow. I don't know what manners he has, but he is very good-looking. Well, girl, what do you say?"
> "Well, I like him, and if you will permit it, I shall marry him."

Immediately she wrote him a letter. He should come right away so that her mother and her father could meet him, so that she could see if she liked him or not. . . .

"Well, my beloved Annus, I have come . . . so that we can talk alone, not just in a letter. Now tell me what you want. Will you come with me or not?"

"Wait," she said. "First I shall speak to Father and Mother. I shall come only if they permit it."

The old ones were called in immediately and the fellow was full of glee.

"Do not reject this luck for I believe you will not regret having given me your daughter."

"My son, I don't hold her back if she wants to go. Whom she loves she should join, for girls ought to marry! . . ."[26]

Situations similar to this, which should lead to a heroic deed, are pointed up even in tales that are laid at the court of a king: *I Don't Know, The Snake Prince, The Twelve Robbers.* In these tales the narrator often had to disgress in detailed descriptions of persons and unknown places which need an explanation.[27] Great care was expended in the description of the plush adornments of the princess—which the village cannot imagine—and the narrator lingered with the supernatural powers in their realms beyond our own world, with descriptions of royal palaces and luxurious gardens. She used extravagant colors when she described magic wonders, and the concept living in her fancy became reality. She was able to do this thanks to an unusual psychological compassion for the characters of her narration and for her listeners.

Should we concentrate here on the single, sensitive descriptions of inner emotions, on the descriptions of personalities in the individual tale passages, on the tricks of the trade with which Mrs. Palkó slowed down the action and at the same time increased the interest of her listeners, we would have to quote entire pages, perhaps entire tales. In the following we will examine a few characteristic passages and texts, and then refer to the single *märchen* in the Appendix. The type of subjective narrator who, while retaining the traditional structure of the tale type, is able to create a new form, not by combining motifs or dissolving and reshaping a new form, but by including subjective feeling originating in the experiences of her own life and from living with the tale, is indeed a rarity.

The means which Mrs. Palkó used include descriptions of states of mind, conflicts of conscience, battles between good and bad impulses, of the pain inflicted upon the innocent, of love and faith—which are the feelings that accompany the hero through the tale. Mrs. Palkó, an excellent judge of the human soul, knew very well how to present her accounts to the public in a credible way, because unconsciously she lived all the situations with her tale heroes.

An exceptional development of the psychic processes her heroine has to undergo is shown in the tale of *The Serpent Prince:* she has to accustom herself to the thought that a monster will become her husband. We shall quote here only the passage which contains her reaction to the news that she is being given in marriage to a serpent:

> "I would rather have my throat cut and be buried somewhere than become his wife. . . . What in tarnation have you been thinking of? I should marry a serpent? Why have you fetched me and brought me here? Why did you not tell me what kind of son you have? I don't care if he is good a thousand times over—I don't need him. I shrink from looking at him, he is an abominable, an awful beast. I should lie down in bed next to him? I'd rather kill myself."
>
> She ran from one window to another. There were bars, iron bars on them. There was no possibility of escape.
>
> The King and the Queen left the house and locked the door, leaving the girl where the serpent was.
>
> She ran around in the house as if she could find something to comfort her. She ran upstairs and wept, wringing her hands. How could she escape? What to do? The day will pass, but what am I going to do at night? She weeps, she sobs bitterly, but nobody has pity on her and lets her out.
>
> In the evening the Queen brings her something to eat. But she only watches the door, ready to spring when it opens. But the Queen immediately locks the door with the key; she cannot get out, she must stay in there. She (the Queen) has just put down the dinner. And in the morning she still saw it standing there, for she [the girl] did not need to eat. She had run to and fro all night long, sobbing bitterly, and in the other room everybody heard how the girl wept. And they left and did not let her out. Thus it went a whole week long, but the girl did not eat a bite, never laid down, and always ran around in circles in the castle. . . .

How powerfully could Mrs. Palkó describe the sorrow of the parting of the brother and sister in *The Princess!* Heart-rending is the story of the hungry children in *Margit*, which finally drives the father to steal. The tragic ending of the tale *The Glass Casket,* when the Devil brings "desperation" on the heroine (i.e. scares her to death), shakes her audience. We could go on indefinitely, yet every single example would only serve to confirm that Mrs. Palkó's descriptions of situations, which show so much psychological insight serve the real content. They explain how what the tale relates can really happen. The narrator lived in her tales, and with these tricks she also induced the listeners to enter the tale world and observe the happenings from that viewpoint. With help from Mrs. Palkó, we were actually able to identify with the situations, unimaginable in reality. The transformation of the Serpent Prince into a handsome young man becomes not only believable but natural, just as do the devouring of people and the changing of the devil into a man in the tale. And it occurs in such a way that the listener feels that this was the only way it could have happened.

Among all the female narrators described in the international folklore literature, Mrs. Palkó can best be compared to Vinokurova. Azadovski reports that this narrator concentrated her attention mainly on the representation of real life and of psychological developments, and that this makes her different not only from the Siberian narrators but from other Russian storytellers.[28] The flow of action did not interest her as much as the local and psychological aspects, on whose account she shortened or lengthened the action, something that cannot be said about Mrs. Palkó.[29] "In the development as well as in the description of an episode, the attention of the storyteller is not directed to the outward motivation, or the strict sequence of facts, but upon the inner drive for the action. Here, too, she develops unusual capabilities and observes with the sharp eye of a psychologist."[30]

Both Onchukov and the Brothers Sokolov have already pointed out in their collections that the female storytellers like to weave their own life stories into their tales. They also state that feeling, finesse, tenderness, and sentiment are prevalent in the tales of the female narrators.[31] Unconsciously, the tales mirror their usual living conditions and the things which occupy them,[32] and they never can remain as factual as the male narrators. And just as Vinokurova's preference was for the slandered, persecuted, and suffering heroines, Mrs. Palkó always described them with the utmost empathy. Like Medvedjeva, she was thinking of her own fate, and moved the listener when she wept over the rejected bride[33] and when she, like Vinokurova,[34] painted the mother's picture with special tenderness, thinking of the raising of her own children and her own widowhood. Haiding, too, mentions a storyteller who fills the sad fate of the mother in the tale *The Girl Without Hands* with true and living emotion.[35] It is worthwhile to point out the corresponding variant of this tale from Mrs. Palkó. In the tale of *The Twelve Robbers*, Mrs. Palkó conveyed in many passages the sorrow of the mother. It is a remarkable instance in which her own voice could be heard, even in a tale laid out in royal surroundings. The description of the Prince's mother, the Queen Widow, is convincing and characteristic. It is Mrs. Palkó's own compassion which shows in that of the mother when the Prince brings home the crippled girl.

> The mother—she was the King's widow, immediately appeared.
>
> "Look, Mother, what I brought you!"
>
> "Where did you pick up this girl, my dear son?" the queen said. "She cannot work."
>
> "I did not bring her here to work. Permit me, my dear mother, to make her my wife."
>
> "Oh, but what do you mean, my dear son. This is out of the question, she does not fit you. It does not make any difference where she comes from, who her ancestors are, but she has neither hands nor feet. Are you not worthy of anyone better? You could choose a princess."
>
> "Mother," the King said, "whatever you say; I can see for myself that she has neither hands nor feet, but I still like her. Permit me to marry her, for if you don't I'll go out into the wide world and leave you."
>
> "Just think, my son, what you are doing," she said. "You will go for a walk where all the newly-married men take their wives, and you cannot do it. And what will the people say when they hear what kind of wife you have taken? What will the country say?"
>
> "Mother, I don't care what the country or the people say; permit me to marry her, or I'll leave."
>
> The mother thought the matter over. She would rather give in than let her son go. "Well then," she said, "take her—but I hope you won't be sorry. You are young. You don't think ahead; you will be sorry, but then it will be too late."

This uneasiness appears in the course of events, and the boundless love of the mother also extends to the young queen. Her happiness is overflowing when the child is born. When a forged letter informs her that her son wants to repudiate his wife and child, she nearly goes out of her mind with sorrow. She bombards her son with desperate letters in order to move him, and when she is not successful she threatens suicide.

When the mother read the letter, she became nearly distraught. "What has gotten into my son," she said; "How he loved her, how after I told him don't marry her, you'll be sorry, but he said no, never. And now he writes me such things. But now I won't permit her to be taken away. What do you think, do you really believe I'll permit this sweet child to be dragged from the castle? Then I too will die!" In her reply to him she wrote: "If you don't have pity for her, at least think of the child!"

When the old queen received the letter, she broke into tears. "Oh, my God, what am I to do now?"

She was so sorry for her daughter-in-law and also for the child, that it nearly broke her heart. And again the queen wrote, "My dear son, don't break my heart entirely. There's only a sliver of it left. When you brought her home you did not obey me, and now I won't contradict you. But what do you mean—having her and the child taken away—is there no God in heaven?"

Let us return to Mrs. Palkó's tale structure. We have already said that she builds up her tales with considerable logic. Nothing or very little changes in the structure even when a tale is told several times; the plot remains in the main logical, while the variations depend on the continually changing applications of the realm of reality, the realistic motif. These variations are not uniform: some tales change essentially at each recital and others do not change at all. Even within the tale itself there are parts which are always repeated verbatim, and others which are constantly changed.[36]

As to the motif structure, only *The Three Princes, Ej Haj, The Turk,* and *The Twelve Robbers* seem to contain important individual innovations, but we cannot be completely sure of this since we did not have occasion to hear these same tales from other narrators in Kakasd. It may therefore be that Mrs. Palkó adapted these forms as she told them. It is especially interesting to watch how her style of narration uses and adapts the stereotyped forms.

Mrs. Palkó possessed a very outspoken feeling for form. Every one of her *märchen* was carefully composed, and she did not have poor texts. Whatever she was not quite sure of or had forgotten, she would not even begin to tell. Occasionally, with a few pieces her delivery would be weaker than usual, and we would have heard her tell the tale with much more color at other times. But it never happened that any of her tales were out of proportion, poorly done, or unfinished. Her careful formation is felt in every tale. She always adhered to the law of motif combination and commonplace formulae, using generalities, stereotypes, and repetitions, apart from the introductory and closing formats which, although learned from her brother, she seldom used. "My brother also started the *märchen* this way: that there were two goats and the devil knows, I don't know. He said, 'Always start the tales so that people laugh!' But I am not very good at it." Mrs. Palkó knew very well the tricks of the trade and used them consciously, but she rejected anything she did not like or was not in the mood for. Her composition was done consciously; she did not merely adapt what she had once heard somewhere but followed the rule of tale construction. She knew very well what really belonged and what had no business being in the text, and as a result of this knowledge her *märchen* became consistent.

Some of the most logically constructed tales are *Józsi the Fisherman, Anna Mónár,* and *Nine.* In them we find, through repeated deliveries, changes in phraseology. Sometimes we find astonishing similarity in the choice of words and in the rendition of motifs which also occur in other tales, while the same *märchen* is shown on different occasions in a completely different form. One time she would linger on one incident, and then again on another incident, and embroider other details according to her whim.

The formation can be minimal, as in the tale of *The Lazy Young Woman* (listed in *Folktales of Hungary* as *Lazybones*). In the first recorded variant, the husband returns his wife to her mother rolled in a straw bundle. In the version noted five years later, the mother takes pity on her daughter and dresses her again; the husband forgives her and takes her back, and from then on the young woman no longer burns her dresses.

More important were the modifications of the tale *The Murdering Istéfán* when the text was recorded for the second time after an interval of four years. The delivery had grown more rhythmical, as the fate of the robber was told three times: the first is when the robber himself relates it to the boy; the second, when the boy tells it to Lucifer in hell; the third when the robber relates it to the priest and asks his advice. The content and meaning of the tale had also deepened; the initial story was lengthened. The mother of the hero in the story is a poor peasant girl who has two suitors. She is not allowed to take the poor one but is forced to take the noble suitor, for "it is better that she should follow the prince than the poor man." Thus the tale motif originates in the contrast between the rich and poor. The poor girl curses her misfortune and wishes the child she is expecting to hell; this curse must be dissolved by the boy. The modification is achieved by Mrs. Palkó when she explains an inexplicable thing—the girl marrying someone she does not love—and makes it real, thus achieving a rapprochement between the traditional tale and her own reality.

In order to show how a tendency changes and thus affects changes in the extent of a tale part, we shall cite here a very striking example. The three variants of the beginning of one tale, *Peti and Boris*, are characteristic not only of the change in the form but in the content. We noted the first text in 1948 and the second in 1954. The third text was published in the same year by Gy. László. Even though this writing comes from a newsman, rather than an expert, we can consider it accurate in this connection since we are so well acquainted with Mrs. Palkó's style.[37]

### VARIANT A

Once there was a young man. And then he had land, a farm. The husband always went out into the fields, the woman always stayed home, but then they had enough. The husband was never satisfied. . . .

### VARIANT B

Once upon a time there was a young man and a young woman. They had a field and they also had cows. They were quite nicely fixed. They also had a little boy. The woman always went into the field; she never had anybody with whom she could leave her child, so they took him along. They had much to do. They had to go and hack and so they laid the little boy under a bush where it was cool so that nothing should happen. But the boy stayed only until they had bedded him down. He was about a year and a half. When they had started with their work, he rose, wept and cried constantly so that your heart could break, for the ants and flies bothered him and the thorns pricked him.

"Listen, Peti, this was the man's name, "I shall go home with the child, this is no good. It is better for me to stay home for I don't get anything done this way," said the woman.

"Good," the man answered, "at least I won't have to listen to all that crying."

Well, then Boris, that was the woman's name, went and took up the child. She fed it, washed it, and put it down in a cool place, and it fell asleep when she rocked it to sleep. Within herself she thought, "This is not bad, my husband will get along by himself.

I have enough to do here; a woman's work is never done, all her life."

She milked the cow, fed corn to the pigs, fed corn to the ducks, gave water to the chickens, laundered the small things, heated the stove, made butter, baked bread, cleaned the yard and the house. She cooked dinner and when Peti came home, she gave him something warm to eat. They all ate dinner and then laid down to sleep.

When dawn broke Boris said, "Peti, get up, you have to go out into the field."

"This is easily said, Boris, for it is easy on the woman, she is in the cool all day long while we must sweat in the fields."

### VARIANT C

Once upon a time there was a young couple. They were good peasants. They had a field, they had cows. They had only one child, a two-year-old girl. Time came for hacking and they had to go out to work. They had to take the little girl along, they could not leave her in any place. But as the little girl was not accustomed to being in the field, she ran after her mother, cried and wanted to be taken on her lap. The man's name was Peti, the woman's Boris.

Then, one day Peti said to his wife, "Tomorrow you will not come out with me, you remain at home with little Juliska. For," he said, "it is more damage than use, for the little one is trampling down all the maize."

Then Boris said, "Sad enough, for the hacking is urgent. What will you do alone?"

"What I'll do? I shall hack by myself, so I won't hear the crying."

Said Boris, "It is true, I have enough to do at home. A woman's work is never done, all her life long!"

It became evening. They went home and Boris had to prepare dinner. When they had eaten, they laid down to sleep. The woman said, "Get up Peti. It is dawning; you have got to go hacking."

He had his breakfast and she gave him lunch so he did not have to come home. Peti went hacking alone. The woman stayed home. The poor thing hardly knew where to begin, there was so much to do. First she gave maize to the pigs, then some bran. Then she ran into the stable, cleaned it, and fed the chickens, milked the cows; then she ran back into the house—the little girl was still asleep—she made the beds, used the broom, then finished the breakfast. When the little girl arose, she had finished. Then she tackled the rest of the work. She always had things to do; she was a skillful and able woman. When the husband returned home, all work was done. She had milked the cow, fed the pigs, prepared a good dinner, and was ready when her husband came home.

"Well, Peti," she said. "Rest, wash your feet, eat your dinner."

Peti washed his feet, then he said, "My you women have it so good!"

Originally, the introductory part of the tale consisted of only one sentence, in which the facts are stated. Apparently this was the way Erzsi Matyi had told it. Mrs. Palkó had first deepened the following part of the tale by funny, dramatic particulars; the main accent was on the adventures of the husband unskilled in housework. In time, however, the description of the couple's situation seemed too limited, for the more the common work load is stressed—the labor of the woman in the field and in the house and the care of the child—the clearer the message of the tale appears: the life of the woman is more difficult than that of the man.

Changes of this kind were quite frequent with Mrs. Palkó, and in time a form emerged which was final and which she did not change again.

We mentioned above that similar incidents in different tales, narrated in the same fashion, will often match word for word. This does not mean that there is no essential difference in the parallel passages, but the form is always the same. This, too, is part of Mrs. Palkó's art of delivery. To illustrate, we shall quote parallel passages from different tales.

Our first example, the order to torment the magic horse, occurs almost literally in all three of the tales, but differs according to the intent of the individual tale types.

### I Don't Know

"Uncle, Uncle Soldier, what is the matter with this pony, why is it so thin?"

"Well, my child," he said, "that's the way it is." Then he said, "Why does this pony not eat like the others?"

"Well, we don't give him what the others get," he said, "not what the other horses get."

"But why do we not give him the same things?"

"My child," he said, "this pony," he said, "*when the others get hay he gets oats. And when the others eat oats, then he gets hay. You never must give him what the others get or what he demands. For he demands that which he wants at the moment. But you never must give him*," he said, "*the same which the others are getting.*"

### THE SKY-HIGH TREE

Then the dragon said to János, "Well, you know, János, feed these, give them to drink, and curry them. *But the pony which lies there, you do not need curry, you do not need to give him what the others are getting; but when he demands hay, give him oats, when he wants oats, give him hay; if it demands hay give him water, but never give him what it demands!*"

### EJ HAJ

Well so Ej Haj had gone home. "Stop, you bundle of misery, you lied to me! I am going to show you!"

Then he said to his servant, "See here, my son, *when this horse demands hay, give him water, when it wants water, give him oats; never give him what he wants!*"

In two of the tale passages the same thing is treated: the hero meets the magic horse. And yet there is a difference. In the first tale the hero and the horse are the victims of one and the same sorcerer and are joined by a common interest; in the second tale the hero takes up service with the dragon, and with the help of the magic horse rescues the heroine. In the third tale the situation is quite different: the hero himself is changed into a horse, out of revenge, by the sorcerer.

The following examples will show how the same kind of thinking, expressed in the same words, is applicable to similar situations. With Mrs. Palkó each tale follows its own theme, but similar themes lead to similar forms. We shall select the moment when the queen has died and the hero or (heroine) has become an orphan. The suffering of the king and the words of consolation originate in the same sentiment and thus are expressed in the same way.

### THE SKY-HIGH TREE

But the king was so sad, he did not eat or sleep for days; he wept over his wife. But the little girl always comforted him.

"*You know very well, we are not born all at the same time and we do not die at the same time. One has to accept God's will.*"

The King reflected, "My God, how young is this girl, I should not weep so much. I cannot resurrect her with it." One day the father said, "My child, I shall never marry again, I declare. I shall never find a woman such as was your mother. That doesn't exist. I would rather stay the way I am!"

"*Dear father, don't stay the way you are, for I shall not stay here forever, and what will you do alone then?*"

Then the King said, "It does not matter, my child. But I shall never remarry. I would rather stay a widower!"

## THE FLEA PRINCESS

. . . day and night he mourned his wife. Whenever the girl entered she found her father weeping.

"Why do you weep, Father?"

Then he said, "How should I not weep," he said, "that your mother was not loath to leave me behind! Such a wife I never shall get again, and that I cannot forget."

"But surely you will get a wife, Father. There are beautiful and very good ones. . . . Dear Father," she said, "I do not want to see you so sad!" She said, "Marry," she said. "This is much better for you and forget my mother, or she will not find any rest. *God had wanted it this way, so it has to be.* Even if I leave you behind when God gives me happiness and I leave you here, you will be even sadder. It is better you marry again as long as I am still at home!"

"No, my child, I told you, I shall never marry again!"

## I DON'T KNOW

Oh, how the king is mourning, he is weeping night and day. No dinner, no sleep, all he does is weep. He cannot restrain himself. There was a beautiful photograph of the queen in a room, like a statue. So, every day which God allowed to be, the King knelt before it and prayed for the repose of her soul, but for sobbing and weeping he could not pray and always started to wail.

The king had a steward and this steward he always believed to be very just. Well, he went to him every day for he knew that he would find the king always weeping, and he comforted him.

"Great King, why do you weep so much? *You must know that we are not all born at the same time and shall not die at the same time. Accept God's will that He let the queen live until now and let her die now.* You, my gracious King, will marry again, take another wife, and continue to live. Why then weep so much?"

Thus he comforted the king day after day, but he continued to weep for his wife for he said that we would never get again such a beautiful and good wife as was his first wife.

One day he wept again, wept so much that he nearly choked. And the steward again went to him and said, "Gracious King, restrain yourself. Do you want to ruin yourself? What shall become of the little boy if he loses his father too? Even if you want to die of your great sorrow, have mercy on your little son!"

"It must be, it must be," he said. "I must accept my fate, for I see she doesn't return much as I weep, even if I commit suicide. . . ."

"I say," he said, "that I cannot forget her, for when one really loves one's wife one should not forget her! *But do accept it that we are not all born at the same time and that we shall not all die at the same time.*"

### THE PRINCESS

. . . Well, so, her father the king wept day and night so much that his eyes were never dry, so much did he weep for his wife.

"My dear child, I shall never marry again, for such a woman as your mother, I shall never find her again. So, I shall stay as I am until I die!"

And in his sorrow the king became so ill that he had to die. . . .

Our third example is supposed to show the masterful variation of one and the same theme. We want to put in juxtaposition the descriptions of the same scene from five different tales. In each we see the pomp of the royal entourage. Through the colorful, artistic style, Mrs. Palkó fully displayed her rich imagination. The pomp is often described in the same words and sentences, and yet each description is different and far exceeds the model of the tale motif. Mrs. Palkó's individual shaping was molded to the traditional material. Nowhere is anything out of place, nothing remains undigested; the richly embroidered episodes do not distract from but rather complete the formal perfection of the *märchen*. We shall select from the first two tales the moment in which the hero and heroine make themselves known, the moment of the triumphant entry in the royal palace. Both state the same things and yet they are different.

### THE THREE PRINCES

There he had a dress the like of which eyes never beheld, it was so beautiful. From the shoes to the chako, everything.

"Well," he said, "now, my dear, you will get your bridal dress!"

And then he had his attire. They went into a room with a mirror on each side so they could see themselves from head to toe. Then they dressed, put on their clothes. They were so beautiful, especially the bride, that they were more like angels than people. Then the girl went outside and whistled and the coachman came up. She ordered him to harness *four heavy black horses before a glass coach. The harness was of pure gold, there was more gold on it than leather.* Then the coachman stopped in front of the door. The tip of the whip, too, was of solid gold. Then she put on the veil and preened herself as a bride, took a beautiful bouquet of flowers into her hands.

"And now," she said, "we can go."

They took their seats in the coach, in front a footman, and off they went. The top of the coach was closed so they did not get any dust. When they approached the castle of the father, the wedding was going full tilt. When they were quite close *the telephone rang that a guest was coming*, but who it was they did not know, four horses harnessed one after another, but *they thought it was an emperor*, they never had seen such beautiful horses. From the gate to the door of the castle *were ranged two rows of guards*, and at the door there were soldiers on each side in dress uniform. Well, then, the coach had arrived and the lords came out of the castle. They waited to see who had come with such beautiful horses, in such a beautiful coach. The old king arrived, the coach stopped, *the top was removed*, a beautiful couple. The king nearly fell over backward when he recognized his son.

"My son," he said, "where have you been so long?"

The father took his son by the arm and led him and his bride, arm in arm, took them into the castle and sat them down at the table, but the other two brides were only ridiculous next to this one, everybody had eyes only for her. A bushelfull of gold pieces was emptied on the table; the old king said he would give it to the bride who could sweep them off the table with her hair. Well, then the bride of the older prince tried it but not a single gold piece fell down, for she had only very short hair, and the other too. The third, the bride of the youngest, then went but her hair reached to her heels. She swept everything in one swoop and everything belonged to her. . . .

## I Don't Know

. . . A coach should be here, it is *all made of glass* and the edges and trim of diamonds. The golden coach must be made of glass, and the wheels of gold and the axle of God knows what.

He decided everything and said how it should be. And four horses should be harnessed to it, *four black horses, black like blackthorn*. Their coats must be shining, and all four should be harnessed one after the other. "All the rings of the harness must be of diamonds," he said," and of gold, and the knob of the whip must be of solid gold and an extra dress coachman should be sitting on the cab, for we are going now," he said, "to see my father-in-law. There we will celebrate my wedding. It will be as beautiful as I said."

He had hardly spoken when the glass coach stood before him. It was so that only God knows what was on the windows. Such a coach no human being had ever laid eyes on, how beautiful it was! And *four black horsese were harnessed* to it, they were decorated with flowers, and in *beautiful harness all decorated with diamonds*. The horses were even more beautiful. Never had anybody seen anything so beautiful.

"Well, woman," he said, "let us get dressed, I want a completely new wedding dress brought for me, a gown for my wife. We only want to get dressed and then we shall go."

He hardly had said it when everything was there. A royal gown such as kings wear, with red and gold tassels. My God, how they looked, it can hardly be told. . . . The beaked helmet also was of pure gold. Well, from head to toe, even the spurs, everything was so shiny one could hardly look at it. And the bride, the wedding gown she had! Nobody ever could have seen such a one. One could not find out if it was velvet or silk or what it was. It was so beautiful. . . .

The bride's wreath so beautiful and charming, *the wedding rose* in *her hand* when she goes to the wedding. They were well fitted with everything as they looked at each other. They went and stood before a large mirror. When one looked at the other, they could not stop marveling how beautiful they were. Well, then they took their seats in the coach, in front the footman, and started up. They went and arrived at this place, *there where those soldiers stood, the palace guard* on either side, they expected the guests, that is, they received the guests when they arrived. Well, suddenly they saw that the coach approached. But such a coach nobody had ever seen before. How beautiful was the coach, how beautiful the horses. *Not for a king but like for an emperor.* Many people had been here before, there were many balls and weddings and everything, but such a coach as the one that came now, never had come to the king's palace. *They quickly telephoned the palace that a guest was arriving but they did not know was he an emperor or what,* but ever since they had received their eyesight they never had seen anything the like. What horses, and what a coach—it could only be an emperor who was arriving. The guests, too, got up from the tables and went into the entrance to wait for the arriving couple. The band played so that the earth trembled. They played a welcome march.

Well, then, they come, they enter through the gate, slowly. They opened eyes and mouth when they saw what was entering. Who could it be, then, even the king trembled, what unexpected guest could arrive now, that one, that, that, that . . . that is a foreign emperor and who knows where he comes from? The arrived coach stopped in front of the palace door. All the mighty of the realm surged up to look. *The top was lifted.* When the king saw his son, and his daughter next to her husband, he did not recognize them. . . .

There is another way of describing all that pomp: a poor man has become rich. For this we shall select three tale passages: the persons are similar in all three; only the situations vary.

### DEATH WITH YELLOW LEGS

[A poor man improves his financial position by taking Death as a godfather.]

Well, with this he had become so rich that he bought a three-story palace and lived in it. Even the youngest son wore a gold ring, this shows what lords they had become. In the cellar money was kept in barrels, and the drawers were full of it. . . . A beautiful castle, a beautiful flower garden, everything was there that was needed, *the money was kept in barrels in the cellar* . . . the youngest son even *wore gloves on his fingers.* . . .

[When Death comes to fetch him, he tries to bargain with him and shows him his riches, trying to move his heart.]

"Come with me into the cellar so I can show you what I earned."

"Well, I'll do it."

He took him to the cellar, all barrels were full, two rows of barrels.

"See, Godfather, I have much to live for and you are calling me away from the living? Do you not have pity on the poor children? Should I leave them here without a father?"

"No, cousin, they have enough to live on. You have broken your word; you must die."

"Then, at least permit me to show you into my flower garden."

There was a fish pond with glass-clear bottom and in the middle there was *a well with a hand pump and on top of it an elephant and from it flowed the water in a gold chute.*

"See, Godfather, all this is mine!"

### PEASANT GAGYI

*Peasant Gagyi* becomes a rich man by donning a magic belt. A man "three span high" brings everything he orders. We shall list three of his commands and their execution.

"I order that tomorrow there should be a castle here at the end of the bridge which is fastened to the bridge with three gold chains.

It must have 300 windows and 150 doors but the window and door frames must all be of pure gold, and the door handles of diamonds. And the steps must be of pure gold, the entrance. . . . I order that everything that belongs in a king's palace should be there— furniture, beds, tables, that all furniture be the most beautiful in the world . . . and the closets should be full of things. Pictures— the house must have everything. I will add that the courtyard should be paved with marble and around the castle there should be a flower garden the like of it there is nowhere in the world. In it all sorts of flowers should be planted with the best fragrance and around it there should be a row of trees, there should be fruit trees, of all kinds of fruit, of the best in the world. . . .

"I order that right here in the middle of the courtyard should be a well. *But a well that has a pump, and on top of it a lion, from his mouth the water should flow and through the pump come down in a chute.* And on the other side of the courtyard there should be another well, one from which the cattle can drink, but there the chute should be of round concrete and enough water, and in every chute the water should flow from another source. . . .

"I order that around the courtyard, that on the sides of the yard all around there should be buildings. First the stables, the horse barns, for the foals first, then the roans, then the geldings, then the oxen, then the cows. But for each a separate stable, and the water chutes on the side, and the floor too, everything must be of glass. . . . And then, after the stables, should be the barns, wheat barns, so that every kind of grain is separated and brought into a barn. . . ."

Well, and then the mother had become such a fine lady, that *she wore gloves* and went around with gold bangles on her arms and gold rings on her fingers. . . .

### GÁBOR NÉMET

In the tale of *Gábor Német* we find the concept in a completely different environment. The factory owner bequeathes his fortune, his stables and barns, and his money to the hero, the diligent worker. He shows him everything that one day will be his. The style is remarkable, rhythmical, and the sequences are closed by the refrain, "All this belongs to you."

First he took to the factory where he had worked. Then to the glass factory and on to the iron works, from there to the weaving plant, and so, one after the other. There were so many factories, it was frightening how many, it was nearly impossible to go through all of them.

"Look here, my son, all this is yours. Come along now, I want to show you the stock."

He showed him the stockpile of ready-made furniture. "Well, my son," he said, "this is all yours. Now you have to sell it and turn it into money."

Then he took him to the glass factory. There were loads of the finest glasses, jugs, glass plates, the best of the best! "Look here, my son, all this is yours!"

Then they went to the warehouse where the enameled pots and pans were kept and where cooking utensils were made. This warehouse was well stocked, too. "Look here, my son, all this is yours; you can sell it all."

Then he took him to the warehouse of the iron works. There were iron utensils, locks, moldings, God knows what, many different objects made of iron. "Look—all this is yours."

Then they went to a big hall where the finest luxury cars were lined up. "Look, my son, all this is yours."

Then he showed him where the railroad cars, the freight cars, were standing, to take the goods out of the factories. "Well, my son, this, too, is yours."

Then he took him to the dress shop warehouse, which was chock-full of ready-made dresses and men's suits, sewed and not yet sewed, so that one hardly could move around. "See, this too is yours. Here the workmen buy their clothes." And then he continued, "Now I have shown you everything, but I still want to show you the granaries."

They went into the stables. My goodness, what beautiful stables, with double stalls, all with double rows of troughs! And the troughs from which the horses were feeding had mirrored walls, bottoms, *everything was mirrors.* So heavy and well-fed were the horses they nearly died from laziness.

"My lord, why is it that the troughs are made of mirrors?"

The factory owner answered, "This is so the horses can see each other when feeding, then they eat more. They should see that another horse starts forward to feed, and they hurry over to eat themselves. They have more appetite this way and that's why these horses are so fat."

Then they went to the brood mares and there, too, the troughs were of mirror glass. Then on to the foals. "All this, my son, is yours!"

On to the *oxen and the calves, each one in separate stables.*
"Well, my son, all this is yours."

Three examples should suffice to show that, within a limited circle of possibilities, the narrators, even though they are bound by form, shape differently motifs which essentially coincide.[38]

At this point we must also discuss the extension of the tale, the question of the narrator's verbosity. The tale plot is an outline which harbors eventful incidents and details one event as it happens. Delivery traditionally permits the narrator only a formalized, threefold repetition. Where, then, can a narrative talent, while holding to the outline of the tale, best display itself? Only in the embroidering of detail.

As already pointed out in Chapter 5, in consideration of the fact that the mark of a literary work is the description of situations, the insertion of descriptive passages and characterization, the opinion has crystalized that the narrator who, through his own verbosity, deviates from his topic, spoils the *märchen*. On the contrary, we have become convinced that it is inflexible devotion to one version which spoils a tale. The creative and talented storyteller has no way of proving his talent other than through smaller or more considerable modifications. The situation is different for narrators who have specialized in realistic stories and anecdotes. Their public prefers to hear as many of the short and funny stories as possible. With these narrators the accent is not on the artistic shaping of the text but on dramatic performance and delivery of the punchline. Today, this type of storytelling is by far the most prevalent in Western Europe and the United States. In contrast to this, the good narrator of magic tales must prove his art within the framework of the tale by including his own thoughts and weaving his personal opinions into the tale. He not only adheres faithfully to the regular three-part construction, retaining the threefold repetition, but he is so skillful in his explanations, in paralleling the world of the tale to the world of reality, that he is able to extend the tale topic to twice or even three times its original length.

Does this extension enhance the tale? We have already mentioned Vinokurova and Kalin, who, at first glance, appear to tighten the tale rather than lengthen it.[39] But these narrators really do not tighten: while they tighten or contract the traditional frame, or theme, they lengthen and embroider in passages that are closest to their own experience.[40] Most of the excellent storytellers like to talk, and the attention which the audience offers them contributes to the utmost to the drawing out of the story. Many narrators are said to have stated that it depended only on them how long a tale was going to be. Mrs. Palkó related with considerable pride that she had told one tale from early afternoon until dawn of the next day. Our experience has led us to believe that the ability to tell a particularly long tale is a special gift, though those who reproach the narrators with verbosity are also often right. There are, of course, narrators who, through unnecessary verbosity, dissolve their tales and render them shapeless. This happens for the most part with the moralizing, hyperclever types. Among these is the laborer mentioned by Henssen who completely destroyed the form in his tale, which comprised eighty pages.[41] Another such tale can be found among those of Péter Pandur[42] and other more recently investigated Hungarian narrators such as L. Ámi and M. Ordódy, discovered, respectively, by S. Erdész and I. Dobos.

Mrs. Palkó's *märchen* in general are long, since she consciously strove for greater length; her feeling for form and her realistic art dictated this. The more she identified with the tale, the more she deepened the parts she most preferred. How far she could go in extending a tale is revealed in *I Don't Know*. She has extended the content, which comprised only a few pages in Elek Benedek's version, to forty printed pages, and it cannot be said with certainty how long it took her to accomplish this. This is the longest of her tales recorded by us, followed by *The Twelve Robbers* and *The Turk*. Her magic tales fill, on the average, twelve to fifteen pages; only the anecdotes are shorter, even though these, too, are relatively long. But this does not reveal very much about the true length of a *märchen*. Mrs. Palkó and informants have assured us that during a wake she had told the following tales from six o'clock in the afternoon until daybreak: *The Psalmsinging Bird, Anna Mónár, Prince Sándor, The Fawn*, and *The Sky-High Tree*.[43] Since tales we recorded did not take up this much time, we must conclude that they are not constant in length, but variable. The fact that a few tales, for example *The Flea Princess, The Strong János*, and *The Three Princes*, are quite concise may be attributed to unfavorable circumstances during their recital. We often could state, ourselves, that our informants had not exaggerated the extent of the long tales mentioned above, when we heard one and the same tale under different circumstances. Here a case is worth mentioning which did not take place in the usual village surroundings. When Mrs. Palkó had received the State Medal, she was fetched away from the buffet table at the House of Parliament by two reporters who asked her to tell one of her tales into the microphone. Though there was much going on in the hall, Mrs. Palkó began to tell the *märchen* of *Anna*

*Mónár.* In our notes the *märchen* takes up eight pages, but here, after an hour and a quarter, she had only told a quarter of the tale, and had to stop because the tape had run out. The reporter had not counted on a tale of such length. We can see therefore that the extent of the tale changes according to mood, to feelings, and to the opportunity for extending it with small details.

It also happens that a tale becomes uneven through this extension. *I Don't Know*, for instance, passes through four instead of three adventures, and the description of these four adventures is not symmetrical. When the narrator arrived at a detail she liked especially well, she made it more colorful. But this does not make her verbose. There is not a single moment which does not serve the form, the flow, the movement of the action, the increase of tension, the interest of the listener. This is why Mrs. Palkó's extensions, even though they increase the bulk of the tale, bring tradition essentially closer to the listener of today. We can only repeat that the realism of the storyteller is also apparent in this.

The episode of the mixed-up letters in the tale of the *Twelve Robbers* illustrates this point. The traditional tale motif is extended by Mrs. Palkó to a threefold exchange of the letters. On the whole she cites twelve letters, the real ones and the counterfeit ones, and never, thanks to the masterful and logical structure of her tale, makes a single mistake. To give an idea of this correspondence, here is one exchange of letters between mother and son, including both the real and the forged versions:

. . . "My dear son, be of good cheer, for joy has entered our castle. Such a great joy I cannot even tell it. You have a son beautiful as gold, and we can rather look upon the sun than upon him. Do not worry, your wife is fine; she is well cared for and does not have pains, doctors are with her; so don't worry and that the good Lord may bring you back home."

. . . "Well now you got it, my dear son," she wrote. "When you return home, you will really have a ball. Your wife has given birth, but she has brought two puppies into the world. Write what I should do with her. There is nothing but weeping and wailing in the castle. I have to remember how I beseeched you not to take her for your wife. What will become of you now when you come home and see all this?"

"Mother, you ask what you should do with her. I only tell you, what is born is born, and it is God's creature. Take care of her until I get home. Once home, we shall see what we can do. Until then do not do any harm either to the puppies or to my wife, but rather take good care that nothing happens to them!"

... "Dear Mother, order two soldiers to take the basket and take my wife back from where they had brought her, for I do not want her any more."

These letters are artfully built into the story. On every occasion Mrs. Palkó tells how the letter carrier is made drunk and describes the wiles of the tavern keeper's daughter and the despair of the old queen. The threefold mix-up of the letters is no senseless longwindedness; on the contrary, through it the tragic moment of the conflict is heightened and the fate of the unsuspecting innocent woman and the golden-haired child is sealed. Correspondence is a means of communication for Mrs. Palkó's heroes, although she is illiterate. The written word has magic for her. Characters in her tales frequently express their feelings in their letters, as cited above in the case of *Anna Mónár*. In *Fairy Ilona*, guided by the similarity of the situation, Mrs. Palkó includes letters almost identical to these of the *Twelve Robbers*.

We have so far touched only lightly on the question of Mrs. Palkó's manner of delivery. The listener was first attracted by her beautiful Szekler dialect and by her style. The style of her *märchen* was flexible and conformed completely to the nature of the tale itself. It was lyrical and poetic when the tale demanded it, hard and concise if necessary. It could also be tortuous, epic, dramatic, satirical, or full of humor. The examples cited bear testimony to her great richness of expression and fine stylistic sense. We shall mention such outstanding features in the comments on the tales, here we wish to speak exclusively of her manner of delivery.

Mrs. Palkó's strength is not in a dramatic performance of the tales. She was far removed from Chicherov second type, whose main virtue is not the working out of the text but the art of vivacious reproduction. Mrs. Palkó's talent is, in the main, epic; and the narration is the important thing for her. She used few gestures or movements of her body. Her delivery could be called dramatic only insofar as she lived with the story as it went along, making reflex gestures in her identification with the hero. It was only with her anecdotes that her gestures became more vivacious, though even there she usually was under the influence of the story herself.

As we have stated, the interruptions and calls from the audience are a part of the act of storytelling. Mrs. Palkó explained unknown concepts without the questions being called out to her. She often asked us, while telling a story, "Do you know what this is? This is the way the Szeklers say it." "In former times even the poor herdsman could become a rich king."[44] Beyond these outward explanations—informing the ignorant listeners—she let her heroes explain what she wanted to say. This is one of the most important methods of achieving credibility and realization. The passage in which *I Don't Know* is initiated into the secrets of the royal kitchen demonstrates this.

> . . . The king had the chief cook called in and said to her, "Look at this child. I entrust him to you, he shall be on hand to help you. . . . Take him first into the larder and show him everything; tell him, in this chest is this and in the other that; in this sack there is wheat flour, in the other rice; here are the dried prunes, here the figs and Heaven knows what else; here are almonds, there oranges, and much more of everything."
>
> She showed him everything, "See here, my son, something is here and another thing there." On every sack there was a label and all you had to do to know what was in it was to read the label. . . .

Or, in another place:

> "Little I Don't Know, would you permit me to go to church? I never have time for it. . . . You don't have anything to do but watch the fire. The soup is on the stove . . . I have sieved it and put every-thing in it which belongs into it, only a little salt is still missing. Half an hour after I leave put the salt in . . . a tablespoon full, just enough that the soup continues to simmer with the salt. . . . But you must watch carefully; the fire must not burn too well, the soup must only simmer with a small fire under it, then it gets fatter. . . . Put one or two sticks of kindling on the fire, so that the soup only simmers. . . ."

Mrs. Palkó's explanations were not as explicit as those of Péter Pandur. When the magic horse recounts all the difficult tasks the hero has to solve, he takes care to repeat minutely the exact hours, minutes, and seconds.[45] It is characteristic of Mrs. Palkó's anecdotes that she dished out moral teachings for her listeners as well as advice and instruction for the hero. Thus she admonished to the village community to behave cor-rectly. In the tale *The Uncouth Maiden*, the mother teaches the daughter as follows:

> "Well, now, Mother, I have come so that you can tell me, that you teach me how to talk to a fellow."

"Well, now, my girl, if he comes, if he enters, receive him just as we do. Give him a chair, please sit down, I know you are tired. Then sit down next to him," she says, "ask him how he came to this village. Well, now here you want to woo a girl, or maybe you already had a sweetheart? Keep your voices down so we don't hear you, we old ones, so the young man need not be ashamed. Do, my girl, this is the way you must talk to a fellow. Then, when he goes out the door, look after him and follow him. If you want him to come back to you, you must say, 'If you want to come with good intentions, come; if you want to come only for show and then leave me, don't come.' So—this is the way you must talk," she said. "If he wants to kiss you, kiss him back, show him that you love him. This is the way you must talk with a fellow."

Mrs. Palkó usually has the events told; that is, she herself does not tell them but describes them through the mouth of her heroes, through dialogue. The framework of the events is always epic; she never digressed from this framework, and all her dramatis personnae spoke within it. The extent of the dialogues depended on the kind of tale. In the magic and adventure tales the narration formed the main part of the story; dialogues animated the jokes. The relationship between dialogue and the narrative sections appeared in the short passage from the tale of *The Turk:*

### THE TURK

On the way home the hero meets with two riders.

"What is your hurry? Why are you pushing these poor animals; don't you see how hot it is?"

"We were in a hurry, we saw you, that we can meet you."

"But when they talked this Turk noticed that they were not native Turks, for their tongues always stumbled over the Turkish words. But he knew Turkish as well as if he had been born a Turk. He said:

"Who are you, where do you come from?"

"Well," so they said, "we come from this and this city."

"Well, what is your nationality?"

"We are Hungarians. We have served for ten years, now we are on our way home."

"Well," he said, "so you are Hungarians?"

"Yes."

"Well, I too am Hungarian. Where do you come from?"

"From Hungary," they said.

"Well, I too come from Hungary."[46]

"Well, then, let the three of us walk together."

Well, then the two were happy that they had found a comrade. They saw that he was a well-built man, a strong man. They let their horses canter, rode in one row side by side and talked with each other. Once one of the comrades said, "Comrade, it would be good to look for some shelter, so that we are not underway during the night."

"I think so too," the Turk said; "I think so too," said the other. "I think we should rest and also rest the horses for the night."

From afar they saw that they were nearing a city. So the Turk said, "Do you see the city? There we shall ask for shelter for the night."

Then they ranged the horses one after the other, fell into a trot, and reached the city before sunset. So they went to the very first house and stopped. They tied the horses to the post and all three of them went in. Then they saw that there was a young woman who was working at the stove. They said, "Good evening." The young woman greeted them. Well, then the Turk asked her, "Do you have a husband?"

"Yes."

"Where is he?"

"In the forest, but he will soon be home," she said. "What do you want?"

So he said, "We would like a shelter for the night, for three horses and three men. Can you take us in?"

Then the young woman said, "You are welcome to come in. I shall give you a good dinner, a good bed, you can rest here until morning. For the horses we have a good stable."

"But your husband is not at home," the third of them said. "Will he not be mad if you take us in?"

"Oh no, he won't be mad," she said. "We are of the same opinion."

"Well," the two men said, "let us stay here."

Said the third, "Let us go on, where the master of the house is at home."

Said the two men, "Why, then? She likes to take us in, she gives us a good dinner, a bed, what else do we need?"

"Listen," the third man said, "if you want to stay, so stay—but I won't stay here."

"Why then? You see she takes us in of her own free will."

"But," he said, "I won't stay."

Then he got up, wished them a good night, and went away.

The relationship between the narrative passages and the dialogue is similar in the magic tales in which the hero and his counselor are at the center of the events. Here the advice and the description of the hero's execution of it are in full accord with each other.

Very often Mrs. Palkó did not even need the commentary of the third person, for the happenings were so eventful that the dialogue of the heroes was sufficient. The more exciting, the more dramatic an event, the less need there is for explanations. In the tale of *The Twelve Robbers*, for instance, one of the fellows meets his little sister, of whose existence he was ignorant, and learns of the relationship only through the dialogue.

"Where do you go, little girl?"
"I go to see my brothers," said the little girl.
"And where are your brothers?"
"In the forest."
"What are they doing there?"
"They are felling trees."
"And to whom do you belong?"
"To father and mother."
"And what is the name of your little mother?"
"Mother."
"And of your father?"
"Father."
He could not get any more out of her, nor could the little girl tell her name.
"Listen," said the young man, "who told you that you had brothers in the forest?"
"Yes, I have brothers, twelve of them."
"From whom did you learn this?"
"From my mother. My mother said that the little brothers sent money, and the little dog brought it, and so I am going with the little dog to see my brothers."

In the same way, an explanation is unnecessary when the *Turk* reveals his identity. This scene forms the climax of the tale. Noteworthy here is the realism, for the dialogue also delineates the woman's character. The storyteller has psychologically structured her dialogue and thus makes the encounter especially exciting:

. . . The woman stepped aside, she was ashamed. Then the stranger said, "Why do you step aside?"
"For me it is all right here."

"I heard you are a widow?"

"Sure, since twenty years."

"What did your husband die of, what illness?"

"The wolves devoured him."

"That should be true? Maybe it is not true. Who saw it?"

"It is true," said the woman.

"And if I should say that your husband is alive?"

The woman started to laugh out loud. "Well, my husband was swallowed by the earth, his body is nothing but dust."

"But if your husband were alive, what would you say? I am telling you that he did not die."

She said, "Oh, I don't believe it. Nobody can make me believe this. I have the death certificate. My man should be alive?"

Then he said, "Did he have any marks, your husband?"

Then she said, "He had one."

"What was it?"

"A mole below the left arm."

Then the man opened his shirt and showed it to her. "Such a one?"

"Just such a mole had my husband."

"Well, woman, be convinced that I am your husband, we have both pronounced the vows before the altar, we were married together. It was a mistake that the wolves devoured me, for they have not torn me apart. . . ."

The anecdotes are different, in that the accompanying text forms merely the inessential framework. The essential parts are to be found in the dialogues, which describe situations as well as events. Here Mrs. Palkó used dialogues in quick succession, as for example in *Katyika and Matyika*, where we find continuous dialogues. We quote here in part:

. . . "Who put the many pots into the garden?"

"I, Matyika, I."

"Where did you get the many pots?"

"I bought them."

"What did you pay for them?"

"Golden money!"

"I told you not to touch that!"

"I have not touched it, not I. It was the potter who dug out the money."

"How did the potter know what there was? You must have shown him."

"Well, I did not only buy pots, but also pans and plates."

"I told you not to say anything. What shall I do now? What shall we live off in our old age?"

"But you did not say so! You should have told me before, then I would not have done it, would not have bought pots!"

"But I told you that you must not touch the money, for we must put it away, so we have something when we get old."

"Well, if you had told me before I would not have done it. Matyika, I tell you, let's go after him, somewhere we shall catch up with him and take back our money. . . ."

*The Wager of the two Godfathers* is an anecdote which seems like a stage comedy. This anecdote, too, is couched in dialogue from beginning to end. The persons in it are the traditional comedy characters who present a true comedy even without the active dramatic presentation of the storyteller. The classical comedy types, such as the man who feigns death to test his wife and the mourning wife who is already looking for new adventures, render the style of the storyteller dramatic right from the start. The accompanying prose text is so short that it might be considered as stage directions.

The woman ran home. There her husband was on his back in bed, his eyes closed. The woman rushed to the bed.

"My darling, dear husband, open your eyes, your comrade is coming." The man did not answer. "What's the matter with you? You have not passed away, have you?" the woman wailed.

The man did not open his eyes, of course. She tried his chest with her hand, but he did not breathe.

"Oh, my, oh my God, my husband died." She cried as if her heart was breaking.

"Why did you send me away? Now I did not see you die!"

With this the comrade came through the door.

"Good God, please open your eyes, speak to your buddy. He liked you so much and now you won't speak to him?"

The man stepped over to the bed. "What's the matter with you, buddy? Say something to me. You sent for me and here I am."

The man did not say a word. Then his comrade picked up his hand, felt his pulse, and made a sad gesture.

"What is it, neighbor? Is he dead, maybe?"

"Yes, my dear, he will never again speak to us."

Then the woman threw herself over her husband, wept desperately, and tried to awaken him, but all in vain.

The comrade then said, "Listen, neighbor, don't cry so much, it won't bring him back. Once dead, always dead. You better give me the razor so I can shave him, and put on some water for his bath, for I must bathe him."

But the woman cried and cried and did not want to leave her husband's side. What was to become of her? How could he leave her alone when they had enough to live, enough work? Why did he choose such a strange house where I cannot get in? So she went on wailing so that it resounded all through the house.

We have tried to show that Mrs. Palkó was an extraordinarily gifted storyteller, that she took her material from the traditional tale body, that she did not deviate from the linguistic, stylistic, and formal convention of the Hungarian folktale but filled it with new life. Although we have quoted only a few examples to point out the characteristics of her art and indicate her great talent, each and every one of her *märchen* are worthy of special treatment.

# 10

# Görgy Andrásfalvi,
# Mrs. Anna Sebestyén,
# and Márton László

## György Andrásfalvi[1]

WE HAVE ALREADY MADE THE ACQUAINTANCE OF THE SECOND outstanding storyteller of Kakasd, for we have founded our statements about the function of the folktale in Kakasd to a great extent upon his opinion and his remarks. Andrásfalvi has given detailed explanations of the tale occasions and the customs of storytelling. We have repeatedly quoted his opinions about the social and economic conditions and about the historic tradition in old Andrásfalva and in Kakasd. All this shows that Andrásfalvi is a many-sided personality who knows many things and is an ideal informer for the folklorist. Not only could this small and deformed hunchback give information about the spiritual treasure of the village and about the social conditions, he could also furnish exact information on all questions of material culture. He even took up a pencil and illustrated what he was explaining. His disposition, the family heritage, the social conditions, and his deformity all contributed to form his personality, and all this had its part in the formation of a storyteller's profile.

We know that he inherited from his grandfather the inclination to tell tales, and that he was indebted to his father for his love for books, his thirst for knowledge and education. He lost his father when barely fifteen years old, and being the youngest of the family, he stayed with his widowed mother while his sisters and brothers married and went away. In his weak body was lodged a strong will and he took extraordinary pains to prove that he was anybody's equal. In addition to seasonal labor in the Moldavia region, he tried a variety of other occupations: he planted onions and cabbage, fed the pigs, went out for daily labor, worked as a handyman, caught fish, wove baskets. There is no work he would not accept in order to butter his dry bread.

He tried to balance the disadvantages of his weak body by becoming a jack-of-all-trades. He was not able to become a soldier or found a family like the others, and thus he looked for something that might compensate. Thus he came to books and found consolation in reading. He read everything that came under his eyes, as we have mentioned. His interest in history was especially great; he preferred historical novels and books on Szekler history. He also followed political events with great attention, reading the news with great interest, and he liked to talk politics at friendly gatherings. He had already become accustomed to his bodily deficiency when an unexpected event changed the course of his life. Late in life, at the age of forty, coincidence brought him together with his contemporary, Erzsi Mátyás (Matyi). Erzsi had likewise not been very lucky in life; though she came from a powerful family, she had stayed single because of her eye ailment, had not inherited anything, and made her living sewing and spinning for hourly wages, repairing stoves, folding shirts and skirts, and accepting any kind of occasional work. When Andrásfalvi and Erzsi got together, they owned only one and a half acres of land; later, in Kakasd, they received nine acres because they had two children. We have already mentioned that Andrásfalvi and his wife were bitter because the influential and respected kin people did not help them in resettling and had not defended them. As a result, Andrásfalvi's house was not what he would have liked to have. They had hoped to be able to start a life in the new home which would compensate them for the demeaning past. Even though Andrásfalvi would have expected more from society, his reputation had been steadily growing since resettlement. When we knew him, he was no longer the miserable churl from the poor part of town; his word carried weight. He was well liked in company and meetings, and he himself liked to be among people. It was difficult to find an evening on which he was at home. He not only visited the neighbors, he met respected people and discussed with them politics and other questions of importance to the village. His thinking was clear and logical, and even if he recognized the backward, religious-magic belief world of the Bucovina, he experienced his life more consciously than Mrs. Palkó. Being a man, he was influenced by other experiences and his thinking was more rational. His knowledge of literature and his historical consciousness delimited his tale treasure, which is founded upon traditional material.

In a way, on the basis of his texts, we may count Andrásfalvi among those "legend tellers," discussed in Chapter 1, who consciously upheld historical tradition. Watching him tell an episode out of the history of Hungary, it was easy to observe how a legend is born. In his texts we find the simple account of the event, the simple relation of the event, containing one or two incidents, but also the completely polished text of the legend. At a gathering after a meeting of the ministers of foreign affairs in Berlin, he not only repeated literally the broadcast speeches but evaluated them and judged the problems of the divided Germany according to his sound instincts. It was most astonishing to see that he presented reality in poetic form, including in it his own observations, within his own horizon, just as he introduced his historical knowledge into his legends. Andrásfalvi lived the history of the Szekler, and through it he lived politics which protect the rights of the poor. Whatever he learned through listening or reading, the new and the old, were expressed by him and formed according to his opinions. In spite of his relative youth, Andrásfalvi, the legend teller, had a place among the old and respected men. As a teller of legends he exhibited a different attitude from that of the storyteller; his texts tried to be realistic and he treated them differently than a *märchen*. At the same time, Andrásfalvi might be counted among the reading storytellers. In Chapter 7 we spoke about his reading material and also about his activity in a reading to others. His tale material as well as the recitals in company and in the houses at wakes doubtless strengthened respect for him. He does not belong to those who lecture on morals based on religious literature: he himself liked to read religious texts, but he did not use them. He rather employs history or novel-like narratives.

One cannot say that Andrásfalvi was not religiously inclined: this would hardly be possible in the Kakasd atmosphere; yet religious reading material was only of secondary importance to him and had only an outward influence. Andrásfalvi kept his obligations to the church in the same way. He went to church because it was customary, but his wife could get him to do no more. He went to wakes only "to tell stories; he does not pray, he cracks jokes." We do not want to draw any further conclusions from the fact that twice in his tales the priest is treated in an anti-clerical way, but in this matter he is unique among the Kakasd storytellers.[2] This we can state, however; Andrásfalvi's thinking is sober and rational, and sometimes—perhaps unconsciously—he found himself in disagreement with the usual thinking at Kakasd.

The same can be said about his attitude toward folk belief, though he knew a great many belief stories which had "happened" to him or to other reputable men.[3] Though he himself had seen the incubus, the malevolent demon in the shape of the beautiful woman, and the revenant, though he believed in healing through magic formulae, he still mentions many occasions on which the revenant turned out to be a shadow, or a bull turned loose. In the *Fisherman's Adventure* he describes expertly how he set out one evening to catch fish. He claims never to have felt fear and, in contrast to others, that he never encountered the horrible apparitions except on one occasion, and that he relates. The fact that he scarcely believes in ghosts, or would not believe in them if he had this experience today, becomes clear from the explanation which he adds to the story: the "ghost" that had scared him turned out to be his own dog![4]

The ghost story set during the nightly catching of fish seems to coincide with Mrs. Palkó's story No. 14. The story comes from Mrs. Palkó's father, and in order to make it more believable, Andrásfalvi "adapted" it as his own experience. While Mrs. Palkó deepened the magic atmosphere of the story, Andrásfalvi simplified it as a story which he certainly heard as an experience of his grandfather, and gave it a background of reality.

Characteristic in this respect is the passage from the story *The Twin Rods*, mentioned in Chapter 7, in which woman turns to the witch for advice. When we add that the woman only dares to visit the witch behind her husband's back, that is, while he is at church with the children, and that the results of the complicated witching procedure are successful, it is not difficult to recognize Andrásfalvi's religious belief. He himself was not caught in the naive folk belief inherited from his forebears; he, on the other hand, strove to come to a clear understanding through his sober and simple thinking processes. Yet his non-religious reading materials did not tend to destroy the magic belief world, for he himself never went so far as to doubt traditional belief: he was governed only by his feeling for reality, and his fancy remained close to reality. The fanciful, novel-like narratives, the romantic pieces, and the chapbooks penetrate in part his narrative material and, insofar as their nature permits, his *märchen*.

Andrásfalvi, therefore, was a teller of *märchen*, of legends, and was considered a well-read man in Kakasd society. But how is one to characterize him as a narrator?

We know that he, as well as Mrs. Palkó, was always welcome at wakes. Since he was more mobile, he appeared more often than Mrs. Palkó did. As he admitted himself, he had not been telling tales for a very long time, the older narrators from whom he had learned were until recently still living, and as a result he had few occasions to tell stories. In addition, he was not old enough for a storyteller. "When I began to get older and began not to be so much ashamed, I began to tell *märchen*" —these are his own words.

When we survey the tale material of György Andrásfalvi before us, we first note its inconsistency. We see voluminous *märchen*, carefully formed, which can easily compare with the best pieces of Mrs. Palkó. Beside these we see moralizing texts which clearly deviate from the style of the *märchen*, and insignificant texts reduced to a mere list of contents. Of his seventeen pieces (not counting the historical tales and belief stories), eleven texts are complete, the rest only fragments. Of many tales he himself said that he once knew them but in the meantime had forgotten them. At wakes, and in company, he continued to tell his most beautiful tales (Appendix, Nos. 64, 65, and 66); the weaker ones no longer belonged to his repertoire, and he would narrate them only when urged by the collector. To these, in addition to the unpublished fragments, belong Nos. 67, 70, and 72, which show clear traces of forgetfulness. This makes us wonder why a narrator who showed brilliance in his Nos. 64, 65, and 66 had such a bad memory and why his repertoire was so small.

Andrásfalvi's *märchen* come from his home environment, and his sources were the same as Mrs. Palkó's were. In most cases, however, he no longer clearly recollected from whom he had learned his tales, with the exception of *Ilona Beautiful*, which he traced back to his grandfather, and *The Discharged Soldier*, which he had heard from János Zaicz. The villagers thought that *The Nine Kernels of Grain*, *The Beautiful János*, and *The Twin Rods* also came from the two Zaicz narrators. Márton László's influence consisted in giving him books to read, which explains why the narratives from *Poncianus* are not second hand but come directly from the reading matter. It would therefore be wrong to suppose that he forgot the older narratives and remembered only the more recent ones.

When we talked about the storytelling in Andrásfalva, we mentioned that Andrásfalvi participated in male storytelling sessions—at the shoe-maker's for instance, or in the tavern—and that he listened to the spinning women at his mother's invitation. He entered the company of the village spinning rooms only after he was married. His first appearance as a storyteller probably took place on a male storytelling occasion: one person said something, another added something, and they recalled tales to each other's memories. His narrative talent soon became apparent, and it was he who was preferred by the listeners. He himself spoke about the old storytelling occasions and what he used to know, and how these themes had taken shape in his memory, when it was his turn to tell a story.

> If someone is present who would listen until morning—like Gergely at the moment—the tales flow from my mouth when somebody pays attention. I have to leave out much because there is so much to write. It will take another two hours. I have told it at the shoe-maker's, in the tavern; they said, "Well, another one, it is only ten o'clock." Well, so I started again. Well, then, they fetched a bushel of apples from the ground, and what I could not finish I ended on the next day. And so it went.

This statement indicates that Andrásfalvi's tales depended greatly on his listeners' attention; they become longer or shorter according to how the listeners' wishes. It was his conviction that the greatest gift of the storyteller is the ability to lengthen his tales at will. According to Andrásfalvi, real storytelling took place at home in the Bucovina; today its possibilities are considerably more restricted. He renders his opinion several times in the course of his tale *The Beautiful János:* "You know, if I could tell this in the Bucovina manner, one can still load more, so it can be well rounded out." One has to encourage him and talk to him, and he will remember his *märchen,* as the following shows.

> A year ago we went to see the László Kovács family. The story-telling then goes this way: if I can do it and tell one, then he tells another and then I pay attention to his tale and remember much myself, then I give such a piece that somebody else cannot tell. One had to reflect, and then I could add something. One can stick to this.

Andrásfalvi put the blame for his forgetfulness on the scarcity of storytelling occasions. He considered the wakes the most adaptable places for storytelling. He cited titles of tales for the wakes which he could no longer recite because he could not remember them any more.

I know many tales, but they are recalled only with difficulty.
I have to ponder *The Golden Wand* and *The Golden Apple*. If I
reflect I shall remember them. A princess had three marks, and yet
there was somebody who found her out. There was a musician—it
[the tale] is very funny. There is another; the king had three sons,
and one of his eyes laughed and the other wept. I knew another:
there was a man changed into a duck and he came to a fish pond,
and the mother wanted to catch it and drank the whole fish pond.
But I do not recall it. And the nicky thaler [lucky penny], that
was a nice one too, but when was this? When did I tell this tale?
Then we did not have so many worries. . . . It takes only a little
while until one starts one, then the tales are coming. If I could
only succeed in telling *Péter Szápári;* it is such a long time since
I last told this tale. Then there is also the *Discharged Soldier*, a
nice tale. But for this you must drink two glasses of wine—for this
is a little funny [i.e., obscene]—so that I am not ashamed. They are
laughing about this the same way at wakes. This too, is nice: the
*Twin Rod*, a couple in poor conditions; that is the beginning.

First we believed that Andrásfalvi might have been able to tell all
these tales in an atmosphere similar to the wake, and that the presence
of the collector upset him. But this assumption was wrong. With our
prodding he reflected on the tales cited—only three of them are part of
his repertoire—and tried to piece them together, but he did not succeed.
We often had occasion to hear him tell stories at wakes and elsewhere,
but even there he always chose one of the same stories: *The Discharged
Soldier, The Twin Rod, Ilona Beautiful,* or *The Nine Kernels of Grain*.
From conversation with other people present we found that he preferred
to tell these stories.

We thus have to content ourselves with the fact that Andrásfalvi was
a very popular storyteller whom people liked to hear, in spite of the
small quantity of his standard material. We also have to add that he was
popular not only for his marvelous *märchen*, but—as we mentioned before—because he was a well-read man who was able to hold the listeners'
attention with historical, novel-like stories as well. This did not preclude
the possibility that later on, under the influence of a storytelling community or under some other unforeseeable circumstance, he might be
able to fashion *märchen* which at the moment escaped his memory. He
tried everything to satisfy the collector; he was full of good will, for as
a well-read man he recognized the aims of the folklore collector to the
fullest. We had to explain thoroughly to him how the collected material
was to be evaluated, and he showed great readiness to do his part to

insure our success. It is due to his efforts that weak, lifeless pieces were also recorded, even though it was not our aim to increase the stock of these.

The *märchen* which formed Andrásfalvi's constant repertoire are voluminous and well constructed. The shorthand notes of the *märchen*, *The Twin Rod*, ran to thirty typed pages; the tape recordings of *Ilona Beautiful* and *The Nine Kernels of Grain* correspond to between twenty-two and twenty-six typewritten pages. The fourth magic tale, *The Poor Blind Beggarman*, is only a fragment and rather uncouth, even though it shows traces of individual formation. However, the tale of *The Discharged Soldier*, which is like a novella in style, is quite different, for here we are dealing with a city craftsman's *märchen*. The two *Poncianus* novellas and No. 70, which also have a classical origin, show a very definite peculiarity of style and clear adherence to reading matter. His only true individual anecdote is No. 71, where he uses the accents of a sharp village satire. Even though Andrásfalvi's narrative repertoire is not very extensive, even though part of his texts are only fragmentary, and even though traces of foreign influences are discernible, his narrative talents are worthy of recognition.

There are more innovations in the *märchen* construction and the linking of motifs in Andrásfalvi than in Mrs. Palkó. The construction of his most beautiful and harmonious *märchen*, *The Twin Rod*, may be termed felicitous and absolutely individual. It is worth considerable discussion. It can be assumed for certain that Andrásfalvi received only a sketch of the material, and that he then proceeded to introduce, after his own taste, episodes and even completely fashioned motif units from other tales. Andrásfalvi here has combined the elements of five tales which have a close affinity to each other, by ordering their sequence individually, and has enlarged his tale beyond these by adding new incidents of his own.

The composition of this *märchen* is completely individual and deviates strikingly from the usual linking of motifs. Though the *Twin Brothers* type forms the tale framework, a new form emerges in which a series of tale motifs is blended. The episode of service of the witch (AT 556F*)—often linked to type AT 552 (554/B*)—is the only one which remains whole and rounded out, because our narrator likes it very much. In the *märchen* where this episode originally belonged, in the Hungarian oicotype of *Ilona Beautiful*, it is executed according to his best knowledge, and is here by necessity transformed. The three good deeds are left out, and since the precondition for them is also dropped, the hero makes helpers out of the animals by accidentally touching their magical body parts. Andrásfalvi's sense of proportion is also shown in the fact that he omits the Grateful Animals at the dragon slaying, as well as the impostor. There is no need for them here, since the hero accepted service with the witch in order to prepare himself for this adventure. He already possesses a magic sword and a magic horse; he has ability of his own and does not need others' help to acquire a reputation. In order to emphasize the superiority of the tale hero, Andrásfalvi includes here the motif of the simpleton-hero (AT 314A) instead of following the course of AT 303 (*The Twins* or *The Blood Brothers*), to which the general plot of his tale belongs. The youth keeps his heroic attire deposited with an old woman and, in turn, he does menial work at the court of the king as a baker's apprentice. This contrasting behavior of the hero follows logically his initial characterization as the foundling who left home for adventure and acquired a magic horse and sword for his stepbrother as well. It also enhances the virtues of the central hero, better illuminating the superiority of the poor boy. Up to this point there is no break in the course of the young man's adventures, no conflict; this will come only with the appearance of the second youth (the brother). Such composition bears witness not only to Andrásfalvi's clearly expressed sense of tale construction, it reveals his vast knowledge of motifs. He is at home in the world of the *märchen* and he uses it according to his own taste.

Andrásfalvi also handles well the traditional formulae, and the most consequential tale in this regard is *Ilona Beautiful*. We find introductory and final formulae more frequently with this narrator than we do with Mrs. Palkó. (See, for instance, No. 68, *The Discharged Soldier;* No. 70, *The Beautiful János;* and No. 66, *Ilona Beautiful*.) Considered closely, the tale of *The Nine Kernels of Grain* (No. 65) is not quite as finished in form: the missing parts—obviously forgotten by the narrator—are often replaced by clever innovations. We can also find structural changes in the tale of *The Poor Blind Beggarman* (No. 67). Just as with Mrs. Palkó, we find most of the changes and embroidering in Andrásfalvi in those parts of his tales which describe reality.

Realism is one of the most characteristic features of Andrásfalvi's narrative art, as it was with Mrs. Palkó's. But his realism is of a different quality; it is conscious, and the narrator takes a position vis-à-vis the tale world. While Mrs. Palkó subjectively lived what she narrated during her storytelling, we sense the distinction between the atmosphere of Andrásfalvi's tale world and the real world. His most beautiful tale also starts from everyday life in the village, where the description of reality is consciously elaborated. When the hero enters the world of the *märchen*, which is governed by a different kind of law, the narrator continues to describe the world as viewed by village people only to point out possibilities of reality in the world of the *märchen*. To show how this is done we shall quote the description of reality in *The Twin Rod*.

The initial situation in the everyday life of the village and the slow transition to the world of the *märchen* is the same in Mrs. Palkó's stories, as we have seen, and most significantly so in her magic tales where the village milieu is essential and not merely a background or point of departure, as in *The Fawn* and *The Smoking Kalfaktor*. This is the way Andrásfalvi also fashions his *The Twin Rod*, and we can even say that here the dual world view so typical of the *märchen* is more apparent than usual. The action of the tale, or rather the wanderings of the hero, alternate between the two worlds of village reality and *märchen* reality. By an unusual and extraordinary event, the hero enters the magic world through a wood leading to the *märchen*-world and away from the familiar environment. The two run parallel, and the hero even comes back to the reality of the peasant village from time to time, until the tale ends with the unification of the two worlds. It is an unusual mixture of the two.

The miracle that starts the *märchen* action happens during an ordinary, everyday occupation of people in Kakasd. A young couple is working outside in the fields; the little child is sleeping in the shade:

> Thus an hour and a quarter passed while she gathered hemp at her husband's side. Suddenly he stood up and said, "Woman, what are you doing? Where is the child?"
>
> "I nourished it," she said, "and then it fell asleep, and so I came to gather hemp in order to get it over with quicker."
>
> "Fine, fine woman, but all the time we paid no attention to the child, what it is doing. Well, no lizard should have crept into his nose or ears."
>
> The woman got up and hurried away; when she arrived she cried out in despair, "Man, man come quick!"
>
> "What happened? I told you something would happen to the child!"
>
> "Thank God, nothing bad has happened, but a miracle! I cannot recognize mine, for there are two infants!"
>
> Then the man joined her and both were astonished.

This still is not a *märchen* miracle, for the couple finds a solution that is fitting for ordinary village people:

"Well, woman, let the gathering of the hemp go; you take one infant and I take the other. The city hall is on our way home. Let us report there what happened."

This they did, and as said, they went to the city hall. The mayor was just about to go home, for soon the bell would sound for the noonday meal.

"Mr. Mayor, something strange has happened; stay another moment!"

"What's up, Pista?"

"What's happened to us! This morning we started to gather hemp. We worked steadily, and my wife deposited our gift from God along the border of the meadow, and when she went to look after it, she found two infants one next to the other. This is why I came. We had only one child and now there are two. We are reporting and if somebody should seek this one he can find his child right away and so we would like to leave it here, and the Mr. Mayor should do the rest."

"This is impossible, Pista my son. Should I worry about it? Nor is my wife nursing, what should I do with it? I have no time for coddling and cradling. Take it home and care for it until somebody claims it."

Even the following instance of the event leading up to the *märchen* still remains in the real world of the village. The couple brings up the two children, and year after year passes. The mother is haunted by the question of which one is her child and which the foundling. What can she do in order to find out but turn to the wise woman, who, as was pointed out in a preceding chapter, helps the people of Kakasd. The magic practice which Andrásfalvi first ascribes to the old woman and then—varying it further and increasing the tension—describes in detail, is as follows:

"Where are they now?"

"They went to church with their father."

"This is even better. Before they come home, you will look for a rod, a branch which has two twigs, a twin rod. The two sprouts have to be of equal length; what kind of rod is not important, but it must be a twin rod. You cut them off; you need not even clean them. You keep them behind your back, and before they come in you go out to meet them as far as the fifth or sixth house, and hide yourself behind a small door. When they approach wait until they are close; then come out and follow them without being observed, and hit the one as well as the other over the head with the twin rod, but quite strongly. They will be frightened and start to weep; they are just coming from church, they never hurt anybody, and they will be greatly offended. One of them, on coming home, will run into the shed and sit down on the cutting block; the other will hide in a corner of the room. Then take a pair of scissors and make a sign either on the one who is outside or the one who is inside. He who is inside is your own son, the one you have borne."

By such means Andrásfalvi heightens the tension of the story toward the climax. The next step again is very logical: the woman cannot keep the secret, and as the two brothers start quarreling, it comes to light. The injured one, the strange boy, goes out into the world. Up to this point the events follow each other the way a simple man would expect; it may happen this way; it might be true. What happens beyond this point in the *märchen* is the *märchen*. But the two worlds continue to exist side by side until the very end. This is borne out in the scene when Sándor comes home after his first heroic deed with his magic sword and horse to show them to the villagers—a scene which is extremely important to Andrásfalvi—in order to enjoy his fame. Here also he inserts the Life Token motif (E 761.1.3).

There is one more lively dramatic scene played in the village, in which the second brother is the hero.

One fine day there was communal digging in the neighborhood. The neighboring farmer had built a barn and asked his neighbors on the street on which he lived to come and carry earth. Miska too was asked. The men turned out in great numbers with their horses and wagons, and by evening they had carted a great deal of earth. The peasant for whom the earth moving was done also had a grown son, who went for the Gypsy band to play dance music in the barn. A barrel of wine was broken out and people drank and danced. But Miska did not dance; he only went there to look around. It was close by in the neighborhood, and from time to time he ran home to look at the hole, to see if blood was flowing from it. Finally, he saw a thick and rich stream of blood oozing from the hole. He said nothing to his parents, but ran into the closed livingroom, put on his valiant's outfit which Sándor had given him, girded himself with the sword, and went out and saddled his horse. Miska opened the gate and gave the horse its head—it would carry him to the right place.

After this the real home world turns up only in the final episode.

Andrásfalvi's dual outlook on the world becomes apparent in the description of the outward appearance of the hero in his adventure with the dragon. The hero behaves during his activity in the world of the tale just like a village boy; he checks in at the king's court in order to take up service.

Sándor dressed like a baker's apprentice and went away, reported at the king's court in the kitchen, with the head cook, asking if he could enter his service. There should certainly be much work when three daughters were to be married. The pots had to be washed, wood to be cut, water to be carried, and who knows what else? The kitchen master was glad to engage him. The cook had not said how much the wages for a day, a week, or month would be, but Sándor did not care; he was glad to get work. The first job he got was cutting wood. He was sent out to fetch dry wood, to hack it and cut it up for kindling. . . . In the meantime Sándor had finished cutting wood. He packed a bundle, put it on his arm, and went into the kitchen. Then they sent him out to get water, two buckets full, for something had to be washed out.

And it is the same hero who, when he is famous, hurries, dressed up in his valiant's attire, to the rescue of the maiden just about to be sacrificed to the dragon.

He went home to the old woman where his horse was. There he tore his baker's duds from his body and put on his fight gown, saddled his horse, and leading it by the reins, he slowly walked out on the flowery hill which was not very far from there, and sat down next to his horse. Suddenly he pricked up his ears, for accompanied by loud music and dirges, sound of trumpets and rolls of drums, there came the oldest daughter of the king, the bride. The girl's eyes were covered by a white handkerchief and the escorts who had led her so far, returned to the palace and left her alone. The cortège stopped on top of the hill of flowers. Then Sándor rose and, leading his horse by the rein, went to the princess, took the cloth from her eyes, and asked why she had been brought here.

"Brave knight, do you not see that I shall be married? I am wearing a veil on my head."

"To whom are you being wed?"

"To the dragon with twenty heads."

While the two were talking to each other, the horse began to neigh. Then Sándor shortened the strap below his belly and fastened it. Then he shook the girl's hand and sprang onto the saddle. . . . When the princess saw that the dragon had only two heads left, she threw the pleated skirt over her head in the manner of a peacock displaying his feathers, and ran back home to the palace. When the King saw her he nearly had a stroke. It had hardly been a quarter of an hour that one had led his daughter away . . . and here she was again.

"Oh, my daughter," the king said, "is your father's word not sacred to you? Do you want this land to be burnt down to the last wooden spoon?"

"But Father," the girl cried, "a strange knight has killed the dragon!"

"How do you know that?"

"I know because I talked to him—and then I watched as he cut off the dragon's heads one after the other."

"When did you leave him?"

"When the dragon had only two more heads left."

"Why did you not wait to the end to see if the hero was going to win, then I could have thanked him and asked him to appear at my court, to know who he is and where he comes from. You, however, left him standing like Paul did to the Walachs. This was not nice of you."

In this tale Andrásfalvi gives a good example of the conscious formulation of a double realism. In this duplicity of reality and imagined reality his art appears most clearly. The examples cited show that Andrásfalvi's realistic description does not result from his identification, as it does with Mrs. Palkó, but from an excellent gift of observation, from experience and knowledge of people. Empathy with the situation of the individuals can hardly be noticed. His recital, too, is much more objective; he does not stop the action to describe details and psychological situations. With Andrásfalvi everything flows on, and the colorful variety charms and holds the attention of the listeners.

Monsters and other superhuman beings of the tale world always behave like people in Andrásfalvi's descriptions. The giants in *The Nine Kernels of Grain* differ from the villagers only in size.

> Then he thought to himself; he is not afraid any more, at twenty paces' distance, for the man had wide trousers. . . . He sees that the man has a moustache just like the one his father sports or the Reverend. . . . He crept up on all fours and pulled the trouser seam with his hands, for he wore such a nice, billowing pair of Hungarian trousers. . . .

Even though the adoptive father of the hero is a giant and his wife is the daughter of a fairy, their life parallels the way of life of newlyweds in the village. The passage in which the fairy wife gets her clothes and flies back to fairyland is essentially a description of a dance in Andrásfalva:

> . . . Then the giant gave them money so that they could plan and did not have to stop under way but could go where the amusement

was. Where there are many lords, kings, princesses, in the cinema or the theater. So they left. They came to an enormously big city. There was a big dance, big amusement. They said it was such an entertainment, a contest. There was much money at stake, and there were a big crowd of people invited. Whose dance was most pleasing was acclaimed by applause, then he was embraced and brought to a table and the price which was established, was put into his saddlebags. So they too went there. Well, they were curious. Everybody turned around dancing: the king danced and the princesses, gentlemen and girls, young women. But nobody was applauded. When the young pair of giants, holding each other, was standing around looking, a fellow came up to them and bowed to the young woman. He turned to the young husband and asked him to be so good as to permit that they danced a Danube waltz together. To which the giant said, "I don't mind it if she likes to!"

So they went. Well, now the Danube waltz started and they danced it so beautifully like nobody else and whoever had a soft heart thought it would break. . . .

Even more striking, perhaps, are the human customs of the three dragon brothers-in-law in the tale of *Ilona Beautiful*. On her table, prepared for dinner, are a "good duck soup, boiled rice, and with it hashed meat of hare." "They eat and drink, they drink wine," while the dragon admits to the fellow that in his youth he had also fallen in love with the picture of the girl, the picture which caused the hero to fall into a deadly faint.

Believe me, my little brother-in-law, had I not eaten you up seven times and vomited you out seven times, you would now be asleep for all eternity. I also know why you fell asleep there. I too once fainted, but since I have a dragon's nature I could bear it. This girl has put you to sleep. Me too. Now you have just seen her life-size picture, but when you see her alive in all her vivacity, you will not only fall into a dead faint, but first dirty your finely pressed linen underpants. I was not lucky enough to make her my wife, and thus your sister became my wife who resembles this girl as to face and figure. But let us go, the soup is getting cold. At table I shall tell you more about her.

All these examples illuminate the realism in Andrásfalvi's tales, the arbitrary linking of reality and fantasy. We can see that his rational view of life never fades and that his cleverness and sobriety never leave him while he is telling stories. He never loses contact with the everyday world, and often, in order to inject life into the tale situation, he recalls memorable events which happened to living persons, or he refers to important events of the near past such as resettlement and arson at Kakasd. Thus he concludes a tale with the following words: ". . . And thus they founded a beautiful realm, in fairyland, as we have it in the Tolna county."

When we spoke about Kakasd society it became readily apparent that Andrásfalvi possessed a strongly developed sense of self-consciousness. We also know that he was politically active and took a clear and unequivocal stand. We do not meet with the subjective lamentation of the poor which we find so often in Mrs. Palkó, and not only because he told fewer tales in which the contrast between rich and poor occurred. Even though this conflict is evident, it is not stressed by Andrásfalvi. The aim of his tales is entertainment; the colorful, varying narration in the well-liked and frequently read chapbooks in his example. This literary influence prevents this excellent narrator from being as personal as a poor peasant who weaves himself into the tale. As we have said, Andrásfalvi does not himself live in the tales; while he remains to some degree rather impersonal, his sharp gifts of observation are apparent. When, by placing his tales in the village, he brings them closer to the listeners, he is acting not from inner experience but from observation.

In only one of his tales, *The Rich Peasant and His Wife* (No. 71), does Andrásfalvi sharply oppose the rich peasant and the poor neighbor. He shows the moral superiority and harmonious family life of the poor man and the decadent morals of the rich peasant woman. This realistically rendered tale does not follow the usual conventional description of a flighty woman that is common to jokes, but has a deeper foundation and is much more bitter; the events in old Andrásfalva lend it such reality as to break through the framework of the anecdote. On the one hand, it is a lively mirroring of the former conditions of life of the carters of Andrásfalva; on the other, it is a true mirroring of the social contrasts between poor and rich. The rich peasant takes his poor neighbor into service. When the two wagons are returning home after a long haul, the rich peasant goes to the tavern. It is raining and a driving wind is whipping around. The poor neighbor has to guard the horses while the rich peasant warms himself inside, eating and drinking. This is brought to the attention of a stranger who addresses the man who is shivering in the cold, and during the conversation the humiliating reason for his humble behavior comes to light: the poor man is dependent on the rich one, who pays the wages which assure the poor man a living.

"You both drove the wagon?"

"Yes," the man answered.

"Why don't you too have a drink then? Why don't you order a cup of good, hot tea?"

The man replied, "My master ordered me to watch the wagon outside."

"You stick faithfully with your master?"

"Yes, sure, because I am a poor man and I get my daily wages for diligence and faithfulness."

"And did you keep faith?"

"Yes, I sure did!"

"And your master won't offer you even a cup of tea?"

"No," the other said, "so far he has never done so."

Still, the poor man is the positive hero of this story; even though he lives under hard conditions he is morally superior; he reveals the unsavory facts of the rich peasant's family life. The confirmation of the wife's unfaithfulness and her punishment form the actual content of the tale, but we cannot laugh about it as we are accustomed to doing, with jokes of this kind. The tale does not contain any situational fun but a rottenness which causes bad feelings. The end is formed by an idyllic situation: the even-tempered, clean family life of the poor man.

This tale is domiciled in the old Szekler world, but Andrásfalvi judges and presents it from the modern viewpoint; the simple anecdote has become a social satire with deep-felt meaning.

Andrásfalvi's speech, both in conversation and during narration, was less archaic than Mrs. Palkó's. There are some inconsistencies within the dialect, for he, in contrast to general usage in Kakasd, uses a great many erudite words. This unusual mode of expression may be traced to his reading material, for it can be found principally in the pieces which were originated by the classic novellas: *The Beautiful János*, *The Faithful Widow*, and *The Young Shrew*. The stage for these texts is a foreign world, and the expressions as they occur are organic parts of the narrative. They remain with the texts of the literary stories and they do not enter the word treasure of Andrásfalvi, for the narrator does not use them in other tales. In a scene in the office of the Beautiful János he says, for example, . . . "he kept a Negro as a house servant, who tidied up his office"; "I propose to you"; "I have such a taste for roast hare"; "he should have it put into the newspapers that he wants to marry." Andrásfalvi's travels outside the village during the last fifteen years and his experiences had made a use of this kind of expression possible. Richest in this regard is probably *The Discharged Soldier,* in which the city atmosphere is only natural. In addition to the family of the king, the discharged soldier, the tavern keeper, and the "piano-building master" play a part. The hero is entertained in the tavern "of the Lion"; in a "separate cell," he asks "a million crowns" from the king; "the chambermaids go in to make the beds"; the hero "regulated it according to his wristwatch, for he had a wristwatch."

But in other tales, too, we find expressions which do not stem from the tale atmosphere. For example, the hero coming to a far land is asked, "What push did you have to come here?" (*Ilona Beautiful*). Sometimes the narrator is very choosey in his manner of expression. The tale figures do not speak, they "consult" each other (*Ilona Beautiful*). Yet we can say that this occurs only rarely. A much greater part is played by folk language comparison, as for example: "He was desperate like Mrs. Rákocsi's hen"; "he burst like Pista's frog"; "he left him standing like St. Paul did to the Walachs" (*The Twin Rod*), and others. If Andrásfalvi's language is not as rich as that of Mrs. Palkó, even if it shows numerous foreign expressions and unusual forms, it cannot be characterized as spoiled. That he is following the style tradition—and we have discussed this in the foregoing chapters—can be best judged by observing how the style of the pieces read develops toward the Szekler style, even if these texts could not penetrate in full the Kakasd tale tradition, when they disintegrate or when they slip into oblivion. The best example of this is Andrásfalvi's tale of *The Faithful Widow.* Though the story parallels its model feature by feature, it is an essential innovation in that it has been placed by the narrator in a village setting. In its original shape the peasant audience would have rejected it. However, in the modified form it was believed as an affair that could easily happen among the well-to-do peasantry, and it could even be believed that those people passed the time playing dominoes.

> A rich young peasant had taken for his wife a suitable peasant girl. For two years they lived together blissfully. They loved each other so much it is hard to describe. So, on a Christmas Eve, he said, so that they should not pass the evening in boredom, "Let us take out the dominoes; we can pass the time with them." "Good man." The husband liked the game very much, and they started to play. Whoever could not pair up the stones—whatever eyes remained on the stones—he received that many blows on the hand. It had just happened to the wife to remain the last one and she could not put the stones together in pairs. The husband had a stick

in his hand and with it he struck his wife on the palms of her hands. But since they loved each other very much, his blows were very light and tender. But the husband also had a penknife in his hand which he had seized together with the little stick, and as he dealt out the six blows, he scratched the tip of her little finger with the knife so that a little drop of blood appeared. When the husband saw this he fainted away. . . .

The representation so far shows that Andrásfalvi's recital is quite varied. In his most beautiful tales he speaks colorfully and vivaciously. He uses description for the presentation of situations, but less often than did Mrs. Palkó. In the tale of *Ilona Beautiful*, the dragon becomes nervous when he senses danger; he does not like the wine any more, and the cigarettes do not taste good. His unrest affects the listener, who knows something is about to happen. The wanderings of the hero across the forest in *The Nine Kernels of Grain* is similarly described. The listener is thus psychologically prepared for coming events. But more often the narrator presents the turbulent events by means of dialogue; he makes his heroes speak. The most carefully worked out dialogues are to be found in the witch episodes in *The Twin Rod* and *Ilona Beautiful*, as well as the fairyland scene in the tale of *The Nine Kernels of Grain*, where the three girls are expecting the arrival of the hero and three times put him to the test. Not only are the dialogues in these scenes of artistic beauty, free from superfluous bombast they are also told in the true tone of the *märchen* and are dramatic in form as well as in content.

Andrásfalvi was a better performer than Mrs. Palkó. While he was telling a story he would rise and underline what he said by gestures and mimicry. In the ballroom scene of *The Nine Kernels of Grain*, he demonstrated how the fairy danced and stooped humiliated and be- wildered in the middle of the floor, with downcast eyes; when the girl had flown away he made a gesture with his hand as if he would like to hold her back. When he told a story, the listeners did not crowd in closely about him but left a space open, because they were accustomed to his rising and moving around while telling a story. When we heard him tell stories in the wakes he was seated in the middle of the room and his listeners were in a semicircle about him. If he was invited somewhere, he occupied the main place at the table, with the listeners sitting near the stove opposite the table, on both sides of the beds, and on small hassocks. Only at home did Andrásfalvi sit before the stove and stoke the fire while he told stories, for the place of honor belonged to his guests. While he was narrating, he would smoke and drink a glass of wine. But he never drank more than two or three glasses, not for any-thing in the world, for "in the warmth the wine gets warm and the words do not come any more to my lips."

Summing up, we can say that Andrásfalvi belongs with the extremely gifted storytellers. Apart from his gift for telling legends, and in spite of his small *märchen* repertoire, we can compare him to the Russian narrator personalities like Ganin and Sigov. Even if he cannot compete with Mrs. Palkó when it comes to realism, ability to compose, narrative talent, and dramatic construction, there are resemblances between the two narrators. Andrásfalvi's tales are less personal and his texts do not betray the fact that they all originated from the same hand. His individual pieces show great stylistic differences. Further observation will reveal the future development of the storytelling situation in Kakasd. It will reveal whether Andrásfalvi's repertoire remained narrow, was further polished, or was enlarged and enriched. There is a possibility for development in either direction.

## Mrs. Anna Sebestyén (Geczi) née Mézes[5]

Vivacious, eighty-one year old Mrs. Sebestyén had lived with her daughter in Tabód since 1953. She did not say much about her own life except that she was an orphan, a foundling taken in by neighbors of the Zaicz family. Her fate was that of the village poor: daily labor, seasonal labor in the Moldavia region, work as a servant girl or hired help—the struggle for subsistence. She did not want to talk about the past—"nothing interesting in this"—"we lived as it was possible." When her husband died in 1940 she went to live with her son, Benedek Sebestyén, where she stayed until a short time before we first met her in 1950.

Mrs. Sebestyén was a typical community narrator, without conscious artistic pretensions, who took advantage of every occasion for story-telling just because she was fond of the *märchen* and liked to entertain company. Such occasions were communal work—almost exclusively work done by women—such as spinning; family gatherings, including the circle of children from the family; and wakes when a child had died. She was often called to the wake for a child, as we mentioned in Chapter 6, to banish sadness with her funny tales so that "even the little one may find comfort in its casket." In addition to Mrs. Sebestyén there were several other female narrators of this type in Kakasd; we chose her because she had the greatest repertoire. We have recorded twenty-six of her texts. We also chose her because a certain independence appears in her tales, though Mrs. Sebestyén herself belongs to the bearers of tradition, the personalities who conserve and reproduce a tale.

She could neither read nor write, but in the course of her life she had heard a great many tales. She had listened to both the Zaicz story-tellers, she heard Marcika Pintyer and much of Mrs. Palkó's narration, and she liked to listen carefully to the words of other narrators. She herself only told stories when there was nobody else around who could do it better.

As to the relative number of her belief stories, magic tales, and jokes, these are distributed nearly evenly, a fact reflecting her personality. We shall investigate these three kinds of narratives more closely in the following paragraphs.

### Belief Stories

AMONG THE BELIEF STORIES of Mrs. Sebestyén, there is only one, *The Devil's Midwife*, which in construction and form bears the characteristics of a *märchen*. We have referred to it earlier in Chapter 3 in our discussion of the relationship between *märchen* and folk belief. The other texts of a similar nature are "true stories," that is, the events described in them are personal experiences that have happened either to the narrator herself or to neighbors, acquaintances, or relatives. At the beginning of each story the source is quoted: "In our neighborhood a man had died. . . ." "My father was haunted by this spook. . . ." "Well, so, my mother-in-law was going home. . . ." "Once it happened to me. . . ." Persons known to everybody are always cited by their full names. Every story is short, hardly more than twelve to fifteen lines; the decisive words are put into the mouth of the demon, the villain, or the victim, and yet it is not they who tell the story but the narrator herself who recites them in a very dry manner. This is the usual narration technique of belief storytellers, who relate in a factual, objective manner one "case" after another when the occasion arises in the community. Mrs. Sebestyén is not guided by artistic principles and will not clothe her stories in the form of polished legends; her aim is to tell her audience about as many hair-raising events as possible. Mrs. Sebestyén's belief stories are not sharply delineated; rather, they flow one into the other. We can feel that she has been telling them one after the other, almost without stopping to take a breath, just as they came to her. Sometimes she even inserts a new one, which she cannot expand upon, but which she thinks worth telling because it is an extraordinary experience. Thus, for instance, the following example can hardly be called a narrative and is simply an account: "Formerly there were witches around. They sat down on coal shovels and flew over the village. The neighbor woman, too, was such a witch. Gergely told us so. They braided the manes of horses."

We noted down Mrs. Sebestyén's belief stories one after another in the spinning rooms. Younger and older women were gathered there, and two or three, taking turns, also told belief stories. Only two women presented the same story. The women behaved exactly like the members of the storytelling sessions described by Brinkmann, to which we have referred at various times. In Kakasd the belief-story communities form themselves *ad hoc*, especially in the work groups of the women (we never met men who told belief stories during their communal work). Someone turns the general conversation in this direction, and then—as Vajkai reports from Cserszegtomaj—one story calls for the next and nothing else is discussed the whole evening long. Mrs. Sebestyén can hardly be counted among the specialists in belief stories in the sense of Vajkai,[6] in spite of her inclination toward the magic stories and preference for telling about the revenants, ghosts, and miraculous happenings. She likes to entertain her company with other narrative genres as well.

## Magic Tales

WE RECORDED eight texts which can be called magic tales. Mrs. Sebestyén usually told them in the family circle, or to the children, or during a wake. In general it can be said that her texts follow subject more or less faithfully, or at least stick to the most essential parts, because very often she had already forgotten the complete *märchen* text. In spite of this, the beauty of her language, the supple form of her recital, and the individual embroidering of certain parts place her high above those who, without feeling, relate excerpts of contents. Mrs. Sebestyén was not avid for storytelling fame. Her knowledge only meant to her that she could recite one or another *märchen* when the occasion arose. She spoke highly of the outstanding storytellers who knew many tales, as for instance János Zaicz and Mrs. Palkó, and also admitted that she learned, or at least heard, many tales from them. We indicate in the Appendix how far she was influenced by Mrs. Palkó's *märchen*, several of which she adopted. The following still played a part in her repertoire: *The Princess' Picture, The Advice of the Rooster, The Galuschka Cooking.* Two more texts also stem from Mrs. Palkó, but Mrs. Sebestyén, when we knew her, was no longer able to finish them: "I also knew the one where they cut off her arm, [of the girl] who had twelve robbers for brothers." And "the gypsy girl throws her into the well." She selected only one episode each from *The Advice of the Rooster* and *The Galuschka Cooking*, but even these merit consideration. The text has not lost its meaning, has not become a wilted fragment, but is so well rounded as to be able to stand on its own; in this regard her ability for independent creative action is shown. *The Princess' Picture*, by contrast, closely follows the subject of Mrs. Palkó's *märchen*, *The Princess*. Even though Mrs. Sebestyén's variant is much shorter, it is symmetrical and well formed and could well pass for a live text. To prove this we would like to compare side by side a short paragraph from the renderings of Mrs. Palkó and Mrs. Sebestyén.

The preliminaries of the *märchen* vary in the two versions. With Mrs. Palkó, the king and the queen are dying, and the dying father impresses on his son to take care of his sister and to marry her according to her station in life. The prince has photos made of his sister and of himself so that they should not forget each other even if separated, and he starts out to seek a bride, one who should come close to his sister's beauty.

Mrs. Sebestyén does not mention the parents, but the prince wants to marry his own sister, who declines and urges him to go out and look for a suitable bride.

The comparison of the two texts reveals the difference between the extraordinarily gifted narrator and the run of the mill community storyteller.

| MRS. PALKÓ | MRS. SEBESTYÉN |
|---|---|
| . . . "Dear Sister, I want to get married, but for whose hand I am to ask I don't know. I decided to go away and leave you behind, and I shall not return before I have found a girl who is like you. And if I don't find her I shall not marry." So the girl said, "Dear Brother, what shall I do in the meantime?" "God will not forsake you. Here are your guards and your major domo; he will pay attention. I say, if I find a girl I shall return soon, but if I do not find her I shall roam the whole world. But before I leave let us go to the city to have photos made of ourselves." They went to the city to a photographer. | Once upon a time there was a fellow, a prince, and a princess. And the girl was so marvelously beautiful that it cannot be described. She had gorgeous golden hair, blue eyes, and red cheeks—well, she was beautiful. When she walked, roses sprang up under her feet. <br><br> Well, her brother loved her very much and said to her, "I take you as my wife." "Oh, my Brother, this is not possible, we are brother and sister, and that is a grave sin. But you," she said, "if you want to get married, go look for a bride that would fit you." Well, then the fellow was sad, he considered what he should do. He had a |

And the Prince said, "Make a photo of my sister, but such as you see her in the flesh, that it breathes and lives; it cannot speak, but you have to shoot her as you see her. Whatever you ask I shall pay you, but take a picture as you see her." Well, so the photographer made the picture and she was just like in life only it did not talk. She could not talk. He gave it to the girl and took the one of the girl himself, for he had a picture made of himself too. He put a gold chain on it and took the picture and put it around his neck. And he carried it so he could see his sister all the time. Well, they go home. He collected everything and got ready so that he could leave the next morning. In the morning he said, "Well, dear sister, we say goodbye now. Don't weep," he said, "for I shall return while I am alive. Do not weep, God will help you." They took leave of each other and the fellow mounted his horse, a magic horse and let it run. They went together as far as the door, and the girl looked after him as long as she could see him and when she could not see him any longer, she returned weeping. She was weeping all the time.

Well, so, the fellow wanders and wanders so long until he comes to the neighboring kingdom. He goes into the king's city and just where the castle stands he stopped on the side of the road, he tied the horse to a photo made of the girl, a big picture, and this he took along so that as long as he was wandering, he could also see his sister. The fellow then started on his way, went wandering; he wanted to wander around until he found a girl such as his sister was.

Well, as he is wandering around, he is getting tired and comes to a king's castle, and lies down on the wall, putting the photo next to him. Well, it happens that a prince was leaning out of the window and seeing the photo on the fellow's chest. He ran from the castle, and walked to the fellow and said, "Hi, there, my friend, where did you get this marvelous photo? She is so uncanningly beautiful that I never have seen the like of it." Then the fellow said, "I did not get it anywhere, I had it made, for this is my dear sister." Then the prince asked, "Where is your sister?" "At home." "Well, where are you going?" "I left and I shall wander around until I find a girl like my sister, and if I can't find her I shall never marry, never take a wife." Then the prince said "Be nice and come back with me, show me your sister, show me where she is." "Well," he said, "I have come from far and now I should go back there?" "Come on," he said, "just show her to me for I want to marry her." . . .

tree and thus he stood and reflected where he should turn
now. And just in this country
the prince stood at the open
window of the tower. He wondered about the fellow and saw
the board around his neck. Well,
he was standing so far and
could not see the board well,
so he calls a soldier and tells
him to send the fellow to him.
"Who are you?" he said. "Be
good enough to come and see
the king's son." Well, so he
went. He put the soldier next
to the horse so it could not un-
tie itself, and went before the
king. The king descended from
the tower and came to meet him.
They shook hands and he said,
"Who are you?" He then said
he was a king's son and this and
that. He said, "I too am a prince,
the heir to the throne." "But this
photo, is it for sale? Why do
you carry it around your
neck?" "No, this is not for sale,"
he said. "Nobody could give me
so much that I could give it
away." "Well, who is the girl?"
"She is my sister." "Well, where
are you going?" "I am wandering. I have made up my mind to
wander until I find a girl like
my sister," he said, "and then I
shall marry her." "Well," he
said, "look here, if she is as
beautiful as she is on the photo.
. . ." "She is even more beautiful—alive, she is even more beautiful," said the prince. "See, I
beg of you—I am looking for a
bride. If I like her, I shall take
her as my wife." . . .

There are more *märchen* in Mrs. Sebestyén's repertoire which she did not learn directly from Mrs. Palkó and which probably belong to the Kakasd tale tradition and therefore are also to be found in Mrs. Palkó's repertoire. They too show traces of individual shaping by the narrator, but we cannot present absolutely certain examples because we do not know the sources. In spite of this we may assume in the majority of cases that certain innovations come from Mrs. Sebestyén. Thus it is characteristic for her, having a preference for magic tales based on belief stories, that AT 365 as well as AT 365A belong among her favorite tales, and that both, indeed, are individual, deviating in form from those of Mrs. Palkó and from every other known Hungarian variant. In both her versions the background belief world is clearer in expression than it is usually found to be. Especially in the *märchen* of *The Dead Lover*, it is noteworthy that the young man appearing in the spinning room is nobody else but the goose-footed incubus (*lüdérc*), well known in folk belief.

> ... This other girl hid together with her lover, they wanted to know where the fellow went. Then they chatted who knows how long, then he left the girl, somersaulted and shitted fire, and disappeared like the wind. This the other boy and girl saw to the end, then they too went home. In the morning the mother of the girl whom the incubus had visited came to the neighbor girl and asked her, "Dear girl, was this fellow here?" "He sure was." "And what kind of a fellow was he—what do they say?" "Well," she said, "mine invited him to play with the others, he rose and jostled him and saw that he had a goose's foot." Well, then the woman took fright. "When he accompanied her home, which path did they take?" "Well, they chatted a little longer, then the fellow made a somersault, started to let out fire, and disappeared like the wind!" Well, the woman was afraid, she went home weeping, she told her husband and asked what she could do for the girl had been seized by the incubus, how could she prevent their getting together? ...

Mrs. Sebestyén's tale of *The Cabinetmaker's Apprentice* was told by Mrs. Palkó's under the title of *Gábor Német*. Mrs. Sebestyén heard it from Marcika Pintyer. We are dealing here with a very good, taut variant, which bears the signs of being one of her favorite *märchen*. In her recital we can discover individual traits of the storyteller which do not change the subject or its structure, and yet let us recognize the narrator. The names are not the same—here the young people are called Feri and Iluska, rather than Gábor and Juliska—and the use of tale formulae and generalities are more evident in the more compact, sober presentation. Mrs. Sebestyén's fancy is not as sweeping and encompassing as the fancy of Mrs. Palkó, who so ably transferred the environment of the king to the stage of the city and the factory. The factory owner here corresponds perfectly to the well-to-do peasant. He receives the young man in search of work with the same words which the patriarchal king of the magic tale uses:

> . . . He [the tale hero] continues walking along here and finds a factory. He then went to the door and asked the guards. They let him enter. He went to the owner of the factory. The factory owner asked him, "Well, my son, what do you want?" "What I want, my father? If I could find some service somewhere, or some work!" "All right, my son," says the factory owner, "you have come to the right place; if you want to work, there will be a job for you." . . .

The property of the factory owner does not correspond to Mrs. Palkó's description, which is partly from the folktale, partly from the village milieu:

> . . . He went with the man and the man showed him everything. He took him along, showed him the stables, the one was full of big oxen, full of mares, the other full of milk cows, another full of horses, small calves, foals, pigs, an uncanny amount of grain. He also had three hundred acres of land. "Well my son," he said, "starting from now I place it all in your hands and you care for it." . . .

There are two more *märchen* which belong in this group: *Jutka in Ashes* and *The Twelve Ravens*. Both come from a schoolbook and are only short resumés of contents.

### Jokes

As SEEN from the community's point of view, Mrs. Sebestyén's function as a teller of jokes was her most important one. Mrs. Sebestyén liked to laugh a great deal herself, but she also liked to see others laugh and she had an acute sense of the comic and could imitate others well. She had a sharp tongue and could express "her opinion" in a few words. In the company of women talk would soon veer to the newest sensation, to gossip—and Mrs. Sebestyén could hold her own in this too; from there it was only a step to comical anecdotes and jokes. In the center of the sharply aimed anecdotes which she related for the amusement of the spinning woman there is for the most part a ridiculous or damnable quality. She tells of lazy, stupid, or boasting women who know neither cooking nor baking and cannot spin, of girls who are simple, dirty, slow, lazy, and inattentive, of women and girls who have to pay for their mistakes. All anecdotes are short but very effective, are excellently recited, and show a lively dialogue. As to dramatic rendering, No. 90 is especially notable. This anecdote is about a woman who does not want to spin and sends her husband into the forest to get wood for the spinning rod. So as not to be discovered not having spun anything, she hides behind a tree and cries out with a ghostly voice, "Leave the wood go, or you won't live another six hours." All through the narration there is the masterful imitation of the woman, of her cry, her voice, and the voice of the man. Here it is not the story itself which is essential, but its presentation. While the narrator recited the events in the forest she imitated the movements and the words of the man.

In this scene we could follow not only the imitation of the voices but also the presentation of the acts, accompanying the words of the actors. The narrator had taken to herself the role of the credulous husband. Hearing the unexpected voice, she suddenly raised her head, rubbed one ear as if she wondered if she had heard right, looked around to see where the voice was coming from, and then recited how the man returned to his work, dropped it again; she put her kerchief around her shoulders as if it were a fur and approached the door. This interpretation earned great applause for the narrator. Often it happened that the woman guided her to an especially well done anecdote. "What did you say, Aunt Anna? How have you imitated the awful girl?" She remembered exactly how they laughed about certain anecdotes.

Among the jokes we should mention above all *The Poor Fisherman and The Rich Neighbor*, a text which patently deviates from other variants. This should be worth considering not only because of its excellent recital but because of its content. Nowhere does the narrator enlarge, never does she leave the simple action, but its formal containment, the elegant, lively dialogue, and the beauty of the language are outstanding. There is not one superfluous sentence in this story; the succinct presentation is also suggested by the well-established content. The luck of the poor man, the envy of the rich, this is the theme which, as in Mrs. Palkó's tale of *The Two Brothers*, equalizes the social injustices which constitute a problem very near to the heart of the narrator. Here we can see true compassion in Mrs. Sebestyén; here she no longer merely tells a story, but she lives it deeply within herself and submerges herself in the miseries of the poor man, in the sad family circumstances. She approaches Mrs. Palkó's descriptions at the corresponding point in the story of *Death with Yellow Legs, The Fawn,* and *Margit:*

> The poor man went fishing every day that God allowed to be, but he did not catch even the tiniest fish. When he came home his children cried that his heart was breaking, what should they eat, there was nothing for them to eat. Once the poor man said, "What could I do with you, since I cannot give you anything? The poor man too, wept. Then he said to his wife, "I shall try once again today, maybe I can catch a little fish." So he went and fished until dusk, but he could not catch anything and wept bitter tears, for what was he going to do, how long since his children had eaten anything, and he had not even a small fish to bring home to them. It was becoming night but he told himself, I shall try once more, will cast out the nets once more and if God decides this should be it. He draws the net, draws again, but cannot manage it. My God, he tells himself, now there are so many that I cannot haul them in. What am I to do, how can I draw my net out of the water? He works hard for a long time until he finally gets the net out of the water, but again there was nothing in it, nothing at all except a small diamond. Then the fisherman told himself that this was God's will, I shall take the little stone out of the net and bring it home. He did not know what kind of a stone it was. He went home, the children cried, what was he to do with them? The man wept together with the children, because he could not give them anything to eat." ...

Once the poor family has become lucky, the interest of the narrator turns to something else; for justice to be complete the rich man has to be ruined. The well-to-do peasant brings the king old cats, and they ruin everything in the most beautiful room of the castle; then the rich peasant gets what he deserved.

This is the portrait of an average female narrator who is very popular at the communal work of women. She wanted to entertain her listeners, brought gaiety into the spinning rooms, roused their attention with her belief stories, and dispensed comfort during the wakes for children.

## MÁRTON LÁSZLÓ (MARCIKA PINTYER)

HUNGARIAN FOLKLORE so far has not discovered any folk poet who could be compared to Márton László. We cannot actually count him among the storytellers, for we know only very few of his tales and have never heard him tell them—we only know him from the remembrances of others, for he was no longer alive when we put together our collections. Even taking his handwritten book, which is eight hundred pages long, as the basis for our investigations, it is questionable whether the folklorist should take him into serious consideration. Is it really possible that the work written by him and distributed in handwritten copies can be made the object of an investigation into folklore, into the folktale?

In the preceding chapter we pointed to the necessity of a thorough consideration of the influence of literature on folklore. We have considered our material, the tale stock of Kakasd, from this point of view. We mentioned that the Kakasd folktale is at its best during the wakes, during which the narrator and the song leaders who are conversant with the religious usages, and hence "educated" or "well-read" men, are equally important factors. But when we consider more closely these factors that serve the same purpose but have different origins, it appears that the impetus came from Márton László, and that it not only founded the present-day tale treasure but contributed to a widening of the most important tale occasion still extant. The previous statements show that our narrators learned tales from him, that they received books from him, that his tales penetrated the folk tradition, that his *Book of the Dead* represented a guide to a ritual that was binding for the whole society, and that the rites during wakes were preserved and kept alive through his book. This is the reason why we must occupy ourselves with Márton László in connection with the storytelling of Kakasd, even though his person should be counted equally among the literary and the folklore figures.

Outside of the information already listed, we know very little about his life. He was poor and went to work in the Moldavia region. He liked to tell stories, read much, and developed a special faculty: whatever captured his attention in what he heard or read, he put down on paper in a new form.[7]

György Andrásfalvi said about him, "He led the groups. We went to them to hack turnips and he wrote down what he had heard, he learned much from them. He also asked me: 'Hey Gyurka? Don't you know something?'" "Such a man he was," said János Mátyás, "that when he heard something, he put it together in rhymes." "He formed much according to his own mind," says Mrs. Palkó. Not only did he ask others for tales, stories, and songs, not only did he learn what they told him as worth knowing, he also showed passionate interest in books.

His son, János László, relates, "He sometimes had fairytale books come from Budapest. He looked up books where he could find the titles, in the house of the priest, and then sent for them to Pest. He had the books brought in. Even from the Bucovina he wrote to Pest and they sent them. He even begged the priest in the Bucovina for books."

These statements show the sources, the two-fold starting points of his education: folk tradition and church literature. We know that Márton László also had a function as song leader, reader, or storyteller during wakes. Mrs. Palkó said that he liked to tell "funny tales" for the women and during wakes he liked to make people feel jolly. Everybody thought him extremely gifted, and his word carried weight everywhere. Today it is difficult to state with precision how good a storyteller he actually was. It is a fact that he knew many stories, but we still believe that he would not have been able to hold his own in competition with the two Zaicz storytellers. He preferred to tell tales with a religious moral which, as we shall see, he recited with much humor. Mrs. Palkó learned the greater part of such tales from him. When his name was mentioned in the village, people did not think of him foremost a storyteller but as the author of the *Book of the Dead*, and only when a person stopped to think a little was his storytelling also mentioned. He was known through his *Book of the Dead*. Everything he ever heard, or read, or learned, he collected and put down in his original form. With unending patience he wrote one book after another, many of them on order.

In Chapter 7, we discussed the origin of books for wakes; we raised the question whether they were influenced by the Franciscans in the Csík, whether we were faced with a late survival of a medieval codex type of church literature genre, or whether we were dealing with the individual creation of a devout literate peasant who had a literary bent, and who provided a written guide to serve a ritual of his people. It would be difficult to take a definitive stand in view of the paucity of sources, for we are not informed about the local and folkloristic aspects of the scarce material in our hands. There are different opinions prevailing to the material available. Many state that Márton László alone wrote the *Book of the Dead* and that his book was in use everywhere in the Szekler villages of the Bucovina. No one else had ever written a manual for wakes, and during wakes the old, well-known songs were sung under the direction of the songleaders. The songleader had also led the prayers, and it usually happened afterward that stories were told for entertainment, though this was unplanned. Others are of the opinion that there were other manuals for wakes by different authors. But when we looked for the places mentioned, we always found the books to be copies of Márton László's *Book of the Dead*. This was the case with the book of Ambrus Sebestyén and with the one copied by József Mátyás, a very fragmentary volume which is in the possession of his daughter, Mrs. Szakács. How precious the book by Márton László still is today is shown in the fact that Mrs. Sebestyén-Boda,[8] who is in possession of the only complete version, will loan her copy only on very rare cases; many villagers come to her house to make excerpts from it on the spot. During the winter of 1959 the songleader József Palkó copied out the dirges from it.

Though hymn and prayer books for the rites at wakes were possibly written before Márton László, certainly no others wrote any while he was alive and no copy of an earlier form was in circulation. Therefore, in the absence of reliable information, we must leave open the question of whether there had been a similar handwritten book of folk literature existing before him, or even of previously written church manuals of rites. Whatever the case may be, one thing is certain: the *Book of the Dead* compiled by Márton László is an individual work.

The copy which we are familiar with was made in 1934. Up to this date, Márton László, according to a note on page 803 of the book, had copied twenty-six of them.

I, myself, Márton László or Marcika Pintyer, have written many beautiful *Books of the Dead*. Such books are in

| | | | |
|---|---|---|---|
| Andrásfalva | 15 | Marosludas* | 2 |
| Hadikfalva | 2 | Csernakeresztur* | 1 |
| Istensegits | 2 | Székelykeve | 1 |
| Déva* | 2 | Józseffalva | 1 |

Márton László wrote these books on order. "He was a poor man," János Mátyás says. "He had a little house, and during the summer he earned money for the winter; during the winter he was occupied with these books, even at night. What he had put together was bought and he got a few pennies. Jóska Palkó [the elder, Mrs. Palkó's husband] took his songs from it."

János László says,

He only sang at wakes, and when he had time he wrote these *Books of the Dead*. He was able to write as he spoke. He was so very gifted. He copied from books, and searched for the best. That he spread through the village so they could learn from it. They did

* Transylvanian villages where people from Andrásfalva had settled.

not fit with the Church. He got books also from the priests and copied from them and added from his own mind so it could be read. Would he still be alive he might be able to tell so much, to write so much! He wrote many books, but they remained in the Bácska. He wrote these books for money and they paid him for ink and pens so that he did not write for nothing. They read in them; when he was no more, it should be in the house where the wake was. Into every book he wrote different things. He was able to tell stories like Mrs. Palkó, he knew them as well, and my father knew them even better, even without a book. Everybody knew he could tell stories and he was invited. If he did not go out to tell stories or sing, they went to his house and called him. What kind of books my father would have been able to write if he had been told to write!

All this shows that Márton László's book filled a definite need. He manufactured these books according to a general wish (as we shall see when we closely examine the contents). During the rites people read from the book, sang from it, or freely recited from it, according to the capabilities of the individuals present.

For such a book to come into existence, a personality with unusual gifts was necessary, one who knew the folklore tradition well, who could read and write fluently and was well acquainted with questions of religion.

As mentioned elsewhere, the devout Kakasd storytellers of a religious-mystical inclination explained the Bible and functioned as songleaders during wakes. Márton László also belonged to this type; he matched the zeal of the lay singer Ádám Sebestyén in keeping closely to the church ceremonial.

From the above we may deduce that Márton László was a conscious author, for he possessed the self-importance of a writer. He put a high value on his work, for on the very first page of his book he wrote: "In this book are written down a great many beautiful songs for the dead and at the end there are marvelous texts." On the second page: "This book was written by Márton László or Marcika Pintyer during the months of October and November 1934 in Andrásfalva. He who does not know how to sing or read well, should not take up the book to leaf through it, for it is worth it to pay good attention to this book."

As far as we can judge from the fragments which have come to hand, the content of each book is indeed somewhat different and sometimes even greatly changed. The differences appear mostly in the ordering of the material. The most consistent are the legends and exempla, and the useful notations are also to be found in all the books, but the moralizing, joking, half-comical, anecdotal thoughts and the rhymed jokes are not always the same. It seems as though the author reserved the last pages for stinging jokes and colloquialisms, for the three faulty copies which we had access to all contained different anecdotes in this position. The author also had jotted down for whom he had written the copy, as for instance, "This *Book of the Dead* belongs to Mrs. Marie Jordáki, written 1940." By comparison we could state that the consistent texts did not coincide word for word but were similar in content. This, of course, is mostly due to the form. The tighter the form, the greater the coincidence. The texts in verse form are the most consistent, and the differences in the versified prose texts are also minimal.

Today we may assert that Márton László became something of a collection point for a certain kind of folk tradition through his ability to read and write. Besides, he contributed greatly to the enrichment of tradition by his free variations of his literary experiences. He had melded the folklore and the literary tradition and made them a source of new folklore tradition. The essential fact is that he wrote down his work and thus spread his knowledge, a fact which had never before occurred in folk tradition. We knew popular poets, literate peasants whose ambition was to write poetry, prose diaries, memoires, chronicles, expressing themselves in writing.[9] There were also guides for wedding ceremonials for popular use, written by village teachers and craftsmen, but we never before had heard of any Hungarian peasant who wrote a book of ceremonies (rites) about traditional usages, and thus renewed the very usage itself, enriching the traditional folklore form contained in it. As a consequence, the literary work of Márton László was spread in two ways, by reading aloud and by free reciting, a fact which accounts for its return to the oral tradition.

It would be well worthwhile to subject Márton László's *Book of the Dead* to a study in comparative literature, to trace its predecessors in medieval literature and to correlate the single items to earlier parallels both in content and form. Such a study would be very helpful in throwing light on the share of originality and adaptation in Márton László's *oeuvre*. However, here we must limit ourselves to the folkloristic evaluation, and we shall only touch on questions that are important in the consideration of the Kakasd tale body. The subject under scrutiny is doubtless a late survivor of a very old literary genre whose preservation can be attributed to the peculiarity of the archaic culture of the Bucovina Szeklers.

When Márton László compiled his work, he must have had literary models before him. This is apparent from the arrangement of materials included in the book. Márton László makes certain that the reader will find what he is looking for; this is why the pages are numbered and a table of contents is found at the beginning of the manuscript. In addition he inserts a guide for the use of the book in the first pages: "Who is looking for songs or texts in this book will find them in front, in the table of contents. There is also a list of songs and a list of texts, it can be found easily, it is not necessary to leaf through the whole book to find a single song or text." The table of contents lists fifty-seven songs and forty-two texts, but when we counted we found there were even more: sixty-four songs and eighty-three prose texts.

There is not much that can be be said about the first part, the group of songs for the dead. These are the texts of old, popular church hymns—often even with indication of the melody—which were sung during wakes according to the custom of Andrásfalva. There is a great variety in the lament songs, according to age, sex, social status of the deceased, cause of death (accidental, long illness), and other specific circumstances. Every song is accompanied by a corresponding remark: "this song for young people"; "this song is fitting for old people"; "this song fits a father or a mother who leave behind a marriage partner or children." The songleader at wakes makes his choice according to these indications.

The content of the second part has a great many variations. It seems as if Márton László wanted to make his books more interesting through the variations in sequence. Nearly every prose piece is prefaced, "This is a different text," and then he explains, as in the chapbooks, what it is all about. Sometimes, in order to make the following piece even more important he adds, "It is not I who say so but the Holy Writ."

The material of the different versions of the *Book of the Dead* consists, of course, of entertaining reading matter that is religiously colored and devout, but wherever possible the author tried to shape it in an interesting way. The terrible tortures of the Saints and Martyrs, new miracle stories, bloody slaughter, exciting adventures, dangerous undertakings follow each other in breath-taking swiftness, and in between occur the unexpected rescue or the divine miracle. These stories satisfy the craving for sensation of the simple man just as do the tabloids, pulp magazines, and cheap paperback novels, or as did the thrilling adventure stories in the chapbooks. The only difference consists in the author's providing religious edification at the end of each story, to admonish the readers to become devout. But in the religious atmosphere of old Andrásfalva this is no detriment to the effect of the adventure stories of the chapbooks: the people of Andrásfalva enjoy the illusion of devout spirituality and are filled with satisfaction. In addition there are many sermon-like meditations about the human weaknesses and sins so often scourged by the Church; everyone can apply these to himself. Márton László tries efficiently to actualize them. As simple as his means may be, he applies their morals to the conditions of his native village.

There can also be found useful information, communications about the extraordinary facts; there are tales and jokes, which lighten the oppressive atmosphere of the wake and trigger a liberating laughter in the course of varied, exciting, and sentimental entertainment.

When we examine the *Book of the Dead* with a view to its numerical composition, we see that religious legends and Bible stories occur most often, altogether numbering twenty-six pieces. Among the religious legends is a series of martyr legends (including, for example, those of St. Eustache, St. Helen, St. Julia, St. Vincent, the Hermits, St. Peter and St. Paul, St. Anthony, St. Augustine, St. Philip, St. Martin); among the biblical stories are the most interesting ones from the Old and the New Testaments, for the greater part apochryphal, such as Genesis and the Fall, Salome, Samson and Delila, Saul, David, the Temptation of Jesus, the death of Caiphas and of Pilate, the life of the Holy Family in Egypt. Religious stories are represented in great numbers in the volume, numbering altogether twenty. They are about sin, the Our Father, dissatisfaction, wrath, the Rich Man, Fortune, and the soul. Numerous as well are the examples of incidents of recent times— the wounded soldier, the nun who likes to look into the mirror, the spoiled girls, the chaste couple, the conversion of the prodigal son— which number fourteen. In addition to eight tale texts, there are also useful reports about the settling of the village, of Andrásfalva, about village life, and about the Catholic church; starting with 1880 Márton László had noted from memory the names of the priests, the teachers, the lay singers, the judges, and the church members. There are also bits of news about technical innovations, interesting facts from the natural sciences, a chronology of Biblical events, informative pieces about prophets and about the age of the inhabitants, death statistics, a list of church feasts, information about the lives of the Old Testament kings, and so forth. These are followed by miscellaneous things: the Catholic and the Calvinistic ABC, notes about outlaws, funny remarks about second marriages, figures of speech and proverbs.

Characteristic of this book, whose contents are so varied and colorful, is the constant parallel of the oral and the literary. Although the relationship between the two is quite uneven, one thing is certain: very little in this voluminous handwritten manuscript cannot be traced back to a literary source. In fact, we would hesitate to say that any one piece is not literary in origin. At the same time, this work does not contain a single text which does not show traces of folkloristic reshaping. Only of a few religious legends can we say that Márton László copied them from a book; but even in these instances, individual shaping is revealed in moral teachings deduced from them.

Márton László's personality may be seen in his language and style rather than in the individuality of his tale formation. The expressive Szekler language is so prominent that it appears in the spelling, which follows the dialect, as well as in usage and sentence structure. A particularly characteristic sign of his poetic gift is the fact that nearly all prose pieces are written in a kind of measured prose. As we had never found in another *märchen* text in Hungarian folklore, or in a story or any other prose narrative, rhymed lines of different length,[10] we tried without much success to trace models to which he could have had access. We found this form only in two Protestant sermon texts. One, by the preacher Sámuel Diószegi, originated in 1673. We also found a volume which was written in a kind of rhymed prose, but since it had no beginning and no end, we could trace neither the author nor the date of the edition. To judge from the print and the four-line pairs of the rhymed text, the book probably originated at the end of the eighteenth century. It contains eighty orthodox Protestant texts for edification. Since rhymed prose may not have been unknown in church practice, Márton László may easily have had models. Thus we can say that Márton László's rhymed prose, which he had garnered from religious reading material and applied accordingly, is very remarkable.[11]

If only occasional pieces of the *Book of the Dead* were written in this form, or if it were restricted only to one genre, it might have been assumed that the author had taken over rhymed chapbook novels, and that the rhymes had become halting and uneven because of his lapsing memory. There are examples of this: we know peasants who can recite by rote versified chapbook novels. That this is not the case with Márton László, that the texts contained in his book were not originally in this rhymed prose, is witnessed by the frequency of the rhymes. There are a negligible number of texts which do not contain rhymes. Among these are mainly a story of edification, a biblical story, a tale, and a legend. Since the majority of these genres, however, are presented in rhymed form, since the style, when compared to the chapbooks, is completely folkloristic, and since the language is the archaic language of the Bucovina Szeklers, there can be no doubt about the fact that the rhyme comes from Márton László. His very irregularity is an indication of this. In most of the texts appears unconscious inclination toward rhyme, which, however, is never very consequent. Some sections fall apart; others rhyme very well. In some of the stories, the sentences which are put in the mouth of the speaker will rhyme; in others, there is not a single rhyme in the entire story, except in the opening and closing phrases which give the moral. This bears out the assumption that Márton László had taken over stories and actualized them himself. But there are also pieces which rhyme from beginning to end. From this unevenness we can conclude that the extent of the rhymed version depended on how much Márton László had edited the texts, and on the extent to which he had worked over the traditional version, since the rhymed version nearly always goes hand in hand with a transformation of language, vocabulary, and style.

The peculiarity of Márton László's style is the rhyme, but it has not been constructed with workman-like craft. This is revealed by the traditional and variable forms in his account of "News Worth Knowing," forms which in the Hungarian original have a tendency to create rhymes.

> There were two King Mátyás, but the Just King Mátyás was born in 1443 and died 1490; he brought the art of printing to our homeland. King Mátyás is dead and dead is Justice. This word will be true as long as lasts the world.[12]

He uses the same formula, changed according to the subject, for two different pieces of information:*

> From the earth up to the sun there are 20 million kilometers and to the moon 385 thousand and he who does not believe it need not believe it/ we shall need no tribunal for this/ and we shall not be condemned to the wheel,/ I have not measured it, but there are those who have measured it/ they have noted it down/ and if you do not believe me, go and ask them/ you need not go far/ only here, to Budapest.[13]
>
> With every breath, with every gasp, a soul ascends to the judgment seat of God/ so much dying is done every minute/ dying

---

* In this and the following quotations from the *Book of the Dead*, the punctuation is faithful to the handwritten copy. Slashes indicate where rhymes fall in the Hungarian.

never ends/ and all that is written here/ as it is printed in the Holy
Scriptures/ and as it is recommended by the Holy Popes/ and who
does not believe it/ need not believe it/ we need no tribunal for this,
and we shall not be condemned to the wheel/ and whoever does
not want to believe it at all/ we have no need to go on talking to
such a smart-aleck/ the Lord Jesus himself never made friends
with such a clever one/ with such big-minded Pharisees.[14]

Passing on to the contents, we want to point out some pieces and
characteristics of the texts which are worth considering because of their
peculiar Kakasd slant. In spite of his deep religious feeling, Márton
László liked to scoff, and often liked to give a humorous background to
religious edification. A good example of this is the text which describes
the virtues with which a poor man could live happily, because it was not
worthwhile to wait for a "baked pigeon."* As soon as he touched upon
the pigeons, Márton László continued the thought as follows:

> . . . and it is written, and that's the way it is, that a baked pigeon
> will not fly into our mouth; once in the old world there were
> fabulous times/ so that a baked pigeon flew into the mouth of every
> man,/ but it is a long while since this happened/ it happened once
> like the dog market of Buda at the time of King Mátyás,[15] which
> is still being mentioned today/ and thus it is with the baked pigeons,
> but it may be that in the old world the pigeons flew around baked,
> so that the people could live easier./ But now we cannot see that
> they are flying baked/ but how good would it be if this were the
> case now/ a man would close his jaws on them and get away/ but
> today they do not fly around baked/ or maybe there are none/
> the devil take them/ how much we would need them/ there are
> enough mouths to feed/ once I opened my mouth real wide/ if a
> baked pigeon would come and fly into my mouth/ I looked here
> and I looked there/ I paid close attention but I waited in vain/ I
> had to close my mouth/ for I did not see a single one/ and I am
> not at all lucky even if I wait/ for my stomach rumbles mightily/
> I can see that, until they come we have to start working so as not
> to go hungry/ and we must not wait for the baked pigeons/ for
> they have been delayed somewhere/ and hereabouts they may
> come only tomorrow/ my stomach cannot wait any longer/ I have
> to do something. What shall I do, I must work./ Nothing can be
> changed./ If man wants to live he cannot wait for the baked
> pigeons/ but it is still good to be on the lookout/ so we do not fall

---

* An old Hungarian saying, "Baked pigeons do not fly into your mouth,"
meaning that it is necessary to urge a lazy man to work.

asleep in the meantime/ for then we would regret it./ I can see I
have to work/ and cannot wait for the baked pigeons.[16]

To the moral application of a poem which obviously comes from
religious writings, Márton László adds the following joke:

God save us from the Christian merchant*;
from the poor who became a judge;
from the beggar's intentions;
from a woman who is strong like a man
and from the old maid become wife.
For they want to learn the bad
like the discharged soldier;
they are full of whims
like a little dog full of fleas;
he who wrote this, is an old man, who has seen enough sorrow;
in the whole world there is no brave man who would teach this.[17]

Márton László is especially fond of making fun of women. His son
János relates, "He wrote a long tale about his own fate." After the death
of his first wife, Márton László married again very soon, but he soon
separated from his considerably younger, lazy, quarrelsome, and flighty
wife. In order to entertain at wakes, he has put his own misfortune in
the form of an anecdote and put it into a "serious" framework. The lines
which praise the second marriage are repeated as a refrain in a poem,
though neither the rhymes nor the original manuscript indicate that
Márton László actually wanted to write a poem. It is well worth noting
the vital sense of humor:

This is a lesson and a teaching about the good medicine for eye
sores. This little piece of writing tells us of such a medicine/ which
cannot be bought in the Likman store,[18] nor in the pharmacy/
Do let us see what kind of medicine this is/ and what's its name/
that is supposed to be so good for sore eyes./ It is true that it is not
good for anything else/ only for the widower whose eyes are
hurting./ Always I have heard from the old ones/ and from the
wise old men/ that the widower, when his eyes are sore, should
not spend his money for a thousand medicines/ for he will spoil
his eyes even more with these medicines/ for it is well known that
the best medicine for sore eyes is a second marriage./ And if you
are a widower, go ahead and marry and don't be afraid, for you

* Local general store owners, horse dealers, etc., as a rule were Jews.

will regret it only once/ for if you are a widower and your eyes are hurting/ they might be pasted shut/ do not be afraid for this medicine will open them shortly./ Oh, this second marriage, what a powerfully good medicine it is!/ If you have a wild hair in your eye, this medicine will get it out/ so that your head will start spinning/ and if your eyes are bloodshot and even running,/ this medicine will clean them up./ It will open them so much/ that they will become big like potatoes./ What a good medicine, indeed, is this second marriage/ when your eyes have a trachoma you don't need to have them operated for this medicine will heal them/ so much that even your hair will be taken off./

You widowed man, if you get a speck in your eye, get married; then you don't need to cool your burning eye with cold, wet compresses, nor paste it with the white of an egg/ and you don't need to put any honey into it, for this good medicine will cleave your speck that you will remember exactly the very day./ Boy, oh boy, how good and useful is this medicine, this second marriage,/ we have already heard/ what useful medicine we have found. Then the widowed man when his eyes hurt him, does not need to torment himself blind, he should marry,/ then he need not run to the pharmacy for medicine/ for much as his eyes might have been pasted over before/ his second marriage will open them for him/ and if you could gauge them/ it does not hurt,/ you need not go around with a blindfold/ for the second marriage opens them for you/ so that your soul will soon be damned/ and if during your widowhood a cancer is breaking up on your behind/ the second marriage will get it out by the roots/ so that it won't take long that you get crazy with it/ and what is it that heals all kind of pain through medicine? The second marriage./ All those who tried it know/ for their eyes do not hurt any longer/ and even if they hurt/ the poor man cannot mention it/ for in front of the wife he cannot regret anything,/ and you should not complain for nothing/ for the heart of the second wife is harder than a rock./ Yes, it really is good medicine, this second marriage/ . . . he who has written this/ has burdened himself plenty with his second marriage,/ for quite often he was at the point/ of hanging himself/ and often he has deliberated/ where he should hide./ Many more are helped by this medicine, the second marriage./ End.[19]

Among the funny pieces in the *Book of the Dead* there are some pointed anecdotes and even some frivolous ones. But what is more interesting is that the zealous Márton László himself originates jokes which make fun of priests. What is astonishing is that they are not encountered elsewhere in Kakasd. On the last page of Mrs. Jordáki's copy of the *Book of the Dead* we can read the following fragment: "When the priest preaches and addresses the women, he opens both his arms as if for an embrace/ but when he addresses the men he threatens with his balled fist!/" The copy we have on hand at this writing reads as follows on page 804:

> Once upon a time the priest and the singer were at a funeral to-gether and when on the way home,/ they stopped at a tavern/ for a glass of wine/ it was cold and they were freezing/ but they did not have any money about them, so the priest said to the Jew Mikhel, fill up two glasses of wine, I shall send the money pres-ently, immediately, said the Jew, I shall fill them but charge them, yes charge them, said the priest but do not put down my name for I am ashamed if somebody learns/ that the priest owes money to the innkeeper/ so, Mikhel write it down, but wrote it this way:
>
> | Dominus vobiscum | 6 leu |
> | etkum spirituo | 5 leu |

Márton László's world concept, insofar as it is revealed in his texts, is unique. There is hardly another storyteller in whom we can discern so clearly, and who expresses in such an unvarnished and self-important manner, the view of justice for the poor man that we can see in the religious-didactic texts of this completely mystical-religious minded nar-rator. The moralizing in his tales reminds us of the edifying tracts of the preachers in Hungarian literature. In them, insofar as they express the hopes and desires of the people, can be found the same plebian tone as in Márton László, when he has secured the Kingdom of Heaven for the poor man. The poor man is a good man. God loves him and assures him and his fellow suffers that their situation will improve in the Beyond; even though injustice on earth cannot be eradicated, they will be happy in Heaven. The rich will be the ones to suffer, and their suffering will be forever. God will mete our justice. These thoughts are in many re-spects well known from the old Hungarian church literature. But Márton László re-creates these familiar church lessons for his own milieu, and makes them understandable to the people of Andrásfalva. We shall mention one of the most characteristic of the many edifying tracts.

A variant of the sermon on Lazarus (Luke 16:19–26) much in use among Protestant preachers indicates that we should not rebel against our fate. Both the poor and the rich are necessary; we must bear our fate in peace, and rewards will be given only in the Beyond.[20] This well known false moral, born of misery, is transformed by Márton László as follows:

> . . . there you will be much happier, much richer than anybody else who has money and is standing in line before us. They were so only in this world, but that was all; they could not take it with them into the other world, here they had an abundance of every-thing, but in the Beyond they will have to content themselves, for it is written that we cannot live twice a whole life . . . they have lived well down here/ they waded in milk and butter/ they had money to burn./ I think that in the Beyond we shall not want to change places with them, there I would not like to be in their shoes. God only knows what will happen to them . . . this world is short, short like the tail of the cottontail, once it will come to an end, short as it was, but Beyond is forever and all those who had so much money and were rich, where will they be?"[21]

The rich man deserves hell for his godlessness, and Márton László gives an example from his own experience:

> . . . a rich man, I don't put his name down, I shall only write that he lives in the village, below the church, he just had put out potatoes and a woman said, "With this we have done our part, God may bless it, so that something will become of it and we can also give something to the poor" and the peasant said, "is this why I put them out, is this why I worked so hard that I have to distribute them among the poor—I wish they would rather rot in the ground than be distributed among the poor?" In spite of this God gave His blessings and there were so many that he could hardly take them home, but God is still waiting that He be thanked for his benefi-cence.

In the following he comforts his fellow sufferers with the thought that money alone does not make one happy:

> Our King Ferenc Jóska [Emperor Franz Joseph], who died in 1916, had everything he wished and needed as a King and Emperor and yet he was not happy, to the contrary, much more unhappy than anyone else, for the bad news which caused him so much sorrow, came on him from every part. One day he heard that one of his brothers, Lipot [Leopold], had fallen off his horse and broken his neck; the other day he heard that his brother Miska [Maxi-milian] and his family, eleven persons all together, had died, all of a sudden a big stone palace had crumbled and had buried them all

as they sat at luncheon. This news gave him much sorrow, and his own children also died suddenly, and later his son, the successor to the throne, Rudolph, also died suddenly in 1889, of whom the world knows that he committed suicide by shooting. After that his wife Queen Elizabeth, all of a sudden the kind and charming, innocent woman died in 1898, an Italian stabbed her in the heart in the middle of the city, and she died immediately, and not long afterwards the war of 1914 broke out. All these were great sorrows for our King and he was right when he said that he was more bitter than any other man on this earth and even though he had everything which could give pleasure, he had so much sorrow, he never could consider himself happy, to the contrary, he complained about his kingdom. In his bitterness he even said, Mother, it might have been better if you had borne me somewhere in a ditch, it would have been better if I had to beg for my daily bread than that I should have so much sorrow in my old days. . . .[22]

But Márton László also cites examples which are much closer to the poor villager. The man who owns a lot is not always happy:

. . . This lucky man says to the rich man, oh, these earthly goods do not mean happiness, but slavery, serfdom, for possessions mean much worry and much work. Day and night one has to work, there is much damage and sorrow, and there is a lot of bitterness. The rich man is only the slave of his cattle, of his possessions, he has no rest not even when he eats and drinks, he is always hurrying, never knows what to do first;—many rich people gain bitterness instead of joy, where is happiness? I can only say that a clever, sensible poor man lives much better than many unskilled and reckless rich people, for this poor man even if he works hard for his daily bread can eat it in peace and quiet and what he earns laboriously he even saves, he eats and sleeps in peace, not only his life but also his death is more quiet as that of the rich man, and in the Beyond his fate is easier than that of the rich man for he has less to atone for, and his sufferings will be less, because the rich man will be presented with a long bill and even after death he finds no rest, or his son or daughter or son-in-law damn him over the distribution of his goods, but there is nothing to curse the poor man for when he dies, and even under the earth he is better off than the rich man. . . .[23]

In another text in which the topic is equality before God, Márton László takes "the big clans," the rich families of Andrásfalva, as an example:

. . . why does one person look down upon the other, he himself is made of the same dust: the last beggarman is on an equal footing with you, he only goes about in a better dress than the beggar, you, too, are only dust, like him, and why then, do you despise him, why do you denounce him, why are you ashamed of the company of the poor man—the only difference is that one has a fortune, cattle, nice clothes, and the other a big family, but what did your family come from, it did not come from the stars, if you have a nice dress, it remains here, they leave you only a shirt and a pair of pants, and all your cattle will stay here, your fortune too remains here on earth, what then are you taking into the other world, you will need something there, which can relieve your soul, but you do not take along anything, for everything that is here only reaches as far as the grave, then you cannot claim it any longer as your own. Your family, your friends and neighbors will accompany you to your grave, then they cover you up and leave you to yourself and go home and when they prepare the dinner for the wake, they will guzzle well and stop thinking of you any longer.[24]

These examples will show that Márton László, in commingling the popular literary tradition and interpreting it, is a characteristic representative of the Bucovina Szekler culture. His personality blends perfectly into the picture, into the atmosphere from which have grown the world view and the tale treasure of the people of Andrásfalva. Beside Mrs. Palkó, the teller of magic tales, beside György Andrásfalvi, the historically inclined type, stands Márton László's devout and religious, literate personality. His religious experiences fill his storys, leading to complete one-sidedness. Strikingly few texts have a historic concern. It is unusual that a man from the Bucovina should be so little interested in any history except that of the church. In addition to the considerable biblical data, the often reliable notations of belief stories, and the great amount of genealogical data, there is only one text in existence which concerns Hungarian history. There is a single short notice about King Mátyás (quoted above); other historical figures mentioned include Attila, King of the Huns, mighty biblical Kings, and conquerors of antiquity (Nebuchadnezzar, Alexander the Great, Kings David and Darius). In another context he also mentions the regime of Franz Joseph, which during his time did not yet belong to history. There is no doubt that Márton László's interest had become one-sided through his deep concern for Catholicism, which also shaped his tales.

When we count the pieces which the Kakasd storytellers ascribe to him with certainty, there are eighteen *märchen*. Only five of them show no religious coloring: The two Poncianus novellas (*Prince Sándor* [Nos. 27 and 97], *A Woman Who Could Sing Well* [No. 101]); the anecdote, *The Dog Market of Buda* (No. 100); and two short, popular jokes. Of the others, three could pass as genuine *märchen*: *Józsi the Fisherman* (No. 22), *The Two Hermits* (No. 38), *The Son of the Wheelwright* (Nos. 98 and 28). These tales may have been contained in Benedek's collection of Hungarian tales and legends, but may also have lived as well in oral tradition. The rest of the texts have an obvious literary origin: *The Prodigal Son* (No. 99), *Listen How Dancing and Pipe-Smoking Started* (No. 104), *János the Smith* (No. 41) (older ones); *Gábor Német* (Nos. 58 and 96), *Margit* (No. 63) (newer ones).

On further consideration we arrive at the following conclusion: Márton László's tale treasure shows the same characteristics as his other works; and in it we can observe the enrichment of folk tradition through the addition of literary elements. Since we do not know Márton László's sources, we cannot say with certainty to what extent the texts taken from non-folk sources had been transformed by him, whether he had taken them all from books, or whether such texts occur particularly in his repertoire because he was especially interested in them. It is certain, though, and this can be seen from his text examples, that he recited his *märchen* in his own words and never took them over slavishly. Here, as in the majority of the texts that are not tale-like, there can be found dialect words, together with the rhymed form and the rhythm of the prose style so characteristic for the popular *märchen*. This is the Szeklers' manner of speaking, shown also in the spelling. Most removed from this style are *Prince Sándor* and *The Son of the Wheelwright*, but even in these we can find harmonizing lines.

*A Woman Who Could Sing Well* does not show rhymed form. The style is less solemn than that of the two tales just mentioned, but it is quite folkloristic and full of popular sayings. Here the rhymes are very unsteady, even though they occur not merely in two or three places, as is the case with our other examples, but accompany the tale to the end. The fresh, popular tone is prevalent, though Márton László apparently did not make use of the oral variant of the tale type AT 1536/B, known in Kakasd, but followed a chapbook version. The place of action is far away, and the horses killed are thrown into the Tiber. The theme is so close to traditional jokes that it was adapted completely. There are such passages as the following:

. . . Well, some time passed, a few years passed, but finally there was smoke from every chimney, no spoon fell down without noise; however this may be, this couple lost their heads over something, they probably know why they quarreled. . . .[25]

And at the end comes the popular moral. Márton László teases the women; he deduces a moral from the excellent tale, exactly as he does from pieces in the *Book of the Dead*, by adding one:

. . . and if he had denied it, it still would have been for nothing/ for they were already caught in his claws/ the woman was recognized as a great sinner, for the law knows/ what the woman has in mind and in her heart/ for this it is necessary to be a man to drive it out of her/ and what her mind is hatching out/ she will not rest before she has finished it/ and if it does not go the way she wants it/ the house will stand on its head.[26]

Extremely interesting is the style in the tale of the *Prodigal Son* (AT 838), a tale text little known in the Hungarian material. Even though it bears the character of the written word, its language is quite popular—there is not one sentence which would indicate the influence of the chapbook or other literature. Its solemn character and its pathos result from its being written down. It is striking that, in contrast to the unrhymed parts of the narration, the words of the characters are cast in rhyme. Especially tight are the words in which the youth sentenced to the gallows takes his leave of the world. These lines in rhymed pairs, corresponding to the usual popular dirge, deviate from Márton László's own style:

> Látod anyám, látod, mi lett énbelölem,
> A rossz növelésvel én hova kerültem.
> Én most ezt csak neked köszönhetem.
> Hogy az ifju életemet akasztófán végzem.
> Mikor gyermek voltam, mindent megengedtél
> akármit tehettem, te nem fenyitettél
> mert ha kiskoromban nem kényeztettél volna
> mint más anya jóra tanitottál volna
> Most erre a fára nem kerültem volna.*

*Do you see, my mother, what has become of me, what has become
    of me because of the bad raising.
  It is you to whom I can owe
  That I end my life on the gallows.
  As a child you let me do anything,

We should mention, in addition to *The Dog Market of Buda*, another piece which also belongs to the religious as well as to the etiological legends: *Listen How Dancing and Pipe-Smoking Started*, a spirited, well-fashioned tale. Even though this tale had been a part of the folklore tradition for a long time, Márton László's individual style is easy to discern. The naive concept is expressed in a near-medieval way: the first men, devils, and angels are described as if they were ordinary beings. The narrator describes the first men, their customs, and their relaxations the way he imagines "life without sin" would be. In the ideal world people are good and God-fearing, they speak of holy things, they sing devout songs, they do not know gluttony, nor what brandy is, nor what dancing or smoking are—they live in quiet concord.

Very precious are the many figures of speech, the pertinent language, the easily flowing rhymes. Special attention should be paid to the plastic description of the dance. The moral, the lesson, which is not omitted here, either, is completely folkloristic and reflects the Szekler way of thinking.

Finally, we want to mention two tale-like texts which we have not included in our tale collection but which deserve attention as individual formations of Márton László. They have religious coloring, and are partially legend and partially belief story.

We might assume that either text occurred in one form or another in the chapbook, but they could also have come from folklore tradition in their present form. The most probable assumption is that they represent a fundamental transformation of material of a literary origin. One text tells about a young man who had fallen heir to a fortune. Disguised as a valet, a devil joins him and persuades him to play cards. The young man gambles away his fortune, and when nothing is left, the devil one night leads him to Lucifer. The prince of hell asks him to deny God as the price of restitution of his fortune. The man shrinks from this and goes away. In the end he gets everything back. The devil as a servant (anecdote) and the denial of God as a test (belief story) are well-known motifs in the folklore tradition. Style and language correspond to the style of the realistic peasant tale. We quote here the dialogue between the devil-servant and the young man who lost his fortune, and the meeting with Lucifer:

> Whatever I did you did not punish me.
> If you would not pamper me in early youth
> But teach me to be good as other mothers
> I would not have gotten into the hands of the henchman.

... The servant sees that his master is so sad and thus he asks him once: "Lord why are you so downcast?" and the fellow says, "Oh, you child why should I not be downcast, when you know what kind of fortune I had before and now I don't have a piece of bread, so I must be desperate/ how shall my life end/ I shall depart from here even today/ and will always follow my eyes/ I never worked/ I never learned to steal—I am at my wit's end/" Then the child answered: "My dear master, do not be desperate/ not everything is lost yet,/ if you will listen to me you will be rich again/ that you will not want to exchange places with the king."/ Then the fellow answered smiling: "How can this be possible? That I can get rich through something while I do not have anything to eat today."/ Then the child said: "This can happen easily,/ you only need to listen to me/ and follow my advice./ During the night I shall lead you to a place/ where you will get an awful lot of money,"/ Well, so the day passed and it was night and when the clock struck ten the child said: "Master, now we can go, we shall go into the forest/ and there we shall find a lot of money."/ Then Satan arrived in the guise of a man and the child said to Lucifer: "Master, I have been serving this fellow for many years,/ I hope to get my wages for my services/ but now he has become very poor and is depending on your help," and then the Lord of Hell said:/ "I shall help you but only if your fellow will deny before me the Almighty God; when you want to be a very rich man, I shall give you so much money that you shall be richer than your father and all your relatives,/ you only have to deny the holy Godhead"/ but the fellow was very scared and did not want to do it and the child said to him:/ "My dear master, consider it well/ don't you see the misery in which you are living/ you do not have anything to eat/ you have fallen on such bad days/ is it really so much of a thing to pronounce this one word 'I deny you'? Say only this one word and immediately all your wishes will be granted". . . ./[27]

Another text is an apochryphal legend, *How the Holy Family Fared in Egypt*. The peasant coloring is striking. The Holy Family lives in exactly the same way as poor people live in the countryside. They build their own hut; they accept any kind of work that is available. Joseph, as carpenter, puts a broken-down cellar into order:

... for a while the dwelling of the Holy Family had neither a roof nor a door/ the wind could blow in/ at will/ but the Holy Family did not stop to consider it/ under the circumstances it was all right./ Joseph carried the tumbled-down debris outside/ he somehow repaired the bad cellar/ since he knew his craft as a carpenter/

so he improvised a door from some kind of pieces/ the roof where it had caved in/ he covered with rubbish and weeds./ But no palace came from this, of course/ but even a camp guard had his own hut. . . .[28]

Joseph accepts work in construction; Mary sews and spins just like the poor women of Andrásfalva:

. . . and so the Virgin Mary said: "Don't be angry, Joseph: I can spin and weave and I can sew dresses/ this will help towards some small income/ the people who now do not like us/ maybe it will be different once they get to know us/ for little money I can work well for them/ and thus God will help us."/ "And I am looking around," said Joseph, "A house is built in part, I have seen, many poor people are working there, maybe they can use a good master."/ . . . But Joseph worked already/ he was missed on the construction work/ his co-workers liked him and respected him very much/ and they did not envy him for what he got paid. . . .

Even the little Jesus lived like the poor children in Andrásfalva, and at an early age helped around the house:

. . . when Mary had finished her sewing/ she had it put away by the little Jesus/ . . . on his side he carried a small satchel/ and in his hand a tiny handbag/ which he brought home packed full of groceries; and whoever had something to spin or to sew, brought it to the lovely Maria/ so he could see the divine child/ . . . .

The legend tells how the little Jesus, gathering flowers for his mother, loses his way. He encounters a shepherdess who is spinning for her master while she watches the herd. The little Jesus asks the girl to lead him home, but the girl is afraid of the wrath of her master: "I am a servant and my master gets angry." Nevertheless the girl takes the little boy home. When she returns she sees that a miracle has happened. The cattle have not done any damage and what had to be spun lay finished at the bottom of the basket.

These examples will suffice to illustrate certain types of Márton Lász-ló's *märchen*. His storytelling and his *Book of the Dead* greatly influenced the magic-religious world view of the people of Kakasd and had a lasting effect upon its *märchen* and tale treasure.

Márton László's *Book of the Dead* and other similar folklore creations diffused through folk manuscripts and their oral transmission point to the importance of the study of the influence of literature on folklore. In archaic regions we are still able to find among the peasantry primitive stages of literary life, comparable in many respects to the Hungarian literature of the sixteenth to the eighteenth centuries, in which written and oral tradition are not yet strictly separated from each other. Márton László's style shows the pathos and the solemnity of literary tradition and at the same time the flexibility and immediacy characteristic of oral tradition. The texts taken from books are not fossilized; they are full of vigor and life, as behooves folklore. We can sense with nearly every piece that it is alive, that it belongs to a series of variants, and that it does not have a definitive form. It is the reborn, individual creation of an eminent representative of folk tradition, and it provides incentive and a point of departure for new forms of oral tradition. To unearth the clerical and secular writings in print which diffused the old literary forms and preserved them for a long time among the people is a task for the literary historian. Such an undertaking might well produce priceless information concerning not only single genres and themes but the question of form.[29]

# A P P E N D I X

# The Kakasd Tale Body:

# A Survey

FOR THE READER'S INFORMATION we shall list in the following, according to narrator, the tales in the Kakasd stock. The expert will find here everything worth knowing about the *märchen* referred to in the study. After giving the Aarne-Thompson number of the individual tales (AT) and a general reference to international parallels* and to the Hungarian tale indices by J. Berze Nagy (BN) and/or J. Honti, we shall list the Hungarian variants, point out their most characteristic traits—especially those of ethnic significance—and indicate the stylistic features of individual narrators.

Concerning Hungarian variants, we checked all the printed *märchen* collections, but, with the exception of our own manuscript collections, we did not include archive material. Therefore the quantity of the variants in many cases does not reflect accurately the *märchen's* popularity and frequency in the whole of the Hungarian language territory. Consequently, the small number of our variants has no relation to the richness of the living tale body. The collection contains many *märchen* which we are certain are well known in almost every Hungarian village, though they have rarely been written down. In the past, collectors did not even record tales that were obscene or antireligious, or which they felt were indecent, and these were seldom added to archives. In arranging the notes on belief stories which are not contained in the Aarne-Thompson index, we have noted Thompson's *Motif-Index* (MI) in referring to international parallels, and H. Bächtold-Stäubli's *Handwörter-*

* See Bibliography and List of Abbreviations for complete citations.

*buch des deutschen Aberglaubens* (BS). For the Hungarian variants we also used the Ethnological Archives of the Ethnographical Museum in Budapest (EA) and the Archives of the Folklore Institute of the University of Budapest (FI).

The literature cited with the individual tales does not exhaust all variants of the type in every case but is concerned solely with those which are close to the Bucovina Szekler version of the *märchen* and which may be considered immediate variants. This is true especially for those *märchen* in which individual shaping has combined motifs of different tale types, or for those which show a great variability within the framework of the tale type. Unfortunately, we cannot completely rely on the Hungarian type indexes; there are many inaccuracies and mistakes in Honti, and in Berze Nagy's type index. Very often different *märchen* types are erroneously grouped together because of the similarity of an inessential motif or incident, or, conversely, different variants of the same type are separated for the same reason. The new classification being done by Á. Kovács and associates is still under way, although the classification of animal and numbskull tales is available in mimeographed form.

## Mrs. Palkó's Tales

1. *The Iron Laci* (1956) A peculiar combination of some closely related tale types, essentially it follows AT 301/A (*Quest for the Vanished Princess*), linked to 552/A (*Three Animals as Brothers-in-law*). The initial incident follows type 408/I (*The Three Oranges*). Berze Nagy included the story with a more or less arbitrarily formed group of tales under BN 468ˣ (*The Damned Sister*). Some of the texts included in this group also indicate a relationship with type 590/A (*The Treacherous Wife*). The diverse connections of the tale are indicated in BN I, 243-250, 566-577, 639-642, and II, 183-188. The closest variants of Mrs. Palkó's text are Majláth, pp. 187-202, and Kálmány, *Szeged* I, 121-123, where the name of the hero is also the same. Berze Nagy rightly points to the affinity of this tale with the characteristic Hungarian ethnic type BN 319ˣ (AT 328/A; Dégh, 1964, pp. 15-28, 306-307), which can also be corroborated by a version of P. Pandur (Dégh, 1940, pp. 32-46) in which a hero is also named Iron Laci.

Mrs. Palkó had heard this tale half a year before, during a visit to her sister in the neighboring village of Mucsfa. It was being read aloud "from some kind of old book." This must have been a popular adaptation of Majláth's version by Benedek (1894, III, 174-188). As in the case of other newly acquired tales, Mrs. Palkó did not have the time to adapt this story completely to her own style, although she did tell it quite often during the winter following her visit. Sometimes she followed the original almost verbatim, even to identical expressions; in other places she modified it considerably according to her own taste. One small incident compared to the original printed version would well characterize her style of immediate creation:

BENEDEK

The boy arrives home and his sisters are just playing ball. He joins them too, but the girls agree on hitting him always on the head with the ball, in order to pay him back once and for all for his naughtiness, for his pranks with which he harrassed them so much. Laci got really angry when he saw that they all hit him with the ball and in his fury yelled at the girls, "If the earth would only swallow you!" Immediately the earth opened and the three princesses disappeared.

MRS. PALKÓ

The three princesses went out to the yard to play ball, to enjoy themselves. One of the girls tells the other two, "Listen, when Laci comes back from school, he will want to play with us. But," says she, "all of us just hit him with the ball, let us beat him real hard, to make him angry." Hardly were these words spoken when Laci was back home. He did not rush in to eat but joined them to play ball. But the girls did as they decided, each struck him, beat him with the ball. Laci at last became annoyed when he realized that they were only making fun of him. Then he said to them, "I wish the earth would swallow all three of you!"

As he uttered these words the earth broke open under them and swallowed all three. But nobody ever saw where they had disappeared. Lunchtime came then and the girls were nowhere. They went out to look for them, search for them, but they could not find them. Evening came but the girls still were nowhere. Once the king said, "I wonder where the girls might be, where do they stay for so long? They never did this before. No lunch, no supper, how can they stay away without eating?"

There was great sorrow in the King's court. They were searching for the princesses everywhere, all over the world but could not find them, did not know where to look for them. . . .

And surely they awoke to a new morning, but the girls still were nowhere. Now the king sent soldiers after them to search for them, to find them. They looked through the whole world but they did not find them. They did not see the girls anywhere, there is no trace of them. The king is in tears and so is the queen! How could they disappear from the face of the earth without a trace that nobody can tell about their whereabouts?

2. *The Three Princes and the Man with the Iron Hat* (1948)   AT 304 (*The Hunter*) + 723\* (*The Hero Binds Midnight, Dawn and Midday*) + 401/A (*The Enchanted Princesses*) + 402 (*The Mouse as Bride*); Honti, pp. 13, 18, 19, 28; BN I, 283; BP, II, 30, 318, 366, 503 and III, 114. For the motif of the binding of celestial bodies see Frazer, *The Golden Bough* I, 318; BP, III, 288; MI, D 2146.2.2 and H 1128.

VARIANTS: Gaál, *Magyar népmese* II, 154, 214; Majláth, p. 343; Erdélyi, 1855, p. 7; Nyelvör, 1899, p. 418; *MNGY* VI: 369, VII: 467, IX: 15, XII: 95, XIII: 357; *Ethn.*, 1931, p. 40; *Pesti Napló*, Jan. 4, 1931, p. 31; Berze Nagy, 1940, II, 86, 114; Dégh, 1942, I, 171; Nagy-Faragó, p. 71; Ortutay, Dégh, and Kovács I, 374, 381.

Only two or three of the variants mentioned above can be said to be close to our text. On the other hand, we know a great many in which the one or another episode of our *märchen* can be found. Therefore only those were mentioned here in which the course of the action or several episodes are coincident with our *märchen*. Even though the type 723\* (or coupled with 304 or 402) was formed specifically in the Hungarian folk tradition, the tale before us, which combines elements from different tale types, is very seldom found in this form. It could much better be compared to pieces in older tale collections (Majláth, Gaál, Erdélyi) or even to the much older *Story of the Three Wandering Princes*, which is contained in the eighteenth century manuscript tale collection at Sárospatak. As many other of our tales, this text bears witness to the fact that the tales of the Bucovina Széklers reflect a much earlier time, since they did not play any part in the development of the *märchen* within the whole of Hungary.

The combination in Mrs. Palkó's tale is a very felicitous one, for this is to be counted among her best constructed, most fanciful hero tales. Basically it follows type 402. But here, as well as in the adjacent types 304 and 401, the motif of the two brothers' treachery is absent. Here Mrs. Palkó borrows from the tale type 551 (*Water of Life*) and from her own tale, *The Psalmsinging Bird*, which she regards very highly.

3. *I Don't Know* (Tape recording, 1949)   AT 314 (*Goldener*) + 532 (*I Don't Know*); BN, I, 336; BP, III, 94, 340; Katona, 1912, I, 244-248; Solymossy, 1918, pp. 277-286, and 1919, p. 66; Thompson, 1946, pp. 59, 61.

The motifs which occur in various combinations in the Hungarian material of the tale type marked *I Don't Know* can be found in the AT type index in two different, well-known, and popular tale families. They are the tale types of 314 and 530–32 which Lajos Katona, who first constructed type sketches for a Hungarian tale classification, designated with the name of *Tuhkamo*. Katona indicates another related type in the Hungarian material, and Sándor Solymossy correctly follows the two mentioned. The tale is the male redaction of AT 510 (*Cinderella*), the so-called Male-Cinderella. In spite of the similarity in topic development and the frequent intermingling of elements, Aarne did not recognize the connection between these three *märchen* themes, which vary among themselves, when he made his international type determination. Thompson writes that it is hard to determine if the *I Don't Know märchen*, (a close variant of our text), which can so frequently be found in Eastern Europe could be designated by 532, or if it should merely be considered a variation of 314. According to him the *märchen* is of Russian origin, has spread from the Russian language field, and has become popular most of all in Finland, Hungary, and the Baltic States. Since all three *märchen* have a common basis, that of the simpleminded hero (or one who pretends to be simple-minded) who carries out menial work as a hired hand, who is derided and looked down upon by everybody, Solymossy arrives at the conclusion that we are dealing with three variations of one basic story. These three *märchen* have sprung within recent history from a common foundation, an archetype (in which the character of *I Don't Know* and also the magic horse might have occurred). One thing is sure: the three *märchen* and their variations blended with each other thoroughly and are extremely popular in folk tradition, even though there is not the slightest literary influence discernible in them. A monograph on this subject could search out their origin and paths of development. The assumption of an Eastern European origin is borne out by the facts that the popular variants are widespread to this day, and that all three types are frequently represented, especially in the Slavic language territory. There are indications in the variants of this particular tale that it might have originated, and have maintained itself, in countries where serfdom and other features of feudalism were surviving anachronistically. Rejecting W. Anderson's opinion on the origin of the stupid hero who figures in this tale, Meletinski (1958, pp. 64-160) seeks an explanation in the stages of social evolution.

VARIANTS: Gaál, 1822, p. 25; Gaál, 1857-1860, I, 139, and II, 133; Erdélyi, 1846-1848, II, 367; Pintér, p. 101; Istvánffy, p. 86; Merényi, 1862, I, 1; Nyelvör, 1876, p. 419, 1886, p. 326, 1889, p. 330; *MNGY* IX, 55, 69, and XIII, 70, 344; *Ethn.* 1918, p. 246; Ortutay, 1940, p. 243; Dégh, 1942, II, 16; Kovács, 1943, I, 165; Végh, p. 151; Faragó-Nagy, p. 103.

The most striking parts of the *märchen* are the following: (1) comforting words for the king, preparation for war, and the increasing meanness of the major-domos; (2) the conversation in the stable between *I Don't Know* and the soldiers; (3) the horse instructs *I Don't Know*; (4) description of the city, the people in the streets, the royal family, and the girl; (5) the cook; (6) the scorn of the brothers-in-law; and (7) the description of the pageantry when *I Don't Know* and his wife make their entrance into the royal palace. (German translation: Ortutay, 1957, pp. 227-275.)

4. *Ej Haj* (1948) AT 325 (*The Magician and His Pupil*); BN, I, 407; BP, II, 60; Benfey, *Pantchatantra;* E. Cosquin, "Les mongoles et leur prétendu

role dans la transmission des contes indiens vers l'occident européen," pp. 497-612; Azadovski, 1926; Thompson, 1946, pp. 69-70.

VARIANTS: Gaál, 1857-1860, III, 180; *MNGY* III, 362, VI, 277, IX, 67, and XIII, 432, 435; BN, 1940, II, 112; Dégh, 1942, I, 220.

Mrs. Palkó's *märchen* is to be counted among the most complete and most colorful of the Hungarian variants. Usually the incident of the boy learning the secret magic, which he subsequently uses, behind the back of his magician master, remains vague or obscure. Because of this the master, who does not want his pupil to outdo him, takes his revenge. This motif (MI, D 671 and 672) with Mrs. Palkó leads to the tale type 313 (*The Magic Flight*). Here too the sorcerer's daughter assists the hero to outwit her father. An entirely new incident also figures in the tale: the prince, who is about to go to his wedding, borrows the horse into which the magician has changed the hero. This might be Mrs. Palkó's invention and might be derived from the magic horse motif of the *Sky-High Tree* (tale No. 23). It is well worthwhile to compare Mrs. Palkó's variants with those of the likewise creative narrator Péter Pandur. He uses broader brush strokes for some of the incidents (for example, the father puts the son three times into service for three years—the service and the bargain appear three times), but Mrs. Palkó's text is livelier. It is worth mentioning that Diószegi (1954, pp. 56-58, and 1958, pp. 96-120) sees in Pandur's description of learning magic by being chopped into slices an element of shaman practice.

Regarding the name of the magician (which in Hungarian means a sigh), we should observe that in the international variants the devil is summoned by the ejaculation "oh" (BP, II, 963). See also Schullerus (p. 36) regarding the same thing in Rumanian *märchen*. It is possible that the name, "Ej Haj," was inspired by Elek Benedek's variant *János Teddneki* (III, 220). Here the King of Devils is called "Hájháj." Benedek's *märchen* otherwise varies considerably from this. Again, Diószegi (1958) relates the word *Haj* to the Vogul shaman's *Xai*, an invocation to the supernatural at ritual ceremonies.

5. *Pihári* (1956)  AT 326 (*The Youth Who Wanted to Learn What Fear Is*); BP, I, 22; BN, I, 411; Katona, 1912, I, 283; Thompson, 1946, pp. 105-106.

VARIANTS: Erdélyi, 1846-48, III, 289, 315; Kálmány, 1914-1915, I, 15, and 1881-91, I, 8; Merényi, 1882, II, 191, 215; Gaál, 1857-1860, p. 40; *MNGY* IX, 37, and XIII, 47; Nyelvör, I, 376, and XIII, 186; Pintér, p. 133; Berze Nagy, II, 29, 30; Gönczi, p. 311; Nagy, p. 202.

The "old book" from which an old man had read and to which Mrs. Palkó refers at the end of the *märchen*, could only be a household tale book, as with the *Iron Laci*, in the manner of Benedek. Mrs. Palkó's remark is an indication of the preciousness of such books. The book has already been ruined, but from the torn pages "they want to make a new one." The Benedek variant can be traced back to a text by Erdélyi (1846-48, III, 289), in which the hero is likewise called "Pihári," and with which it completely coincides.

Mrs. Palkó does not deviate from the book tale in any way. Only her rich language lends special flavor to the *märchen*.

6. *Zsuzska and the Devil* (1948)    AT 328 (*The Boy Steals the Giant's Treasure*). The international index does not indicate the female version of the tale which is very popular in Hungary. BP, III, 33; BN 328¹* (I, 426).

This *märchen* is closely related to type 327/A (*Hansel and Gretel*); they are often coupled together. The male variation is also very well known in Hungary. Just as does AT 327/A with type 510 (*Cinderella*), the type AT 328 often pervades tale AT 531 (*Ferdinand the True and Ferdinand the False*).

VARIANTS: Arany, 1862, p. 213; Nyelvör, 1873, p. 279; *MNGY*, IX, 83, and XIII, 266; BN, II, 117; *Ethn.*, 1928, p. 196; Végh, p. 149; Ortutay-Dégh-Kovács, I, 411. *Rébinka*, in my own manuscript collection is told by the 17-year-old Ida Kása from Sára in Zemplén county (1943). The *Sea-leaping Shoes*, also from my collection, is told by the 56-year-old József Fejes.

Our variant here is closest to that of László Arany. The title is the same, and the deviations result solely from Mrs. Palkó's style. Her experiences as a servant girl in the house of wealthy burghers are well detailed in the story of the poor peasant's daughter.

7. *Death With the Yellow Legs* (1948)    AT 332 (*Godfather Death*); BN, I, 447; Thompson, 1946, pp. 46-47; Christiansen, pp. 70-82.

VARIANTS: Erdélyi, 1855, p. 17; Gaál, 1822, p. 72; Merényi, 1861, I, 175; Berze Nagy, 1940, II, 127, 128, 130; Fél, p. 193; *Death as Brother-in-law*, related by the 59-year-old András Ferencz, Csikmenaság, 1952 (FI).

Our variant follows its type, although the trick ending with the Our Father prayer, which usually forms the high point of the tale, is missing. Instead of this we have the somewhat brutal beheading of the poor man by Death.

8. *The Dead Lover* (1948)    AT 365 (*Lenore*); MI, E 215; BN I, 484; Child, V, 60; Thompson, 1946, p. 41; Peuckert, 1955; Benkö, 1934, and 1936, p. 26; Dános, 1938, p. 107; Ortutay, 1940, p. 396.

VARIANTS: Pap, 1865, p. 94; *MNGY*, I, 207, and XIII, 253; *Ethn.*, 1901, 315, 1908, 297 (*cantefable*), 1928, 54; Benkö, 1934, p. 22 (+ 407); Ortutay, 1935, p. 236 (+ 407); Berze Nagy, 1940, II, 135, 137, 139; Fél, pp. 139, 143; Banó, 1941, p. 243; Dégh, 1942, I, 284; Balassa, pp. 133, 524-25 (twelve versions in manuscript); Dobos, 1962, p. 172. This tale also is included in a popular collection by Elek Benedek, *Székely népmesék és balladák* (*Szekler Popular Tales and Ballads*), p. 111.

In Mrs. Palkó's text, as in many of the other Hungarian variants, we can feel that the belief foundation for the *märchen* is still alive, for it is made a reality for the people of Andrásfalva through folk religion. Being familiar with Mrs. Palkó's magic practice, we can see her as the "old neighbor lady" who occurs so often in her *märchen* and who advises the girl of this tale. This case is not unusual and not unbelievable (compare the belief stories below about revenants: Nos. 10-14, 73, 74, 75). The headless horse is a well-known spook in folk belief (see below, No. 14).

9. *The Glass Coffin* (1950)   AT 407/B (*The Devil's [Dead Man's] Mistress*); BN, I, 558; BP, II, 125, 485, and III, 259.

It was only in the last revised edition of the international tale catalogue that this *märchen*, which is one of the most popular stories in Hungary, was included as an independent type. However, the area of distribution seems to be relatively small. Hungarian researchers who so far have been concerned with it usually join it to type 365 above (*Lenore*). Since there is an affinity between the two and since there are cases where the motifs are mingled, they consider this version a variant of this type. László Benkö, in his study of 1934, is of the opinion that all the types with miraculous resuscitation are related to the legend of *Lenore*, for example AT 720, 403, 407, etc.

In our opinion, the relationship between 365 and 407 alone can be assumed, in that both are based on the belief that the dead or the spirits of the dead appear when they are mentioned, and that they take their revenge. This belief is an element of the common European pre-Christian folk belief still alive today. In our two variants (see Nos. 77 and 78 by Mrs. Sebestyén), the strength of the victim declines from day to day because of the vampire-like apparition of the Evil One. This demon spirit is widespread in the legends and belief concepts of the Hungarian ethnic groups in the Bucovina as well as in the Moldavia region (compare Hegedüs, 1952, pp. 50, 60, 101, 156, 265) and along the southwestern borders of Hungary. Since this form of vampire belief is known especially among Poles, Slovaks, and Russians, and to a lesser extent among Balkan Slavs and Rumanians, we may conclude that the Hungarians who were residing in ethnically mixed regions, or contact zones, had taken it over from them. We may also add that Mrs. Palkó had heard this *märchen* from a Rumanian girl. For the connection of this *märchen* with folk belief, see Ortutay, 1940, pp. 396-397; Berze Nagy, 1940, II, 493; Dégh, 1964, pp. 285, 349; Dégh, 1965, pp. 83-85.

VARIANTS: Arany, 1862, p. 153; Nyelvör, 1873, p. 421, 1879, p. 328, 1893, p. 475, 1895, p. 332; Lázár, p. 613; *MNGY*, XIII, 190; Kálmány, 1914-1915, I, 73; *Ethn.*, 1929, 201, 1935, 72; Ortutay, 1935, p. 236; Berze Nagy, 1940, II, 153, 156; Fél, p. 147; Benkö, 1934, p. 22; Hegedüs, 1946, p. 40; Ortutay, 1940, p. 269 (two versions in English translation Dégh, 1964, p. 46); Banó, 1941, p. 65; Dégh, 1942, I, 236; Hegedüs, 1952, p. 162. Balassa, pp. 144, 526, lists six more unpublished variants; Dobos, 1962, p. 174. A manuscript version was narrated by the 17-year-old Ida Kása from Sára, Zemplén county, in 1943 (in my personal collection). Concerning hiding from the Evil One as it occurs in this *märchen*, see Kálmány, 1914-15, I, 60; Dégh, 1942, II, 67.

Mrs. Palkó's *märchen* is well rounded and perfectly balanced. In her recital and her tone of voice she differentiates clearly between the incidents anchored in belief and claiming credibility of the village public, and the miraculous adventure of the king with the girl as a flower. The most beautifully recited is the last scene: the king asks his wife to accompany him to church. The indescribable fear of the wife and the moment when she sees the Evil One are graphically rendered in the narration. One does not know if she really sees something terrible or if all this is only a figment of her imagination, and if it is the terrible fear that in the end brings about her despair, that is, her death. Our two variants differ in their tragic ending from the more usual form of the *märchen*, which has a happy ending.

10. *The Restless Dead Man* (1949)  The foundation of Mrs. Palkó's "experienced" or "heard" stories is the belief that a dead man who is wept over cannot find any rest and that his pillow is wet with tears. This same belief can be found both in the medieval literary exempla and the *märchen* (BS, IX, 330; MI, E361; BP, II, 485; Child II, 234). For the meeting of the dead see *MI*, E 491, BS, IV, 1503. For the money of the dead man see *Ethn.* 1907, 293; BS, III, 1907. For making one a beggar see Berze Nagy, 1940, III, 231. For the sickle see L. Kovács, p. 101. For the belief that one must not shed tears over a dead man, for his casket gets wet and his angel's wings become moist, see Gönczi, p. 356; Berze Nagy, 1940, III, 227; *Ethn.*, 1928, 115, and 1938, 143.

11. *The Midnight Mass of the Dead*  MI, E 492; Christiansen, 4015; BS I, 1070; BP, III, 472; Thompson, 1946, p. 257.
  HUNGARIAN VARIANTS: *Ethn.*, 1895, 48-49, 417, 1895, 138, 1901, 315, 1917, 231; Ipolyi *Magyar Mytholgia*, II, 118; *The Diary of Mihály Cserei*, p. 225.
  Mrs. Palkó tries to make this "case," which joins the preceding one, believeable by attributing it to a foreign priest. It is quite possible that, in the multi-ethnic town of Andrásfalva, she had heard it from a Polish girl.

12. *The Count and János, the Coachman* (1948)  *MI*, E 371; BS IX, 574 (return from dead to reveal hidden treasure) + E 415; BS 574 (the dead cannot rest until a certain work is finished) + E 463 (living man in dead man's shroud). BN 322* (I, 405); Aarne, 1918, p. 114; Harva, p. 27; Beke, pp. 340-349; *Midwest Folklore*, 1952, p. 47.
  VARIANTS: Erdélyi, 1846-1848, III, 289, 315; *MNGY*, I, 447 (the same is in Elek Benedek, V, 199); Dégh, 1964, p. 291. More distant variants—*Ethn.*, 1904, 41; *MNGY*, XIII, 438; Ortutay, 1940, p. 235—The Hungarian versions, and Mrs. Palkó's text among them, are essentially legends of belief, of which several less well-formed variants are also known as actual stories about revenants. The motif of the hero sleeping in the shroud is close to the motif in the tale of the youth who wanted to learn what fear is (AT 326). The two

plots are often mixed up with each other, as in the more distant variants. In connection with the type see also Chapter 7.

According to folk belief the return of the dead is often connected with hidden money. Mrs. Palkó adds to the above another example which completes our text in several regards:

> The dog sees the dead man and is afraid of him. My mother told us that she was in service at a certain place where there was a bad woman. No hired man could stand it longer than one day with her. When Mother got there, the woman died. She was buried, and she went home. She says that she saw her, as she came out of the furrow, the dog saw her. But he was so afraid of her, he barked fearfully, not as if he would bark up a living person. But how long it lasted, I don't know. From the furrow she passed into the garden. There was something hidden there. She was waiting that somebody would force her to say why she was waiting. That is this way, whoever hides something quickly, hides money, has no rest, one only has to remove it from where it is hidden. If only somebody had forced her to speak!

*MI*, E 371; BS IX, 574 (returns on account of the money + *MI*, B 733 (an animal sees the dead man); BS, IV, 473 (a dog sees the dead man).

The explanation in the form of a tale added to the *märchen* to explain the return of the dead leads to another rich field of folk belief. See Solymossy, 1919, p. 131; Bán, 1915, pp. 28, 86; Szendrey, "Magyar népmonda tipusok és tipikus motivumok," *Ethn.*, 1922, 49; *MI*, N 532; BS, VII, 1005 (fire is the sign) + N 553, 2, BS, VII, 1007 (disregard of the command for silence). One has to throw something upon it: BS VII, 1008; Gönczi, p. 228. Boots: *Ethn.*, 1896, 378. Shirt: *Ethn.*, 1896, 176. Children's shirts: *Ethn.*, 1893, 217; Ipolyi, I, 199. Prayerbook or some other holy object: Versényi, p. 29. Talk to the revenant: Balassa, pp. 285-86, No. 157, and pp. 185, 582, No. 29. Female revenant: Balassa, pp. 270, 186-188, 308, 370, 374, No. 187.

13. *Fasting* (1954)  This case of the revenant (poltergeist) who throws objects around but does not break them follows Mrs. Palkó's *märchen* mentioned above. Here, however, the restlessness has other causes: the dead is rendered restless because the survivors forced him to return by fasting, a custom well known with Szeklers. "The woman began fasting so as to harm her husband. The man had beaten the woman badly and she was very bitter about it and then started to fast, and then he had to stay in bed for twenty years." This practice is widespread among the Szeklers in Transylvania and the Rumanians, whom the Kaluger monks unwittingly helped. See BS, II, 1241; *Ethn.*, 1891, 253; Balassa, pp. 268, 312, No. 155.

14. *My Father's Adventure* (1949) *MI*, C 225, 3; BS, II, 1205, IV, 1117 (the cat of the witch) + F 491 (incubus) + G 211, 13, BS, V, 625 (frog)

+ G 211, ii; BS, IV, 1615 (ghost in horse's guise) + E 424.1.3 (dressed-up-woman) + D 2070 (fainting spell). In the Hungarian material, the incubus spreads fire: *Ethn.*, 1891, 204, 1914, 324, 1928, 97, 1927, 47; Nyelvör, 1902; p. 530; Turista Közlöny, 1917, pp. 53, 56, 62. Witch's frog: *Ethn.*, 1890, 287, and 1938, 184 (Balassa, No. 127.)

In this narrative the belief in witches is coupled with that in the revenant. Both combine here: the witch cannot find rest because of her evil deeds and has to return. As a ghost she takes the forms in which, while alive, she ruined people by leading them astray or by "driving them to despair" (Balassa, pp. 64-65).

15. *The Beautiful Erzsébet* (1956)  AT 400 (*The Swan Maidens*). For variants, see notes to tale No. 65 below.

SOURCE: Benedek, I, 211, whose original is Kriza's *Fairy Erzsébet* (*MNGY*, XII, 15). It is worthwhile to compare this variant with Andrásfalvi's tale *The Nine Kernels of Wheat*, which is a much more individualized and original reworking of the same source. Mrs. Palkó was faithful to the version which she had learned about half a year before, when it was read aloud to her. Though she knew Andrásfalvi's version she was in no way influenced by it. She considered it as his tale, and one of his the most favored pieces in his repertoire. Mrs. Palkó's recital here is relatively awkward. She starts at the wrong place and corrects herself only after some time by telling the tale again, from the beginning. The heroine's name, Fairy Erzsébet, she also often confuses with the more common name of the type, Fairy Ilona. In order to check the stylistic difference between Kriza's pseudo-popular Szekler language, Benedek's literary adaptation, and Mrs. Palkó's unsure, not yet established, but natural oral style, we shall quote one single incident. Mrs. Palkó instinctively corrects the sophisticated book story creatively. The incident tells about the hero coming closer to the fire and beholding the sleeping giant. The narrator repeated the scene when she began the story again. It is worthwhile to give both versions, although Mrs. Palkó shortened the second because of the repetition.

| KRIZA | BENEDEK |
|---|---|
| . . . and lo, there is the fire he saw but what a bunch of log burnt there, the flames reached the sky. He started towards it; coming to the fire, behold, a big man encircles the fire, placing his head on his foot. He was covered with a big cloak. He muses, what to do, should he lay down outside or inside of the man? For if he stays outside, he | He approaches the fire and what does he see, good Lord! Nothing but a terribly big giant, stretched out around the fire, but he is so big that his body completely surrounds the fire, he laid his head on his foot sleeping like this. The youth lays down outside of the giant, he catches cold, if he lays down inside, the giant will find him and kill |

will catch cold, if inside, he will be burned. He neatly slips into the sleeve of the big cloak and there falls peacefully asleep.

him. What else could he do but creep into the sleeve of the giant's jacket and fall asleep there and did not move till morning.

### Mrs. Palkó 1

As he walked toward the fire what a sight his eye caught. Three cord of wood on the top of each other were burning and a big giant slept beside it. The giant was so big that he surrounded the whole fire. So big was the man he put even his head on his foot. This is how big he was, he could place his head on his foot after encircling the fire. The youth went closer and looked down upon him. O my God, I have never seen such a big man. "I am tired, I would like to rest," he said, "but where could I lay down? If I go inside of him and he wakes he will throw me into the fire. And if I lay down outside, I will be cold." The youth collected his wits and climbed up high into the sleeve of the giant. Into the sleeve of his cloak and in there he fell asleep.

### Mrs. Palkó 2

And then he caught sight of a big fire, there was a big fire and the giant slept there. "O my God, tell me what to do now? I would like to warm up myself because I am cold. But if I go inside, I might wake him," he says, "and he flings me into the fire. And if I lay down outside," says he, "I am freezing." The man was so big that he encircled the fire and still managed to put his head on his foot. The giant was asleep and he climbed up into the sleeve of his cloak.

16. *The Princess* (1950)   AT 403/A (*The Wishes*); BN, I, 548; BP, I, 99, II, 278, III, 82; Arfert, 1897; Thompson, 1946, pp. 117-119; Karl, 1909, I, 73; Eckhardt, 1937, pp. 11-13; Kardos, (n.d., pp. 76-78, 273. Although this tale can be traced in its constituent elements back to classical antiquity and shows a parallel development both in oral and written literature across Europe, the basis of the Hungarian redaction seems to be the French Bertha legend shaped around the late twelfth century. It is the romantic story of *Berthe aus grans piés*, the forsaken bride in the Charlemagne cycle, who was a fictitious Hungarian princess. The close relationship between Hungary and France in the late Middle Ages accounted for the specific popularity of the tale. The motifs of this *märchen* are easily linked to other related types which also center around the persecution of the innocent heroine; that is, the episodes of *märchen* of similar content are easily included in this tale. The closest affinial types are *Little Brother and Little Sister* (450), which probably shares the same source, and the types of *Cinderella* (510), *The Three Oranges*

(408), *The Girl Without Hands* (707), and *The Talking Horse's Head* (533). See also Thompson, 1946, p. 117.

Mrs. Palkó's text contains a motif which deserves special attention: the girl who weeps pearls (*MI*, D 1454.4.1.) S. Solymossy, 1917, p. 225 in his study on this motif of oriental derivation, states that it has found entry as a secondary motif into the tale of *The Kind and Unkind Girls* (AT 480). Turóczi-Trostler informs us about an exemplum from 1763 and refers to European and French literary editions which have influenced Hungarian oral narratives (*Historiák és méses fabulák*, pp. 80-81). The model for the heroine possessed of fabulous qualities comes from India and has penetrated into this tale of origin through paths that can scarcely be traced today.

VARIANTS: Majláth, p. 318: Gaál, 1857-1860, II, 54; Arany, pp. 83, 99; Pintér, p. 173; Kálmány, 1914-1915, II, 70, 98; *MNGY*, VIII, 56, 57, 58, 65, X, 218, 227, and XIII, 249, 295; Ortutay, 1935, p. 149; Berze Nagy, 1940, II, 150; Fél, p. 149; Bözödi, p. 7; Ösz, p. 186; Dégh, 1942, II, 137 (only the motif of the girl who sheds pearls as tears); Kovács, 1943, I, 209 (+510), 216 (+510) and II, 68; Hegedüs, 1952, p. 102; Bözödi, 1958, p. 5. A scant variant of our text also occurs in Elek Benedek (I, 470).

It is a very well recited, poetic *märchen*. Its beginning is quite unusual; the good quality of the girl, for which she is rewarded with the extraordinary ability, is missing. In this tale, too, the descriptions, characterizations of persons, and situations merit special attention. The young king—though he is a background figure in the tale—is suffering the long prison term practically as a martyr for justice. In this *märchen* the thought is recurrent that there is no difference between people and that the only difference between rich and poor lies in the way they dress. The king, liberated from prison, puts on his royal garments and is immediately the one he was before imprisonment.

17. *Rosemary* (1959) AT 403 (*The Black and the White Bride*). For details of the tale see above. This tale belongs also to the old repertoire of the storyteller. However, after the Kakasd settlement Mrs. Palkó preferred to relate the other one in public. This accounts for its more hesitant narration. Among her favorite stories about persecuted heroines, Mrs. Palkó had a special liking for the variants of the "pearl-weeping girl" story, which is clearly shown by this tale. She adapted three strongly divergent variants from the old Andrásfalva tale body, of which only one could survive since the audience selected only one worth listening to. Thus the other two disintegrated. This one, in spite of memory lapses and unnatural, abrupt ending, has striking qualities. A significant deviation from other Hungarian variants is the inclusion of I.c. motif on AT 613 (*The Two Travelers*). However, the girl's transformation into a dove and the flower growing in her path are not unknown motifs; the capturing of the dove is in accordance with AT 707 (*The Three Golden Sons*). On the other hand, the successful escape of

the heroine and the regaining of her eyesight are almost identical with *The Princess*. Mrs. Palkó's dramatic style is exhibited in the double structure of the tale (for details see No. 18 below).

18. *The Fairy Princess* (1950)   AT 408 (*The Three Oranges*); BN, I, 566; BP, II, 125, and IV, 257; Thompson, 1946, pp. 94-95.

VARIANTS: Gaál, II, 186, 254; Erdélyi, 1846-1848, II, 345, and III, 252; Merényi, 1861, II, 35; Arany, p. 128; Nyelvör, 1871, p. 374, 1875, p. 473, 1878, p. 182, and 1885, p. 519; Istvánffy, p. 39; *MNGY*, IX, 213, X, 96, and XIII, 297, 301; *Ethn.*, 1922, 77; Berze Nagy, 1940, II, 158 (+301): Kovács, 1943, II, 161 (complicated coupling of six tales); Gönczi, p. 290 (+510); Dégh, 1940, p. 44 (+707); Hegedüs, 1946, p. 60; P. Szentmártoni, p. 124; Végh, p. 74. In my manuscript collection there are two variants, related by the 22-year-old Julis Puskás and by the 45-year-old Ferencz Sebök of Piricse, Szabolcs County, 1938.

This text belong to the category of tales which bases its action on the preparations for the dramatically conducted revelation. In this tale the narrator has the events pass twice before our eyes: once when they occur; the second time when the hero or his spokesman (his child, the young hero) relates them as his own experience. This construction is done consciously and logically in *The Three Oranges* (compare also Dégh, 1940, p. 44) and in the *Golden-Haired Twins* (see Banó, 1941, p. 222, and 1939, p. 159). It may also occur in other tales in which the heroine is besmirched (see above *The Twelve Robbers*, No. 35, and *Ilona Beautiful*, No. 36, as well as Ortutay, pp. 140, 278). Varying with the inventiveness of the storyteller, the twofold narration can also be used elsewhere (Dégh, 1942, I, 171). Here the narrator is presented with an excellent occasion, under any conditions, to present dramatically the increased restlessness and the final annihilation of the unmasked schemer, bringing it to a moving climax in the second telling.

Mrs. Palkó, as well as János Nagy who narrated the Bodrogköz variant, presented a lively storytelling situation exactly like that of their own village community. The spinning bee is held at the queen's quarters in the royal palace, where the royal and princely ladies and girls are assembled to do fine needlework and "everyone told a tale in turn, they were amused about it and laughed . . . ;" "now it is your turn to tell"; "all right then please, listen to me carefully . . . ;" "they put her in the middle, around her sat the noble ladies, and in their midst they put her on a chair." The arrangements and the preparations correspond exactly to those at a wake, when the invited story-teller tells a story.

19. *The Two Sisters* (1959)   AT 403 + 480 (*The Kind and the Unkind Girls*). A fragmentary text includes only the *I–III* incidents of the type and does not seem to be close to any of the known variants. Though the initial

episode of this story is missing from both of the related types above (Nos. 16 and 17), in all probability it does not belong to them but is part of a long forgotten type brought to light by association in the memory of Mrs. Palkó.

20. *The Serpent Prince* (tape recording, 1950) AT 425/A (*Cupid and Psyche*); BN I, 583; L. Katona, 1912, I, 218-229; BP, II, 223, 245, and III, 37; Koechlin, 1945; Swahn, 1955.

VARIANTS: Gaál, 1922, p. 364; Gaál, 1857-1860, III, 86; Merényi, 1861, I, 3; Pap. 101; *MNGY*, VII, 394, X, 116, 123, and XIII, 238; *Ethn.*, 1929, 53; Berze Nagy, 1940, II, 163, 166; Dégh, 1942, I, 260; Hegedüs, 1952, p. 268; Nagy-Faragó, p. 75; Bözödi, 1958, p. 425; Nagy, p. 76.

This tale is numbered among the most beautiful of Mrs. Palkó's pieces. It is colorful, poetic, and very lyrical. Not only is each situation well defined, but the state of emotion of the heroine is delineated with great insight and compassion. We want to point out especially the following parts: (1) Introduction: the grief of the royal couple over being childless (compare the same in the tale of *The Turk*); (2) treatment of the misbegotten child; (3) the bride's being won by a ruse and her sufferings in the castle, then her gradual acceptance of what cannot be changed; (4) the advice of the wise woman (see also the *Glass Casket, The Dead Lover, Rupcsen-Hencsen, The Murdering Istéfán, The Twin Rod*); (5) the twitching of the hazel bush (compare the *Tannhäuser* motif, further down, also in *The Murdering Istéfán*); (6) the motif of the sleeping potion, which is an organic part of type 407. English translation: Ortutay, 1962, p. 84.

21. *The Fawn* (tape recording, 1950) AT 450 (*Little Brother and Little Sister*) (403 IIIa, IVa, Va); BN I, 607; BP, I, 79-96; Thompson, 1946, p. 118; Arfert, 1897.

There are no great differences among the variants: in most cases the starting point for the tale is the fact that the father takes a second wife and that the stepmother plots to have the children killed. The cannibal motif (*MI*, G 36)—the starving parents' plan to slaughter their own children—usually occurs not only in the Hungarian but quite frequently in Slovak and Polish versions. In both the international and the Hungarian material the rhymed decoy call of the brother transformed into a duck can be found frequently.

VARIANTS: Erdélyi, 1846-1848, III, 274; Arany, p. 100; Lázár, pp. 597, 616; Nyelvör, 1884, p. 429, and 1902, p. 115; Kálmány, 1914-1915, I, 73; *MNGY*, IX, 238, 334, 342, and XIII, 303, 307; Berze Nagy, 1940, II, 175; M. Ferenczy László, p. 95; P. Szentmártoni, p. 71; *Ethn.*, 1937, 356; Konsza, pp. 68-69 Manuscript versions of *The Little Prince Miklós* in my collection narrated by the 63-year-old Emera Balázs, nee Virág, of Rimóc, Nógrád County,

1938, by Julis Krivács, 21, of Piricse, Szabolcs County, 1957; by András Ferencz, 59, of Czikménaság, 1942; by Zsófia Halász, nee Éles, 34, and by János Nagy, 63, of Sára, Zemplén County, 1943. In Elek Benedek (1894) under the title *The Beautiful Czerczeruska*. This text, which was often reprinted in juvenile books, has influenced folk tradition and even Mrs. Palkó. English translation: Ortutary 1962, p. 255.

22. *Józsi the Fisherman* (tape recording, 1950)   AT 465/C (*A Journey to the Other World*) + 750/A (*The Wishes*); BN, I, 635; Thompson, 1946, p. 93; comparative literature: Berze Nagy, 1940, II, 496, Note 60.

VARIANTS: Gaál, 1857-1860, III, 234; Nyelvör, 1887, p. 377; Kálmány, 1814-1815, II, 75; *MNGY*, XII, 189; Berze Nagy, 1940, II, 189, 192; Kovács, 1943, II, 70 (+ *The Frog Woman*); Ösz, p. 135.

As far as the plot is concerned, Mrs. Palkó's text corresponds to Kriza's *Józsi the Fisher* (*MNGY*, XII, 189), which is also taken over by Elek Benedek (III, 281). As to style, however, it is much more colorful. The tale may be regarded in its entirety as an original invention of the storyteller. She has recreated and formed every element anew with deep insight. The only unevenness may be found in the fact that the hero may be counted either among the lazy stupid types (*Male Cinderella*, see No. 3 above) or among the strong types as AT 650 (*Strong John*). The tale dramatically points up the life-and-death struggle between the youthful serf and the lord of the manor. The fisher boy who caught a goldfish can only hope to be relieved of his forced labor for three days. But lo and behold, he is the proprietor of a "princely" fortune. How could the lord of the manor, who has come as a guest, tolerate this? He does everything to ruin this serf who had outdistanced him, and for this he has to do relentless penace. The lord is not able to do what his serf can do with the assistance of supernatural powers, because he owes his dominion to the unjust world order.

Mrs. Palkó's narrative gifts are especially apparent in the scene where the fisher boy and the lord of the manor meet for the first time face to face, as well as in the dialogue between the lord and the bricklayer.

23. *The Sky-High Tree* (1948)   AT 468 (*The Princess of The Sky Tree*) + 302 (*The Ogre's Heart in the Egg*). This tale is one of the most characteristic ethnic types and is known throughout the Hungarian language territory; its origin has long been of concern to many scholars. (Solymossy, 1922, pp. 38-45, and 1930, p. 61; Harva, pp. 34-39; Szücs, p. 23; Berze Nagy, 1958; Diószegi, 1954, pp. 24-28, and 1958, pp. 149-168, 270-277). On the basis of a profound analysis of forty-five Hungarian variants and twenty-eight variants from neighboring countries, we came to some conclusions concerning the extent, variation, spread, and origin of the type. Taking into account the fact that the tale seems to be known exclusively among Ukranians; Transylvanian Rumanians; Saxons and Gypsies; Serbs; Croatians; Slovenes; Austrians;

and Hungarian-Germans ("Swabians"), we might be justified in assuming that the story must have originated on Hungarian soil and have reached the folk literature of other peoples through oral transmission alone. Probably its adoption was furthered by the fact that the sky-high tree motif has been linked up with such widely popular European tale incidents as types 301, 302, 400, 531, 532, 552, and 556/F$^x$. Characterically, the episodes surrounding the basic plot are of such diversity, as a result of the impact of different ethnic contacts, that the resulting tales vary from three to sixty pages in length.

In spite of this great variety, we believe that the story framed by the sky-high tree motif originated mainly in a specific combination of two tale type clusters: *The Man on the Quest for his Lost Wife* and the *Male Cinderella*. The tree story, however, which appears most frequently in the form of a skeleton story for other tales, shows a solid composition. The hero has to climb a tree which reaches up to the sky. He climbs it either to bring its fruit to the sick king, who will be rejuvenated by tasting it, or to rescue the princess who has been carried up the tree. To climb the sky-high tree requires superhuman effort, and only the tale hero is equal to the task. This incident, as the oldest and basic component of the tale, was traced back to the initiation ritual act of the shamans of the pre-conquest (1960 A.D.) Hungarians, parallels of which are known from related Uralic and Altaic peoples in Siberia. Besides the tale adaptation, the theme also survives in contemporary belief legends.

VARIANTS of Mrs. Palkó's tale (a combination of AT 468 and 302): (1) Benedek: *Székely mesemondó* (1880, p. 57); (2) *MNGY*, X, 426; (3) variant told by I. Mihály Rigó in Ketesd, Transylvania, collected by A. Kovács in 1942, manuscript in EA 3912/B 513; (4) variant told by P. Lakatos, collected by A. Béres in Rozsály, Szatmár county, 1947, manuscript in FI; (5) variant told by Gy. Ferencz in Csikmenaság, Transylvania, 1942, collected by L. Dégh, manuscript in FI; Ortutay-Dégh-Kovács II, 87; (6) variant told by V. Korolevich in Strabichevo (Mukachevo region), 1960, collected by P. V. Lintur, manuscript in FI in Ukrainian; Ion Creangă Calendar 1912, II, 141-153, in Rumanian. The only consequent affiliation of *Sky-High Tree*, this tale is probably due to the popularity of Benedek's storybook not only among Hungarian peasants but among other nationalities of the former Austro-Hungarian Empire. It is worth noting that the variants listed were all collected in the Eastern Hungarian language area.

24. *Rupcsen-Hencsen* (1950) AT 500 (*Rumpelstilzchen*); *MI*, H 1027 + 221 + H 521 + C 432; Berze Nagy, I, 660, 663; Katona, 1912, I, 287-290, No. XIV; BP, I, 490; von Sydow, 1909 and 1943; Thompson, 1946, p. 48.

VARIANTS: Arany, p. 31, *MNGY*, XII, 162, and XIII, 165; Benedek, I, 202; *Földrajzi Közlöny*, 1893, p. 278; Konsza, p. 106.

This tale is rare in the Hungarian tale stock, is limited nearly exclusively to Transylvania, and does not occur in more recent collections. Mrs. Palkó's text is a complete and faithful variant; only single elements are individually varied. The influence of her motif stock known from her other tales can be felt clearly. The motif of giving away the newborn child (AT 303 and 756/B), for example, is inserted here, as it is in the tale of the *Murdering Istéfán* (No. 37). The part of the local witch assumes more weight than required by the *märchen*. In this tale also as in *The Fawn, The Snake Prince, The Fairy Princess*) a heroine in distress becomes happy. Regarding the second recital of the tale see the notes to *The Fairy Princess* (No. 18).

The source for Mrs. Palkó's *märchen* might be the variant published in the collection of the Grimm brothers, and may have come to her from the Germans settled in Andrásfalva who had close ties with the Szeklers. We come to this conclusion because of the long name Rupcsen-Hencsen, which otherwise does not occur in the Hungarian versions and which phonetically resembles the name of Rumpelstilzchen which appears in the Grimm tale. The text is nearly identical, except that the wise woman is included by Mrs. Palkó.

*25. The Blackmantle* (1956)  AT 507/A (*The Grateful Dead Man*); BP, III, 83; BN, II, 670; Liljeblad, 1927, Thompson, pp. 50-53.

VARIANTS: Turóczi-Trostler, p. 39; Gaál, III, 127; Istvánffy, p. 28; *MNGY*, IX, 492; Nagy and Faragó, p. 65 (only the frame story). I recorded one version from P. Pandur in 1956.

In spite of its wide popularity in Europe, this type was only sparsely recorded in the Hungarian language area. However, it seems to be quite old and consistent in its structure, having been written down first by an eighteenth century Hungarian poet, Csokonai, who put it into the mouth of a storytelling farmhand in his drama of 1795. *Tempefői vagyis as is bolond aki poétává lesz Magyarországon* (*Tempefői, a Fool Who Becomes a Poet in Hungary*). Two motifs in Mrs. Palkó's tale figure in the oldest variants: the black cloak of the grateful dead in the one mentioned above, and the hero's mother sending her son on the search for a wife as beautiful as herself, in Gaál. These two moments indicate that the story belongs to the old Szekler stock. The incest motif (mother-son) as the initial situation in this version has only father-daughter parallels in AT 510/B (see next tale).

Mrs. Palkó's tale is more dependent on the fear of the returning dead, indigenous to Kakasd society, than on the magic tale plot. She had known the tale long since, but it had dropped from her memory. In contrast to her usual accuracy in such matters, she could not remember where she had heard it. This was not among her favorite tales, which probably explains why it came back to her only under intensive questioning. We cannot exclude the possibility that a storybook version of Andersen's tale had affected her indirectly some time before. At any rate, we assume that she heard a corrupted version or retained only fragments of the tale and completed it on her own. Whatever the tale plot lost, the legend gained. Mrs. Palkó not only colored it with dramatic dialogues between the hero and the revenant but included essential motifs, at the same time adjusting it to local folk belief. For a detailed analysis see Chapter 7 and Dégh, 1957, pp. 307-318.

26. *The Flea Girl*  AT 510/B (*Cap O'Rushes*); BN, II, 15; BP, I, 165, and II, 45; Rooth, 1951.

VARIANTS: Pintér, p. 101; Nyelvör, 1889, p. 283; *MNGY*, IX, 173, 230, 238, and X, 218, 360; Ortutay, 1939, p. 149; Berze Nagy, 1940, II, 204, 208; Ferenczy, p. 77; Ortutay, 1940, p. 172; Dégh, 1940, p. 64; P. Szentmártoni, p. 87.

Mrs. Palkó's tale is unusually short; when I went to see her I interrupted her intensely busy housework. There was a constant coming and going of people interrupting her tale; though she could not concentrate enough, she insisted on finishing her story. In spite of this, the *märchen* is well-rounded, and the absence of the last episode (revenge of the father) is not bothersome. Any malevolent feeling of the father is absent from this variant: the last wish of the dead mother—to marry whom her shoes will fit—must be carried out. Since the king makes the mistake of commanding his daughter to commit "the crime," to marry him, he develops a guilt feeling. As a consequence his revenge is left out; on the contrary, he asks forgiveness of his daughter, who had fled in face of the terrible command.

27. *Prince Sándor and Prince Lajos*  AT 517 (*The Boy Who Learned Many Things*) +516/C (*St. James of Galicia*); BN 520 + 932; Rotunda, P 311; Katona, 1912, I, 263-267, No. VI; BP, I, 323; Wesselski, *Märchen des Mittelalters*, p. 221; *Tegethoff*, I, 124; Thompson, pp. 112, 138-139.

The basis for this *märchen* is formed by the Moses legend, different medieval editions of which were known all over Europe. According to Thompson, it was popular in oral tradition mostly in Eastern Europe, Hungary, and the Baltic countries. In this monograph *The Faithful John*, E. Rösch treats in detail (pp. 161-173, 198-199) the connection between the tale type of *Amicus and Amelius* (516/C) and of *The Faithful Servant* (516). According to his view, the legend which had spread in the West, since the beginning of the eleventh century was combined in Southern Hungary with the tale containing the child sacrifice originating in the East. Concerning the sword motif see: Heller, 1905, p. 257, and 1906, p. 214; Solymossy, 1919, p. 68. For other connections regarding the boy who understands the language of the animals see Aarne, 1914. When considering the frame of our *märchen* we notice that it is related to type 725 (*The Dream*).

VARIANTS: Gaál, 1857-1860, I, 3; Erdélyi, 1855, p. 114; Kálmány, 1914-

1915, I, 42; Dégh, 1942, II, 51; Hegedüs, 1952, p. 185; Kriza, 1956, II, 280; a manuscript variant from Hévizgyörk, Pest County, told by the 18-year-old Örzsi Tóth, 1939, FI.

Both the variants above and those collected in Kakasd seem to have literary origins. Even though the *märchen* is known in Europe in oral tradition, in Hungary it has entered folk tradition through the translation of the famous Latin novella collection, *The Seven Sages of Rome*. The tale in question is the fifteenth story in this collection. Its Hungarian variant, *The Story of Poncianus*, has appeared at various times since the first Viennese edition in 1571. G. Heinrich in his critical edition (1898) mentions one rhymed version, *Igaz barátságnak és szives szeretetnek tüköre* (*Mirror of True Friendship and Hearty Love*), which appeared eight times, between 1762 and 1848. The last chapbook edition which we know is generally disseminated and was annually reprinted between 1864 and 1911 (see Chapter 7).

Mrs. Palkó's text, well narrated and artistically shaped, can refer to two sources. One is the Erdélyi variant mentioned above which also appears in the well-loved Elek Benedek collection (IV, 411); the other doubtless is the one occurring in Márton László's *Book of the Dead*, even though Mrs. Palkó refers to the telling of the story by one of her daughters-in-law. Though Mrs. Palkó's style in spots recalls the literary source, and though the strongly moralizing character of the tale has been conserved, her turn of phrase and her impressive language make it much more lively and pliable. For a long time this tale enjoyed great popularity in Márton László's *Book of the Dead*. He himself also told it.

Comparative analysis of the versions of Mrs. Palkó and M. László is very instructive, showing the difference between the simple, natural but powerful artistry of the oral narrator re-creating a new form from the awkward book tale. We can witness here the process of folklorization, the adaptation of a written story to folk literature. The two texts are almost identical in their content. Mrs. Palkó changes ideas that are incomprehensible or unknown to her only where they play a part or where she can find an acceptable and persuasive possibility for explaining facts or conflicts to herself and to her audience. Minimal as the actualization might be, it mirrors the peasant view of the world. The following are examples of such modifications: (1) in Mrs. Palkó's tale the hero is the child of "simple peasants," while in the other he is the son of a nobleman; (2) the hero suggests his friend marry the princess instead of doing so himself because his own lowly peasant antecedents do not permit such a union for him; (3) in order to have the boy study, his father sends him to the priest (in the other, to a scholar), for in the eyes of the Bucovina society the "learned man" is the man who has studied, the one they know from close contact—the priest; (4) the sermon-like speeches are omitted and the only religious "action" that remains in the text is the miraculous healing of Prince Sándor, forced by fasting and praying.

28. *András Kerekes* (1950)   The frame of the tale coincides with AT 517–
671 (*The Three Languages*). (For literature see Note 27). It includes motifs
from the following tales: 725 (*The Prophecy*) + *MI*, T 671 and R 131 (*The
Disowning of the Strange Boy;* also see No. 64, *The Twin Rod*) + 756/B
(see No. 37 below, *The Murdering Istéfán*). We know of only one variant
with the same combination of motifs, that in Nyelvör, 1798, p. 228. This is
the reason that Berze Nagy lists it in his type index under fate stories and
assigns a new number to it as a new story: 939. Elek Benedek adapted the
Nyelvör version and restyled it extensively (IV, 92; *Itt sem volt, ott sem
volt mesevilág,* Budapest, 1888, p. 49). It is only natural for this devout tale, so
fitting for a wake, to have found entrance into Márton László's *Book of the
Dead* as well as into the repertoire of Mrs. Palkó, the star storyteller of wakes.

Mrs. Palkó's tale is the ideal of natural simplicity itself. Her artistic rendering was helped greatly by the fact that she did not have to dictate but could
speak freely for the tape recorder. By and large, Mrs. Palkó's story does not
deviate from Márton László's text and she does not embroider it with new
episodes; in spite of this it is individual and full of dramatic dialogues. All
traits that are alien to a *märchen,* all artificiality, all elements which do not
fit the logical system of the tale are simply dropped. Mrs. Palkó does nothing
more than use the mother tone of the *märchen,* which everybody understands. In this way all the incidents of the unknown *märchen* are understandable. It is only the outstanding storytellers who can tell so much in such
simple terms. The envy of the lord's son is only a scant episode in the written
variant; the young man's departure results from it. Mrs. Palkó is not satisfied
with this. She adds, with a good sense of proportion, a scene which frequently appears in the tales of *Three Golden Sons* and *The Twins of Blood-
Brothers* (AT 707 and 303) in which the boy learns that he is only a stranger
in the house. In order to heighten the dramatic impact of the scene, Mrs.
Palkó relates it twice. (For these tricks of the trade see notes to *The Fairy
Princess,* No. 18.)

29. *The Psalmsinging Bird* (1948)   AT 550 (*Search for the Golden Bird*) +
551 (*The Waters of Life*); BN, II, 102, 109; BP, II, 394; Thompson, 1946,
p. 107.

The oldest variants of our *märchen* come from Oriental sources; its elements are also contained in *One Thousand and One Nights* (literary variants:
Bolte and Polívka, I, 511). Paralleling the literary versions, it is well known
in European folk tradition. The types 550 and 551 differ only in as much as
the three princes in one tale are looking for the magic bird and in the other
for the Water of Life. Since both the life- and death-bringing water and
the magic bird symbolizing happiness are old elements of folk belief, they are
often interchanged and melded (*Motif-Index* E 80; Wunsche, 1905). Bátky
(1928, p. 105) calls special attention to the drinking vessels in forms of birds.

He writes, ". . . the glasses used for religious or ceremonial occasions symbolize birds who guard and bring the water of life, rejuvenation." The tale, which is founded on primitive religion, has taken a twofold development in the course of time. Thus the two types were able to emerge, even though contact and mixing of the two is very infrequent, as the variant shown here makes clear.

VARIANTS: Erdélyi, 1846-1848, II, 364; Gaál, *Magyar népmesék*, II, 3, 188, and III, 1, 35; Majláth, p. 255; Merényi, *Dunamelléki*, I, 71; Pap, p. 108; Pintér, p. 79; Arany, p. 7; *MNGY*, IX, 72, 486, and XIII, 118; Kálmány, 1881, I, 1; Berze Nagy, 1940, II, pp. 228, 232, 326; Berde, *Székely népmesék*, p. 22; P. Szentmártoni, p. 40; Dégh, 1940, pp. 32, 100; Kovács, 1943, I, 183; F. Kovács, p. 88; Nagy, 41, Konsza, p. 87; variant told by 34-year-old Mrs. Mária Bónis, née Bogil, of Sára, Zemplén County, in 1943 (PI).

Our *märchen* exhausts to a large extent the motifs of both types but also deviates from them in essential traits. The motifs of the three enchanted maidens is inserted (AT 401/A; also see above *The Three Princes and The Man With the Iron Hat*, No. 2), but the love motif is completely absent, as is the figure of the girl from Fairyland who reveals the betrayal of the brothers. In our *märchen* we find the ring which forecasts misfortune, a motif which organically belongs to other *märchen* (*MI*, E 761; see György Andrásfalvi's tale *The Twin Rod*), and the gouging of eyes for food (*MI*, M 265, AT 613). But all this is not Mrs. Palkó's individual formation: she received it in this form from Elek Benedek (under the same title in III, 179, and *Itt sem volt, ott sem volt mesevilág*, p. 85). The changes in content made by Mrs. Palkó are minimal—she merely smoothed out some of the unevenness of the written source—hence her formal shaping is most important. This appears especially in the introductory motif, in the adventure of the search for the bird, in the betrayal of the brothers, and in the embroidering of the adventure of the disguised hero.

30. *Peasant Gagyi* (tape recording, 1950)   AT 560 (*Aladdin*); BN, II, 152; BP, II, 455; Aarne, 1908, pp. 3-82; Thompson, 1946, p. 70.

VARIANTS: Gaál, 1857-1860, III, 116; Arany, p. 220; Merényi, 1861, I, 3, and 1862, I, 63; Nyelvör, 1886, p. 89, 1887, p. 277, and 1903, p. 42; Istvánffy, p. 43; *MNGY*, IX, 187, X, 168, and XIII, 179; Berze Nagy, 1940, II, 271; Ortutay, 1935, p. 79; Bözödi, p. 20; Banó, 1941, p. 156; Ösz, p. 57; Dégh, 1942, II, 86; Dégh, 1940, p. 86; Kovács, 1943, I, 165 (+ 314 + 552); Beke and Katona, p. 41; Gönczi, p. 309; Hegedüs, 1952, p. 3; Nagy and Faragó, p. 75 (+ 425 A); Ortutay-Dégh-Kovács, II, 463. There is one manuscript variant, told by the 67-year-old András Kása from Sára, Zemplén county, 1943, FI.

The starting point for most of the variants is the tortured animals and the gift of the snake. These motifs are missing entirely from Mrs. Palkó's *märchen* and therefore the motif of the grateful animals after the princess is carried off does not play any part, as it does in the other variants. Here Mrs. Palkó's *märchen* puts the motif of the simpleminded youth (squandering of a fortune for some nonsense) at the start of the tale, and the pact with the birds takes the place of the grateful animals (type AT 328 A\*, *Three Brothers Steal Back Sun, Moon, and Star*). It is closest to Arany's variant which also has the title of *Peasant Gagyi*. Both tales may have the same origin, but it is also possible that Arany's version appeared first in a chapbook or a schoolbook. Be this as it may, Mrs. Palkó's *märchen* is much more beautiful, goes much more into detail, and is more plastic. Especially lively points are the exchange of letters between the hero and the princess and the conversation with the crows. Just as she does in other *märchen*, Mrs. Palkó gives a graphic description of the glamour (quoted in Chapter 7). Special attention should be paid to the comments of the listeners which accompany the whole tale to its end, since they are proof of the audience's lively interest, which is the result of the colorful recital of the storyteller (Chapter 6). There were about twenty people present.

31. *The Golden Egg* (tape recorded, 1956)   AT 567 (*The Magic Bird Heart*) + 566 ( *The Three Magic Objects and The Wonderful Friends*); BN, II, 179; BP, I, 528, and III, 3; Aarne, pp. 143-200; Thompson, p. 75.

VARIANTS: Gaál, 1822, p. 195; *MNGY*, IX, 358, X, 21, and XIII, 276 (+ 566); Nyelvör, III, 517; Dégh, 1942, I, 156 (+ 303); Hegedüs, 1952, p. 83; Ortutay, Dégh, and Kovács, II, 514; Dégh, 1960a, p. 38 (three manuscript versions analyzed).

In the Hungarian material the first part of the *märchen* (the heart and the stomach of the golden bird) are connected in general with AT 303; the other part on the three magic objects (AT 567) usually occurs independently. Mrs. Palkó had heard this tale only a year before in Mucsfa. The fact that she had incorporated it into her repertoire is probably due to the circumstance of her heightened reputation as a storyteller. In spite of this the tale had not been unknown in the village, for other storytellers knew it. The Moldavian version noted by Hegedüs in 1950 is very similar to that of Mrs. Palkó, though the emphasis in hers is more on the second part. Especially detailed is the scene of the funny punishment of the shrewish princess and her maid.

32. *Nine* (1950)   AT 650 (*Strong John*); BN II, 218; BP II, 285; Thompson, 1946, pp. 85-86.

The Hungarian variants are as variable as the international ones, often intertwined with 301/B, which might account for a distant common origin. The strong servant outwitting and ruining his master is a topic especially favored in Eastern Europe, where feudal remnants survived well into the twentieth century.

VARIANTS: Merényi, 1861, I, 123, and 1863, II, 93; Kálmány, 1881, I, 128, and 1914-1915, I, 79; Nyelvör, 1887, p. 428, and 1899, p. 234; Pintér, p. 163; *MNGY*, VI, 343, X, 35, 261, and XIII, 19; Ortutay, 1940, p. 352 (Note p. 450); Kovács, 1943, I, 196; Végh, p. 15; Ortutay and Katona, p. 318; Hegedüs, 1952, p. 110; Nagy and Faragó, p. 144; Bözödi, 1958, p. 95; Nagy, p. 130; Konsza, p. 115.

First publication of our text: Ortutay and Katona, p. 185. A faithful variant of Merényi's text (1863, II, 93, *A kilencz*), it was also included in E. Benedek's storybook (II, 426). With regard to the hero's name, the symbolical number-naming referring to the strength and huge appetite (that of nine persons) also occurs in the international variants (BP, II, 288). Concerning the visit to the devils' mill, our *märchen* touches a motif of the tale of *The Murdering Istéfán* (765/B). See Berze Nagy, 1940, II, 501, Note, p. 89.

33. *The Strong János* (1950)  A variant of the preceding *märchen* using some other motifs.

VARIANTS: *MNGY*, IX, 301, X, 384, and XIII, i; Kálmány, 1914-1915, I, 79; Ortutay, 1940, p. 262 (in another connection, an itinerant brings in the whole crop in order to help an old peasant); Berze Nagy, 1940, II, 266; Dégh, 1940, p. 64; Ortutay and Katona, p. 280; manuscript version of the 80-year-old János Halász of Sára, Zemplén county, 1947, FI.

34. *The Red-Bellied Serpent* (tape recorded, 1950).  AT 670 (*The Animal Languages*); BN, II, 233; BP, I, 132; Aarne, 1914; Thompson, 1946, pp. 83-84; Solymossy, 1919, p. 66.

VARIANTS: The oldest Hungarian variant was preserved in the form of a popular illustration from the beginning of the fourth decade of the last century. The picture shows the sheepherder, lost in thought, sitting at the table; his nagging wife; the stupid dog; and the clever cock. The legend says, "Great is the sorrow and the battle with his conscience of the shepherd who understands the language of the animals, for he is to die if he betrays the secret; but as he cannot resist the insistent curiosity of his wife. . . ." The rest is illegible. (Reprinted in Viski, ed., *Magyarság Néprajza*, III, between pages 144 and 145.) *Merényi*, 1863, II, 165; Nyelvör, 1874, p. 227; Lázár, p. 618; *MNGY*, VI, 294, 301; Fél, p. 141; Berze Nagy, 1940, II, 267; Gönczi, 1948, p. 287; Hegedüs, 1942, p. 187 Konsza, p. 125; Ortutay, Dégh, and Kovács, II, 690; *The Fiery Serpent*, told by the 67-year-old András Kása from Sára, Zemplén county, 1942 (FI).

The closest to our variant is the version by Berze Nagy mentioned above. A new contribution in Mrs. Palkó's *märchen* is the figure of the hero as a sheepherder's hired hand who can obtain the hand of the chief herdsman's daughter only if he can acquire enough standing (i.e. substance). This is the point of departure of the *märchen* and everything which follows is based upon it.

35. *The Twelve Robbers* (tape recorded, 1954). AT 706 (*The Maiden Without Hands*) + 451/I (*The Maiden Who Seeks Her Brothers*); BN, II, 242; BP, I, 295; M. Schlauch, *Chaucer's Constant and Accused Queens;* Thompson, 1946, pp. 120-121; Däumling, 1912; Solymossy, 1919, p. 67. The tale of *The Maiden Without Hands* is closely related to the type of *The Three Golden Sons* (707). In both tales the heroine is accused of having given birth to a dog, which gives rise to the course of the *märchen* and its solution. The starting point of our *märchen* can be different. In the Hungarian variants it is mostly the father who carries out the mutilation, because the heroine does not want to become his wife (see also notes concerning a similar motif in AT 507, 510/B, Nos. 25, 26). The circumstances of the girl's mutilations are not unknown in the European variants, but this is the first occurrence in the Hungarian material.

As mentioned earlier, our storyteller had heard this tale from a Rumanian girl in the Rumanian language while she herself was still a young girl. We can no longer find out how this variation went and how much Mrs. Palkó had changed. Yet there is no doubt that the disowning of the heroine goes back to the influence of a Rumanian variant, because the episode inserted here is known in the Rumanian redaction of the tale but is completely missing in the Hungarian. In a variant recorded in 1953 in Racsa (Oas Territory, Rumania), two youngsters, a brother and a sister, received a present from their aunt—a golden horse and a dog of the same color. The boy marries the daughter of the emperor, who hates her sister-in-law bitterly and tries to kill her. Therefore she murders, one after another, first the golden horse, then the dog, and finally her own golden-haired child, and hides the knife under the pillow of the girl so that she can accuse her of the murders. After the third murder the boy condemns his sister to death, but since no weapon can wound her, he cuts off her hands and her feet and leaves her lying on a tree trunk. (Due to the gracious help of Sabin V. Dragoi, the manuscript could be checked in the manuscript archives of the Bucharest Folklore Institute, where it is listed under Nos. 14 and 149.) The rest of the tale follows the type. The introduction with the beginning of type AT 451 seems to be Mrs. Palkó's individual invention; instead of the brothers being turned into ravens, we find them as robbers, a portrayal that better corresponds to her rational viewpoint.

Variants: Erdélyi, 1846-1848, II, 195, 212; Istvánffy, p. 62; *MNGY,* IX, 173, 203, XII, 107, and XIII, 331, 335; Ortutay, 1935, p. 158: Berze Nagy, 1940, II, 345; Banó, 1941, p. 222; Kovács, 1943, II, 132; Bözödi, 1958, p. 113; Konsza, p. 73; manuscript of the 45-year-old gypsy, Ferenc Sebök, from Piricse, Szabolcs county, 1938; two variations from Csikmenaság, related by the 27-year-old Károly Péterfi and the 18-year-old Annamária Ferencz, 1942 (FI).

This tale was among Mrs. Palkó's favorites. She usually told it during wakes, embroidered as a "nice long" tale. The tenor of the tale and its style correspond to the style of stories in which the heroine passes through hard tests of fortune; they gain impact on second telling and keep the listeners spellbound, no matter how many hours the narration lasts.

36. *Fairy Ilona* (tape recorded, 1956)   AT 707 (*The Three Golden Sons*); BN 707 + 707 x I, (II, 248, 267); BP, II, 380; Thompson, pp. 120-122.

The Hungarian redactions of this tale, as indicated in the BN catalog, differ from the outline of the AT plot. In one of the subtypes the golden-haired daughter rescues her ill-fated, golden-haired brothers, and a magic bird reveals the truth to the king. In the other, the golden-haired brother and sister are helped by the fairy bride of the brother, whom he acquired by tricking her into a fabric shop aboard a ship. There is much intermingling and blending of the two themes; clusters of related types are also often included. Mrs. Palkó's tale belongs to the second subtype, of which we possess the following Hungarian variants: *MNGY*, X, 313, and XIII, 312; Kriza, 1956, II, 250; Ortutay, 1940, p. 109; Gunda, 1956, p. 144 (told by a Hungarian Gypsy). However, the fairy incident is not exclusively Hungarian but is also known in the Serbo-Croatian, both in narrative songs and in tales (Bošković-Stulli, 1962, 15-36).

Mrs. Palkó's text is very well shaped, and the manner of recital and use of formulae coincide those of her tales that belong to related types (see Nos. 35, 21). The audience present also remarked about this: "The tale is similar to *The Fawn*!" "I have already heard this tale!" "It is exactly like *The Twelve Robbers*." Unfortunately, the interruptions impeded the recital of the *märchen* as it usually is done, and thus the repetition of the story was omitted (the part where the son of the innocent, suffering heroine reveals the true facts), and the storyteller only mentioned in passing that all of it should be told over again.

37. *The Murdering Istéfán* (1949)   AT 756/B (*The Devil's Contract*): MI, M 211 + F 82.4 + Q 521; BN 757* (II, 312); BP, III, 463; Andrejev, 1927, and 1924.

The Hungarian variants are closely related to the North Slavic, especially the Ukrainian, Great Russian, and Polish, local redactions. This is borne out by the definitely slavic-sounding names occurring in the tales: Marajz, Bojnyik, Mádaj (and also from the misspelling of the last: Kádár and Máté), Palinkó, etc.

VARIANTS: Merényi, 1863, II, 127; Nyelvör, 1877, p. 469, and 1886, p. 569; Lázár, p. 622; *MNGY* IX, 59, XII, 109, and XIII, 424; *Ethn.*, 1919, 82; Berze Nagy, 1940, II, 292; Ortutay, 1935, p. 141; manuscript variant narrated by the miller Imre Bándi, Csikmenaság, 1942, FI.

Mrs. Palkó's *märchen*, which is well known and well liked among her audience, follows Kriza's version. It was from Kriza that Elek Benedek took it for his big edition (I, 304), and through Benedek's collection it was spread in Andrásfalva.

Attention should be paid to the advice which the clergyman gives throughout: he does not incite him to religious, pious, or devout deeds, but to the forms of exorcising generally known among the people, to the practice of magic actions (see Szendrey, 1938, p. 35). The motif of the magic circle is contained in AT 810; the smoking out of the devils from hell also belongs in type 650, as we pointed out in connection with the tale of *Nine* (No. 32).

38. *The Two Hermits* (tape recorded, 1951) AT 859 (*The Angel and the Hermit*); BN, II, 323; Beledi, pp. 326-335; Binder, 1892, p. 281, and 1893, p. 130; György, p. 191; Heller, 1945, pp. 45-47; Katona, 1900, pp. 145, 199, and the annotations to his edition of the *Gesta Romanorum*, Régi Magyar Könyvtár, 18; Lázár, 1891, p. 130; Rohde, 1894; Solymossy, 1919, p. 62; Turóczi-Trostler, pp. 88-89.

Literary and popular forms are known all over Europe. In spite of the great differences in time and place, there are no great deviations, and only the deeds of the angel are varied. (They can be found in Hungary as early as the sixteenth century in the exempla collections of P. Temesvári and Osvát Laskai, as well as in the Debrecen and Ersekujvár codices, *Nyelvemléktár* X, 149 and XI, 142). The first Hungarian translation of importance goes back to the year 1695. It is contained in János Haller's translation of the *Gesta Romanorum* (Nos. 80 and 127). It is presumed that most of the later literary and oral versions are based on this edition, though each one shows deviations of varying degrees from the original. Since the first oral versions collected in Transylvania and published by Balázs Orbán in 1882 (*MNGY*, III, 384), many folklorists have investigated the question of their connection with the literary predecessors. Lajos Katona, in his study mentioned above, compares the Hungarian versions. According to his opinion, the folktale does not stem directly from the Haller translation. He refers to a rhymed chapbook variant which appeared in 1870 (*The Hermit Who is Seeking God's Justice*, or *The Hermit Delivered from His Doubts*, Tatár Péter regekunyhója, No. 114) which doubtless had literary sources even earlier than the folktale. Unfortunately all older variants are of literary character and thus we cannot determine whether the folk tradition which arose in the wake of the medieval sermons assisted the literary influence. The new variants which have been published since Katona's study show a waning, as do tales whose actuality has passed and which are still remembered but no longer told. Only the *märchen* of Mrs. Palkó shows a deviation in this respect.

VARIANTS: *MNGY* III, 384, 411; *Ethn.*, 1895, 260, 1909, 165, and 1910, 360; Berze Nagy, 1940, II, 296 (comparative literature in Notes 108, 505). In 1949, I noted a variant in Tiszakarád, told by the 80-year old Mrs. Mokri.

It may be assumed that Mrs. Palkó's variant stems from the collection of B. Orbán, which also appeared in Benedek's storybook (I, 342).

39. *The Three Archangels* (tape recorded, 1956)  Benedek, III, 245, indicates this tale as coming from *MNGY* I, 490. It is possible that the funny story of Adam and Eve's expulsion from Paradise came to the Bucovina along this route. The Szekler's anecdote renders a magnificent characterization of the three archangels and gives them a national character. Gabriel, the Rumanian archangel, can be treated to food and drink; Raphael, the Hungarian archangel, can be persuaded by talk—he is so soft-hearted that he even asks God for mercy. Only the third, Michael, the German archangel, carries out the command, after consuming the proffered eats and drinks. With the cry; "*Marsch hinaus* (Out with you)!" he drives the first human couple out through the gate. We do not know any other variants, but this belongs to the topic around *MI*, A 1331 (*Paradise Lost*).

40. *The Smoking Kalfaktor* (1948)  AT 812 (*The Devil's Riddle*); BN, 831\*, II, 368; BP, III, 12; Thompson, 1946, p. 43.
   This *märchen*, which is popular chiefly in Germany and in the Baltic countries, occurs in different variants, depending on the way the hero gets rid of the devil. In the center of the Hungarian variants is the deciphering of the figure symbols (*MI*, H 543). The deciphering of the figures one to seven, one to nine, or one to twelve as the difficult task to be solved is very frequent in folk literature (BP, III, 15; BN, 1939, p. 114; Heller, 1940, pp. 250-252; Domokos, pp. 357-366). This motif can be found with Caucasian Moslems and Indian Buddhists, and in the rites and the conversation of Jews on the eve of Passover as well as in European medieval legend collections. Its tendency is both didactic and entertaining. This twofold role is also contained in the Hungarian variants.
   Kriza mentioned that it was customary at weddings, while the terms of the dowry were determined, to ask for the significance of numbers; the text for questions and answers was even to be found in printed popular wedding guide books. Volly (1937, p. 465) observed that these questions are posed by a singer in the form of songs during weddings or funeral meals, with all the guests answering in song lead by another singer. We think that the insertion of this custom into the *märchen* has its origin in the Middle Ages (there is a variant in the *Legenda Aurea* of 1260: here St. Andrew answers the devil instead of the man interrogated). This is the origin of the religious coloring which this *märchen* shows in contrast to others, in which the hero is liberated either by solving impossible tasks or by destroying the devil.
   VARIANTS: *MNGY*, XII, 219; *Nyelvészeti Füzetek*, pp. 17, 65; Nyelvör, 1872, p. 328; Berze Nagy, 1940, I, 576, 578, and II, 331, 332; Banó, 1941, p. 284.

The outstanding quality of this *märchen* is its realism. Its tenor is not at all tale-like but is very close to real life, just like the "true story." The *märchen* gives a good picture of the Andrásfalva way of life—wooing a girl, the life of the young people, and the primitive form of hunting practiced there, the "game hitting" (hitting the game with a flat piece of wood). In this atmosphere the "miracle" happens—but it does not belong with the true miracles of the *märchen*, for the hero does not become rich. All he gains are victuals, something with which he can prepare a wedding feast.

The name for the devil, "Kalfaktor" (here used in the sense of trouble-maker), also occurs in other *märchen* (see *MNGY* XIII, 34).

41. *János the Smith* (1949)   This is an unknown *märchen* not listed in the type indexes. It is closest to AT 821. The devil, impersonating the smith who had baited him, carries out a robbery in the church and only at the last minute saves the smith from the gallows. This *märchen* does not follow either the tale tradition of Andrásfalva or the religious or moralizing booklet reminiscences. The moral of the tale is that not only God and the saints deserve respect but the devil, for he too can punish man. The Devil has his portrait on the wall among the saints. Even though there are genuine folklore motifs in this tale (such as the exchanging of places on the gallows), it is still possible that its origin is a storybook. The recital is witty and well formed.

42. *A Mother's Atonement* (1948)   This is a typical tale for wakes, where Mrs. Palkó learned it. Essentially it is a religiously-colored variant of AT 838 (see, farther on, Márton László, No. 99), which certainly originated under the influence of some church teaching or example. For the scene in hell see *MI*, Q 560.

43. *The Proud Princess* (tape recorded, 1956)   AT 900 (*King Thrush-beard*); BN, II, 404; BP, I, 443, Philippson, 1923; Krohn, 1939; Thompson, 1946, p. 104.

VARIANTS: Merényi, 1863, I, 136; Kálmány, 1914-1915, II, 109; *MNGY*, IX, 376; Berze Nagy, 1940, II, 351; Dégh, 1942, II, 153; Konsza, p. 130. For the motif of scattering the hidden food while dancing, see other *märchen* types, for example Dégh, 1942, II, 5. A manuscript version from Piricse, Szabolcs county, was told by the 61-year-old Mrs. S. Hunyady, FI.

Mrs. Palkó's realism shows up very clearly in this *märchen*. In other variants of the tale it seems quite incredible to us that the proud princess who can pick and choose sons of kings, and finds none of them good enough for her, goes away with the dirty, ragged fellow of low birth. P. Pandur, just as Mrs. Palkó, finds it necessary to explain this contradiction. In this tale the king is so furious about the choosiness of his daughter that he vows to give her as a bride to the first comer. Then the prince appears, disguised as a beggar as had been decided beforehand. The two royal families set up this "trick," since it is in their interest that the two young people should meet. In Mrs. Palkó's version, the prince arrives as a notary who attracts the attention of the moody, willful princess with a piece of jewelry, and she goes with him not because she has fallen in love with him but because she has paid a high price for the ring. She "covers herself with shame" and knows very well that her father will have no mercy once she is discovered; she therefore has to flee the king's court. This is why she leaves with "the potter's son," and why she bears all her humiliations.

44. *Lazybones* (1950) Here we have one of the anecdotes with didactic tendencies for the edification of the village girls. Mrs. Palkó's *märchen*, a short version of which also occurs in Mrs. Sebestyén's repertoire, shows the place of the woman in village life and her correct behavior, and also contains a moral. The starting point of the tale coincides with two others by Mrs. Palkó (*The Dumb Girl*, No. 55 and *The Uncouth Girl*, No. 54), but transcends them. The youth does not immediately shrink from the bad qualities of the girl; he marries her in spite of her laziness—on account of her fortune which later on she squandered lightheartedly. Industry is a prime virtue of women in peasant society, and she who burns all her clothes and linen because she does not know how to do the laundry will be punished.

Only the last motif is known in the international material: the naked young woman, wrapped in straw, is carried into her parent's house (AT 902\*). The tale rouses laughter and belongs with the anecdotes about girls stood up by their suitors (types AT 1450–1474). The motif of burning the clothes can also be found in the Hungarian material (Hegedüs, 1952, p. 160). Otherwise this tale has no parallel in the Hungarian. English translation: Dégh, 1965, p. 142.

45: *The Turk* (tape recorded, 1953) AT 910/B (*The Servant's Good Counsels*); Rotunda 7.21.2; BN, II, 407; Katona, 1912, I, 267-270, No. VII; Thompson, 1946, p. 164; Katona, ed., *Gesta Romanorum*; György, p. 196; Seiler, pp. 51-70.

Haller's translation in the *Gesta Romanorum* (1695) may be considered for the first among the Hungarian variants (Exemplum No. 103). Surely the tale has contributed to the dissemination, in oral tradition, of the three counsels which have become popular figures of speech, as is shown by proverb collections (see András Dugonics, II, p. 148). The tale however, has only a handful of published Hungarian variants: Gaál, I, 857, I, 222; Nyelvör, 1878, p. 87; *MNGY*, X, 141; Berze Nagy, 1940, II, 354, 356; Kovács, 1943, I, 162 (remote variant). It can also be found in Benedek, IV, 339.

Mrs. Palkó's *märchen* is more complete than the Hungarian variants known so far and differs from them in several other respects. It is only here that the reason for the young man's departure for the great wide world turns out to be his childlessness. The service in Turkey is likewise a new element in the tale and might stem from other ethnic groups living in the Bucovina. The motif of the service having to last until the sandal is worn out is part of another tale: the discharged soldier works in hell; he has to heat the kettle under the damned souls until his sandals are worn out (AT 811). The magic feature of the sandal being indestructible does not fit into the tale, which otherwise is quite rational and in which no "miracles" occur. The ending, too, represents a new incident in the *märchen:* both sons become priests and the father finds the culmination of his happiness in the consecration of his two sons. The addition of this motif to the *märchen* is probably due to Mrs. Palkó, for in her concept, becoming a priest equals "being a great lord" (see *András Kerekes* and *The Murdering Istéfán*). For the rest, the adventure-like recital with its thrilling details is Mrs. Palkó's own invention. The structuring of the story and the strange atmosphere of the foreign country heighten the story. Motifs like the "Turkish" dress of the hero, the liberation of the condemned men, the pistol test, and the passport are all specific interminglings of old and new, from which stem both folk tradition and newer book experiences. This *märchen* type does not belong with the fantastic tales but is rather a humorous guide to human self-control, to clever balancing. Therefore the variants are restricted only to the sober confirmation of the experiences of the servant or the discharged soldier on his way home. Mrs. Palkó, on the other hand, enlarges the three tale incidents (comprised of the three counsels) into exciting adventures— though the extent of each of the three episodes is not the same—by embroidering through colorful recital the mysterious service in Turkey, and the concluding reward—the happiness of the sons, the cutting of the bread.

46. *Anna Mónár* (1948)   AT 956/B (*The Clever Maiden Alone at Home Kills the Robbers*) + 955 (*The Forty Thieves*); BN, 955, II, 432; BP, I, 373; Thompson, 1946, pp. 173-174.

The *märchen* has two fundamental types, which it can be assumed with certainty have developed from a common mold: the one (AT 955) in which the courageous girl discovers and catches the robbers, and the other one in our text. The first is better known and more common; the second can be added as a sequence to the first. Less frequently it occurs by itself. In the form by Mrs. Palkó in which AT 954 is added, we know only three variants: (1) the manuscript variant of A. Herrmann from Sorkitótfalu; (2) Berze Nagy, 1940, II, 375, 3; and (3) E. Benedek, I, 312. Since we can find similarities in composition with our tale only in the three examples cited, and the heroine is a miller's daughter only in these (she is usually an innkeeper's daughter), we must assume that the common source is the variant from Elek Benedek's collection which frequently has been incorporated into storybooks.

OTHER VARIANTS (we quote here only those that contain one or the other of the two composite parts): *MNGY*, X, 163, and XIII, 441; *Ethn.*, 1922, 79; Berze Nagy, 1940, II, 276, 369, 373; Ortutay, 1935, p. 203; P. Szentmártoni, p. 79; Dégh, 1942, II, 165; Kovács, 1943, II, 33; Konsza, p. 138; manuscript version of the 34-year-old swineherder Imre Kádár and of the 29-year-old Anna Angyal Hován from Piricse, Szabolcs County, 1938, FI.

Here Mrs. Palkó's feeling for dramatic tension comes to the fore. The part which precedes the arrival of the robbers is outstanding. The old people have gone to the wedding and the young girl remains alone at home. She is reading quietly, and yet we feel that there is something in the air, that it is laden with tension, and that something is going to happen. Mrs. Palkó's realistic attitude toward her tales also appears here; the girl disables the robbers with the sabre, but somebody might ask how a sabre was to be found in the miller's house. She feels that an explanation is needed here, otherwise the tale would sound incredible. "The old miller had seen military service with the hussars, and had brought home the sabre as a keepsake." Other interesting incidents of the tale are the exchange of letters (see *The Twelve Robbers, The Seprent Prince, Fairy Ilona*), the manner of the winning of the bride, the strange wedding parade, and the self-immolation of the old woman. They all surround and stress the bravery of the girl in the center of the action.

47. *The Sly Servant* (tape recorded, 1956)   AT 1000 (*Bargain Not Becoming Angry*) + 1005 (*Building a Bridge or Road*) + 1685 (*The Foolish Bridegroom*) + 1017 (*Covering the Whole Wagon with Tar*) + 1132 (*Flight of the Ogre with His Goods in the Bag*) + 1120 (*The Ogre's Wife Thrown into the Water*); BN, II, 440, 441; BP, II, 288.

VARIANTS: Jókai p. 63; *MNGY*, II, 5; Nyelvör, IV, 84, VIII, 464; *MNGY*, X, 35; Berze Nagy, 1940, II, 177-178; Kovács, 1943, I, 201 (she adds five variants from Ketesd: *A kalotaszegi mesekincs*, 1944, p. 27); Nagy and Faragó, p. 149; Nagy, p. 82; Konsza, pp. 118, 122, 139.

"When there was the fair in Mucsfa, in October, I heard it there. From the daughter of my sister, she read it from a book. Here I have told it so often; in the evening they call for me to come and tell a story," says Mrs. Palkó. The *märchen* read aloud certainly came from *MNGY* II, 5, for it was taken over by many storybooks. In spite of this Mrs. Palkó's tale is a complete and well-formed unit and very witty, which shows that during the five short months since she had learned it, she had formed the text to a great extent herself.

48. *The Wager of the Two Comrades* (tape recorded, 1950)   AT 1350 (*The Loving Wife*); MI, T 231.3 + H 1556.I; Rotunda, 492.2. Berze Nagy assigns it the number 1459* (II, 526) and equates it erroneously with type

1510 (*The Matron of Ephesus*), to which it is close but with which it does not coincide; see Ziegler, 1937, below, notes to György Andrásfalvi's tale *The Faithful Widow*, (No. 72). The only Hungarian variant known so far appeared in Nyelvör, 1904, p. 58.

It is a popular anecdote, originating in medieval literature, about the fickleness of women. An earlier variant occurs in the *Pentamerone* and in the *Seven Sages of Rome*. The fable of Mozart's famed opera *Cosi Fan Tutte* also belongs in this cycle of themes.

Mrs. Palkó's text is a realistic, popular peasant story from any point of view. It is one of her polished masterpieces. Construction, dialogues, turns of speech, and recital are excellent. The joke is sharp and her satirical tone is quite believable, as if she were relating an event which had just happened in the village.

49. *The Szekler Bride* (1959)   AT 1365/B (*The Obstinate Wife*); BN 1363 + 1164, II, 509, 470; Thompson, pp. 209-210. An anecdote of literary origin, known through Europe since the Middle Ages, it is among the latest acquisitions of the narrator, learned from her sister's daughter in Mucsfa. We have two versions (*MNGY*, III, 355; Kriza, 1956, II, 354) very close to ours, which makes it probable that one of Benedek's storybooks contained the Kriza tale. Though Mrs. Palkó stuck to the form heard at the time of recording, she had much success with the tale; it quickly became almost as popular as *Peti and Boris* (No. 52).

50. *Katyika and Matyika* (1950)   AT 1387 (*The Woman Goes to Get Beer*) + 1371\* (*The Woman Is to Pile Up the Pottery*) + 1291 (*One Cheese Sent To Bring Back Another*) + 1653/A (*Guarding the Door*); BP, I, 316, 521.

VARIANTS: Nyelvör, 1903, p. 48; Kálmány, 1914-1915, II, 191; Nyelvör, 1887, p. 327; *MNGY*, IX, 524; Kálmány, 1914-1915, II, 121, 186, 190, 191 + Merényi, 1861, I, 195; *MNGY*, VIII, 444; *Ethn.*, 1939, 162; Berze Nagy, 1940, II, 442, 450; Banó, 1941, 270; Dégh, 1942, II, 185; Kovács, 1943, I, 225, and II, 76; Konsza, pp. 157, 159, 160.

The episodes of our tale are generally known in Hungarian oral tradition, but since the single episodes and adventures form a complete unity in themselves, they often become independent and/or join with each other in various sequences. Generally, in the anecdotes the motif coupling happens much faster and more easily than in the magic tales. It may even happen that all the stories belonging to this type cycle will combine into one tale, just as it may happen that one single episode is formed into an independent tale. This is why the elements of our *märchen* can be found in the most varied compositions. Yet there are very few close variants. The first and the last episodes of Mrs. Palkó's *märchen* belong with the tales of the stupid husband and only very rarely refer to women. The recital of our narrator is full of humor, as are also two related anecdotes, *Könyvenke* (No. 53) and *Peti and Boris* (No. 52).

51. *The Nagging Wives* (tape recorded, 1955)   This is an unknown anecdote which belongs to the type cycle of the foolish married couple. The funny recital provided hilarious moments for the women with their children who came to Mrs. Palkó in the evening, bringing their distaff and spindles. The two quarreling women turn their behinds to each other and neither wants to stop, because then she would be the losing party. But in order for the bread to be baked, the stupid husband takes turns with his wife. Mrs. Palkó's sense of humor is expressed in the rhythmical dialogue proceeding to the climax, as the husband from time to time announces to his nagging wife how far he has got in the preparation of the bread. She did not value this joke highly. "Isn't it something?" she commented. "I told this for women but it was not for children to overhear. I would have beaten up that woman who was stupid enough to show her behind. . . ."

52. *Peti and Boris* (tape recorded, 1949)   AT 1408 (*The Man Who Does His Wife's Work*) + 1210 (*The Cow on the Roof of the House*) + BN 1409 (*Husband Does Not Recognize Himself*) + BN 1411 (*The Man Who is Hatching Eggs*) BN, II, 476, 516, 518, 519; BP, I, 321; Thompson, 1946, p. 194.

The basic plot of this tale is known all over Europe. It varies greatly, combining the motifs of different anecdotes and changing them slightly. According to the whim of the moment, the narrator chooses freely from the anecdotes belonging to related groups around AT 1387 and 1696 (*What Should I Have Said?*) or to the anecdotes of the foolish boy and girl.

VARIANTS: Kálmány, 1914-1915, I, 118; *MNGY*, VIII, 444; Kovács, 1943, II, 9; Ortutay and Katona, p. 351; Nagy, p. 188; Konsza, p. 161.

In spite of the small number of variants, we are of the opinion that this tale is very wide spread and that it was very sparsely collected. It seems to be especially popular with the Szekler ethnic group. One variant from Kászonimpér coincides not only in the text but also in name (*Pepi and Boris*) with ours from the Bucovina. An element which often occurs in our anecdotes is that of the cow lifted onto the roof of the house to graze there: Ballagi, *Magyar példabeszédek* II, 352; Kálmány, *Koszoruk*, II, 178, and 1881, II, 132, 1914-1915, I, 115; Nyelvör, 1906, pp. 428 429, and 1907, p. 332; *Nyelvészeti Füzetek* 33, 37, 38; *Ethn.*, 1912, 108; Berze Nagy, 1940, II, 397. For summing-up literature see György, p. 221. Berze Nagy considers the man hatching eggs as an independent tale type on the basis of *MNGY* X, 432, and XII, 123.

This tale is greatly applauded by Mrs. Palkó's audiences. I have heard it several times when she told it to her guests; the young women in particular like *märchen* of this kind. She herself liked it very much, was greatly amused, and laughed with her listeners. When I first took it down in shorthand, the narrator could not keep the tempo which I needed. As an excuse she explained that it was a trick, just with anecdotes of this kind, to tell it quickly and to recite it in a quickly flowing language, for otherwise the nagging of the woman and the uncouthness of the man "do not come to light so well." It is astonishing to see how much the women like this tale, which in the end raises its voice against the position of women in the old patriarchal family structure of the backward peasant village.

53. *Könyvenke* (1950)   AT 1450 (*Clever Elsie*) + 1384 (*Husband Hunts Three Persons as Stupid as His Wife*) + 1245 (*Sunlight Carried in a Bag into the Windowless House*) + BN 1284* (*The Woman Who Beats the Hen for Refusing to Breastfeed the Chicks + The Woman Who Cuts Off the Hands of the Child*) + 1288 (*Numbskulls Cannot Find Their Own Legs*) + BN 1334* (*The Human Chain*). Essentially, the *märchen* consists of the type 1450 + 1384; BN, II, 512, 523; BP, I, 335, and II, 440; Thompson, 1946, pp. 193, 210; in addition episodes about stupidities which the narrator selects at will. According to Thompson, the tale originates in the Orient and his literary beginnings; from there it came into folk tradition through medieval European chapbooks and jest collections.

VARIANTS: Arany, p. 64; Nyelvör, 1874, p. 31, and 1879, p. 89; Kálmány, 1914-1915, I, 113, 115; Kálmány, 1881, III, 166; Berze Nagy, 1940, II, 412, 413, 414; Konsza, p. 155. *The Woman Who Beats the Hen* (BN 1248*) occurs in one variant: Berze Nagy, 1940, II, p. 414. Several folklorists analyzed the type of the human chain (BN 1334*). See Katona, 1912, I, 282-283, No. XIV; György, p. 117. Variants: Nyelvör, 1876, p. 179; *Ethn.*, 1895, 128, 1903, 468, and 1928, 29; Berze Nagy, 1940, II, 404.

Arany's text mentioned above has appeared in several of Elek Benedek's collections, for example, *Itt sem volt, ott sem volt mesevilág.*

In Mrs. Palkó's humorous story, type 1288, (*Numskulls Cannot Find Their Own Legs*), well known in the international tale body appears for the first time in the Hungarian language. The second and third "stupidity" are well known in the Hungarian; the episode of the stupid woman who is about to cut off the hand of the child caught in the fence seems to be Mrs. Palkó's own invention.

54. *The Uncouth Girl* (1950)   BN 1458** (*Puella pedens*); BN, II, 526. There are a great many anecdotes about girls not knowing how to behave and revealing hidden defects when the suitor arrives, known ever since the sixteenth century, and also in written literature (BP, III, 237). This story, which has only one parallel classified by Berze Nagy (Nyelvör, 1873,

p. 41), deals with the girl who cannot withhold breaking wind and who, being afraid to bring water from the well in the dark, urinates into the cabbage while the suitor watches from under the bed.

This magnificant anecdote and a few more mentioned in the notes to No. 44 (*Lazybones*) were used in Andrásfalva as educational devices. It was told in the circle of women and girls in the spinning rooms or at other gatherings. Just as she did with the following similarly aimed story, Mrs. Palkó gave this anecdote a masterful form.

55. *The Dumb Girl* (1950) This anecdote cannot be connected with any of the established tale types, unless to AT 1459*. In this text not only are the local customs and ethical order revealed, but Mrs. Palkó's sense of humor and her ability to make her listeners laugh are given scope. The dialogues are very lively. The girl who does not know how to talk to the suitor speaks nonsense and offends him by obscene language in spite of her mother's warning (Chapter 7).

56. *The Five Brothers* (tape recorded, 1954) AT 1525/E (*The Thieves and their Pupil*); Rotunda K 306. In all probability it stems from type 1525/A (*The Master Thief*), and is especially popular in Northern Europe (Bp, II, 393; Thompson, 1946, pp. 174, 175). We do not know of other Hungarian versions of this particular tale.

Mrs. Palkó's construction is not faultless. Only the first and last of the adventures is worked out. The middle one is mentioned but not carried out.

57. *The Two Brothers* (tape recorded, 1950) AT 1536/D* (a tentative addition to the general type 1536: *Disposing of the Corpse*); BN, II, i; Suchier, 1921; Solymossy, 1919, p. 66.

In the widely varied kinship of this anecdote that stems from a common nucleus, the smuggling in and out of the corpse has been known in Europe since the Middle Ages. Among the many variants, the most popular is the story of the dumping of the often killed, skirt-chasing priest (such as M. László's text; see below, No. 101) or that of the carrying about of the corpse of the greedy priest. Both are well known in Hungarian folk tradition. The tale told here, however, introduces something new: at the center of attention we have social injustice. The uneven distribution of earthly goods leads in this story, as in so many real cases in peasant society, to family quarrels and lawsuits concerning the share in the inheritance. The unjust division which leaves everything to the older brother and disinherits the younger is changed by the latter with corresponding alacrity. We know only of two similar, but not identical, variants of this story (F. Kovács, p. 62; Dégh, 1942, I, 80-81, and II, 178). By means of the tale P. Pandur demonstrates the most brutal kind of justice that is known in Hungarian folk narratives. There is no trace in this of the devout moral—that the good man will get his reward and the bad man will be punished. It is not a question of good and bad, but of rich and poor, lucky and unlucky, and of a correction of the unjust distribution of goods. A poor man saves the life of a boy, and out of gratitude the boy takes everything away from the rich neighbor—and carries the rich neighbor's possessions into the house of the poor man. The boy's deed is done in the name of the "restless" revenant, and he also causes the striking down of the priest who comes to bless the house. The summing up of the tale justice in the end goes this way: "The poor man became an extremely wealthy one, and the rich man became extremely poor . . ." (Dégh, 1942, II, p. 185). The other version is a shorter one in which the servant ransacks the house and takes the possessions of the nobleman whose dead brother he is supposed to bury. Mrs. Palkó's *märchen* has the same moral. The only difference lies in the fact that here we have two brothers. Even though the younger is lazy and a drunkard, tale justice demands that he get the same part as the diligent brother. The necessary goods must not be doled out according to human qualities, but each person must get his just share. If distribution was unjust it has to be corrected. Mrs. Palkó makes the difference between rich and poor very plausible: the two brothers' relationship actually resembles that of master and hired man which triggers the conflict. We have already shown in Chapter 2 that even with the Bucovina Szeklers where sib relationship plays such an important role, there were many cases where difference in possessions divided sisters and brothers. Mrs. Palkó knows these cases very well. She describes reality, when the poor brother explodes in view of the full granaries of his rich brother, saying, "Is this justice?" The sly expedient for the rightful distribution is based on the folk belief in the revenant, and the superstitious brother immediately falls for it. "God's justice" is carried out by the younger brother, who divides everything equally to the last wooden spoon.

58. *The Poor Man and the Gypsy* (1954)   This story, which can be inserted in the group of *MI*, J 1510, does not belong to the typical Gypsy anecdotes so common in Hungary in this connection. We know only one single Hungarian variant: Ösz, pp. 118-119. The case of the poor man outwitted by the barber was indeed very close to the people of Andrásfalva who made their living felling wood and hauling. When the barber takes wagon and horse as well as the logs for his money, the Gypsy gets even with him by forcing him to shave his donkey.

59. *The Gypsy King* (1959)   AT 1640 (*The Brave Tailor*); BN, II, 563-566; BP, I, 128; Bødker, 1957, pp. 1-23; Thompson, p. 144.

The stable form of this widely known tale is probably due to the popularity of the Grimm version. Most of the Hungarian versions do not include the whole chain of motifs and many are combined with the themes of *The Stupid Ogre*. Our text contains one single episode (AT 1640/V: *The Coward War Hero*) which seems to be otherwise the least stable part of the whole in European tradition. There are only two Hungarian versions—both Transylvanian—to which it shows clear affinity (*UMNGY*, VI, 176; Konsza, p. 122).

As treated thoroughly elsewhere (Dégh, 1959), the tale of Mrs. Palkó belongs to the old repertoire of Andrásfalva, having been latent for a long time. She learned it shortly before the telling from her son, József, who heard it, he stated, from his grandfather when a child. Some incidents of the story—the army headed by the Gypsy substituting for the king, making a bridge of green twigs and stealing sandals for getting through the marshland, scaring away the enemy by pulling down trousers, exposing back parts which are mistaken for dogheaded Tartars by the enemy—are probably local inventions.

60. *The Old Witch* (tape recorded, 1954) AT 1641 (*Doctor Know-All*) + 1530* (*The Man and His Two Dogs*). It is a variation of an episode of a type known all over the world. See *MI*, N. 611, 2 (*The Woman Counts Her Yawns*); BP, II, 412.

*Doctor Know-All* is frequently represented in the Hungarian: BN, II, 566; Katona, 1912, I, 285; György, pp. 166-167; Berze Nagy, 1940, II, 523, Note 237. We only know a close version of our own variant (*Ethn.*, 1922, 84) with annotations by Solymossy, according to whom the anecdote, which is unknown in Eastern Europe, probably stems from a literary collection or has come through the channels of oral tradition from Western Europe.

Mrs. Palkó's variant deviates: it is more witty (the eaten plums are counted by the old woman) and is extended by the episode of calling the dogs by their ambiguous names (see *Magyarság néprajza*, IV, 62).

61. *Lawyer Virág* (tape recorded, 1954) AT 1675 (*The Ox as Mayor*); BN, II, 583; BP, I, 59; Rotunda K 491. Although frequently occurring in Hungary, it is mentioned only by Berze Nagy, 1940, II, 441, Note 524, and Ortutay, Dégh, and Kovács, III, 868.

62. *Gábor Német* (tape recorded, 1950) This is an unknown tale of a new type of which we have not yet found variants, with the exception of those in the Andrásfalva version. It may well be that this story, which in its structure and concepts is a magic tale but which is set in an industrial scene, describing a peasant lad on the way to becoming a skilled worker, was inspired by popular reading matter. This might account for the fact that the actors have family names, and that the name of the village in which the story starts is also given, something which does not occur in folktales.

It might well be that the elements which have led to the formation of the *märchen* stem from one of the many books which were distributed among Hungarian minority groups. One thing is sure: the *märchen* in its present established form is completely folkloristic and typical for the Bucovina.

Mrs. Palkó formed the *märchen* well. She had learned from M. László, but often heard it from her father and her brother. Not only in the concepts is the peasant world-view expressed, but also in the style. The tale formulae penetrate the commonplace action (dialogue with the watchman, conversation of the factory owner with the boy when he hires him, the rhythmic prose as the factory owner shows the plant and his property, the description of wealth, the transfer of the idea of the folktale king to the factory owner, the proud bearing of the body in front of the girl, etc.). The story must have been passed on and polished before it reached our narrator. The *märchen* shows that Mrs. Palkó has told it often and with pleasure. Her individual shaping is apparent mostly in the characterizations. That of the proud judge and his family is excellent. The haughty landowner and the wealthy family of the judge stick together. Against them stands the wife of the landowner, who herself has become a victim of the unwritten law of the peasant society that property decides and not the affection of the young people. She revolts when the happiness of her daughter is at stake. The story of the lovers' separation because of class difference often occurs in popular songs and ballads, and its happy ending is finally the theme of this *märchen*. See also the variant of Mrs. Sebestyén (No. 96).

63. *Margit* (tape recorded, 1950). This is not a *märchen* but a story which takes its topic from the life of the agricultural laborers in the Bucovina. It is possible that it came from reading matter of religious origin. I consider it more reasonable, however, that it is founded on a true story which gave an account of a common occurrence with the migrant agrarian workers who were unemployed during the years of agrarian crises. Mrs. Palkó knows the misery of the peasants who were most run down, for she herself had experienced it, and this tale is characteristic of it. In the tragic fate of one family Mrs. Palkó indicates the way of the poor peasant which leads to ruin. The realism of the narrator reaches its climax in the description of the old world and strict, cruel rules of the peasant life.

## György Andrásfalvi's *Märchen*

64. *The Twin Rod* (1948) *MI*, T 671, K 131 (*The Stepchildren*) + AT 303 (*The Twins or Blood Brothers*) + 556F (*The Shepherd in the Service of a Witch*) + 300 (*The Dragon Slayer*) + 314 (*Goldener*) or 510 (*Male Cinderella*) + 400/V d. (*The Ring Baked into Cake*) + 552 (*The Animal Brothers-in-law*). In addition to this rich motif coupling, the frame of the

*märchen* ultimately belongs with type 303; this type is varied by the story-teller and greatly enlarged. BN II, 260; BP I, 528; K. Ranke, 1934; Thompson, 1946, pp. 24-33.

The basic form of the *märchen* of the *Twin Rod* is the *Dragon-Slayer* type, which is simply enlarged by three episodes: (1) two identical boys; (2) the life token; (3) the service of the witch. This *märchen* belongs with the most common and most variable European tales. That is why the Hungarian redaction is also full of ethnic deviations and even individual innovations. Since it would be difficult to enumerate the intricate structures belonging here, we will point only to the close relatives of Andrásfalvi's tale: *The Twins or Blood Brothers:* Erdélyi, 1846-48, I, 495, and III, 241; Merényi, 1861, I, 79, and 1862, I, 149; MNGY, XIII, 56, 59, 70. *The Foundling:* Berze Nagy, 1940, II, 76, 79, 82; Ösz pp. 142, 168; Banó, 1941, p. 239; Dégh, 1942, I, 146, 156; Nagy, p. 152. *The Witch in the Forest:* MNGY, XII, 113; Nyelvör, 1875, p. 231; Bözödi, p. 101. *Hero Disguised as a Baker, The Ring Baked into Cake:* Dégh, 1942, I, 252. *In the Service of the Witch:* Ethn., 1936, 93; Ortutay, 1935, p. 43; Kovács, 1943, II, 161; Ortutay and Katona, I, 87. Other variants belonging here are mentioned below in the notes to György Andrásfalvi's tale *Ilona Beautiful* (No. 66), because the episode of 556 F* belongs organically in that type. For the motif of the sword of chastity (*MI*, T 351), see note to *Prince Sándor and Prince Lajos* (No. 27). For that of the life token (*MI*, E 761.4.1): Ethn., 1919, 68-69. The prophesy through laying out beans: Ethn., 1913, 87.

This tale, to which numerous references were made above, belongs among the richest and most colorful pieces of our Kakasd collection. Andrásfalvi links into a smooth, independent, and individually shaped whole the motifs taken from different though related tales. It is a good example of the way in which the natural elements from different tale types, having affinial relationship to each other, can be coupled by the joy of storytelling, the power of shaping, and the inventive art of the outstanding narrator.

65. *Nine Kernels of Wheat* (tape recorded, 1950)  AT 400 (*The Man on a Quest for His Lost Wife*) + 313 (*The Magic Flight*) + *MI*, G 531.5.i (*Giants*) + P 271, N 812 (*Friendship Between the Giant and the Hero*) + D 832 (*Acquisition of Magic Objects by Tricking the Fighting Heirs*); Berze Nagy, I, 492; BP, I, 442, and III, 406; Holmström, 1919; Aarne, 1930; Soly-mossy, 1919, pp. 65, 70 Thompson, 1946, pp. 88-100; Ováry, p. 23.

The story of the swan maidens, of which the Hungarian *Argirus märchen* (an oral tale derived from the literary tradition of the Renaissance) is a variant, occurs in three well-known related *märchen* as an incident: in the types AT 313, 400, and 465/A. Well known is the subtype in which the hero follows the swan maiden after overcoming her (400) and her hostile father forces him to solve many difficult tasks (313). It is much rarer—though

Andrásfalvi's *märchen* belongs here—that the motif of the disappearance of the swan wife and the quest for her is inserted (465/A). A special Szekler variant developed of the quest and the tests by the fairy wife.

VARIANTS: Arany, 163; *MNGY*, IX, 249, 269, and XII, 170 (this version closest to our text; see also Notes 456-457); Ortutay, 1935, p. 110; Berze Nagy, 1940, II, 94, 98; Banó, 1941, pp. 197, 251; Kovács, 1943, I, 83, 139, 217, and II, 45, 142; Bözödi 1958, pp. 156, 162; Nagy, p. 142; Dégh, 1965, pp. 28, 307, in English. Two manuscript versions from Sára, Zemplén County, were narrated by the 45-year-old cobbler András Berkó and by the 34-year-old Mrs. Mária Bónis, in 1943; one from Csikmenaság was narrated by the 29-year-old shepherd Gyula Ferencz, 1942 (FI).

As stated in Chapter 6, recording of the tale took place before a big audience and it is because of the keen interest that Andrásfalvi succeeded so well with his piece. Among all the variants available in Hungarian folk tradition, only the one by Kriza can be called closely related (see also *Fairy Erzsébet* of Mrs. Palkó, No. 15). This tale in a stylized form was spread through E. Benedek's famous collection (see I, 211) and therefore it might possibly have influenced Andrásfalvi's text, but only indirectly. The comparison of the two forms however, shows characteristic differences illuminating the essential transformation by way of oral tradition. In the version of Andrásfalvi, the initial motif—the service of the three brothers for the field of wheat, and the return of the youngest son and his wife to the parental roof—are missing. This loss, however, is replaced by felicitous additions, including the episode of the devils quarreling over inherited magic objects and the scene in Fairyland (arrival in the cloak which makes one invisible, the three tests of the fairy which add considerably to the retardation of the climax). It is characteristic that the narrator extends several scenes according to his own taste and embroiders them, and on the other hand that he restricts others to the very minimum. In order to give an idea of the handling of the subject by Andrásfalvi, here is a segment for which we quoted samples from Kriza, Benedek and Mrs. Palkó (two samples) in No. 15 above:

> Well, then, his eyes could perceive that it was fire, indeed. And he sees that the hind leg of an ox was on the top of the fire, on the top of the glowing embers. It was about a glowing twenty-meter fire of acacia tree. On the top of it was roasted the leg of an ox and a wheat loaf as big as an ordinary millwheel. And such an enormous giant laid around the fire, that is, he surrounded the fire, that his heels reached the crown of the tree. He was able to encircle the twenty-meter live coals. He snored so strongly near the fire that all dry leaves that remained on the tree were trembling as if the wind would have blown them and immediately fell down.
>
> Well, he thought at a distance of twenty steps, he would not be scared, that he saw that the man was in his underwear. He thought to go down on his fours and creep slowly closer. Well, he did what he thought, went down

on all fours and crept there. The closer he got the stronger was the snoring. Well, he held himself by grasping the dry leaves, once here, once there, arriving at the spot. Now he sees the roasting ox leg on the fire and that huge loaf of bread. And my, the man has a mustache like his father or like that of the reverend father, but it did not matter what it looked like. Now, the boy figured, it would not be wise to wait until the old man got up, but rather to find out what to do. Still on all fours he crept close, right to his heels, and pulled his pants leg, he had a nice wide pair of Hungarian pants, and the boy climbed up right to the hips of the giant man. High up the hips of that big, strong man. There, at the bottom of the pants he sat down, jumped in and sat down and kept there in silence.

By comparions with Mrs. Palkó's adaptation we can see that if the good storyteller is not influenced by knowledge of the source, he feels free to twist his tale according to his own taste and fantasy. The recital of the tale in general is uneven. There is no connection between the crow that steals the wheat and the birds who advise the hero; there is no action in the episode of the quarreling devils—it is merely restricted to advice. Excellent and psychologically well prepared is the wandering around of the youth in the forest, and his encounter with the fearsome giant. Here, too, the realism in the magic world of the tale is apparent in the description of the mustache, the pen knife, the garment of the giant, the account of a ball in the township, and so on. The description of the situation in fairyland is very dramatic, as the young woman in her desperate situation awaits the return of her husband, laying a plate for him at the dinner table.

66. *Ilona Beautiful* (tape recorded, 1950)   AT 552/A (Ic, IIa, IIIa) + 552 (*Three Animals as Brothers-in-law*) + 554 (*The Grateful Animals*) + 302 (*Ogre's Heart in the Egg*); BN, II, 118; BP, I, 134, II, 19, 198, 451, and III, 426; Thompson, 1946, pp. 55-57.

The root of our *märchen* is the simplest form of the *Animals-as-Brothers-in-law* type, which very early passed from folk tradition into written literature. This *märchen*, whose essential part consists of the animal brothers-in-law helping the hero by giving him a particle of their own bodies (552), was probably extended in Eastern Europe, with the closely related episode of the grateful animals (554), and further through addition of the fitting incident of 556F* (*The Shepherd in the Service of a Witch*), which otherwise is little known in European folk literature except in mostly Slavic, Rumanian, and Hungarian language areas. The way of the monster's stealing the girl seems to be a specifically Hungarian invention (basic motif occurs in type 302), as well as this special construction of the tale. The Hungarian variants are numerous and, though they are composed of many various motifs, all show astonishing logic in composition. It happens that the motif of the *Animals as Brothers-in-law* is supplanted by the motif of the *Sky-High Tree* (468; see above No. 23), and sometimes by that of the *Dragon-*

*Slayer* (300). The formal steadiness of the *märchen* appears in the fact that the dialogue between the magic horse and his master, the monster, shows a fixed formula in most variants, just as the conversation between the grateful animals and the dragon brothers-in-law is nearly rhythmically repeated. In the Hungarian variants the monster is often named Holofernus, Hollóferjös, or Hollófernyiges, certainly a truncated form of the biblical name Holofernes, as confused with the Hungarian word *holló* (raven). The name Tündér Ilona appears for the first time in Transylvania in a letter dated March 8, 1554: "God be with us, and may guide me out of this *Tündér ország* (fairyland); even though I do not have yet my Ilona, I would gladly go away."

VARIANTS: Majláth, p. 257; Erdélyi, 1946, III, 241 (*Service with the Witch*); also Népmesék, p. 7; Merényi, 1862, II, 1; Nyelvör, 1885, p. 375; Kálmány, 1881, I, 131, and 1914-1915, II, 31, 164; manuscript in Magyar Tudományós Akadémia, 990/IV.9; *MNGY*, VI, 320, VII, 435, IX, 29, 43, 127, 277, X, 422, and XIV, 196; Beke and Katona, p. 54 (*The Sky-High Tree*); Dégh, 1945, p. 12 (+ *In the Service of the Witch*); Ortutay, 1935, p. 43 (+ *The Sky-High Tree*); Banó, 1941, p. 45 (+ *The Sky-High Tree*); Kovács, 1943, I, 165 (+ 314, 560), and II, 97 (+ *The Sky-High Tree*), 161 (+ *In the Service of the Witch*); Ethn, 1936, 93 (+ *In the Service of the Witch*); Virány, p. 34 (+ *Sky-High Tree*). The following parts of the well-formed *märchen* are outstanding; the lively dialogues with the dragon brothers; the description of the place; the scene when the hero falls in love when looking at the picture of the fairy; and the compassion of the dragon with the hero (compare No. 36). It is worth noting that the use of 556F*, which organically belongs to this tale, shows the storytelling quality of Andrásfalvi when compared with the inclusion of the same episode in *The Twin Rod*. Another lively scene is the hero's dialogue with the helpful fish, based on his own experience as a fisherman.

67. *The Story of the Poor Blind Beggarman* (1950)  AT 571 ("*All Stick Together*"); BN, II, 194; BP, II, 39; Thompson, 1946, p. 154.

VARIANTS: Arany, p. 223; *MNGY* XII, 128; Kálmány, 1914-1915, I, 18, 110; Ortutay and Katona, I, 87; Hegedüs, 1952, p. 107. It is contained in several popular *märchen* collections of E. Benedek, for instance in *Itt sem volt, ott sem volt mesevilág*, p. 48.

Andrásfalvi's *märchen* departs from the variant above. The point of departure certainly came from another tale and the composition is not always felicitous, for the tale does not build up organically. Instead of the golden lamb or another animal, a self-propelled wagon plays an important part here, which is not to be found in other oral tales but in the popular books. We deem it possible that it was transferred from reading matter into the folktale, possibly even from an edition of the chapbook tale *The*

*Miracle Wagon* (published by K. Rózsa, Budapest, 1895). The other parts of the *märchen* follow the type and the details are pretty, even if rather simple in expression.

68. *The Discharged Soldier* (1948)   AT 854 (*The Golden Ram*); Rotunda K 1341.I; BN, II, 384; BP, I, 446; Thompson, 1946, pp. 157-158.

VARIANTS: Erdélyi 1846-48, II, 348; Nyelvőr, 1900, p. 42; *MNGY* IX, 411, 415, and XIII, 33; Ortutay, 1940, p. 360 (only the beginning; fragmentary version); manuscript variant, narrated by the 34-year-old Mrs. Zsófi Halász from Sára, Zemplén County, 1943, (FI).

A typical soldier's tale which Andrásfalvi had heard from a discharged soldier.

69. *The Young Shrew* (1948)   Our *märchen* corresponds to the eighth novella of the Poncianus chapbook *Tentamina* (*The Patience of the Husband*); see *Poncianus*, Régi Magyar Könyvtár 5, pp. 124-132. Here this novella appears for the first time in folk tradition. Though the original text was retained essentially without change, the individual marks of the narrator's style can be easily discerned. In spite of this we do not dare to designate this tale as completely folklorized. Andrásfalvi does not quote his sources, but it may be assumed that a cheap edition of the *Seven Sages of Rome* (Poncianus) was well known to him.

The text is close to type AT 901 (*The Taming of the Shrew*); *MI*, X 31. It also occurs in the Italian novella literature (Rotunda T 296).

70. *The Beautiful János* (1948)   AT 1426* (*Man with Unfaithful Wife Comforted*); BN, 977* (II, 437); see Solymossy, 1916, p. 275 for international parallels; see also Wesselski, 1925, I. Also contained in the Italian novella literature, Rotunda J. 882. i.

Lajos Katona had already pointed out that the action of this *märchen* was identical with the frame tale of the *Arabian Nights* (*Revue des traditions populaires*, 44). In his treatment of the international variants, Solymossy endeavors to find the key to the origin of the first Hungarian variant, from Transylvania in 1882, published by B. Orbán. After comparing the different Oriental and European variants, mostly stemming from literary sources, he concludes that the Hungarian oral text has come to Hungary from the Orient, but not through the *Arabian Nights*. This *märchen* took roots in the West, and also in Hungary, not through the intermediary of literature but through oral tradition.

So far all we know are two Hungarian variants. The first is that one collected by B. Orbán (*MNGY*, III, 393), also printed in one of the popular collections of E. Benedek (*Székely népmesék és balladák*, 1885, p. 193). The other (J. Ösz, p. 24) occurs not much later. It is striking to see that, including Andrásfalvi's, all three texts come from the Szeklers, differing only as far as the style peculiarities of the narrators differ, though seven decades lie between the recording of the first and the third. It may well be that Benedek's reworked edition has helped the spread of the *märchen*, at least in the limited sphere of the Szekler land, for it seems to be unknown in other regions of Hungary. We failed to find the first literary version which precedes the oral one. As a consequence we have to accept as probable Solymossy's thesis that it was transmitted by way of oral tradition from the Orient. The tale, however, did not spread very widely but was limited to a narrow area. It might have belonged to an early repertoire of the Szekler tale tradition, like many other *märchen* preserved in the Bucovina which were contained in old collections but today are either unknown or occur in the Hungarian tale body in altered forms.

71. *The Rich Peasant and His Wife* (tape recorded, 1954)    AT 1360 (deviate) is a variant of this type family, so far unknown to us. It also occurs among the Italian novellae, Rotunda Q 487*.

72. *The Faithful Widow* (1954)    AT 1510 (*The Matron of Ephesus*). There are numerous literary editions. Griesbach (1889) traced the spread of the story of the faithless widow through world literature. It also occurs in the Italian novella literature: Rotunda K 2213. i. According to Thompson (1946, p. 209) the *märchen* never became popular but gave rise to a series of similar anecdotes about women's faithlessness (see AT 1350; also Mrs. Palkó, No. 48).

The Hungarian variants are generally nourished by two sources: the translation from the *Seven Sages of Rome* (XIV, novella: Vidua (*The Comfort of the Widow*) and from Voltaire's *Zadig* (2nd chapter), Lafontaine's edition. The literary works of some eighteenth and nineteenth century Hungarian authors, Verseghy, János Kis, Dugonics, Jókai, and others are based on the latter; the popular versions came into their own through the spread of the Poncianus version in the form of chapbooks. For these editions see Nyelvör, 1904, p. 32, and 1906, p. 58; *Ethn.*, 1926, 153. Literature of the Hungarian variants: Heinrich, p. 406; Tolnai, p. 902; Krausz, pp. 263, 311; Weber, p. 455; Solymossy, 1926, p. 153; György, pp. 119-120; Gálos, 1908, pp. 125-126. Recently E. Brandon (1965, pp. 37-41) treated the subject and compared Andrásfalvi's text to the novella in *Seven Sages of Rome*.

73. *The Return of the Damned Soul* (1950)    *Ml*, E 411; BX IX, 573 (does not find rest because of guilt) + E 425. 1, L; BX, IX, 349 (woman dressed in white) + B 733; BS, IV, 473 (an animal senses the dead person).

We have mentioned several times, in discussing Mrs. Palkó's belief legends, the epic formation of the popular folk belief concerning the revenant and the insertion of this concept into the *märchen* (see notes to Nos. 8-13). A variant of this tale is mentioned in Notes to No. 12.

74. *The Witch Appears in the Guise of the Lover* (1950)  *MI*, D 2070 (as a nightmare) + D 658.2; BS, IV, 511 (in the shape of a seductive woman). Similar tales in Hungarian are *The Pressed Victim Is Rendered Speechless* (Gönczi, P. 159; Berze Nagy, 1940, III, 340; *Ethn.*, 1928, 42; Komáromy, p. 64 and *The Witch Torments, Chokes* (*Ethn.*, 1892, 72, and 1909, 312; Komáromy, p. 78).

75. *The Fishing Adventure* (1948)  *MI*, F 491 (The nightmare). For Hungarian parallels see *Ethn.*, 1891, 205, 1914, 324, 1927, 47, and 1928, 97; Nyelvör, 1902, p. 530; *Turista Közlöny*, 1917, pp. 53, 56, 62; Balassa, pp. 64-66 (summary).

This story of superstition is very characteristic. It illuminates the origin of an epic form based on folk belief. The supernatural power which causes harm always appears in the midst of some rational action. In this version, Andrásfalvi tells of a nightly fishing expedition during which the "extraordinary case" occurred. This is a variant of No. 14.

## Mrs. Anna Sebestyén (Geczi)

76. *The Witch Shoed as a Horse* (1950)  *MI*, G 241.2.1 (witch transforms person and rides him) + G 211.1.2 (witch as horse shod with horseshoes); BS, III, 1881. This is a widely popular belief legend with a well-rounded, stable frame. This is why Berze Nagy mistakenly included it in his tale type index under 335[xx] (I, 453-455). The Hungarian redaction, the blacksmith's wife, who transforms the apprentice into a horse by hitting him with a bridle and rides him to the witch's Sabbath, where she is unmasked by the other apprentice, is turned into a horse and shoed. This story in a more or less complete form has been known since the Middle Ages and is still popular in today's peasant villages: Thury, p. 197; Komáromy, pp. 228, 231, 327, 336, 562, 593, 660-663; S. Dömötör, 1939, p. 210; Katona, 1891, p. 62; Binder, 1891, p. 167.

VARIANTS: Merényi, 1861, II, 167; *Ethn.*, 1895, 233, 331, 1898, 139, 1929, 193, and 1936, 45; Kálmány, 1914-1915, I, 60; Ortutay, 1935, p. 240; Fél, pp. 191-192; Berze Nagy, 1940, II, 131; Ortutay, 1940, p. 298 (Note p. 401); Hegedüs, 1952, p. 238; Balassa, 1963, p. 249 (Balassa added fifty-three more manuscript versions from the EA in his notes).

77. *The Dead Lover* (1950)  See Mrs. Palkó's *märchen* No. 8. Though we have here a rather fragmented, sparse variant, it differs considerably from Mrs. Palkó's text, and might have a different origin, which may have con-

tained more and different rhymed parts than the ones which are generally known:

Másfél ember és egy lófej;
Trop, pinkalup, ajtó-ablak nélkül való kápolnát majd elérjük;
Aluszol-e hótt pajtás?
(One and a half man and a horse-head;
Klop-klop, we soon arrive at the door-and-windowless chapel;
Are you asleep, comrade Dead?)

For parallels see K. Ranke, 1955, III, 255, in a riddle.

The scene at the grave was missing and was replaced by another, nightmarish scene put together from horror tale motifs—the ghostly vision of a ruined chapel in the woods and the horse changed into the hanged man.


78. *The Incubus* (1950)   See Mrs. Palkó's tale No. 9 (*The Glass Coffin*) for a detailed treatment. This text deviates considerably from Mrs. Palkó's *märchen*. Here it is the incubus itself who—in keeping with the living village belief—takes the place of the dead bridegroom. In the exposition of this tale we have another proof for the interaction of the *Lenore* (AT 365) type. In this *märchen* the dead man returns because his love is mourning him, but no longer as the beloved sweetheart. He becomes a devilish avenger, who takes the girl with him. This tale also deviates from the usual version in that it is the neighbor's daughter who identifies the former lover at the request of the girl's mother, who then turns to the wise woman for advice.


79. *Stories of Revenants* (1950)   The "cases" reported here are additions to the belief stories related so far of the restless dead. They confirm the strength of the psychological basis for *märchen* types 365 and 407. In connection with the following notes, see also Mrs. Palkó's texts No. 8-14 and Andrásfalvi's text No. 73.

These belief stories were told one after the other in the spinning rooms, as one brought another to mind:

A. *MI*, E 451, BS, IX, 574 (*Unsettled Business*) + E 425.2 (*In the Shape of An Old Man*);
B. *MI*, E 425.3. (*In the Shape of a Child*);
C. *MI*, E 371, BS, IX, 574 (*Finding of the Hidden Treasure*);
D. *MI*, E 321. (*The Visit of the Dead Marriage Partner*);
E. *MI*, E 265. BS, I, 710 (*Meeting with a Ghost Leads to Sickness*) + E 411.0.3, BS, IV, 1032 (*The Horse Cannot Draw the Wagon*); and
F. *MI*, E 421.1. BS, VIII, 1453 (*The Invisible Ghost*).

Similar stories were told by other narrators. The spinning girls and women identified so closely with the ghost stories that nobody had the courage to investigate when they heard a thump from the other room. The cat locked in the "clean" room had bumped an apple off the table, and when this was discovered later, everybody laughed in relief and assured us that nobody today would believe in such nonsense, i.e. that ghosts were abroad today.

80. *Three Miraculous Stories* (1950)  These stories concern people who are born deformed as a sign of God's punishment or for other mystical reasons. We are quoting these three "cases" solely as an illustration of the belief world of the village. *MI*, D 196, BS, V, 623 (child in the shape of a frog); *MI*, E 423.i.5 (child in the shape of a hog).

81. *The Picture of the Princess* (1950)  A variant of Mrs. Palkó's tale No. 16, *The Princess*.

82. *The Twelve Ravens* (1950)  AT 451 (*The Maiden Who Seeks Her Brothers*); BN, I, 616; BP, I, 70, 277, 427; Thompson, 1946, p. 110.
    VARIANTS: Merényi, 1863, I, 115; Nyelvör, 1874, p. 468, and 1875, p. 517; *MNGY*, VII, 430, IX, 216, 223, and XIII, 331; Kálmány, 1914-1915, II, 40; Berze Nagy, 1940, II, 178, 182, Dégh, 1942, I, 274; manuscript variant from Sára, Zemplén county, related by the 34-year-old Mrs. Mária Bónis, 1943 (FI).
    This is a short excerpt whose recital is confined solely to the facts of the tale action.

83. *Jutka in Ashes* (1950)  AT 500 (*The Name of the Helper*) + 501 (*Three Old Woman Helpers*). The coupling of the two related *märchen* can be found in other variants as well. This text is completely independent of Mrs. Palkó's variant but follows precisely the version taken over from L. Arany by Benedek; even the title is the same. For another close parallel see Kriza, 1956, II, 179. Otherwise see Mrs. Palkó's *märchen* No. 24, *Rupcsen-Hencsen*.

84. *The Devil's Midwife* (1950)  AT 476* (*In the Frog's House*), type established following BN 476ˣ (I, 648) on the basis of eight Hungarian variants. The story, however, belongs among the belief legends rather than with the *märchen*. Christiansen notes it as a migratory legend: 5070 (*Midwife to the Fairies*). The general outline is as follows: Woman/man carelessly promises to be midwife to frog/best man to devil. She/he liberates souls, tends to newborn child, acts in wedding ceremony in hell, is rewarded by worthless objects (coal, trash, bricks, etc.) that turn into gold.
    VARIANTS: Pap, p. 125; *MNGY*, I, 429; Nyelvör, 1874, p. 139; *Ethn.*, 1891, 302; Berze Nagy, 1940, II, 196 (in a horror tale), 197; Dégh, 1965, pp. 296, 300 (in English).
    Mrs. Sebestyén's text deviates considerably from the variants and the plot indicated by Berze Nagy. A promise given on the spur of the moment leads to the adventures in hell. The deliberation of boiling souls, a motif

belonging to tale type 756/B, is missing and is replaced by another, the taking away of the dishes from the poor by magic. The magic power of the pronounced word, the transformation of worthless objects into gold, and the exchange of the child are belief concepts generally known, but new with Mrs. Sebestyén in this context. The pin thrust into the infant's head occurs with the Cheremis (Beke, 1958, pp. 317-318). Since the tale-like turn is lacking in Mrs. Sebestyén's account, her recital is rather an abruptly presented belief story with possibilities for transformation into a *märchen* (see Chapter 7).

85. *The Cock's Advice* (1950)   See Mrs. Palkó's *märchen* No. 34 (*The Red-bellied Serpent*). This is a fragment of the type but a well-rounded, independent story in itself.

86. *The Potato Boiling* (1950)   An unknown anecdote, this text may be included with AT 902 (*The Lazy Woman*) as well as with 1370 (*The Lazy Wife*), the type which reports the exemplary atonement of the young women who are lazy or greedy or have other bad qualities. The relentless procedure is reminiscent of Andrásfalvi's *märchen* No. 69, and its similarly brutal solution. The quarrelsome wife is tamed by sprinkling hot potatoes over her naked body. Two other remotely related variants are known in Hungarian folk tradition: Berze Nagy, 1940, II, 408; and a manuscript from Kishartyán, Nógrád country, narrated by the 57-year-old József Gregus, 1952 (FI).

87. *Work, Cat!* (1950)   AT 1370 (*The Lazy Woman*); BN II, 510.
   VARIANTS: *MNGY*, III, 356, and XII, 137; Kálmány, 1914-1915, I, 28, 117; Kriza, 1950, II, 370. The *MNGY*, XII, 137 variant became popular with the Szeklers as it spread through E. Benedek's storybook (II, 94). It was also included in schoolbooks. There are many editions, rhymed versions, and *märchen* plays.

88. *How Many People Eat Today?* (1950)   This anecdote also belongs with the type cycle AT 1370, based on the moral, he who does not work may not eat. It is known in this form only in two versions: Kriza's posthumous work (1956, II, 3680), and Bözödi (1958, p. 182.) It seems to remain a local variant in the Szekler country.

89. *The Galushka [Dumpling] Cooking* (1950)   A short variant of Mrs. Palkó's text No. 54 (*The Uncouth Girl*).

90. *The Lazy Spinning Woman* (1950)   AT 1405 (*The Lazy Spinning Woman*), BP, III, 128; Thompson, 1946, p. 207.
   It is possible that the variant of this anecdote about the woman who

threatens her husband from behind a tree from cutting wood for a spinning reel, very popular in Eastern Europe, comes from the rich Rumanian tale stock and reached the Szeklers either in the Bucovina or in the Moldavia region. AT 1380, *God's Word from Behind the Tree*, also contains the same trick.

Both of the two Hungarian variants can be found in Berze Nagy, 1940, II, 409 and Konsza, p. 183.

91. *Three Girls and the Suitor* (1950)  AT 1452/A (*The Bride Test*). This is a new variation of the theme in BP, III, 238. In Hungarian there are two other Szekler variants: Ortutay, 1955b, III, 520; and Konsza, p. 157.

92. *The Blind Girl* (1950)  AT 1456 (*The Blind Fiancée*); BP, III, 237. This was never included in Hungarian tale collections, though it is not unknown. It probably did not find acceptance in the published collections because of its obscene climax. The episode also occurs independently, as a village anecdote in which the girl makes fun of her simple-minded beau by turning toward him her backside, which he mistakes for her mouth. Erzsi Matyi told a similar story of the stupid fellow who went to his wedding with his best man, and since he had forgotten to ask a kiss from his bride, wanted to kiss her through the window—and thus came off second best.

93. *The Girl Without Underwear* (1950)  Essentially a slight variation of type AT 1458. Its tendency is different from that of the other known versions. Here two bad qualities are scourged: slovenly dress—the reason why the boy throws hot porridge over the girl's naked body; and, of secondary importance, unclean cooking. Hungarian variants: Berze Nagy, 1940, II, 564; Banó, 1941, p. 192.

94. *The Poor Fisherman and the Rich Neighbor* (1950)  AT 1689/A (*Two Presents to the King*); Honti 1533[1] (*The Round Stone*); BN 905* (II, 406).
The old form of this anecdote is as follows: a cat is brought into a mouse-infested country by a man who is subsequently made rich for this by the king. Another man is envious of this fortune and wants to try his own luck by offering more precious presents, upon which he is rewarded by the king with cats. The story was included in *Gesta Romanorum* and in Italian sources in the thirteenth century. From these the story develops in two directions. One development, by contamination, evolved the famous *märchen* which is connected with the name of the Lord Mayor of London, Dick Whittington (about 1400), as well as the variants of this tale (see BP, II, 75). The other development of the story leads to our variant. Essentially it relates the success of the poor man and the failure and shame of the greedy rich man. For variants see BP, III, 170-192; Rotunda J 2415.1.

Two logical forms have evolved in the Hungarian stock. Both have oral and literacy variants. For a listing of the latter, see György, pp. 171-173. Both are often connected with the name of King Mátyás, the Righteous.

VARIANTS: Merényi, 1861, I, 143 (also published in E. Benedek, II, 252); Nyelvör, 1903, p. 181; Kálmány, 1914-1915, I, 205; *Ethn.*, 1922, 54, and 1926, 83, B. Tóth, *Magyar anekdotakincs*, I, 122, 151; Jókai, pp. 7-9, 10-11; Dugonics, I, 52-53; J. Vajda, *Magyar bors*, 4-5; Erdélyi *Közmondások*, p. 57; Berze Nagy, 1940, II, 352, 569, 582; Kovács, 1943, I, 273; Konsza, p. 133.

Mrs. Sebestyén's text belongs with the tale type of the poor fisherman who fishes up a diamond, and of the rich man who gives loads of cats to the king. For the other form also occurring in Hungarian folk tradition, from which the proverb of the Buda dog market originated, see below, Márton László, No. 100.

95. *Ág* (1950) *MI*, G 61 (human flesh eaten unwittingly). See the introductory episode of the tale *The Fawn* (No. 21). The cannibal element also occurs in some of the variants of the tale AT 720. For this tale as a riddle tale see Berze Nagy, 1940, II, 18.

96. *The Cabinetmaker's Apprentice* (1950) This is a well-rounded, very good variant of Mrs. Palkó's tale of *Gábor Német* (No. 62). By comparing the two texts and taking into consideration the storytelling abilities of the two narrators, we may try to come to a conclusion as to the original source. Even though the extent, the form, and the turn of language deviates a great deal, the theme is developed logically, for it follows closely the sequence of the plot:

## MÁRTON LÁSZLÓ'S HANDWRITTEN TALES

97. *Prince Sándor Book of the Dead*, pp. 201-247. For annotations to this text see Mrs. Palkó, No. 27. The freely adapted text of Márton László probably comes from a very old, unknown source, which accounts for its archaic features. Márton László's handwritten piece has an individual, definitive style, in which its origin within the folk tradition can also be felt. The moralizing, didactic tendency and the occasional long windedness are rather an indication of peasant shrewdness and selectivity than of sticking to an original literary text.

98. *The Son of the Wheelwright Book of the Dead*, pp. 179-193. For a variant see above Mrs. Palkó, tale No. 28, In comparison with their source, E. Benedek's collection, the texts of Mrs. Palkó and of Márton László are obviously much more carefully formed and filled out. The written version, destined for reading as a storybook tale, is completely folklorized, even

though the natural process of transformation was distinctly controlled by the knowledge of the source as well as by the written version. Therefore it is rather laconic and is shortened in the second half. At the end we find a moralizing tone which is alien to the *märchen*.

99. *The Bad Rearing*   AT 838 (*The Bad Rearing*); BN 779 I[x]. The exemplum of Oriental origin appears a second time in Hungarian folk tradition. The first one (Kálmány, 1914-1915, II, 148) probably comes from quite a different source. Its content has changed considerably: the erring young man encounters his father in the woods and in revenge skins him alive.

We know numerous Hungarian literary variants which go back to the medieval Christian exemplum. It is contained in the seventeenth century collection of fables by Gábor Pesti as well as that by Gergely Marosvásárhelyi; P. Pázmány mentions it in a sermon, and it is also known in anecdote collections of the eighteenth century. For a summary of the sources see György, p. 90.

We deem it possible that our variant entered Márton László's book quite early by way of sermons. Our variant has the traditional form of the exemplum: first the story is told, then its teachings are pointed out. It might be a part of the several centuries old popular literary tradition that had been preserved by the Bucovina Szeklers to this day.

In a recent publication of medieval and oral folklore versions, Röhrich (1962-67, vol. 2, pp. 279-90, 471-74) includes a German prose translation of our text, disregarding other Hungarian variants as well as the related story of Mrs. Palkó.

100. *The Dog Market in Buda*   Book of the Dead, pp. 194-200. See Mrs. Sebestyén's tale No. 94, above, for another variant of the basic story and for the international and the Hungarian variants.

Márton László's *märchen*, fixed in writing, is of course limited by its form and its use. Even though the style is elaborate and we can feel the influence of the reading matter (the *märchen* repeatedly appeared in chapbooks, most recently in 1909 in Book 9 of the popular library of Kálmán Rózsa and his wife), the fresh, popular style of the author appears to great advantage. This tale belongs with the best pieces of rhymed prose.

101. *A Woman Who Can Sing Well*   Book of the Dead, pp. 279-285; AT 1536/B; BP, III, 238; Bédier, 1893; Pillet, 1901; B. Heller, "Barát-Kádencziák," pp. 842-851; and Heller, *Ethn.*, 19 (1908), 272; Gálos, *Ethn.*, 18 (1907), 1-18, 65-73, and *Ethn.*, 22 (1911), 382.

The Hungarian variants, just as other European oral versions, go back as far as the "Amantes" novella in the *Seven Sages of Rome*. Here the point is no longer the humiliation of the three hunchbacks—and the husband—but the murder of the three knights (monks in some versions) who went out to seek romance. The first Hungarian version was included in the Poncianus chapbook as its twelfth novella (pp. 154-161, 229). It also occurs in the anecdote collection of Samuel Andrád, *Elmés és mulatágos rövid anekdoták*, 1790, II, 255. In oral tradition it does not occur earlier than the second half of the last century. These are all rustic stories on the smart peasant woman outwitting amorous parsons and discharged soldiers. This is why Berze Nagy included the versions in his Hungarian type index under 1726A$^x$.

VARIANTS: Nyelvör, 1874, p. 369, and 1904, p. 297; Lázár, p. 625; Berze Nagy, 1940, II, 453. The low number of variants is deceptive as to the frequency of the anecdote. It is one of the best known in the whole Hungarian language area, and there is hardly a collector who has not noted it down. Berze Nagy also notes (1940, I, xvi, i), "The tales of the three hunchbacks and the shamefaced young wife are the most popular." The anecdote is equally popular in manuscript collections and in the oral tradition. Its rare ocurrence probably results from the obscenity of its variants.

Márton László's version does not stem from folk literature but directly from the Poncianus novella, with which it coincides in every respect.

102. *The Priest and the Cantor  Book of the Dead*, p. 804. This anecdote, which was unknown so far, may be listed with the group about parsons and sextons (AT 1775-1824). The parson and the sexton, being without money, ask the inkeeper for credit on drinks. To avoid being found out, he notes the debt under "Dominus vobiscum" and "et cum spiritu tuo."

103. *The Woman from Hadik  Book of the Dead*, p. 805. A slimy anecdote about the naked legs of a young washing woman, so far unknown, which served as entertainment, together with the devout readings, during wakes.

104. *Listen How Dancing and Pipe-smoking Started  Book of the Dead*, pp. 506-516. This is one of the etiological legends, which certainly were church-inspired. We think it possible that this story, which in taste and concept is a pure folk narrative, originated in the wake of a sermon from the pulpit. The church proclaimed for centuries the devilish origin of the dance, and presented it as a terrible sin for which awful punishment lay in wait in the Beyond (see Réthei Prikkel, pp. 9-16). The same judgment was pronounced on other worldly pleasures such as smoking and the consumption of alcoholic beverages. Legends telling that tobacco comes from the devil are quite well known (Nyelvör, 1889, p. 424; Kálmány, 1891, III, 179; Berze Nagy, 1940, II, 604). We could find only one parallel to our text: Kálmány, 1914-1915, I, 175-186. (The devil goes to a tavern in order

# NOTES

## List of Abbreviations

| | |
|---|---|
| AT | Aarne and Thompson |
| *Acta Ethn.* | *Acta Ethnographica* (Budapest) |
| BN | Berze Nagy |
| BP | Bolte and Polívka |
| BS | Bächtold-Stäubli |
| *DtJb* | *Deutsches Jahrbuch für Volkskunde* |
| EA | Ethnological Archives of the Ethnographical Museum, Budapest |
| *Ethn.* | *Ethnographia, A Magyar Néprajzi Társaság Folyóirata* (*Journal of the Hungarian Ethnographical Society,* Budapest) |
| FFC | Folklore Fellows Communications (Helsinki) |
| FI | Archives of the Folklore Institute, Budapest |
| IFC | Irish Folklore Commission |
| *JAF* | *Journal of American Folklore* |
| MI | *Motif-Index* (Thompson) |
| *MNGY* | *Magyar Népköltési Gyüjtemény* (*Anthology of Hungarian Folk Literature*) |
| PMLA | Publication of the Modern Language Association of America |
| *Sov. Etn.* | *Sovietskaia Etnografia* |
| *UMNGY* | *Uj Magyar Népköltési Gyüjtemény* (*New Anthology of Hungarian Folk Literature*) |

## Preface

1. Wolf, 1964, p. 48.
2. Ortutay, 1947, pp. 50-55.
3. Belényesy, 1958; *Acta Ethn.*, 1959, 159-162.
4. Dégh, 1950, pp. 127-128.
5. The first volume of the Kakasd tales containing forty-nine texts of Mrs. Palkó was published in 1955. The second, issued in 1960, included

another thirteen tales from her along with twelve from Gy. András-falvi, twenty-eight from Mrs. Sebestyén, and thirteen from M. László. A selection of thirty tales from the collection of Z. Kelemen, a local teacher, was published with my introduction and comments in 1965.

6. Dégh, 1963, pp. 1-12.
7. Utley, 1966, pp. 70-84.


## PART I

### Chapter 1. History of the Szeklers

1. According to Hungarian chronicles containing the legends of their origin, the brothers Hunor and Magyar were the original fathers of the Huns and the Magyars. The Huns, who, after the fall of Attila and the decline of their immense empire, had retired to the province of Transylvania, are—according to popular conception—the predecessors of the Szeklers. For the Hungarian origin myth, see Róheim, pp. 11-29.
2. Györffy, 104-116.
3. Imreh, p. 9.
4. Imreh, pp. 11-22.
5. Szádeczky, pp. 103-114.
6. Sántha, p. 5.
7. Szádeczky, p. 123.
8. Sántha, pp. 12-15.
9. This is an error. Joseph II, who supported the settlement in the Buco-vina, reigned later; he followed his mother, Maria Theresa, to the throne after her death in 1780.
10. Szádeczky, pp. 240-241.
11. Sántha, p. 10.
12. Szádeczky, p. 239; Sántha, p. 19.
13. Ibid.
14. Sántha, p. 23.
15. This is a mistake: at that time Moldavia region did not yet belong to Rumania.
16. The *Bukovina* as a territory on the eastern slope of the Carpathian mountains existed for 170 years. It was annexed by the Austrian Empire in 1774 and was allotted to Rumania in 1918. The region north of the river Siret fell to Russia in 1944. Beck, pp. 5-9.
17. *Fogadj isten* means "God, accept us!"
18. *Isten segíts* means "God help us!"
19. Kis-Várday, pp. 131-133, 137.
20. Belényesy, p. 16.
21. Sántha, pp. 57-58.
22. Belényesy, p. 16.
23. An error resulting from the fact that after the settlement in the Buco-vina, the Szeklers went across the border into Rumania to do seasonal labor.

24. The fact that the informant is listing the Bucovina village names with regard to the settlement in Moldavia proves how vivid the conception of the unity of the former Szekler communities has remained. This explains why the villagers strove to be settled together at Tolna and Baranya.
25. The informant, who hails from Andrásfalva, begins at this point to relate the tradition about the founding of his village.
26. Kis-Várday, p. 133.
27. Jancsó, p. 4.
28. Oberding, 1939, pp. 9 ff.
29. Oberding, 1939, p. 10.

## Chapter 2. Social and Economic Life in Old Andrásfalva

1. Belényesy, p. 26: "Though the property conditions in Andrásfalva were the most favorable compared with the other four villages at the time of settlement, the increase in population led to economic ruin because of the lack of sound material foundations and the absence of any possibilities for realizing better conditions."
2. Oberding, 1939, pp. 13, 21.
3. Brockhaus, *Konversationslexicon*, 1894, III, p. 714.
4. Oberding, 1939, pp. 9-10.
5. Kis-Várday, p. 137.
6. Oberding, 1939, p. 11; Sántha, pp. 82-83.
7. Oberding, 1940, p. 21.
8. Oberding, 1939, p. 13.
9. Halász, p. 104. For variations of the second verse with melody see Balla, p. 135.
10. After World War I the Austro-Hungarian monarchy was dissolved and the Bucovina fell to Rumania.
11. For a description of fishing in the Suceava see the tales of Mrs. Palkó (Appendix, No. 14) and of Andrásfalvi (Appendix, No. 75).
12. See Andrásfalvi's tale *The Rich Farmer and His Wife* (Appendix, No. No. 71).
13. Belényesy, pp. 28-29.
14. Halász, p. 104. Belényesy, p. 39, describes how the Rumanians by the beginning of the nineteenth century, had already blended with the Szeklers. She also quotes cases of her informants.
15. Oberding, 1939, p. 10. Mrs. Palkó's grandmother on her mother's side was of Polish origin.
16. Told by György Andrásfalvi.
17. Told by Ferenc Farkas; also see Oberding, 1939, p. 11.
18. Told by Ferenc Farkas.
19. Belényesy, p. 32. When giving exact figures of the ethnic variety of Bucovina, Beck (pp. 84, 86-98) confirms the Szekler characterization of the other nations. He emphasizes that Bucovina was a miniature "united Europe" composed of Rumanians, Ukrainians (Ruthenians), Huzuls,

Lipovani (an exiled Russian sect), Jews, Germans, Poles, Hungarians, Gypsies, and Armenians, who, while maintaining their own cultures, together shaped another specific culture.

20. The Bucovina Szekler sib and kinship system and its maintenance in Transdanubia is discussed in detail in Fél, pp. 85-97. Interesting in this connection is the study terminated in 1949 by E. Sergő, in which the author lists the connections of 180 members of the Mátyás family. (The manuscript is to be found in the Folklore Institute of the University of Budapest).

21. Bakó, 1941, pp. 146-147, quotes characteristic cases from Istensegits.

## Chapter 3. *Resettlement Procedures (1883-1941)*

1. Belényesy, pp. 18-19.
2. Szádeczky, pp. 1-7.
3. Sántha, p. 90.
4. As Márton László relates in his ritual book, the *Book of the Dead* (pp. 194-195), "In 1890 the first settlers went to Déva; in Csernakeresztúr they settled in 1912, in Marosludas in 1904. In 1906 the first family left for Canada."
5. Oberding, 1939, p. 13.
6. Oberding, 1939, p. 23.
7. Oberding, 1939, pp. 11-17.
8. Belényesy, p. 21. Mrs. Zsók says that the brotherhood of Hungarians and Rumanians had changed "when Hungary made demands upon Rumania, they said, '*Dutyle Budapesta* (Go to Budapest)! After the war of 1914 the people were incited one against the other. Until then they lived peacefully with each other."
9. The property of the well-to-do had lost its value because they could not take the land with them but had to sell it cheap (Sántha, p. 129). Our informants assure us that all the poor people were glad to leave the Bucovina. "Those with more than eight acres would much have preferred to stay, if those with three acres had not insisted on leaving," György Andrásfalvi says.
10. The names of the settlements were Andrásfalva, Andrásföldje, Andrásnépe, Bácsandrásháza, Andrástelke, Bácsandrásszállás, and Andrásmezö (Sántha, p. 130).
11. Belényesy, p. 22.
12. Sántha, p. 128.
13. Fejér county had the largest Church-owned manorial estates. The Church, like the landed aristocracy, refused to cut parcels for the landless peasantry from these estates.
14. Referring to Marshal Miklós Horthy, who was Governor of the Kingdom of Hungary between 1920 and 1944.

## Chapter 4. *The Settlers of Kakasd*

1. See Weidlein, pp. 1-25, for the origin and removal of this German group.
2. See Belényesy, p. 22, for the same statement. These reports all originate

around 1955, a fact which seems to be essential for correct understanding of the change of social structure within the period in question.

3. See Dégh, 1950, regarding the social realignment of groups.
4. Belényesy, p. 12.
5. Oberding, 1939, pp. 21, 22.
6. Mátyás Mátyás. Márton László's *Book of the Dead* enumerates priests, teachers, and church singers from 1860 on. The same enumeration can be found in Sántha, p. 49.

## PART II

### *Chapter 5. Survey of the Results in Folktale Research to the Present*

1. Some bibliographical summarization of works done so far is to be found in Peuckert and Lauffer, 1951, pp. 130-176, and Röhrich, "Märchen-forschung," *passim*. New trends attempted and results of works in progress are encompassed by the reports of three congresses of the International Society of Folk Narrative Research: that in Kiel-Copenhagen (1959), that in Athens (1964), and the meeting at Liblice in 1966 (*Fabula*, 9 [1967]).
2. Bolte and Polívka (IV, 41-94) put together such quotations. See also Jahn, 1914, p. 23.
3. To cite only the best-known example: Ch. Perrault, *Contes de ma mère l'Oye* (Delarue, 1954, pp. 1-22).
4. Cf. Gonzenbach, 1870; Bladé, 1886; Campbell of Islay, 1860-62; Radloff, 1866.
5. Săineanu, 1895. A. E. Vasiliu collected the material for his work, *Povești și legende* (Bucharest, 1928), from 1897 to 1914. In his introduction he follows Săineanu's suggestion and names his narrators, describing their narrative style.
6. Kriza, 1911, pp. 327-328; Faragó, 1967. János Kriza, who was influenced by Herder, had been collecting in Szekler country since the beginning of the nineteenth century.
7. Greguss, p. 319.
8. Pintér, p. 63.
9. Aarne (1910, pp. 23-29) distinguishes between the conscious and the unconscious individual variation. Krohn opposes the opinion that folk poetry is a collective creation (1926, pp. 23-24).
10. Petsch, 1900; Bolte and Polívka, IV, 17-36; Speiss, pp. 62-66; Löwis of Menar, 1912; Berendsohn, pp. 129ff; Mackensen, pp. 313, 315. See also the Czech researchers influenced by the Germans: Tille, 1902, 1937, pp. 612-621; Polívka, 1916, 1936, pp. 5-16. Kubín grouped all his *märchen* collections according to the narrators.
11. Wesselski, 1935, pp. 219-220.
12. Vikár, 1905, p. 443.
13. Sebestyén, p. 591.
14. Berze Nagy, 1907, pp. x-xi, 226-227; 1915, pp. 104-105; 1942, pp. 67-68.
15. Ortutay, 1939, p. 222.

16. This simile comes from Lajos Katona (1912, p. 200) who constructed twenty-one type sketches based on the Hungarian folktale body.

17. We do not intend to enumerate the classification works published since the early attempts of Hahn and Gomme, because they are known to the experts. We are confining our remarks to the present state of cataloging and classification of the Hungarian *märchen*. Honti's catalog (1928) is already outdated. Berze Nagy's classification prepared between 1914 and 1938 was based on materials collected before 1924, though published only in 1958. We have great expectations for the new catalogue, which is still being compiled at the time of this writing, because it will considerably aid our own research. (Á Kovács, 1955, pp. 443-447; 1958, *passim*; 1966, *passim*.

18. Von Sydow, "Popular Prose Traditions and their Classification," 1948, pp. 127-145.

19. Ibid., "Folktale Studies and Philology," pp. 207-219.

20. Ibid., "The Folktale from the Ethnic Viewpoint."

21. Ibid., "Geography and Folktale Oicotypes," p. 46.

22. Ibid., pp. 44-46.

23. Ibid., "Folktale Studies and Philology; On the Spread of Tradition," pp. 203-205, *passim*.

24. Evaluation of the corresponding work by von Sydow is in Peukert and Lauffer, 1951, pp. 155-65; Swahn, 1955, pp. 421-431.

25. See Thompson (ed.), 1953, p. 282; O'Sullivan (O'Suilleabháin), 1963, pp. vii-x.

26. The practical application of von Sydow's theoretical considerations is seen mainly in the works of his disciples. Of these we shall mention the monographs of Liljebald (1927), Rooth (1951), and Swahn (1955). Regarding the latter, the comments by W. Anderson on the foundations of the method deserve recognition: Anderson, 1955, pp. 118-130; 1956, pp. 115-118; Swahn, 1956, pp. 111-115. With respect to a dependable fieldwork method inspired by von Sydow, see Tillhagen, 1948, and Tillhagen, 1959.

27. Christiansen, 1953, pp. 70-82.

28. Many researchers have debated about the existence of an "archetype" and the possibility of tracing one. In this connection we wish to mention especially the considerations by Károly Marót. *Ethn.*, 1940, 151; 1954, pp. 5-6; 1956, pp. 123 and 125; and similar statements by de Vries, 1954, pp. 12-13. On this question the great representative of the Finnish school, Stith Thompson, is opposed to W. Anderson. Thompson, too, expresses doubt whether the early form of the *märchen* can be isolated, and whether it makes sense to search for it: ". . . though I have concerned myself for half a lifetime with the history of narrative motifs, I am very sceptical of any success in working out what we may call the prehistory of a particular tale . . . the ultimate origin . . . must remain a mystery . . . it is merely impossible to recapture the needed facts" (1955, p. 486). The validity of "types" has been contested several times since they were established. Since the publication of the second revised

edition of Thompson's international type index of 1961, some folktale scholars have expressed doubt concerning its usefulness for modern research; on the other hand, the number of new national index projects has increased as never before. Desiring to develop a system of morphological classification as reliable as Linné's plant classification, Propp (1927) worked out his structural model of the Russian magic tales, which almost parallels the classification system of tale types and motifs (Levin, 1967). Recent structural form and content analysis following Propp's work after a lapse of more than thirty years has developed into an exciting new trend, though it is not yet ripe enough to replace the type system which forms the basis of current international cooperation. Dundes, 1964; Taylor, 1964, pp. 121-129; Holbek, 1965, pp. 158-161; Roberts, 1965, pp. 229-235; Greverus, 1965; Jacobs, 1964, pp. 319-22; 327-32; Jacobs, 1966, pp. 413-427; *Fabula*, 1967, *passim*.

29. Eberhard and Boratav, 1953, pp. 16, 24.
30. Korompay, 1941, pp. 176-177.
31. Krohn, 1926, p. 25.
32. Gorki, 1950, pp. 389-407; Sokolov, 1945, pp. 13-16; Ortutay, 1941, pp. 161-181; Marót, 1947, pp. 162-164, and 1956, pp. 39-40; and Lintur, 1953, p. 8, all refer to similarities and differences between oral and written literature.
33. F. Ranke, "Das Märchen," pp. 257-258.
34. Sharp, 1907, pp. 110-115. Berze Nagy (1942, pp. 66-67) arrives at similar conclusions.
35. Anikin, *Sov. Eth.*, 1953, pp. 80-87. The same is expressed by E. Pomerantseva, 1952, III.
36. Marót (1947, p. 165) states, "everything is production, even the seemingly automatic reproduction . . . thus we can say that the artfully 'reproducing' singers or narrators of the Brothers Grimm, of V. Randloff, or of Ortutay can already be considered conscious authors." Bascom (1955, p. 248) gives folk literature a new label, "verbal art," and sees a new production in each reproduction: "where the narrator is supposed to introduce original variation . . . a tale may very markedly differ even from one telling to the other by the same narrator. In such cases, each telling of a tale must be regarded as a unique event. . . ." Ortutay (1948, pp. 42-43) says that each topic which is orally transmitted assumes a new color, and that this verbal *Zersagen* (R. Weiss's expression modeled after the term *Zersingen* in folksong research) offers a gifted personality on occasion to make it blossom.
37. Henssen, 1941, p. 40.
38. Chichevov (1946, p. 29) states, "Tradition and authorship are inseparable." Gorki, "Dissolution of the Individuality," *Collected Papers*, 1905-1916; Anikin, 1953, 4, p. 86.
39. Ortutay, 1937, pp. 66-67; Marót, 1947, p. 165.
40. Brinkmann, 1931, 12, pp. 23-24.
41. Wesselski, 1931, p. 178; Weiss, 1946, pp. 34-35; Zender, 1935, xxiii.
42. Wisser, 1926; Haiding, 1953; Haiding, *Träger*, p. 24.

43. Uffer, 1945, pp. 25-26.
44. The *märchen* is always tied to one gifted individual, as stressed also by Koechlin, pp. 9, 96; Mackensen, p. 315; von Sydow, 1948, pp. 20, 44; Ball, pp. 172-173; de Vries, p. 42; Henssen, 1951, p. 41; Weiss, p. 285; Bîrlea, 1963, p. 352.
45. Tillhagen, 1948, pp. 268-269.
46. Jahn, 1891, p. xi; Löwis of Menar, 1921, pp. x-xi; Sokolov, 1945, p. 241; Azadovski, 1926, pp. 25-32; Thompson, 1946, pp. 16-17, 411, 454; Colum, p. xii; Delargy (O'Duilearga) 1945, pp. 26-29; Bolte and Polívka, IV, 6; von der Leyen, 1953-54, II, 271.
47. Bîrlea (1963, p. 349) mentions one exceptional case in Rumania: a group of masons in Transylvania hired a woman to tell stories after World War I.
48. Berendsohn, p. 129. For observations regarding the outstanding representatives of Hungarian folktale creation, see Marót, 1939, pp. 273-277, 1940 (*Egyet. Phil. Közlöny*), 230-231, and 1945, p. 7; and Ortutay, 1940, pp. 18-19.
49. Ortutay, *Parasztságunk élete*, p. 18; Berze Nagy, 1915, pp. 104-105; Lintur, 1953, p. 8.
50. Delargy, 1945, p. 13; Thompson (ed.), 1953, pp. 300-301; Bascom, 1955, p. 249.
51. Sharp (p. 30) states, "Variation is the product of the individual; whereas Selection is the act of the community" and (p. 16) "The suggestions, unconsciously made by the individual singer, have at every stage of the evolution of the folksong been tested and weighed by the community, and accepted or rejected by their verdict."
52. Ortutay, 1948, pp. 25-29; 1940, 10. For a summary of criticism of the Hungarian editions, see Dégh, "*History of Hungarian Folklore*," pp. 75-79.
53. Berze Nagy, 1907, pp. viii-ix; Sebestyén, pp. 591-592.
54. Such as the tale texts recorded for linguistic magazines such as *Nyelvör* and *Nyelvészeti Füzetek*, or the narrative collection of the dialectologist Horger (1908).
55. As Brinkmann notes, the rounded-out pieces of the existing collections give an inaccurate impression of the living tale treasure (p. 1). The striving for reliability is emphasized more in Grudde; Zenker-Starzacher, pp. 10-17; Delarue, 1947, pp. 117-118; Thompson, 1946, pp. 346-351. For many statements about the relevant directions in the new Hungarian research see Dégh, *History of Hungarian Folklore*, p. 30, and Dömötör, 1947, p. 267. The step toward the observation of the natural environment of the tale was the realization that the collector should not disturb the narrator (Uffer, 1945, pp. 8-9), and that collecting should be done in the narrators' natural surroundings (Schwietering, pp. 72-73).
56. Concerning tape recording of reports see Lindgren, p. 350; Thompson, 1946, p. 411; Delargy, 1945, pp. 8-9, 30; Thompson (ed.), 1953, pp. 3-12. The Hungarian radio had started to record folktales as far back as

1936 (Ortutay, *Magyar Szemle*, 1938, 11ff). Tillhagen pointed out the hopelessness of the task of recapturing in writing the narration of folktales. There is just as much difference between the written tale and the tale which is narrated as there is between the typed play and the play performed on the stage. The tale should therefore be captured on sound film (p. 271). Henssen worked with magnetophon and 11 mm. film (1951, p. 9; see also *Hessische Blätter*, XLIII, 8-9). Haiding paid special attention to the gestures and the facial expressions of the narrators (*Oesterreichs Märchenschatz*, 1953, pp. 404, 412; see also 1955, *passim*). Ball writes that the recordings should fix the narrator and the listeners at the same time (pp. 170, 171). For the efforts of Hungarian, Rumanian, and Czech researchers in this field, see Hegedüs, 1946 and 1952; Bîrlea, 1963, pp. 342-343; and Jech, 1956, pp. 55-57, to name only a few.

57. Fiedler and Hoerburger (pp. 6-15) sum up their experiences in trying to capture the performance of the narrators on film. In this regard see also Jech, 1965; Satke, 1958; W. Werner, 1966-67, and Sándor, 1963. More recently, Á. Kovács is experimenting with the recording of the rhythm and metric of the tale (1967). Principles of collecting methods based on the experience of Dorson (1964, pp. 1-20), Goldstein (1964, *passim*) and Dundes' article advocating collection in context (1966) are extremely useful in the formation of a more adequate fieldwork technique.

58. Malinowski, pp. 29-30, 34-35, 54.

59. Ibid, pp. 125-126.

60. Lindgren, pp. 350, 361; Bascom, 1953, pp. 283-290. American anthropologists have developed through the successful combination of Malinowski's ideas and Boas' field research methods and diffusion concept a study of personality and culture which is largely socio-psychologically oriented. Although American anthropologists were not particularly concerned with creative personalities and their social role in little communities, their approach to the individual, as representative of a group, helped in the formation of the method of the present study. The writings of Redfield, Herskovits, Jacobs, DuBois, Benedict, Barnouw, and Honigman, in general, and of Hallowell (1947), Bascom (1954), and Lowie (1958, 1959), in particular, are suggestive for the fieldworker in folklore. Fischer's condensed survey of the socio-psychological analysis of the folktale (1963) is an attempt to bring together anthropologists and folklorists; however, only a handful of the so-called "anthropological folklorists" make use of the folkloristic approach (*The Anthropologist Looks at Myth*, special issue of *JAF*, vol. 79, 1966; Crowley, 1966). See also Dorson, 1959 (*JAF*, vol. 72), pp. 198-199.

61. Peuckert, *Märchen*, 1906-8.

62. F. Ranke, 1933, pp. 203-211.

63. Mackensen, pp. 315-36; Peuckert, 1938, pp. 3-5, 65-67; Peuckert and Lauffer, pp. 142-146; Weiss, pp. 33-34; Hain, 1962, pp. 2563-2568.

64. Thompson, 1946, pp. 449-455; von der Leyen, 1953-54, II, 284-285.

65. Sokolov, 1945, pp. 224-225.

66. Eberhard, *JAF*, 1954, p. 232. Eberhard's concern is emphasized in his collecting of Turkish minstrel tales (1955).

67. Dobroliubov, 1934, pp. 432-433.

68. For the research methods of Hilferding, Rybnikov, Grigorjev, Markov, and others, see: Azadovski, 1926, pp. 5-8; Sokolov, 1927, pp. 161, 172, 219. See Chistov, pp. 5-29, concerning Onchukov's collection, *Folktales from the North.*

69. In 1914 Zelenin's collection entitled *Velikorusskie skazki Permskoi gubernii* was published, followed a year later by his *Skazki Viatskoi gubernii.* At the same time, the brothers Sokolov published a voluminous collection, *Skazki i pesni Belozerskogo Kraia.* These three are some of the most important of the collections treating several outstanding narrators.

70. Systematic collecting of folktales was conducted in the tale-rich regions, especially around Archangel, Vologda, and Olonec, in Pskov, Orel and the surroundings of Tambov, and in the isolated regions of Siberia and the Ural mountains. In 1936 Novikov and Ossovetskii published first 56 and then 120 folktales of the famous Kupranika (or Barishnikova). In 1938 Nechaev published the tales of Korgujeva. Azadovski and Eliasov (1940), Novikov (1941), and Gofman and Minc (1941) all followed this example. Narrators such as Nerhov, Bogdanov, Suslov, Semionov, and Vinokurova, to mention only the most famous, became well known (Sokolov, 1927, pp. 218-219; Pomerantseva, 1964, pp. 598-603, 614-616). For the Russian method and storytelling among Slavic peoples, see Polívka, 1932, pp. 5-12.

71. Here the name of A. G. Nikiforov must be mentioned especially; cf. Azadovski, 1938, p. 32. P. V. Lintur (1953, p. 9) demands the complete penetration of a storytelling community.

72. Azadovski, 1926; also in *Literatura i folklor*, a chapter about "Russije skatzoschniki i russkije skazki," 1938; also 1932, "Russkaja skazka, Isbrannije mastera."

73. Chicherov, pp. 229-240.

74. Lintur, 1953; also 1957, *passim.*

75. *Folklore of the Soviet Epoch* (Moscow, 1952).

76. V. S. Bakhtin, pp. 153, 2, pp. 154-163; Nechaev and Rybakov, 3, pp. 134-141; Anikin, *Sov. Eth.*, 86, to mention just a few of the many reports, discussions, and articles.

77. Astakhova, 1954, 2, pp. 112-115.

78. Anikin, 1953, p. 57; Pomerantseva, 1954, p. 241.

79. Recently V. Propp (1963, p. 104) mentioned the preference of "masters of narration as a reason for neglecting the study of retold storybook *märchen.*

80. Anikin, 1964, pp. 350, 359; Péter, 1965, pp. 120-125.

81. Ulrich Jahn, xi-xii, xv-xvi.

82. Bünker, vii-ix, x-xi; cf. the appreciation of Lajos Katona in *Ethn.*, 1907, pp. 251-253. Encouraged by Bünker, S. Graf collected the entire material of a Heans narrator (1914, p. 20).

83. Wisser 1926, pp. ix-xxviii.
84. G. F. Meyer, 1925.
85. Hertha Grudde, 1931 and 1932.
86. Merkelbach-Pinck, 1939; Zenker-Starzacher, 1941. For further summing-up, see Peuckert and Lauffer, 1951, pp. 141-146; Röhrich, "*Märchen-forschung*" II, *DtJb*, 1956, 299-304.
87. Schwietering, pp. 66-68, 71-78.
88. Schwietering and his disciples have investigated peasant communities by always concentrating on an ethnographic or folkloristic phenomenon as the particular item lives. M. Bringemeier (1931) observed the communal role of the song repertoire of a folksinger; Brinkman (1933) recorded the narratives of a village while carefully observing the opportunities for telling tales. Worthy of mention are the work of M. Hain (1951), in which the communal function of the proverb and folk speech is investigated, and the monographs by Györgypál-Eckert (1941), on the tale treasure of a Swabian village in Hungary (apparently social and psychological aspects of the study are the result of the influence of her teachers, A. Spamer and R. Thurnwald).
89. Brachetti, 1930, p. 202. See, in a similar vein, Röhrich, "*Märchen-forschung*" I, *DtJb*, 1955, p. 282.
90. Brachetti, 1930, pp. 209-210.
91. Henssen, 1936, pp. 12-22; See also *Hessische Blätter*, XLIII, 5-29.
92. Bringemeier, 1931, p. 4, writes that "not the individual but the community is the bearer of the folk treasure."
93. Henssen, 1936; also 1951. See the review of Weiss, 1946, pp. 129-130.
94. Uffer, 1945, 1961.
95. Haiding, *Österreichisches Zeitschr, fr. Vk.* 1953, pp. 24-36. See also 1953 for a summary of the research results so far. Preface by Henssen.
96. Langstroff, 1953; Sareyko, 1954.
97. Cammann, 1961; Oberfeld, 1957, 1958; Werner, 1966-67.
98. Two examples of the many Brachetti (1935), who wrote her dissertation on the basis of Grudde's and Wisser's collections, and Krause-Siebert (1947), who used the material of Grudde.
99. I have dealt with the topic, summing up the results to date: Dégh, 1965; Matičetov, 1961; Bošković-Stulli, 1963; Sirovátka, 1965; Pop, 1965.
100. Dégh and Jech, 1957, pp. 567-808; Dégh, 1960; Domokos, 1967.
101. Ranke, 1955. Three volumes of the collection have appeared so far.
102. We find very early notes on the Irish tale material and storytelling (Bolte and Polívka V, pp. 52-64), above all by Thomas Crofton-Corker (Dorson, 1955, p. 2). Campbell of Islay and Douglas Hyde, during the second part of the nineteenth century, aroused the scientific interest (Delargy, 1945, p. 5; Dorson, 1966, pp. v-xxxii).
103. Delargy, 1938, pp. 37-40.
104. Delargy, 1945, pp. 46-47. Here we must mention that the Hungarian folklorist János Honti investigated the Irish folk material and recognized its decisive role in the formation of a European tale body (1936, pp. 33-39). See also Honti, *Helicon*, pp. 65-73.
105. O'Sullivan, 1942; Thompson (ed.), pp. 3-12; Thompson, 1938, pp. 53ff;

also 1946, pp. 407-408; Delargy, 1945, pp. 8-9; Loomis, 1949, I, p. 200.

106. Thompson (ed.), 1953, p. 282; Murphy, 1938, p. 216; Jackson, 1936, pp. 265-293; Lindgren, 1939, pp. 335-336.

107. Delargy (1963) summed up his result in a more recent article. Of the publications of the Irish Archive materials in independent volumes and the journal *Béaloideas* mention should be made of the publication of the repertoire of three outstanding storytellers, that of Shéain O'Chonaill, Thomás O'Criomhthain, and Séan O'Sé (Delargy, 1948, 1956, 1961). As a result of the carefully planned collecting techniques developed by the IFC, the recently published folktale catalog became the most authentic of its kind, on the basis not only of an imposing number of versions but of texts collected with regard to their bearers. O'Sullivan-Christiansen, 1963.

108. In Northern Europe we should also mention the work of Tillhagen along with the Irish collections (1948). He collected and evaluated, following similar principles, the legends and *märchen* of a Swedish migrant Gypsy tinker. His observations led to new recognition of the personality of the storyteller.

109. Satke, 1958; Jech, 1959; Noy, 1963 and 1965; Massignon, 1965, Crowley, 1966.

110. For a detailed bibliographical review, see Bîrlea, 1963, pp. 335-352, and Pop, 1965. A volume of essays in preparation on the East European folk narrative (Indiana University Folklore Institute Monograph Series) includes the studies of O. Nagy, T. Brill, and J. Faragó on storytellers and their social role in Rumanian villages.

111. Anthropologists, following Boas' teaching, collected narratives extensively among the North American Indians, with comments on individual narrators and audiences. The non-Indian folk prose tradition of America, on the other hand, has hardly advanced over the collecting and publishing method of the brothers Grimm, to say nothing of lack of attention paid to the narrators. See *The Folktale, A Symposium* (1957), particularly Dorson's article. Dorson from the early 'fifties on develops in extensive fieldwork a method of research on storytellers and their social setting. His approach (1956; 1958; 1960; *Fabula*, I; 1961, 74-83) launched the trend and encouraged similar studies from his Bloomington school.

112. Kálmány, 1914-1915, II, VI-VIII. For review of this work, see Berze Nagy, 1915, pp. 93-115.

113. Marót, 1931; 1940 (*Ethn.*); 1940 (*Egyet. Phil. Közlöny*); 1945; 1947; and finally 1956.

114. Ortutay, 1940, pp. 8-9.

115. Banó, 1941.

116. Dégh, 1942.

117. Kovács, 1943.

118. Ortutay, 1955, pp. 56-65. Ortutay's theoretical considerations concerning the principles of oral transmission in European peasant culture have been especially suggestive in recent years. He points out the processes of

variation through integration and disintegration and through the interaction of individual and community, and discusses invariant cases and
the creative results of affinity among folklore forms. Ortutay, 1959,
1961, 1965.

119. Since the publication of the folktale texts of the present study (in two
volumes—Dégh, 1955 and 1960), three more collections have been published in the series of the *New Collection of Hungarian Folk Literature*.
In the first, Dobos has edited the tale body of a peasant family which
covers the tradition chain in the lifetimes of four generations (1962).
I reviewed this collection in *Fabula* 6 (1964), 265-270. In the second
collection Balassa has published the legend stock of a village, emphasizing the role of legend-tellers of different types (Balassa, 1963). The
third book encompasses the body of tales of the village of Rozsály and its
raconteurs (Béres and Kovács, 1967). For the works in progress, see
Á Kovács, 1958. For an evaluation of the achievements of this series
and the future tasks, see Dégh, 1963, pp. 1-12.

## Chapter 6. *The Tale Occasions*

1. Thompson, 1946, pp. 5, 7, 13, 454.
2. Wesselski, 1931, pp. 37-63; de Vries, p. 43. The simple forms created
   by the different functions of mental expression were first recognized
   by A. Jolles, although his considerations were for the most part rejected by folklorists. K. Ranke's reinterpretation on an ethnological
   basis corresponds with our ideas (K. Ranke, 1961, pp. 1-11). Recently
   in an address (Prague, 1966), the same author coined the term *homo
   narrans* to express the sum total of Man as narrator and tradition bearer
   who shapes the different basic forms of narration by expressing desires,
   dreams, and fears common to mankind (Ranke, 1967).
3. DeVries points out that the different narrative forms are composed of
   the same narrative material, and that the similarity of the motifs is not
   equivalent to equality of the genres (p. 155). The fact that type motifs
   which are found in contemporary folktales also belong to the heroic
   legends only proves that they were known simultaneously (pp. 49-50).
   DeVries is speaking here about the "same building blocks," and he
   shows how the same motif can be fitted into myth, legend, and *märchen*
   (pp. 51-100).
4. Unfortunately, we know very little about the narrative genres either
   of antiquity (Bolte and Polívka, IV, 41-47; Peuckert, "Märchen," pp.
   1772-1773) or of the aborigines (S. Thompson, 1957-58). Most researchers have failed to give us a delimiting and clear separation according to genres. Only recently, through the influence of Malinowski (pp.
   20-30), can we discern efforts to separate narrative forms according
   to their use and meaning for the informants (Hallowell, 1947, pp. 547-
   548; Herskovits, 1958, pp. 13ff.; Bascom, 1954, p. 336; Bascom, 1965, pp.
   3-20; Lowie, 1958, and Lowie, 1959). R. E. Mitchell, doctoral student
   in folklore at Indiana University, Bloomington, distinguished narrative
   forms according to their function in his Trukese collection of an out-

standing narrator (1966). Students in my classes, among them Ashraf Siddiqui (Pakistan) and Kinishi Yamashita (Japan), gave detailed descriptions of the function of different narrative genres. We also find evidence that storytelling in primitive or non-European societies often coincides with storytelling customs in Europe (Bascom, 1949, pp. 1-16; Krug, p. 348; Weeks, pp. 39-48, 76-84, 121-130, 361-370; Himmelheber, 1951, pp. 9-10; Harva, p. 287; Crowley, 1966). Röhrich's evaluation of storytelling in aboriginal societies is significant for analogies with the origins of the European *märchen* (1956, p. 115).

5. Thompson, *JAF*, 1955, 487-488.
6. Thompson, 1946, pp. 13-30.
7. Carpenter, 1946; Trencsényi-Waldapfel, 1953, pp. 491ff.
8. Marót, 1956, pp. 44-45.
9. Trencsényi-Waldapfel writes that the mythos "may take its path among the less controlled regions," as for example in the folktale. Not every myth has developed into a folktale, but there are some which developed into folktales very early (1936, pp. 309, 310).
10. Thompson widely discusses the European tale material, which, since the age of discovery, has spread to all parts of the world, transforming the traditional material of primitive peoples (1946, pp. 283-293).
11. Röhrich, 1958, pp. 246-247.
12. "They differ somewhat in their behavior, it is true, but they are alike in their disregard of originality, of plot, and of pride of authorship" (Thompson, 1946, p. 5). The same opinion can be found in Thienemann, 1931, pp. 102, 109.
13. Thienemann, 1931, p. 115.
14. Kardos, n.d., p. 19.
15. In the fifteenth century, the Italian court historian, Galeotto, in the court of the Hungarian renaissance king, Mátyás, remarked that the language of the poets was the same as that of the peasants, the burgher, and the lord, and that therefore they understood each other.
16. As far back as the twelfth century the "unknown scribe," Anonymus, of the Hungarians, referred to a folktale in his historical chronicle: "Etsi tam nobilissima gens Hungariae primordia sue generationis et fortia queque facta sua ex falsis fabulis rusticorum vel garrulo cantu joculatorum, quasi sompniando audiret, valde indecorum et satis indecens esset. . . . Si scriptis presentis pagina non vultis . . . credite garrulis cantibus joculatorum et falsis fabulis rusticorum"* (Incipit prologus et gesta Hungarorum anonymi p. magistri. In Emericus Szentpétery, ed., *Scriptorum Rerum Hungaricarum*, I, 1937, 14ff.). For

---

* "If the very noble Hungarian nation would, as if in a dream, hear of its first beginnings and of its many heroic deeds from the false tales of peasants or from the prattling songs of buffoons, this would be a very embarrassing and indecent matter . . . if you do not like this writing on this page, give credit to the songs of the prattling minstrels and the false tales of the peasants. . . ."

its folkloristic evaluation see J. Honti, *Anonymus és a néphagyomány* [*Anonymus and Folk Traditions*], Minerva Library 60, Budapest, 1942.

Early Hungarian documents refer for the most part to the secular song poetry, to lute players, and to violin players. We can hardly find anything before the sixteenth century, in addition to the expressions of the times mentioned above, except the transformation of the popular *märchen* motifs into secular literature in sermons. The scourging of storytellers and those who listened to them is first recorded in the sermons by Bornemisza, who, among others, objected to the popularity of lies in *märchen*. During the following two centuries there is more such evidence to be found.

17. The description of tales in early times as *fabellae aniles*, and later as "lying gossip," and the condescending smiles which it evoked apparently resulted from its confrontation with literature which claimed to be truth; with reference to the heroic tales of the court singers this was so, but the *märchen* never claimed that it should be believed.

18. Sokolov, 1945, pp. 164-165; Löwis of Menar, 1912, p. xi.

19. For instance, in the narrator Novopolzev (Pomerantseva, 1952, II). We have evidence, starting with the beginning of the twelfth century, of the storytelling of the serfs which went on at the courts of the rich lords, noblemen, and rich landowners in Russia (Sokolov, 1945, pp. 256-257; Pomerantseva, 1954, pp. 230-232).

20. In the *Disciplina Clericalis* we read that the fabulator of the king told five tales every evening. Several sources mention the storytellers at the courts of the knights and noblemen and later in the bourgeois salons (Bolte and Polívka, IV, 4-7; Peuckert, "Märchen," pp. 1777-1779; von der Leyen, 1953-1954, II, 271-272). Delargy cites sources according to which the poet-narrator Forgall is said to have told a story every evening from November first to May first for his master at the court of Mongánn (1945, p. 18).

21. Bolte and Polívka IV, 4; Löwis of Menar, 1921, XI; Solymossy, 1938, p. 42.

22. Pomerantseva, 1954, p. 231.

23. F. Ranke speaks about the circulation of the folktale during the course of history (1935, I, 256-257).

24. Thompson, 1946, p. 18.

25. Von der Leyen, 1953-1954, II, 272.

26. De Vries (p. 178) writes that a "folktale easily found its way to the low classes" and had an important part to play there as a sort of wishful poetry. Then he points out that the function of the folktale was a different one in the circle of the people from what it was at the court of the dukes (p. 175). See also Pomerantseva, 1954, p. 232; von der Leyen, 1953-54, II 272; Sieber, pp. 28-30; Steinitz, pp. 321-342; Danckert, pp. 221-266.

27. For a summary of these work occasions see Bolte and Polívka, IV, 8; von der Leyen, 1916, pp. 409-410; Bartlett, pp. 164-293; Lindgren, pp. 362-366; Wisser, 1926, XVI; von Sydow, 1948, pp. 13-15; Sokolov, 1945,

p. 266. For the Hungarian material see Dégh, 1942, I, 57-61, and 1955, pp. 131-134; and Béres, pp. 433-443.

28. F. Ranke, 1935, p. 249.
29. Mackensen, p. 317; Zaunert, pp. vi-viii.
30. Langstroff, p. 131.
31. Zender, pp. xxii-xxiii.
32. A summary of the literature known so far may be found in Röhrich, 1956, pp. 162-164.
33. Viidalepp, p. 167.
34. Jech, 1961, pp. 511-526.
35. Cammann, p. 15.
36. Bîrlea, p. 120. Similar proofs are in de Vries, pp. 42-43; and Penavin, p. 336.
37. As Wisser said, "Among peasants and the so-called educated classes, one seldom meets people who know these stories. Among the 240 not more than maybe a dozen belong to that class" (1927, p. xvi).
38. Uffer, 1945, pp. 16-17.
39. Henssen, 1951, p. 41.
40. K. Ranke quotes 154 narrators in his book, among whom approximately 42 are craftsmen; 35 work in agriculture as handymen, day laborers, and shepherds; and only 9 are listed as "peasants." It is possible that the numbers are unreliable through the inaccuracy of the collectors. Occupation is seldom listed for women, but in spite of this they should be considered (1955, pp. 351-354).
41. In addition to the small craftsmen of the village, the following play a definite role: shoemakers, tailors, woodcutters, street laborers, construction laborers, carpenters, miners, seamen, fishermen, millers, carters (Haiding *Märchenschatz*, p. 388).
42. Campbell, 1890, p. VI, Sokolov, 1945, p. 226; Haiding, *Zeitschrift*, p. 28, and *Märchenschatz*, p. 640. Haiding mentions the tailor Brückner, who does not narrate during work but only after finishing it.
43. Sokolov, 1945, p. 226.
44. Azadovski, 1926, p. 24.
45. Tillhagen's gypsy narrator relates how stories were told in the barracks while pots and pans were repaired (pp. 261-262). This is also mentioned by Christiansen in Thompson (ed.), 1953, p. 298. For the storytelling of Hungarian skillet-repairing gypsies, see Gunda, 1956, p. 142; and Gunda, 1963, pp. 96-99, 101-102.
46. Campbell (1890, p. VI.) quotes from a letter of 1860 that young people in Pool-Ewe, Rosshire in the West Highlands of Scotland used to assemble on long winter evenings when tailors and shoemakers came to the village. While they made the new quilts and shoes for the villagers, they told tales all night. Zender reports similarly the great storytelling occasions which resulted when a shoemaker, tailor, wheelwright, or carpenter came into the house. Storytelling was part of his trade, and the family and the neighbors would sit down together (p. xi). Uffer's best narrator, Spinas Plasch, was an itinerant shoemaker

who told stories to people in the house until he had finished his work (1955, p. 75; also p. 67). Henssen, too, describes a shoemaker who had a great influence on the young Gerrits (1951, pp. 2-3). Henssen photographed another storytelling shoemaker while he worked (1936, pp. 8-9). In the same place he also reports about the storytelling of men who had come together at the shop of the maker of wooden shoes (pp. 6-7). For storytelling in the shoemaker's workshop, see Merkelbach-Pinck, 1940, p. 12; and Cammann, pp. 9, 15.

47. Brinkmann, p. 9; Uffer, 1955. Henssen reports on storytelling during the building of a canal (1951, p. 5). Nedo reports an investigation of the specific tale treasure of the stonecutters (p. 36). See also Delargy, 1945, p. 20.

48. Kovács, 1943, p. 29; Dégh, "History of Hungarian Folklore," p. 402. Anyone who came to András Berkó to have his shoes repaired waited while it was done. Several people thus would gather in the house, and while he repaired their shoes, Berkó told stories to those who waited. He always asked the collector to his house, for this was the way he liked best to tell his stories. The same situation was encountered in Tiszamogyorós, in Szabolcs County, in 1962. I stayed at the house of the local cobbler, Lajos Báró, and recorded tales from early morning till midnight in his workshop, while the customers waited barefoot for the boot repair to be completed. In the bigger workshops in the city the apprentices and helpers took turns singing and telling stories—the shoemaker István Beke from Székesfehérvár reported about this in 1954.

49. Compare the narrative occasion of the Bag community (Pest county), Dégh, 1942, I, 57. Pandur's father was also a carpenter. He himself had worked nearly all his life as a street laborer, ditchdigger, and construction apprentice, and told stories in the barracks near the place of work, before going to bed. In many places even today stories are told while construction work is going on; here the old craft tradition meets the peasant culture.

50. In Drégelypalánk, Nógrádszkáll, Szécsény, and other northern Hungarian villages we still find gifted storytellers among the construction workers. These workmen have conformed completely to a half-peasant, half-craftsman way of life. In 1953 I had an occasion to listen to József Pityí in Dunaujváros, the industrial center which was being erected; in the evening after dinner he told stories to the members of his work gang. S. Dobos, (1958), published a volume of narratives collected among construction laborers at the same place. They told their stories in their barracks after evening meals.

51. See also the observation cited above from Uffer. Röhrich gives a summary treatment of the occurrence of craftsmen in folktales (1956, p. 164).

52. Among the many documents available we want to point out only numbers 6 and 24 in the tale collection of Péter Pandur (Dégh, 1942), in which the description of the prince disguised as a craftsman is completely unvanished.

53. Bogdál, F., "Egy munkásdal változatai" ("Variations of a Workman's Song"), *Ethn.*, 64 (1955), 277-278.

54. Haiding, Zeitschrift, p. 28; Polívka, 1932, pp. 21-23; Langstroff, p. 59.

55. Haiding, *Märchenschatz*, pp. 397-402.

56. Ibid., p. 401.

57. Ibid., p. 389.

58. Bolte and Polívka, IV, 5-6; Sokolov, 1945, p. 226; Haiding, *Märchenschatz*, pp. 388, 395-396. In addition they are mentioned at least briefly in every specialist's tale collections.

59. Kolos, p. 64. Solymossy (1938, p. 10) mentions that Gaál asked one of his friends, a colonel, to collect tales among the soldiers under his command. The colonel proclaimed the order that each soldier had to write down a folktale, and thus many of the handwritten manuscripts start: "Soldier János Kovács obediently reports to the Sir Colonel that once upon a time there was. . . ."

60. Kálmány, 1914-15, II, viii.

61. Katona, 1912, I, p. 195.

62. "Oh mother! Haven't you brought me up to be a big brute of an ass who hasn't even been taught to tell a tale." It is said in Sára that the man who cannot tell a story has to shout this into the stove (Dégh, 1943). It may also happen that one is ordered to sit on the edge of the bed and to stay there until the tale is completed (see Kovács, 1943, I, pp. 31-32). Béres, too, mentions something that happened at the end of the 'thirties. The oldest man in the room asked, before going to bed, "Well, who can tell a story? Nobody? Well, then the one whose bed is on the outside will start" (p. 440). Another storyteller relates that the one who could not tell a story had to drink up a whole panful of water. See also Dégh, 1944, p. 135, and "History of Hungarian Folklore," p. 44.

63. Graf, p. 22.

64. Mentioned by O. Penavin, pp. 335-37.

65. U. Jahn, 1891, p. x; Petsch, 1900, p. 47; Bolte and Polívka, IV, 8.

66. Katona, 1912, I, 1973.

67. Delargy, 1943, p. 20.

68. Solokov, 1945, pp. 225-226.

69. Dégh, 1944, pp. 235-236.

70. Beke and Katona, pp. 91-92; Penavin, p. 335.

71. Cammann, pp. 10-11.

72. F. Ranke, 1935, p. 249.

73. Azadovski, 1926, pp. 26-35; Sokolov, 1945, p. 259. Rather similar was the role of Armenian guerilla fighters sheltered by villagers in Turkish Armenia (Hoogasian-Villa, p. 38).

74. Delargy, 1945, pp. 24-26.

75. Haiding, Zeitschrift, p. 127; Gunda, 1963, p. 103.

76. Merkelbach-Pinck, 1940, p. 13; Á. Kovács, 1943, I, 28.

77. Kovács mentions those who go to market (1943, I, 30). In his handwritten work, I. Bereczki cites the words of a cowherder from Dévaványa: "When we went home from Akasztó or Töviskes Estate,

somebody would ask, 'Who can tell a story?' Then one started to tell a story. We were going home—there were fifteen or twenty of us. But we got home so fast [14 to 15 kilometers] we hardly noticed it." Zenker mentions a German-Hungarian storyteller from the Vértes region who told stories without interruption all the way home from the field. The peasants started in the evening, and when day broke at their arrival at home, he had not yet finished the story. So they sat down in front of the church and left only when the story was finished (p. 36). Azadovski reports that one of his favorite narrators was the miller Ananjev, who told stories to the women who waited their turn. In the work of the brothers Sokolov published in 1915 they write that the wait in front of the mill often lasted for days, and that stories were told during this time. It was here that the narrator Filipov had learned his stories. In Hungary, too, up until fifteen or twenty years ago, we know of similar entertainment at the mill. This kind of storytelling, "Story-Telling as a Pastime among Travelers Found Together on the Road," is characterized by Sol Tax as quite usual among the Indian city-dwellers and merchants in Guatemala (*JAF*, 1949, 123-135). For similar notes see Merkelbach-Pinck, 1940, p. 12; Bîrlea, p. 126; Sébillot, 1881, II.

78. Gunda, 1963, pp. 96-99.

79. For a summary of earth laborers see I. Katona, pp. 103-105.

80. Bolte and Polîvka, IV, 8; Zenker-Starzacher, pp. 27, 37; F. Ranke, 1935, p. 252. Bîrlea, p. 116; Grudde, 1932, pp. 14-15; Haiding, *Märchenschatz*, p. 390; Zender, XIII; Sébillot, III; Kovács, 1943, I, p. 49. Pomerantseva (1965) mentioned that this custom has survived to our day. The bemedaled Kolchos brigadier, Kovalev, for example, would tell stories every evening in the place he spent the night, and when he became the head of the village reading circle, the listeners followed him there. Béres (1955, p. 437) writes that in Rozsály, in Szatmár county, children are broken in to work through storytelling. "The boy could hardly wield the hatchet, but he wanted to hear the story. So he went reluctantly down the rows of sunflowers in order to listen to the story. Mostly the story of the lion prince was told, for he liked it best; it did not have an end. Sometimes his father, sometimes one of his brothers, was the storyteller. If he stopped hacking, they stopped telling the story. Thus he learned hacking during storytelling without being aware of it himself."

81. Dégh, 1944, p. 134; see also *Ethn.*, 1947, p. 96.

82. Kálmány, 1914-15, II, VII.

83. Berze Nagy, 1957, p. 226; Erdész, 1961-62. The visits of storytelling shepherds and night watchmen are always welcomed by the women working in the barn.

84. Massignon, pp. 12-13.

85. Kovács, 1943 I, 30-31; Ortutay, 1940, pp. 41-43. Zenker-Starzacher also mentions two old men who entertained the harvesters in their barracks until late at night. Cammann describes the storytelling of West Prussian threshers hired for winter work. Ten to twelve men slept in the stable,

which was warm from the cattle. Storytelling went on for seven weeks. Whoever fell asleep while the narrator spoke was fined one quart of brandy or the equivalent in money (Cammann, pp. 11-13).

86. Azadovski, 1926, pp. 24-25.
87. B. and J. Sokolov, p. 225.
88. Chetkarev, 1955.
89. Haiding, *Zeitschrift*, pp. 28-29.
90. This information was provided by Sabin V. Dragoi.
91. Ortutay, 1940, p. 41.
92. Szendrey, *Ethn.*, 1931, pp. 197-198.
93. We have considerable evidence of storytelling being stopped when someone fell asleep. With the woodcutters, the formula was: "Bones"; "Bricks" (Ortutay, 1940, pp. 41-42). In the barracks of the construction workers in Budapest it was "Bones"; "Meat." "With this they put us to sleep" (Dégh, 1942, I, p. 59). With the soldiers it was "Bones"; "Meat" (Béres, p. 440; Dégh, "History of Hungarian Folklore," p. 44). According to a French document storytelling was the entertainment that soothed men after work. The narrator says "Cric" before he starts to narrate, and the listeners answer "Crac," signifying that they are ready to listen (Felice, pp. 442-446). For similar checking of the attention of the audience for formulaic responses, see Crowley, pp. 19-22.
94. Faragó, J., "Kurcsi Minya, havasi mesemondó" ("Minya Kurcsi, Storyteller of the High Mountains"), *Ethn.*, 1967, pp. 238-260.
95. Kolos (p. 64) cites Mailáth's words: "The Magyar storytellers are one of the many traces of oriental origin of that people. Just like the night fabulators of Arabia, they can narrate for hours on end, even through the night, without their listeners getting tired. Most of them are to be found among sheepherders and soldiers. Folktales which in other countries can be found only in the spinning rooms and the nurseries, up to our own times, were rescued from oblivion in Hungary around the watch and campfires of the herders and the night work in the fields."
96. Bîrlea, 1956.
97. Arany, 1904, p. 188; Kovács, 1943, I, p. 30-31; Dégh, *Ethn.*, 1947, p. 96. Béres (p. 438) reports on the early life of the youngsters who herd the cattle in the open. In Rozsály, twenty to thirty youngsters would drive the oxen to the grazing lands, playing and telling stories, and they would be delighted when a real connoisseur of folktales joined them, one who had been around.
98. Á. Kovács, 1943, I, p. 58.
99. Kovács reports that the spinning rooms in Ketesd now provide only a second-rate storytelling occasion because of the other entertainments for the young people (1943, I, p. 28).
100. Berze Nagy, 1907, p. xi. See also Petsch, 1934, p. 47.
101. Storytelling for entertainment during communal work in winter appears at the same time as storytelling around the fireplace. These "circles" exist in Ireland from the middle of September to the middle of March, a fixed time period mentioned by many: Delargy, 1945, pp. 19-20;

Colum, pp. xiii-xv. In olden times in Aran Island, storytellers told their tales between the last week of October and Christmas; fishing commenced in January (Messenger, p. 202). See also Mühlhausen, pp. 8-9. Similar to this is the *veillée* of the French peasants, which lasts from five o'clock in the afternoon to midnight (Carnoy, pp. ii-iv); or the *Maisstube* mentioned by Merkelbach-Pinck in 1940 (p. 12), and Langstroff (pp. 71-72). Similar also are the visits in winter described by Haiding (*Märchenschatz*, pp. 391-392, 401-402). For similar evidence see Zender, p. xiv; Henssen, 1936, pp. 4-5; and Hoogasian-Villa, pp. 38-40. Although the rhythm of seasonal labor, which is the occupation of storytelling people, appoints the time for narration in European folk society, we know of no restrictions or taboos such as those in several Asian, African, and American Indian cultures, where snakebite, damage to the crops, disease, or death might be the consequence of telling or listening to tales during the daytime.

102. Berze Nagy, 1957, p. 226; Gunda, pp. 103-104.
103. Since these are known all over Europe, we have selected only a few of the Hungarian documents: Ortutay, 1950, p. 41; Kovács, 1943, I, 24-27; Béres, 1954, pp. 435-437 (he stresses especially the so-called "communal work" which the women do together on invitation, for example flax combing, husking and kerneling of corn, and spinning). Béres also reports on the storytelling of gypsies while they weave baskets and mats during the winter (p. 440). In summary, see F. Ranke, 1935, p. 249; Petsch, 1934, p. 41; Brinkmann, p. 8; Zenker-Starzacher, pp. 27, 37; Hoogasian-Villa, pp. 38-40.
104. Haiding, *Zeitschrift*, p. 29; on the "Märchenabend," see Cammann, pp. 16-19.
105. Uffer, 1945, pp. 21-22.
106. Brinkman, pp. 8, 9.
107. Zenker-Starzacher, pp. 36-38. Sewing and weaving in the family circle are also mentioned in Delargy, 1945, p. 20.
108. Cammann, pp. 9-10, 14.
109. Von Sydow, 1948, p. 13.
110. From Tillhagen we heard about this at Christmas, at Easter, and at baptisms and funerals (pp. 271-276). See also Haiding, *Märchenschatz*, p. 390; Bîrlea, p. 116; Béres (at weddings), p. 439; Jech, 1961 (baptism, marriage, birthday parties); Penavin (pig-killing); Erdész, 1961-62 ("evening-making").
111. Tömörkény, 1914, p. 98.
112. Ortutay, 1940, p. 41.
113. The former day laborer, Mrs. Tóth, fifty-three years old and a native of Somogy county, returned to her village after the land reform. Ilona Dobos noted down a great many of her tales and also her autobiography (Dobos, 1962).
114. For a similar incident see Dégh, 1942, I, p. 54; see also Gy. Andrásfalvi, Chapter 10.
115. Dégh, 1944, p. 135.

116. Honti, 1942, pp. 238-239.
117. Cammann, p. 9.
118. Banó, *Ethn.*, 1944, 178.
119. Ibid.
120. Ortutay, 1937, pp. 21-26; Eberhard and Boratav, pp. 12-13.
121. Dégh, "Népmese és ponyva," 95-97.
122. Fedics, too, did not allow anyone to tell his tales; he was offended and treated competition condescendingly (Ortutay, 1940, pp. 58-59).
123. Bolte and Polívka, IV, 32-34, offer exhaustive comparative material. See also Petsch, 1900, p. 63, and Brachetti, p. 204. Henssen reports the reason why it was always Gerrits's turn when the neighbors got together: though many were present, only very gifted narrators told stories (1951, p. 15). The terminating formulae show that such competitions were spread all over Europe.
124. We know many examples of the fact that the traditional tale text was considered an awe-inspiring heritage from a forebearer and that everybody strove to reproduce it unchanged. For the success of this practice, see Chapter 8.
125. L. Arany, 1904, p. 188.
126. Lázár, 1896, p. 56.
127. This was said by F. Czapár, the fisherman, in Sára in 1943 when he was forty-five years old (Dégh, 1944, pp. 135-136).
128. The control question in Sára went this way: "How many asses did I say?" And when someone did not know, the answer was: "You are the second" (Dégh, 1944, pp. 135-136).
129. Azadovski, 1926, pp. 30-31. Sokolov (1945, p. 227) reports about storytelling that went on through whole nights and several days.
130. "The tale grows longer and more complicated; they could even fill an evening, even the evenings of a whole week. . ." (Christiansen, 1938, p. 326). "Tradition exists in many places of stories which took several nights to tell. These were romances or hero-tales, or the popular tales. . . . A man . . . fell asleep by the fire and found a story going on when he awoke the next morning. . . . I heard of a beggarman who took seven nights to tell a story" (Delargy, 1945, p. 21.) See also Thompson (ed.), 1953, p. 5; Messenger, p. 202. At the convention of the Hoosier Folklore Society, in October 1966 in South Bend, Indiana, my colleague, Ilhan Basgöz, mentioned the performance of the coffee house storytellers of Anatolia (Turkey). The telling of minstrel tales is very similar to that of Hungarian magic tales in the men's work community. The narrator asks his audience where he had stopped the previous night and from that point he continues the tale, night after night.
131. For Hungarian examples and summaries of several international documents see Dégh, 1944, p. 134, and *Ethn.*, 1947, 96; also "History of Hungarian Folklore," p. 44. In spite of these documents one must not generalize, for we do not yet have a sufficient number of proofs. In some places, for example Germany and Rumania, the reverse is the case, and experience shows that the community loves variety. To be able to

judge this phenomenon equitably we need still more collecting. A general summation of the length of storytelling is given by Cammann, p. 12.

132. Banó, 1947, pp. 83-90.

133. Dégh, 1944, pp. 134ff.

134. I had occasion to listen to such a "frame tale" in a storytelling community of fishermen in Sára. The hero was a prince who wanted to look for a tale, and started on his way to find the most beautiful folktale; at each stage one member of the storytelling community had to tell a tale. For a description, see Dégh, 1944, p. 136.

135. Petsch, *passim*; Bolte and Polívka, IV, pp. 23-24; Sokolov, 1945, pp. 257-258; Laport, pp. 7-9; Thompson, 1946, pp. 457-458.

136. The narrators which I met used to embroider tales with their extremely long and often rhymed introductory and final formulae, not only when they related in public but also before the collectors. The Irish "runs" are very similar in many respects.

137. Berendsohn had already drawn attention to this (p. 129).

138. These very functions of the *märchen* led to various theories, for folklorists usually used to stress only one of these and did not consider the others (Thompson, 1955, p. 487).

139. Dömötör, 1947, p. 168.

140. Bolte and Polívka, IV, 17-20.

141. "It is essential to the understanding and interpretation of folklore to know whether a given tale is regarded as historical fact or fiction. This bears directly upon the explanation of folklore as a form of amusement or as 'literature' . . ." (Bascom, 1954, p. 336). Legend experts since the Grimm brothers usually try to define the folk legend by contrasting it to the tale, stating that the tale is poetical and will entertain, while the legend's intent is to teach or to recount an event (Lüthi, 1961, pp. 22-48).

142. Kovács, 1943. Such notes are to be found elsewhere as well. "Can you lie well?" many a peasant inquired when an itinerant craftsman asked for a night's shelter, and what he meant was tell a tale. When the right ones got together, they often told tales all night long. (Haiding, *Zeitschrift*, p. 28). According to Henssen, the concept of "lie" here means artistic creation or invention (*Hessische Blätter*, 43, 18). An early evidence of the ambivalent meanings of lie and tale is Martin Luther's use of the word *Lügende* for *Legende* (tale narration), at the Council of Mantua in 1537.

143. Berze Nagy, 1907, pp. x-xi.

144. Schwietering, 1955, p. 71.

145. Honti, 1943, pp. 110-112; Pomerantseva, 1954, pp. 249-250.

146. Bolte and Polívka, IV, 20; Röhrich, 1956. pp. 178-186.

147. Bolte and Polívka, IV, 26-32.

148. Brinkmann, pp. 19-22.

149. Dégh, 1942, I, 66-68.

150. Ortutay, 1940, p. 62. Similar explanations are given by Bîrlea (p. 118) and by Delargy, 1945, p. 8.

151. The frame of mind after the immediate effect of the tale and the wakening to reality is well characterized by Lázár in his report of the role of the excellent narrators in the spinning rooms: ". . . to arrange a tale session with such a narrator is not an every-day pleasure: the rapture with which the listeners are filled is understandable. Many a one stops, the spindle in her hand, and many a sentimental one breaks into tears; and 'this is only a tale, unfortunate one!' and he slaps him on the back, and brings him back with a rush into real life" (Lázár, 1896, pp. 56-57).

152. Ortutay, 1940, p. 68.

153. Ibid., pp. 73-75. "Between this 'possibility of happening' and actual happening there is still a difference," writes Peuckert (*"Märchen,"* 1958, p. 1775). In general the question of the *märchen* versus reality and the residue of belief in the *märchen* has recently been treated quite seriously. Several works have appeared concerning these questions in addition to that of Röhrich cited above. See also Rörich, II, 1956, 304-305.

154. "He also knows how to differentiate between his stories and those narrated by others. Many tales are not told by him because they belong to tale treasure of somebody else. On the other hand he is well aware of the fact that his own stories are never told by anybody else as they really are, which means as he is able to relate them" (Uffer, 1945, p. 13).

155. We treat the learning of tales in general in Chapter 8. See also von Sydow, 1948, pp. 13-15, and Brachetti, 1930, pp. 205-206. Haiding writes that the grandparents immediately transmit the *märchen* tradition to the grandchildren (*Zeitschrift*, p. 30).

156. Malinowski (1926, p. 26) was the first to observe this: "Every story is 'owned' by a member of the community. Each story, though known by many, may be recited only by the 'owner'. . . . " For a similar observation see Nippold, pp. 348-349.

157. "As long as a folk-tale traditor remains in his district, anyone else will hardly try to tell *his* tales, for in this they like to observe a kind of literary copyright. Not until he is gone can we reckon on someone else assuming his mantle" (von Sydow, 1948, p. 49).

158. "The *märchen* which he is wont to tell his listeners, this is his *märchen.*" (Kálmány, 1914-15, II, viii).

159. Berze Nagy, 1915, pp. 105-106.

160. Uffer, 1945, p. 75.

161. "Each district had its very own in addition to the general tale treasure. Thus one narrator leaves to another the tale which he 'possessed,' so to say, as the first owner. He continued to be respected as the proprietor" (Merkelbach-Pinck, 1950, p. 12). See also Brinkmann, pp. 26-27, and Grudde, 1932, p. 13.

162. "The sense of rivalry is strong with these *Shannechas*. The best way to get one of them started with telling a particular tale is to remark that a certain rival has told it well. He will then insist that you have never heard the story really told as it should be and he then proceeds to demonstrate" (Thompson, 1946, p. 454). Delargy also reports that sixty to eighty years ago the single villages were in competition with each other;

in some house marked beforehand, the narrators would take each other's respective narrative measure (1945, pp. 18-19). Such natural competitions have, of course, nothing to do with the organized taletelling competitions in the communist countries (Jech, 1961, pp. 527-528).

163. Röhrich, "Die Märchenforschung," II, 221.

164. Delargy, 1945, pp. 20-21.

165. Ibid., 1945, p. 26.

166. Let us remember Perrault's fictional Mother Goose and all the tale poets who put their *märchen* into the mouths of old woman or wet nurses, remembering the narrators of their childhood. A good picture of this is drawn in the list (mentioned above) of Bolte and Polívka. In examining Gorki's popular sources, Piksanov (pp. 3, 31) mentions Grandmother Akulina Ivanovna Kaschirina and the wet nurse Jevgenia, both extremely gifted narrators. Pushkin, too, recorded the tales of Arina Rodionova.

167. Thimme, p. 10. Behrendsohn enumerates one by one the storytellers of the brothers Grimm. Despite the presence of so many female storytellers, he considers the role of women as storytellers as negligible (pp. 15-16).

168. Hahn is one of the first to ascribe to women the ability to tell stories. When he was a consul in Greece, he had listened mainly to women narrating stories at their places of work and in the spinning rooms. In his opinion, men, while drinking wine, are entertained mostly by jokes (I, 114-115).

169. Zenker-Starzacher, pp. 22-26.

170. Kovács, 1943, I, 33, 50-51.

171. Pintér, p. 65. We often heard that children would sneak in and listen to the storytelling unobserved from the dark corners. Almost all of the excellent storytellers remember how they succeeded, when children, in getting to listen to a story. See also Henssen, 1936, p. 4, and Delargy, 1945, p. 26.

172. Pomerantseva, 1952, XV.

173. Bolte and Polívka, IV, 9, 10.

174. Mackensen, p. 316.

175. Wisser, 1927, pp. xiv-xv.

176. Wisser, 1927, pp. xxv-xxvi.

177. Meyer, p. xxii, writes that out of 224 narrators only 28 were women. Zender counts 88 per cent men and 12 per cent women; he states that the women never pointed to their mothers as teachers, but to their fathers (p. xxii). Henssen says that in the Münster country the tale occasions for women were unfavorable, and that in contrast to 77 men, only 16 women told him stories. In judging the Merkelbach-Pinck collection, Langstroff (p. 134) points out that 24 women and 17 men had told stories to the collector, and that he concluded from this that she had met rather with women than with men. There are 110 male and 44 female narrators in K. Ranke's Schleswig-Holstein tales (1955, pp. 351-354).

178. Henssen (1936, p. 4) writes that among even the best female narrators, none knew more than 20 tales, whereas the men knew 60 to 70. Langstroff (p. 134) says that in the book of Merkelbach-Pinck the women are in the majority, but that among 105 tales only 45 originated with women, and that only 10 women know more than one story to tell.

179. Walker and Uysal, p. 2.

180. Uffer, 1945, pp. 17-18; Merkelbach-Pinck, 1940, pp. 11-12; Langstroff, pp. 133-34; Polívka, 1932, pp. 5-16; Schwietering (based on Grudde and Wisser), 1935, p. 73; Haiding, 1953, pp. 384-386; Henssen, 1936, p. 4. Based on Grudde, Henssen confirms that the story materials used by women were a derivative of the tale treasure of men (*Hessische Blätter*, 43, 18; Sareyko, pp. 4-15; von der Leyen, 1953-54, II, 271). For a discussion of this question, see Dégh, "Népmese és ponyva," pp. 89, 97; "History of Hungarian Folklore," 36-37.

181. Thompson, 1946, pp. 407, 454-455; Delargy, 1945, p. 7.

182. Cammann, pp. 9-10.

183. Sokolov, 1945, pp. 232-233.

184. Azadovski, 1926, p. 12.

185. Zenker-Starzacher, pp. 39-40. This does not mean that women did not take part in listening to stories when they had the time and the occasion. They all know the general tale treasure but they do not narrate. "While women do not take part in the storytelling, not a word of the tale escapes them, and if their relatives or close friends make any slip or hesitate in their recital, it is not an uncommon experience of mine to hear listening women interrupt and correct the speaker" (Delargy, 1945, p. 7).

186. Kovács, 1943, I, 35, and Henssen, 1936, p. 4, give such proof. We must not, of course, conclude from this that there once existed a secret male community where women were excluded and tales were its derivate, as Á. Kovács claimed; rather that storytelling had long been a custom in the community of men, and that the free language used there was not destined for the ears of women.

187. Cammann (pp. 9-10) considers that when women took over storytelling as family entertainment, it became almost a middle-class pastime.

188. Swahn, 1955, pp. 437-438.

189. Dégh, 1950, pp. 180-181.

190. She refers to Márton László (Marcika Pintyer) the author of the *Book of the Dead*.

191. This means to all the houses on one street, in the neighborhood.

192. Brinkmann's examples of occasional storytellers correspond to these.

193. The growing interest in the new forms of folk narrative is indicated by some suggestive articles: Bausinger, 1958; Dobos, 1964; Neumann, 1966.

194. Haiding, too, writes that his best Burgenland storyteller was awakened late at night and asked to come tell stories, because everybody would fall asleep while stripping feathers ("Träger," 1953, pp. 27-28).

195. Dégh, 1942, p. 32; Kovács, 1943, I, 47.

196. Delargy speaks of storytelling dynasties, of inherited tale treasures, and

even of conscious tradition: the tradition is preserved for 130 to 160 years, through three generations (1945, p. 21). See also Haiding, *Märchenschatz*, pp. 384-385. Zenker, in his frequently mentioned work, gives an excellent report of storytelling which does not exceed the family circle. Grandparents, parents, and children are the bearers of tradition. In the storytelling of the women, we recognize a typical storytelling custom which is important even if limited to a modest audience, for there is always the latent possibility that a person of better-than-average storytelling talent will emerge and will develop into a storyteller for the whole village community (pp. 22-26, 36-39). József Faragó in his discussion of the discontinuance of *märchen* telling in Mezöség: "Here the fairy tales are considered 'child's play not fitting for adults' and that is why they are told at home, in the family circle. In front of a bigger audience joke-like tales and anecdotes are preferred" (1954, pp. 20-31). Erdész, 1961-62, also reports this.

197. Ágnes Kovács investigated the storytelling of children and distinguished between stories that are told for children and those told by children (1943, I, 46-50; II, 106-141). Pandur, too, says: "In my childhood I told stories also to other children" (Dégh, 1942, I, 59). My experience was that school children between the ages of eight and fourteen could give accounts of adult tales that circulated in the community. As unobserved listeners they thus led me to the individual narrators.

198. We have evidence about the custom of wakes all over Hungary, though they differed in detail from those of the Bucovina and especially from those of the Transylvanians and the Szeklers. Mostly it is the women who hold the wake. They sit in the room with the dead and sing dirges until midnight, or even all night long (Luby, 1935, pp. 185-186; *Ethn.*, 1894, 183; 1957, 185). When men, too, are at the wake, they sit in another room and entertain each other. Some of the motifs of the Andrásfalva wakes are also known elsewhere, but in general do not carry such a traditionally maintained social weight as here. The reason for this may be sought in the well-known ethnic conditions.

199. Storytelling during wakes is an internationally known custom. To mention only a few proofs of importance for our study, Uno Harva (p. 287) writes, "It is a custom of the Kalares that the relatives do not go to bed for three nights after the interment but stay awake by telling each other stories." Sartori (pp. 42-44) mentions storytelling at wakes as a pastime among the Ostyaks and with Turkish-Tartar tribes, in which the sorcerer also plays a role. Herskovits (p. 237) mentions this custom from Trinidad. Among the Irish "at funeral wakes the night is whiled away by tales told now by one, now by another of the gifted *shannechas*" (Thompson, 1946, p. 454; see also Delargy, p. 20). Delargy (p. 17) reports in connection with a narrator, "Wherever there was a wake, it was there he would surely be. They used to set him to tell a story to shorten the night. I saw him once for two nights running telling stories at the same wake." For a monographical description of amusements (storytelling among others), see O'Sullivan (O'Súilleabháin), 1967. We

also have two German documents: Merkelbach-Pinck, 1940, p. 12, and Zender, p. xii. For the telling of funny and serious stories, see Bächtold-Stäubli, V, 110. We have only a few documents about storytelling at Hungarian wakes: from Hegyhát, Baranya county (*Ethn.*, 1901, 28-29); from Kisküküllö county (*Ethn.*, 1918, 98-99); and from Rozsály (Béres, p. 438). Gunda (1958, p. 142) reports that it can also be found among Gypsies in Szatmár county.

200. In the house of mourning, the party games of the younger people are best known. Nemes-Népi Zakál reports from Örség on a funny game played in 1818 (*Ethn.*, 1917, 111-112). In Baranya county, storytelling alternates with games. Gönczi (p. 360) reports on jokes and games, "the latter without any connection with the sorrow of the relatives who are mourning for the dead."

201. See also *Ethn.*, 1894, 334; *Ethn.*, 1897, 292-293; Gönczi, p. 360.

202. The men's entertainment consists for the most part in playing cards: *Ethn.*, 1895, 51, 224, 296; *Ethn.*, 1938, 131; Lázár, 1896, p. 94.

203. In most places it is the women who sing; the song leader is usually found among Presbyterians (Luby, 1935, pp. 185-186; Lázár, 1896, p. 94; Végh, p. 208).

204. Dégh, *Ethn.*, 1950, 181.

205. This is stressed by Malinowski (p. 20) as well as by Bascom (1954, p. 336). See also Note 4 above.

206. To cite the experience of two observations: "Thus narrators and listeners are in constant 'cross-fertilization.' The listener thus is not only passive, but, like the narrator himself, an active link in the chain. Only when this cross-effect, which is caused by the spiritual fusion of all those concerned, becomes apparent, when they are all atuned to each other, the true mood materializes" (Merkelbach-Pinck, 1940, p. 7). Graf's narrator Ofenbeck was "bagged" for poaching by the village constables one winter evening, just when he had started to tell stories. The listeners begged the constables to wait so they could hear the end of the story. "The policemen seemed to like being in the warm room; they sat down and the brigadier asked Ofenbeck to continue, and so he went on telling his story as if nothing had happened. He knew to make it so thrilling that hour after hour passed without anybody being aware of it. It was far beyond midnight when he finished. The story had its effect also upon the police so that they let him go after he promised them that he would never again lay hand on a gun" (Haiding *Märchenschatz*, pp. 396-397). Henssen (1954, pp. 21-22) directs attention to the art of listening to a story.

207. The conditions under which Henssen took his tape recordings were no more favorable than ours. The only electric current available was at the inn where he lived, and thus there could be no question of a natural "storytelling community." "His [the storyteller's] young neighbor, Theodor Röckers, who came and went daily like a son of the house, kept him company. Other listeners also drifted in. Expressions of ap-

proval, remarks, questions, and hints contributed to the course of a tale as it corresponded to what was done at home" (Henssen, 1951, p. 9).

208. Satke (pp. 32-66) tried to capture the performance of the storyteller in the community while being hidden with his movie camera. Crowley's Bahamian tales "were collected in their natural settings, at the same times and places at which they would have been told without the presence of the investigator" (Crowley, p. 6). Recently I. Sándor (1964, pp. 523-556) summarized the problem of the dramaturgy of storytelling. For the technique of narration in Rumania, see Vrabie, pp. 606-613.

209. The connection between the *märchen* and actual problems is characteristic. During my stay at Kakasd nine cases of arson had happened one after another. The whole village was terrorized by a freely operating arsonist, and while the police were investigating, the villagers kept a vigil every night.

210. The magic of the story was apparent when Mrs. Palkó once visited me at my quarters in Kakasd. She dropped in while two neighbor women were also around. One of the women reminded her of one of her favorite stories, which Mrs. Palkó immediately started to recite. It was an extremely long story (*The Twelve Robbers*) that lasted for hours. Although restless because her five children were left alone, the woman could not take her eyes off the lips of the narrator and urged her on continually: "Proceed, Aunt Zsuzsi, proceed." When she came to her senses after the tale was finished, I asked her whether she had heard the story before. She knew it almost by heart, having heard it many times; still she was charmed by the tale.

211. Lázár (p. 56) likewise points to this when he speaks of the "impatient young boys" who wish for a livelier entertainment and who have no taste for long drawn-out entertainment.

## Chapter 7. The Tale Material: The Narrative Body of Kakasd

1. Zender (p. xxiii) has confirmed this for the area in which he collected.
2. Henssen, too, calls attention to it: "The functions of the different narrative forms can be recognized only when the whole, regardless of its being a *märchen*, legend, anecdote, or contemporary true story close to reality, is being judged. This points to the necessity of covering all the complete narrative treasure" (Henssen, I, 1939, 134).
3. Ortutay, 1935, pp. 20-23, and 1940, pp. 64-73.
4. Vajkai, pp. 55-68.
5. Honti, 1947, pp. 21-24, and 1941, pp. 86-90; Henssen, 1939, p. 134.
6. For a general discussion of the topic, see Hand, 1965, p. 441.
7. Langstroff (pp. 75, 132) has treated the connection between the pious belief in miracles and the popular belief concepts, as well as the connection between piety and folk belief in the *märchen* and legend material. Schwietering (p. 71) writes to the point: "The strongest community-building power is here based on belief in the supernatural. This belief is a communal belief and not an individual one."

8. For discussion of popular piety, see Ortutay, 1938, pp. 70-73, 102, 103, 140.

9. Ibid., pp. 45-51. For discussion of peasant types, see Ortutay, 1948, pp. 16-27.

10. Dégh, 1942, I, 68-69.

11. It is quite characteristic that Mrs. Palkó should invest the sum she received on occasion of the state medal in a "burial dress," as soon as she alighted in Szekszárd. Similarly, it is characteristic for her to believe that she owed me great thanks for the distinction, and for her to have expressed her thanks by having a mass said for my sake.

12. For healing by casting water, see Lörincze, pp. 36-47. Ákos Szendrey's *Hungarian Dictionary of Customs* (in the archives of the Ethnographical Museum, Budapest) reports it from twelve location. On going for water without speaking, see Gönczi, *Göcsej*, p. 268, and *Ethn.*, 1907, p. 82; Kiss, *Ormányság*, p. 151.

13. Berze Nagy, III, 267; Szendrey (*Dictionary*) quotes fifteen examples.

14. Szendrey (*Dictionary*) indicates a wide distribution of the magic children's disease *aggos* (senile), spread all over the Hungarian language territory; he also reports it from Transylvanian and Bucovina Szeklers. I recorded the magic procedure of symbolical cooking of the infant in the Csík-Szekler village of Csikszentdomokos in 1945, which came very close to the description given by Mrs. Palkó. Nine naked women by the same name go around the house in this case, nine times.

15. *ebagos* (*eb* = dog, *agos* = senile). *Magyar Tájszótár* [*Hungarian Dialect Dictionary*], Budapest, 1893, I 448, p. 13: *ebagos*, "a child born with dense hair or with big, hairy ears" (the so-called changeling); *agos* = an infant born with hair covering its body and suffering from malformation. In the dictionary quoted, both data sources were the Szeklers. *Magyar Entymologiai Szótár* [*Hungarian Etymological Dictionary*] (Budapest, 1914-30, I, 20) defined *megagosodik* as "getting senile," in the sense of "getting hairy." The proofs collected by Magyary-Kossa coincide with the things heard in Kakasd concerning the historical material as well as the signs of the sickness and its cure. Páriz Pápai writes in his *Pax Corporis* (1701, p. 325): " 'Ebag' is a sickness of children; while they eat and drink enough nothing is noticeable, but they dry up, become weak, and lose weight day after day. In some places in Hungary this is called 'eb-ag.' This sickness is caused by a subcutaneous worm that is as thin as a single hair, it cannot even be seen except in bathing. . . ." Magyary-Kossa writes further (I, 355-357): "Concerning the meaning of the word *ebag*, I have to note that the expressions *ebag, ebaga, abag, ebagos*, and *agos* still exist in various places in the country, even though infrequent, and the people use them to designate the English sickness and its various signs. The description of a superstitious healing, which has come down to us from the eighteenth century, mentions an old-looking child; there is not a question that we have to do with a case of rickets. According to a description from the year 1794, thin and sickly children with the English sickness in Somogy County were 'boiled,'

which means that the child was put naked into a big earthen container next to the range. An old woman holds the child with one hand; with the other she moves a wooden spoon around it. The mother of the child meantime walks around the house, then she puts her head into the kitchen door and asks the woman who boils the child, 'What do you cook?' 'An old man,' she answers. The mother replies, 'A young should come from it.' This is done three times, and then the boiling is finished."

16. Dégh, 1942, I, 25-26.

17. See Thompson, *Motif-Index*, G 225, p. 4.

18. AT 1353. Von Sydow ("Folktale Studies and Philology," 1948, pp. 197-198) connects this tale with the medieval examples of old women bringing misfortune and compares it with similar Oriental types. He does not touch relations to the belief-world.

19. Honti, 1945, p. 69.

20. Vajda, 1944, I, 184-185.

21. Kovács, 1943, pp. 184-185.

22. Bolte and Polívka, IV, 36-40; van Gennep, 1910, p. 28. Sokolov (pp. 253-54) calls the stories originating from the witch and ghost beliefs *bilički* ("past happening").

23. Von Sydow, 1934, p. 261; Tillhagen, 1964, p. 9-17; Röhrich, 1958; Dégh, 1965; Blehr, 1967.

24. Vajkai, p. 58.

25. Vajkai, pp. 58, 59 also Peuckert, "Sage," 1958, p. 1746.

26. In addition to the quoted work by Brinkmann, the dissertation by L. Brixius (1939) is also concerned with the function of belief stories, the narratives embodying popular belief. Peuckert and Lauffer, I, 129: The aim is an investigation, through individual narrators, of the function of belief stories within a community.

27. The three cycles described by Brinkmann, for instance, show this form. Observation of legend-telling confirmed the fact that even the simple legends are usually performed with the lively participation of the community (Dégh, 1965, pp. 85-86).

28. Vajkai states that belief stories, like the magic tales, could be grouped according to types, as von Sydow (1934) and Peuckert ("Sage," 1958, p. 1759), but he does not distinguish between the loose and the more stable compositions.

29. Vajkai, p. 60. Honti (1947, p. 27) expresses this as follows: "The belief story is a report about popular belief in narrative form, a religious legend or a report about traditional material, but without the traditional form and narrative appearance; it is a part of the general narrative and appears when the question is expressed or even when it is not expressed." For a discussion of the form and definition of the belief story, see Beitl, 1953, p. 652. The formal features of the belief legend and its correlation with actual folk belief and ritual are dealt with in detail in Dégh, 1965, pp. 80-85.

30. We must refer once more to the reportorial character of the belief story as pointed out by von Sydow. Brinkmann details clearly that the narrator

does everything he can to be believed. He quotes sources when he has not experienced the event himself; he cites old, respected, and trusted men, and often reaffirms his credibility by saying, "I myself would not have believed it, had I not heard it from my parents." Often he also cites time and place, and the "evidences" are sometimes most elaborate. It also happens that the teller of *märchen* does the same thing, but for reasons of artistic credibility (see Chapter 8). Here, however, the "evidence" is an indispensable ingredient of the genre, localization in general being synonymous with credibility. See Peuckert, "Sage," 1958, pp. 1751, 1757; Dégh, "Processes of Legend Formation," p. 86; Lüthi, 1961.

31. F. W. Schmidt (pp. 129-143, 230-244) has set out to prove the artistic value of the popular legends; however, even the best narrators recorded in recent years (Balassa, 1963; Dégh, 1965) cannot match the artistic presentation of the *märchen*.

32. Similarly Henssen (1951, p. 41) says in discussing Gerrits: "These narrators, in general, have less importance in the development and transmission of legends. Such stories are too simple and unadorned for them, and they have no occasion to show off their art as it is revealed in the embroidering of the varied and colorful action of a *märchen*."

33. The Hungarian belief legend types and cycles are grouped in Dégh, "Processes of Legend Formation," pp. 334-351.

34. Jolles, pp. 240, 243; Lüthi, 1961, p. 47; Lüthi, 1966.

35. Honti, 1947, p. 28.

36. Liljeblad (pp. 98-99, 102-103) indicates how the belief elements can become *märchen* elements. Pomerantseva (1954, pp. 245-246), too, lists the mythological elements and arrives at the following conclusion: the magic tales lost their mythological character at a very early time and were transformed qualitatively, although they still retained a few elements of mythological thinking. The reality of life penetrated the magic tale and helps to keep up the popularity of the tale. Peuckert ("Sage," 1958, p. 1756), however, warned against considering the *märchen* simply an extended development of the legend form. And Eliade (p. 200) emphasizes that the "coexistence, the contemporaneousness of myth and tales in traditional societies raises a question that, though difficult, is not insoluble."

37. Solymossy (1938, III, 372-78) refers to the fundamental differences existing between the supernatural beings in *märchen* and those in belief stories (monsters, witches, sorcerers). Similarly, Röhrich (1956, p. 13) lists the supernatural beings of both types.

38. "We certainly do not deny the fact that age-old belief and customs continue to live in the *märchen*, but this is so because they have become the everlasting and unexchangeable property of all mankind. They continue to live and are transformed in content and form, lose their original religious meaning and may spring up every moment as motifs in the products of fantasy" (De Vries, p. 34). A vast literature exists about the similarity of or the differences between *märchen* and the legend from

the content point of view. This is summarized in the work by Max Lüthi (1961). He compares the performance of similar themes in legend and in *märchen* form. Röhrich's (1956, pp. 9-27) thorough and methodical comparison of the two types is also very instructive.

39. It is interesting to note that this *märchen* type is closer to belief stories, with the resettled Csángó's of Moldavia, than to the *märchen*, as if the elements of the actual folk belief had taken the upper hand and had essentially dissolved the artistic form of the *märchen*. See Hegedüs, 1952, pp. 156, 265.

40. Ortutay, 1940, pp. 268-285; Dégh, 1942, I, 236-245; Dégh, "Processes of Legend Formation," tales No. 4 and 66. For discussion of the legend form of the theme, see Dégh, 1965, pp. 83-85.

41. Liljeblad, pp. 105-117.

42. Dégh, 1942, II, 67-68; Balassa, *passim;* Dégh, "Processes of Legend Formation," pp. 291-302.

43. I recorded one example in Hévizgyörk (Pest county) from a servant girl, Örzsi Tóth. It starts with the preparation of a St. Lucy's stool, continues with the midnight mass of the dead, then develops the adventures of a man who is running after a witch horse, and finally ends as *märchen* type AT 300.

44. See Appendix, No. 84.

45. Mrs. Palkó, Appendix, No. 20.

46. Andrásfalvi, Appendix, No. 64.

47. Honti, 1947, p. 24.

48. Ortutay, 1935, p. 32.

49. Vajkai, p. 59. See also Banó, 1947, pp. 239-240. The relationship between tales and legends was touched upon in historical depth by two papers presented at the Liblice meeting of the International Society of Folk Narrative Research, September, 1966: Jiří Horák, "Remarks about the Relations between Fairy Tales and Legends"; and M. Lüthi, "Urform und Zielform in Sage und Märchen." Lately Boratav (1966) has paralleled tales with their legend counterparts.

50. Ortutay, 1940, pp. 63-75.

51. Lüthi, 1953-54, pp. 321-326.

52. Majland (pp. xii-xiii), too, for example, tried to convince his readers that the Szekler reading material had no influence whatever upon the folk poetry.

53. Berze Nagy, 1940, I, xv.

54. Dégh, 1946, p. 148.

55. Christiansen, 1953, p. 71.

56. Ortutay, 1935, pp. 18-19. In this collection the *märchen Koplaló Mátyás* (*The Hungry Matthew*) and *A kutya* (*The Dog*) come from a chapbook.

57. Ortutay, 1941, p. 164.

58. Especially in the second volume (Banó, 1941) we find many such texts which come from chapbooks or storybooks, for example Nos. 5-7. See also Ortutay, 1940, tale No. 18 of M. Fedics. Though Pandur's style was

greatly influenced by his early reading matter, there is only one such text of his to be found, No. 50. From Ágnes Kovács' collection, only the transmissions from children's storybooks belong here. I. Dobos' informants learned partly from jest books and children's fairytale editions. Newer collections, though, are showing that we have to contend more and more with book-tale influences.

59. Dégh, 1942, I, 73-79.

60. It is quite conceivable that Marie, the old nurse of the Wild children, who was drawn by Ludwig Grimm reading with her glasses on her nose, told her stories not only from memory but from storybooks (Bolte and Polívka, IV, 423-433). Berendsohn also stated that a part of the Grimm *märchen* are originally book tales (Hagen, 1955, pp. 392-410), as is also shown by Lüthi's study on Rapunzel (1961, pp. 64-79).

61. Colum, p. xv.

62. Jahn, 1891, pp. xvi-xvii.

63. Azadovski, 1926, pp. 60-61, and Azadovski, "Skaritel'stvo," pp. 5-28. See also Wisser, 1926, p. xviii. A very thorough analysis of a noted storyteller's reading matter and literary sources has been issued lately by Pomerantseva (1965, pp. 265-275).

64. Henssen, 1951, pp. 16-21.

65. Ranke, 1951, pp. 126-133. Here we must point out the literature which has been concerned with the influence of the Grimm *märchen*, both inside and outside Germany—Röhrich, II, pp. 308-313; and the anniversary volumes in memory of Jacob Grimm by two leading German journals: *Hessische Blätter*, 54 (1963), and *Deutsches Jahrbuch*, 9 (1963).

66. Rumpf, 1951; Delarue, 1951; Hagen, 1954.

67. Haiding, *Märchenschatz*, p. 418.

68. Peuckert and Lauffer, p. 145.

69. Langstroff, pp. 47-56.

70. F. Ranke, 1938, pp. 123-133. See also Pomerantseva, 1952, p. 256; Rath, pp. 131-144. For a summing up of this question, see Peuckert and Lauffer, pp. 142-143.

71. Bîrlea, 1963, p. 343.

72. Until now research has paid very little attention to the different stages of literary influence. Little distinction has been made, for example, between the immediate reading aloud of a tale and the further second- and third-hand, etc., retelling of a former book tale which gradually looses its literary character—the process of transformation by continuous retelling. The simultaneous presence of reading and narration is characteristic for the present state of the East European peasant culture. Some narrators read, but the tale is transmitted orally and not by lending books—that is, the transmission is still communal. In this way, the literary influence enters folk tradition. A characteristic example of this is the Szekler *Book of the Dead*, which we discuss in Chapter 10. Proof that it was not absolutely necessary to be able to read in order to cultivate and preserve literary tradition within an oral culture can be found

in the preservation of their voluminous literature among the completely illiterate Irish. Colum writes (p. xv), "The Irish have remained an oral rather than a literate people . . . the academic poetry of the seventeenth and eighteenth century was confined to farmers and fishermen; one could hear a recital of the poems . . . in the thatched cottages a hundred years after the poets were dead and gone. And the oral memory held matter that went much farther back than the eighteenth and nineteenth centuries." Robin Flower remembers a man who sang of Ossian while hacking potatoes: "Without further preamble or explanation he fell to reciting Ossianic lays. For half an hour I sat there while his firm voice went on. After a while he changed from poetry to prose. . . . So far as the record goes, this matter in one form or another is older than the Anglo-Saxon Beowulf, and yet it lives in the lips of the peasantry" (*The Irish Tradition*, cited by Colum). Delargy (1945, pp. 26-30) goes into more detail about the continuation of the literary tradition in folk poetry.

73. Among such narrators belongs the shoemaker named Spinas Plasch, who also narrates from his reading matter, but he thinks it is different when one hears a story told (Uffer, 1955, pp. 75-79). Sokolov (1945, p. 231) mentions a case in Jerchov of a similar "learned" narrator. Kovalev, a modern Russian raconteur, is a good representative of this type (Pomerantseva, 1965).

74. See Sokolov, pp. 145, 228, concerning a narrator type who has read many romantic and adventure novels. It must be recorded that these narrators generally cherished their reading matter, and that they would much rather recount word for word than narrate. Merkelbach-Pinck (1940, p. 14) writes: "There are good narrators who can retain a story, once read, all through their lives nearly letter-perfect and can recite it regardless of whether it goes back to a school reader or to the entertainment section of a weekly paper. . . ."

75. This was expressed in a similar way by János Nagy from Sára, when I asked him about historical traditions of the War of Independence of 1848. See Dégh, *Ethn.*, 1947, p. 233.

76. See also Végh, pp. 181-182; Dégh, 1948, pp. 206-207.

77. For evaluation see Chapter 8.

78. Sándor Dömötör, *Hetedhét országón tút*, No. 86 in the series Nemzeti könyvtár.

79. For instance, *Zsuzska*, Appendix, No. 6, and *Peasant Gagyi*, Appendix, No. 28.

80. Ortutay, 1935, p. 19.

81. Á. Kovács, 1943, I, 6off; 1961, pp. 431-444.

82. Heroes of Hungarian historical legends.

83. *Book of the Dead*, pp. 800-801. Manuscript in my possession.

84. The stories of *Prince Sándor* and the *Sorcerer Virgil* penetrated folk tradition quite easily. See Appendix, No. 25.

85. Poncianus, *The Seven Sages*, II (Budapest, 1911). A chapbook published and printed by Kálmán Rózsa and his son-in-law.

86. *Kulak:* In Russian, a well-to-do peasant. The use of the word indicates that the Communist class distinctions among the peasantry became known around 1950 in Kakasd community life.

87. Since the title page is missing we cannot state where it was published and what the exact title is.

88. Lajos Varga, *A lagrégibb irodalom nyomán a szentéletü Genovéva érzékeny, szomoru, szivreható története* [*On the Tracks of the Oldest Literature About the Sentimental, Sad, Heart-stirring History of St. Genevieve*], 1908. A chapbook.

89. Ortutay, 1935, pp. 33-34; Banó, 1941, pp. 18-19; Dégh, 1942, I, 56-57, 66, 73-79; Zenker-Starzacher, pp. 43-44.

90. Nechaev and Rybakova, 131-141; Pomeransteva, 1953, pp. 3, 142-144, 1965, pp. 272-273; Röhrich, 1956, 191-199.

91. Dégh, 1942, I, 77-78; Sokolov, 1945, p. 228; Banó, 1939, p. 8. Banó points out that the influence of the book undermines the healthy folk style of the *märchen.*

92. Mackensen, p. 316.

93. F. Ranke, 1938, pp. 47, 129-130.

94. Ibid., p. 133.

95. Regarding the role of the anecdote, see T. Kardos, 1953, pp. 135-150; T. Dömötör, pp. 29-32.

96. Nagy and Faragó (pp. 20-30) talk about the fact that in today's Hungarian villages in Transylvania, it is the anecdotes which hold the center of attention. In a similar way, Peuckert (1930, pp. 151-175) sums up the Western European situation where the magic tale in general has faded from the tale treasure. See also Peuckert-Lauffer, p. 177.

## Chapter 8. The Storytellers

1. Lintur, 1953, p. 15.

2. Kovács, 1943, I, 42-60.

3. "To shed light upon the role of the individual in folklore we absolutely have to collect the entire tale body of a community. The collectors, however, in most cases do not go beyond recording the tales of one or two storytellers. In order to get a clear picture of the märchen tradition of a village or a region, the repertoire of the outstanding folk narrators has first to be isolated and noted down, then the texts of the less famous narrators have to be recorded too" (Lintur, 1953, p. 9). He carried out these principles when doing fieldwork in the village of Gorinchevo. Between 1939 and 1951 he met two famous masters, three gifted, and several mediocre storytellers. He recorded altogether 150 *märchen* plots, sufficient for a conclusion regarding the *märchen* tradition of the village (1957, pp. 3-4). Henssen (1939, pp. 136-137) also aimed at this, as well as the Irish folklorists (Thompson, ed., 1953, pp. 2-6, 282).

4. Ortutay (1940) cites illiteracy or, better, verbal transmission as the characteristic fact for the survival of the folktale and (1965, pp. 3-4) of all folk literature. Furthermore, B. Heller (1945, p. 43) refers to several famous storytellers; it was illiteracy which conserved the whole Gaelic-

Irish tale collection. Bulgarian folk epic was preserved because under Turkish rule oral folklore was the only literature that could survive for centuries. We must, of course, not generalize, for research in the newer European folklore of the modern, civilized world also has found examples of storytellers who themselves have written down their *märchen*. Today literacy is no rarity. Some narrators of Merkelbach-Pinck wrote down their stories. Similar manuscripts exist in the Czech and Slovak folklore manuscript collection archives, which shows that knowing how to read and write did not necessarily mean the death of storytelling. For a general summary on the memory factor in storytelling, see Hunter, pp. 144-183.

5. Thus the brothers Grimm, when they mention Mrs. Viehmann, their great narrator. Bünker and S. Pintér also stress this. Such narrators were the most precious for the investigators of tale types who required only the skeleton of the variants. As Tillhagen (pp. 267-268) puts it, these storytellers were simple bearers of tradition: "These transmitters—for this is the way it was generally assumed that transmission of a tale happened within a certain cultural area—once learned their material and reported it consequently to others who, on their part, learned the tale, and so on. I do not believe that it was as simple as this. The storyteller probably played a much more important role. He is not like the relay runner who passes on his staff—his *märchen*—from one generation to the other. We should rather compare him to a gardener who selects from the many wild flowers those he specially loves, cares for them and cultivates them, and thus grows more beautiful and durable species which he can transmit to posterity. If he does not do so, they revert to wildness and are lost in generalities." According to R. Weiss (p. 285), "The creator of tales, though, is an artist even if he uses the traditional magic motifs, and even the märchen carrier and märchen teller needs a special gift in order to render logically the often highly complicated combination of motifs and to imbue the whole with fascination. At any time there were only single individuals who appeared within a village as the outstanding märchen tellers. They have their own, personal narrative style and some of them are able to form new märchen variants from the traditional form transmitted to them."

6. Zenker-Starzacher, pp. 39-40.

7. We have learned from József Faragó's information that Bágyi stuck closely to the composition of his repeatedly recorded *märchen*. "He clung to his *märchen*, not only in details, from sentence to sentence, but also in composition and structure. Coming to the motif about the woman in the city, the narrator excused himself, not willing to hurt the feelings of the women present. He refused to tell it at all because he felt that nothing could be changed in a *märchen*."

8. Bünker, pp. 420-436; Haiding, *Märchenschatz*, pp. 367-388.

9. Ortutay, 1940, pp. 15-16.

10. Zenker-Starzacher, 1941, p. 40.

11. Henssen, 1951, p. 38.

12. Yates, p. 2. The situation might be similar to that of the Gaelic narrator Macdonald mentioned by Ettlinger (p. 56).
13. See Chapter 6.
14. Grudde, 1932, p. 102. For an evaluation of the problem, see Henssen, *Hessische Blätter*, XLIII, 18; Sareyko, pp. 5-9.
15. Marót, 1945, p. 3. In other words, ". . . no tale, no matter how sacred or traditional, can be told twice in exactly the same way without improbable feats of memory, variation both intentional and accidental . . ." (Crowley, p. 1).
16. Bolte and Polívka IV, 8-9; F. Ranke, 1935, p. 355; Henssen, 1936, pp. 14-16; U. Jahn, 1891, p. ix; Sokolov, 1945, pp. 226-227; Satke, 1958; Bîrlea, 1963, p. 348; Noy, p. 19; Dorson, 1956, p. 4.
17. Kovács, 1958, pp. 454-457.
18. As noted already in Chapter 6. See also Delargy, pp. 15-16; Thompson (ed.), 1953, p. 113.
19. Viidalepp, pp. 159-160.
20. Jech, 1959, p. 523.
21. As mentioned in Chapter 6, the narrators would come forward only in a favorable situation or after the passing of other outstanding storytellers. Only then did they recite the *märchen* they had heard since early childhood; from passive carriers of tradition they became active narrators.
22. Such a rare case is András Albert from Csíkszentdomokos, who was only thirty-six years old when he told his seventy tales, and was already well known in the whole region. We find young storytellers among the narrators of Merkelbach-Pinck as well as among the Irish.
23. Wisser, 1926, xv; Uffer, 1945, p. 8; Haiding, *Märchenschatz*, pp. 385-386; Zender, p. xxiv; Delargy, 1945, p. 23. The best Hungarian storytellers were already old when their *märchen* were recorded. Fedics was eighty-six, Pandur sixty, J. Lacza seventy, Ámi seventy-four, Mrs. Tóth over fifty; the storytellers of Sára were fifty to sixty years old. It is worth mentioning that most of the narrators, when quizzed about their sources, referred to old people—family members, old villagers, or old itinerants whom they had met somewhere at some time.
24. Henssen, 1951, pp. 12-13.
25. Haiding, "Träger," p. 30. For similar examples, see Haiding, *Märchenschatz*, pp. 383-384.
26. See also Chapter 6 and von Sydow in connection with active and passive carriers of tradition. It is important to note that the storyteller hears the pieces of his repertoire (or the raw material) continuously, and that the tale tradition of his environment penetrates his memory. Walter Anderson (1923, pp. 399-401) has repeatedly pointed this out when emphasizing the law of *Selbstberichtigung* as causing the remarkable stability of folktales (1935, pp. 22-24; 1951, p. 334; 1954, pp. 3-4). It is important to know here where the storyteller has learned his tales. Delargy (1945, p. 22) writes, "The vast majority of the storytellers known to me personally, or to our collectors, learned the greater part of their tales from members of their family, usually father or grand-

father, a few from their mothers and grandmothers. But they have learned many tales also from neighbors, from beggarmen, and occasionally during their work as migratory laborers, in neighboring countries." See also Henssen, 1936, pp. 6-10; Brachetti, 1930, pp. 205-206; Langstroff, pp. 135-136.

27. "The tale is such that its end can be beyond the forest or right here at the door of the hut," says Fedics (p. 84). For similar notes on Pandur, see Dégh, 1942, I, 58, 59-61. See also statement of Czapár in Chapter 6.

28. "An outstanding storyteller can improvise an excellent long and richly embroidered tale from the most meagre motif" (Ortutay, 1940, p. 82).

29. Sándor Varró (*A népkötemények kezdeményezéseiröl* [*On the Origins of Folk Poetry*], 1866, p. 492) expresses the general opinion: "The authors of folklore, the folk poets, do not strive for laurels, as the opinion goes. They create for the pleasure of the community, and they silently agree that their song and not their name be on everybody's lips."

30. Among the many references to the self-consciousness of the storytellers, see Merkelbach-Pinck, 1940, p. ii, and Kovács, 1943, I, 69.

31. Marót, "Idios en koinoi," p. 226. For his own self-respect, the storyteller must do everything he can to enlarge his repertoire. He will undertake long journeys in the hope of hearing new tales, and is not deterred by bad weather, as Delargy writes. And what he has once heard, he will never forget. He repeats it to himself as he travels or as he drives the cattle home (Delargy, 1945, p. ii).

32. Pandur often mentioned this, and Fedics expresses himself as follows: "There are not as many hair on me as I know tales" (Ortutay, 1940, p. 61).

33. Statement of J. D. Suggs; Dorson, 1956, p. 4.

34. Statement of J. Schwili; Noy, 1963, p. 19.

35. Parallel cases are known from different famous narrators. Delargy (1945, p. 22) mentions one who continued through a whole winter with a new tale for every evening. Campbell (I, 189-93) mentions a Scottish itinerant craftsman who knew a different story for every night. "Wenn de te Gänge kömp, de kann drei Daga un drei Nächte an eenen Stück vertelln" (Henssen, 1936, p. 9). The same is true of the Gypsy Taikon (Tillhagen, 1948, p. 256).

36. Dégh, 1942, I, 31, 53.

37. Ortutay, 1940, pp. 60-62.

38. Dégh, 1940, I, 66.

39. Von Sydow, "On the Spread of Tradition," in *Selected Papers* (1948), pp. 13-15. It is a pity that collectors were only seldom interested in recording complete autobiographies like that of Mrs. Tóth. See Dobos, 1962, pp. 105-148. In this matter the life history recording method would be rewarding to adopt from social anthropologists (Langness, 1965, *passim*).

40. Bünker, p. viii.

41. Kálmány, 1914/15, II, vii-viii.

42. Dégh, 1940, I, 32-53. (Pandur's biography is in a separate narrative.)

43. The international motif treasure is transmitted to the narrators by ethnic tradition (Eberhard and Boratav, p. 24; De Felice, p. 460). Restrictions in the liberty of shaping the *märchen* were dealt with recently by M. Lüthi (1963, pp. 1-14).
44. Azadovski, 1926, p. 17.
45. B. and I. Sokolov, 1915; Pomerantseva, 1954, p. 234.
46. Azadovski, 1926, pp. 25-32, 36-37.
47. Sokolov, 1945, pp. 227-228.
48. Ibid., pp. 228-233.
49. Pomerantseva, 1954, p. 235.
50. Pomerantseva, 1952, p. 4, and 1965, *passim*. For a summary, see Pomerantseva, 1966, pp. 614-617.
51. Chicherov, 1946, p. 2.
52. Ortutay, 1940, p. 17.
53. Ortutay, 1940, p. 7.
54. Henssen, 1936.
55. Banó, 1939, pp. 6-9.
56. Banó, 1941, pp. 17-18, 20-23.
57. Uffer, 1945, pp. 10-15, 19-21.
58. Haiding, *Märchenschatz*, pp. 407-408, and "Träger," p. 28.
59. Henssen, 1936, pp. 11-12; Langstroff, pp. 75-77. See also Brachetti, pp. 206-208; Zender pp. xxv-xxvi; R. Weiss, pp. 284-285; Röhrich, 1958, p. 665.
60. Bîrlea, 1963, pp. 248-252; Jech, 1961, pp. 526-528.
61. De Felice, p. 457ff.
62. Bolte and Polívka, IV, 260; Brinkmann, pp. 13-15; Kovács, 1943, I, 26-31; Uffer, 1945, pp. 78-79; Thompson (ed.), 1953, p. 294, summarized in Dégh, 1959, pp. 68-69.
63. Lázár, 1896, p. 56.
64. János Arany (1817-1882), one of the greatest Hungarian poets and one of the initiators of the popular classical trend in poetry, was deeply interested in folklore. His son László Arany, whom we have already mentioned, was, as a result of his father's inspiration, among the pioneer tale collectors.
65. In a book review about the tale collection of L. Merényi, J. Arany's works, vol. 6 (Pest, 1861), p. 428.
66. Eberhard and Boratav, p. 16. Aarne (1913, pp. 69-70) notes, when sketching the reasons for the variation of tale texts, that the method of formulating them is associated with both reason and fantasy. Mackensen (*Zeitschr. f. deutsche Bildung*, 1930, 353) points out that the changes can be caused by forgetting and misunderstanding just as well as by creative capacity. Halliday (p. 134) cites pertinent examples that conscious and unconscious variants sometimes cannot be separated.
67. Swahn, 1955, p. 349; Halliday, pp. 133-134.
68. F. Ranke, "Das Märchen," p. 253.
69. Kovács, 1943, I, 60-71.
70. Bartlett, pp. 30-47; Hunter, pp. 144-183; Lindgren, pp. 370-371; Ander-

son, 1951, pp. 5-6, and "Meine Antwort," *passim;* Dundes, pp. 243-247; Glade, 224-236.

71. Ortutay, 1959, 1961, 1965; Voight, 1966.

72. Jech and Rychnová, 1954, pp. 209-218.

73. Dobos, 1961.

74. Jech, 1965, pp. 199-208. The tales were first collected by J. S. Kubín some fifty years ago. See also Dégh, 1960, pp. 37-39.

75. Halpert (1957, p. 61) writes "How much do storytellers change their versions of stories? Tests should be made by recording tales from the same narrator at different intervals. Do some kind of stories . . . have more stability than others? Do some lend themselves more readily to improvisation? How much do storytellers vary among themselves in the same kind of stories? What stories lend themselves to change and what factors cause the change?"

76. Brunvand, 1961.

77. Katona, pp. viii-ix, in introduction to Berze Nagy, 1907.

78. Szendrey, *Ethn.*, 1931, pp. 45, 92.

79. Ortutay, 1940, pp. 82-83.

80. *Ethn.*, 1939, p. 226.

81. Tillhagen, pp. 264-265. With a similar method Wisser (1926, p. 16) proves the creativity of his narrator Hans Lembke. Since then several folklorists have pointed to the necessity of repeated recordings, as for instance Astakhova in the preface of her work *Bylini Severa* (1938); Václavek, 1947, p. 18; Sirovátka, pp. 50-51; and Satke, 1958.

82. Eberhard and Boratav, p. 17.

83. Ranke, 1955, p. 7.

84. Dégh, "History of Hungarian Folklore," pp. 44-48.

85. Spiess, pp. 60-67. He shows numerous examples of the role which befalls a narrator in renewing a motif chain. He mentions the "workshop secrets" so well guarded, in the field of composition, and the tricks of the trade which the narrator uses to impress his listeners.

86. Bødker mentions that he heard a narrator recite five times, each time in front of a different community, and that he adapted the text each time to fit the circumstances (in Thompson, ed., 1955, pp. 290-291). The same case is also mentioned by Halpert (p. 61).

87. Skipping or changing an element or coupling motifs in a different way causes the change of a whole chain, as Mackensen writes (Pessler, II, p. 313). See Eberhard and Boratav, p. v, for discussion of new *märchen* that thus came into existence.

88. It is worth mentioning that János Mailáth discussed this matter in 1864: "Often a narrator fuses two and three märchen into one; sometimes he divides one into several, embroiders it, and changes it as the mood strikes him or the mood of his listeners seems to require" (quoted in Kolos).

89. We have already pointed this out in Chapter 6 in connection with János Nagy and the narrators from Sára.

90. Thompson (ed.), 1935, p. 5; Halliday, pp. 135-136.

91. Dégh, 1961, p. 69. Here we wish to mention that in 1956 we suceeded in tape recording the entire tale treasure and the biographies of the narrator, since deceased. The evaluation of the material and the weighing of the changes which have occurred within the span of the last fifteen years is being carried out. It will suffice here to say that the tale repertoire has changed very little. Altogether 15 per cent of the tales have disappeared. The new pieces number scarcely more than 20 per cent, but the great majority of the texts have been transformed and newly formed. Only a small proportion have followed the original text to the letter.

92. Pandur changed a tale with a negative end after one of our remarks: "Don't worry . . . we shall resurrect him [the dead hero] again, then we shall make a good end for the tale. Jancsi will fetch his father and his mother [poor old people] to Fairyland" (Dégh, 1942, pp. 1, 216). Henssen (*Sammlung und Auswertung*, pp. 28-29) says of his blind Büning that he watered down one of his *märchen* so much that he had forgotten the details. When the collector called his attention to this, the narrator confessed that in order to show his gratitude for the cigars he was given, he had enlarged on the tale. We want to add Gunda's (p. 144) instructive example. His Gypsy narrator started a tale differently on telling it a second time. To the question, "Which beginning was the right one?" he replied, "It can be this way, but it also can be the other way."

93. Ortutay, 1940, p. 84.

94. Zender, p. xxvii.

95. Solymossy, *Ethn.*, 1919, 57.

96. Solymossy, 1920, p. 17.

97. Ibid., p. 6. Solymossy's concern in another study with the phenomenon of motif linking is similar (*Ethn.*, 1922, 30).

98. Anatole France writes ("Contes et chansons populaires," in *La vie littéraire*, IV, Paris, 1898, 74-75), "Nous savons que l'humanité toute entière s'amuse, depuis son enfance, d'un très petit nombre de contes dont elle varie infiniment les détails sans jamais en changer le fonds puéril et sacre. . . . Mes ces vieilles, ces éternelles histoires en passant dans chaque contrée, s'y colorent des teintes du ciel, des montagnes et des eaux, s'y imprègnent des senteurs de la terre. C'est là justement ce qui leur donne la nuance fine et le parfum; elles prennent, comme le miel, un gout de terroir. Quelque chose des âmes par lesquelles elles ont passé est resté en elles, et c'est pourquoi elles nous sont chères. This statement does not need any explanation. "Nearly every collection offers examples for local color, and such connections with place and time are not negligible . . . traits, but are quite significant for the reality concept of the tale and the teller" (Röhrich, 1956, p. 155).

99. Thompson (ed.), 1953, pp. 317-318; Röhrich, 1956, p. 156.

100. Mackensen, "Das Deutsche Volksmärchen," p. 312; Henssen, 1951, p. 20; Löwis of Menar, pp. 20-29; Sareyko, p. 24; Röhrich, pp. 164-165, 172-173.

101. Honti, 1937, p. 14; Lüthi, 1962, p. 81; Dégh, 1961, pp. 70-71.
102. Mackensen, "Das Deutsche Volksmärchen," p. 317. Steinitz (pp. 333, 335) stresses the democratic tendency of the tale and the storyteller. Röhrich demonstrates in many examples the social criticism present in the *märchen*; he shows how powerful is the confrontation of rich and poor, how strongly the injustice or social differences appears (1956, pp. 165-169). Social protest might be expressed by landless peasant storytellers in forming their versions. This does not mean that the *märchen* as a genre would originate in class conflict. The tale adventure and the victory of the hero carries a more general message that cannot be restricted to nineteenth and twentieth century peasantry.
103. Azadovski, 1926, pp. 16-17; Sokolov, 1945, p. 259; Pomerantseva, 1954, p. 229; Zenker-Starzacher, p. 45; Ágnes Kovács, 1943, I, 34-35, 62-63, 64-68; Henssen, 1951, pp. 20-24.
104. It is significant that the "big tasks" in the tales almost always stem from the local occupations or crafts or originate in individual experience: the heavy peasant work of the hired men, buggy-drivers, herders, harvest hands; experiences from the wandering years or from military service. Azadovski (1926, p. 14), for instance, writes that the cabinetmaker working for the forest spirit received good dishes to eat; in the tale about the manor hands the three strong men appear as harvest hands. From a tale in Kalotaszeg we can follow the work cycle of the seasonal laborers (Ortutay and Katona, I, 280). In Azadovski's narrators the popular occupations of the Vecholensk region are mirrored (1926, pp. 34-35).
105. Pomerantseva (1954, p. 250) talks about the description, in the tale, of the heavy labor on the earth, the dross of the poor people. Azadovski (1926, pp. 58-61) relates how his Siberian storyteller wove her own experiences from the time she was a servant girl into her tales, and how often she speaks of the way of life of the poor people.
106. See Sokolov, p. 258; Pomerantseva, 1954, pp. 229-230; Löwis of Menar, 1921, pp. 20-29; Azadovski, 1926, p. 14; Bolte and Polívka, IV, 20-24; Eberhard and Boratav, p. 12; Sareyko, *passim*; Ortutay, 1940, pp. 98-102; Dégh, 1942, I, 84-98.
107. Ortutay, 1940, p. 105.
108. Thompson, 1946, pp. 455-457; Lüthi, 1961, pp. 49-56, and 1963.
109. Ball, pp. 172-173. Sokolov (1945, p. 227) and Wesselski (1936, p. 241) stressed the importance of investigation of the narrative style. In Hungary Ortutay gave a good example with his detailed investigation of the style of Fedics (1940, pp. 88-96).
110. Thompson (ed.), 1953, pp. 290-292; Halpert, p. 61.
111. Christiansen can trace this style tradition in Norway back 200 to 250 years (Thompson [ed.], 1953, pp. 217-218). Delargy (1945, p. 21) traces the genealogy of such a chain of transmission even further back. Style traditions within one family is essentially the subject of some of the text analyses: Merkelbach-Pinck, 1939, p. 226; Sareyko, pp. 4-20; K. Ranke, 1955, p. 7.
112. Chapter 6, Note 207, gives an account of new interest in the style and

dramatic delivery of the narrator. A stimulating method is to tape record narrators' opinions on their art of narration, performance, style, and technique (Crowley, pp. 137-141).

113. Ortutay, 1940, pp. 88-96; Tillhagen, pp. 265-266. Hain (p. 127) calls attention to the investigation of formulae: "We can already say at this point that the dialect narrator constantly falls back on proverbs, pictures and formulae as building blocks for his märchen, inserting them more or less into the different narrative formulae and fabrics, and thus relies on them to render the character of a situation."

114. Thus the narrators from Sára. Henssen (1951, p. 20) calls Gerrits one of them.

115. Azadovski, 1926, pp. 64-68.

116. Ortutay, 1940, p. 103.

117. Instead of quoting many well-known proofs, we wish to refer to one of the pioneer Hungarian authors, István Lázár (1896, p. 56) who speaks about the natural and unconscious dramatic art of the narrator: ". . . his recital quickly becomes dramatic; he forgets himself and his environment, he lives completely within the event recited; with a sobbing voice he can move to tears when he mourns the bitter fate of his hero; but he laughs all over his face when he follows a funny scene; he takes a compassionate part in virtue's struggles, and when the misdeed is punished he adds with deep satisfaction: 'served him right!' With a funny tale he makes a serious face so that the comical fact has a greater effect." See also Jahn, 1891, pp. xi-xiii; Petsch, 1934, pp. 57-58; Azadovski, 1926, pp. 44-46; Zenker-Starzacher, pp. 33-34; Ortutay, 1940, pp. 92-94; Dégh, 1942, I, 93-95; Kovács, 1943, I, 72-74; Henssen, 1951, pp. 24-25; Pomerantseva, 1954, p. 235; Haiding, 1955, pp. 9-10; Delargy, 1945, p. 16. István Sándor (p. 526) categorizes as follows the functions of gestures in storytelling: (1) imitative or descriptive; (2) symbolical, referring to feelings or state of mind; (3) associative, bringing environmental objects into the action; (4) explanatory.

118. Henssen, 1951, pp. 36-37. For a bibliography of similar attempts, see István Sándor, 1964, pp. 531-533.

119. Haiding, "Träger," p. 31.

120. Satke, pp. 57-66; Noy, 1963, p. 18.

121. When the narrator was in a good mood, he acted out the tales more than he recited them. With the Kölderascha tribe it was the custom to tell stories during work, and often the plot of the tale was represented in drama form. "Sometimes there were four of us or even five who told tales. One was the wolf, the other the prince, a third was a giant, or caliph, or whoever was needed. This was real theater, do you understand? It could start in the midst of work. The others of course went on working, but in time when the action got more and more exciting, they did not care a bit for anything else and did nothing but listen, waiting their turn. For the farther the *märchen* progressed, the more people appeared. So, one, for instance, was to be the judge and immediately he sat down, his legs folded under him, twirled his moustache,

and making a solemn face he started judging and talking wildly. And there was the accused standing before him, bowing deeply and full of fear. And there were the guards, and people and God knows what else!" (Tillhagen, pp. 260-261) In this connection, see also Christiansen's statements in Thompson (ed.), 1953, pp. 297-298.

122. Cammann, pp. 15-16.

123. This coincides with the statements of Löwis of Menar (1921, p. 6): "Every narrator possesses his own material from which he creates and beyond which he does not dare to go. Hand in hand with this we find an outspoken narrative style which characterizes the individualities of the speakers and gives rise to observations."

124. For conclusions concerning the Kakasd tale stock, see Dégh, 1959, *Rheinisches Jahrbuch*, p. 23-39.

## Chapter 9. Mrs. Zsuzsánna Palkó, nee Zaicz

1. Maxim Gorki (p. 391) writes, "The fundamental thought of the working man is the attempt to lighten the work burden and to increase productivity."

2. "Does the king live here?" she asked. "There is no king anymore, Aunt Zsuszi." "But the land is governed from here, is it not?"

3. Ortutay, 1940, pp. 53-54.

4. A similar statement is made by Lintur (1953, p. 8) in connection with Kalin's concept of the world.

5. Described in detail in Chapter 3.

6. Here she is thinking of the apparent advantage represented by the greater amount of actual money the poor man possessed. The rich people had hardly any cash on hand; they bartered produce, and the carters did not sell their wares for money but battered them for important articles.

7. Dégh, 1959, pp. 28-29.

8. Viidalepp, pp. 165-166; Delargy, pp. 21-22; Zenker-Starzacher, p. 42; Henssen, 1951, pp. 12-13, and 1936, p. 6-10.

9. She expressed herself in the same sense on other occasions. See Chapter 6.

10. Mrs. Palkó also recalled tales of her brother's which she did not like and of which she could remember nothing more than fragments. "János also related this, but I would rather not pull it out. Why should I tear it to pieces? A woman had twins, she went out to work in the fields, and a lioness kidnapped one child. The other a wolf, but I cannot tell it, it is a long time since I heard it. Also of *Red Valiant* I know only a little bit."

11. Both texts are published in Dégh, 1959, *Rheinisches Jahrbuch*, pp. 23-39.

12. The analysis of the world view and cosmic concepts of storytellers as gleamed from tales and by questioning was attempted recently by two folklorits: Erdész (1961, 1963) and Noy (1965).

13. Related in detail by Martha Bringemeier, pp. 11-58.

14. Sokolov, 1945, pp. 229-230.

15. Ortutay, 1940, pp. 56-57.
16. Ibid., pp. 102-103.
17. Azadovski, 1926, pp. 14-15.
18. For experiences of a servant girl in the city, see also Vinokurova in Azadovski (1926, pp. 58-59) and Röhrich (1956, 1964).
19. See Siebert, pp. 24-25, for literature on this question.
20. Azadovski, 1926, pp. 59-61; Röhrich, 1956, pp. 163-166.
21. Dégh, 1956, pp. 166-168.
22. Dégh, 1950, pp. 172-191.
23. Similarly with Vinokurova (Azadovski, 1926, p. 68) and Medvedjeva (Sokolov, 1945, p. 232).
24. Röhrich (1956, p. 164) judiciously remarks that the social reality recently depicted in the *märchen* is not a consequence of conscious realism but rather an "unconscious adaptation of the narrator to the reality in which he lives."
25. This is in agreement with K. Ranke's opinion (1958, p. 647) that in the adventure related in a folktale, the central hero is "a wanderer between the worlds," and thus the elaborate description of the first scene is of eminent importance.
26. See Appendix, No. 46. Note the masterful creation of atmosphere in preparation for events which follow.
27. In order to find out more about the extent of her imagination we questioned Mrs. Palkó about the details of the magic tales—characters, objects, events—and about the locales she had never seen except in her mind's eye. After the tales were told we discussed, in a relaxed conversation, how she imagined the king's garden, yard, kitchen, and people in *I Don't Know*, fairyland, and the talking horse, and so on. A methodical questioning of storytellers in this manner would help us to find out the relationship between the images sketched in the international tale types and the presentations of the narrators. See Dégh, 1963, p. 6.
28. Azadovski, 1926, p. 43. But Mrs. Palkó is not far from Miazi-Moam, the favorite storyteller of Haiding (1955, p. ii).
29. Azadovski, 1926, pp. 37-41.
30. Ibid., pp. 46-47.
31. Solokov and Solokov, 1915, 62.
32. Ibid., p. 242.
33. Ibid., p. 232.
34. Azadovski, 1926, pp. 62-64.
35. Haiding, "Träger," pp. 32, 36.
36. Dégh, 1960, p. 36.
37. *Esti Budapest*, 1954, No. 7 (*Literary Supplement*).
38. Lüthi, 1963.
39. Lintur, 1953, p. 14.
40. Azadovski, 1926, pp. 55-58.
41. According to a letter to me from Gottfried Henssen.
42. Dégh, 1942, II, 86-100 (with notes about origin). A new type of story-

teller seems to have emerged in recent years, one that breaks away from the traditional tale topics as a result of the impact of modern urban influences: books, movies, and television. The tales of such narrators are composed of traditional *märchen* motifs but cannot be fitted into any of the established types. These narrators, all gifted people, reached the limits of folk culture. The community does not accept them fully yet, nor are they yet authors of literature (Dégh, 1960, pp. 41-42; Pomerantseva, 1965).

43. For information about the length of the tale in Europe in general, see Cammann, 1961, pp. 12-13.
44. Henssen (1951, pp. 26-27) writes the same about Gerrits.
45. Dégh, 1942, I, 92.
46. She means that he is not a Hungarian from Transylvania or the Bucovina.

### Chapter 10. *György Andrásfalvi, Mrs. Anna Sebestyén, and Márton László*

1. He was born in 1904. After resettlement in 1941, he changed his name from Zaicz to Andrásfalvi. The same was done by many other Szeklers who, according to their names, could be considered of foreign extraction (Gruber–Gábori, Rancz–Rózsa, Daradics–Darabos).
2. The one is the *Young Shrew*, in which the hopeful lover of the young woman is the priest. The other is *The Poor Blind Beggarman*. In this tale the priest and his adherents fly through the air clamped to three naked girls, and Andrásfalvi points out that here they are priests of a non-Catholic confession.
3. See Appendix, Nos. 73-75.
4. Zender (p. xxi) cites similar cases. Such rational outcomes of traditional belief stories are quite common with nonbelieving narrators.
5. Mrs. Lajos Sebestyén acquired the name Geczi through her husband from her father-in-law, whose name was Gergely and nickname Geczi. According to Szekler custom, men are usually called after their father's first name and women after their mother's. Thus Mrs. Sebestyén acquired through her husband, "Lajos Geczi," the nickname "Mrs. Lajos Geczi" (in Hungarian, Geczi Lajosné).
6. Vajkai, pp. 5, 8.
7. Through Merkelbach-Pinck (1940, pp. 13-14) we know of narrators who write down their tales so as not to forget them. The Institute of Ethnography and Folklore in Bratislava keeps the personal handwritten tale noted by a Slovak storyteller. We too received three voluminous tales in a letter from András Albert, the outstanding storyteller from Csíkszentdomokos. With increasing formal education, there are more and more examples of this.
8. We were able to copy the one by Mrs. Sebestyén-Boda, and we used it as the basis of our investigations.
9. Among the best-known products of folk writing known in Hungary from the late nineteenth century are the peasant letters, songbooks,

guides for wedding ceremonies, and collections of gnomes, proverbs, and sayings. The writing of diaries and village chronicles was no rarity among the wealthy peasants of the great Hungarian Plains. The folk poet as a specific personality is well characterized by many authors: Bözödi, p. 61; Tamási, pp. 205-231; János Nagy-Czirok, *passim;* László, pp. 89ff. There are a great variety of chapbook and broadside authors (Takács, 1951, pp. 1-49, and 1955, pp. 419-422). Among the peasant author types, there is a certain similarity between Márton László and István Orosz, the deeply religious author and publisher of church hymns, as is shown in his works edited by S. Bálint (1940).

It would lead us too far to cite here the corresponding European parallels, but that of the Czech *Pismáci* is self-evident. (The concept originally was equivalent to "reader of the Bible.") A typical manifestation of a centuries-old literate peasant culture with a traditional folk literacy, these personalities are chroniclers of everyday village events, writers of memoirs, poets, and both recorders and reshapers of folk customs; they are natural philosophers who have an inner drive to put down their thoughts in writing. The qualities of the *Pismáci* as presented by Jech (1956, p. 6, and 1957, p. 84) and B. Slavik (1940) are comparable to those of Márton László, as well as to those of the Irish *seanchas,* a narrator type that both preserves and passes on literature and folklore but which, because of a peculiar situation, has never learned how to read and write (Delargy, 1945, pp. 29-30).

10. The rhymed prose forms have extensive roots in Oriental folk literature. Goldzieher (pp. 19-20) points out that "in the makam type of recitation, which the literature of some Moslem (Persians, Turks) people have taken over from the Arabs, and the solemn use of which is still exercised during the Friday calls to the mosque (khutba), the prose rhythm is called sadsh . . . in contrast to kafijat, which is used for the verse rhyme." Marót points out that this form without doubt originated in the desire for a certain solemn, mystical, and magical atmosphere. This is the explanation for its sometimes seeping into the folktales of certain people, for it occurs in oral tradition but not in writing. (Rhymed prose occurs most frequently in the Russian folktales, but it can also be found elsewhere, as for example in the Irish "run" and in the Hungarian introductory and concluding formulae.)

11. During our investigations we could find this form neither in the written literary tradition nor in the folklore tradition. Conversations with scholars of literature from both Hungary and Transylvania convinced us, however, that this form must have existed, even though no traces of it have been discovered so far.

12. *Book of the Dead,* p. 201. "King Mátyás is dead and dead is Justice," a generally known popular saying deriving from the justice of the renaissance king, led to the formation of countless anecdotes and legends and probably was spread by them.

13. *Book of the Dead,* pp. 201-202.

14. Ibid., pp. 402-403.

15. This saying originates with a specific Hungarian variant of an international migratory anecdote (see Appendix, No. 100).
16. *Book of the Dead*, pp. 518-520.
17. Ibid., p. 553.
18. Lichtmann, the general store owner from old Andrásfalva.
19. *Book of the Dead*, pp. 335-340.
20. The Lazarus Sermons are to be found in Hungarian literature for the first time in the writings of György Kultsár, Péter Bornemisza, and Gáspár Károli.
21. *Book of the Dead*, p. 407.
22. Ibid., pp. 411-414.
23. Ibid., pp. 414-416.
24. Ibid., pp. 438-441. Note in this connection the joke of Márton László quoted in Chapter 2.
25. Ibid., p. 283.
26. Ibid., pp. 284-285.
27. Ibid., pp. 387-401.
28. Ibid., p. 389.
29. In this regard we wish to mention Max Lüthi's address, "Folklore and the Study of Literature," presented at the International Congress on Regional Ethnology at Arnhem in 1955 (1956, pp. 116-120).

# BIBLIOGRAPHY

NOTE: In entries of works by Russian authors published in languages other than Russian, the foreign spelling of the author's name is given in parentheses.

Aarne, Antti, *Estnische Märchen- und Sagenvarianten*. FFC 25. Hamina, Suomalainen Tiedeakatemia, 1918.

———, *Leitfaden der vergleichenden Märchenforschung*. FFC 15. Hamina, Suomalainen Tiedeakatemia, 1913.

———, *Die magische Flucht*. FFC 92. Helsinki, Suomalainen Tiedeakatemia, 1930.

———, *Der tiersprachenkundige Mann und seine neugierige Frau*. FFC 15. Hamina, Suomalainen Tiedeakatemia, 1914.

———, "Vergleichende Märchenforschungen." *Mémoires de la Société Finno-Ougrienne*, XXV, 3-82. Helsinki, Druckerei der Finnischen Literaturgesellschaft, 1908.

———, *Verzeichnis der Märchentypen*. FFC 3. Helsinki, Suomalainen Tiedeakatemian Toimituksia, 1910.

Aarne, Antti, and Stith Thompson, *The Types of the Folk-Tale; a Classification and Bibliography*. FFC 184. Helsinki, Suomalainen Tiedeakatemia, 1961.

Abrahams, Roger D., *Deep Down in the Jungle . . . . Negro Narrative Folklore from the Streets of Philadelphia*. Hatboro, Pa., Folklore Associates, 1964.

Ahlström, Axel, "Europeiska sagor; Sago-studier," *Folkminnen och Folktankar*, 21 (1934), 76-107.

Anderson, Walter, *Kaiser und Abt: die Geschichte eines Schwanks*. FFC 42. Helsinki, Suomalainen Tiedeakatemia, 1923.

——, "Meine Antwort." *Hessische Blätter für Volkskunde*, 47 (1956), 115-118.

——, *Eine neue Arbeit zur experimentellen Volkskunde*. FFC 168. Helsinki, Suomalainen Tiedeakatemia, 1956.

——, "Eine neue Monographie über Amor und Psyche." *Hessische Blätter für Volkskunde*, 46 (1955), 118-130.

——, "Der türkische Märchenschatz." *Hessische Blätter für Volkskunde*, 44 (1953), 111-132.

——, *Ein volkskundliches Experiment*. FFC 141. Helsinki, Suomalainen Tiedeakatemia, 1951.

——, *Zu Albert Wesselskis Angriffen auf die finnische folkloristische Forschungsmethode*. Tartu, K. Mattiesens Buchdv., 1935.

Andrád, Sámuel, *Elmés és mulatságos rövid anekdoták [Droll and Jolly Little Anecdotes]*. Pécs, 1790. 2 vols.

Andreev, N. P. (Andrejew, N. P.), *Die zwei Erzsünder*. FFC 54. Helsinki, Suomalainen Tiedeakatemia, 1924.

—— (——), *Die Legende vom Räuber Madej*. FFC 69. Helsinki, Suomalainen Tiedeakatemia, 1927.

——, *Ukazatel' skazochnykh siuzhetov po sisteme A. Aarne*. Leningrad, 1929.

Anikin, V. P., "A szóbeli költöi alkotás, a variáns és a verzió a folklór kollektivitás-elméletének megvilágitásában" ("Oral Creation; the Variant and the Version in the Light of the Theory of Communal Authorship in Folklore"), *Ethn.*, 75 (1964), 350-359.

——, "Ob izdaniiakh narodnoi poezii," *Leningradnaia Gazeta*, 1953, 57-59.

——, "O spetsificheskikh osobennostiakh narodnogo tvorchestva," *Sov. Etn.*, 1953, No. 4, 80-87.

*Arany János Minden Munkái [Complete Works of János Arany]*. Pest, Ráth, 1861. 6 vols.

Arany, László, *Magyar népmese-gyüjtemény. [Hungarian Folktale Collection]*. Pest, 1862.

——, "Magyar népmeséinkröl" ("Concerning our Hungarian Folktales"), in Vol. 52, *Magyar Remekirók*. Budapest, 1904. Pp. 131-191.

Arfert, P., *Das Motiv von der unterschobenen Braut*. Schwerin, Hofbuchdruckerei, 1897.

Astakhova, A. M., *Bylini severa*. Moscow, 1938.

——, "Voprosy narodnogo poeticheskogo tvorchestva," *Soveshchanie v Institute Russkoi Literatury Ak. Nauk SSSR (ANSSSR)*, 2 (1954), 112-115.

Astakhova, A. M., I. O. Dmitrakov, and A. N. Lozanova, *Ocherki russkogo narodno-poeticheskogo tvorchestva Sovetskoi epokhi*. Moscow-Leningrad, 1952.

Azadovski, M. K. (Asadowskij, M. K.), *Eine sibirische Märchenerzählerin*. FFC 68. Helsinki, Suomalainen Tiedeakatemia, 1926.

——, *Russkaia skazka. Izbrannie Mastera*. Leningrad, Izdatel'stvo Akademia, 1932.

——, "Skazitel'stvo i kniga," *Jazyk i Literatura* (Leningrad), 8 (1932), 5-28.

Azadovski, M. K., and L. E. Eliasov, *Skazki Magaia*. Leningrad, 1940.

*Az Isten igazságát kereső, vagy: a kételyekből kigyógyult remete* [*The Seeker of God's Justice, or: the Hermit Who Was Healed of His Doubts*]. No. 114 in Tatár Péter Regekunyhója (The Story-Hut of Péter Tatár). Pest, A. Bucsánszky, 1870. A chapbook.

Bächtold-Staubli, Hanns, and Eduard Hoffmann-Krayer, *Handwörterbuch des deutschen Aberglaubens*. Berlin, De Gruyter, 1927-42. 10 vols.

Bakhtin, V. S., "O nekotorykh problemakh fol'kloristiki," *Sov. Etn.*, 1953, No. 2, 154-163.

Bakó, Elemér, "Leánylopás a bukovinai székelyeknél" ("Bride-theft among the Szeklers of Bucovina"), *Ethn.*, 92 (1941), 146-147.

Balassa, Iván, *Karcsai mondák* [*Legends of Karcsa*]. UMNGY XI. Budapest, Akadémiai Kiadó, 1963.

Bálint, Sándor, *Egy magyar szentember* [*A Hungarian Evangel*]. Budapest, 1940.

Ball, John, "Style in the Folktale," *Folklore*, 65 (1954), 170-172.

Balla, Péter, "Népzenei gyüjtés a bukovinai magyar falvakban" ("Folksong Research in the Hungarian Villages of Bucovina"), *Ethn.*, 46 (1935), 126-141.

Ballagi, Mór, *Magyar példabeszédek, közmondások és szójárások gyüjteménye* [*Collection of Hungarian Parables, Proverbs, and Figures of Speech*]. Szarvas, 1850. 2 vols.

Bán, Aladár, "A kincskeresés a néphitben" ("The Treasure Hunt in Folk Belief"). *Ethn.*, 26 (1915), 28-40, 86-93.

Banó, István, *Baranyai népmesék* [*Folktales of Baranya*]. UMNGY II. Budapest, A Budapesti Egyetem Magyarságtudományi Intézete és a Franklin-Társulat Magyar Irodalmi Intézet és Könyvnyomda, 1941.

———, "Egyéniség és közösség szerepe a népmese életében" ("The Role of the Individual and the Community in the Life of the Folktale"), *Ethn.*, 55 (1944), 26-33.

———, "Két szëm magyaró" ("Two Hazelnuts"), *Ethn.*, 50 (1939), 159-161.

———, "Mesemorfológia, meseélettan" ("Folktale Morphology, Folktale Biology"), *Ethn.*, 58 (1947), 85-90.

———, "Szlovákul hallott mese magyar elmondásban" ("A Tale Heard in Slovak, Retold in Hungarian"), *Ethn.*, 59 (1948), 117-120.

Bartlett, F. C., *Remembering*. Cambridge, 1932.

———, "Some Experiments on the Reproduction of Folk-Stories," *Folklore*, 31 (1920), 30-47.

Bascom, William R., "Folklore and Anthropology," *JAF*, 66 (1953), 283-290.

Bascom, William R., "The Forms of Folklore: Prose Narratives," *JAF*, 78 (1965), 3-20.

———, "Four Functions of Folklore," *JAF*, 67 (1954), 333-349.

———, "Literary Style in Yoruba Riddles," *JAF*, 62 (1949), 1-16.

———, "Verbal Art," *JAF*, 68 (1955), 245-252.

Bátky, Zsigmond, "Pásztor ivócsanakok a Néprajzi Múzeumban" ("Herdsmen's Drinking Vessels in the Ethnographical Museum"), *Néprajzi Értesítő*, 20 (1928), 97-105.

Bausinger, Hermann, "Strukturen des alltäglichen Erzählens," *Fabula*, I (1958), 239-254.

Beck, Erich, *Bucovina, Land zwischen Orient und Okzident.* Freilassing, Pannonia-Verlag, 1963.

Bédier, Joseph, *Les Fabliaux: études de littérature populaire et d'histoire littéraire du moyen âge.* 2nd ed. Paris, E. Bouillon, 1893.

Beitl, Richard, *Wörterbuch der deutschen Volkskunde.* Stuttgart, Kohlhammer, 1953.

Beke, Ödön, *Tscheremissiche Märchen, Sagen und Erzählungen.* Helsinki, 1938.

Beke, Ödön, and I. Katona, *A magyar nép meséi. Csalóka Péter* [*Folktales of the Hungarian Folk. Péter Csalóka*]. Budapest, 1947.

Beledi, P. Miksa, "Keleti motivumok egy nyugoti mesében" ("Oriental Elements in a Western Folktale"), *Ethn.*, 3 (1892), 326-335.

Belényesy, Márta, *Kultúra és tánc a Bukovinai székelyeknél* [*Culture and Dance of the Bucovina Szekler Enclaves*]. Budapest, Akadémiai Kiadó, 1958.

Benedek, Elek, *Magyar mese—és mondavilág* [*The World of Hungarian Legends and Folktales*]. Budapest, Athenaeum irodalmi és nyomdai Kiadó, 1894. 5 vols.

———, *Székely mesemondó* [*Szekler Storyteller*], Budapest, 1880.

———, *Székely népmesék és balladák* [*Szekler Popular Tales and Ballads*]. N.d.

Benfey, Theodor, *Pantschatantra: fünf Bücher indischer Fabeln, Märchen und Erzählungen.* Leipzig, F. A. Brockhaus, 1859.

Benkő, László, "Adalékok a halott vőlegény balladatipus történetéhez" ("Contributions to the History of Ballad-Type of the Dead Bridegroom"), *Ethn.*, 47 (1936), 26-34.

———, *A halott vőlegény története* [*The Story of the Dead Bridegroom*]. Marosvásárhely, 1934.

Berendsohn, Walter, *Grundformen volkstümlicher Erzählerkunst in den Kinder- und Hausmärchen der Brüder Grimm.* Hamburg, W. Gente, 1921.

Béres, András, "Mai mesélő alkalmak" ("Narrative Occasions Today"), *Ethn.*, 66 (1955), 433-444.

Béres, András, and Ágnes Kovács, *Rozsályi népmesék* [Folktales of Rozsály]. UMNGY XII. Budapest, Akadémiai Kiadó, 1967.

Berger, Dorothea, "Die Volksmärchen der Deutschen von Musäus, ein Meisterwerk der deutschen Rokokodichtung," *PMLA*, 69 (1954), 1200-1212.

Berze Nagy, János, "Banó István: Baranyai népmesék" ("István Banó: Folktales of Baranya"), *Ethn.*, 53 (1942), 65-69.

———, *Baranyai magyar néphagyományok* [*Hungarian Folk Traditions from Baranya*]. Pécs, Kiadja Baranya Vármegye Közönsége, 1940. 3 vols.

———, *Égigérő fa* [*The Sky-High Tree*]. Pécs, Tudományos Ismeretterjesztö Társulat Baranyamegyei Szervezete, 1958.

———, "A finnek Meseosztályozása" ("The Finnish Folktale Classification"), *Ethn.*, 24 (1913), 65-82, 147-160.

————, "Kálmány Lajos új mesegyüjteménye ("Lajos Kálmány's New Tale Collection"), *Ethn.*, 26 (1915), 93-115.

————, "A 'katekizmusi ének' és a néphagyomány számszimbolikája" ("The 'Catechism Song' and Number Symbolism of Folk Tradition"), *Ethn.*, 50 (1939), 111-135.

————, *Magyar népmesetipusok* [*Types of Hungarian Folktales*]. Pécs, Baranya Megye Tanácsának Kiadása, 1957.

————, "Mese" ("The Folktale"), in Vol. III, *A Magyarság Néprajza*, Károly Viski, ed. Budapest, 1938. Pp. 226-289.

————, *Népmesék Heves-és Jász-Nagykún-Szolnok megyéböl* [*Folktales from Heves and Jász-Nagykún-Szolnok Counties*]. MNGY IX. Budapest, Az Athenaeum Részvény-Társulat Tulajdona, 1907.

Binder, Jenö, "Megjegyzések 'A Gesta Romanorum hatása a magyar népköltészetre' cz. dolgoazatra" ("Notes on the Work 'The Influence of the Gesta Romanorum on Hungarian Folk Literature' "), *Ethn.*, 3 (1893), 281-285.

————, "Párhuzamok magyar meséinkhez" ("Parallels to Our Hungarian Folktales") *Ethn.*, 2 (1891), 167.

————, "A zarándok és az isten angyala" ("The Pilgrim and the Angel of God"), *Ethn.*, 4 (1893), 130-134.

Bîrlea, Ovidiu, "Cercetareă prozei populăre epice" ("Collection of Folk Literature"), *Revista de Folclor*, I (1956), 109-134.

————, "Die Erforschung der Volkserzählung im Rumänien," *DtJb*, 9 (1963), 335-352.

————, "La fonction de raconteur dans le folklore roumain," *Laographia*, 22 (1965), 22-26. Paper presented at the Athens Congress in 1964.

Bladé, A., *Contes Populaires de la Gascogne*. Paris, 1886. 3 vols.

Blehr, Otto, "The Analysis of Folk Belief Stories and their Implications for Research on Folk Belief and Folk Prose," *Fabula*, 9 (1967), 259-263. Paper presented at the meeting of the International Society for Folk Narrative Research, Liblice, September, 1966.

Böckel, Otto, *Psychologie der Volksdichtung*. Leipzig. B. G. Teubner, 1913.

Bødker, Laurits, "The Brave Tailor in Danish Tradition," in W. Edson Richmond, ed., *Studies in Folklore*. Folklore Series No. 9. Bloomington, Indiana, Indiana University Publications, 1957. Pp. 1-23.

Bolte, Johannes, and G. Polívka, *Anmerkungen zu den Kinder-und Hausmärchen der Brüder Grimm*. Leipzig, Dieterich, 1913-32. 5 vols.

Boratav, Pertev Naili, "Zur Beziehung zwischen Märchen und Sage," *DtJb*, 12 (1966).

Bornemisza, Péter, *Ördögi kisértetekröl, avagy rettenetes útálatosságáról a megfertöztetett világnak* [*On the Temptation of the Devil or about the Horrible Dreadfulness of the Afflicted World*]. Sempte, 1878.

Boškovic-Stulli, Maja, "Regionalna, nacionalna i internacionalna obilježa narodnih pripovijedka" ("Regional, National and International Traits of Folktales"), *Filološki preglad*, 1963, 83-93.

————, "Sižei narodnih bajki u hrvatskosrpskim epskim pjesmama" ("Subjects of Folktales in Serbocroatian Epics"), *Narodna Umjetnost*, 1 (1962), 15-36.

Bözödi, György, *Az eszös gyermök; Bágyi János meséi* [*The Clever Child; Tales of J. Bágyi*]. Bucharest, Állami Müvészeti és Irodalmi Könyvkiadó, 1958.

———, "Irásos népi müveltség" ("Written Folk Literature"), *Termés*, 1943, 56-59.

———, *A tréfás farkas; Bágyi János meséi* [*The Witty Wolf; Tales of János Bágyi*]. Budapest, 1942.

Brachetti, Mathilda Agnes, *Studien zur Lebensform des deutschen Volksmärchens*. Baden, 1935.

Brachetti, Mechtilda, "Das Volksmärchen als Gemeinschaftsdichtung," *Norddeutsche Zeitschrift für Volkskunde*, 9 (1931), 197-212.

———, "Das Volksmärchen als Gemeinschaftsdichtung," *Nieder-deutsche Zeitschrift für Volkskunde*, 8 (1930).

Brandon, Elizabeth, "Le sorte d'un conte: AT 1510," *Laographia*, 22 (1965), 37-41. Paper presented at the Athens Congress, 1964.

Bringemeier, Martha, *Gemeinschaft und Volkslied*. Münster, Aschendorff, 1931.

Brinkmann, Otto, *Das Erzählen in einer Dorfgemeinschaft*. Münster, Aschendorff, 1933.

Brixius, Lothar, *Erscheinungsformen des Volksglaubens*. H./Saale, M. Niemeyer, 1939.

Brunvand, Jan H., "An Indiana Storyteller Revisited," *Midwest Folklore*, 11 (1961), 5-14.

Bünker, Reinhold, *Schwänke, Sagen und Märchen heanzischer Mundart*. Leipzig, 1906.


Cammann, Alfred, *Westpreussische Märchen*, Vol. 3, *Fabula* Series A. Berlin, W. de Gruyter, 1961.

Campbell of Islay, F. J., *Popular Tales of the West Highlands, Orally Collected with a Translation*. Edinburgh, 1860-62. 4 vols.

Campbell, John Francis, *Popular Tales of the West Highlands. Orally Collected*, 1890.

Carnoy, Emile Henry, *Littérature orale de la Picardie*. Paris, Maissonneure et Cie, 1883.

Carpenter, Rhys., *Folk-Tale, Fiction and Saga in the Homeric Epics*. Berkeley and Los Angeles, University of California Press, 1946.

Cazan, Ion C., *Literatura populara din Drăguş*. Bucharest, 1947.

Chetkarev, K. A., *Mariiskie narodnye skazki*. Ioshkar-Ola, 1955.

Chicherov, I. V., "Traditsiia i avtorskoe nachalo v fol'klore," *Sov. Etn.*, 1946, 2, 29-40.

Child, Francis James, *The English and Scottish Popular Ballads*. Boston, Houghton Mifflin Company, 1882-98. 5 vols.

Chistov, K. V., "Zametki o sbornike N. E. Onchukova Severnye skazki," *Trudy Karel'skogo filiala Ak. Nauk SSSR*, VIII (1957), 5-29.

Christiansen, Reidar Th., "Further Notes on Irish Folktales," *Béaloideas*, 22 (1953), 70-82.

———, "Gaelic and Norse Folklore," *Folk-Liv*, 2 (1938), 321-335.

———, *The Migratory Legends*. FFC 175. Helsinki, Suomalainen Tiedeakatemia, 1958.

Colum, Padraic, *A Treasury of Irish Folklore*. New York: Crown Publishers, 1954.

Cosquin, Emmanuel, "Les mongoles et leur prétendu rôle dans la transmission des contes indiens vers l'occident européen." *Revue des Traditions Populaires*, 27 (1912), 497-566.

Crowley, Daniel J., *I Could Talk Old-Story Good: Creativity in Bahamian Folklore*. Berkeley and Los Angeles, University of California Press, 1966.

Danckert, Werner, *Unehrliche Leute; die Verfemten Berufe*. Bern, Francke, 1963.

Dános, Erzsébet, *A magyar népballada* [*The Hungarian Folk Ballad*]. Budapest, Magyar Királyi Udvari Nyomda, 1938.

Däumling, Heinrich, *Studie über den Typus des Mädchens ohne Hände*. Munich, 1912.

Dégh, Linda, "A Néprajzi Intézet gyüjtőmunkája" ("Fieldwork Report on the Work of the Folklore Institute"), *Ethn.*, 61 (1950), 127-8.

———, "Az AaTh *449/A mesefipus magyar redakciója" ("The Hungarian Subtype of AaTh *449/A"), *Ethn.*, 71 (1960), 277-296.

———, "Adalékok a hálás halott epizód meséi és mondai formálódásához" ("'The Grateful Dead' as a Tale and a Legend Incident"), *Ethn.*, 68 (1957), 307-318.

———, "Adatok a magyar parasztság irodalmi életéhez" ("Contributions to the Literary Life of the Hungarian Peasantry"), in *Magyar Századok. Irodalmi müveltségünk történetéhez*. Budapest, 1948. Pp. 299-315.

———, "Adatok a mesekeret jelentöségéhez" ("Contributions to the Meaning of the Folktale Frame"), *Ethn.*, 55 (1944), 130-139.

———, "Beszámoló az 1848-as néphagyománygyüjtés eddigi tapasztalatairól" ("On the Present State of Research Work Concerning the Relics of the Revolution of 1848 Among the Folk"), *Ethn.*, 58 (1947), 230-235.

———, *Bodrogközi mesék* [*Folktales of Bodrogköz*]. Budapest, 1945.

———, "Az egyéniségvizsgálat perspektivái" ("The Perspective of Research on the Personality of the Story-Teller"), *Ethn.*, 71 (1960), 28-42.

———, *Folktales of Hungary*. Chicago, University of Chicago Press, 1965.

———, "History of Hungarian Folklore," *Folia Ethnographica*, I (1949), 72-98.

———, "Ismeretlen tipusú népmese a dunántúli székelyeknél" ("An Unknown Folktale Among the Szeklers in Transdanubia"), *Ethn.*, 61 (1950), 172-192.

———, *Kakasdi népmesék* [*Folktales of Kakasd*]. Vol. 1: *Tales of Mrs. J. Palkó*; vol. 2: *Tales of Mrs. Palkó, Gy. Andrásfalvi, Mrs. L. Sebestyén and M. László*. UMNGY VIII, IX. Budapest, Akadémiai Kiadó, 1955, 1960. Reviewed by Ingrid Schellbach in *Fabula*, 4 (1961), 278-282.

398 · Bibliography

——, "Latenz und Aufleben des Märchengutes einer Gemeinschaft," *Rheinisches Jahrbuch für Volkskunde*, 10 (1959), 23-39.

——, "Népmese és ponyva" ("Folktale and Folk-Book"), *Magyar Nyelvör*, 1946: 68-72; 1947: 4-7, 43-45, 88-92.

——, "A népmesekutatás új útjai" ("New Methods of Folktale Research"), in Vol. I, *Néprajzi tanulmányok*. Budapest, 1949. Pp. 36-52.

——, *Pandur Péter hét bagi meséje* [*Péter Pandur: Seven Folktales of Bag*]. Budapest, Officina, 1940.

——, *Pandur Péter meséi* [*Péter Pandur's Tales*]. UNMGY III-IV. Budapest, Budapesti Egyetem Magyarságtudományi Intézete és a Franklin-Társulat Magyar Irodalmi és Könyvnyomda, 1942. 2 vols.

——, "Processes of Legend Formation," *Laographia*, 22 (1965), 77-87. Paper presented at the Athens Congress, 1964.

——, "Die schöpferische Tätigkeit des Erzählers," in *Internationaler Kongress der Volkserzählungsforscher in Kiel und Kopenhagen*. Berlin, W. de Gruyter, 1961. Pp. 63-73.

——, *A szabadságharc népköltészete* [*Folk Poetry of the War of Independence*]. Budapest, Akadémiai Kiadó, 1952.

——, "Az Uj Magyar Népköltési Gyüjtemény tanulságai és soron következő feladatai" ("The Results of the New Collection of Hungarian Folk Literatures, and Future Goals"), *Ethn.*, 74 (1963), 1-12.

——, "Válasz Banó Istvánnak" ("Reply to István Banó"), *Ethn.*, 58 (1947), 90-98.

Dégh, Linda, and Jaromír Jech, "Příspevek k studii interethnických vlivů v lidovém vypravování," *Slovenský Národopis*, 5 (1957), 567-608.

Delargy, James H. (O'Duilearga, S.), "Cnuasach Andeas; Scéalta agus Seanchas Sheáin I Shé ó Ibh Ráthach," *Bealoideas*, Vol. 29 (1961), No. 1963.

——, *The Gaelic Story-Teller. Proceedings of the British Academy*. London, 1945. Rhys Memorial Lecture.

——, "The Irish Folklore Commission and its Work," in *Travaux du I*er *Congrès International de Folklore*. Tours, Arrault, 1938.

——, "Irish Tales and Story Tellers," in Hugo Kuhn and Kurt Schier, eds., *Märchen, Mythos, Dichtung; Festschrift zum 90. Geburtstag Friedrich von der Leyens, am 19. August 1963*. Munich, C. H. Beck, 1963.

——, *Leabhar Sheáin I Chonaill Sgéalta agus seanchas ó Ibh Ráthach*. Dublin, Folklore of Ireland Society, 1948.

——, *Seanches O'n Oileán Tiar Tomás O'Criomhthain Dalheachtaigh Robin Flower*. Dublin, 1956.

Delarue, Paul, "Les Contes merveilleux de Perrault et la tradition populaire," *Bulletin Folklorique d'Ile de France, Nouvelle Serie*, 13 (1951), 195-201.

——, "Les contes merveilleux de Perrault; faits et rapprochements nouveaux," *Arts et traditions populaires*, 1954, 1-22, 251-274.

——, "Receuils de contes et de légendes," *Les Mois d'Ethnographie Française*, 1947, 117-118.

Diószegi, Vilmos, "A honfoglaló magyarság hitvilága ('ösvallásunk') kutatásának módszertani kérdései" ("Methodological Problems of the Research of the Religion of the Magyars at the Time of the Conquest"), *Ethn.*, 65 (1954), 20-68.

———, *A sámánhit emlékei a magyar népi müveltségben* [*Shamanistic Elements in Hungarian Folk Culture*]. Budapest, Akadémiai Kiadó, 1958.

Dobos, Ilona S., *Egy somogyi parasztcsalád meséi* [*Tales of a Peasant Family of Somogy County*]. UMNGY X. Budapest, Akadémiai Kiadó, 1962.

———, "Az 'igaz' történetek müfajának kérdéséröl" ("On the Problem of the 'True Story' as a Folk Narrative Form"), *Ethn.*, 75 (1964), 198-215.

———, *Szegény ember vizzel föz* [*The Poor Man Cooks with Water*]. Budapest, Magvető, 1958.

Dobroliubov, N. A., *Polnoe sobranie sochinenii.* Moscow, 1934.

Domokos, Pál Péter, "A Népmüvészeti Intézet újabb gyüjtéseiből" ("From the New Collections of the Institute for Folk Art"), in *Emlékkönyv Kodály Zoltán 70. születésnapjára.* Budapest, 1953. Pp. 338-372.

Domokos, Sámuel, "A kétnyelvü mesemondás problémái" ("Problems of Bilingual Storytelling"), *Ethn.*, 78 (1967), 547-53.

Dömötör, Sándor, "A boszorkányok gyülése a magyar néphitben" ("The Witches' Gathering in Hungarian Folk Belief"), *Ethn.*, 50 (1939), 210-211.

———, "A mesemondó egyénisége" ("The Personality of Folktale Tellers"), *Magyarságtudomány*, I (1942), 443-449.

———, "Titokzatos-e a mesealkalom?" ("Is the Occasion of Storytelling Mysterious?"), *Ethn.*, 58 (1947), 226-269.

Dömötör, Tekla, *Régi magyar vígjátékok* [*Old Hungarian Comedies*]. Budapest, Szépirodalmi Könyvkiadó, 1954.

Dorson, Richard M., *Buying the Wind.* Chicago, University of Chicago Press, 1964.

———, "The First Group of British Folklorists," *JAF*, 68 (1955), 1-8, 333-340.

———, "The Folktale Repertoires of Two Maine Lobstermen," in *Internationaler Kongress der Volkserzählungsforscher in Kiel und Kopenhagen.* Berlin, W. de Gruyter, 1961. Pp. 74-83.

———, *Negro Folktales in Michigan.* Cambridge, Mass., Harvard University Press, 1956.

———, *Negro Tales from Pine Bluff, Arkansas, and Calvin, Michigan.* No. 12, Folklore Series. Bloomington, Indiana, Indiana University Publications, 1958.

———, "Oral Styles of American Folk Narrators," in Thomas A. Sebeok, ed., *Style in Language.* Cambridge, Mass., M.I.T. Press, 1960. Pp. 27-53.

———, "Standard for Collecting and Publishing American Folktales," *JAF*, 70 (1957), 53-57.

———, "Tales of a Greek-American Family on Tape," *Fabula*, I (1957), 114-143.

———, "A Theory for American Folklore," *JAF*, 72 (1959), 197-215.

Dugonics, András, *Példabeszédek és jeles mondások* [*Figures of Speech and Pithy Sayings*]. Szeged, 1820. 2 vols.

Dundes, Alan, "Metafolklore and Oral Literary Criticism," *The Monist*, 50 (1966), 505-516.

———, *The Morphology of North American Indian Folktales*. FFC 195. Helsinki, Suomalainen Tiedeakatemia, 1964.

———, ed., *The Study of Folklore*. Englewood Cliffs, N. J., Prentice-Hall, 1965.

Eberhard, Wolfram, *Minstrel Tales from Southeastern Turkey*. Berkeley, University of California Press, 1955.

———, Review of *Modern Greek Folktales; Chosen and Translated by R. M. Dawkins*. *JAF*, 67 (1954), 231-236.

Eberhard, Wolfram, and Pertev Naili Boratav, *Typen Türkischer Volksmärchen*. Wiesbaden, Steiner, 1953.

Eckhardt, Sándor, "A Berta-monda" ("The Bertha Legend") *Ethn.*, 48 (1937), 11-13.

Eliade, Mircea, *Myth and Reality*. New York, Harper and Row, 1963.

Erdélyi, János, *Magyar közmondások könyve* [*Book of Hungarian Proverbs*]. Pest, 1851.

———, *Magyar népmesék* [*Hungarian Folktales*]. Pest, 1855.

———, *Népdalok és mondák* [*Folksongs and Legends*]. Pest, 1846-48. 3 vols.

Erdész, Sándor, "The Cosmological Conceptions of Lajos Ámi, Storyteller," *Acta Ethn.*, 12 (1963), 57-64.

———, "Téli estézés egy nyírségi faluban" ("Evening Making in Winter in a Village in the Nyírség"), *Józsa András Muzeum Évkönyve*, IV-V (1961/62), 115-128.

Ettlinger, Ellen, "International Conference on Celtic Folklore," *Folklore*, 65 (1954), 56-57.

Faragó, József, "Kurcsi Minya, havasi mesemondó" ("Minya Kurcsi, Storyteller of the High Mountains"), *Ethn.*, 78 (1967), 238-260.

———, "Lörinczi Elek árkosi népmesegyüjtése" ("Elek Lörinczi's Folktale Collection from Árkos"), *Nyelv és Irodalomtudományi Közlemények*, 11 (1967), 49-60.

Faragó, József, and J. Jagamas, *Moldvai Csángó népdalok és balladák* [*Moldavia Csángó Folksongs and Ballads*]. Bucharest, 1954.

Fél, Edit, *Kocs 1936-ban; néprajzi monográfia* [*Kocs in the Year 1936, an Ethnographic Monograph*]. Budapest, Pázmány Péter Tudomanyegyetem Magyarságtudományi Intézet, 1941.

———, "Some Data Concerning Kinship Institutions Among the Szeklers of Bukovina," *Acta Ethn.*, 8 (1959), 85-97.

Félice, Ariane de, "Contes traditionnels des vanniers de Mayun (Loire-Inferieure)," *Nouvelle Revue des Traditions Populaires*, 2 (1950), 442-446.

Ferenczy, László Marcella, *Székely népmesék* [*Szekler Folktales*]. Brassó, 1957.

Fiedler, Alfred, and Felix Hoerburger, *Beiträge zur Aufnahmetechnik und Katalogisierung von Volksgut*. Leipzig, F. Hofmeister, 1956.

Fischer, John L., "The Sociopsychological Analysis of Folktales," *Current Anthropology*, 4 (1965), 235-295.

Földyné, Judit Virány, *A Bodrogközi Láca Népmeséiből* [*Folktales of Láca in the Bodrogköz*]. Sárospatak, 1957.

Fraenger, W., and W. Steinigtz, eds., *Jacob Grimm zur 100 Wiederkehr seines Todestages*, Vol. 9, *Deutsches Jahrbuch für Volkskunde*. Berlin, 1963.

Frazer, James. G., *The Golden Bough; A Study in Magic and Religion*. London, 1907-15. 12 vols.

Gaál, György, *Märchen der Magyaren*. Vienna, 1822.

———, *Magyar népmese-gyüjtemény* [*Anthology of Hungarian Folktales*], ed. by Kazinczy Gábor and Toldy Ferenc. Pest, 1857-60. 3 vols.

Gálos, Rezso, "A három pupos meséjének egy magyar származéka" ("A Hungarian Derivative of the Tale of the Three Hunchbacks"), *Ethn.*, 18 (1907), 1-18, 65-73.

———, "A Historia Septem Sepientum elterjedéséhez" ("On the Spread of the Story of the Seven Sages"), *Ethn.*, 19 (1908), 125-126.

———, "A póruljárt szerelmesek meséjéhez" ("On the Tale of the Deceived Lovers"), *Ethn.*, 22 (1911), 382.

Gennep, Arnold van, *La Formation des légendes*. Paris, E. Flammation, 1910.

Glade, Dieter, "Zum Anderson'schen Gesetz der Selbstberichtigung," *Fabula*, 8 (1966), 224-236.

Gönczi, Ferenc, *Göcsej népköltészete* [*Folk Poetry of Göcsej*]. Zalaegerszeg, 1947.

Goldstein, Kenneth S., *A Guide for Fieldworkers in Folklore*. Hatboro, Pa., Folklore Associates, 1964.

Goldzieher, Ignác, *A pogány arabok költészetének hagyománya* [*The Tradition of Poetry among the Heathen Arabs*]. Budapest, 1893.

Gonzenbach, Laura, *Sizilianische Märchen aus dem Volksmund gesammelt*. Leipzig, W. Engelmann, 1870. 2 vols.

Gorki, Maxim, *Irodalmi tanulmányok* [*Literary Studies*]. Budapest, 1950.

Graf, Samuel, "Hianzische Märchen," *Zeitschrift des Vereins für Volkskunde*, 24 (1914), 20-31.

Greguss, Ágost, "A népköltészet ügyében" ("Concerning Folk Poetry"), *Vasárnapi Ujság*, 1863, 319.

Greverus, Ina-Maria, "Thema, Typus und Motiv zur Determination in der Erzählforschung," *Laographia*, 22 (1965), 130, 139. Paper presented at the Athens Congress, 1964.

Griesbach, E., *Die Wanderung der Novelle der treulosen Witwe durch die Weltliteratur*. Berlin, 1889.

Grudde, Hertha, *Plattdeutsche Märchen aus Ostpreussen*. Königsberg, 1931.

———, *Wie ich meine "Plattdeutschen Märchen aus Ostpreussen" aufschrieb*. FFC 102. Helsinki, Suomalainen Tiedeakatemia, 1932.

Gunda, Béla, "Die Funktion des Märchen in der Gemeinschaft der Zigeuner," *Fabula*, 6 (1963), 95-107.

———, *Néprajzi gyüjtőúton* [*On a Folklore Collection-Trip*]. Debrecen, 1956.

Györffy, György, "A székely társadalom" ("The Szekler Society"), in György Székely, ed., *Tanulmányok a parasztság történetéhez Magyar-*

*országon a XIV. században* [*Essays on the History of the Peasantry in 14th Century Hungary*]. Budapest, 1953. Pp. 104-116.

György, Lajos, *A magyar anekdotakincs története* [*The History of the Hungarian Store of Anecdotes*]. Budapest, 1931.

Györgypál-Eckert, Irma, *Die deutsche Volkserzählung in Hajós, einer schwäbischen Sprachinsel in Ungarn*. Hamburg, 1941.

Hagen, Rolf, *Der Einfluss der Perraultschen Contes auf das volkstümliche deutsche Erzählgut und besonders auf die KHM der Brüder Grimm*. Göttingen, 1954.

———, "Perraults Märchen und die Brüder Grimm," *Zeitschrift für deutsche Philologie*, 74 (1955), 394-410.

Hahn, Georg, *Griechische und albanische Märchen*. Leipzig, 1864. 2 vols.

Haiding, Karl, *Österreichs Märchenschatz*. Vienna, Pro Domo Verlag, 1953.

———, "Träger der Volkserzählungen in unseren Tagen," *Österreichische Zeitschrift für Volkskunde*, 1953, 24-36.

———, *Von der Gebärdensprache der Märchenerzähler*. FFC 155. Helsinki, Suomalainen Tiedeakatemia, 1955.

Hain, Mathilde, *Sprichwort und Volkssprache; eine volkskundlich-soziologische Dorfuntersuchung*. Giessen, W. Schmitz, 1951.

———, "Die Volkskunde und ihre Methode," in Vol. III, *Deutsche Philologie im Aufriss*, W. Stammler, ed. Berlin, Erich Schmidt Verlag, 1962. Pp. 2547-2570.

Halász, Antal, *A hazatértek; a bukovinai magyarok 200 esztendeje* [*The Repatriated; 200 Years of the Bucovina Hungarians*]. Nagyvárad, 1941.

Haller, János, *Hármas História; Gesta Romanorum*. Régi Magyar Konyvtár 18. Budapest, 1900.

Halliday, W. R., "The Welsh Gypsy Folk-Tales," *Journal of the Gypsy Lore Society*, 7 (1928), 131-136.

Hallowell, A. Irving, "Myth, Culture and Personality," *American Anthropologist*, 49 (1947), 544-556.

Halpert, Herbert, "Problems and Projects in the American-English Folktale," *JAF*, 70 (1957), 57-62.

Hand, Wayland D., "Status of European and American Legend Study," *Current Anthropology*, 6 (1965), 439-446.

Harva, Uno, *Die religiösen Vorstellungen der altaischen Völker*. FFC 129. Helsinki, Suomalainen Tiedeakatemia, 1938.

Hegedüs, Lajos, *Moldvai csángó népmesék és beszélgések; népnyelvi szövegek moldvai telepesektöl* [*Moldavia Csángó Tales and Conversation: Dialect Texts from Settlers of Moldavia*]. Budapest, Közoktatásügyi Kiadóvállalat, 1952.

———, *Népi beszélgetések az Ormánységból* [*Folk Conversation Texts of the Ormánység*]. Pécs, Nyomda és Könyvkiadó, 1946.

Heilfurth, G., and B. Martin, eds. "Dem Gedenken der Brüder Grimm am 100. Todestag von Jacob Grimm, 20. Steptember 1963," *Hessische Blätter für Volkskunde*, 54 (1963).

Heinrich, Gusztáv, "Az ephesusi matróna a magyar irodalomban" ("The Widow of Ephesus in Hungarian Literature"), *Egyetemes Philologai Közlöny*, 1878, 406ff.

Heller, Bernát, "Barát-Kádencziák" ("Monk Anecdotes"), *Egyetemi Philologiai Közlöny*, 29 (1904), 842-91.

——, "Kard a hálótársak közt" ("The Sword Between the Bedfellows"), *Ethn.*, 16 (1905), 257-268; 17 (1906), 214-218.

——, "Még néhány szó a katekizmusi énekröl" ("A Few More Words on the Catechism Song"), *Ethn.*, 91 (1940), 250-252.

——, "A póruljárt udvarlók meséjének magyar nyelvü és magyar vonatkozású változatairól" ("On the Hungarian and Related Variants of the Tale of the Baffled Lovers"), *Ethn.*, 19 (1908), 272-274.

——, "Uj magyar népköltési gyüjtemány I" ("New Collection of Hungarian Folk Literature I"), *Ethn.*, 56 (1945), 41-48.

Henssen, Gottfried, "Sammlung und Auswertung volkstümlichen Erzählgutes," *Hessische Blätter für Volkskunde*, 43 (1952), 5-29.

——, *Stand und Aufgaben der deutschen Erzählforschung*. Offprint from *Festschrift Richard Wossidlo*. Neumünster, 1939.

——, *Überlieferung und Persönlichkeit: Erzählungen und Lieder des Egbert Gerrits*. Münster, Aschendorff, 1951

——, *Volk erzählt; Münsterländische Sagen, Märchen und Schwänke*. Münster, Aschendorff, 1954.

——, "Volkstümliche Erzählkunst," in *Beiträge zur rheinischen und westfälischen Volkskunde in Einzeldarstellungen*, 1936, No. 4.

——, "Wesenszüge der westfälischen Volkserzählung," *Rheinisch-Westfälische Zeitschrift für Volkskunde*, 5 (1958), 75-105.

Herskovits, Melville J. and Frances S., *Dahomean Narrative; a Cross-Cultural Analysis*. Evanston, Ill., Northwestern University Press, 1958.

——, *Trinidad Village*. New York, A. A. Knopf, 1947.

Heyden, Franz, *Volksmärchen und Volksmärchen-Erzähler zur literarischen Gestaltung des deutschen Volksmärchens*. Hamburg, Hanseatische Verlagsanstalt, 1922.

Himmelheber, Hans, *Aura Poku; Volksdichtung aus Westafrika*. Eisenach, E. Röth, 1951.

Holbek, Bengt, "On the Classification of Folktales," *Laographia*, 22 (1965), 159-161. Paper presented at the Athens Congress, 1964.

Holmström, Helge, *Studier över svanjungfrumotivet i Vǫlundarkvida och annorstädes*. Malmö, Maiander, 1919.

Honti, János, "Dégh Linda, Pandur Péter meséi" ("Linda Dégh; Péter Pandur's Tales"), *Ethn.*, 53 (1942), 328-340.

——, *Az ismeretlen népmese* [*The Unknown Folktale*]. Budapest, Officina, 1947.

——, *A mese világa* [*The World of Märchen*]. Budapest, Pantheon, 1937.

——, "Notice sur le conte égyptien du Prince Prédestiné," *Oriens Antiquus*. Budapest, Magyar Keleti Társaság Kiadványai, 1945.

——, "Notices sur la légende populaire," in Alexander Scheiber, ed., *Heller Bernát emlékkönyv*. Budapest, 1941. Pp. 86-90.

——, "Pásztor Árpád meseközlése a Pesti Naplóban" ("Árpád Pásztor's Tale Publication in the Pesti Napló"), *Ethn.*, 42 (1931), 45-46.
——, *Verzeichis der publizierten ungarischen Volksmärchen auf Grund von Antti Aarnes Typenverzeichnis.* FFC 81. Helsinki, Suomalainen Tiedeakatemia, 1928.
Honti, John T., "Celtic Studies and European Folk-Tale Research," *Béaloideas*, 6 (1936), 33-39.
——, "On a Type of Saga Incidents," *Helicon* (Debrecen), IV (1942), 65-75.
Hoogasian-Villa, S., *100 Armenian Tales and their Folkloristic Relevance.* Foreword by Thelma G. James. Detroit, Wayne State University Press, 1966.
Horák, Jiří, "Remarks on the Relations Between Folk-Tales and Legends," *Fabula*, 9 (1967), 254-259.
Horger, Antal, *Hétfalusi csángó népmesék [Csángó Folktales from Hétfalu].* MNGY X. Budapest, Athenaeum, 1908.
Hunter, Ian M. L., *Memory.* Revised ed. Harmondsworth, Middlesex, England, Penguin Pelican Books, 1964.

Imreh, István, *Majorsági gazdálkodás a Székelyföldön a feudalizmus bomlásának idején [Farmstead Economics During the Decline of Feudalism].* Bucharest, 1956.
Ipolyi, Arnold, *Magyar Mythologia.* Budapest, 1929. 2 vols.
Istvánffy, Gyula, *Palócz mesék a fónoból [Palocz Tales from the Spinning-Room].* Liptószentmiklós, 1890.

Jackson, Kenneth, "The International Folktale in Ireland," *Folklore*, 47 (1936), 263-293.
Jacobs, Melville, "A Look Ahead in Oral Literature Research," *JAF*, 79 (1966), 413-427.
——, *Patterns in Cultural Anthropology.* Homewood, Ill., Dorsey Press, 1964.
Jahn, Erich, "*Die Volksmärchen der Deutschen*" *von J. K. Musäus.* Leipzig, 1914.
Jahn, Ulrich, *Volksmärchen aus Pommern und Rügen.* Norden, D. Soltau, 1891.
Jancsó, Elemér, *A bukovinai magyarság [Hungarians of the Bucovina].* Kolozsvár, 1938.
——, "A bukovinai magyarok mai helyzete" ("The Bucovina Hungarians Today"), *Magyar Szemle*, XXII (Sept., 1934.), 14-21.
Jech, Jaromír, *Lidová vyprávěni z Kladska [Folktales of the Glatz].* Prague, 1959.
——, "Lidové povídky zapsané Věnceslavem Metelkou," *Československá etnografie*, 5 (1951), 66-84.
——, "O přesný zápis nářečniha textu folklorního, folkloristického a ethnografického," *Československá etnografie*, 4 (1956), 55-67.
——, *Tschechische Märchen.* Berlin, Rütten und Loening, 1961.

———, "Zur Methode der wiederholten Aufzeichnung von Volkserzählungen," *Laographia*, 22 (1965), 119-208. Paper presented at the Athens Congress, 1964.

Jech, Jaromír, and Dagmar Rychnová, "O proměnlivosti lidového prozaického podání. Rozbor zápisů o turcich lidojedech," *Český lid*, 41 (1954), 209-218.

Jókai, Mór, *A magyar nép élce szép hegedüszóban* [*The Joke of the Hungarian Folk in Beautiful Fiddle Notes*]. 14th ed. Budapest, 1914.

Jolles, André, *Einfache Formen*. Halle, M. Niemeyer, 1930.

Kálmány, Lajos, *Hagyományok* (*Traditions*). Vácz, Kiadja a Néphagyományokat Gyüjtő Társaság, 1914.

———, *Ipolyi Arnold mesegyüjteménye* [*Arnold Ipolyi's Tale Collection*]. MNGY XIII. Budapest, Athenaeum, 1914.

———, *Koszoruk az Alföld vad virágaiból* [*Wreaths of the Wildflowers of the Lowland*]. Arad, 1877-78. 2 vols.

———, *Szeged népe* [*Folk of Szeged*]. Arad-Szeged, 1881-1891. 3 vols.

Kardos, Tibor, *Középkori kultúra, középkori költészet: a magyar irodalom keletkezése* [*Medieval Culture, Medieval Poetry; the Beginning of Hungarian Literature*]. A Magyar Történelmi Társulat Könyvei 7. Budapest, c. 1940.

———, "A magyar vigjáték kezdetei" ("The Beginning of Hungarian Comedies"), in *Kodály-emlékkönyv*. Zenetudományi Tanulmányok I. Budapest, 1953.

———, "A Trufa; egy régi magyar irodalmi müfaj jellege és európai összefüggései ("The Jest; Character and European Relationships of an old Hungarian Genre"), *Filológiai Közlöny*, 7 (1955), 11-138.

Karl, Lajos, "A Berta-monda" ("The Bertha Legend"), *Ethn.*, 20 (1909), 1-20, 73-82.

Katona, Imre, *A magyar kubikosok élete* [*The Life of the Hungarian Excavator*]. Budapest, 1957.

Katona, Lajos, *Irodalmi Tanulmányok* [*Literary Studies*]. Budapest, 1912. 2 vols.

———, "La bel homme trompé par sa femme. Conte Hongrois." *Revue des traditions populaires*, 1889, 44ff.

Katona, Lajos, ed., *Gesta Romanorum*. Régi Magyar Könyvtár No. 18. Budapest, 1900. A critical edition of the work by János Haller, Kolozsvár, 1695.

———, "Párhuzamok magyar meséink és népies elbeszéléseinkhez" ("Parallels to our Hungarian Folktales and Popular Stories"), *Ethn.*, 2 (1891), 12-16, 58-62.

———, "A remete és az angyal" ("The Hermit and the Angel"), *Ethn.*, 11 (1900), 145-154, 199-211.

Kelemen, Zoltán, and Linda Dégh, *Tolna megyei székely népmesék* [*Szekler Folktales from Tolna County*]. Szekszárd, Szekszárdi Nyomda, 1965.

Kiefer, Emma Emily, *Albert Wesselski and Recent Folktale Theories*. No. 3, Folklore Series. Bloomington, Indiana, Indiana University Publications, 1947.

Kis-Várday, Gyula, "A bukovinai székely falvak" ("The Szekler Villages in Bucovina"), *Ethn.*, 44 (1933), 131-139.

Koechlin, Elisabeth, *Wesenszüge des deutschen und des französischen Volksmärchens; eine vergleichende Studie zum Märchentypus "Amor und Psyche" und zum "Tierbräutigam."* Basel, B. Schwabe, 1945.

Kolos, István, Gróf Mailáth *János [Count János Mailáth], 1786-1855.* Budapest, 1938.

Komáromy, Andor, *Magyarországi boszorkányperek oklevéltára [Archive of Witch Trials in Hungary].* Budapest, 1910.

Konsza, Samu, *Háromszéki magyar népköltészet [Hungarian Folklore from Háromszék],* ed. J. Faragó. Marosvásárhely, Állami Irodalmi és Müvészeti Kiadó, 1957.

Korompay, Bertalan, "Népköltési kiadványainkról" ("On our Publications of Folk Literature"), *Ethn.,* 52 (1941), 169-179.

Kovács, Ágnes, "Benedek Elek és a magyar népmesekutatás" ("Elek Benedek and Hungarian Folktale Research"), *Ethn.,* 72 (1961), 431-444.

————, "The Hungarian Folktale-Catalogue in Preparation," *Acta Ethn.,* 4 (1955), 443-477.

Kovács, Ágnes, ed., *Kalotaszegi népmesék [Folktales of Kalotaszeg].* UMNGY V-VI. Budapest, Budapesti Egyetem Magyarság Tudományi Intézete és a Franklin Társulat Magyar Irodalmi Intézet és Könyvnyomda, 1943. 2 vols.

————, *Magyar állatmesék tipusmutatója [Type-Index of Hungarian Animal Tales].* Budapest, 1958. Mimeographed.

————, "Népmüvészeti és népköltési gyüjtés a baranyamegyei moldvai székely telepesek között" ("Folk Art and Literature Collecting Among the Szekler Settlers from the Moldavia in Baranya County"), *Ethn.,* 65 (1954), 197-209.

————, "Rhythmus und Metrum in den ungarischen Volksmärchen," *Fabula,* 9 (1967), 169-243. Paper presented at the Liblice meeting, 1966.

————, "Die ungarische Märchenforschung der letzten Jahrzehnte," *DtJb,* IV (1958), 453-466.

Kovács, Ágnes, and L. Maróti, *A rátótiádák tipusmutatója. A magyar falucsúfolók tipusai (AaTh 1200-1349) [Index of Hungarian Numskull Tales (AaTh 1200-1349).]* Mimeographed. Nézprajzi Muzeum-MTA néprajzi Kutatócsoport. Budapest, 1966.

Kovács, Ferenc, *Iratosi kertek alatt. Kisiratosi népköltészet [Folklore of Kisiratos].* Bucharest, Állami Müvészeti és Irodalmi Könyvkiadó, 1958.

Kovács, László, *A kolozsvári hóstátiak temetkezési szokásai [Burial Customs of the People of Hóstát in Kolozsvár].* Kolozsvár, 1944.

Krause-Siebert, Anna, *Der ostpreussische Volkscharacter wie er sich in ostpreussichen Märchen widerspiegelt.* Kiel, 1947.

Krausz, Sámuel, "A hütlen özvegyasszony irodalmáról" ("On the Literature on the Unfaithful Widow"), *Ethn.,* 15 (1904), 265-272, 311-314.

Kriza, János, *Székely népköltési gyüjtemény. Összesitö válogatás a kiadott és kéziratos hagyatékából [Compilation of Szekler Folk Poetry, from his Published and Unpublished Manuscript Remains, Emended by] P. Gergely and Á Kovács.* Budapest, Magvetö Könyvkiadó, 1956.

————, *Vadrózsák, Székely Népköltési Gyüjtemény, II rész* [*Wild Roses; Anthology of Szekler Folk Poetry, Part II*]. MNGY XII. Budapest, Az Athenaeum Részvenytársulat Tulajdona, 1911.

Kriza, János, Balázs Orban, Elek Benedek, and Jób Sebesi, *Székelyföldi gyüjtés* [*A Collection from the Szekler Land*]. MNGY III. Budapest, Az Athenaeum Részvenytársulat Tulajdona, 1882.

Krohn, Kaarle, *Die folkloristische Arbeitsmethode*. Oslo, H. Aschehoug & Co., 1926.

————, *Übersicht über einige Resultate der Märchenforschung*. FFC 96. Helsinki, Suomalainen Tiedeakatemia, 1931.

Krug, A. N., "Bulu Tales," *JAF*, 62 (1949), 348-374.

Kubín, Josef Stefan, *Lidové povídky z českého Podkrkonoší*. Vol. I: *Podhoří západni;* Vol. II: *Ukrají východni*. Prague, Česka Akademie Věda Uměni, 1922, 1926.

————, *Povidky Kladské*. Prague, 1908-10. 2 vols.


Langness, Lewis L., *The Life History in Anthropological Science; Studies in Anthropological Methods*. New York, Holt, Rinehart and Winston, 1965.

Langstroff, Karl Heinz, *Lothringer Volksart; Untersuchung zur deutsch-lothringischen Volkserzählung an Hand der Sammlung von Angelika Merkelbach-Pinck*. Marburg, N. G. Elwert, 1953.

Laport, George, *Les Contes populaires Wallons*. FFC 101. Helsinki, Suomalainen Tiedeakatemia, 1932.

László, Gyula, "Verses szerelmeslevelek" ("Popular Love Letters in Verse"), *Termés*, 1943, 89-95.

László, M., "A bukovinai és moldvai csángók" ("The Bucovinian and Moldavia Csángó"), *Földrajzi Közlemények*, 1877, 53-68, 193-199.

Lázár, Béla, "A 'Gesta Romanorum' hatása a magyar népköltészetre" ("The Influence of the 'Gesta Romanorum' on Hungarian Folk Literature"), *Ethn.*, 2 (1891), 232-237.

Lázár, I., *Alsó-Fehér vármegye magyar népe* [*The Hungarian Folk of Alsó-Fehér County*]. Nagy-Enyed, 1896.

Levin, Isidor, "Vladimir Propp: An Evaluation on his Seventieth Birthday," *Journal of the Folklore Institute*, 4 (1967), 32-49.

Leyen, Friedrich von der, "Aufgaben und Wege der Märchenforschung," in *Aufsätze für Kultur-und Sprachgeschichte*, 1916.

————, "Die Volkssage," in Vol. I, *Die deutsche Volkskunde*, Adolf Spamer, ed. Leipzig, Bibliographisches Institut, 1935. Pp. 203-215.

————, *Die Welt der Märchen*. Düsseldorf, E. Diedrichs Verlag, 1953-54. 2 vols.

Liljeblad, Sven, *Die Tobiasgeschichte und andere Märchen mit toten Helfern*. Lund, A.-B. Ph. Lindstedts Univ. Bokhandel, 1927.

Lindgren, Ethel John, "Collection and Analysis of Folklore," in F. C. Bartlett, M. Ginsberg, E. J. Lindgren, and R. H. Thouless, eds., *Study of Society*. London, K. Paul, Trench, Trubner & Co., 1939.

Lintur, P. V., "Zakarpatskii skazochnik A. Kalin. Probleme traditsii i novatorstva v ustnom narodom tvorchestve," Uzhgorodskii Derzhavnii universitet, *Naukova Zapiski*, 24 (1957), 45-73.

————, *Zakarpatskii skazochnik Andrei Kalin. Problema traditsii i lichnogo nachala v tvorchestve skazochnika.* Uzhgorod, 1953.

Lőrincze, Lajos, "A tolna-baranyai (volt bukovinai) székelyek névadási szokásaihoz" ("On the Naming-Customs of the [Formerly Bucovinian] Szeklers in Tolna-Baranya County"), *Ethn.*, 59 (1948), 36-47.

Löwis of Menar, August Arthur von, *Der Held im deutschen und russischen Märchen.* Jena, E. Diederichs, 1912.

Loomis, Roger S., "Celtic Folklore," in Vol. I, Funk & Wagnall's *Standard Dictionary of Folklore, Mythology, and Legend.* New York, Funk & Wagnalls, 1949. Pp. 200-205.

Loschdorfer, Anna, "Bakonyi német (sváb) falvaink szerepe a magyar népi hagyományok megörzésében" ("The Role of our German [Swabian] Villagers in the Bakony in the Preservation of Hungarian Folk Traditions"), *Ethn.*, 46 (1935), 76-79.

————, "Veszprémmegyei népmesék" ("Folktales of Veszprém County"), *Ethn.*, 47 (1936), 91-104.

Lowie, Robert H., "Individuum und Gesellschaft in der Religion der Naturvölker," *Zeitschrift für Ethnologie*, 83 (1958), 161-169.

————, "The Oral Literature of the Crow Indians," *JAF*, 72 (1959), 97-104.

Luby, Margit, *A parasztélet rendje [The System of Peasant Life].* Budapest, Centrum Kiadóvállalat, 1935.

Lüthi, Max, "Aspekte des Volksmärchens und der Volkssage," *Germanisch-Romanische Monatsschrift*, XVI (1966), 337-350.

————, "Freiheit und Bindung im Volkmärchen," in Hugo Kuhn und Kurt Schier, eds., *Märchen, Mythos, Dichtung; Festschrift zum 90. Geburtstag Friedrich von der Leyens, am 19. August 1963.* Munich, C. H. Beck, 1963.

————, *Die Gabe im Märchen und in der Sage; ein Beitrag zur Wesensfassung und Wesensscheidung der bieden Formen.* Zurich, 1945.

————, "Gattungsstile (Sage und Märchen)," *Wirkendes Wort*, 1953-54, 321-327.

————, *Märchen.* 2nd ed. Stuttgart, Metzlersche Verlagsbuchhandlung, 1964.

————, "Urform und Zielform in Sage und Märchen," *Fabula*, 9, (1967), 27-41.

————, "Volkskunde und Literaturwissenschaft." *Actes du Congrès international d'ethnologie régionale*, 1956. Arnhem, Rijksmuseum voor Volkskunde: Het Nederlands Openluchtmuseum, 1956. Pp. 116-120.

————, *Volksmärchen und Volkssage: zwei Grundformen erzählender Dichtung.* Bern, Francke, 1966.

Mackensen, Lutz, "Das deutsche Volksmärchen," in Vol. III, *Handbuch der deutschen Volkskunde*, Wilhelm Pessler, ed. Pp. 303-326.

————, "Zur Märchenforschung" ("To Folktale Research"), *Zeitschrift für deutsche Bildung*, 6 (1930), 339-353.

Magyary-Kossa, Gyula, *Magyar orvosi emlékek; értekezések a magyar orvostörténelem Köréböl [Written Hungarian Medical Documents; Papers from Hungarian Medical History].* Budapest, 1929. 2 vols.

Majland, Oszkár, *Székelyföldi gyüjtés [Collection in Szeklerland].* MNGY

VII. Budapest, Az Athenaeum Részvény-Társulat Könyvnyomdája, 1905.

Majláth, János, *Magyar regék, mondák és népmesék* [*Hungarian Legends and Folktales*]. Pest, 1864.

Malinowski, Bronislaw, *Myth in Primitive Psychology*. London, 1926.

Marót, Károly, *A görög irodalom kezdetei* [*The Beginning of Greek Literature*]. Budapest, Akadémiai Kiadó, 1956.

———, "Idios en Koinoi; Gondolatok Fedics Mihály meséiről" ("Thoughts on Mihály Fedics' Tales"), *Egyetemes Philologiai Közlöny*, 64 (1940), 224-235.

———, "A magyar néprajzkutatás feladatai" ("The Tasks of Hungarian Ethnographical Research"), *Ethn.*, 51 (1940), 272-308.

———, "Mi a 'népköltészet'?" ("What is 'Folk Literature'?"), *Ethn.*, 58 (1947), 162-173.

———, "Ritus és ünnep" ("Rite and Festival"), *Ethn.*, 51 (1940), 143-187.

———, "Survival és Revival" ("Survival and Revival"), *Ethn.*, 96 (1945), 1-9.

———, "Szent Iván Napja" ("Saint John's Day"), *Ethn.*, 50 (1939), 254-279.

Massignon, Geneviéve, *Contes traditionnels des teilleurs de lin du Trégor, Basse Bretagne*. Paris, A. et J. Picard, 1965.

Matičetov, Milko, "Gefahren beim Aufzeichnen von Volksprosa in Sprachgrenzgebieten (An slowenischen Beispielen dargestellt)," in *Internationaler Kongress der Volkserzählungsforscher in Kiel und Kopenhagen*. Berlin, W. de Gruyter, 1961. Pp. 179-187.

Merényi, L., *Dunamelléki eredeti népmesék* [*Original Folktales from the Banks of the Danube*]. Pest, 1863-64. 2 vols.

———, *Eredeti népmesék* [*Original Folktales*]. Pest, 1861.

———, *Sajóvölgyi eredeti népmesék* [*Original Folktales from the Valley of the Sajó*]. Pest, 1862. 2 vols.

Merkelbach-Pinck, Angelika, *Lothringer Volksmärchen*. Kassel, Bärenreiter Verlag, 1940.

———, "Wanderungen der Märchen im deutschsparchigen Lothringen," *Folk Liv*, 3 (1939), 224-231.

Messenger, John, "Joe O'Donnel, *Seanchai* of Aran," *Journal of the Folklore Institute*, I (1964), 197-213.

Meyer, G. F., *Plattdeutsche Volksmärchen und Schwänke*. Neumünster, 1925.

Mitchell, Roger Edward, *A Study of the Cultural, Historical, and Acculturative Factors Influencing the Repertories of Two Trukese Informants*. Unpublished Ph.D. dissertation, Indiana University, 1967.

Mühlhausen, Ludwig, *Diarmuid mit dem Roten Bart; Irische Zaubermärchen*. Eisenach/Kassel, E. Röth, 1956.

Müller, E., *Psychologie des deutschen Volksmärchens*. Münster, 1928.

Murphy, Gerard, "Folklore as a Halo to the Understanding of the Irish Fionn," *Folk-Liv*, 2 (1938), 211-216.


Nagy, Olga, *A három táltos varju; Mezőségi népmesék* [*The Three Magic Crows. Tales of the Mezoseg*]. Bucharest, Állami Müvészeti és Szépirodalmi Könyvkiadó,

Nagy, Olga, and J. Faragó, *Elöbb a tánc, azután a lokoma; mezöségi népmesék* [*First the Dance, then the Feast; Folktales of Mezöség*]. Bucharest, 1954.

Nechaev, A. N., and N. Rybakova, "O nekotorykh problemakh fol'kloristiki," *Sov. Etn.*, 1953, 134-141.

Nedo, Pawol, *Sorbische Volksmärchen*. Bautzen, Domovina, 1956.

Neumann, Siegfried, "Arbeitserinnerungen als Erzählinhalt," *DtJb*, 12 (1966), 179-190.

Nippold, Walter, *Rassen- und Kulturgeschichte der Negrito-Völker Südostasiens*. Göttigen, 1936. 2 vols.

Novikova, A. N., and N. A. Ossovetskii, *Skazi Kupriianikhi*. Voronezh, 1937.

Novikov, N. V., *Skazki Filippa Pavlovicha Gospodareva*. Petrozavodsk, 1941.

Noy, Dov, *Contes populaires racontés par des juifs du Maroc*. Jerusalem, Organisation Sioniste Mondiale, 1965.

Noy, Dov, ed. *Jefet Schwili erzählt, hundertneunundsechzig jemenitische Volkserzählungen aufgezeichnet in Israel, 1957-1960*. Vol. 4 in *Fabula*, Series A. Berlin, W. de Gruyter, 1963.

———, "The Universe Concept of Yefet Shvili; a Jewish-Yemenite Story-Teller," *Acta Ethn.*, 14 (1965), 259-275.

Oberding, János György, *A bukovinai magyarság településtörténeti és társadalomrajzi vázlata* [*A Sketch of the Settlements and Social History of Hungarian Bucovina*]. Offprint from *Hitel*, 1939, No. 3-4. Kolozsvár, 1939.

———, *Az órományiai magyarság* [*Hungarians in Early Rumania*]. Pécs, 1940.

Oberfeld, Charlotte, "Heinrich Lüttecke, ein Erzähler aus dem Waldecker Lande," *Hessische Blätter für Volkskunde*, 48 (1957), 31-43.

———, "Magisches Denken und moderne Zivilisation; ein schwälmer Märchen und sein Erzähler," *Hessische Blätter für Volkskunde*, 49 (1958), 207-214.

Onchukov, N. E., *Severnie skazki*. Petrograd, 1908.

Ősz, János, *Csudatáska* [*The Wonderful Pouch*]. Kolozsvár, 1940.

Ortutay, Gyula, "Begriff und Bedeutung der Affinität in der mündlichen Überlieferung," in *Internationaler Kongress der Volkserzählungsforscher in Kiel und Kopenhagen*. Berlin, W. de Gruyter, 1961. Pp. 247-252.

———, *Fedics Mihály mesél* [*Mihály Fedics Tells his Tales*]. UMNGY I. Budapest, Az Egyetemi Magyarságtudományi Intézet Kiadása, 1940.

———, *Hungarian Peasant Life*. Budapest, Officina, 1948.

———, *Magyar népismeret* [*Hungarian Folk Science*]. Budapest, 1937.

———, "A magyar népköltési gyüjtemények története" ("The History of the Hungarian Folk Poetry Collections"), *Ethn.*, 50 (1939), 221-237.

———, *Magyar népköltészet* [*Hungarian Folk Poetry*]. Budapest, Szépirodalmi Könyvkiadó, 1955. 3 vols.

———, *A mai magyar belsö vándorlás és a néprajzi kutatás* [*The Modern Intra-Hungarian Migration and Ethnographical Research*]. Budapest, 1947. Two lectures.

———, "Népköltészet és müköltészet" ("Folk Literature and Art Literature"), in Sándor Eckhardt, ed., *Ur és paraszt a magyar élet egységében* [*Lord and Peasant in the Unity of Hungarian Life*]. Budapest, Király:

Magyar Pázmány Péter Tudományegyetem Bölcsészeti Karának Magyar-ságtudományi Intézete, 1941.

——, "Népmese, népdal, néprajzi hanglemez" ("Folktale, Folksong, Folk-lore Recording"), *Magyar Szemle*, 11 (1938).

——, *Nyíri és rétközi parasztmesék* [*Peasant Tales from Nyír and Rétköz*]. Gyoma, Hungary, Keszült Kner Izidor Konyvnyomdájában, 1935.

——, *Parasztságunk élete* [*Our Peasants' Life*]. Budapest, 1938.

——, "Principles of Oral Transmission in Folk Culture," *Acta Ethn.*, 8 (1959), 175-221.

——, "The Science of Folklore in Hungary between the Two World Wars and During the Period Subsequent to the Liberation," *Acta Ethn.*, 4 (1955), 5-89.

——, "A szájhagyományozás törvényszerüségei" ("Regularities in the Oral Transmission of Folk Tradition"), *Ethn.*, 76 (1965), 1-9.

——, *Székely népballadák* [*Szekler Folk Ballads*]. Budapest, Egyetemi Nyomda, 1948.

——, *Ungarische Märchen*. Berlin, Rütten & Loening, 1957.

Ortutay, Gyula, and I. Katona, *Magyar parasztmesék* [*Hungarian Peasant Tales*]. Budapest, Szépirodalm. Könyvkiadó, 1951-56. 2 vols.

Ortutay, Gyula, Linda Dégh, and Á. Kovács, *Magyar népmesék* [*Hungarian Folktales*]. Budapest, Szépirodalmi Könyvkiadó, 1960. 3 vols.

O'Sullivan, Seán (O'Suilleabháin, Seán), *Folktales of Ireland*. Foreword by R. M. Dorson. Chicago, University of Chicago Press, 1966.

——, *A Handbook of Irish Folklore*. 2nd ed. Hatboro, Pa., Folklore Associates, 1963.

——, *Irish Wake Amusements*. Cork, Mercier Press, 1967.

O'Sullivan, Seán, and Reidar T. Christiansen, *The Types of the Irish Folk-Tale*. FFC 188. Helsinki, Suomalainen Tiedeakatemia, 1963.

Ováry, Z., " 'Rózsa és Ibolya' Arany János népmeséje" (" 'Rózsa and Ibolya,' János Arany's Folktale"), *Ethn.*, 34 (1924), 23-30.


Panzer, Friedrich, *Die Kinder- und Hausmärchen der Brüder Grimm in ihrer Urgestalt*. 1913.

Pap, Gyula, *Palócz népköltemények* [*Palócz Folk-Poetry*]. Sárospatak, 1865.

Penavin, Olga, "Die ungarische Volksmärchenforschung in Jugoslavien," *Laographia*, 22 (1965), 335-337. Paper presented at the Athens Congress, 1964.

Péter, László, "A népköltészet változatokban él" ("Folklore Lives in its Variants"), *Ethn.*, 76 (1965), 120-125.

Petsch, Robert, *Formelhafte Schlüsse in Volksmärchen*. Berlin, 1900.

——, *Wesen und Formen der Erzählkunst*. H./Salle, M. Niemeyer, 1934.

Peuckert, Will-Erich, *Deutsches Volkstum im Märchen und Sage, Schwank und Rätsel*. Berlin, 1938.

——, *Lenore*. FFC 158. Helsinki, Suomalainin Tiedeakatemia, 1955.

——, "Märchen," in Vol. III, *Deutsche Philologie im Aufriss*, W. Stammler, ed. Berlin, Erich Schmidt Verlag, 1962. Pp. 2677-2726.

———, "Däs Märchen," in W. E. Peuckert and Otto Lauffer, eds., *Volkskunde; Quellen und Forschungen seit 1930.* Bern, Francke, 1951.

———, "Sage," in Vol. III, *Deutsche Philologie im Aufriss,* W. Stammler, ed. Berlin, Erich Schmidt Verlag, 1962. Pp. 2641-2676.

Philippson, Ernst, *Der Märchentypus von König Drosselbart.* FFC 50. Greifswald, Suomalainen Tiedeakatemia, 1923.

Piksanov, N. K., "Gorkii o fol'klore," *Sov. Fol'klor,* 1935, 2, 331-341.

Pillet, Auguste, *Das Fabliau von den Trois bossus Ménestrels und verwandte Erzählungen früher und später Zeit.* Halle, 1901.

Pintér, Sándor, *A népmesékröl. XIII eredeti palóczmesével* [*Concerning Folktales; with Thirteen Original Palocz Tales*]. Losonc, 1891.

Polívka, Jiří, *Povidky lidu opavského a hanáckého* [*Tales of the People of Opava and Haná*]. Prague, Nákl. České Akademie Císaře Františka Josefa pro rědy, Slovesnost u Uměni, 1916.

———, "Úvod; Východoslovanské pohádky," in Vol. 1, *Slovanské pohádky.* Prague, Nákladem Slovanského Ustavu, u. Komisi Nakladatelstri Orbis, 1932.

Pomerantseva, E. V. (Pomeranceva, Erna V.), "J. F. Kovalev, ein belesener russischer Märchenerzähler," *DtJb,* 11 (1965), 265-274.

———, "Nekotory voprosy izucheniia narodnogo tvorchestva sovremennosti," *Sov. Etn.,* 1953, No. 3, 142-144.

———, *Skazki Abrama Novopol'tseva.* Kuibyshev, 1952.

———, "Skazki," in P. G. Bogatyrev, *Russkoe narodnoe poeticheskoe tvorchestvo.* Moscow, 1954. Pp. 228-257.

———, (Pomeranzeva, Erna V.), *Russische Volksmärchen.* Berlin, Akademie-Verlag, 1964. 3rd ed., 1966.

Poncianus (P+oncziánus), *A hét bölcs mester, vagy: miként ajánlja Poncziánus római császár fiát Dioklecziánust a hét bölcs mester nevelésébe, kik a nemes tudományokra és bölcseségre tanítják és továbbá: mint hurczoltaték az hétszer akasztófára, mostoha anyjának hütlensége s példázatai miatt; de mindannyiszor megszabadul a haláltól a hét bölcs mesternek szép hasonlatai által, s majd hatalmas császára lesz a római birodalomnak* [*The Seven Wise Masters, or, How Poncianus Commended Diocletian, Son of the Roman Emperor, to the Up-Bringing of the Seven Sages, Who Taught Him High Arts and Wisdom, and Further, How He Was Dragged to the Gallows Seven Times Because of Treachery and the Insinuations of His Stepmother, and How He Evaded Death Each Time with the Beautiful Answers of the Seven Wise Men, and then Became a Yet Mightier Emperor of the Roman Empire*]. Budapest, 1911.

*Poncianus históriája.* Vienna, Bécs, 1573. Critical edition: G. Heinrich, ed. Régi Magyar Könyvtár 5. Budapest, 1898.

Pop, Mihai, "Caractere nationale şi stratificări istorice în stilul basemelor populare" ("National Character and Historical Stratification in Folktale Style"), *Revista de Etnografie şi Folclor,* 10 (1965), 3-11.

———, "Caractéres nationaux et historiques dans le style des contes populaires," *Laographia,* 22 (1965), 381-390. Paper presented at the Athens Congress, 1965.

Propp, Vladimir, "Märchen der Brüder Grimm im russischen Norden," *DtJb*, 9 (1963), 104-112.

Radloff, Wilhelm, *Proben der Volksliteratur der türkischen Stämme Südsibiriens*. St. Petersburg, 1866. 5 vols.

Rădulescu-Codin, C., *Ingerul Românului; povești și legende din popor*. Bucharest, Socec & Co., 1913.

Ranke, Friedrich, "Aufgaben volkskundlicher Märchenforschung," *Zeitschift für Volkskunde*, 42 (1932), 203-211.

——, "Kunstmärchen im Volksmund," *Zeitschrift für Volkskunde*, 46 (1937), 123-133.

——, "Das Märchen," in Vol. I, *Die deutsche Volkskunde*, Adolf Spamer, ed. Leipzig, Bibliographisches Institut, 1935. Pp. 249-262.

——, "Märchenforschung; ein Literaturbericht," *Deutsche Vierteljahrschrift für Literaturwissenschaft und Geistesgeschichte*, 14 (1936), 246-304.

——, *Volkssagenforschung; Vorträge und Aufsätze*. Breslau, Maruschke & Berendt, 1935.

Ranke, Kurt, "Betrachtungen zum Wesen und zur Funktion des Märchens," *Studium Generale*, 11 (1958), 647-664.

——, "Einfache Formen," in *Internationaler Kongress der Volkserzählungsforscher in Kiel und Kopenhagen*. Berlin, W. de Gruyter, 1961. Pp. 1-11.

——, "Einfache Formen," *Journal of the Folklore Institute*, 4 (1967), 17-31.

——, "Der Einfluss der Grimmischen Kinder- und Hausmärchen auf das volkstümliche deutsche Erzählgut," in *Papers of the International Congress of European and Western Ethnology, Stockholm, 1951*. Stockholm, 1955. Pp. 126-133.

——, "Kategorienprobleme der Volksprosa," *Fabula*, 9 (1967), 4-12. Paper presented at the meeting of the International Society for Folk Narrative Research, Liblice, September, 1966.

——, ed., "Papers Presented at the Liblice Meeting of the International Society of Folk-Narrative Research, September 1-4, 1966," *Fabula Zeitschrift für Erzählforschung*, 9 (1967). W. de Gruyter.

——, *Schleswig-Holsteinische Märchen (Aa-Th 300-402)*. Kiel, F. Hirt, 1955. 2 vols.

——, *Die zwei Brüder; eine Studie zur vergleichenden Märchenforschung*. FFC 114. Helsinki, Suomalainen Tiedeakatemia, 1934.

Rath, E., "Volksbuch und Volksmund; zur Quellenfrage steirischen Erzählgutes," *Zeitschrift des historischen Vereins für Steiermark*, 45 (1954), 131-144.

R. Berde, Mária, *Székely népmesék* [*Szekler Folktales*]. Budapest, 1924.

Réthei Prikkel, Marián, *A magyarság táncai* [*The Dances of the Hungarians*]. Budapest, 1924.

Roberts, Warren E., "Collection and Indexes: A Brief Review," *JAF*, 70 (1957), 49-52.

———, "Holbek on the *Type Index:* A Rejoinder," *Journal of the Folklore Institute,* 2 (1965), 229-235.

Rohde, O., *Die Erzählung vom Einsiedler und dem Engel.* Leipzig, 1894.

Róheim, Géza, *Hungarian and Vogul Mythology.* Seattle and London, University of Washington Press, 1954.

Röhrich, Lutz, "Die deutsche Volkssage; ein methodischer Abriss," *Studium Generale,* 11 (1958), 665-691.

———, "Märchen mit schlechtem Ausgang," *Hessische Blätter für Volkskunde,* 49-50 (1958), 236-248.

———, *Märchen und Wirklichkeit; eine volkskundliche Untersuchung.* Wiesbaden, F. Steiner, 1956.

———, "Die Märchenforschung seit dem Jahre 1945," *DtJb,* I (1955), 279-295; II (1956), 274-319; III (1957), 213-224.

———, *Erzählungen des späten Mittelalters und ihr Weiterleben in Literatur und Volksdichtung bis zur Gegenwart. Sagen, Märchen, Exempel und Schwänke mit einem Kommentar.* Franke Verlag, Bern und München, 2 vols. 1962 and 1967.

Rooth, Anna Birgitta, *The Cinderella Cycle.* Lund, C. W. K. G. Kerup, 1951.

Rösch, Erich, *Der getreue Johannes.* FFC 77. Helsinki, Suomalainen Tiedeakatemia, 1928.

Rotunda, Dominic Peter, *Motif-Index of the Italian Novella in Prose.* No. 2, Folklore Series. Bloomington, Indiana, Indiana University Publications, 1942.

Rumpf, Marianne, *Rotkäppchen; eine vergleichende Märchenuntersuchung.* Göttingen, 1951.

———, *Ursprung und Entstehung von Warn- und Schreckmärchen.* FFC 160. Helsinki, Suomalainen Tiedeakatemia, 1955.


Sadovnikov, D. N., *Skazki i predaniia Samarskogo Kraia.* St. Petersburg, 1884.

Săineanu, Lazar, *Basmele Românilor. Studiu comparativ cu legendele antice.* Bucharest, Academia Română, 1895.

Sándor, István, "A mesemondás dramaturgiája" ("The Dramaturgy of Storytelling"), *Ethn.,* 75 (1964), 523-556.

———, "Világos és Arad a magyar néphagyományban" ("Világos and Arad in Hungarian Folk Tradition"), *A Magyar Tudományos Akadémia II Oszt. Közleményei,* 1953, 105-186.

Sántha, Alajos, *Bukovinai magyarok* [*The Bucovina Hungarians*]. Kolozsvár, 1942.

Sareyko, Hans Ulrich, *Das Weltbild eines ostpreussischen Volkserzählers.* Marburg, 1954.

Sartori, Paul, "Erzählen als Zauber," in *Volkskundliche Studien, Friedrich Wilhelm Ott zum 70. Geburtstag dargebracht.* Berlin and Leipzig, 1930. Pp. 40-45.

Satke, Antonín, *Hlučinský pohádkář Josef Smolka* [*Josef Smolka, Storyteller of Hlučín*]. Ostrava, Krajské nakl., 1958.

Savushkina, N. I., *Ideino-khudozhestvennye osobennosti bytovoi skazki i ee obshchestvenno-vospitatel'naia rol' v sovremennosti.* Moscow, 1956.

Schlauch, Margaret, *Chaucer's Constant and Accused Queens.* New York, The New York University Press, 1927.

Schmidt, Friedrich Wilhelm, "Die Volkssage als Kunstwerk; eine Untersuchung über die Formgeschichte der Volkssage," *Niederdeutsche Zeitschrift für Volkskunde,* 2 (1929), 129-143, 230-244.

Schmidt, Kurt, *Die Entwicklung der Grimmschen Kinder- und Hausmärchen.* H./Salle, M. Niemeyer, 1932.

Schoof, Wilhelm, "Neue Urfassungen Grimmscher Märchen," *Hessische Blätter für Volkskunde,* 44 (1953), 65-88.

Schullerus, Adolf, *Vereichnis der rumänischen Märchen und Märchenvarianten.* FFC 78. Helsinki, Suomalainen Tiedeakatemia, 1928.

Schwietering, Julius, "Volksmärchen und Volksglaube; Dichtung und Volkstum," *Neue Folge des Euphorion, Zeitschrift für Literaturgeschichte,* 36 (1935), 73-78.

Sebestyén, Gyula, *Dunántúli gyüjtés [Transdanubian Collection].* Budapest, Atheneum, 1906.

Sébillot, Paul, *La Littérature orale de la Haute Bretagne.* Paris, Maissonneure, 1881. 2 vols.

Seiler, F., *Ruodlieb, der älteste Roman des Mittelalters.* Halle, A. S. Verlag der Buchhandlung des Waisenhauses, 1882.

Sharp, Cecil James, *English Folk-Song; Some Conclusions.* London, Simpkin & Co., 1907.

Sieber, Friedrich, "Wünsche und Wunschbilder im späten deutschen Zaubermärchen," *DtJb,* III (1957), 11-30.

Sirovátka, Oldřich, "Obraz Josefa Hybeše v lidové tradicii na Rosicko-Oslavansku," *Česky lid,* 43 (1956), 49-56.

——, "Zur Erforschung der nationalen Eigenarten des Märchens," *Laographia,* 22 (1965), 517-526. Paper presented at the Athens Congress, 1964.

Slavík, Bedřich, *Písmáci selského zapsané lidu.* Prague, 1940.

Sokolov, B., and Sokolov, Iu., *Skazki i pesni Belozerskogo Kraia.* 1915.

Sokolov, Iu., *Le folklore russe.* Paris, 1945.

——, "Po sledam Rybnikova i Gilferdinga," in *Khudozhestvennyi fol'klor.* Moscow, 1927.

Sokolov, Y. M., *Russian Folklore Introduction and Bibliography,* Felix J. Oinas, ed. Hatboro, Penn., Folklore Associates, 1966.

Solymossy, Sándor, "Az 'Égbenyúló fáról' szóló mesemotívumunk" ("Our Tale Motif 'The Sky-High Tree'"), *Ethn.,* 41 (1930), 61-62.

——, "Az ezeregy-éj" ("The Thousand and One Nights"), *Ethn.,* 30 (1919), 45-73.

——, "Keleti elemek népmeséinkben" ("Oriental Elements in our Folktales"), *Ethn.,* 33 (1922), 33-44.

——, "A magyar ősi hitvilág" ("The Ancient Hungarian Belief World"), in Vol. III, *A Magyarság Néprajza.* Budapest, 1938. Pp. 340-382.

——, "Mese a Jávorfáról" ("The Tale of the Maple Tree"), *Ethn.,* 31 (1920), 1-25.

——, "Mesehősnő, aki 'gyönyyöt sír és rózsát nevet'" ("The Folktale Heroine; 'Pearls Wept and Roses Laughed'"), *Ethn.,* 28 (1917), 223-237.

————, *A népmese és a tudomány* [*Folktale and Science*]. Budapest, Kis Akadémia, 1938.

————, "Népmese-tanulmány" ("Folktale Study"), *Ethn.*, 29 (1918), 277-286.

————, "A 'Szép ember' meséje" ("The Tale of the 'Beautiful Man' "), *Ethn.*, 27 (1916), 257-275.

Speiss, K., *Das deutsche Volksmärchen.* Leipzig/Berlin, 1917.

Stahl, Henri H., *Nerej, un village d'une region archaïque.* Bucharest, Institut de sciences sociales de Roumanie, 1941. 3 vols.

Stefanuca, P. V., "O familie de poveştiri din Jurceni (Basarabia)," *Anuarul Archivei de Folclor,* 6 (1939), 77-100.

Steinitz, Wolfgang, "Lied und Märchen als Stimme des Volkes," *Wissenchaftliche Annalen,* 4 (1955), 321-378.

Suchier, Walter, *Der Schwank von der viermal getöteten Leiche in der Literatur des Abend- und Morgenlandes.* Halle, 1922.

Swahn, Jan-Öjvind, "Bekenntnisse eines Ketzers; Kurzgefasste Erläuterungen anlässlich einer Besprechung," *Hessische Blätter für Volkskunde,* 47 (1956), 11-115.

————, *The Tale of Cupid and Psyche* (*AaTh 425 + 428*). Lund, C. W. K. Gleerup, 1955.

Sydow, Carl Wilhelm von, *Finsk metod och modern sagorforskning.* Lund, 1943.

————, "Kategorien der Prosa-Volksdichtung," in *Volkskundliche Gaben, John Meier zum siebzigsten Geburtstage dargebracht.* Berlin and Leipzig, W. de Gruyter, 1934. Pp. 253-268.

————, *Selected Papers on Folklore.* Copenhagen, Rosenkilde and Bagger, 1948.

————, *Två Spinnsagor; en studie i jämförande folksaga forskning.* Stockholm, P. A. Norstedt, 1909.

Szádeczky, L., *A székely határöség szervezése* [*Organization of the Szekler Border Guards*] *1762-1765-ben.* Budapest, 1908.

Szendrey, Zsigmond, "A halottak, szentelmények és eljárásmódok a varázslatokban" ("The Dead, Sacraments and Usages in the Practice of Magic"), *Ethn.*, 49 (1938), 32-46.

————, "Munkanóták" ("Worksongs"), *Ethn.*, 42 (1931), 197-198.

————, *Nagyszalontai gyüjtés* [*Collection in Nagyszalonta*]. MNGY XIV. Budapest, 1924.

————, "Pásztor Árpád meseközléséhez" ("On Árpád Pásztor's Tale Publication"), *Ethn.*, 42 (1931), 92.

Szentmártoni, P. Kálmán, *Székely népmesék* [*Szekler Folktales*]. Kolozsvár, n.d.

Szentpétery, Imre, ed., *Gesta Hungarorum. Scriptores Rerum Hungaricorum I.* Budapest, Academia litter, hungarica atque societate histor. hungarica, 1937.

Szücs, Sándor, "Az 'égbenyúló fa' a sárréti néphitben" ("The 'Tree Reaching to Heaven' in the Folklore of Sárrét"), *Ethn.*, 56 (1945), 23-25.

Takács, Lajos, "Nepi verselők, hírversírók" ("Popular Verse-Makers: Writers of Broadside Poetry"), *Ethn.*, 62 (1951), 1-49.

―――,"Occasions et débit de récitations épique populaires chantées sur des événements d'actualitiés," *Acta Ethn.*, 4 (1955), 419-442.

―――, "A rendes pipázás privilégiumjai" ("The Privilege of Real Pipe-Smoking"), *Ethn.*, 65 (1954), 210-222.

Tamási, Áron, "Igaz történet elbeszélése" ("The Telling of the True Story"), *Pásztortüz*, 1929, 205-207.

Taylor, Archer, "The Biographical Pattern in Traditional Narrative," *Journal of the Folklore Institute*, I (1954), 114-129.

Tax, Sol, "Folk Tales in Chichicastenango," *JAF*, 62 (1949), 125-135.

Tegethoff, Ernst, *Märchen, Schwänke und Fabeln.* Munich, 1925.

Thienemann, T., *Irodalomtörténeti alapfogalmak [Basic Concepts of Literary History].* Pécs, 1931.

Thimme, Adolf. *Das Märchen.* Leipzig, W. Heims, 1909.

Thomka, Viktor, *Egy aldunai székely község szociográfiája [Sociography of a Szekler Community on the Lower Danube].* Magyar Kisebbség, 1939.

Thompson, Stith, *The Folktale.* New York, Holt, Rinehart & Winston, 1946.

―――, ed., *Four Symposia on Folklore; Held at the Midcentury International Folklore Conference.* Bloomington, Indiana, Indiana University Press, 1953.

―――, *Motif-Index of Folk-Literature, a Classification of Narrative Elements in Folktales, Ballads, Myths, Fables, Medieval Romances, Exempla, Fabliaux, Jest-Books, and Local Legends.* FFC 106-109, 116, 117. Helsinki, Suomalainen Tiedeakatemia, 1932-36. 6 vols. New edition based on doubled materials: Copenhagen, Rosenkilde and Bagger; Bloomington, Indiana, Indiana University Press, 1955-1958.

―――, "Myths and Folktales," *JAF*, 68 (1955), 482-488.

―――, "The Study of Primitive Storytelling; Its Present Status and Future Directions," *Folk-Liv*, 21-22 (1957-58), 185-190.

―――, "Tale-Collection in Ireland," *Southern Folklore Quarterly*, 1938, 53-58.

Thury, Etele, "Bornemisza Péter könyve az ördögi kisértetekről" ("Peter Bornemisza's Book about the Temptations of the Devil"), *Ethn.*, 24 (1913), 195-205.

Tille, Václav, *Povídky, jež sebral na Moravském Valašsku.* Prague, 1902.

Tillhagen, Carl-Herman, "Ein schwedischer Märchen- und Sagenerzähler und sein Repertoire," *Rheinisches Jahrbuch für Volkskunde*, 10 (1959), 9-22.

―――, *Taikon erzählt.* Zurich, 1948.

―――, "Was ist eine Sage?" *Acta Ethn.*, 13 (1964), 9-17.

Titiev, Mischa, "Two Hopi Myths and Rites," *JAF*, 61 (1948), 31-43.

Tömörkény, István, "A tanyai ember Ág Illese" ("Ág Illés [Achilles] of the Farmsteader"), *Ethn.*, 25 (1914), 97-101.

Tolnai, Vilmos, "Az ephesusi matróna irodalmához" ("The Literature about the Widow of Ephesus"), *Egyetemes Philológiai Közlöny*, 19 (1896), 902 ff.

Tóth, Béla, Magyar anekdotakincs [Hungarian Anecdote Treasury]. Pest, 1898-1903. 4 vols.

Trencsényi-Waldapfel, Imre, "Bellerophontes," in Magyar Tudományos Akadémia I. Osztály Közleményei, II (1953), 1-14.

——, Mitológia [Mythology]. Budapest, 1956.

Turóczi-Trostler, József, Históriák és mesés fabulák [Stories and Fabulous Fables]. Gyoma, 1939.

Uffer, Leza, "Märchensammler in Romanisch Bünden," in Robert Wildhaber, ed., Alpes Orientales. Basel, 1961. Pp. 129-147.

——, Rätoromanische Märchen und ihre Erzähler. Basel, Schweizerische Gesellschaft für Volkskunde, 1945.

Underhill, Ruth Murray, The Papago Indians of Arizona and their Relatives the Pima. U. S. Department of the Interior, Office of Indian Affairs, Sherman Pamphlets No. 3, Lawrence, Kansas, 1940.

Utley, Francis Lee, "Folktale, Folkteller, and Folk Milieu," Journal of the Folklore Institute, 3 (1966), 70-84.

Václavek, Bedřich, Písemnictví a lidová tradice [Literacy and Folk Tradition]. Prague, 1947.

Vajda, László, "Csodálatos történetek pásztorokról és állatokról" ("Remarkable Stories of Herders and Animals"), Ethn., 55 (1944), 139-143.

——, "A néprajzi anyaggyüjtés módszere és jelentősége" ("The Meaning and Method of Collecting Folklore Material"), Ethn., 65 (1954), 1-19.

Vajkai, Aurél, "Az ördöngős molnárlegény" ("The Devilish Miller-Boy"), Ethn., 58 (1947), 55-69.

Vasiliu, A. N., Povești și legende. Bucharest, 1928.

Végh, József, Sárréti népmesék és népi beszélgetések [Folktales and Popular Conversation from Sárrét]. Debrecen, 1944.

Viidalepp, Richard, "Von einem grossen estnischen Erzähler und seinem Repertoire," Acta Ethnologica (Copenhagen), 3 (1937), 158-173.

Vikár, Béla, "Élö nyelvemlék" ("Living Language Relics"), Néprajzi Értesítő, 2 (1900), 131-142.

——, "Somogy megye népköltése" ("The Folk Poetry of Somogy County"), Ethn., 10 (1899), 25-34.

——, Somogymegye népköltése [Folk Poetry of Somogy County]. MNGY VI. Budapest, Athenaeum, 1905.

Viski, Károly, ed., A Magyarság Néprajza [Ethnography of the Hungarians], Vol. 4. Budapest, 1937.

——, Magyarság Néprajza. 2nd ed. Budapest, Királyi Magyar Egyetemi Nyomda, 1941-43. 4 vols.

Voigt, Vilmos, "A variáns, invariáns és affinitás fogalmainak definiciója" ("The Definition of Variant, Invariant, and Affinity"), Ethn., 77 (1966), 136-138.

Volly, István, "Katekizmusi ének" ("Catechism Song"), Ethn., 48 (1937), 465-468.

Vrabie, Gheorghe, "Sur la technique de la narration dans le conte roumain," *Laographia*, 22 (1965), 606-615. Paper presented at the Athens Congress, 1964.

Vries, Jan de, *Betrachtungen zum Märchen*. FFC 150. Helsinki, Suomalainen Tiedeakatemia, 1954.

Walker, J. W., *The Truth about Robin Hood*. Wakefield, 1952.

Walker, Warren S., and Ahmal E. Uysal, *Tales Alive in Turkey*. Cambridge, Mass., Harvard University Press, 1966.

Weber, K., "Die Novelle der treulosen Witwe in Ungarn," *Ungarische Rundschau*, 1913, 455.

Weeks, John H., *Congo Life and Folklore*. London, The Religious Tract Society, 1911.

Weidlein, Johann, "Hessen in Ungarn," *Hessische Blätter für Volkskunde*, 45 (1954), 1-25.

Weiss, Richard, *Volkskunde der Schweiz*. Erlenbach-Zürich, E. Reutsch, 1946.

Werner, Waltraut, "Porträt eines ungarndeutschen Märchenerzählers an einer Tonfilm-Aufzeichnung des Institutes für ostdeutsche Volkskunde. 'Wie Markus Schaffer das Märchen vom Fürchtenicht erzählt,' " *Jahrbuch für ostdeutsche Volkskunde*, 10 (1966-67), 120-141.

Wesselski, Albert, "Die Formen des volkstümlichen Erzählguts," in Vol. I, *Die deutsche Volkskunde*, Adolf Spamer, ed. Leipzig, Bibliographisches Institut, 1935. Pp. 216-248.

———, *Märchen des Mittelalters*. Berlin, H. Stubenrauch, 1925.

———, "Probleme der Sagenbildung," *Schweizerisches Archiv für Volkskunde*, 35 (1936), 131-188.

———, *Versuch einer Theorie des Märchens*. Reichenberg i. B., F. Kraus, 1931.

Wisser, Wilhelm, *Auf der Märchensuche; die Entstehung meiner Märchen sammlung*. Hamburg, Hanseatische Verlagsanstalt, 1926.

———, *Plattdeutsche Volksmärchen*. Jena, E. Diederichs, 1927.

Wlislocki, Heinrich von, "A zarándok és Isten angyala" ("The Pilgrim and the Angel of God"), *Ethn.*, 3 (1894), 260-265.

Wolf, Eric R., *Anthropology*. Englewood Cliffs, N. J., Prentice-Hall Inc., 1964.

Wunsche, A., *Die Sage vom Lebensbaum und Lebenswasser*. Leipzig, 1905.

Yates, Dora Esther, *A Book of Gypsy Folk-Tales*. London, Phoenix House, 1948.

Zaunert, Paul, *Deutsche Märchen aus dem Donaulande*. Jena, Diederichs, 1926.

Zelenin, D. K., *Velikorusskie skazki Permskoi gubernii*. 1914.

———, *Velikorusskie skazki Viatskoi gubernii*. 1915.

Zender, Matthias, *Volksmärchen und Schwänke aus der Westeifel*. Bonn, L. Röhrscheid, 1935.

Zenker-Starzacher, Elli, *Eine deutsche Märchenerzählerin aus Ungarn*. München, 1941.

Ziegler, Wilhelm, *Die Frau im Märchen*. Leipzig, 1937 .

# INDEX OF MOTIFS

(Motif numbers are from Stith Thompson, *Motif-Index of Folk Literature*, 6 vols.; Copenhagen and Bloomington, Ind., 1955-58)

# INDEX OF TALE TYPES

(Type numbers are from Antti Aarne and Stith Thompson, *The Types of the Folktale*, Helsinki, 1961; and from János Berze Nagy, *Magyar Népmesetipusok*, Pécs, 1957)

# GENERAL INDEX